KEN WILLIAMS

Ken Williams

A Slugger in Ruth's Shadow

Dave Heller

McFarland & Company, Inc., Publishers
Jefferson, North Carolina

ISBN (print) 978-1-4766-6535-1
ISBN (ebook) 978-1-4766-2583-6

Library of Congress cataloguing data are available

British Library cataloguing data are available

Front cover image of Ken Williams courtesy National Baseball Hall of Fame Library, Cooperstown, New York

Printed in the United States of America

McFarland & Company, Inc., Publishers
Box 611, Jefferson, North Carolina 28640
www.mcfarlandpub.com

In memory of my grandfathers:

Joe Heller, a sports fan who followed
both the Philadelphia Phillies and A's,

and

LaVerne Lyon, a former semi-pro baseball player
and Yankees fan who once saw Babe Ruth bunt for a hit.

Table of Contents

Acknowledgments

It isn't often one will lead off thanking an entity, but here it is the case. After all, the Internet has provided a great boon to researchers. I once had a boss who said we had the greatest resource in the history of the world at our fingertips, and he was so very right.

The Internet—and all that is housed there—has brought the past to our doorstep. Or, at least our computers. While not every piece of information is available, I was able to read newspapers from Boston to Honolulu, find United States census reports from five decades, and read articles from magazines as far back as over 100 years.

And it isn't just words from the long ago which the Internet is able to provide. It also can lead to finding people. Doing a search—I can't remember exactly what I was looking up—somehow I discovered a message board post about Ken Williams written by a Larry LaBeck, who happened to be a distant cousin of the former ballplayer. The post was a few years old, but again thanks to the information superhighway, I was able to find Larry's phone number (thank goodness for landlines, which the majority of people actually still had in the early 2000s).

Larry was a wealth of information on the Williams family history and was able to provide a number of photographs which appear in this book. He also was able to put me in contact with Ken Williams's son, Jack. And Jack put me in touch with his older brother, Ken Jr.

I can't thank the Williams brothers enough for their time and patience. They granted numerous interviews and offered up as much information as they remembered or knew. How much do people really know about their father, they had wondered. In their case, their parents didn't talk much about Ken Williams's baseball career or their past. But they had a point of view and information that no one else would. I know at times it must have seemed like they were just humoring me—Jack had mentioned others had made a claim of writing a book on their dad and none had come to fruition. It took longer than expected, but they were a big part of this book's being published. They provided a direct link to their dad as only they could.

There were other people, too. Tamara Vidos at the University of Oregon's Knight Library was very helpful on my visit to Eugene. I spent days in that library taking advantage of their extensive microfilm of late 19th- and early 20th-century Oregon newspapers.

I would be remiss if I didn't mention the group of librarians at the Shorewood Public Library for being the library nearest to me that had a microfilm machine. They probably never imagined someone would be in there hours upon hours, day after day, week after week, year after year, poring over microfilm. I'm not saying I was in there a lot, but it had a Norm at Cheers feel. It got to the point after many sojourns over there that I was able to explain how to order microfilm to the newer librarians. For those who were there the entire time and put up with my numerous requests, and then the subsequent phone call to tell me the microfilm was in, followed eventually by the next order and me returning the research saying, "This one can go back," I can't thank you enough for your patience and time. And for having a microfilm machine (actually a few) so I didn't have to go downtown and pay for parking.

Not to say the Milwaukee Public Library wasn't a help. The requests filtered through them to their lending libraries, plus I spent a day there going through their archives of magazines, such as *Baseball Digest*.

Then there are the people I never met or talked with. If not for a friendly librarian, Janet Craig, at the Regina Public Library, perhaps my research would have come to a halt. I requested microfilm from them, but they had a policy in which they don't lend to libraries in the United States (they had problems in the past getting materials back, for whatever reasons). I pleaded my case and even offered to use my credit card as a deposit in case something went wrong. She acquiesced and made an exception for me, sending the microfilm to the Shorewood Library—and never took my card number. Without being able to read the accounts of Ken Williams's first year-plus of professional baseball, I shudder to think what else I could have done. So much information was gleaned from those long-ago pages, all because a librarian in Western Canada took a chance on me.

Others to thank include those who corresponded with me: Dwayne Isgrig, who sent me some information I couldn't access; SABR's Fred Brillhart, Dave Baldwin (a former ballplayer helpful in matters of contracts) and Trent McCotter; Greg Hanberg of the *Grants Pass Daily Courier*, who sent me his 1987 articles on Ken Williams; Jack O'Connell of the BBWAA; Don Thomas of the Josephine Country Historical Society, who sent me a bunch of information; and author Richard Huhn and Marc Kollbaum from Jefferson Barracks.

Of course, are those I will never forget—my family. My parents, Mel Heller and Elaine Lyon, have always, shall we say, put up with my intense love of sports, and hearing their reaction when telling them a book is going to be published is priceless. My older brother, Steve, helped foster that love of sports, and baseball in particular, with our many days playing whatever game we could get our hands on, and was also a trivia partner.

I got to relive the joy of baseball through my sons, Laben and Kieran, as they played in their youth. It is probably too much to ask that they become as interested in baseball's history as I am, but hopefully I can open a window here and there for them with a book like this. Or maybe they'll appreciate it when they're older, like most kids.

Finally, there is my wife, Shelly. I couldn't do any of this without her understanding. She married a sports nut and probably never fully realized what she got herself into, but she never questioned my sanity for going to Oregon, or making all those trips to the library, or sequestering myself in front of the computer to transcribe notes and write a bunch of words on a blank document which turned into this book. She did it knowing the outcome would not be my being able to buy a summer house with the book's profits, but that I did this passion project for the pure joy. If that's not true love, I don't know what is. And I mean that from both directions. Thank you for allowing me to pursue my dreams and supporting me 100 percent of the way, no questions asked. Who could ask for anything more?

I've done all I could to preserve the memory and playing career of Ken Williams. I hope you enjoy it even a tenth as much as I did researching and writing it.

Who is the rooter's joy and pride?
Who gives the pesky pill a ride?
And separates it from its hide?
Ken Williams

—L.C. Davis, *The Sporting News,* May 11, 1922

Preface

Many an hour were spent in my youth talking baseball, and a lot of that time revolved around trivia. Whether it was with my brother at home, with friends—or even teachers—at school, it was always a good day when I could stump someone.

There were a couple of go-to baseball trivia questions whenever someone new entered the fray. One was: Who was the only player to pinch-hit for Ted Williams? I sometimes amended this to: Who was the only player to pinch-hit for Ted Williams *and* Roger Maris? It gave it a little more oomph. (The answer: Carroll Hardy.)

The other, more popular question, asked by those who had delved into baseball trivia, was: Who was the first player in history to hit 30 home runs and steal 30 bases in a season? Or, more simply: Who was baseball's first 30–30 player? The answer, of course, is Ken Williams. As a kid, that was enough information for most. But not me.

As a lifelong fan of the Baltimore Orioles, I discovered at a young age that they were once the St. Louis Browns. So as someone who quickly became interested in the history of baseball, I became a fan of them as well. (Or, more specifically, since I was born nearly two decades after they left St. Louis, I became interested in their history.) I was the one at the cafeteria lunch table who argued that George Sisler was a better first baseman than Lou Gehrig. Someone had to defend the Browns, I reasoned, and living in Central New York, I was far from anyone else who would do such a thing.

Thus Ken Williams became more than a trivia answer to me. I could look up his statistics in the *Baseball Encyclopedia*—this was the late 1970s and early 1980s—but beyond that, information was hard to come by.

A few decades later, there was still little readily available information about Williams. Most of what I read discounted his slugging feats because of the ballpark he played in, Sportsman's Park in St. Louis, which had a closer-than-usual right-field fence. The left-handed-batting Williams thus could, it was suggested, take advantage of that situation.

But was Williams really just a product of the place where he happened to play the majority of his baseball games? Was his apparent power in fact a mirage? There were other questions, too. Why, for instance, did he get such a late start in the major leagues? Most of his big league career unfolded after he turned 30.

The search was on to find as much about Williams as possible. And thanks to the Age of Information that we live in, many of my questions—including those asked above—were answered.

Williams was not a self-promoter, however, and he seldom talked about himself to others.

If asked, he'd be happy to talk about the baseball of his day, but otherwise he kept his thoughts to himself. The things that he was never specifically asked about, then, such as why he batted left but threw right, are likely to remain unknown. We can guess, but not even Williams's own sons knew the answer. And nothing in the available sources so much as broaches the subject.

Reputations can sometimes be falsely made. George Sisler was known as a gentlemanly ballplayer, likely because he was a collegian, an all-around good player, and, as star of the team and later manager, more accessible to journalists. Williams was said to be irascible, primarily because he was quick to argue a call with an umpire, and that reputation followed him throughout his career. Williams loved to hit, and if a strike were called on him that he believed to be a ball, he'd complain. He would do the same in the field and on the basepaths when calls went against his team. But, except for one instance in semi-pro ball, he never got physical with anyone. (Unlike Sisler, the collegian, who once waved his bat at a pitcher and another time hit an umpire.) The point here is that reputations require careful handling by the biographer, particularly when they took form on the printed page more than 100 years ago.

It has also been reported that Williams was a loner, with few friends or none in baseball. He might have kept things close to the vest, but there is no evidence that he lacked friends or was disliked. In fact, the situation appears to have been quite the opposite. Williams was often asked to play in exhibitions and barnstorm, and even managed one of the teams—hardly evidence of someone who had no friends in the game. At old-timers' games and reunions, he was right in there mixing it up with former players, not shunned and off in a corner. No one is around to offer first-person accounts and the truth likely, as usual, falls in between, with a mix of reputation, myth and fact.

If there is anything to the belief that Williams was taciturn or moody, could an incident from his first stint in the majors shed light on it?

While some information about him appears to have been lost to time, as it often is for players of the nineteenth and early twentieth centuries, I've done all that I can to fill in the picture of Williams as both an athlete and a man. In the course of researching this book, I pored over newspapers and magazines from every year of his amateur and professional career, along with those published in the years since. I also spoke with members of the Williams family and dug into the available archival material.

It is my hope that in the pages that follow, the reader will learn much more about Williams than the papers of his day, his contemporaries, or even our advanced statistics alone can reveal.

Chapter 1

Grants Pass and the Semi-Pro Life

They came to see baseball heroes past and present. The dais included Hall of Famers Frankie Frisch, Rogers Hornsby and George Sisler, eventual Hall of Famer Jess Haines, and present-day superstars and future Hall of Famers Stan Musial and Red Schoendienst.

But those at the $10-a-plate dinner honoring the all-time St. Louis all-star team saved their biggest applause of the night for someone who thought he'd been forgotten. The former ballplayer, who had played his last game in the major leagues nearly 30 years prior—and when he did play, was in the shadow of others who played in St. Louis, Sisler and Hornsby, not to mention the immortal Babe Ruth—and who played the majority of his career on a team which no longer existed, took in the unexpected reaction.

Years later in recalling the event, his son, Jack, said his father "never thought that people paid that much attention to him. He didn't realize how well known he really was."[1] Overcome with emotion, the former St. Louis Browns outfielder cleared his throat and managed to utter his words of appreciation: "This is the most wonderful thing that ever happened to me."[2] Ken Williams wasn't forgotten after all.

◆ ◆ ◆

Ken Williams was born June 28, 1890, although for much of his life people thought he was born in 1893. But more on that later.

While there was no generic path to becoming a baseball player in the early 20th century, Williams's journey certainly was different. First off, he was born in Oregon, hardly a hotbed of baseball talent, but also not a very populous state.

The 1890 census shows 317,704 people residing in Oregon—or nearly 30,000 fewer than in Rhode Island. By 1910, that number rose to 672,765, but that still put Oregon far down the list, as 31 states had a population of over 1,000,000, including Oregon's bordering states, California and Washington.

Coincidentally, Ken Williams's father and mother both came to Oregon at roughly the same time. Robert Trimble, Williams's maternal grandfather, moved his family from Iowa—by way of Missouri—to Oregon on ox teams in 1852, settling in Douglas County near Canyonville. Similarly, Williams's paternal grandfather and his family, which included a young son, Brit, headed to Oregon in 1852, settling in Benton County near Corvallis.

Both families took advantage of the Donation Land Act, which provided 320 acres of land to those who were "willing to live upon the land and develop their claims into homes and farms"[3] in the Oregon Territory, which consisted of what we now know as Idaho, Oregon, Washington and part of Wyoming.

Brit Williams, father of Ken Williams. He held many jobs over the years, from gold prospector to teacher to hotel owner (courtesy Larry LaBeck).

Gold fever struck in Oregon around this time. In 1851, it was discovered in the Josephine Creek as well as several other towns in what would soon become Jackson County. In 1859, Oregon became a state. In 1860, Robert and Clementine Trimble had a daughter, Carrie. In 1870, Robert took his family to Josephine County—which had split from Jackson County in 1856—and they settled 10 miles north of the town of Grants Pass.

No one seems to know why Grants Pass is called what it is. Some claimed it was named after Ulysses S. Grant, who had passed through the area. In actuality, Grant never traveled to southern Oregon. No matter; the name stuck (although at first perhaps as Grant's Pass).

The Rogue River traverses Grants Pass, which had to be a draw to gold seekers. Its ideal weather—mild temperatures in the winter and little rain from March to November—would later have the town promote itself with the phrase "It's the climate," which can still be seen on a large sign in the city limits.

Whether for mining gold, the accommodating weather or other reasons, people started to migrate towards south Oregon, although hardly in droves. In 1851, there were 865 people in Josephine County; by 1875 it had increased to 1,400.

Robert Trimble died just a month after arriving in Josephine County, so he would not see the marriage of his daughter seven years later, in 1877, to Brit Williams. According to family legend, special permission was needed for the nuptials to take place, as Carrie Trimble was just 16, ten years younger than Brit. Brit Williams would later dabble in teaching, real estate and hotel management. But early in his marriage, he, like many others in the area, had the gold bug.

Brit and Carrie had a son, Edward, in 1879. In 1880, the three were living with a man named Edward Good in Leland, Oregon, roughly 20 miles south of Grants Pass. In the 1880 census, Good is listed as Williams's partner in the gold mining business, hardly a rarity in Leland, as many occupants of the town listed gold mining as their occupation.

How successful—or unsuccessful—Brit Williams was at mining gold is not known, but his stay in Leland did not last long. The Williams family would move to Merlin, which is roughly 9 miles north of Grants Pass. More sons would follow as well—Henry in 1881, Claude in 1883 and Charles in 1888. There was another son, Wally, who likely died at a young age.

By 1890, the Williamses settled in Grants Pass, which had built up quickly. The town wasn't incorporated until 1887, but there had been a stagecoach station established there in

The Williams boys. Left to right, back row: Henry (b. 1881) and Edward (b. 1879); middle: Claude (b. 1883); front row: Charles (b. 1888) and Ken (b. 1890) (courtesy Larry LaBeck).

1864 and a post office in 1865. Gold would continually be found nearby (it was estimated in 1893 that "$100,000 of gold bullion shipped annually from Grants Pass"[4]), helping establish the town as a city of commerce and entertainment.

By 1892, Grants Pass—now known as the City of Grants Pass—had an opera house, the First National Bank of Southern Oregon, and a store which sold dry goods, boots and shoes. Agriculture, mining and lumber were its primary resources. A dam was built in 1889 to help generate electricity, leading to street lights being installed in 1893.

An 1892 article in the *Oregon Observer* noted, "In 1884, Grants Pass contained but a single habitation; today at 2,500 people."[5] Yet, this was still the 19th century and the majority of people in the United States lived east of the Mississippi. Grants Pass was a product of its time.

When Ken Williams was a child, the streets were dirt roads. This would create a muddy or dusty walk, not to mention having to avoid the droppings from any horse or ox which

might have preceded pedestrians down the street. At the same point, Grants Pass was like any town. People worked at their jobs and kids went to school. The Williams family was no exception.

In 1890, Brit ran a hotel. His sons Ed (fireman), Henry (blacksmith) and Claude (salesman) worked as well, while Charles and Ken attended school. At one point, Ken's fifth grade class was moved to City Hall, where the boys took to throwing rocks at the jail cells below. Since Ken was later noted for his strong arm as an outfielder, one wonders how many prisoners were on the wrong end of a stone hurled by Williams.

Also, and more importantly for Ken, like other towns across the country, Grants Pass had a fascination with baseball. And in 1903, Grants Pass joined the Southern Oregon Baseball League. Soon, Ken Williams would be spending his time not in the classroom, but on the ballfield.

Top: **Ken Williams (right), six-and-a-half years old, with his brother Charles (courtesy Larry LaBeck).** ***Bottom:*** **The home and boarding house owned by Brit and Carrie Williams (courtesy Larry LaBeck).**

Like any small town in America at the turn of the 20th century, there wasn't a lot going on in Grants Pass. Yes, they had an opera house—which would also host traveling acts, such as Maro, the Prince of Magic—and on occasion the circus would eventually pass through (The Greater Norris & Rowe Circus brought "scores of wild trained beasts"[6]).

But Grants Pass was a working, blue-collar town. While gold camps would sprout up around southern Oregon, Grants Pass was mainly a lumber town. There was also a sawmill, a couple of box factories and outfitting shops, plus a number of saloons. There were a large number of saloons before the laws started to limit how many alcohol-serving establishments were allowed until eventually Grants Pass—and Josephine County—became dry on July 1, 1908.

As the *Rogue River Courier* noted on the last night liquor was allowed to be sold, "The ten saloons in Grants Pass closed Tuesday night with a drunken orgie [*sic*] unequalled in the history of the city ... boys as young as 16, who were staggering about the streets in a state of beastly intoxication from 10 o'clock until after the hour of closing, uttering oaths and vulgarity regardless of the passing of ladies and children, in a manner beyond belief in a city which has been heretofore noted for its usual quiet, notwithstanding its ten saloons."[7]

Pity the poor drunkard who passed out in the city's roadways, as in retaliation for losing the ability to sell alcohol, saloon owners helped shoot down a bond to pave the streets. The busy Sixth Street, where a number of shops were located, would not be paved until 1910.

Brit Williams (arrow) and Ken's brother Edward (middle, seated left of Brit) among those pictured in a Grants Pass group photograph (courtesy Larry LaBeck).

Logging was an important industry in Grants Pass and Oregon. Ken's cousins (third and fourth from right) were loggers (courtesy Larry LaBeck).

It is not known if Ken Williams was involved in such debauchery, but he was 18 years old and known to imbibe, like most ballplayers of his era, so it would not be a surprise if he partook in a few last legal drinks.

While the pastime of whiling away the hours drinking was now dead in Grants Pass, another was flourishing—the playing of baseball. There were no major-league teams anywhere near Grants Pass—Major League Baseball wouldn't hit the West Coast until 1958. But baseball was still big, thanks not only to a large number of minor leagues but also amateur and semi-pro community leagues and teams. The local leagues would come and go as town teams folded, reorganized or decided to play elsewhere.

In 1903, when Grants Pass joined the Southern Oregon Baseball League, it did so with Ashland, Medford and Jacksonville. In 1906, with telephones sprouting up all over Josephine County, Roseburg entered the group and Grants Pass was calling its team the American Athletic Club (A.A.C.).

At 16 years old, Williams was not ready for the A.A.C. team just yet. He likely played for the Grants Pass Junior baseball team, made up of high school–aged players—although not necessarily in high school, as Williams stopped attending school after the eighth grade. If coverage was slim for the A.A.C. team in the local papers, it was nonexistent for any team of lesser caliber.

The intrastate games proved to be wildly popular. Players weren't necessarily from the

If Ken Williams hadn't been a baseball player, perhaps he would have gone into logging, like his brother Edward (arm on engine) (courtesy Larry LaBeck).

given town—the star Grants Pass player was Henry Pernoll, who started out with a team in his hometown of Applegate before landing with Grants Pass—but that didn't lessen the enthusiasm.

For a June 12, 1906, game, in which the A.A.C. team beat Ashland 11–0, the *Rogue River Courier* wrote: "The grandstand was packed and literally running over with visitors from the different valley towns and many had to be turned away for lack of even standing room."[8] Led by Pernoll, Grants Pass would win the league in 1906, leading to "a great deal of enthusiasm"[9] for the A.A.C team in 1907.

That enthusiasm obviously did not spread to the players, a number of whom did not return to the team. Perhaps these players went to other local teams. Certainly, Grants Pass wasn't above poaching players from nearby community clubs. After the A.A.C. lost on the road to Medford 14–4 on May 12, after barely winning the week before against the same club at home 8–7 in 11 innings, Grants Pass signed Medford's catcher.

But the star of the A.A.C. team was still Pernoll. It was reported that he had 17 strikeouts in a 5–3 win over Ashland on June 23. In a 2–1 14-inning loss to Medford in the team's season-ending game July 11, Pernoll allowed just two hits and struck out 23—or it might have been six hits and 21 whiffs, depending on which report is to be believed accurate.

These local games could attract some top-quality players. Pernoll's opponent in that Medford game was George "Curley" Cooper, who toiled on various minor-league teams from 1897 to 1904, including the Oakland Oaks of the Pacific Coast League. This also meant that these games could draw the attention of the organized leagues.

Grants Pass is roughly 250 miles from Portland. It also was on the train line to San Francisco, where the Portland Beavers (also known previously as the Portland Giants and Portland Browns) would play PCL games.

In late June, the Beavers stopped at Grants Pass on one of those trips. When they left, Portland had acquired the services of Pernoll, who would join the team in late July when they made the trip through southern Oregon again.

Surely, residents of Grants Pass awaited the news and statistics of Pernoll's foray into professional baseball (and he was big news in town, even years later. When he was sold by Portland to Aberdeen in 1909 for $4,000, it was front-page news in the *Rogue River Courier*). They'd find out he pitched in 21 games, finishing with a 7–12 record and 2.92 ERA.

But, more importantly for Ken Williams, he found out you could be paid to play baseball. And in 1910, when Pernoll debuted for the Detroit Tigers, he'd see that even a guy playing small-town baseball in Oregon could make it all the way to the major leagues. However, first he had to make the local nine.

In 1908, the baseball season began with Fred Roper elected manager and the Grants Pass team—no longer referred to as A.A.C.—holding a 16-player tryout April 3. There is no mention of any names of those who attended the tryout and coverage of the team in the local papers was less than usual that year, but Williams likely attended, as on May 3 his name appeared for the first time in print, playing right field and batting seventh.

The 9–3 win over the Roseburg "Models" was "reported as interesting," according to an article in the *Umpqua Valley News*, "although in some instances the playing on both sides was of the ragged nature."[10]

Williams's name does not appear in any other game stories, of what there were, for the rest of the season, but then again nor does anyone else's. Grants Pass did play a number of games, though, up until September 11, when it beat a team comprised of players from Gold Hill and Jacksonville 4–1.

In 1909, however, it was getting hard to keep Williams's name out of the newspaper. The season began with something of a coup for Grants Pass. The Portland team in the Northwestern League—referred to as "Casey's Colts" after player-manager Pearl Casey—was training in Medford, which is located 30 miles east of Grants Pass. Manager Roper convinced Casey to stage an exhibition game in Grants Pass against the local team.

This wasn't as much a game as it was an event. Many local shops closed during the game so more people could attend. And more people would be needed, as this was not an act of charity by Casey. To help pay the costs of bringing the Portland team slightly west, the cost of grandstand seats was raised from a quarter to 50 cents, although "general admission, which includes the bleachers, remain at 25 cents."[11] A brass band was present and played throughout the game. The Grants Pass team showed up in their new uniforms of "light grey and blue."[12]

The game itself was, of course, no contest. It was indeed a team of professionals, which included 19-year-old Jack Fournier, who would eventually hit .313 over 15 major-league seasons, against small-town amateurs. Portland would win 18–3, but Williams did get mentioned in the *Morning Oregonian*'s roundup. In the third inning, "Williams found an opening and shot one safe"[13] and would eventually score Grants Pass's second run (alas, Portland had scored six times in its first three innings).

Williams would continue to hit for Grants Pass, and he was established as the team's leadoff hitter while playing shortstop. However, the team's results were mixed. Williams had a pair of doubles in the season opener April 4, but Grants Pass lost at home 9–3 to Medford.

In an 8–2 loss at Jacksonville, Grants Pass had only three hits, Williams with one of them. There was instability in the Oregon League as well. Medford drew only 27 people to its 10–6 win over Grants Pass on May 16. On May 19, a new league was announced, of which Grants Pass would be a part.

But these were not concerns of Ken Williams any longer. There were leagues all over the country like the ones Grants Pass played in. These were amateur leagues, meaning players were not paid, but there were ways around that.

In California, the Siskiyou County Baseball League was formed May 2. Four teams would play in the league and an 18-game schedule was established with a promise by league president Chas H. Johnson of "good clean games, free from rowdyism."[14]

Among the four towns in the league was Hilt, which was just over the Oregon border. Hilt wasn't as much a town as it was a lumber camp. Cabins were strewn up in a line in this small town, with a railroad running right next to them. A hotel was on one far side of the town with a few other shops and businesses along the way.

In the middle of the few businesses standing was a baseball field with a small set of wooden bleachers behind home plate. Fans could look out upon the game and the hill in the background, with the cabins and railroad at their back. With little, if any, other entertainment in town, the baseball games were a popular venue for the townfolk, and a brief respite from the hard life they led.

"Everybody at Hilt seems to turn out when there's a baseball show on," according to a report in the June 3 *Siskiyou News*. "It's only a little burg, having only two short streets, in addition to the woods and mill camps, but the grandstand was well filled...."[15]

How Ken Williams made his way to Hilt is not known. He could have been recruited, or heard about the league and ventured on his own. There was a Grants Pass connection to Hilt as well, since in 1902 John Hilt sold his property to four men from the town.

But still, why would Williams move 60 miles from his hometown and be away from his family and friends to live in a small lumber town and play amateur baseball? Probably because the baseball was of the "amateur"—wink, wink—level.

Towns like Hilt would set up players like Williams with jobs—in Williams's case, a position in a box factory. Usually these jobs were easier than most, a security guard for example. But it's not like some players didn't have hazardous duty.

One of Williams's teammates and co-workers, "Curly" Davidson, lost two fingers on his left hand while working on a planer. Less than three weeks later, Davidson was back on the ballfield with a bandaged hand—and he went 2-for-4. Fortunately, Williams didn't have Davidson's misfortune at work and it didn't take him long to establish himself as Hilt's best hitter.

In the team's opening game—an 11–6 win at Yreka (a lumber town roughly 30 miles south of Hilt)—Williams played shortstop and batted second, going 4-for-5 with a double, two triples and a stolen base. Williams was moved to third base for the next game, a 10–3 home win over Yreka, and the local paper dubbed him "a cracker-jack"[16] at that position.

Despite the glowing review of his defense, fielding ground balls would be an issue for Williams throughout his baseball career. It's doubtful he ever had a game worse in the field than he did June 6, 1909, when he committed four errors (Hilt made seven in total, but still beat Hornbrook 10–7).

Even with his occasional difficulties on balls hit on the ground, Williams could be counted on making a number of spectacular plays on those hit in the air. In Hilt's 8–3 win at Hornbrook—which was also the return to action of "Curly" Davidson—Williams made a running catch of a foul fly hit by a batter named Wells (whose first name is lost to time). "It was a hard run," wrote H. Bleacher, a Hornbrook fan, "way over by the fence ... and not many amateur third basemen would have got it."[17]

Williams kept compiling hits no matter his defense. He had one in the above-mentioned win at Hornbrook, another in a 3–1 loss to Sisson (and he scored the lone run). On July 4, Hilt administered a 23–10 shellacking of Hornbrook in which the losers gave up after eight innings, then came back a couple hours later to play Kennett. Trailing 2–1 after seven innings, Hilt took the lead in the eighth with Williams contributing a two-run double. Williams had an RBI hit and scored a run in the ninth as Hilt tallied seven times in winning 16–4.

Hilt had a powerhouse team. They kept winning and Williams kept hitting—he had an RBI double and a steal in a 4–1 win over Yreka on July 18, which would turn out to be the final game in the Siskiyou County Baseball League.

Sisson, which had beaten Hilt twice, had trouble playing its games because it was the furthest of the four cities in the league. The other three teams were grouped together, while Sisson, now known as Mount Shasta, was 60 miles from Hilt and 40 from Yreka. Also, teams just couldn't keep up with the expenses—even in an "amateur" league there was travel and equipment to be taken care of.

But the Hilt team wanted to keep playing baseball. So they'd get townspeople to pony up some money in winner-take-all games. A three-game series was scheduled against, ironically in Williams's case, Grants Pass. Hilt lost the first game 5–3 in 12 innings on July 25 and a $500 purse ($250 from each town) was at stake in the rematch August 1. Williams had a rare 0-fer, going hitless in four at-bats, but Hilt won anyway 6–0.

The rubber match was scheduled to be played August 15 in Medford. But a week before the game, Williams and a pitcher named Wick left the Hilt team. Seeing as how Williams was back in the lineup a week later (and getting two hits as Hilt beat Grants Pass 6–3), whatever differences (likely monetary) there were had been resolved.

Including league games and those played for money, Hilt went 17–6 and, according to the *Siskiyou News*, were "the undisputed champions of Northern California and Southern Oregon."[18] One hopes Williams savored this championship, because he never got another opportunity to properly celebrate a title.

After the season in Hilt ended, Ken Williams retreated back to Grants Pass, as he would do after every baseball season henceforth. While readying for the weather to turn and a return to the diamond, Williams did try his hand at football. In one game in 1910 played just after the new year, Williams was noted for playing "good ball"[19] at halfback in a 0–0 tie against Central Point.

But baseball was Williams's game, and with the dissolving of the Siskiyou County Baseball League, he was back at it in his hometown, playing for the Grants Pass Rogue Valley Merchants team. Williams was established as one of the team's best hitters and fielders, batting third and usually playing third base but also catcher, to likely take advantage of his strong arm.

A 14-game schedule was highlighted by a 5–4 win in 11 innings on June 5 over a Medford team that entered with a 12–0 record. The *Rogue River Courier* dubbed the match "perhaps the best game of baseball ever witnessed in Southern Oregon, and without a doubt the best played in the city."[20]

But the highlight for Williams in 1910 came two weeks later when Portland manager Walter McCredie offered to give the Grants Pass native a tryout when he returned back through the city after a road trip which took his team to California. Portland had a strong team—the Beavers would win the Pacific Coast League championship—and nothing became of it, but Williams was clearly the class of Grants Pass and someone who was playing at a level above his amateur teammates and opponents.

Twelve years later, McCredie recalled seeing Williams for the first time: "The Oakland Oaks had an outfielder on the sick list, and somebody suggested they send to Grants Pass to get Williams to fill in. What a big, gawky, overgrown kid he was! He didn't even know how to wear a baseball uniform and he had a home-made pair of baseball shoes through which he had driven spikes. He was the funniest looking ballplayer I ever saw. But none of us laughed at him the first time he went to bat. All he did was to bust four balls on the nose in as many successive times at bat, every one of them a screeching line drive."[21]

However, when the 1911 season in southern Oregon began, Williams was still playing for Fred Roper and Grants Pass. The first recorded home run for Williams came during a game against the Medford Invincibles at Grants Pass on April 30, 1911. It was noted by the *Medford Daily Tribune* that "Williams of Frants Pass [*sic*] featured the game with a home run in the eighth inning over the right-field fence."[22]

A story told years later by the town's elders claimed that once, in a close game, Williams's father B.A. fainted after seeing his son hit one over the fence. Perhaps the tale stemmed from

A Grants Pass team with Ken Williams (back row, fifth from left), unknown year (courtesy Larry LaBeck).

this late-inning shot. The *Daily Tribune* said Williams played "a star game"[23] in a 6–5 Grants Pass win over Medford the next week when he went 2-for-5 with a double.

Medford was the opponent yet again May 14, and even though Grants Pass lost, Williams was rewarded with a pair of shoes (he chose Paelcards) and some cigars from local businessman H.L. Truax, who among other things was the manager of the Grants Pass opera house, for hitting a home run over the fence in the fifth inning.

Williams continued his hot hitting in the next game against Medford, a 3–2 loss on May 28, with a pair of singles. He also was referred to in the *Medford Daily Tribune* as "Crab"[24] Williams. This was not based on his love of seafood or a peculiar way of walking, but rather Williams's penchant to complain and be upset with umpiring. This was the first time such a trait was pointed out in a newspaper, but it was far from the last. At the tail end of his major-league career, a veteran American League umpire would have this to say about Williams: "The worst moaner I ever worked around was Ken Williams. He got himself in the mood where he thought he couldn't get a close decision. I have seen him running to first base three steps behind the ball and although he knew he was out by two yards he would start yelling—'No! No! No!'—when he got near the bag. He has something to say about every strike that is called on him but he has been talking so long the umpires don't give him a tumble."[25]

It wasn't a crab-like performance Medford saw from Williams in a June 18 game, but more like a bull. In the seventh inning, in front of "the best crowd of the year,"[26] Williams, on first base after singling, took out the Invincibles' popular shortstop Joe McCarthy on a force play. Williams was clearly trying to break up a double play, but according to reports he was out by at least five feet and his hard slide upended McCarthy with such force the shortstop did a "complete somersault."[27]

McCarthy's teammates rushed at Williams while the Grants Pass team, led by the bowler-wearing manager Roper, tried to pry Williams—who was quick to defend himself with his fists—from the melee. Williams got no sympathy other than from his teammates. The Medford team, obviously, went after him; the Invincible fans weren't happy to see one of their favorites treated that way; the umpire—who was from Grants Pass—called Williams out; and the Medford paper was none too kind, calling it "one of the dirtiest plays seen on the diamond this season."[28] There was some praise, though, in a column in the *Medford Daily Tribune* titled "Scoops Around the Infield" written by someone named Arabella.

"Third sacker Williams ... is in my estimation the best infielder in the local ranks," wrote Arabella, "but he has one drawback—his disposition. Always chewing the rag, raising a lick and slipping in a dirty one when he can, he mars what would otherwise be a splendid baseball machine. When he cuts out the rough stuff the fans will be forced to be with him."[29]

Perhaps it was Williams's disposition that was partly responsible for his remaining in the amateur ranks. After all, a few weeks earlier teammate Al Baker, the team's catcher, was reported to have been signed by Boston of the American League and assigned to play in Sacramento of the Pacific Coast League for the rest of the season—which he did, although records indicate he only played in four games with two at-bats and never made it to the majors. Baker would be reunited with Williams soon enough, however.

For his part, Williams kept playing stellar baseball both at the plate and in the field. He was even called on to pitch for Grants Pass in a double-header split with Medford on July 3. The *Rogue River Courier* remained impressed with Williams, as well as a couple of his team-

A Grants Pass team with Ken Williams (front row, second from right), unknown year (courtesy Larry LaBeck).

mates, writing, "The playing of Raber, Weckler and Williams should be cheered until the evening of one's lifetime … and the eye of Williams should be cherished until [*sic*] the field."[30]

A four-team baseball league with teams from Ashland, Central Point, Grants Pass and Medford was to commence starting in late July, but the plans took a hit as Williams and his Grants Pass teammates stood around waiting on the July 23 opener for Central Point to appear, which it never did. A week later, Medford proclaimed, due to a hotter-than-expected summer, it wouldn't play baseball again until September. Ken Williams's baseball playing for 1911 appeared to be over. However, he was soon to rejoin his former teammate Baker.

Sacramento outfielder Jimmy Lewis had been hit in the head by a pitch in early July. While he tried to pinch hit, the *Sacramento Bee* reported that Lewis "is not yet in good condition. Whenever he exercises violently he suffers from pains in the head."[31] The Solons (or Senators, as they were often also called) were in need of some help. As it happens, they were headed to Portland for a six-game series with the Beavers, who had just taken over first place in the PCL (Sacramento was 67–73, in fifth place in the six-team league).

Ken Williams had an offer to play for Sacramento. Williams—who was recommended to Boston by someone named Doyle of Medford, Oregon—had been contacted by Red Sox scout Frank L. Dickinson in early August and signed a contract. Two weeks later he received a telegram from Sacramento player-manager "Patsy" O'Rourke to report to Portland.

The *Rogue River Courier* reported that Oakland of the PCL—on the recommendation of Hub Pernoll—had tried to get Boston to release Williams from his contract so he could sign with the Oaks, but to no avail. Either way, Williams was going to the minors. And just like Baker, he was going from amateur baseball to the Pacific Coast League, one of the highest—if not the highest—caliber minor league. Unlike Baker, Williams would get an opportunity to play.

Williams was put up in a hotel in Portland and was on hand at the Beavers' Vaughn Street Park for the opening game of the series August 22. Clearly he was an unknown quantity among his teammates—save Baker—and manager; reports sent from Portland to the *Sacramento Bee* claimed Williams "has shown considerable class in the small brush around Grant's [*sic*] Pass, Oregon."[32]

With Sacramento losing 5–0 in the ninth inning, Williams stepped to the plate as a professional baseball player for the first time, sent in to hit for outfielder Al Heister—who batted fifth in the lineup—with two runners on base and two out.

Williams stepped to the plate with a familiar batting style, described by the *Rogue River Courier* as "a thousand times like [Hall of Famer Nap] Lajoie's, except the great Frenchman bats right handed."[33] Never intimidated with a bat in his hand, Williams, who had a keen batting eye during his entire career, walked. His professional career didn't start with a bang, but it wasn't a whimper, either.

Williams was back on the bench for the second contest in the series, but he got into the game earlier than the previous day. In the sixth inning, O'Rourke inserted Williams in left field for Heister. He made the most of his opportunity. Williams, who at the time was deemed a "'straight-away' hitter,"[34] had two hits, singling in the sixth and socking a triple to open the ninth inning, and eventually scoring a run. He also made a great running catch on a drive by Portland's Tommy Sheehan in yet another Sacramento loss, this time 5–2.

The game caught the attention of the *Sacramento Bee*, which included Williams in its headline for the game's recap. "NEW OUTFIELDER IS THE BRIGHT STAR OF THE GAME" blared the headline. "Williams, Sacramento's new outfielder is the bright star of the Senators in yesterday's game at Portland."[35]

The Portland paper, the *Oregonian*, which was at the game covering the Beavers, also took notice, writing, "O'Rourke has an awkward individual named Williams doing substitute duty as an outfielder, and the 'greeny' can hit the ball, if nothing else."[36]

Reporters weren't the only ones noticing. Williams caught the eye of O'Rourke as well. Even with Lewis returning to play left field August 24, O'Rourke put Williams in center to replace not Heister, but 40-year-old Deacon Van Buren. Reports later indicated Van Buren was "indisposed,"[37] which could mean Van Buren was ill or Sacramento just wanted to give Williams a chance and this was a way to save face. As both Van Buren and Williams batted left-handed, these are the two most likely scenarios. (Williams did everything else right-handed and both of his sons were right-handed. "I never could understand how he did it, but that's what he did," Ken Williams, Jr., said. "No, he never did [explain it to his sons]."[38]) There was no indication in any of the game reports of an injury to Van Buren.

Regardless of his reason for getting in the lineup, Williams was placed sixth in the order but went 0-for-3 while making one catch in center in yet another Sacramento loss, this time by the score of 5–1. Sacramento went with the same outfield the next day—with Williams again batting sixth. The Solons were handcuffed by Portland's Benny Henderson, who struck out nine (including Williams in the second inning). Sacramento managed just three hits off Henderson, but Williams had one of them—a single—as he went 1-for-3 and made a couple of more plays in the field.

"This chap Williams, who is some awkward [player] right now, looms a most promising ballplayer," wrote the *Oregonian*'s W.J. Petrain. "As soon as the greenness works off he is likely to shine, for he can hit the ball."[39]

Despite being 3-for-8 in his limited time—including a triple and having just one of three Sacramento hits in the previous game—Williams was not in the lineup August 26 as Van Buren returned and Chris Mahoney took Heister's place in the outfield along with Lewis. The game turned out to be a Portland blowout—12–3—and player-manager O'Rourke took some players out of the game early, including himself, but he left his outfield intact.

"Patsy O'Rourke got tired of playing in the sixth inning and sent all of his substitute players into the game except Williams," reported the *Oregonian*. "Why he did not send in Williams, Patsy neglected to explain."[40]

Williams sat out again as Portland won its sixth straight over Sacramento, 3–2 on August 28. The Solons headed out of town and back home for a series against Vernon, with Williams remaining behind. There was no chance Williams was going to be making that trip to Sacramento. It was obvious he was brought in just to fill in while the Solons were in Portland.

Before heading out to Portland, O'Rourke had been talking with the San Francisco Seals about obtaining outfielder Tommy Madden—a 27-year-old left-handed hitting outfielder who appeared in a handful of major-league games in 1906 and one game in 1910. With the brief road trip to Portland, negotiations could continue and Sacramento wouldn't have to use any extra travel expense to get Madden there.

While Sacramento was headed back home, the team announced it had bought Madden. Williams had been thanked for his service, and was told to return to Grants Pass and await further instructions from the Boston Red Sox. The *Sacramento Bee* reported Williams "is under contract to report to Sacramento when the training season opens next year."[41] Or was he?

Williams had been paid for his time with Sacramento that week plus expenses for hotel and his travel to Portland. His salary was prorated at a rate of $150/month. There was no base minimum salary in 1911 for players in the Pacific Coast League, but if there was one, that would be it. That rate over a season—roughly six months—would be $900. In Williams's case, it was one week–$37.50. Williams wanted more than that. He wanted a salary from the Boston Red Sox starting from August 28—the date his payment ended—until the end of the season.

Baseball's governing body at that time was the National Commission, a three-person board made up of the American League president, the National League president and a chairman. In 1911, those three would be Ban Johnson (AL), Thomas Lynch (NL) and August Herrmann (chairman and owner of the Cincinnati Reds). Johnson and Herrmann would be on the commission for its entire existence, from 1903 to 1920, with the board coming to an end when a baseball commissioner was hired.

Williams certainly was putting himself in a precarious position. First, he was an unknown player, an amateur from Oregon who happened to play in a handful of minor-league games. Second, he was taking on a major-league team—the Red Sox—with those deciding his fate all part of the major leagues. Third, he had no agent or lawyer to represent him. He could just state his case and hope for the best. Fourth, in an era of gentlemen's agreements, getting blackballed from organized baseball was not out of the question.

Was risking a potential major-league future worth a few paltry dollars? Certainly

Williams couldn't see the forest for the trees—he was back in Oregon, and the major leagues must have seemed like the furthest of potential realities.

Williams made his claim and the decision was made in November. Apparently not in question were that a Boston scout did contact him and he did play for Sacramento. However, the odds were stacked against him. Boston president Jimmy McAleer claimed to have no idea who Williams was—the team had never heard of him until notified of his claim of due salary. (Of course, McAleer hadn't taken over as president until September—after Williams played for Sacramento—when he bought controlling interest from John Irving Taylor, who had served as the team's president before McAleer.)

McAleer said the Red Sox scout was never given the authority to give Williams a contract. Sacramento, it turns out, had made all the payments to Williams but "paid him for actual service up to the time he was dismissed."[42] *The Sporting Life* reported that "without a contract from or service to that club his demand for pay is dismissed. As neither club asserts title to him the player is declared a free agent by the National Commission."[43]

In other words: No additional pay from the Red Sox and no spring training invite with Sacramento. Just right back to square one, back in Grants Pass as an amateur baseball player and box factory worker. That would have to do, for a little while longer at least.

Chapter 2

O Canada: The Path to Pro Ball

There was always baseball to be played in Grants Pass and Ken Williams could take advantage of that. With his request for more money from the Boston Red Sox denied and no other professional prospects, Williams once again took the field in 1912 for his hometown team once the weather permitted.

He would play where needed—third base and pitcher, thanks to his strong arm, and first base as well. The *Rogue River Courier* even featured a cartoon of Williams with the caption "Playing First Base is Easy for 'Dinkey'"—Dinkey, or Dinky, being an ironic nickname as Williams was 6 feet tall in an era when the average male his age was 5-foot-8—"He refused to accept renumeration for his artisty."[1]

Williams easily could have been called "Dinky" in the next stop on his baseball path—after all, he was taller than anyone else on the team (most of them by at least 4 or 5 inches)—but he would pick up a new nickname, one which befit his prowess at the plate: Home Run Williams.

In addition, he also found a way to get paid to play baseball—at least indirectly. In late June, Williams headed to Weed, California, to play for that town's team. Weed, like Hilt, was a lumber town. It was estimated that in 1910 there were 1,500 to 1,800 laborers in Weed, which has a view of nearby Mt. Shasta. But this was not a town for families to settle, but a town of purpose. And that purpose was lumber.

"The Weed Lumber Company has one mill running daily and expects to have both running soon," according to an article in the *Siskiyou News* in 1910. "The company is now shipping from eight to twelve carloads of shook and doors daily to Southern and Eastern points. The company is building a new warehouse for additional room for the door department, and on top of it is to be installed an up-to-date electric searchlight.... [This] will prevent many small and petty robberies which are continually being committed in Weed."[2]

Williams would play baseball while also working in one of these lumber warehouses—the Weed Lumber Company store, which had "W.L. Co. Store" emblazoned on the team uniform. "Weed is one where they hired you so you could play ball. You worked, but not real hard,"[3] recalled Jack Williams, Ken's youngest son.

Williams quickly gained the reputation as a longball hitter, and the fans were disappointed when he didn't hit a home run. And, at times, he was, too. After a rare loss by Weed—18–7 at home to Yreka on July 28—the *Siskiyou News* reported, "Home Run Williams could not connect with the little pellet although the grandstand and bleachers urged and implored him to live up to his past performances. In his last appearance at the rubber, after popping a foul to Calkins [the third baseman], he turned in disgust and deliberately flung his bat high over the grand stand and into the tall pines beyond. A bit of a temper, eh?"[4]

Williams's reputation as one who "crabs" had followed him as well, although he kept his temper in check during an August 4 game at Medford, much to the chagrin of some spectators. Williams went 3-for-4 (or 2-for-5, depending on the report, one of which ruled an error on one of his hit balls), scored a couple of runs and drove in another while playing spectacular defense in front of a crowd of around 1,000, including 150 from his hometown of Grants Pass.

But, as T.F. Handley wrote in the *Rogue River Courier*, "Williams also perturbed old friends by his elimination of crabbing, behaving with the urbanity of a cavalier and the dignity of a lord chief justice."[5] The hometown faithful needn't have worried, though, as Williams "ragged a little" in an August 18 win at Weed over Medford, "but that's his way and the fans enjoyed it."[6]

The fans also enjoyed his hitting and the winning—Weed won a number of games and was pronounced the "Champions of Northern California and Southern Oregon" in a postcard displaying the team members.

Williams's 1912 season in Weed was a successful one, and in 1913 he would once again head south to join an amateur/semi-professional team. But that detour would be a short one. The direction would take an unexpected turn, as he was finally about to embark on his professional career. Williams would end up not traveling south to play pro ball, but north. Far north. In fact, he'd be leaving the United States.

◆ ◆ ◆

The Weed baseball team, self-proclaimed champions of Northern California in 1912. Ken Williams is fourth from the left (courtesy www.sportingoregon.com).

The town of Regina, Saskatchewan, was looking to get back in the baseball business. The city had fielded a team in the Western Canada League in 1909 and 1910. But teams came and went from the WCL and Regina was without a team in 1911 and 1912.

The Western Canada League only had four teams in 1912 and was looking (once again) to reorganize. Two of its franchises—Bassano and Red Deer—were not going to return, although the management of those clubs made sure to reserve their players' contracts so they were not free to sign with anyone else, as was teams' right.

"The Western Canada League might readily be called 'The League of Uncertainties,'" wrote *The Sporting News*. "Uncertain each year as to what cities shall comprise its circuit, for as yet no two years have we witnessed the same circuit; uncertainty on various occasions as to whether the organization could weather the storm and finish the season, and uncertainty on the part of the players in different cities, as to whether their pay check would be forthcoming."[7]

Regina was undergoing a major reconstruction. A cyclone in June 1912 wiped out much of the town. But buildings were quickly being rebuilt or restored in what the *Regina Leader* described as the "greatest development in the history of the city of Regina."[8]

With the renewal of Regina came the desire of having a baseball team to root for by the city's inhabitants, even in an uncertain league like the WCL, which operated on the lowest rung of organized baseball's ladder.

Almost to prove the point that city residents were behind a team, this was a public offering. Shares in the team were being sold at the rate of $25 with a total of 800 shares the goal. By March, Regina had raised $20,000 in capital—all 800 shares had been sold. Regina, along with Medicine Hat, Moose Jaw and Saskatoon, would join holdovers Calgary and Edmonton for the 1913 WCL season.

For a manager, it was announced on March 3 that the team hired Billy Hamilton, who just happened to have an interesting past. For one thing, his name was really Billy Hulen. Hulen played mostly in the minor leagues during his playing career, but he did get some time in the majors and still holds the record for most games played at shortstop by a natural left-handed thrower (a record which likely will live on in perpetuity) when he appeared in 78 games at that position for the 1896 Philadelphia Phillies.

After a few years in the minors—with a brief stint back in the majors in 1899 with Washington—Hulen bought the Colorado Springs franchise in the Western League. As he collected money from local boosters, he promised a winning team. Instead, he reportedly played school-aged kids and the team floundered. Hulen sold the team the next year and left with a nice-sized profit, much to the chagrin of the town faithful.

In 1902, Hulen said he was headed home to Ashland, Oregon, where he owned a ranch, to visit his wife. Only he never showed up and was presumed dead. Instead, he was playing baseball under the name Billy Hamilton until he was found out in 1906.

Hamilton, or, Hulen, did have experience managing in the Western Canada League, as he helmed Medicine Hat in the league's 1909 incarnation. But he had been out of baseball ever since, opening up a cigar store in Roseburg, Oregon, as well as holding interests in several mining companies around Southern Oregon.

The *Regina Leader* paraphrased a letter dated from Hulen (signed as Hamilton), reading, "He is confident that he can get a first class team together although he will not guarantee to land the championship."[9] Apparently, Hulen had learned a small lesson from his time in Colorado Springs.

All Hulen needed now was players for a team which hadn't existed a year earlier, thus had no one under contract. Some teams in the WCL scouted the camps of higher minor-league teams and awaited their castoffs. For Hulen, who once owned a ranch in Ashland and was now setting up shop in nearby Roseburg (about 100 miles to the north), Oregon was a logical spot to set up base.

A good number of the players Hulen secured under contract he found in Oregon. There was Al Baker, the catcher who played for Grants Pass and had a brief foray with Sacramento; Earl Hill, a first baseman from Portland; D.W. Rankin, who had pitched semi-pro ball around Oregon; and the Hargraves brothers—Art and Jack—born in Canada, but who most recently had played semi-pro in Roseburg. There was also a D. Williams—as in Dinky—an outfielder from Grants Pass.

◆ ◆ ◆

Ken Williams was actually in California when he was asked to join the Regina team. He was planning on yet another year of semi-pro baseball, playing for Woodland. He didn't get the chance to see too much action, but the little he did see made quite an impression. A decade later it was remembered, "Williams poled out three home runs in his first three steps to the plate and after that the opposing pitcher kept the ball far out of his reach."[10]

While some players held out for more money—it was called the "Rube Marquard effect,"[11] after the New York Giants pitcher who held out for more money following a 26–11 season in 1912—Williams was one of those who signed on early with Regina.

The salary wouldn't be great. The Western Canada League had troubles in the past with teams spending too much. In 1910, for example, the league had an $1,800 per month limit—for the entire roster. Yet teams quickly went over $2,000 and later up to $2,700. For 1913, the WCL was imposing a cap of $1,500/month.

So if everyone made the same salary (which was doubtful), Williams would pocket around $428 (roughly $107 a month with a 14-man roster), assuming he stayed healthy. According to the Bureau of Labor Statistics, that would equal the buying power of $10,434.25 in 2016. This was, after all, Class D ball, the lowest class of organized baseball. But it sure beat working in a factory during the week and only getting to play baseball on the weekends.

Williams left California and headed back to Grants Pass to collect his things. He missed by a week the opportunity to play for Grants Pass against the Chicago American Giants, a traveling Negro Leagues team led by the enigmatic Rube Foster. But he did make it back to Grants Pass in time to play for the local team against Portland of the Northwestern League.

In the top of the 10th inning and the score tied at 1, Williams fielded a ground ball with the bases loaded by future major-league pitcher Carl Mays and threw home to Baker for the force, but Baker's throw to first base to complete the double play sailed into right field and two runs scored.

In the bottom half of the inning, Williams stepped to the plate with two outs and Baker on second base with the score still 3–1. Mays, who won 22 games the previous year for Boise in his first season of pro ball and who would win 208 games in the majors, was on the mound.

The hometown faithful "called for 'Dinky' Williams for one of his old, familiar home runs for his farewell before he left to join Regina."[12] On Mays's second pitch, Williams obliged, knocking the ball well over the right-field fence, sending the crowd into a frenzy.

There was just one problem. Before the game, fearing a Portland hitting assault, Grants

Pass had asked that any ball hit over the fence count only as a double, to which Portland agreed. Williams's hit thus had only made the score 3–2, and when the next batter grounded out, the game was over. (This didn't stop the *Oregon Observer* from calling the game a 3–3 tie.)

Ken Williams's days as an amateur ballplayer were over. It was now time to start his professional career. Regina held its first workout April 11 in Roseburg. There would be practices twice a day, in the morning and early afternoon. On April 15, Regina played its first game, heading to Corvallis to play the Oregon Agricultural College (later to be known as Oregon State).

Williams might have wondered if he was still playing semi-pro ball. Playing against a college team on a field befitting the poorest of amateur clubs, the teams combined for 18 errors (and just 14 hits, seven apiece). Williams, though, had no miscues and went 2-for-5, singling in his first two at-bats, and made a couple of catches in left field.

It didn't take long for Williams to stand out among his peers. Just two days after the game, he was widely praised in a report in the *Regina Leader*. He was called the "'moose' of the squad," and it was noted that he "showed up well in gathering fast grounders and in whipping the ball around the bases. But it was in batting that Williams shone.... [He] hits it hard, and is one of the best sluggers on the squad."[13]

The paper already surmised Williams would make the team, although what position was unknown. Third base was seemingly occupied by Jimmy Irwin. Williams had a strong arm, so he could pitch. But outfield was his likely destination.

Rain played havoc with Regina's training, but even when the team could play, it was only against college teams and on fields which weren't in the best of condition. Nevertheless, Williams's talent was evident and as the team wound up its training, it was noted that he "appears to be a fixture in left field."[14] The team broke camp May 2 as Hulen released three players—including third baseman Irwin—to get down to 15 players and headed to Medicine Hat for the season opener.

"With the WCL salary limit I work on I could not get National or American League ballplayers, but I got the next best thing,"[15] Hulen said with his usual bluster. The fact was most of the players on the Regina team had never played in organized baseball. The *Edmonton Journal*, however, picked Regina as well as Edmonton and Saskatoon for best bets on finishing in the first division.

But money certainly was going to be an issue. Dominion Park, where Regina would play its home games, was in need of serious repair. The town had hoped to raise money to fix it up with season-ticket sales—$10 would be good for admission to 50 events at the park—but purchases were slow. Eventually $300 was accumulated and put forth for repairs, with work beginning immediately so the park would be in shape for when Regina opened its home season May 8.

Hulen did pay $5 each for the team's jackets to go with their uniforms for the team now known as the Regina Red Sox. The coats were "maroon with large white buttons,"[16] while the jersey was gray with maroon stripes and "Regina" in red letters across the chest.

Paying $5 for a coat was fine, but $4 for a hotel proved to be too much. Upon arrival in Medicine Hat, the team took up at a hotel and had dinner. But after eating, they were told the rate of $4 a night. Regina's budget was already thin, so Hulen had the team pack up and find an establishment with a cheaper rate.

The opener in Medicine Hat on May 5 was preceded by an automobile parade at 1:30 p.m. with the game beginning at 3. Fans lined the streets and the stadium with megaphones in hand, many wearing the orange and green of the hometown Hatters.

As expected, Ken Williams was in left field in his first opening day as a professional. He also was batting fourth, demonstrating that indeed he was considered among the best of the hitters on the club. Williams went 0-for-3 in that game and even made an error (one which was deemed "excusable, the condition of the grounds being mainly responsible"[17]), but unlike his brief time with Sacramento in 1911, he was on the winning side.

The cold weather was fine for fans in the opener, but only 600 turned out for the next game, with Williams again in left field. He got his first hit—a single—but was doubled off first base following a pop out. In the eighth, Williams collected his first RBI with a triple, but Regina fell 6–4.

Getting doubled off first base was a part of Williams's game—he was aggressive on the basepaths. He showed the positive side to that in Regina's third game when he went from first to third on a sacrifice bunt. He also showed off another part of his game—power—rapping a double and triple, both of which scored runs in a 5–3 win.

The Red Sox would leave Medicine Hat after the game and wouldn't arrive in Regina until 5 a.m., but they had to feel buoyed after taking two of three in their first series. They arrived to a city hungry for baseball.

May 8 was declared a city holiday by Regina Mayor Robert Martin, declaring all businesses must be closed at 4 p.m., 30 minutes before the first pitch. "Baseball may not be the national game," Martin declared, "but it is certainly the most popular game in Canada today."[18]

At City Hall, Martin welcomed the team to the city and made other grandiose statements. Then, at 3:30 p.m., a parade to the Dominion Park began. The Imperial band led the way with players following behind in automobiles. It was noted that the players were all smiles, but with the frigid temperatures, perhaps their mouths were frozen open.

Dominion Park was being worked on feverishly for this opening game, but it was not quite ready. The grandstand was not completed—the roof still needed some work—although two bleachers had been erected. A grandstand seat would cost a patron 50 cents—25 cents to get onto the grounds and another 25 cents for the seat. Children's tickets were discounted at 10 cents. And on opening day, people paid.

With professional baseball back in Regina, nearly 5,000 people packed the park. There weren't enough seats to house the fans, many of whom "wore miniature red and gray socks, had streamers of like color and holding megaphones."[19] Many fans lined up on the first-base side, others around the outfield. The crowd included some women, as it was noted that "all the ladies in the vicinity of left field were agreed that Mr. Williams certainly has a fine voice."[20] As was custom in the day, it was decided if a ball was hit into the crowd, it would count as a double.

The game itself was not well played. The weather was brisk and the field not in great shape. Nevertheless, the large crowd went home happy as Regina won 13–10, with Williams scoring four of those runs and going 3-for-4 with a triple.

The crowd wasn't as large on May 9, but the paid attendance was still 1,450. Once again, Williams put on a show with his daring base running and pure power. After walking to lead off the second inning, Williams was picked off, yet again a little too aggressive. But that style paid off in the fourth as he went from first to third on a bunt and scored as the throw to third was wild.

Then it was time for Williams to flex his muscles. He led off the sixth inning with a triple—the fourth consecutive game in which he had a three-bagger—and scored. In the seventh he hit a deep fly to left field that bounced off an automobile parked in fair territory, causing the *Regina Leader* to grouse, "Just because the rooters are allowed to bring the 'bull' inside is no reason why auto owners should bring their car in and crowd up the fielders. Why not leave the cars on the outside?"[21]

Regina won the game 7–3—Williams scoring three times—to give the Red Sox a 4–1 record. As the team left for Moose Jaw, little did they know this would be their high point of the season. Starting in Moose Jaw and moving on to Edmonton and Calgary, Regina lost six straight games. Williams, while still hitting (.354, third in the league), made a couple more outs on the basepaths, including being thrown out at home trying to score on a fly ball and getting injured in the process (although he'd miss just one game and was pinch-run for in another, but he would continue to play in the latter).

In a 13–7 loss May 10 in the first game of a double-header, Williams was used as a pitcher for the first time. He pitched three innings, allowing two hits—including a double that plated two runs—while walking one, hitting two batters and striking out three.

The Red Sox managed to split a double-header against Calgary on May 17, but five straight losses followed—as did a roster shakeup. Johnny Mackin, who had played in Edmonton the previous two seasons but was now umpiring in the Western Canada League, would be brought in to play second base. In addition, it was reported that Hulen was bringing in six other players.

Williams's job, though, was safe. From May 15—the day he came back from his injury—to May 22, he went 10-for-27 (.370). Of course, by May 22, Regina had also sunk to last place. Playing on a cellar dweller certainly didn't help, but being a professional ballplayer did not quash Williams's sometimes temperamental attitude.

Umpire B.S. McDonald was chastised by the *Regina Leader* for his "wretched exhibition of umpiring"[22] in the May 26 game—a Red Sox win, no less. The next day, Williams drew a $5 fine from McDonald for his constant yelling from left field at the umpire, who "insists [the fine] will have to be paid."[23] The *Leader* relayed that McDonald told the paper, "Williams kept directing uncomplimentary remarks at him, and he took it all in good part, although it was very painful. The Regina player was most offensive with his tongue, and was deserving of the punishment meted out to him."[24]

This likely didn't sit well with the fans, and after the May 31 game—another Regina loss, 12–7 to Edmonton—McDonald needed a police escort to a waiting car as fans came onto the playing field and threatened to surround him.

Williams gave fans something to cheer about, albeit briefly, on June 4. In the third inning he hit a ball deep over Saskatoon center fielder Roy "Rube" Mills's head and circled the bases for the first home run of his professional career (and also the first home run by anyone that season at Dominion Park). Williams repeated the trick in the sixth inning, only this time was out at home.

Regina, of course, lost that game, 9–7, and the tide was turning for Red Sox fans. Once grateful just to have baseball being played in their city, now Regina started doing an about-face on its team. The good feeling from opening day just a month earlier was well past gone.

Hulen tried to appease the fans by making changes on the roster. Despite a league mandate to cut down to 12 players, Hulen brought in a few players from Chicago. Originally advertised as former White Sox players, in reality they came from a semi-pro team owned by that team's manager, Jimmy Callahan.

With the changes, Hulen needed a shortstop and moved Williams there for a June 6 double-header. After Williams committed five errors in the two games—including the only three he had hit to him in Game 2—he was back in left field June 7.

Not that these moves helped. With its team getting pounded in an eventual 14–2 loss and dropping to 8–27, Regina fans started to cheer for the Saskatoon team instead. The *Regina Leader*, once in the corner of the franchise, echoed the sentiments being expressed at Dominion Park:

> [The fans] showed that not only has Billy Hamilton Hulen failed to get the sort of ball players that Regina wants, but that he has failed to teach his pupils, such as they are, the first essentials of inside—and for that matter outside—baseball.
>
> Saturday night the Red Sox, such as they are, shot their bolt. They disgraced themselves, and they disgraced the town which has been giving whole hearted, and, best of all, financial support.[25]

Hulen kept making moves, cutting six more players and adding a few more from Chicago, including 17-year-old outfielder Jack Smith, who, like Williams, would enjoy a long major-league career. When Regina took the field June 17, just a month and a half after its first game, only four players were left from the Red Sox opening day roster.

Hulen actually didn't cut enough players, as the mandate was to have 12 players per roster. That drew a pair of $100 fines to the Red Sox from the league and a suspension for Hulen. The latter action got Hulen's attention: he dismissed three more players June 21, and pitcher Calvin Newman was cut a few days later.

Regina wasn't the only one with roster problems. WCL president Frank Gray expelled Saskatoon manager Bill Hurley and the players on that team because they refused to cut down to 12 players. The Quakers were playing with 14 on their roster (13 when they went on the road) and were doling out $1,820 a month, over $300 above the salary limit. Edmonton manager Ray Whisman was suspended for also ignoring the roster mandate and for blatantly exceeding the salary limit as well.

Through all the turnover and turmoil, Williams kept hitting. Back in the outfield—he was rotating between all three spots—he had a 15-game hitting streak from June 9 to July 3 (missing five games in the middle due to an unknown injury). He hit his second home run in a 2–2 tie against Edmonton on June 24. In true Regina luck, the Red Sox took a 4–2 lead in the seventh, but it started raining and the game could not continue, so it reverted back to the sixth-inning score.

Regina—and every other team—was granted a reprieve when it was decided to play the season in two halves. Sasaktoon was declared the winner of the first half (Regina was 13–34, 21½ games out of first place) and would play the second-half winner in a championship series. Teams would begin the second half with a fresh 0–0 record. All suspensions were revoked. A 12-man roster limit was enforced with a $1,500/month salary cap.

A second-half reset wasn't incentive enough for two Regina players who up and left the team. One of those was Earl Hill, one of the four remaining players from opening day. Pitcher Sam Beer, another one of the original four, was then dealt to Saskatoon for three players, as the Red Sox had to now fill a void with two of their 12 gone.

The rebirth worked for Regina for a moment, at least, as the Red Sox won three of their first four games in the second half. Four games or not, it was enough for the *Regina Leader* to declare "Red Sox Take Lead in League Race"[26] in a headline. The good times didn't last. Regina was swept by Medicine Hat in a double-header on July 9 (including making 12 errors in Game 1, although Williams had none), but Williams kept garnering notice, and not just from the local fans.

In the second game of the double-header, Williams smashed a ball—"one of the longest drives ever seen on the local diamond"[27]—to left-center field for a home run. In attendance was a Detroit Tigers scout. The Tigers also had a scout at the Red Sox's June 30 game in Moose Jaw when Regina was two-hit by the Robin Hoods—with Williams collecting one of them.

After the double-header was completed, it was announced that the Tigers picked up an option on both Williams ($1,500) and Jack Smith ($1,000), with the agreement that neither player could be recalled until after Regina's season ended. Williams would write his parents of the transaction and said he was expected to report to Detroit in September. Nothing would come of it, but after playing all those years on Sundays in Southern Oregon and Northern California, it took only a couple of months of professional baseball for Ken Williams to prove he was major-league material. Major-league material, perhaps, but for the time being Williams was stuck with one of the worst minor-league teams in all of organized baseball.

It didn't take long for Regina to fall into last place with a 5–14 record. By that point the Red Sox had a new manager: Hulen resigned July 18, with catcher Heine Krueger taking his place. (Hulen in short time would land a job as a scout for Pittsburgh, causing *The Sporting News* to wonder, "It's odd how a man who can't pick players who will win in Class D can get a job picking them for the majors."[28])

Hulen, Krueger … it didn't matter. The defeats continued to pile up as Regina lost 15 in a row. A losing streak is one thing, but the Red Sox were playing sloppy baseball. After a 10–2 loss to Saskatoon in which Regina committed seven errors and had only five hits, the *Edmonton Journal* wryly observed, "Regina again suffers defeat in the way fans became accustomed to."[29] It was so bad that a 3–11–1 road trip was termed "one of the most successful trips abroad"[30] by the *Regina Leader*.

Williams's hitting wasn't as strong as in the first half when he batted .360, fourth-highest in the WCL, but he proved himself worthwhile in other ways—as a pitcher. At Edmonton on August 22, Williams pitched a rain-shortened seven-inning, two-hit shutout. "Williams signal victory in the box proves him to be one of the best all-round men chasing the hide in the Western Canada League today,"[31] proclaimed the *Edmonton Journal*.

With attendance dwindling in Regina—crowds of 250 were being reported—the team searched for a drawing card. It turned to Williams as the season was drawing to a close. Looking to pack the park in a year-ending double-header, the team placed an ad in the local paper announcing "WILLIAMS will pitch one game."[32]

"The big fellow is very popular with the fans," stated an article in the *Regina Leader*, "and as a pitcher he should be a big drawing card."[33] Williams didn't disappoint, pitching in the first game and beating Saskatoon 8–3 in front of 1,200 fans.

"With speed galore and a fancy assortment of curves, 'Dink' was the man of the hour, and it is doubtful if the Quakers travelling in mid-season form could have fared better than they did Saturday at his hands," reported the *Regina Leader*. "As an all-round player, Williams has (or had) no superiors in the W.C.B.L. and this he proved conclusively when he assumed the role of 'twirler' ... even [Walter] Johnson's record would have been knocked to the boards had he played the role of twirler earlier in the season."[34]

Despite the accolades for his pitching, Williams's true strength was with his bat. Despite slipping in the second half—playing every day and a full minor-league schedule likely taking its toll on someone used to appearing on weekends during the summer—he hit .292, good for 14th in the league. He easily was the best hitter on Regina, which hit just .208 as a team.

In 101 games, Williams had 359 at-bats with nine doubles, 13 triples, and five home runs (of Regina's 11), with 57 runs and 12 stolen bases. Regina, though, was just 16–44 in the second half and there was such lack of interest in the club that the local paper didn't even report the final box scores in the last road trip in early September.

The team's poor finish didn't reflect poorly on Williams, though, who was considered one of the best players—if not *the* best—in the league. He was even tabbed by *The Sporting News* as someone who showed "signs of being worth a trial higher up."[35]

Naturally, after a fine season and nice press clippings, Williams wanted what other players—no matter the era—did: more money. The good news for Williams was the Western Canada League had agreed to up its salary limit from $1,500/month to $1,800/month (manager excluded).

The bad news was Regina hired a new manager who didn't care to put up with holdouts, and the Red Sox had a few (it was also reported the entire Moose Jaw squad was holding out for up to $50 more a month). Charlie Stis, who was a player-manager in Peoria from 1911 to 1912 and played for the St. Louis Federal League team in 1913, was hired by Regina in November and quickly sought out new players to turn the roster over following that dreadful 1913 season.

While Stis (and most managers) did not have patience for a player holding out, it didn't help Ken Williams's cause that he wasn't the kind of player Stis liked to have on his team. Stis didn't drink or smoke, and wanted the same from his players. Williams, like the majority of ballplayers from that era, did both. The *Regina Morning Leader* compared Stis to Connie Mack, and noted Stis also "believes in the intelligent, educated player."[36] Williams, who was done with school after the eighth grade, certainly did not fit that criterion, either.

Slowly the number of holdouts decreased. Ace pitcher Art Bottoroff (or Bottorff or Butteroff, depending on the day and paper) agreed to a "reduced stipend"[37] in mid–February. Outfielder Jack Smith signed on shortly thereafter, and Stis claimed he was fine with an outfield of Smith, Joe Zoellers (who had played with Stis in St. Louis in 1913) and Gilroy (perhaps Thomas Gilroy, who played with Cleveland in the Fed League the previous year).

That left only Williams and pitcher Duke Rankin as returning players unsigned, and that was reduced by one when Rankin informed the club he would be unable to play in 1914. Regina placed him on the suspended list, and Rankin never played professional baseball again. Stis issued an "ultimatum"[38] to Williams in early March. What happened next is a bit confusing.

It was reported in the March 18 *Regina Morning Leader* that Red Sox secretary Pyke, whose main job was as manager of the United Typewriter Company's Regina branch (although he'd resign from his post with the Red Sox in May after being promoted by United Typewriter to its Winnipeg branch), received a signed contract from Williams. This was also about the time Williams was starting to be regularly called "Bill Williams" in the newspaper. His given name, Kenneth, was not deemed masculine enough for a baseball player.

Despite this report, Williams was in Woodland, California, weeks later, having signed and once again playing shortstop for the local semi-professional team there in their Trolley League. But after a handful of preseason games, the *Woodland Daily Democrat* noted Williams was headed north to play in Canada, "having received a flattering offer to play with the same team he was with last season."[39]

Williams made his way to the YMCA in De Soto, Iowa, where the Red Sox team was staying while training in that town. De Soto was about 1,000 miles from Regina, still making it a couple of hundred miles closer than the previous season's training spot.

It didn't take long for Stis to declare Williams would be his right fielder (Smith was in center and Zoeller in left; Gilroy wasn't long for the roster). Williams rewarded the announcement with two hits in an April 14 game against Muscatine and a three-run homer against the same team April 17. He also had a key run-scoring hit in a 3–0 win over Cedar Rapids on April 22 and a two-run double in a 6–4 win over Winona on April 25.

With Regina's Dominion Park in no shape to host a baseball game, the Red Sox began the 1914 season on the road in Medicine Hat. Things started slowly for Williams, who was hitless (0-for-3) in the opener and two days later was put in to pitch in a blowout, and was tagged for seven runs in three innings.

Regina played its home opener May 11 with little fanfare—no parade, no grand speeches—but 3,000 did show up. The fans would recognize just three players from the previous year's team—Williams, Smith and Bottorff (Botteroff/Butteroff). Williams went 2-for-5, his sixth straight game with a hit after that 0-fer to open the season, but for the third straight game he made an error.

On May 15, Regina found itself in an unfortunately familiar spot—last place, with a 3–6 record. Williams was hitting respectably enough (15-for-58, .259), but only had two extra-base hits, a double and triple, although he did have three stolen bases. However, his percentage .824, second-worst on the team to Luther "Casey" Smith, who was at .813 due to 12 errors in 12 games.

Williams flashed some of his defensive prowess May 16, making a spectacular catch in deep right field, and on May 20 from right threw out Edmonton's Jack Goldie at home as he tried to score from second base on a double (Goldie was momentarily frozen, thinking Williams was going to get to the ball).

Through it all, Williams, as would usually be the case for the entirety of his career, continued to hit. In a May 16 double-header sweep of Saskatoon he went 5-for-9 with a triple and a stolen base. In that May 20 game he socked a "mammoth home run drive"[40] to center field. On May 22, he hit another triple and would have stolen home due to a tremendous jump from third base if Casey Smith hadn't bunted him in. In a May 23 double-header, Williams was 4-for-10 with his fourth triple of the season and another stolen base as Regina (8–8) moved into second place.

The tide turned a bit for Williams on May 27. While he did go 1-for-4 with an RBI single, he also was picked off third base shortly after stealing it. In that game, Stis took Jack Smith out of the game and fined him $10 for dropping a fly ball and then not hustling after it (although he rescinded it after Regina ended up winning, 5–3 over Moose Jaw).

Due to the Smith incident and his baserunning error, perhaps Williams was looking over his shoulder the next day when he dropped a fly ball, allowing a run to score. Stis didn't bench Williams, but he did shake up the lineup, moving Williams to third in the order and benching Zoellers.

Things appeared OK for Williams to remain in the lineup. He went 3-for-7 on May 30 as Regina split a double-header with Edmonton. On top of that, Zoellers had taken ill and didn't make a road trip to Moose Jaw; he was rumored to be cut as the Red Sox had to release one player "within a few days."[41]

Regina's road trip did not start well. Third baseman Bill Henry was hit in the head during practice and the Red Sox lost to Moose Jaw 10–1. Williams went 0-for-4, but scored Regina's lone run. Then the rains came, wiping out the next four days' worth of games. But Ken Williams wouldn't be around for the last one.

On June 4, there was a new face in the clubhouse–Miles Netzel, who happened to be an outfielder and, like Williams, batted left-handed. Netzel had been playing with Portland of the Northwestern League and hit .312 with Spokane of the same league in 1911. Netzel also spent a brief time in 1909 with the Cleveland Naps of the American League. Charlie Stis immediately put Netzel's name in the lineup and in right field for the soon-to-be washed out June 4 game. On June 5, Williams was released by Regina.

The *Regina Leader* claimed the Red Sox "expected greater returns but Bill so far has not been batting up to form.... His failure to show up in batting has been a keen disappointment."[42] At the time of his release, Williams was hitting .299, fifth best on Regina—and two of those ahead of him were pitchers.

Without a team, Williams was unsure of his next move. He claimed he had a chance earlier in the season to jump to the Federal League—which was trying to establish itself as the third major league—and there were rumors of offers from clubs in that league. But Federal teams were likely more interested in boosting their image with major leaguers, not a player cut from a Class D minor league—in Canada, no less.

It turned out Williams didn't wait long to land elsewhere, though. Edmonton was in need of an outfielder. The club had released aging Pat Moran in late April; one reason for his poor play was an excuse heard often in the more modern era: "[H]e has too much money and he refuses to put his heart in the game."[43]

Then in early June, the Eskimos saw two of their outfielders suffer maladies: Buss Povey broke an ankle sliding into third, and Jack Goldie stepped on a piece of glass and had trouble even walking. And that's not to mention their shortstop, Foot Ruell, who was hit by a pitch and could barely lift his right arm.

Edmonton was quite the opposite of Regina. They had a nice ballfield—Diamond Park. Regina's Dominion Park was labeled "the worst park in the circuit"[44] by the *Edmonton Journal*. While fans could be scarce at Red Sox games, an oil boom in Edmonton had the town burgeoning (there had been but 15 buildings and a population of 50 just 15 years previous), people flush with money and in good spirits. The Eskimos drew better crowds than the Red Sox despite a worse record and were generally well supported financially.

Even the uniforms of Edmonton were classier. When Williams arrived he was given the home whites, which included over the left breast a blue diamond with a white script 'E' in the center. (The Eskimos' road uniform was blue with gray stripes and EDMONTON spelled downward in the middle of the shirt.)

Rain spoiled Williams's debut, and perhaps he joined his many of his new teammates at one of the vaudeville shows around town. Poor weather limited the crowd to around 750 when Williams did make his first appearance for the Eskimos on June 9. He batted cleanup for Edmonton, obviously in need of a bat, but went hitless in four at-bats, although he took a pitch in the ribs to load the bases in the third. But a new city, same fate for Williams as Edmonton lost 11–2 to Saskatoon.

It didn't take long for Williams to face his old teammates as Regina visited Edmonton for six games (including two double-headers) starting June 12. Williams couldn't hold back his feelings after the Eskimos won the opener 11–6, even though he went 0-for-3 with a walk.

"Bill Williams fairly revelled in the trouncing of his former team mates were getting and was the most pleased man in the lot,"[45] reported the *Regina Leader*. The *Edmonton Journal* wrote, "Much joy among the assembled pen holders, and Bill Williams publicly gave thanks for having the luck to be released by Regina."[46]

The teams would split the six games, but surely Williams would note he went 9-for-24 (.375) in the series—including a two-run homer in a 6–4 win in the finale on June 16—while his Regina replacement, Netzel, was 5–25 (.200).

And as was the case in his previous stops, others were taking notice. "The new player who really shows class is Bill Williams," wrote the *Edmonton Journal*, "who was not good enough for Regina. Since joining the Eskimos, Bill has fielded in a faultless manner and hit the ball hard."[47]

It was true Williams had not committed an error, but that soon would change as he was moved around from right field to second base to left field to first base to third base and again back to the outfield. He also was dropped to fifth—and later sixth—in the lineup after Lou Nordyke had to step down as manager due to an ailing leg, with team president Deacon White taking over as manager and catcher Roy Lemieux acting as field captain.

By August, things had changed not only on the field but also off. Williams was back in the outfield and in the middle of the order, hitting in 21 of 22 games from July 30 to Game 1 of an August 19 double-header. During that stretch he was a scorching 38-for-81 (.469) with four doubles, five triples, three home runs and 10 steals (including three in one game). In a span of nine games from August 20 to 30, he stole seven bases and was a slightly cooled off, but still strong, 13-for-37 (.351).

Again, he was getting to be popular in the newspaper. After his three-steal game in a 7–3 win over Calgary on August 7, the *Edmonton Journal* declared, "Bill Williams is playing the game of his life, and Deacon White is regretting the fact that he did not place the big fellow in centre field right from the start. He pulled off several sensational catches in the south. But his batting has been even better than his fielding."[48]

Williams's home run on August 11 in Edmonton was called "one of the longest drives ever seen at Diamond Park … the ball cleared the right field fence near the scoreboard nearly fully 25 feet. The tremendous drive won Williams sundry boxes, choice cigars, a hat and a pair of trousers."[49]

The home runs came in bunches—he hit all three in a six-game span from August 10 to 14, which "made him [a hit] with the fans and every time he comes to bat he gets a hand."[50] The opposition took notice as well, as Williams started being intentionally walked, something which was very rare in that era.

But the number of fans who were watching dwindled. Edmonton took pride that 40,000 turned out to watch the team in the first half. However, that all changed when Archduke Franz Ferdinand was assassinated June 28, with Great Britain declaring war just over a month later.

This meant many Canadians would set sail to England to help fight–20,000 by one estimate. People stopped turning out to Dominion Park, at least in the numbers they had been.

Crowds of 600 to 1,000 were more commonplace—which would be fine for Regina, but not Edmonton. Citizens would gather in the streets and around the newspaper offices of the *Edmonton Bulletin* and *Edmonton Journal* for the latest news while singing patriotic songs.

The scene was similar in other cities around the Western Canada League; Saskatoon averaged just 300 fans over the last month. Teams were losing money, and a lot of it. It was reported Medicine Hat was in the red $7,500 and Calgary lost $3,500. Edmonton, which had drawn 40,000 over its first 30 games, was relegated to just 18,500 spectators over the final two months.

The war hadn't affected teams in the United States—at least not yet—and the Chicago White Sox sent a letter to White that they wanted Williams immediately, and if he stuck with the club they'd pay Edmonton $1,500—money it could surely use. But the letter arrived after August 26, the deadline for teams to purchase players. After that date, a player had to be drafted. Chicago wanted a player right then and chose not to select Williams (of course, the White Sox had also purchased Braggo Roth from Kansas City in August and could well have been satisfied with his performance, .294 over 34 games).

Williams finished the season batting .315, eighth in the league, with a league-leading 12 home runs. His 209 total bases were second to former Regina teammate Jack Smith, who had 211, while his 43 steals—or 42, depending on the source—also were behind only Medicine Hat's William Daniels. He was listed as having made 14 errors in the outfield for a .929 percentage (the experiment at second base didn't work as well, as he had five errors in his six games at that position). Both Edmonton papers unsurprisingly put Williams on their WCL All-Star teams.

"For right field, Bill Williams stands out like a sore thumb," wrote the *Bulletin*, "though he could be picked for any of the outfield positions. This young player has everything in an outfielder's category, and now that he is taking the game seriously and using his noodle, is one of the best men in the league. It is hard to see how a player with his natural talents can be overlooked by the scouts."[51]

F.M. Germe of the *Journal* wrote, "[T]he only real contestants for the position [of right field] are Bill Williams and Boss Povey, both of Edmonton, and the former is selected by reason of his wonderful hitting and fielding since he joined Edmonton."[52]

The press clippings were a nice resume for Williams, and one he would need. For with the ongoing war not near a conclusion, Williams and the rest of the Western Canada League players would soon be without a team.

Chapter 3

Making a Name for Himself

Ken Williams, as he would do every offseason, paid a visit back to his hometown, Grants Pass, Oregon. While visiting with his parents, he received word from his Edmonton manager, Deacon White, that unless the war in Europe ended soon—an unlikely proposition—the Western Canada League would be in trouble.

Edmonton, like every other team, lost money in 1914; attendance took a drastic turn once there were rumblings of war. White told Williams he would make every effort to sell the player to a major-league team. While going from a Class D league to the majors would be a large jump, White believed Williams was going places, which he reaffirmed to *The Sporting News*, telling the weekly, "Williams and Povey are two fast young outfielders, who will not play here for long."[1]

As it turned out, there wouldn't even be a Western Canada League for Williams to play in. Given permission by the National Commission to suspend operations two weeks prior, WCL teams voted December 3 in favor of doing just that for 1915. As per the commission ruling, teams would retain control of the players, but any who were not sold by February 1 would become free agents.

If Williams had any anxiety as to where his baseball future lay, he didn't have to wait too long to find out. On January 14, 1915—two weeks before he would have become a free agent—it was announced that Spokane of the Class B Northwestern League had purchased Williams from Edmonton. The Indians outbid league rivals Vancouver and Seattle (which finished 1–2 in the league in 1914). Perhaps allowing Edmonton a piece of the sale if Williams were sold to a major-league club sealed the deal.

Spokane was in a salary squabble with Jimmy Lewis, who played left field the previous year. The Northwestern League's salary limit in 1914 was $3,500/month; that was being reduced to $2,500/month in 1915—which was still $500 over the limit of any other Class B league.

Lewis took exception to a pay cut and refused to sign. So Spokane obtained Williams and also traded for outfielder Cy Neighbors, a perennial .300 hitter in the minors, including .315 with 20 steals for Tacoma in 1914.

Not much was known about Williams—the *Spokane Chronicle* barely mentioned the transaction other than one line at the bottom of a story, but the *Spokesman-Review* noted the outfielder was "considered by most of the critics of [the Western Canada League] to be the pick of the entire lot of twilight talent."[2] Of course, Spokane also thought they were getting a younger prospect. For the first time, Williams's age was put in print—21. Except that he was really 24 and turning 25 in June.

WRITE PLAINLY, WITH UNFADING INK. THIS IS A PERMANENT RECORD.

N. B.—In case of more than one child at birth, a SEPARATE RETURN must be made for each, and the number of each, in order of birth stated. This certificate must be filed by the attending physician or midwife with the local registrar within 10 days after birth.

POST OFFICE ADDRESS OF MOTHER

Oregon State Board of Health
Division of Vital Statistics

Certificate of Birth

State Registered No.
Local Registered No.

1. Place of Birth
County Josephine State Oregon
Township or Village Merlin
City Grants Pass No. St. Ward
(If birth occurred in a hospital or institution, give its name instead of street and number)
(If in country, give distance and direction from nearest town)

2. Full name of child Kenneth Roy Williams
If child is not yet named, make supplemental report, as directed

3. Sex of child | To be answered ONLY in event of plural births. | 4. Twin, triplet or other | 5. Number in order of birth | 6. Premature | Full term yes | 7. Legitimate? yes | 8. Date of birth June 28 1890 (Month, day, year)

FATHER
9. Full name William Britton Williams
10. Residence (Usual place of abode) If nonresident, give place and state Grants Pass
11. Color or race White 12. Age at last birthday 82 (years)
13. Birthplace (city or place) Mercer County (State or country) Missouri
Occupation
14. Trade, profession, or particular kind of work done, as spinner, sawyer, bookkeeper, etc. School Teacher
15. Industry or business in which work was done, as silk mill, sawmill, bank, etc. Dist School
16. Date (month and year) last engaged in this work June 1905 17. Total time (years) spent in this work 8 years

MOTHER
18. Full maiden name Caroline Trimble Williams
19. Residence (Usual place of abode) If nonresident, give place and state Grants Pass Ore.
20. Color or race White 21. Age at last birthday 78 (years)
22. Birthplace (city or place) Near Roseburg (State or country) Douglas Co Oregon
Occupation
23. Trade, profession, or particular kind of work done, as housekeeper, typist, nurse, clerk, etc. Housewife
24. Industry or business in which work was done, as own home, lawyer's office, silk mill, etc. Own home
25. Date (month and year) last engaged in this work Sept 1928 26. Total time (years) spent in this work 50

27. Number of children of this mother (Taken as of time of birth of child herein certified and including this child) 4 (a) Born alive and now living yes (b) Born alive but now dead (c) Stillborn

Were precautions taken against ophthalmia neonatorum?

CERTIFICATE OF ATTENDING PHYSICIAN OR MIDWIFE*

I hereby certify that I attended the birth of this child, who was born alive at ... m. on the date above stated.

* When there was no attending physician or midwife, then the father, householder, etc., should make this return. A stillborn child is one that neither breathes nor shows other evidence of life after birth.

Signature Mrs Laura Cook
Mrs Viola Flanagan
(Physician or midwife)

Given name added from a supplemental report (Month, day, year)

Address

Registrar Filed ..., 19... Registrar

Ken Williams's birth certificate proving he was indeed born in 1890 (courtesy Larry LaBeck).

It isn't known when Williams decided to falsify his age, but it is hardly a rare circumstance in the sport. Others before him did it and plenty of others after him, even into the 21st century. The exact reason Williams did it isn't known either, but it isn't hard to figure out: certainly a 21-year-old would still be considered a prospect. At almost 25 (and with only a couple of years in Class D ball), the chances of a team wanting to take a chance and invest in the future of Williams would be slim, if at all.

Regardless, whether he was 21, 24 or 25, Williams would be the youngest of Spokane's outfielders when the team opened training camp. Neighbors was 34 years old, Emil Frisk 40 and Jimmy Lewis—who left for Albany but in the end decided to return to Spokane for a lesser salary—was 32.

Williams arrived a couple of days late for camp, so he was relegated to late sub-in duty in Spokane's training camp opener against Gonzaga on Easter Sunday. He then played for the Yannigans (younger players) against the Regulars on April 5, the same day that Jess Willard beat Jack Johnson in a 26th-round knockout. Williams would prove himself quicker than Willard.

It took only a few games for Williams to be slotted with the Regulars. After he went 4-for-5 with two doubles and a triple in an intrasquad game (a 13–4 Regulars win), the *Spokane Daily Chronicle* noted, "On the form that is being shown by Williams, the slugging outfielder, it is going to be some task to beat him out of a place in the outfield.... [H]e is stinging the apple at a merry clip."[3]

Back in 1913, before beginning his career as a professional ballplayer, Williams just missed out on playing against the Chicago American Giants, but he'd get the opportunity to play twice against the Negro League team as a member of Spokane.

Williams, like everyone else in his era, never appeared in a regular-season game that included an African American player. While Williams was by no means at the forefront of a civil rights movement (in fact, his father would join the Ku Klux Klan when that group rose to some acclaim in Oregon in the 1920s), he never skipped out of an exhibition against a Negro League team. He had also played with a Native American ("Casey" Smith, a teammate in Regina in 1914), and in coming years would also play with and against Chinese players. To Ken Williams, according to his sons, a ballplayer was a ballplayer, no matter the color of his skin.

The *Spokesman-Review* surprisingly noted that "Negroes ... have developed some athletes of major league caliber," but also showed the public racism of the times by referring to the team as "the brunette boys" and "tar babies."[4]

The Giants indeed did feature a number of major-league quality players, among them John "Pop" Lloyd and Pete Hill, both of whom would be inducted into the Hall of Fame. The *Spokesman-Review* said "[Bruce] Petway is claimed by many to be the peer of any backstop in the world. While [Jesse] Barber, [Frank] Duncan and [Frank] Wickware and others have almost equally formidable reputations."[5]

The April 17 game—a 14–13 win for the Giants—lived up to the hype. "It was one of the most remarkable games of ball ever played within these corporal precincts in all these many years," noted the *Spokesman-Review*. "There have been a lot of 1-to-0 errorless games in this town that were not as good. It will be one long to be remembered."[6]

Chicago was down 10 runs, but rallied for nine in the seventh inning after a bungled double-play ball, then scored the eventual winning run on an eighth-inning error. Playing against the strongest competition he had ever faced, Williams, batting third and playing center field, went 4-for-6 including two triples to the right-field fence and a stolen base, making him "the idol of the 1800 bugs."[7]

The second game between the two clubs, on April 18, ended in controversy. With Chicago leading 7–6, Spokane's Jimmy Lewis doubled in the ninth, but hurt his ankle on his way to second base. Cy Neighbors came off the coaching ranks at first base to check on Lewis, and stayed in to run. But then manager Bob Wicker summoned another player to run for Neighbors. With the bases full and one out, Neighbors was sent in to pinch-hit, but the Giants claimed he was ineligible as he had already been used as a pinch runner.

The umpire allowed Neighbors to hit; Chicago manager Rube Foster protested and took his team off the field, with the game being ruled a forfeit. Foster also had to do some smooth talking to calm down irate fans, which, to his credit, he did. The game would not be replayed and would be counted as a loss for the Giants (who went 12–7, including the forfeit, against Northwestern League teams), who also left town with $600 for the two games. Interestingly, the *Spokesman-Review*'s J. Newton Culver sided with the Giants, noting the rulebook states the umpire does not have to announce the substitution; it was official as soon as the ump was notified of it.

Williams continued to prove he could play with anyone, hitting a few deep flies to the fence, which were caught, then tripling to right-center and continuing onto home after the throw by Duncan bounced away from third baseman Bill Francis.

In Spokane's exhibition games, Williams led the team in extra-base hits and total bases. Overall, he hit .405 (13-for-37), second on the club behind Lewis's .457 (the team hit .312), with nine runs, two doubles, five triples and two stolen bases.

Williams's play left little doubt he would be in the lineup for the opener, or at least it should have; Culver did not include Williams in his projected starting nine. But when manager Bob Wicker announced his starters the day before Spokane's initial foray of the 1915 season, he indeed had Williams batting third and in center field.

Williams and the rest of the Spokane players, as well as their adversaries for the day, the Aberdeen Black Cats, took part in an extensive parade. Several local baseball teams, prominent citizens and "fanettes" riding in automobiles, the booster club, a lacrosse team and a high school band proceeded to the Indians' Recreation Park before the April 20 opener.

The Indians had played in Recreation Park, which had the first grass infield in the city, since 1905. The park could hold around 7,000 people and included a large set of bleachers which was claimed to be one of the best in all of the minor leagues and could accommodate roughly 2,000 patrons. The fences at the park were very deep—the exact dimensions are unknown, but all were believed to be beyond 400 feet, which helped account for the fact that few over-the-fence home runs were recorded there (and the first didn't occur until 1908).

It was a chillier than expected day, but around 5,000 fans braved the low temperatures for the opener. Much was expected of this Spokane team, and in the pregame, Wicker was presented with an array of flowers which was clearly labeled with "Pennant 1915."

There were familiar faces on the opposite side of the diamond—Aberdeen's manager was Charlie Stis, who had cut Williams from Regina, and former Regina teammate Jack Smith patrolled the outfield. It was a brief reunion: just a few days later Stis was replaced as manager, and Smith was released because he "couldn't play in the sun field"[8] and landed with Seattle.

Perhaps seeing those two, along with playing in a Class B level, made Williams nervous, as he was described by the *Spokesman-Review*'s Culver. Williams struck out and made an early error, but settled down and ended up 3-for-5 with a triple. He, along with his teammates, would celebrate their 9–5 win in the box seats of the local Loew's Theater, as guest of the manager, Joe Muller, where they would watch various vaudeville acts, contortionists, acrobats, songs, readings and the like.

Williams was providing some sights to see as well. He would open up his time in Spokane with an eight-game hitting streak, although it was broken up during an 11-game stretch as he was sidelined for a few games after injuring his ankle while sliding home with the winning run in the bottom of the 11th inning on April 23. When Williams returned to the lineup April 27, he went 2-for-5 with a double in an 8–7 loss at Victoria and followed that up the next day with his first home run of the season over the right-field fence.

One day after his first hitless performance, Williams, already being referred to as "the much heralded 'home run king' of the Spokane team,"[9] hit a three-run homer in a 6–1 win at Vancouver on May 3. He added home run No. 3 in Vancouver off left-hander Ben Hunt on May 8, causing the *Spokesman-Review* to declare him "the sensation of the season to date."[10] Williams was hitting .390 and leading the Northwestern League in extra-base hits with a double, two triples and the three home runs.

However, by this time, attention was turning away from baseball. On May 7, the ship *Lusitania* had been sunk by German submarines, which got the attention of the United States as President Woodrow Wilson demanded an explanation. In Canada, which featured two

Northwestern League teams (Victoria and Vancouver), tensions were already high as that country was backing Great Britain in the war in Europe. Being of German heritage raised eyebrows in Canada.

The *Spokane Daily Chronicle* reported that Victoria owner Josh Kingham was making sure there were no German players, or anyone who was pro-Germany, on his team. In fact, the Victoria team had recently signed a catcher named Harry Hoffman, but told him not to report if he was of German ancestry. Hoffman said he wasn't German but Dutch—and henceforth was called Dutch Hoffman, just in case there was any doubt.

Williams' place on Spokane wasn't in doubt. The team had to cut down to 14 players by the league-mandated deadline of May 10. Four players were cut, one (a pitcher, Tiny Leonard) was added, and Frank Guigni (or Juney, as he appeared in the box scores) was put on the suspended list. Guigni was hurt, and this allowed Spokane to retain his rights, not take up a roster spot, and also refrain from having to pay him and thus cut into the monthly salary limit.

Already showing off his batting skills, Williams began to demonstrate the other parts of his game as well. His temper was on display May 12 after being called a "busher" by the umpire for sliding into home plate on a force play with the bases loaded. Williams's response to the ump drew a $5 fine.

On the field, the next day, in a 5–0 loss to Vancouver, Williams made a nice running catch to the fence and then threw the ball an estimated 330 feet. After stealing just one base in Spokane's first 16 games, Williams began to show off his speed on the basepaths, swiping 10 bases in the next 15 games, including five—two of third base—in a May 16 double-header sweep over Vancouver.

"[Williams] seems suddenly to have discovered that with all his great speed he might as well be making a bid for the league's base-running honors as well as its batting leadership," an article in the *Spokesman-Review* observed. "He will be on the sacks a whole lot of times, and once he gets the distinction of tomfoolery and legitimate daring he is going to occasion rival batterymen a lot of worry."[11]

George M. Varnell of the *Spokane Daily Chronicle* concurred, writing: "Williams has the speed to get away with his steals and, when he learns to take full advantage of it without playing absolutely headless ball when on the paths, he will be in line to worry the best throwing catchers in the league."[12]

Williams went to sleep on May 29 sitting at sixth in the league in batting average (.327), tied for first in home runs, tied for ninth in doubles and tied for second in stolen bases. He would be knocked out bed around 2 a.m. by a blast that rocked the city. The great explosion was caused by the accidental detonation of ammunition on a nearby docked scow. The blast could be heard as far away as Tacoma and caused an estimated $40,000 damage to shattered plate glass windows around downtown, and $140,000 in overall damage. Theories abounded as to what happened—German angst fueling much of it—but it was never learned what caused the explosion.

Despite the chaos and confusion from the event, 2,000 fans made it out for a May 30 double-header between Spokane and Seattle. Lack of sleep perhaps contributed to a poor offensive showing by both teams. The Indians managed just five hits in the two games, a 1–0 Seattle win and 1–1 tie which was called after eight innings so Spokane could catch a train to Aberdeen. However, Williams did launch a long home run to right field in the second game.

The Indians would win five of eight games in Aberdeen to finish 13–8–1 on their road trip, the best road record ever for a Spokane club. Williams was a big part of it, and according to Spokane president F.C. Farr, the team was getting feelers from two major-league teams about the outfielder. The interest in Williams heated up as the player's performance did the same.

Williams was flashing talent in all areas. On June 9, he did it all, showing off his arm, power and speed. In a 7–3 win at home over Victoria, Williams threw out two baserunners, tripled and made a heads-up hustle play, scoring from third on an accidental bunt down the third-base line. He crept off the bag, waited for the throw to first, then raced home ahead of the relay back from the first baseman, future Hall of Famer George Kelly.

On June 10, it was two more hits—including a perfectly placed single to a vacated second base position on a hit and run—and a stolen base. The next day, he displayed a "fine burst of speed and a long, accurate slide"[13] while swiping home on the back end of a delayed double steal.

After Spokane's June 12 5–4 win over Victoria—the Indians were now alone in first place as well—in which he had a hit, assist and steal, Williams was batting .317 and leading the league with four home runs and 17 stolen bases.

In a June 13 double-header, Williams went 4-for-8, including a double and two triples and accounted for all of Spokane's runs in the opener with a run and two RBI. From June 15 to 18, Williams socked a double and a triple and had a pair of stolen bases. He also made several spectacular catches, including one each in the final three innings of a 2–1 win over Tacoma in 12 innings.

But Williams saved his most impressive feat for Father's Day, June 19. (This game was on a Saturday, not a Sunday, however. Spokane's Sonora Smart Dodd had tried to establish a national Father's Day, the first of which was held in Spokane on June 19, 1910. Thus, June 19 was likely used as Father's Day in Spokane until the third Sunday of each June was used in later years.) The game already was built up as something special with a parade through Spokane's downtown, featuring players and Civil War veterans. Miss Spokane was on hand to throw out the first pitch. Fathers who attended with their children were let into the ballpark for free, while the soldiers were guests of the club. They all witnessed a bit of Spokane history in the third inning.

Facing Tacoma's "Izzy" Kaufman, Williams took a mighty swing at the pitcher's offering. "The crack of the bat and ball startled every soul in sight."[14] The ball set sail for right field. Tacoma's Les Wilson tracked the ball but then gave up and watched with everyone else as he realized the distance it was traveling. The ball cleared the double-deck fence in right by a long margin.

The larger-than-usual crowd, thanks to the Father's Day event, sent up a cheer "that could be heard for blocks. Almost every man in stands and bleachers was on his feet whooping 'er up as big Williams trotted the bases."[15]

It marked just the third out-of-the-park home run since Spokane started playing at Recreation Park in June 1905. Williams's was deemed the most impressive of the three by the *Spokesman-Review*, which wrote: "Considering the fact that the wind was blowing against the batsman, the flag at one time waving toward the grandstand from the center field pennant pole, and that the ball still traveled over a long line, it must be admitted that there was more power in that punch than any that ever cleared this wall, at least." In perhaps of a bit of home-state pride, the *Ashland* (Oregon) *Tidings* a few weeks later would refer to it as "the longest hit in the history of baseball."[16]

One person who did not witness the feat was St. Louis Cardinals scout Eddie Herr, who was in attendance for a double-header the next day. He saw Williams strike out for only the second time at home (the other being on Opening Day) and accumulate just one hit, although he "drove five balls to the outfield."[17] Afterwards, Herr was talking about a Spokane outfielder, but it was Jimmy Lewis, who had seven hits in the two games. Regardless of his double-header performance, Williams was the Northwestern League's best and most feared hitter.

In a June 22 game against Seattle, he was issued a rare intentional walk. On June 26, Spokane was in first place by 6½ games with Williams leading the offense, batting .335—second only to Victoria's Homer Haworth, who was at .345–with a league-leading five home runs and 23 steals. He was also tied for third in the league in triples with five.

Major-league scouts were serving notice that they were on their way to check out Williams. While Herr already checked out Spokane, Dick Kinsella of the New York Giants made his intentions known and asked that no players in the league be sold until he had a chance to look them over. University of Oregon coach Hugh Bezdek, who served as a scout for the Pittsburgh Pirates, said he would be out to look at Williams as well.

Kinsella made it to Spokane in time for the Indians' June 27 double-header against Seattle. Williams definitely made a better impression on Kinsella than he did on Herr. While he went 0-for-3 in the opening game, Williams did have an outfield assist and stole a base. But he really made an impact in the second contest.

In the fourth inning, Williams sent a pitch from Seattle's Frank Eastley over the double deck in right field, just the fourth over-the-fence home run in Recreation Park history, two of those by Williams in the last eight days. Williams had three hits on the day and another assist. When he doubled in two runs to start a seven-run eighth inning, "fans threw several hundred cushions on the field"[18] in celebration.

Needless to say, Kinsella was impressed. He telegraphed New York Giants manager John McGraw a glowing report and met with Spokane president Farr to gauge the price on Williams. The cost apparently wasn't too stiff, as Kinsella said he would check out Williams again when Spokane was in Aberdeen, where the Indians were heading for a six-game series.

Williams struggled in the series at Aberdeen, going 3-for-25. But this did not dissuade scouts or those who had seen Williams play. George Ferris, who played for Spokane and also managed the team briefly in 1906, was still in the city working as an attorney and liked Williams's chances in the majors. "In my journeys back east the last few years I've managed to see nearly every major league club play," Ferris said, "and outside of Detroit, which has [Bobby] Veach, [Sam] Crawford and [Ty] Cobb, I don't believe there is one of the 16 major-league clubs that could not use him right now. I think he has major-league class right now."[19] The Giants were tagged as the frontrunner, but Cincinnati had "not given up hope."[20] Also entering the picture, despite what Ferris thought, were the Detroit Tigers.

Spokane didn't arrive back in town on July 4 until the morning and then played a 13-inning game against Vancouver. If he was exhausted, Williams didn't show it. He stole third base standing up with no throw from the catcher despite pitcher Toothpick Smith's throwing over to second base "eight or nine times."[21] In the 11th, Williams motored to shallow left-center field to rob Tony Brottem of a hit, then made a racing, backhanded catch at the wall to deny Ray Brown of extra bases. In the 13th, he smacked his second double of the game, scoring two, but was out after he overslid third base as he tried for a triple. Watching it all was Tigers scout James McGuire. He quickly set up an appointment with Farr in the morning to discuss Williams.

Over the next two days, in three games, Williams went 6-for-11 with eight runs, a double and two steals. With several suitors at his doorstep, Farr finally decided it was time to sell Williams to a major-league team. Surprisingly, the deal wasn't struck with the clubs who had been aggressively scouting Williams, but rather with the Cincinnati Reds.

The Giants and Tigers both offered $3,000 for Williams. Brooklyn also made an offer for Williams—the amount unknown—but that club was glad to lose out, as it thought it was bidding on a right-handed batter, not having use for another lefty hitter. The Reds basically just outbid everyone else, with the deal being worth as much as $3,500 for Spokane, which would allow Williams to leave for Cincinnati shortly after the purchase.

Spokane, though, wouldn't see all of that upfront money. Based on its deal with Edmonton in obtaining Williams, Spokane had to give half of the proceeds to the dormant Western Canada League team.

Spokane received $1,000 from Cincinnati upon agreement of the deal ($500 of which would be ticketed to Edmonton). Another $1,500 would be paid at some point during the 1915 season, with another $1,000 headed to Spokane if Williams were kept on the Reds' roster after the May 10, 1916, roster cutdown date.

Cincinnati owner Garry Herrmann (front row, second from right), who obtained Ken Williams from Spokane after a deal for Jack Smith fell through (George Grantham Bain Collection, Library of Congress).

The Reds apparently had received a couple of tips on Williams. In May, Tom Colgan, one of Cincinnati's board of directors, happened to be in Spokane and saw Williams play. He went home and informed Reds president August Herrmann about this phenom he had seen. Hermann also received a letter dated June 12 from L.E. Ragsdale of the Western Cereal Company in Spokane. It in part read:

> Having long resided in the vicinity of Cincinnati and been numbered among the faithful, my interest still follows the fortunes of the Reds. Seeing a promising ballplayer ready to "go up," my first wish is that he may be given a try-out by you.
>
> Kenneth Williams, last year with Edmonton, this year Spokane centerfielder, is the best player in this company. Much resembling Bob Bescher [an outfielder who played for the Reds from 1908 to 1913, leading the league in stolen bases four times, and was with the Cardinals in 1915], fully as fast, a slugging hitter who will always top 300 percent in this class, at least, he will surely go to the majors this season. Coming here this spring, he showed remarkable hitting ability, but rough in the field. Under the skillful handling of Bob Wicker, he showed wonderful improvement, and he is now a finished fielder and a fine thrower. His base-stealing of late promises to lead the league in that branch. Your scout should lose no time in looking him over, for he has already attracted big league attention.[22]

The reports from Colgan and Ragsdale might have alerted Herrmann to Williams, and that last line in Ragsdale's correspondence regarding the urgency in signing him could have spurred the Reds to act. But Williams was not the left-handed hitting outfielder Cincinnati had set its eyes on initially.

The Reds had a deal—or at least they thought they did—with Seattle for Jack Smith. The purchase involved Smith's reporting immediately to Cincinnati, as the Reds were looking to bolster their club for the 1915 pennant race. Seattle originally agreed to that, but then changed its mind and decided not to allow Smith to leave at once.

Meanwhile, the St. Louis Cardinals said they owned the rights to Smith, much to the chagrin of Herrmann, who said his team had first claim. However, once Seattle decided it wouldn't allow another team to take Smith until after the Northwestern League's season was completed, the Reds bowed out and the Cardinals, not worried about such limits, swooped in and made the transaction on July 3.

True to its word, Smith played for Seattle the entire season (and helped the team overtake Spokane for the pennant) before appearing in four games with the Cardinals at the tail end of the National League season.

Fortunately for the Reds, Spokane had said it wouldn't make any deal for Williams until at least July 4. This allowed Cincinnati to enter the bidding and snare Williams away from the Giants and Tigers. Despite being in first place, Spokane was willing to let the Reds have Williams as soon as possible.

The Sporting News tried to spin a tale from Herrmann that the Reds all along wanted the attention to be on Smith while Cincinnati snuck in and got the man it really wanted, Williams. That version sounded more like a work of fiction from an owner trying to play up his recent acquisition.

The *Spokesman-Review* reported that Cincinnati, just six games out of first place, although in seventh place, "is badly in need of left hand hitters. Only day before yesterday it purchased Bunny Rogers [Bill Rodgers] from the Boston Red Sox to get a left hand hitter in the infield. President Herrmann requested immediate delivery saying he believed Cincinnati had a chance to move up in the race, and, because of the splendid treatment he had received from the Cincinnati mogul, [Spokane president] Farr decided to yield to Herrmann's wishes."[23]

Said Spokane manager Bob Wicker, who pitched in the majors from 1901 to 1906: "Williams is one of the greatest prospects I have ever seen. Of course I am sorry to lose him, but the kid has a chance in the big puddle and we all look for him to make good."[24]

Williams wasn't quite done with Spokane. He played in two more games on July 8 and 9, going 1-for-3 in the former and 3-for-5 with two doubles in the latter, in which teammate Wynn Noyes also pitched a no-hitter.

Before leaving, Williams tried to buy the bat of teammate Sam Brenegan, which he had been using with success—including both his over-the-fence home runs in Spokane—after his own bat broke. Williams offered as much as $25, but Brenegan wasn't selling.

Williams also was initiated into the Fraternal Order of Eagles prior to his final game. A special noon session was held to accommodate the player, who was headed out of town after the game. Williams's final record at Spokane was a .340 average with six home runs and 34 stolen bases. He would remain the league leader in steals three weeks after departing Spokane.

"Everything considered," wrote a *Sporting News* correspondent, "the record set by Williams, up to the time he left the league, is by far the most impressive of any player that wore a Northwestern League uniform."[25] Now, just three years after wearing the uniforms of semi-pro teams in small towns such as Grants Pass and Weed, Williams was about to be fitted in a Cincinnati outfit.

Chapter 4

A Small Taste of Cincinnati

Kenneth Williams had never been east of Regina in his entire life. Now, having just turned 25 a couple of weeks earlier (although he was still 22 in the eyes of the baseball world), Williams was now boarding a train to Brooklyn, to meet up with his new Reds teammates.

If he was nervous, he wasn't letting on. But he was anxious, excited and confident. "I hope they let me play my regular position, center field," Williams said, "and let me have those two old heads, [Red] Killifer and [Tommy] Leach, on either side of me to coach me on the batters. I realize perfectly that I have lots to learn, but I know I can hit and I'm willing to listen."[1]

The major leagues must have seemed like a dream to Williams when playing on the sandlot dirt fields in Oregon and California. One can only imagine what he thought when he arrived at the Reds' place of lodging, the famous Ansonia Hotel, which had air conditioning—something Williams likely had never experienced before—and boasting of the world's largest swimming pool. The cost of the hotel, which was completed in 1904, was around $3 million—which was probably more than it would cost to rebuild the entire town of Grants Pass.

Williams, along with pitcher Frank McKenry, arrived at the hotel on July 13, shortly after Cincinnati's 5–1 win over Brooklyn. The Reds had shaken up their lineup—Williams was expected to be part of that shakeup—and the result had been a pair of wins (Cincinnati also beat the New York Giants 6–0 on July 12). Nevertheless, Cincinnati was still in seventh place with a 32–37 record, although in a tight pennant race that placed the Reds just 5½ games out of first place.

Kenneth Williams arrived at Ebbets Field on July 14, 1915, as something of an enigma—manager Buck Herzog had never laid eyes on his new player but had high expectations. In describing Williams to its readers, *The Sporting Life* depicted him as a matinee idol, having "romantic eyes and long, black curly hair. He looks, in fact, like a poet about to spring, but denies that there is any poetry, of any amount to speak of, in his composition."[2]

Williams purportedly told the magazine that "about the only poem I could compose, on short notice, would read like this: 'Bat, bat, where's the pitcher at?' And I'm afraid that wouldn't get too far in the Byron-Longfellow stakes."[3]

Penning a composition was the last thing Williams had to worry about. He was immediately placed in the starting lineup, batting seventh and playing center field, and would have to face veteran starting pitcher Jack Coombs.

The right-handed Coombs won 80 games with the powerhouse Philadelphia A's from

Charles "Buck" Herzog, shown in 1912 when he played for the New York Giants. Herzog would be Ken Williams's first manager in the majors in Cincinnati (George Grantham Bain Collection, Library of Congress).

1910 to 1912 (including a 31–9 record and an amazing 1.30 ERA in 1910). He appeared in only four games in 1913–14 due to illness, but was in the midst of a rebirth with Brooklyn in 1915, where he would end the season 15–10 with a 2.58 ERA.

No matter. Williams, as he did against pitchers from his backyard in Grants Pass to the Western Canada League to the Northwestern League, delivered with the bat. In the fourth inning, one batter after Heinie Groh had doubled, Williams laced a Coombs curveball to center field for a single. His first hit also produced his first RBI, as Groh would score Cincinnati's only tally of the game in losing in 10 innings to Brooklyn, 2–1.

Williams hit the ball hard one other time, in the eighth, but it was hit on a line and tracked down by center fielder Hi Myers. That was more action than Williams got in center, as he didn't field one chance.

The *Cincinnati Enquirer* reported that Herzog was "greatly pleased by the appearance of Williams."[4] Herzog also was brimming with confidence in his new-look team, saying he was "willing to stake my season's salary that the club will land in the first division."[5]

Williams's first official fielding play came in his second contest, and it was not a catch, but rather an assist, albeit not on a direct throw. Gus Getz singled to center field to score George Cutshaw. Williams was throwing home in an attempt to get the runner, but pitcher Rube Benton cut it off and threw to second base, where Getz was out.

Heinie Groh, Cincinnati's star third baseman (George Grantham Bain Collection, Library of Congress).

Williams also caught a fly and rapped out another single. The *Cincinnati Enquirer* noted that Williams, along with Bill Rodgers, both "drive the ball with vigor,"[6] and that the outfielder "showed a lot of speed for a big fellow."[7] Despite the praise, in the third game in Brooklyn on July 16, Williams found himself in a new situation—being hit for in a close game and by a fellow lefty, Tommy Leach, no less. Leach took a called strike three as Cincinnati lost a third straight game and fell into last place.

The team moved on to Boston to play the Braves, which were having a new park built. In the meantime, they played their games in the Red Sox's Fenway Park, which had been built just three years earlier.

Despite being hit for in the finale in Brooklyn, Williams remained in the starting lineup and recorded a hit in all five games played in Boston. He scored his first major-league run in the first game of a July 17 double-header on Herzog's third-inning triple, accounted for Cincinnati's only run (again) with an RBI single off Dick Rudolph in a 4–1 loss on July 19, and the next day got his first career extra-base hit with a double.

The Reds lost each time in Williams's first seven games, but he was 7-for-20 (.350), making him a standout on a struggling squad. "He still has something to learn about baserunning," the *Cincinnati Enquirer* noted, "but it may be that he is going to prove a real hitter, an article of which the Reds badly need."[8]

Ironically, it was Williams's baserunning which helped Cincinnati end its skid in the series finale in Boston. He accounted for one of the Reds' runs in a 2–1 win by scoring from third base on a grounder to short, beating the throw to the plate.

Cincinnati was back on a train to Philadelphia after the victory. Along the rails from Boston to Philadelphia, the *Cincinnati Enquirer* reported it was decided that "Kenneth is too refined for Williams to be called by, so the boys have abbreviated it to 'Bill,' which is a more athletic monicker,"[9] a sentiment which harked to his days in Regina. *Enquirer* reporter Jack Ryder concurred, telling the *Spokesman-Review*—which went with "the less fandangled Ken"—that "Kenneth is no name for an athlete."[10]

This would remain the general opinion throughout his career, and was even mentioned in 1924 by a national columnist who wrote, "When his parents christened him Kenneth Roy Williams, they probably had little idea that 'Ken' would some day swing one of the meanest bats in big league baseball. Probably a baseball career was the farthest thing from their thoughts."[11]

Whatever his name, Williams was making a splash. Even those back in Spokane wanted to know how he was doing, calling Frank Smith, owner of a local baseball parlor, each night to find out the latest Williams batting results.

One thing the rooters would find out is Williams was switched to left field, with Red Killefer moving to center. The *Cincinnati Times-Star*'s Bill Phelon, writing in *The Sporting News*, explained: "Williams is all right on flies in front of him, and can range over towards right field very nicely, but when he has to cross in the other direction he flounders. Therefore Buck decided to set him in left field, with instructions to play nearer the foul line than is customary, so that most of his catches would have to be made under conditions satisfactory to the boy."[12]

He immediately acclimated himself to the new surroundings, making a "jumping one-hand catch for a long liner"[13] in the fifth inning off the bat of Fred Luderus as well as a "fine running catch"[14] on Dave Brancroft's foul fly ball.

But Herzog's confidence in Williams might have been starting to wane. The Reds manager took Williams out of the game against the Phillies on July 23, moving Killifer to left and inserting Tommy Leach in center. Leach made an error which allowed Philadelphia to tie the game in the ninth (although Cincinnati would win 3–2 in 10 innings).

The next day, Williams was handcuffed by Grover Alexander (as most of the rest of the Reds were, as Alexander pitched a two-hit shutout) and Eppa Rixey, going 0-for-8 in the Phillies' double-header sweep in Cincinnati.

Williams was given a warm welcome by Reds fans, who were seeing him for the first time. After his initial poor outings, Williams rebounded with a two-hit game in a 4–2 loss July 25 and had an RBI hit in another Reds loss, 6–2, the next day.

Although Herzog again hit Leach for Williams on July 27—against the left-handed Rixey—the rookie outfielder was praised by Phelon for being a "great place hitter,"[15] while *The Sporting Life* noted his ability to bunt, saying Williams "can lay the ball down most artistically."[16]

Williams also kept proving he was useful with more than just his bat. In an August 4 double-header sweep—a season-high fourth straight victory for the Reds—he was part of a double play off a fly out in Game 1 and scored from second base on an attempted pitcher-to-catcher-to-first double play in Game 2. "It was a smart play for Williams to come all the way home from second," observed the *Cincinnati Enquirer*. "He faked [Brooklyn first baseman Jake] Daubert completely, the Brooklyn captain not seeing him until he was almost to the plate."[17]

Williams went on a mini-hitting tear as well, going 9-for-27 while getting a hit in eight of nine games. People were taking notice. Against the New York Giants on August 6, Williams was given the first intentional walk of his career in the ninth inning of a 2–2 tie.

From the recap of the game in the *Cincinnati Enquirer*: "The word went out that he was a dangerous man, and he was deliberately walked in order to keep him from slapping the ball in his well known style.... Kenneth Williams may well be proud."[18] The move didn't work, either, as pinch hitter Tom Clarke singled in the winning run.

Herzog's confidence in Williams appeared to be restored as the next day he moved him to third in the lineup. As it happens, that coincided with Williams's getting to face future Hall of Famer Christy Mathewson, who at 34 was nearing the end of his career. He nevertheless held the Reds to five hits in a 5–4 win.

In Williams's first at-bat against one of the all-time greats, he bunted. But the ball was thrown away and he reached third base. The next time up, he was allowed to swing away and belted his second career triple.

Making the jump from the Northwestern League to the National League, Williams was faring well. His average was now at .256, not eye-popping, but sixth-best on the Reds, who as a team were hitting .253, and he was now seemingly entrenched as the team's No. 3 hitter. He'd bat in that spot in the lineup for the rest of August.

But even on the Reds, Williams's time playing minor-league teams wasn't quite over. The team traveled to Pittsburgh and had a couple of days off, so exhibitions were scheduled against the Wheeling (West Virginia) Stogies and Youngstown (Ohio) Steelmen, both cities within a reasonable distance. The Reds would eventually receive $450 for playing.

Buck Herzog, however, did not make the trip to either game, further alienating him from the team. Herzog wasn't just the manager, he was also the starting shortstop. Yet he wouldn't stay in the same hotel as the other players on road trips. And he tried to emulate the hard-nosed style of New York Giants manager John McGraw, for whom he had played, but Herzog didn't have the experience or history with the players to pull it off. Heading elsewhere while the rest of the Reds had to board a train for a 60- or 70-mile ride and then play some low-level minor-league team surely didn't help Herzog's cause.

"All this talk about Herzog being on good terms with his players is tommy rot," infielder Marty Berghammer, who played for Cincinnati under Herzog in 1914 before bolting for the Federal League's Pittsburgh franchise, told *The Sporting News* in November 1914.

> Why, he doesn't deign to speak to them off the field, and if he happens to meet any of them on the street he passes them with his nose in the air as if there was a mighty big difference between a manager and an ordinary ball player.
>
> He won't ride on the same car with them, and even at the hotel will avoid eating with them in the same dining room if he can. Take it from me, Herzog isn't a popular manager at all, although I take off my hat to him as a ball player and a hustler at that.[19]

The players made the best of the situation with or without the National League's only player-manager. In Youngstown, the team was taken by a bus which was equipped with "an organ that worked the exhaust of the engine and played lively music"[20] from the train station to the ballpark. Outfielder Tommy Griffith took the opportunity to sing songs which he wrote—"Take Me Back to Old Ohio" and "[I'll] Change Your Shadows to Sunshine." (The latter included the lyrics "I'll change your shadows to sunshine—Your life will be as a dream—No more the darkness will enter—Into your heart my sunbeam—Your life to me seems so dark dear—For it I'll try hard to cheer—If you will only believe me—I'll change your life for you, dear."[21])

The Reds won both games, and in the short term all went well for Williams. He had two triples in a 6–4 win over Wheeling and collected two singles as Rube Benton tossed a one-hitter in a 5–0 victory against Youngstown.

But Cincinnati also was able to get a look at a young left-handed outfielder in Wheeling named Earle Neale—better known as "Greasy" and as a future pro football Hall of Famer—which wasn't as good for Williams's long-term prospects. A few weeks after playing the Reds, Neale would send a note to Cincinnati saying he hoped the team would buy out his contract.

Williams was still in left field for Cincinnati in 1915, however. He'd get a hit in 16 of 19 games from August 13 to 28, (excluding an August 22 exhibition against Bridgeport) including

Outfielder Greasy Neale, an eventual NFL Hall of Famer, replaced Ken Williams in Cincinnati (George Grantham Bain Collection, Library of Congress).

a four-hit game August 19 against the Giants. He hit a "resounding"[22] triple which scored two and doubled in another, but both times was thrown out trying to get an extra base off the hit.

It seemed every good play by Williams came with a bad one. He'd make a great play in the field, then lose a ball in the sun. Get a hit, but be out trying to get another base or make a poor decision in trying to steal. For example, in the second game of an August 25 double-header against the Phillies, his RBI single made it 6–5, but after a Leach strikeout he was caught stealing to end the game.

The team went into a slump as well. Shaking things up, Herzog moved Williams to fifth in the lineup, and he responded with a two-run triple in a 4–0 win over the Boston Braves on September 1. But after going 1-for-13 over the next four games, Herzog stopped writing Williams's name on the lineup card (including September 10, which turned out to be the major-league debut of the St. Louis Cardinals' Rogers Hornsby).

Over the next few weeks, Williams's playing time was limited to six pinch-hit appearances and a couple of late substitutions in left field. After a 16-game drought, he was back in the starting lineup against Brooklyn on September 24, and while he managed to go 2-for-4, he also was picked off twice by Sherrod Smith. Once again, the good with the bad.

Cincinnati had just drafted John Beall from Milwaukee of the American Association, and he got the start in left field the next day. Williams would get just two more starts. The first was in Game 1 of a September 27 double-header against the Cubs on a soggy field in wintry conditions. He went 0-for-3 with a walk and strikeout, but did steal a base and score a run. Beall started in Game 2 and went 1-for-4.

Williams and Beall alternated starts again in a double-header vs. Chicago the next day. Beall was 1-for-2 in Game 1 while Williams was hitless in four at-bats and dropped a fly ball (although he also recorded an assist; good with bad yet again).

Williams's final appearance of the season came September 30. With the score tied at 2 in the eighth inning, Williams was summoned to hit for player-manager Herzog, who was slumping with just one hit over his last six games. Williams hit a bouncer over pitcher Johnny Lavender's head that second baseman Alex McCarthy couldn't handle. It was ruled an error, with Heine Groh scoring the eventual winning run.

After the game, Williams and pitchers Frank McKenry and Ray Callahan left the team early (the season ended October 3) and headed home. This was common practice among the Reds, sending players who lived out west home before the season was over. Williams didn't mind leaving, but had some trepidation.

"Just one thing hinders me," he lamented. "Of course I want to go home—and yet if I arrive in my little village home before the end of the season every bug in the place will swear I was fired for failing to make good."[23]

Despite the way the season ended, before leaving Williams signed a contract for 1916 for around $350 a month, or roughly the same amount rookie Rogers Hornsby made ($2,000). For comparison's sake, in 1916 Babe Ruth made $3,500, Joe Jackson $6,000 and Ty Cobb $20,000, while teammate Heine Groh, who was entering his fourth full season in the majors, made $4,000. Williams would eventually be placed on the Reds' reserve list.

Veteran outfielder Tommy Leach lost playing time to Ken Williams with Cincinnati in 1915 (George Grantham Bain Collection, Library of Congress).

Williams managed to hit .242 in 71 games (243 plate appearances), which was good for sixth-highest on the team for players with more than 100 plate appearances. The other starting left fielder, Tommy Leach, hit just .224 with a .275 slugging percentage and would turn 38 in November. Herzog would announce in December that Leach would not be returning in 1916. In other words, the job was Williams's—or someone else's—for the taking. At the World Series, Herzog said, "I'm positive this big Ken Williams can go much better than he showed last season."[24]

According to the *Spokesman-Review*, teammate Groh, who in November was visiting in Spokane, where Williams began the season, was "confident Williams ... will come though big next year."[25]

But all was not positive for Williams. Despite showing prodigious power in the minors, he slugged only .324 with the Reds, hitting 10 doubles and four triples with no home runs.

"Wasn't acclimated, didn't feel halfway right, and am blamed well aware that I didn't play the sort of ball that was expected of me," Williams told *The Sporting News*. "Give me a chance at the start of the season, though, and I think I can deliver."[26]

What Williams didn't say, but a teammate did, was that Herzog had changed Williams's batting style and forced him to go with a lighter bat. Bill Rodgers arrived in Cincinnati around the same time as Williams and held down the second-base job in the second half of the season. He saw the hitting regression firsthand.

"[O]ne day he fell into a slump," Rodgers told the *Oregonian* in 1917, "and after a couple of hitless games, Herzog jumped on him with all feet and made him discard the big bat. Williams is a slugger and not a 'choke bat' artist. A wise manager would not have tried to change his style."[27]

Williams would also have competition. Herzog was clearly impressed with Beall, who just hit .235 in 10 games, saying, "Johnny Beall looked so good that it was plainly a huge mistake to have kept him in the minors for the last five years."[28]

Cincinnati also secured the services of Neale as well as George Anderson, who had played the previous two years for Brooklyn in the Federal League, which had dissolved following the 1915 season.

One thing Williams, Beall, Neale and Anderson all had in common: All were left-handed hitters. Clearly, there was quite the competition underway for Cincinnati's starting left fielder in 1916. All but Beall were also known as having good speed.

After spending his usual offseason in Oregon—where he now had mini-celebrity status, mentioned as being in attendance at a football game in Ashland—Williams met up with fellow West Coasters Red Killefer, Pete Schneider and Frank McKenry on the train to Shreveport, Louisiana, where the Reds were holding spring training. McKenry was worried he would be called back home; he was in the California militia and could be called into service if the U.S., which was trying to hunt down Pancho Villa, went to war with Mexico.

The players settled in at the Youree Hotel—which charged members of the Reds the discounted rate of $3.50 a room—and took a six-minute ride via streetcar to the fairgrounds. The Reds didn't practice in the ballfield in town, as that was being used by the city's Texas League team.

Shreveport, a town of 28,000, didn't have too much to offer for the players other than baseball. It had just banned alcohol (something Williams was used to in Grants Pass), although it did have a movie theater, unlike Alexandria, Louisiana, where the Reds had trained the previous year.

When it came time for baseball, the competition for the left-field spot was quickly in full swing. Herzog was alternating the players at all three outfield positions, with Williams playing in right field (the one secure spot in the outfield, held by Tom Griffith).

As usual, there was the good with the bad. He saw Beall homer in a five-inning intrasquad game, and the next day Williams tripled home two runs in a 21–7 rout over the Shreveport Gassers. But in a six-inning intrasquad game the next day he went hitless (Beall had an RBI single), and then Williams didn't play against Shreveport one day later.

There'd be a 3-for-3 game with a double for the "Colts" against the "Vets," only to be followed by an 0-for-5 game (although with two steals) in a loss to Shreveport. But no one else was making a case for himself, either. By the time the team broke camp March 23, only Anderson had taken himself out of the competition, perhaps partially due to a sore ankle, and he was sold to Omaha on March 28.

In trying to sort out the outfield picture, prognosticators started to peg Beall as the starter with Williams in reserve and Neale hoping to stick around as well. *The Sporting News* said Williams's problems were due to the hot weather in Louisiana, and the cool weather back north would be of help. This was ironic, as throughout his career, reporters would claim the cool weather held Williams down.

Williams's luck began to change in Memphis in a game against the Yankees on March 30. After seeing limited action (and not playing in one game) the previous three days, Williams was given the start in left field. He went just 1-for-4 but hit the ball hard every time up, the victim of three fine defensive plays, and also had an assist in the outfield. His one hit was a double that scored two runs.

He was rewarded with another start against the Yankees back in Cincinnati on April 2.

This time he went 1-for-3 (first baseman Wally Pipp robbing Williams of extra bases on one vicious liner), breaking a 1–all tie in the seventh inning with a two-run single. Williams also stole a base and scored a run, meaning he had a hand in all three runs of 3–1 victory.

Cincinnati closed out its exhibition season with four games against the Columbus (Ohio) Senators, and Williams got the start in left field in each. He didn't fare well at the plate—going just 1-for-11 in the four games—but he did record two steals and three assists, and had seven putouts in one of the contests. He also inadvertently caused the forfeit of the third game on April 6. After Williams was called out at third base on a force, Herzog, who was coaching third base, went into a fit. Herzog was ejected, but refused to leave the field (the same thing had happened a week earlier in New Orleans when Williams was called out at first; on that occasion the police had to be called to escort Herzog out of the park), and thus the game was forfeited.

Herzog obviously didn't hold it against Williams, as he started him in the finale and pronounced Williams would start in left field and bat third on opening day. It was a sunny day for Ken Williams's first major-league opening day on April 12, 1916. He, along with the rest of the Reds players, met at the team office at 11:30 a.m. and headed to the Sinton Hotel for a noon luncheon. From there, they traveled to the corner of Western Avenue and Findlay Street, home of Redland Field. As the players entered, they could hear Weber's Band entertaining the nearly 25,000 fans with a pregame concert.

With 2:37 p.m.—the start of the game—approaching, Williams jogged out to left field and positioned himself in front of the wall, which had "Vote Yes" in large letters (Cincinnati was to vote on appropriating $6,000 for a rail transit system).

Perhaps it was opening day jitters. Or maybe it was playing in such a large crowd (reported as 24,500, then the fourth-largest in team history). Or maybe it was just one of those things. But in the fifth inning, he booted a line drive hit over Herzog's head, the play helping the Cubs score three times in opening up a 5–1 lead en route to a 7–1 win.

Williams did record a hit—he threw the bat at the ball for a bunt single in the eighth—and hit a deep fly to center that Cy Williams made a nice play on, but the error was the play that stood out.

Herzog kept Williams—"Bill," as he was regularly being called in the local papers—in the lineup for the next day's game. And while he made another error in left field, he also singled in two runs in the third inning after faking a bunt to help start a four-run inning. It helped the Reds beat the Cubs 6–3, although only 2,800 fans witnessed it.

Williams walked and scored a run in a 4–2 win over Chicago on April 14, but didn't get a hit, something he also failed to do in the next four games as well. A move to the sixth spot in the lineup—Cincinnati had obtained notorious first baseman Hal Chase and Herzog had him batting third—didn't help, either.

Despite not getting any hits, Williams stopped making errors, had an assist by throwing a runner out at home plate against Pittsburgh on April 17, and stole a base vs. the Pirates on the 18th, although he was also thrown out trying to score from second on a single to left field by Bill Louden (who had replaced Rodgers as Cincinnati's second baseman).

Cincinnati would next play Chicago, but not before facing the Springfield (Illinois) Reapers of the Central League in an exhibition on April 19. Williams, Neale and Beall would all face Springfield's Jesse Haines, a future Hall of Famer.

Playing in left field and batting third, Williams was 1-for-4 with two runs, a double and a stolen base (and also reportedly lost a fingernail sliding into second). Neale played in center and was 3-for-4 with three runs, a triple and a steal. Beall, in right, was 3-for-5 with a run, two triples, a double and a steal.

Reds players gathered at Chicago's new home field at 12:30 p.m. to take part in an opening day parade—as this was the Cubs' first home game at the North Side ballpark. Perhaps Williams wasn't impressed with the park; neither was the owner of the Reds, Gerry Herrmann. Cincinnati's boss declared he "does not think that the Cubs will remain on the North Side for more than a year or two, the stands and the field are both too small for the big league game and the location is not so well suited for the majority of the down-town fans as the old west side."[29]

Williams might have been too disappointed to even notice the size of the field and grandstand, as he found out that Beall would be starting in left field for the Reds. Matters were made worse, at least for Williams, as Beall went 3-for-4 with the first home run hit at what would one day be known as Wrigley Field (not counting Federal League play; the Chicago Whales had played in the North Side park the previous two years, and the Cubs took over residence after the dissolution of the league, at which time the Whales owner, Charles Weeghman, bought the Cubs). Even though the Reds lost that game, 7–6 in 11 innings, Herzog declared the lineup would stay the same for the foreseeable future.

The April 21 game was postponed due to cold, but on April 22, true to his word, Herzog had Williams on the bench and Beall in left. Williams could only watch as Beall went 1-for-5 while striking out three times with men on base. Beall struck out two more times April 23, back in Cincinnati against the Cardinals, but so did Williams, who pinch-hit for Schneider in the 12th inning of a 2–1 loss.

Beall continued to start—going 0-for-3 with another strikeout April 25 and 1-for-3 with a double in an 11–3 win over St. Louis on April 26. Williams got into the latter game as a late substitution in center field for Killefer as Herzog played some backups in the blowout.

Then, suddenly, Beall was gone. Cincinnati was at 23 players and had to get to the league-mandated 21 by May 1. With that deadline looming in a few days, the Reds sold Beall, who hit .333 with two doubles and a homer but with seven strikeouts in 21 at-bats in six games, to Milwaukee before the team headed to Pittsburgh.

Williams was presumably back as the starting left fielder, but that decision would have to wait one more day as the opener against the Pirates was postponed due to rain. That was probably good news to Reds players, who didn't get into Pittsburgh until 2 a.m.—seven hours late—due to a freight train wreck, as well as an additional hour delay in Columbus.

On April 28 the sun was out, there was a game to be played, and indeed Herzog had Williams back in left field and batting sixth. But Williams would soon hope the sun was hidden behind rain clouds.

From the start, Williams had trouble picking up fly balls while stationed in left, the sun field at Forbes Field. He did make one catch, but was slow starting after balls and lost at least two in the sun, which fell for hits. Williams had already struck out in his initial plate appearance—which would also be his last.

In the dugout, Herzog turned to Neale, who had played in just six games and was 0-for-4, and asked if he could play the sun field. "I told him I could," Neale recalled to *The Sporting News* nearly 26 years later. "'All right, get in there,' Buck told me. 'Get a bat and go up and hit for Williams.'"[30]

Nervous, Neale took three pitches down the middle for strikes. But he was flawless in the field, and while he did strike out again, he also rapped a single. He had done enough in Herzog's eyes. Neale remembered Herzog saying to him afterwards, "'The way you've started, kid, you're going to be in there tomorrow.'"[31]

Cincinnati not only had to get its roster down to 21 players, but the Reds also had a $1,000 payment due to Spokane if Williams remained on the roster by May 10. "Charley Herzog had faith in him—lots of it," claimed *The Sporting Life*. "But they say that 'Bull' wrote his own death warrant when he failed to reach a couple of flies on Forbes Field."[32]

The truth was not quite that simple. Herzog probably did have faith in Williams at one point, but he wasn't hitting—perhaps due to Herzog's influence—had already been benched and, finally, looked poor in the field at an inopportune time, when Herzog was just looking for some consistency out of the position.

The math was simple: Williams was struggling (he was just 3-for-27 with no extra-base hits, two walks, and five strikeouts). He also didn't endear himself to his teammates when, during the series against St. Louis, he spotted a friendly face, former Regina teammate Jack Smith, who was now on the Cardinals. As he shook Smith's hand, he heard jeers from his teammates such as "Kiss him!," "Take him out to dinner," and "Why don't you rent a room."[33]

Neale, in his brief time, showed he could handle the sun and helped his cause further with a pair of two-hit games in his first two starts. Herzog also liked the "fighting spirit"[34] of the rookie, who back in Memphis during spring training got in an altercation with teammate Fred Toney, not backing down to the veteran pitcher and ace of the staff. And of course, cutting Williams would save $1,000.

Cincinnati pitcher Fred Toney, the ace of the staff during Ken Williams's short stay with the Reds (George Grantham Bain Collection, Library of Congress).

Herzog informed Williams he was headed back to Spokane. Williams couldn't have been surprised that he was being farmed out, but back to Spokane? That came as a shock. He wasn't the only one surprised. *The Sporting News* as well as syndicated sports columnist Morris Miller expressed shock that Williams would go unclaimed and land back in a Class B league.

"[Williams] certainly is a better man than some of the athletes performing on certain Class A clubs that can be mentioned," Morris wrote, "where the club owners, too, are assuring the fans they are willing to spend millions to strengthen."[35]

Williams and the writers, of course, didn't realize the arrangement between the Reds and Spokane, where the outfielder was technically Spokane property until that May 10 deadline. Certainly this circumvented the rules of the time, but then, players had very few rights in 1916, bound by the reserve clause, gentlemen's agreements, and deals such as this one.

To his credit, Williams didn't badmouth the Reds. In fact, he thought Cincinnati would finish in the first division. (The Reds actually finished in last place. Herzog was traded in midseason to the New York Giants, with Christy Mathewson coming over to manage. Cincinnati also received Edd Roush in the trade, the outfielder finding his place in the starting lineup and eventually the Hall of Fame.) But Williams learned a lesson about the majors: It was nothing like the minors.

"Up there you got to play baseball and deliver or else make way for someone who can," Williams said shortly after his arrival in Spokane. "The old soft soap and salve that figures so prominently in minor league baseball is a thing of the past in the big show. All of the eloquence of a Demosthenes and the oratorical qualities of a Watterson"—this part likely was embellished by the writer, as it is hard to imagine Williams, who didn't get past the eighth grade, making such references—"will not avail you a thing unless you can top it off with a healthy batting average and a good fielding notch."[36]

Recalling the incident with teammates after greeting Jack Smith, Williams said, "The minute you spike the field up there you have to forget that such a thing as a friend exists on the other club. Every enemy that opposes you is looked upon as a venomous enemy, whether he happens to be a college chum of yours or an old crony.... Ride the opposing team from the start of the game, give them old Harry from the time the bell rings until the game is over, holler for every break and play ball up to the standard set and you are liable to stick in the show."[37]

There would be claims later of Williams being an aloof teammate with few friends in the game. No doubt his experience with the Reds would shape how he'd act when he got back to the majors for a second time. But the majors were once again far away, and Spokane certainly represented that, both in geography and its station in the minor-league chain.

Chapter 5

Across the Ocean and Up the Ladder

Kenneth Williams was surprised he was being sent back to Spokane, but once the news was broken to him, he went straight to that city. Familiar with the town, Williams headed to Frank Smith's baseball parlor, whereupon he stumbled upon an argument between two men. One was telling the other how he'd bet Williams wouldn't return to Spokane after being let go by the Reds. Overhearing the conversation, Williams interjected, "I wouldn't be so sure about that."[1] The man offered him the same bet.

"It would be like taking candy from a baby," a straight-faced Williams remarked. Angered, the man said, "You seem to know so darn much, who the devil are you?"[2] Williams informed him and the man then took off out a side door, never to be seen again.

The above story, as reported by the *Spokesman-Review*, is likely apocryphal, used to show the amazement that their best player from a year ago—and someone who didn't belong at Spokane's minor-league level—actually was going to be back in the lineup.

But there was no doubt Williams was a welcome presence in Spokane. The *Spokesman-Review* had a picture of Williams with the headline "Prodigal Son Returns," saying he "is a star performer in this class of company."[3]

There was one little issue, however, before Williams could play for Spokane—he had to agree to terms with the Indians. Williams was making $350 a month with the Reds and wanted the same deal with Spokane. Since the Northwestern League had a salary limit of $1,800 a month, in no way could the team afford to spend over one-sixth of its funds on one player.

Of course, Spokane could use Williams. The team recently cut Cy Neighbors and was using pitcher Dutch Ruether in the outfield. Also, even before Williams was signed, Portland of the Pacific Coast League was making noise that it wouldn't mind acquiring the outfielder.

Thus, only a couple of days after arriving in Spokane, Williams signed a contract with the team. He only missed a couple of games, yet, while residing on the bench, still managed to be thrown out of the first one he attended after signing May 9 (along with manager Nick Williams and two teammates) for arguing multiple calls.

Williams got into his first game with Spokane on May 11 as a late substitute and was in the starting lineup the next day. His impact was felt almost immediately. In an 8–7 win over Butte on May 13, Williams drove in three runs, including two on a double. In a double-header sweep the next day, Williams scored one and drove in one in a 5–4 win in Game 1. In Game 2, when he had two hits, he drew the ire of Butte manager Joe McGinnity after spiking Miners first baseman Ed Kippert while sliding back into the base.

On May 15, in the eighth inning of a 5–4 win over Great Falls, Williams threw a one-bouncer from center field to home plate to nail a runner trying to score from second base in the top of the inning, then scored the eventual winning run in the home half.

However, Williams hurt his knee in the game—an injury he said first occurred when he was in Cincinnati—and was placed on the suspended list, eventually having to go to the hospital to try to hasten the healing process. Williams wouldn't return until June 13—missing 28 games—but that didn't stop inquiries from the Pacific Coast League's Portland team and St. Paul of the American Association as to the availability of the outfielder.

But Spokane was holding on to first place and manager Nick Williams wanted his team to stay there. He made it known that Ken Williams was not available; he was going to be playing for Spokane.

The Indians might have led the Northwestern League, but their offense was struggling. Williams's RBI single in the first inning on June 13—his first at-bat since being injured—resulted in Spokane's first run in 21 innings.

Missing all that time didn't affect Williams's bat. He had a hit in each of his first six games—including four games with two hits—and was noted for making several great catches in center field.

On June 18, after those first six games, Spokane was in first place with a 33–17 record. Vancouver was in second place at just 26–24. Williams and Spokane, however, both went into slumps. On July 2, Williams was hitting just .181, and by July 10, the Indians' lead was down to four games over Butte.

There was still interest in Williams from higher-level minor-league teams, however, but Spokane manager Nick Williams quashed any thought of a deal by saying all offers for his players would not be considered until the Indians clinched the pennant.

Williams was rumored to be in another deal—*The Sporting Life* said Williams, along with Buck Herzog, and perhaps pitcher Clarence Mitchell, were to be traded to the New York Giants, the transaction needing just "the confirmation of the Cincinnati Board of Directors."[4] Perhaps the Reds forgot Williams was not their property, or maybe the magazine had the wrong information. Cincinnati did end up making a trade, though, acquiring Christy Mathewson and Edd Roush for Herzog and Red Killefer.

Meanwhile, Williams started to heat up. From July 4 to 22 he went on a 20-game hit streak, raising his average to .295. In a series at Butte, he hit a home run in both ends of a July 4 double-header and connected again four days later.

After a 6–5 win over Butte on August 1 in which he went 2-for-3 with a double, two RBI and a steal, the *Spokesman-Review* declared, "Ken Williams looked like the hitter who was so much feared by Northwest league [*sic*] pitchers last year.... He took the same old, free swing and met the ball squarely twice...."[5]

On August 9, Williams went 2-for-3 with a triple to "the extreme corner of the right field fence"[6] as Spokane won at Great Falls to increase its Northwestern League lead to eight games. Afterwards, it was announced Williams was sold to Portland of the Pacific Coast League.

Portland owner Judge William McCredie said the team paid "about $1,000"[7] for Williams and agreed the club wouldn't take the outfielder until the 1917 season. Remembering how his team had collapsed the previous season after selling Williams, Spokane president F.C. Farr explained, "We can't afford to break up the club now that the season is so near over and we won't do it.... We have had enough experience on players leaving the team in the middle of the season and we don't care to try it again."[8]

If there was any disappointment for Williams in having to stay in Spokane, he didn't show it at the plate, where he kept smacking the ball, hitting a home run at Great Falls on August 13. A few days later, Spokane relented a bit and said Williams could go to Portland once the Indians' season was completed.

Spokane kept winning and the chances of winning the pennant kept increasing—really, it would take a miraculous collapse for the Indians not to be Northwestern League champs. With Spokane needing just five wins to clinch, Nick Williams left the team to go to Portland on what was described as a "business trip."[9] Able to speak to Nick Williams in person and not just by wire, McCredie convinced the Spokane manager to turn Ken Williams over immediately.

In his last game with Spokane, Williams went out in style. In the10th inning of a 6–2 win at Tacoma with two men on, Williams connected on a Suds Sutherland pitch and sent it far over the right-field fence. "Williams ... knocked what looked to be the longest drive ever seen in the local park," reported the *Spokesman-Review*. "It was still rising when it crossed the right field fence and ought to be somewhere near Hoquiam [roughly 80 miles from Tacoma] by this time."[10]

The local paper, the *Tacoma Times*, confirmed the momentous blast, writing: "The pill soared up into the air like an aeroplane and headed for Oakland station. The small boys are still looking for it."[11]

The game over (and Spokane's magic number to clinch now just at four), Williams boarded a train—fortunate that a proposed railroad strike had not taken place (workers were looking to reduce their work days to eight hours)—and headed the 350 miles to Portland. He arrived at Vaughn Park, the same field he had played on six years earlier—almost to the day—during his brief and somewhat controversial foray with Portland back in 1911, in time for the Beavers' 3 p.m. game against Salt Lake.

Williams was placed in center field and batted seventh. Despite the long past 24 hours, Williams not only played but he also starred. The *Morning Oregonian*'s Roscoe Fawcett wrote, "Kenneth Williams performed brilliantly throughout the game both at bat and in the field."[12]

In his first at-bat for Portland, Williams cracked a double. He also walked three times, scored a run, stole a base and caught all four fly balls hit his way. Williams's lone out was ticketed for extra bases before Salt Lake's Tommy Quinlan "came through with a corking catch."[13]

There was no doubt about it, Portland was glad to have Williams aboard. Not necessarily for any pennant push, as the win put the Beavers at just 57–66 (.463). First-place Los Angeles was 77–55 (.584). Even in a league that played until the end of October, a championship was but a dream.

But Portland had one outfielder, Denney Wilie, nursing a bad knee, and another, Billy Nixon, was ticketed for St. Paul. However, the day after Williams's arrival, St. Paul informed Portland that it had acquired another outfielder and no longer needed Nixon's services.

No matter; Williams was in the lineup to stay. He was in the lineup August 25 and for the first game of a double-header August 26, going 1-for-3 in both games. That was also the day Spokane clinched the Northwestern League title. Williams was a big reason the team won the championship.

He missed the next three games, which included another double-header August 27 which, unfortunately for Williams, was attended by Philadelphia Phillies scout Jim Wolfe. But he was back in the lineup August 29, banging out three hits, including a double, with a walk while stealing a base and recording two assists from his center field position.

After another three-hit game September 1, including another double, Portland released outfielder Billy Speas. He had been with a Portland-based team the previous eight years, but McCredie said he had become expendable with the addition of Williams. In addition to Speas, Portland also got rid of its mascot—a bear cub named Bill, who had started to try to "make a square meal out of several of the Beavers' calves and forearms."[14]

Williams was moved up to the fifth spot in the order as Portland and first-place Los Angeles played three straight days of double-headers. Williams had four doubles, a home run, and a stolen base, and made several nice catches in the six games, drawing the attention of the Angels manager.

"Williams beat us out of several games last week, not only by swatting the ball hard, but by the way he dragged down line drives hit his way," Angels manager Frank Chance would say. "I'd be willing to bet that he went back against the centre field [fence] eight times and robbed us of base hits.

"He certainly looked like a million dollars to me,"[15] added Chance, who was player-manager for the Cubs from 1905 to 1912, winning two World Series and two other National League pennants, as well as the New York Highlanders in 1913–14.

Portland saw Williams's value as well—the team, which had been under .500 for much of the season, was 13–8 since his arrival. On September 9, with seven weeks left in the season, the team and the outfielder agreed on terms which would keep him around for the final two months as well as for the 1917 season, making him the first player to be signed for the following year. The *Portland Journal* reported that Williams "announced that he might as well put his signature to a 1917 contract and get the matter out of his mind."[16]

Of course, Williams, like everyone else in the minor leagues, was eligible for the major-league draft, which was held September 15. Teams gave up $2,500 to draft and claim a player—however, only one player could be drafted per team from Class AA league teams (which included the Pacific Coast League). So when Portland pitcher Wynn Noyes was drafted by the Philadelphia A's, Williams was then deemed off limits to other MLB clubs and could not be selected.

If that turn of events disappointed Williams, it didn't manifest itself on the field. In fact, it might have motivated him, as in a series at Oakland following the draft, Williams went on a tear.

He doubled to open the seventh inning of a 2–2 tie on September 19 and scored the eventual winning run. The next day, he homered off Oakland's Bill Prough, then, following a rainout, went 3-for-3, including a two-run home run. After a 1-for-5 double-header on September 23, while also getting an assist on a fly out double play, he went 3-for-8 in a double-header on September 24. Portland won six of the seven games to move into fourth place.

Williams was hitting .324 with Portland, which was the highest batting average on the team (and second in the PCL to San Francisco's Mike Fitzgerald, who was at .346 in 76 games), and the team was 22–12 in games in which he played.

After watching the Portland-Oakland series, the San Francisco Bulletin's Warren Brown wrote about Williams's prowess as well the businesslike attitude he went about in his game:

> Ken Williams, the biffing center fielder of the Beavers, is about the most serious-looking chap in the league. Ken has played a series in San Francisco [*sic*] and during the entire seven games he hasn't cracked a smile, grinned or displayed any sort of interest in proceedings, outside of an occasional yelp over bad strikes or close plays.
>
> In the course of the series Williams swatted a couple of homers over the right field fence. The average player performing this stunt will job around the sacks grinning from ear to ear. Williams trotted around the paths as if it was an every day occurrence with him. He actually looked bored.
>
> Williams looks like a mighty valuable performer for next year's Beavers, putting aside the strength he has given the club in its final spurt for the present season. He is a hardworking chap, rather awkward, but a result getter, and results are what McCredie likes, or rather demands, from his hired man.[17]

Of course, there was still the 1916 season to finish. In addition to showing off his speed with four stolen bases in a five-game stretch, Williams smacked a long home run into Portland's center-field bleachers against Vernon on October 1.

However, in an October 4 loss to Oakland during the team's final home stand, Williams injured his leg. Beavers manager Walter McCredie said the outfielder would be lost for the remainder of the season, which was scheduled to end October 29. When Williams joined Portland, the team was 56–66. After its 6–0 loss to the Oaks, the Beavers stood at 84–82.

The plan for Williams was to heal and convalesce in Portland, where he wasn't totally without baseball. The Hellig Theater described every play from that year's World Series between Boston and Brooklyn, which began October 7 and ended October 12. But suddenly on October 15, Williams was summoned to California as McCredie didn't want the Los Angeles Angels to clinch the pennant against his Portland team.

Portland split its first two games against Los Angeles and were getting routed in the third game on October 19 when McCredie put Williams into center field in the eighth inning. He called in outfielder Denney Wilie to pitch.

In his first at-bat in 14 games, Williams singled. Then, whether his bad leg was fully healed or not, he stole second and eventually took third on a double steal before scoring Portland's first run in an eventual 15–2 loss. Without Williams, including the game in which he came in as a late replacement, Portland's record was 5–10.

Williams started in left field on October 20 and went 0-for-2, but walked, scored a run and made eight putouts as Portland prevented L.A. from clinching with a 3–1 win. Williams sat the next day as the Beavers won again, but the Angels still clinched the pennant thanks to a loss by Vernon.

Despite having nothing to gain—except trying to finish higher in the standings—McCredie kept playing an obviously not fully healthy Williams, putting him at first base in Portland's final eight games of the season. McCredie was also unhappy with the job Bill Rodgers was doing as a fill-in at first for Ivan Howard, who had torn ligaments in his right arm around the same time Williams injured his leg.

Williams was just 7-for-33 (.212) with no extra-base hits—yet, oddly, six stolen bases—upon being called to California after injuring his leg and thought to be out for the season. That cost him a chance to hit .300, which is where his average was before leaving Portland; he instead finished at .284 with the Beavers. Making matters worse, Portland would stumble to the finish, going 3–5 in its final series in San Francisco to finish at 93–98 and in fifth place out of six teams.

Despite his limited time in the league, both Roscoe Fawcett of the *Oregonian* and Lou Kennedy of the *Portland Telegram*, the latter writing for *The Sporting News*, both put Williams on their 1916 Pacific Coast League all-star teams.

Williams could head home to Grants Pass secure in the knowledge that he could more than hold his own in the top echelon of the minor leagues, was well thought of by many, and didn't have to worry about any contract haggling for next season. Things were looking up as 1917 approached, and it would only get more interesting.

Having already signed his contract, Ken Williams avoided a controversy that developed at the start of 1917. Dave Fultz, a former player and leader of the Fraternity of Baseball Players, an early attempt to unionize, called for players to not sign contracts and eventually strike if their demands, which included "fighting for full payment during incapacitation,"[18] were not met.

This included not only players in the major leagues but also the minors. Portland owner Judge William McCredie speculated about 75 percent of Pacific Coast League players were involved, but the *Oregonian*'s Roscoe Fawcett thought it was less than half. There wasn't much sympathy from owners or reporters. "Barring an occasional injustice, the diamond athletes are fairly well treated by the magnates,"[19] Fawcett wrote.

"Coast League players have had their railroad fares paid to the spring camps, have lived at the best hotels and have drawn more money than we should pay them,"[20] said McCredie, failing to note that players didn't draw a salary during spring training. He also was in favor of cutting the monthly salary allowance of PCL teams from $4,500 to $3,500.

Then, in all seriousness, he added: "We cannot add to our burdens by paying their railroad fares back to their homes in the Fall. They ought to stick it out here for the three or four months between seasons."[21]

Portland players were given additional incentive not to fall in line with the fraternity. McCredie received a couple of offers to host his team for spring training, but one stood out from the rest. Honolulu offered the team $4,000 plus 50 percent of the gross gate receipts to have the Beavers train there. Portland would be the first professional team to have spring training in Hawaii. But players would have to be signed by February 12, or else they were on their own until the team returned to the United States in late March.

"That ought to help break the strike if there is any," said pitcher Byron Houck, one of three players, along with Williams and Bill Stumpf, who were already signed to Portland contracts. "All the boys will want to make that trip and I'll bet Mack has little difficulty signing his players this spring."[22]

Williams quickly acknowledged he would make the trip to Honolulu. "The local owners were not certain … whether [Williams] would care to go," reported *The Sporting News*. "Upon their writing him Kenneth answered by return mail, stating that they could positively count on his going and adding that he would be delighted to have a change from the regular spring grind, which often grows monotonous."[23]

Of course, not everyone was thrilled to make the trip. Portland had made an offer to catcher Joe Kilhullen, who played in the Eastern League in 1916. The United States was not at war, but much of the rest of the world was fighting, and speculation that the U.S. would enter the fray was ripe in the newspapers. Kilhullen decided to sign with Oakland, including with his signed contract a note which read, "I hope that your training camp is in some part of America."[24]

Kilhullen might have feared some anti–German sentiment due to his last name. That certainly was the case for Stumpf. Portland was to leave port in British Columbia, Canada, that country having allied itself with Great Britain, which was at war with Germany.

"We may have some difficulty with the British government with some of our Teuton ballplayers," McCredie said. "I understand they are rather strict. They may grab Bill Stumpf and shove him in a concentration camp for a year or two."[25]

Nevertheless, Stumpf did make the trip to Honolulu, although while he was awaiting to meet the team in Victoria, British Columbia, he hid away at a hotel using the pseudonym Al W. Everding.

In all, 18 players made the trip—three catchers, eight pitchers, four infielders and three outfielders, and many of these were not expected to make the Portland roster for the 1917 season. They were joined by Beavers owner Judge McCredie and his wife, McCredie's nephew and team manager Walter McCredie, and three newspaper reporters. All boarded the ship wearing an American flag pin in their lapels, in part likely to spare them of any abuse on the small chance of conflict with Germans.

It would cost the team $1,500 to assemble the traveling group in Vancouver, where they would leave for Victoria to pick up Stumpf and board the ship *Niagara*. The cost for sea travel would be $4,000, or the entire purse promised to Portland for training in Hawaii.

The *Niagara* left Victoria on February 14 and the voyage, by all accounts, was an easy one, with no rough seas. However, this didn't stop Walter McCredie from remaining in his bunk for the majority of the trip. Judge McCredie also "had a couple of bad days."[26] Shortstop Charlie Hollocher got quite sick when the ship encountered "Devil's Hole" on February 18.

Everyone else tried to while away the time by guessing how far they'd travel each day, or by playing cards or shuffleboard. Once in a while a game of catch would break out on deck, but sooner or later an errant throw would cause the ball to splash in the water down below, thus ending that activity.

It wasn't all fun and games, of course. Each night the ship went dark at night for fear of German submarines (none were spotted). McCredie wasn't even allowed to use the telegraph to inform those in Honolulu that they were close.

Finally, on February 21, the group landed in Honolulu, impressed by their surroundings. Up to the weary travelers stepped Arthur Merrick, the sports editor of the *Honolulu Star-Advertiser* and also a former Portland newspaperman. The key to the city was handed to the team.

The Beavers were taken to Waikiki, where they would stay in groups of two in a dozen cottages which were located just a couple of blocks from the beach. The cottages, which all had unique names such as "Gorilla Rest" and "Swallow Rest" (Williams roomed with Houck in "Beaver Rest"), were constructed in just 5½ days by the Trent Trust Co., and thus were dubbed Trentown.

The cottages were small, estimated at 18 by 26 feet, green and arranged in a circle. There was a plaza in the middle along with a dance hall and a place for the players to lounge about. A large dining hall was built for them nearby as well. It didn't take long for many in the traveling party to exclaim, "Let's go eat!" While local cuisine was partly featured, with papaya a big hit, Williams didn't partake in any, saying, "Not for me. What's the use of getting an appetite for that stuff when you can't get any in the States?"[27]

But the team was in Honolulu to play baseball, and a game was scheduled for the next day against the 25th Infantry team from Schofield Barracks, whom they were to play several times during their stay. Also known as the Wreckers, the team was made up entirely of African Americans, which caused some consternation back in the U.S.

"Cal Ewing of the San Francisco club thinks the league should take action to compel McCredie to cancel the games," reported *The Sporting News*, "but it is the general opinion that the color line can not be officially drawn. McCredie's defense is that the games with the negroes will be big money getters."[28]

The 25th Infantry consisted of future Negro League players "Heavy" Johnson and Dobie Moore, as well as the pitcher who would face them that day, eventual Hall of Famer "Bullet" Rogan.

Rogan offered a rude welcome. It was written by both Fawcett and the *Portland Journal*'s Robert Cronin, who was writing for the *Honolulu Star-Advertiser*, that the Beavers didn't have their "sea legs"[29] yet, thus weren't in proper condition to play. It might not have mattered against Rogan, who struck out 13 and didn't allow a hit until Stumpf bunted for a single in the eighth. Williams had the only other hit, a double in the ninth inning, as Portland lost 3–0.

Portland would get a much-needed day off to train, as well as to enjoy the "perfect"[30] weather, before playing again on Saturday, February 24. This time, behind two hits each by Williams and Ralph Pinelli, the Beavers beat the 25th Infantry, 6–5, in front of a crowd so large that it was reported "half of the $4000 given Portland has been made up."

Williams picked up another hit—a double—the next day, but Portland lost to a team made up primarily of Chinese as Vernon Ayau, who would sign with Seattle, hit a game-winning two-run home run. Judge McCredie was so impressed by catcher Ken Yen's arm, he offered him a contract with Portland (Yen would eventually turn it down, saying he didn't want to leave Hawaii or his job there).

Portland ran into Rogan again February 28 and lost 4–1, although the Beavers loaded the bases in the ninth inning with one out (Williams walked on four pitches with a man on first). But Rogan struck out pinch hitter Robert Marshall, his seventh K, and Moore snared a hard line drive to end it. Williams again accorded himself well, going 1-for-3 with the team's only run, singling, going to third on a passed ball, and trotting home on a Stumpf single. His fielding also continued to be flawless.

When the team wasn't playing or practicing, there was plenty of time to have fun. With the beach nearby, many players took advantage and splashed about. Williams, along with pitchers Kenneth Penner and Gus Helfrich, tried to play the ukulele (Williams playing it with his right hand). Williams—as well as Stumpf—even tried a little surfing.

The team even organized what they called a TrenTown Entertainment Committee, chaired by Bill Rodgers (who in the offseason sold cars, and at some point in 1917 both Williams and Penner bought a Dodge from him). The committee held a party the evening of March 1, with an orchestra, ice cream and refreshments. It was basically a way for the players to meet women.

The *Honolulu Star-Advertiser* noted there were 24 bachelors among the players and newspapermen in town and they "request that all the charming young ladies who can possibly come to be present … and Rodgers wants any young men who come along to bring two ladies and all will be royally entertained."[31] Although Judge McCredie's wife was to chaperone, with 24 bachelors, she certainly couldn't keep her eye on everyone. In fact, the team pitched in and bought a Victrola record player so they could hold a dance nearly every evening.

The partying didn't affect the Beavers in their next game, a 14–4 blasting of Fort Ruger. Portland tuned up St. Louis College 10–3 on March 3, with Williams hitting a home run to deep center which "became tangled up in bicycle wheels."[32] Afterward, Williams said his legs were finally starting to feel good.

But the next day Portland lost again to the Chinese squad, 4–3, with poor fielding dooming the Beavers. For his part, Williams had a hit and made a catch on the only ball hit to him in center field.

Portland's stay on the island wouldn't last much longer, but the Beavers wouldn't lose again. They followed that close loss with a 6–0 win over the 32nd Infantry, which mustered only one hit (Williams was one of four Portland players with two hits). Then, on a day that was "hotter than blazes,"[33] they downed the Chinese team 7–1.

The next day, March 11, it was another game against the 25th Infantry, but there was no Rogan for Portland to face, as the pitcher was on a ship back to the United States. Williams doubled as the Beavers won 3–0. Before the game, Rodgers and Denney Wilie went wild hog hunting. They bagged three, and served it to the team for dinner after the game.

Two days later, with Prince Jonah Kūhiō Kalaniana'ole Pi'ikoi in attendance, Portland beat the Chinese team 9–1. Williams collected three hits and three steals and assisted on a double play.

With the trip winding down and just two games to play—both on March 15—the team went on a shark-fishing tour, with a few of the deadly creatures coming close to the boat. Some were a bit fearful—there were conversations of "hearses and undertakers"[34]—but Williams was said to have had "a wonderful time,"[35] although McCredie would later note "this fellow Williams may not be much on shark hunts...."[36]

Portland finished its trip with a pair of wins, 7–0 over the 25th Infantry and 4–3 over the Chinese team, meaning the Beavers won more games than they lost against both squads. Williams had a hit in both games and finished with a .340 average in Hawaii, the highest on the team (not counting Houck, who was 1-for-2) and his nine runs were second most. He was only one of two regulars to bat over .300—Wilie, who had 10 runs, at .304 was the other—as Portland hit .253.

The trip was deemed a success. The Portland contingent all signed a letter praising their time on the island, while the *Honolulu Star-Bulletin* noted all the attention the city received in the Portland papers. In addition, Portland made around $4,000 in gate receipts on top of the $4,000 given to them to come to Hawaii.

Williams also came out a little fatter, literally, as he gained six pounds—from 178 to 184—on the trip, although he did grumble on "of illness, but as this is an old dodge with him, the players did not take it as serious."[37]

After an uneventful voyage, the Portland team landed in San Francisco on March 20 and as planned met Nick Williams and his Spokane contingent, as well as a few Portland players who didn't make the trip. The teams were supposed head to Stockton to train, but after Nick Williams relayed to McCredie there wasn't much backing for the team there, instead chose to head to Maryville, 100 miles north of Stockton.

The team received two bits of bad news on March 21. In the short term, there were no hotels in Maryville available, as a labor federation convention was ongoing for a few more days. Of more long-term concern, the United States was likely headed to war, with Congress to vote on the issue April 2.

Portland was able to solve the first issue—the team had to split up, with some staying at the local Elk's Club and others taking refuge in the homes of citizens willing to help out.

There was obviously nothing it could do about the second, so the team went about its business.

The Beavers held an intrasquad scrimmage—the infielders vs. outfielders—and played five games against Spokane, going 4–0–1, before finishing up April 1 with the Maryville Trolley League team (which was "bolstered by some major-league holdouts"[38]), losing that game 1–0 in 10 innings.

Portland then boarded a train ready to start the new season with Walter McCredie confident of his team's chances. The Beavers had a lot of new faces on their roster—by one count 10 of the 19 in camp—and by league rule at least four had to have no experience at the Class AA level or higher. Incredibly, despite having played in the major leagues, Williams qualified (something McCredie had argued for in the offseason, claiming Williams had not played a full season at the AA level). McCredie tabbed Williams for the fifth spot in the order behind newcomer Babe Borton and predicted he'd bat around .300.

The Beavers opened in Salt Lake City, where patriotic fervor was in full swing. With the war vote nearing, President Woodrow Wilson was asking for at least one-half million men to be added to the U.S. armed forces. American flags were handed out and "The Star Spangled Banner" was played before the start of the game.

The Senate and the House both voted for the resolution of war and on April 6, Wilson signed it. The U.S. had declared war on Italy. And baseball went on. There wasn't any immediate effect, although one has to wonder what Ken Williams was thinking. The early thought was to make eligible for conscription anyone aged 19 to 25. Williams was listed in this group, although in reality he was 26 going on 27. This plan, if adopted, would end his ruse, and possibly cost him a chance at once again making the big leagues down the line.

Williams had hit in Portland's first nine games, but then went into a slump right around the time the president began to talk of his draft plan. Williams's average dipped considerably, as he was 1-for-his-last-20 and 3-for-30, while Portland was tied for last with Los Angeles at 11–15.

Then, as quickly as he went into a slump, he snapped out of it. It started with an RBI triple to the right-field fence in a loss to Oakland on May 2, followed by a two-run double in a win over the Oaks on May 3. The game was capped by a three-run home run—his first of the season—in the ninth inning, whereupon "the entire bleacher and grandstand gang arose en masse and gave three rousing cheers and a tiger for the husky outfielder."[39] He got a similar reaction the next day when he made an over-the-shoulder one-handed catch, then rammed into the center-field wall but held onto the ball.

He wasn't done. On May 8, in a 7–2 win over L.A., Williams drove in five runs, the first on a triple that went all the way to the right-center field fence, and four more on a grand slam to right field that "sailed so far over the palisades that a boy on an autoped was chasing it down Linton Boulevard at last reports."[40]

Williams had two hits in Portland's next game, its fifth straight win, then homered again on May 10 as the streak reached six in a row.

After a rainout, Portland won its seventh straight, 4–3 in 12 innings over L.A. Williams scored an early run, walking and stealing second and third, scoring on an overthrow on the latter stolen base. In the top of the 12th, he came in from center field on a rundown and ended up throwing out a runner at home. In the bottom of the 12th, he re-tied the game with an RBI single before the Beavers finally pushed across the winning run.

Williams kept pushing his average upwards, and had back-to-back three-hit games at San Francisco on May 15 and 16 (stealing four bases as well in those two games). Shortly thereafter, two important things happened:

President Wilson signed the War Army Bill, and a draft would be held June 5. Men who were aged 21–30 were eligible for conscription. This put Williams as draft-eligible under his real or false age (Williams did use his actual birthdate on his military registration card). While in Los Angeles on May 24, Williams and several other teammates would sign the list and register as absentees—as the majority of the players did not live in Portland. Meanwhile, Judge McCredie declared he could get all the players he wanted from major-league teams in return for Williams or shortstop Charlie Hollocher.

On May 29, with Pittsburgh Pirates scout Hugh Bezdek in attendance (as well as his former manager Nick Williams), Williams hit two home runs in a 6–5 16-inning win at home over Vernon.

A few days later, on June 3, Williams did himself one better, accounting for all of Portland's runs by socking three homers off former major leaguer Roy Mitchell in a 4–3 win in 14 innings over Vernon. He hit a two-run home run in the second inning, tied the game with a solo shot in the ninth and won the game in the 14th. He also doubled in the 11th and was intentionally walked in the 12th.

The fans in the small crowd that attended—there were an estimated 2,500–3,000 on a day in which rain seemed imminent but never fell—threw money at Williams after his homers in the ninth and 14th innings. "If it had been Chinese money," the *Oregonian*'s Fawcett wrote, "Williams would have had to hire a dray to carry it downtown."[41]

The three-homer game made national news, with reports of it in *The Sporting News* and *Leslie's Illustrated Weekly Newspaper*, albeit over a month and half after the fact in the latter. His stellar play wasn't lost on the locals, either.

"Without Williams the Beavers would be in a sorry pickle. The big Grants Pass outfielder covers a lot of ground in the field, is fairly fast on his feet and is a power on the offense,"[42] wrote Fawcett, who predicted Williams and Hollocher would be acquired by a major-league team for 1918. Fawcett's prediction would come true, perhaps sooner than he thought.

St. Louis Browns business manager Bob Quinn went scouting in the Northwest. The Browns manager, Fielder Jones, was quite familiar with Portland, having moved there a decade earlier, running a hotel and eventually scouting Northwestern League teams—including Portland's entry, which was also owned by the McCredies—before becoming league president.

Quinn saw Williams play two games—June 7, in which Williams went 2-for-4 with a stolen base, and June 8, a hitless day in four at-bats. Nevertheless, that was enough for Quinn, and the Browns and Portland made a deal for Williams on June 9.

In 1917, major-league teams didn't have affiliates as they do in modern times. However, MLB teams would have arrangements with minor-league squads to do exclusive transactions with each other. Portland was one of those teams that operated with a particular major-league club.

Up until the 1917 season, the Beavers supplied the Cleveland Indians with numerous players, including outfielders Jack Graney and Buddy Ryan, shortstop Roger Peckinpaugh and pitchers Vean Gregg (a three-time 20-game winner), Rip Hagerman, Spec Harkness, Gene Krapp and Bill Steen—all of whom saw significant playing time with Cleveland. Portland even sold power-hitting first base prospect Louis Guisto to the Indians late in 1916 for, according to the *Oregonian*, seven players and $4,000.

But then Cleveland broke the bond between the two teams, sending three players to Milwaukee in January 1917. "Hereafter Portland will have to deal with Cleveland as it would any other major league organization,"[43] reported the *Cleveland Plain Dealer*.

Portland made a couple of early connections with other teams. On January 19, the Beavers received outfielder Jack Farmer and second baseman Paddy Siglin from Pittsburgh. The next day, the club purchased first baseman Babe Borton outright from the Browns, who had no need for Borton with George Sisler at that position. It was likely no coincidence that those were the two teams who were recently scouting Portland players. Williams had looked "sweet"[44] to Pirates scout Hugo Bedzek, but Pittsburgh was looking for a first baseman. So Quinn swooped in and got Williams.

There was no announcement of what the deal comprised, although Judge McCredie intimated that Portland would receive players and cash. McCredie's nephew and the Beavers manager Walter was not happy with the deal and would continue to voice his displeasure weeks later.

"The Judge tossed a bloomer by letting Williams go for a song," Walter McCredie said. "I wish that he had consulted me, for I know that I could have gotten twice as much for the big slugger. Williams is the greatest hitter this league has ever turned out, yet he did not bring nearly as much money as Louis Guisto did."[45]

Babe Borton, who was indirectly responsible for the Browns landing Ken Williams (George Grantham Bain Collection, Library of Congress).

But what Judge McCredie obviously didn't tell his nephew was that Portland was in some financial trouble, as were all the Pacific Coast League teams. Teams were already faring poorly and the country's heading into war wasn't going to help. There was talk of reducing rosters and cutting salaries to help out teams. Judge McCredie said if players wouldn't cut salaries by even "$25 to $50 a month,"[46] the season might end early by "a month or two."[47]

In addition, Portland still owed money to the Browns for their purchase of Borton—$1,500 to be exact. McCredie suggested Williams as a form of payment instead. While there wasn't an exact date pinned to the delivery of Williams to the Browns, some reports, including the *Oregonian*, said September. The *St. Louis Post-Dispatch* reported it wouldn't be until 1918, as "the Portland club is down in the race and Williams's batting has been the only redeeming feature of the team's plans."[48] Quinn obviously knew he was getting quite the bargain and confirmed the deal.

But for the time being, Williams was still with Portland. There was no celebration for Williams's soon-to-be ascension back to the majors, but he provided his own fireworks.

After going 1-for-3 on June 12 and clubbing a double and stealing two bases the next day, Williams went 4-for-4 with two home runs and a double—barely missing a third home run—in a 5–4 win over Los Angeles at Portland. His performance caused the *Oregonian* to write, "Ken Williams' salary ought to be raised instead of lowered,"[49] and Angels owner Johnny Powers to declare, "We'll win if they conscript Williams."[50] Two days later, Williams homered again (and also "played a star fielding game"[51]), giving him six doubles and six home runs in his last 12 games.

Not everyone was pleased with Williams, however. Williams teased pitcher Walter Mails—who was also known as a bit of a flake—winking at his teammate whenever Mails would remove his cap and brush back his hair while coaching on the bases. Mails finally had enough: he quit the team and went to Seattle, eventually joining a team in the shipbuilders' league.

Mails's leaving certainly didn't affect Williams. He doubled and scored the winning run at Oakland on June 19, then had three hits and stole a base in a 3–1 Beavers win over the Oaks on June 20. He was putting the fear into teams—Oakland intentionally walked him in the June 22 game—and impressed a local writer.

"That one man can make or unmake a ball team was never better shown than Ken Williams, Beaver center fielder, is doing on the bay lots against the Oaks this week," wrote the *Oakland Tribune*'s Carl E. Brazier. "He has developed into the sure-to-death-to-pitchers type of batter—the type that the Coast League has not known since the days when Heine Heitmuller [who played in the PCL from 1905 to 1908] was alive and at his best.... Williams is a worthy successor to the memories of Heitmuller as a man who hits high up around the top in the batting records, and at the same time makes his hits when his club needs them—not just when his batting average needs them."[52]

Through June 24, Williams was fifth in the PCL in batting average at .316 (Portland as a team was hitting just .247), tied for fourth in runs with 46, tied for third in doubles with 19, fourth in stolen bases with 23, and leading the league in home runs with 10, four more than Salt Lake's Early Sheely. Williams's 10 home runs were more than three teams—Vernon had eight, Los Angeles seven and Oakland two—and the same number as San Francisco had.

Williams kept hitting—and hitting home runs—and had no bigger back-to-back games than at Salt Lake on August 10–11. He went 3-for-3 with two home runs and six RBI on August 10 and followed that up with a 4-for-5 effort, including two doubles, a home run, a steal and four RBI, causing the *Oregonian* to dub him "Invincible 'Ken'"[53] in a headline.

On August 26 he was up to a league-leading 21 home runs as well as 45 steals, just two behind the leader, Oakland's Billy Lane. Williams hit for the cycle on September 8 in a 21–1 drubbing of Salt Lake to help Portland get to .500. The Beavers were swept in a doubleheader the next day by the Bees to fall back under .500, but Williams went 5-for-8 in the twin bill.

Not everything Williams did drew rave reviews, however. During a September 16 doubleheader against Los Angeles, it was reported by the *Oregonian*'s James J. Richardson that during a line drive hit over second base, Williams was too busy talking to fans and didn't notice the ball, forcing shortstop Hollocher to run after it, by which time the Angels' Jack Fournier had a double.

Of course, Williams did have reasons to be distracted. He had been drafted, although he wouldn't have to enter the military until the second call for service, expected to be around the new year.

Then in mid–September it was reported that Williams was to be married. He would neither confirm nor deny the report, which said his bride-to-be was Miss Mariam White of Weed, California. The rumor was she was his high school sweetheart, although more likely she was someone Williams met while he played baseball in Weed. There is a record of a 14-year-old Mariam White in the 1910 census from Edgewood, California, which was located just 5 miles from Weed. In addition, the August 29, 1917, *Oregon Observer* noted that a Miss Mariam White had just returned to Grants Pass after visiting Medford for two weeks.

Perhaps this was a decision made on looking to change his draft class—being married with a dependent spouse would move him into a temporarily deferred status. In any case, there is no record of Williams marrying White, nor any marriage talk beyond the September 16 report from the Portland team office.

Williams had another multiple-homer game September 19, knocking two out of the park against Oakland, and hit his final home run—his 24th—of the season in the second game of a double-header against Vernon on September 30.

Even when teams didn't want to pitch to Williams, he did damage. In a September 26 game against Vernon, the Beavers had runners on second and third in the eighth inning of a scoreless tie. With the "fans yelling for a hit from Williams … [Vernon pitcher Art] Fromme started to walk him."[54] However, Williams reached out at the intentional ball and lifted a deep fly to left field, Jack Farmer tagging after the catch for what would be the only run of the game. Fromme protested that Williams stepped over the plate, but to no avail.

Williams would miss the final eight games of the season, which finally ended October 28, but still led the league in home runs (he had six more than Sheely and outhomered every other team in the league other than Salt Lake), finished sixth in batting average (.313), tied for second in steals (58) and second in outfield assists (34). Only one player in all of organized baseball hit more home runs than Williams in 1917—30-year-old Ernest Calbert of Muskogee in the Class D Western Association. The high in the major leagues was 12.

The praise in the local papers was effusive. In a recap of Williams's season, the *Oregonian* wrote: "Other batters have stolen more bases; others have hit more times, and others have hit more extra base hits, but none in the last five years have ranged so close to the top in all of these departments as Williams did during the past season."[55]

Lou Kennedy of the *Portland Evening Telegram* said Williams was the most valuable player of the Pacific Coast League:

> Offensive strength is absolutely necessary for a ball club which wins consistently. Williams constituted the principal point of assault, as far as the Beavers were concerned. In addition to this, however, he had a good record as a fielder, and was one of the best baserunners in the circuit.
>
> The record doesn't show how valuable Williams was in driving in other men ahead of him with his extra base clouts, which won more than one ball game for Portland.…
>
> Williams is in a class of his own on the showing he made. No batter in recent years has been able to show anything like it. Such a record requires a combination of hard hitting and speed on the bases is absolutely required. Some players have topped Williams in one department, and others have topped him in different

> branches, but none of them can show the combination of qualities which have gained him this distinction.[56]

Simply put: Williams had shown he was too big for the highest level of the minor leagues. The major leagues now beckoned him. But with war on the horizon and financial tightening by clubs expected, the question remaining was: just when would he get his chance?

Chapter 6

The Minors, a Major War and the Big Leagues (Again)

Ken Williams had two pressing matters as 1917 turned into 1918: 1. when he would need to report for military duty; 2. coming to a financial agreement with the St. Louis Browns.

Neither stopped Williams from enjoying his offseason, spent, as usual, shuttling between his hometown of Grants Pass and Portland. In December, Williams was initiated into Portland's chapter of the Benevolent and Protective Order of the Elks ("Almost every big man in American baseball today is an Elk,"[1] the *Spokesman-Review* had declared back in 1914). He traveled back to Portland in January to sit at ringside and watch his friend, Battling Ortego, box to a draw against Al Sommer for the Pacific Middleweight title.

Perhaps Williams was buoyed by a report that he likely wouldn't be called by the draft until late in the fall, due to the fact he was 10th on the list of the Class One draft-eligible men in Grants Pass and many in Josephine County had already volunteered their service. (In addition, two of the men in front of him, including teammate Byron Houck, were on the limited service class). Either way, he wasn't happy with the contract he received from the Browns, who were in no mind to hand out big salaries.

St. Louis owner Phil Ball reportedly lost around $25,000 in the 1917 season. Due to the Federal League, salaries had escalated as teams (and leagues) tried to keep hold of their players.

Third baseman Jimmy Austin had been given a $5,000 contract in 1915 to stay with the Browns and not jump to the Federal League. According to *The Sporting News*, the Browns cut his salary to $3,000 for 1918.

Infielder Lee Magee, who had been acquired in a trade from the New York Yankees in July 1917, had a three-year, $25,000 contract, but St. Louis also looked to cut his salary down to $3,000. He was eventually traded to Cincinnati in March. Like Williams, pitcher Bob Groom was displeased with the contract offered to him by the Browns. He was sold off waivers to Cleveland on February 15.

It is with that backdrop that Ken Williams took a look at his contract sent to him by the Browns and refused to sign. From the Browns' vantage point, they weren't going to give big money to a 25-year-old (really 28) outfielder who busted it up in the minors but didn't do too much in his first go-around in the majors with Cincinnati, whatever the reason for his sub-standard play. From Williams's vantage point, the Browns were offering only $75 more a month than he made in Portland—and he played one more month of baseball in the Pacific

Coast League. Pitcher Byron Houck lived in Portland, and as with Williams, St. Louis had obtained him from the Beavers. And, like Williams, he also did not sign his contract.

Browns manager Fielder Jones, who also resided in Portland, took it upon himself to lunch with Williams and Houck on January 24 to discuss the situation. "I'm not registering any kick over the contract, because I know that Fielder Jones will treat me right,"[2] Williams said the day prior to the meeting. Despite the optimism, nothing was resolved. The *Ogden Standard* had a report of the lunch: "Jones said he did not take up the subject of their contacts with them to any great extent, but he intimated that ball players were used to getting all the big money that they could in the olden days and that they had not yet come to realize that in these war times the magnates find it necessary to cut their corners carefully in order to get by.... Neither Williams nor Houck had much to say, but both feel that they would rather stay in the Coast league than play for but a very little more in the majors."[3]

Reports in newspapers of Williams's feelings about his contract situation varied, with terms such as the volatile "incensed"[4] and the more benign "dissatisfied"[5] being used. Meanwhile, in St. Louis, Browns business manager Bob Quinn kept saying he had not heard from Williams (or Houck), and was unaware of any issues. However, with Fielder Jones still in Portland, where he would remain until March 4, the Browns had an agent to deal with Williams.

Houck would agree to terms first, his signed contract arriving at the Browns' office on February 13. That left only four unsigned players: Williams, catcher Hank Severeid, pitcher Dave Davenport and infielder Magee, who as mentioned would subsequently be traded. Quinn expressed optimism that he would receive contracts from all four shortly, and a little over a week later the signed contract for Williams indeed did arrive.

Bill "Baby Doll" Jacobson. Hardly anyone knew the first name of Ken Williams's outfield mate in St. Louis from 1919 to 1926 (George Grantham Bain Collection, Library of Congress).

Williams didn't take the Browns' original offer, and St. Louis didn't exactly break the bank to get the outfielder in the fold. But the team did offer a few hundred more dollars for the season, which placated Williams enough that he signed the contract immediately. On February 26 he sent a telegram to Quinn stating as such: "Have signed contract and mailed it to you today."[6]

It was intimated by the *St. Louis Post-Dispatch* that Williams signed because the Browns convinced him that they could make do without him and were more than willing to let him play in the Pacific Coast League. However, the extra money given to Williams would suggest otherwise. The truth of the matter was the Browns probably needed Williams as much as he needed them. St. Louis was undergoing a complete retooling of its outfield.

Bill "Baby Doll" Jacobson (supposedly given

that moniker in the minors based off the song "Oh, You Beautiful Doll"; Jacobson would claim, "Most people never knew my given name was Bill"[7]), who had played in 148 games in 1917, had enlisted in the Navy, as did Yale Sloan (109 games) and both would miss the entire 1918 season. Slick-fielding Armando Marsans had been traded in July 1917 to the Yankees for Magee. Burt Shotton (118 games) was dealt in December 1917 to Washington along with starting shortstop Doc Lavan for pitcher Bert Gallia and $15,000. Left-handed hitting Ward Miller, who was a starter in 1916 but had only 100 plate appearances in '17, was sold to Omaha and never reached the majors again.

That left the Browns with 27-year-old Earl Smith, who played in 52 games with the Browns in 1917 and 14 for the Cubs in 1916; 34-year-old Ray Demmitt, who hadn't played regularly in the majors since 1914; Tim Hendryx, a 27-year-old who had played sparingly in four seasons with Cleveland (1911–12) and the Yankees (1915–16) before getting a chance to start in '17; and little Johnny Tobin, 26, who was all of 5-foot-8 and 140 pounds, and who spent 1917 with Salt Lake City of the PCL (batting .331) after hitting .213 in 77 games with the Browns in 1916.

Williams, with his impressive minor league statistics and turning just 25 (at least in the Browns' eyes) in June, had to be considered a more-than-viable option for one of the outfield positions.

Jones said only first baseman George Sisler, coming off a year in which he had 190 hits, 37 steals and batted .353, and Smith were assured of starting. Everything else was up for grabs.

"I think I'm safe in saying the team generally is a vast improvement over the one I managed last season because it couldn't be much worse,"[8] said Jones, referring to his team that ended up seventh in the American League with a 57–97 record.

Williams and Houck left Portland together and took a train to Shreveport, Louisiana, where the Browns would hold spring training at Gasser Park, home of the Texas League team. Williams joined St. Louis at an optimal time, as the clubhouse in Shreveport had been updated—it now had hot *and* cold water in the showers.

The players arrived from Portland on March 14 and Williams made quite the first impression. "Kenneth Williams is a great bulk of a man, fast and a sure catch on a fly ball," reported the *St. Louis Post-Dispatch*. "At bat he swings on the ball hard and drives it far into the far corners of the field. It will be difficult to keep him off the team."[9]

In the Browns' first four exhibition games against Shreveport, Williams and Demmitt alternated as starters, and both players were on the "Regulars" team in an intrasquad scrimmage against the "Scrubs" squad.

Williams earned a regular spot in the lineup with his play in an intrasquad game held on March 21 between teams managed by Jimmy Austin and Fritz Maisel, who were each battling for the starting third base position.

The *St. Louis Post-Dispatch* dubbed him the "star of the game ... seven times he ran back almost to the fences and pulled down drives that seemingly were labeled for base knocks. Manager Jones said after the game that Williams is just a great an outfielder as Armando Marsans ever was. Coming from Fielder Jones a compliment like this means a great deal."[10]

Williams followed up that performance by going 2-for-4 with two doubles and a steal in St. Louis's 8–5 win over Shreveport on March 23 and 3-for-3 and two more doubles and a steal the next day in a 5–0 victory against the Gassers. In addition, "Williams also made two great running catches in center field"[11] in the March 24 game, once again earning praise from Jones and comparisons to Marsans.

"He's equal to the best fielder I ever saw," said Jones, who was known as a good-fielding outfielder when he played, making with ease catches over his shoulder. "He times the ball as accurately as the best of them and his ground covering ability is unexcelled."[12]

While Jones compared Williams to Marsans, one newspaper claimed another resemblance. "The writers figure that if Kenneth hits, he will be one of the greatest outfielders of all time, and describes him as a player who fields after the order of Tristam Speaker," reported the *Morning Leader*. "He can go back as far as any fielder in the game and makes catches over his shoulder that are marvels. At going to the side he is even greater and at coming in on a ball we have yet to see his superior.... as a fielder there are few better in the big or little leagues today. The big fellow covers a world of ground, has a great arm and can judge the ball with unerring precision."[13]

But Williams's ascension to the class of Speaker would be derailed—or at least postponed. An illness started to spread throughout the team—outfielder Hendryx, pitchers Gallia, Urban Shocker and Dave Davenport, and catcher Hank Severeid all coming down with the chills and a fever. Severeid had to be hospitalized with what was deemed a severe case of pneumonia, and Davenport would lose 11 pounds.

It was Williams's turn next, just as spring training was coming to a close. He had to be confined to his room and put under a doctor's care and was still feeling ill, complaining of aches and a sore throat, as the team headed back to St. Louis, stopping on the way to play the Texarkana All-Stars.

Williams didn't play in that game, but Jones was hopeful the outfielder would be able to suit up for the annual series against the St. Louis Cardinals, which was held just prior to the start of the season, if not for his fielding, but also for his bat. In 1917, the Browns had just one player (Sisler) slug over .400 who had at least 100 plate appearances. Jones hoped Williams would help put a little more pop into the lineup.

"The coast boy is a wonderful fielder, coming on or going back for a ball with the greatest of ease, and he will develop into a long-distance hitter," Jones said on the eve of the opening game against the National League team. "Williams is a straight-away hitter, one who put a world of force behind his drives, therefore they get past outfielders and are good for extra bases."[14]

But Williams didn't play in the Browns' 4–1 win over the Cardinals on April 7. The weather was cold—it would postpone games until April 12—and with Williams not quite in perfect health, Jones opted to keep him on the bench.

By the time the weather cooperated, Williams had been told he'd been called for the draft and was to report to Camp Lewis, Washington, on April 26. Shortly thereafter, it was already reported that Williams was headed back to Grants Pass and would play on the Camp Lewis baseball team. The squad would be part of the Seattle Shipyards Baseball League, playing double-headers Saturday, then hosting a shipyards team Sunday.

However, after receiving his notice, Williams applied to be inducted closer to St. Louis, rather than near his home of Grants Pass. Permission for this was granted, and Williams, who in reality did not head to Oregon after receiving word of the draft, was home in St. Louis with the knowledge that he'd likely be called for service around May 10.

"I'm ready to go to the army when called," Williams said upon hearing the news. "I haven't played because I wanted to find out first when I was needed for war service. However, since I have found out, I'm willing now to get in and play the best game I can."[15]

The Browns opened up against the White Sox—the game had twice been postponed by rain, which made Williams's arrival seemingly even more fortuitous. However, Williams was a mere spectator, along with the approximately 5,000 fans in attendance at Sportsman's Park, as a band played and soldiers marched. Both were from Jefferson Barracks, soon to be Williams's new home. Afterward, the Browns lost 6–2 to the White Sox, behind Joe Jackson's 4-for-4 day, including a home run and five RBI.

Williams continued to sit—through three games and two rainouts—before finally making his Browns debut on May 2 against the Indians. But he wasn't a starter; instead, he was inserted as a pinch hitter for shortstop Wally Gerber in the seventh inning against Cleveland's Jim Bagby. He hit a hard grounder to first baseman Marty Kavanagh, who raced to the base and beat Williams by a step. The occasion was notable enough for the *St. Louis Post-Dispatch* to run a short headline of "Williams Makes Bow."[16]

The next day, Williams got another chance, again hitting for Gerber in the seventh inning. This time, though, the bases were loaded and the Browns were trailing 5–2. Cleveland brought in Johnny Enzmann to replace Bob Groom and face Williams—this was not a platoon move, as Enzmann was right-handed. Williams walked to force in a run, Enzmann was replaced and the Browns ended up losing 5–4.

Williams wasn't used in the next two games—4–3 and 3–0 wins over the Indians. The Browns then headed out on a road trip and weren't due back until June 1, so Williams was left behind at the Beers Hotel as he awaited military induction.

On May 12, Williams and 554 others from the St. Louis area were inducted into service at Jefferson Barracks, bringing the total number of soldiers there to around 12,000–13,000. Jefferson Barracks served as a training area, a place to get a uniform and initial instruction before heading off to a more permanent camp, and eventually overseas.

But unlike the majority of soldiers at Jefferson Barracks, Williams was a professional baseball player. And, as it happens, Jefferson Barracks had a six-team league and also formed a team to play games around the area in Illinois and Missouri.

Williams had wired home that there were some "fine ball players in his company"[17] and there was some suggestion of his managing a team. There was no evidence that Williams expected to be at Jefferson Barracks long, as he wrote his parents he hoped to make it back to Grants Pass on a furlough before being sent overseas.

Williams was placed on the 16th company team, where one of his teammates was third baseman Eddie Mulligan, who played in 69 games for the Chicago Cubs in 1915–16. When Gene Dale, a pitcher and teammate of Williams's when he played for the Reds, arrived, the 16th quickly claimed him.

League games were played every day on a field with a newly built 3,500-seat grandstand. *The Sporting News* estimated 30 former major leaguers occupied spots on the six teams. The players would leave the barracks to play fundraising games. Cardinal Field hosted an Army-Navy game between Jefferson Barracks and the Great Lakes Naval Station before the Cardinals-Giants contest on July 20. The day was filled with parades and a flag raising as well as the games.

Reports differ on the attendance, but between 15,000 and 18,000 fans watched as Army beat Navy, 6–5, with Williams going 2-for-4 including a key two-out run-scoring single in the eighth inning. The benefit game raised a reported $40,000 for the St. Louis Tuberculosis Society, to be used as a fund for soldiers who contracted the disease during the war.

While more exhibitions and benefits were being scheduled, the players remained at Jefferson Barracks and played in their six-team league. Williams was leading the circuit in batting average (.580), runs (21) and steals (27), and his 16th company team had the best record at 13–2.

A four-game slate between Jefferson Barracks and Great Lakes was announced. The teams would play games benefitting "the development of athletics at Scott Field, the aviation camp near Belleville, Ill., and Jefferson Barracks."[18] Games were scheduled for Alton, Illinois, on August 31, Belleville on September 1, East St. Louis on September 2, and Jefferson Barracks on September 3.

Shortly after the announcement, it was reported that the East St. Louis game already had sold 10,000 tickets. Meanwhile, "plans to make this patriotic ball game the biggest thing Alton has ever attempted in the baseball line were started."[19]

Alton didn't disappoint. A parade was held and several luminaries were introduced to the crowd, including Major Branch Rickey of the gas and chemical service (and also former Browns business manager and field manager). Two pilots provided "an exhibition of flight,"[20] which included one doing a tailspin and another "the loop the loop four times in succession."[21]

There was an overflow crowd of around 5,000, the majority of whom were women. The game itself was won 5–0 by Jefferson Barracks, which had a former major league player or minor leaguer at every position. The highlight was Williams's knocking a fly ball into the overflow crowd for an automatic double, the ball striking a Mrs. Clara Fisher on the head, sending her to the ground and eventually back home (although she was reported to be not seriously hurt).

Rain wreaked havoc with the schedule (the East St. Louis game, for example, wasn't played until September 8 and with only 2,000 in attendance) but still around $4,000 was raised for the war fund.

Next, games were scheduled against Camp Funston, which was located in Kansas. However, the benefit of these games was changing—proceeds would now go to help fund the athletic programs at both camps.

Games were played September 14 and 15, with rain and bad weather holding down the crowd size. Jefferson Barracks won 2–0 on the 14th—the first loss for Camp Funston, which had been 15–0—and lost 3–0 on the 15th.

There was talk of more games, but that was quashed when the commandant at Jefferson Barracks, Col. George K. Hunter, ordered the end of all baseball teams. While the move came as a shock to Charles Cooper, the director of the war camp community service who was scheduling more games, it shouldn't have come as a complete surprise.

Jefferson Barracks was not intended to be a place where soldiers resided for very long. Williams, for example, had arrived four months earlier and was still around—and he was not the longest-term veteran of the baseball teams. "Some of the baseball stars had been retained at the Barracks for six months of more and began to consider themselves permanent institutions,"[22] opined *The Sporting News*.

While the teams had raised some money, Hunter was clearly aware of the potential bad publicity. In June and July, over 500,000 American soldiers were shipped overseas. Names of soldiers killed appeared in the papers daily. And here were a bunch of soldiers still at Jefferson Barracks and in the public eye, playing baseball games. Charitable games while players awaited their orders were one thing, but a proposed service league—and acquiring money to spur athletics—was another.

Nevertheless, Williams, now a corporal, and Mulligan still didn't receive their orders for a couple of more weeks, and even then those were revoked and changed. As October turned into November, it was reported by the *Spokane Daily Chronicle* that Williams was "sent to the northwest ... on a special mission for the war department"[23] which had him visiting Portland as well as making "a quick trip to his home at Grants Pass, Ore."[24]

Williams returned to Jefferson Barracks and, according to his son Jack, was finally ordered to head overseas, but the war ended November 11. "I know he got on the boat and was on his way to Europe when the war ended and they turned the boat around and brought 'em all back, so he never made it over there,"[25] Jack Williams recalled.

On December 14—just over one month later—Ken Williams arrived back home at Grants Pass, officially no longer in the army. He'd spend the rest of the winter back home helping his mother, who leased the Western Hotel just before the end of the year and opened a dining room and charged 40 cents for dinner (50 on Sundays). Williams certainly wouldn't go hungry at that job and his appetite for baseball was only growing as well.

There was no contract squabble for Ken Williams in 1919. The *Grants Pass Daily Courier* reported he got a "considerable advance"[26] from his previous year's salary. In sending his signed document to the Browns, Williams included a note to business manager Bob Quinn that stated Williams expected to win one of the starting outfielder jobs.

The 1918 Browns struggled to a 58–64 record in the war-shortened season. Fielder Jones, who had been so effusive in his praise of Williams's defensive skills, quit as manager 46 games into the season. Third baseman Jimmy Austin took over briefly before Jimmy Burke, a St. Louis native, was hired. Burke was the opposite of Jones, who had set a curfew of 11 p.m. Burke was more player friendly, believing in a good "clap on the back"[27] as a means of motivation.

Fielder Jones as manager of the St. Louis Terriers of the Federal League. He'd move over to the Browns after that league folded and Terriers owner Phil Ball took control of the Browns. He'd manage Ken Williams—briefly (George Grantham Bain Collection, Library of Congress).

Based on the 1918 results, Burke certainly would welcome Williams's bat. George Sisler hit .341 and slugged .440, but the next best regular was outfielder Ray Demmitt at .281 and .370. The Browns as a team hit only five home runs, and one of those was by pitcher Dave Davenport.

Williams wasn't the only player returning. Fellow outfielders Bill "Baby Doll" Jacobson and Yale Sloan were back from the Navy. Pitcher Urban Shocker (army) and catcher Hank Severeid (tank division) were still overseas in France.

Nevertheless, Williams was ready to stake his claim in the lineup. He arrived in

San Antonio, the Browns' spring training headquarters for 1919, ahead of the St. Louis contingent.

During the team's first practice on March 18, it was hard to believe Williams had missed the entire 1918 season, as he was "walloping the ball in the same old fashion as he did last spring,"[28] even hitting the first ball over the fence among St. Louis players.

Williams made enough of an early impression to have Burke station him in center field in the early practices, with Jacobson in right and Johnny Tobin and Earl Smith splitting the duties in left.

"It was remarked by manager Jimmy Burke that something unusual in the nature of a stimulant must have gotten into the system of Kennett [*sic*] Williams since coming to San Antonio, for the speedy outfielder is cutting the grass in the outfield in a manner quite astonishing to his teammates," reported W.N. Norris in the *St. Louis Post-Dispatch*. "Kennett [*sic*] says that there is nothing the matter only that he was feeling very fine when he came here and that this climate has undoubtedly boosted his point of exuberance. Sisler and Williams have both have been pounding the ball hard in the batting sessions, and all of their drives sail straight out on a line."[29]

One reason Williams hit the ball so hard was that he used a heavy bat. Throughout his career in the American League he would use one of the heaviest bats among all the players. Out from under the guise and influence of Buck Herzog in his last go-around in the majors, Williams felt comfortable using the bat he wanted to wield. In San Antonio, when the bat orders were placed, Williams got six Spencer models made of Cuban wood, ranging from 42 to 48 ounces (Rogers Hornsby would later claim Williams at one time used a 54-ounce bat). As a comparison, Jacobson ordered bats between 40 and 44 ounces while Tobin's was 40 ounces.

Whatever bat Williams was using, he was putting it to good use. He had one of four Browns hits in a 3–0 win over San Antonio on March 29 and the next day hit a "mighty HR smash"[30] to right field to score two others ahead of him in a 9–5 victory over the Bronchos.

He then doubled in the first of two intrasquad games and went 3-for-4 in the other, showing his bat control by knocking a single on a hit and run with runners on first and second. But it wasn't just with the bat that Williams was excelling; he was flashing his speed and good defense as well.

"In center field there is nothing to it but Kennett [*sic*] Williams. He has no rival in the field trying for his job, nor is there such a need for a competitor," W.N. Norris wrote in the March 30 edition of the *St. Louis Globe Democrat*. "He is a wonderful fielder and good hitter and in the practice now going on in this camp the big fellow is showing a snap and speed that promise to carry him through several seasons as a major star."[31]

The Browns moved towards St. Louis with stops in Fort Worth and Tulsa for exhibitions. Williams, despite a sore arm, kept playing and hitting. Although he had missed the entire 1918 season save two plate appearances, Williams had shown more than enough in spring training to secure his place in the starting lineup.

But before the regular season began, there was the annual series against the Cardinals. Unlike the previous year, when he was trying to come back from an illness, Williams was among those announced as starters to the crowd by Joe "Biz" Kenney, who did so with an oversized megaphone.

In front of 11,000 spectators, Williams and the Browns took the field at Sportsman's

Park before the game in their new sweaters—which were olive green, despite the team's nickname. Once the game began, the players stood out in their brand new, clean white uniforms with brown and white socks and a white baseball cap with a brown visor.

The visor didn't help Williams, though, as he misjudged a ball in the sun in the eighth inning to allow two runs to score in the opening game. But the play just cost starting pitcher Allan Sothoron a shutout as the Browns won 5–2 with Williams going 1-for-4 at the plate.

The series would shift parks after each game. The Browns took the second game at Cardinal Park 4–0, with Williams collecting a double and triple. The Cardinals won the next two and the Browns took Game 5. Williams had a hit in each game.

The finale was played on Easter Sunday, April 20. Williams went 1-for-4 with a double and a stolen base (as part of a double steal). In the second inning, he showed off his arm by throwing Rogers Hornsby out at third base when he tried to go from first to third on a single. The throw was on a direct line and Hornsby was out by "two yards."[32]

The Browns won the series 4–2 and the teams claimed around $10,000 each, thanks to an approximate 40,000 paid attendance in the six games. Williams tied with Tobin for the team lead in hitting at .333, and also led both teams in steals with four (no one on the Cardinals had more than two).

When the Browns opened their season at home against the Chicago White Sox on April 23, Williams saw a familiar face as Col. George K. Hunter, the commandant from Jefferson Barracks who put a halt to baseball the previous mid–September, threw out the first pitch.

A presentation was also made to St. Louis natives Burke, Tobin and Lefty Leifeld, with each given a bouquet of flowers. Burke was also presented with a "studded diamond watch charm formed by two crossed bats and a ball upon the gold surface. The diamond is placed in the center of the ball."[33] Even White Sox catcher Ray Schalk, who was from nearby Litchfield, Illinois, was presented with flowers—he was given his bouquet before stepping to the plate in the third inning.

As for the game, the Browns were beaten badly, 13–4. Williams was 0-for-3, but did reach on an error and a walk, and also recorded an assist. Over the next three games against Chicago, of which St. Louis only won one, Williams went 5-for-11 with a couple of doubles and two RBI. He also partook in a triple steal in a 9–4 loss on April 26, swiping third as George Sisler raced home while White Sox starter Red Faber went through his windup.

After losing a pair to Cleveland, the Browns headed on a road trip. They beat the White Sox in Chicago's home opener so badly (11–4) that manager Kid Gleason "refused to be interviewed after the game and threatened to lick anybody who persisted."[34] After a rainout, the Browns lost a rain-shortened game 4–2. Williams recorded St. Louis' first hit in the game in the fifth, but in the third inning he and Tobin muffed a chance at the third out on a fly ball which fell between them, with all four Chicago runs scoring after the miscue.

Williams's fielding problems continued in St. Louis's next game, a 6–3 win in 12 innings on May 6 at Cleveland, as he made two errors—a throwing error in the fifth and "a muff"[35] in the 10th inning that re-tied the game. But he also had two hits, including a double, and raced all over the outfield to make eight putouts, which seemingly made up for his earlier mistakes.

"All [Williams] did was to chase around between left and center fields and back to the scoreboard and in by second base, taking down flies, picking up flies and making putouts of what seemed to be real good doubles. He was the whole outfield in himself,"[36] reported the *St. Louis Globe Democrat.*

The *St. Louis Post-Dispatch* agreed, writing, "[T]he old ball game never would have gone into extra innings had it been not for the phenomenal catches of 'Go-Get-'Em' Williams, who robbed the Redskins of one triple and three doubles."[37]

Williams did the improbable the next day, hitting a ball over ball-hawking center fielder Tris Speaker's head for a two-run triple in a 4–2 loss. He also had five putouts, "two of them being bits of actual robbery."[38]

The Browns boarded a 5:20 p.m. train back to St. Louis and arrived back in town to see their game rained out. The down time afforded them the opportunity to attend the parade for the 138th Infantry, which had been overseas for nearly a year and had partaken in the Battle of the Argonne Forest.

It was back to baseball on May 10, but it would be Williams's last game for a while. During a 3–2 loss to Detroit, which left the Browns with a 3–8 record and tied for last place in the American League, Williams got his foot caught in the infield dirt as he tried to steal second base in the fifth inning.

Williams completed the game—he had an assist, but also made the final out, popping out to the catcher with the bases loaded. It turned out he sprained his knee on the steal attempt. While he was fine during the game, the next day he was in so much pain he couldn't even leave his home.

Williams wasn't able to return to Sportsman's Park until May 16, with the thought he would be able to get back in the lineup within a week. But all Williams was able to do was watch the Browns play. He witnessed Boston's Babe Ruth hitting a grand slam in a 6–4 Red Sox win on May 20, but Williams saw the Browns win more than they lost—including a 1–0 win over Washington's Walter Johnson—as Jacobson, who played sparingly when Williams was in the lineup, got hot, driving in 14 runs over 11 games as St. Louis upped its record to 13–11.

With the Browns heading on a long road trip—25 games from May 30 to June 25—Williams was left at home to heal. "It is the invention of manager Burke to give [Williams] complete rest and to allow him to return to the game only when fully convinced that he is capable of playing his best game,"[39] reported the *Globe Democrat.*

That left Williams in St. Louis with a few options. He could watch the Cardinals play. Or perhaps watch Mary Pickford in *Daddy Long Legs,* Blanch Sweet in *The Unpardonable Sin,* or one of Fatty Arbuckle's comedies at one of the local theaters.

There is no record of how Williams spent his free time except for two ways: 1. In mid–June he started practicing at Sportsman's Park with pitcher Dave Davenport, who had been sent home from the road trip to get in condition for the team's return home. 2. On June 19 he got married.

How and when Ken Williams met Ethel Wilkerson is unknown. Surely, though, they met when he was playing baseball or in the army. Wilkerson, who was barely two years younger than Williams, was from Du Quoin, Illinois, which is about 80 miles southeast of St. Louis. She could have easily seen him play for the Browns, or more likely (since Williams saw limited time with St. Louis in 1918) in one of his exhibition games with Jefferson Barracks when they played in East St. Louis or Belleville, the latter about 60 miles from Du Quoin.

"I don't know how it all came about, but they met there, I think, in St. Louis," said Jack

Williams, who wondered how many kids know how their parents met. "And then the season was over and he went home. I mean, it's time to fish! It got right down to where the only way she was going to get him was to follow him out there, and she did. That's my understanding."[40]

Wilkerson decided to hitchhike to Grants Pass and found a friend willing to do the same. Wilkerson, who at 17 had worked as a bookkeeper in a meat shop in Du Quoin, was now working in Grants Pass as a clerk at the Southern Pacific Railroad freight office.

The *Grants Pass Daily Courier* made notice in its June 10 edition that a Miss Wilkinson was leaving for St. Louis to visit her mother and friends. Perhaps the paper had the name spelled incorrectly or maybe it was just a coincidence, but a little over a week later Williams and Wilkerson were married in St. Louis.

When the Browns returned home from their long road trip, the newlywed Williamses declared that his knee was fully recovered. However, the Browns hadn't continued their hot pace on the road: the team returned to St. Louis with a 24–26 record. Burke said he liked the production he was getting from his outfield trio of Tobin, Jacobson and Earl Smith, even though the numbers might not have entirely backed him up. Tobin was hitting .262 with two home runs—which was two more homers than Jacobson and Smith had hit combined. Jacobson at least was batting .283. Smith was at a putrid .229 with a .245 on-base percentage and .271 slugging percentage.

Pitcher Wayne "Rasty" Wright played only for the Browns in his major-league career, 1917–19, 1922–23. He had a career 24–19 record and 4.05 ERA (George Grantham Bain Collection, Library of Congress).

Nevertheless, Williams remained on the bench until June 30, when he was called on to hit for pitcher Wayne Wright in the ninth inning of a 6–1 loss to the Tigers. He watched Ray Demmitt used a pinch hitter instead of himself in games on July 1 and July 3, although he entered as a pinch runner for Demmitt in the former.

Williams got his most extensive action since May 10 in the first game of a July 4 double-header at Cleveland. George Sisler left early and Williams went to center field as Jacobson moved to first base. It wasn't a notable appearance for Williams (1-for-3, made an error and was out at home trying to score) or the Browns (11–1 loss). The most memorable part was when it was announced that Jack Dempsey beat Jess Willard after Willard quit in the third round, causing Burke to throw his cap in the air and eliciting smiles from Cleveland players Tris Speaker and Steve O'Neill, both of whom won money thanks to the bout's result.

Williams was used as a pinch hitter in the second game and Burke had planned to start Jacobson in center field again on July 5 as the Indians and Browns played once again, but now back in St. Louis. However, when Cleveland decided to start Henry Jasper, a right-hander, Burke changed his lineup and inserted Williams in at center field and batting fifth.

The move paid off. Williams plated a run with a grounder in the first inning, hit an RBI double over the first-base bag in the third, and hustled to second for another double in the eighth when Speaker was slow getting to his hit to center. He would move to third on an errant pickoff throw and score on a Wally Gerber ground-out as the Browns won 6–2, Williams accounting for four of the runs. Getting a second straight start, Williams went 3-for-4 with a pair of doubles and a steal on July 6.

The next day, Williams, just a week past his 29th birthday, hit his first major-league home run. It came against Cleveland's Guy Morton in the fifth inning—it not only produced the first run of the game but also was St. Louis's first hit—and it was a monstrous shot. The *St. Louis Globe Democrat* noted that "it was one of the longest drives of the year, and only one other player, 'Babe' Ruth of Boston, has hit one further."[41]

Naturally, Burke kept putting Williams in the starting lineup. Williams paid off the confidence in him. In the first game of a double-header against the A's on July 13, Philadelphia intentionally walked Sisler in the sixth inning to load the bases for Williams, who promptly doubled to left field against lefty Walt Kinney to score all three runs in an eventual 4–3 win. St. Louis would win both games, pushing its record to 8–2 since Williams re-entered the starting lineup. "A slap on the back and a kind word to a discouraged player"[42] is how Burke described his role in the team's recent success.

On July 15, Williams hit another long home run to right field, this one off Philadelphia's Scott Perry, which "was a terrific hit and was caught by a fan standing in the highest row of seats. Had he allowed it to pass it would have fallen upon Grand Avenue."[43]

Left-handed hitting outfielder Ray Demmitt, here shown in a Chicago White Sox uniform, for whom he played in 1914–15, couldn't hold off Ken Williams for a starting job with the Browns in 1919 (George Grantham Bain Collection, Library of Congress).

The Browns would end up losing that game 5–4, allowing four runs in the top of the ninth, including the only major-league home run for Merlin Kopp. But St. Louis would rebound to win the opener of a series against the Yankees, with Williams making a tremendous running catch behind second base on a short fly hit by New York's Sammy Vick. While Williams had been compared to Tris Speaker in the past, Speaker played an extremely shallow center field while Williams preferred to play deep.

No Yankee could play deep enough for Williams on July 17 as he "crushed a ball into the bleachers"[44] for a three-run home run in the eighth inning on the first ball pitched to him by Jack Quinn. It was the first of eight career home runs for Williams off Quinn (8 percent of the 103 homers Quinn, who pitched until he was 50, allowed in his long career). That game would go 17 innings—New York's Hank Thormahlen pitched eight innings in relief while St. Louis's

Bert Gallia went nine scoreless. St. Louis finally won when reserve catcher Walter Mayer laid down a suicide squeeze to score Gene Robertson, who was playing in his first major-league game. Williams filled the box score, going 2-for-8 with the home run as well as a triple, while making two errors but also recording two assists. The game took 4 hours, 5 minutes to play with the winning run scored at 7:35 p.m. The *St. Louis Globe Democrat* put Williams and Sisler, who homered in the ninth to tie it, in a cartoon, calling them "the knockout twins."[45]

Williams closed out the home stand by going 7-for-14 against the Senators as the Browns took three of four games. Since his return to the lineup, the Browns were 14–6 and now 43–37 on the season, although that still only put St. Louis in fifth place and nine games behind the first-place White Sox. During that span of July 5–22, Williams was 28-for-75 (.385) with five doubles, two triples and the three home runs (.613 slugging percentage).

Williams was playing so well and in the headlines so often, that a baby born in St. Louis to Mr. and Mrs. Frank Williams of 6513 Joseph Ave. was named Kenneth Claude Williams—after both the Browns outfielder and the White Sox pitcher.

Ken Williams would face Claude Williams in St. Louis's first road series and hit the first of his three career inside-the-park home runs off the Chicago left-hander. But the White Sox won the game as well as the previous day's, and, despite losing to St. Louis on July 26, the team had already voted on its split of its potential 1919 World Series shares.

The Browns gave the White Sox a lot of flak about that from the opposing dugout the following game, a scorching hot day in Chicago. "Everyone from the bat boy to the last spectator was dripping wet from the heat,"[46] reported the *Post-Dispatch*.

The Browns won the game on July 27 and were fortunate to get on their train to Washington, D.C. While the Browns-White Sox game was going on, just a few blocks from Comiskey Park, an African American boy had drifted too far along the lake, past the dividing line between where whites and blacks were allowed to swim. White boys began throwing rocks at him and eventually he drowned. The incident sparked the worst race riot in Chicago history, which lasted for days.

With temperatures hitting 100 degrees in Washington, Williams slumped a bit, recording his first back-to-back hitless games, although he would go 2-for-3 in the series finale, knocking in the eventual winning run with a ninth-inning single off Dutch Leonard. At the end of July, Williams's batting average was at .308, 15th in the American League. Sisler led the AL with a .360 average while Jacobson was 13th at .311.

The Browns continued their road trip through New York and then Boston. In the latter city Williams prevented two home runs off the bat of Babe Ruth. In the opening game of an August 9 double-header, Williams, who was playing Ruth deeper than usual, went back to the center-field fence, jumped and knocked down a sure home run, although Ruth was still able to leg out a triple. In the second game, on a similar deep fly, Williams made a "remarkable mitt hand side-leaping catch"[47] to likely cost Ruth an inside-the-park homer.

"Babe got a wonderful bit of applause for the crack and it must have made Kenneth feel very good indeed when he came back to the bench and got a wonderfully sustained salvo of applause from the big crowd," reported the *Post-Dispatch*. "Kenneth is some outfielder and made Bobby Roth, one of the most overrated outfielders in the big leagues, look very ordinary indeed as a midgardener."[48]

St. Louis finished up its road trip in Boston on August 12, which also marked the return of Johnny Tobin to the lineup. He had been out since July 21, with a few scattered appearances in August in which he got four plate appearances. Burke had put Jacobson in left field in his stead, and during that time Jacobson had a 16-game hit streak, batting .500 (38-for-76) with six doubles, four triples and two home runs.

Meanwhile, Earl Smith was hitting just .251 with no home runs. With Tobin healthy, Burke put him back in left field. But Smith was now the odd man out and Jacobson put in right field. The outfield of Tobin, Williams and Jacobson would remain in St. Louis for the next five seasons.

The Browns returned to St. Louis for a final home stand, playing 21 games between August 14 and September 3. The *St. Louis Globe Democrat* declared any thoughts of a World Series over after the Browns were swept in a double-header by the Red Sox on August 17, using the headline "Good-By Pennant Hopes."[49]

Johnny "Jack" Tobin, Browns outfielder in 1916, and 1917–25 (George Grantham Bain Collection, Library of Congress).

Ruth pitched in the opener and went the distance in a 2–1 Boston win (Williams went 3-for-4), then homered in the second game to lead the Red Sox to a 6–1 victory. Williams accounted for the only St. Louis run by hitting a home run to right field ("the ball was hit higher into the seats than Ruth's, but lacked the steam attached to the 'Home Run King's' wallop,"[50] wrote the *Globe Democrat*) off future Hall of Famer Herb Pennock. It was the first of just two home runs he'd allow all season in 219 innings (also the first of six HRs Williams would hit off Pennock).

The Browns won the next two games to move into the first division, one-half game ahead of the Yankees. But St. Louis then lost three straight to New York, with Yankees pitcher Carl Mays and George Sisler nearly coming to blows in the finale.

Washington came into town next, and after splitting the first two games, the Browns and Senators were mixed up in a close affair on August 25. Williams accounted for the game's first run in the fifth inning with a home run off Jim Shaw on a 3–2 pitch that bounced off the right-field pavilion roof and bounded onto Grand Avenue.

But Washington came back and led 3–1 going into the bottom of the ninth. Shaw loaded the bases with two outs and Williams coming to the plate. Senators manager Clark Griffith elected to bring in Walter Johnson, who had pitched 2⅓ scoreless innings the previous day, to face Williams.

Johnson threw one of his noted fastballs on the first pitch, but it came in high and tight. Williams ducked out of the way, but moved his body with him. The ball struck him on the hand so hard, it went down to first base, where Joe Kuhel was stationed. Thinking the ball had been hit, Kuhel picked up the ball and touched first base. But the ball had hit Williams, not the bat, and he went to first base, driving in a run. Tobin then won the game with a two-run single.

Williams stayed in the game to run the bases, but he had broken his middle finger. His season was over, as was confirmed when the Browns left for their final road trip and Williams remained back in St. Louis.

Williams ended up playing in 65 games for the Browns in 1919, batting .300 with a .376 on-base percentage and .467 slugging percentage (10 doubles, five triples, six home runs). The .300 mark was fourth best on the team, behind Sisler (.352), Tobin (.327) and Jacobson (.323). His slugging percentage—if he had enough qualifying plate appearances—would have put him eighth in the American League, behind luminaries Ruth and Sisler as well as Joe Jackson and four Detroit Tigers (Bobby Veach, Ty Cobb, Ira Flagstead and Harry Heilmann). His six home runs were the 13th most in the AL. Certainly if Williams had played significant time, there's a good chance he would have finished second in the league behind Ruth's 29 HRs, as three players, including Sisler, were next with 10.

But Williams didn't get more time because he just couldn't stay healthy. He was going to turn 30 in 1920 and his major-league totals consisted of just 138 games and 540 plate appearances. It was beyond time for Williams to play an entire season and show what he could do, or else risk his career in the majors and be branded as someone who was injury-prone.

Williams, with his broken finger, and his bride left St. Louis for Grants Pass in early September and arrived back in Oregon on September 10. The Browns finished out their season, finishing 67–72 and in fifth place in the American League.

Williams likely didn't spend too much time looking at the standings, as he and his wife went on a trip with friends to a couple of different towns in Oregon. Whether he paid close attention to that year's World Series results is unknown. But St. Louis quickly became involved in talk of a World Series fix, with White Sox manager Kid Gleason and business manager Norris O'Neill as well as a Chicago detective visiting St. Louis to meet with some people who were rumored to be involved with a possible scandal.

Not much came from those meetings at first, but the Black Sox scandal would soon become nationwide news, and its results would eventually have an effect on the Browns.

Chapter 7

Getting Established in St. Louis

The talk of a thrown World Series was still just that—talk—as Ken Williams and the Browns prepared for the 1920 season. While there wasn't a big salary squabble for Williams, he was the 28th Browns player to send in his contract to the Browns, with the team receiving it February 18. He would make $3,300 in 1920, which was more than the average American would earn, but over $1,000 less than the mean salary of a major leaguer.

On the Browns, for example, Williams would be paid less than starters shortstop Wally Gerber ($3,500), outfielder Baby Doll Jacobson ($4,000), third baseman Jimmy Austin ($4,200), second baseman Joe Gedeon ($4,800), catcher Hank Severeid ($5,000) and, of course, first baseman George Sisler ($10,000), who was one of the few high-paid stars of the game.

Williams's contract did call for more money than outfielder Earl Smith ($3,000) as well as pitchers Dixie Davis ($3,000), who was acquired in the offseason from Louisville ("I'll wager $200 I'll win fifteen games for manager Burke this year,"[1] he boasted), and Bill Byrne ($1,800), and was the same as Urban Shocker, one of the stalwarts of the starting rotation.

Williams and the rest of the Browns were to report to Taylor, Texas, for spring training. Originally, business manager Bob Quinn had made arrangements to train in Mobile, Alabama, but manager Jimmy Burke "refused to take the Browns there."[2] Quinn acceded to his manager's wishes, and when Taylor's retail merchants made an offer for the Browns to train in their town, Quinn accepted.

Before he headed to Taylor, Williams decided to meet up in Sacramento with Gedeon, who was managing an amateur team in that city. Williams arrived in time to play in the final game and helped Gedeon's team to victory, also clinching the league's championship.

There had been rumors circulating that Gedeon was retiring. He insisted that was not true, but a reason for the rumor would come to light much later when Gedeon's name would come up in the Black Sox scandal.

The trip for Williams and Gedeon to Taylor was not smooth—they missed a train connection and at some point lost trunks that contained various clothes and equipment (Williams would have to borrow a pair of baseball cleats to practice).

Taylor—listed as 33 miles from Austin and 60 miles from Waco—was not exactly a thriving metropolis. But its streets were paved, its baseball clubhouse renovated with showers, and the four-story Blazilmar Hotel, where the team stayed, was built in 1918 and had bathtubs "in practically all rooms,"[3] as well as other modern conveniences (it was also touted as fireproof).

Williams arrived to an outfield situation that was pretty well set. Despite some offseason rumors and talk of Johnny Tobin possibly being dealt, the Browns returned Williams, Tobin, Jacobson and Smith. Ray Demmitt, who played in 79 games in 1919, chose to stay home on his farm in Illinois and play only on weekends for the A.E. Staley team of Decatur—managed by Joe McGinnity—in an industrial league (future Chicago Bears owner George Halas was also on that team). St. Louis had "one outfield that causes no worry,"[4] according to *The Sporting News*.

There was one concern for Williams—how he'd hit after breaking his finger to end his 1919 season. As would be the case for Williams in 1920 and at every spring training for the remainder of his career, as soon as he arrived he was anxious to get to the field to hit.

On February 28, Williams got his chance to swing the bat for the first time since his injury. The Browns set their batting practice order the same way they had their 1919 lineup, in which Williams was fifth (although he would hit fourth, as Sisler was still in St. Louis finishing up a drafting project for General Motors, his offseason job). "Williams wanted to hit all day," noted the *St. Louis Globe Democrat*. "He must have slept on a bat all winter."[5]

The next day, Williams was complaining of a headache—causing the *Globe Democrat* to observe, "Williams is always crabbing about one thing or another, but he's not the 'Hard to get along with sort.' Williams is a fellow who will talk himself into the confidence which brings success."[6]

Unlike Ken Williams, who didn't get past the eighth grade, Browns star first baseman George Sisler went to the University of Michigan (George Grantham Bain Collection, Library of Congress).

And, true enough, despite the headache, Williams stayed at batting practice to hit and hit and hit, knocking ball after ball into the deep recesses of the outfield. "I'm scheduled for the greatest year any ballplayer ever enjoyed," Williams told the *Globe Democrat* between swings. "I sure like to swing on a ball, headache or not. I'm going to larrup one now."[7] And, as the *Globe Democrat* noted, Williams then proceeded to swat a pitch down the right-field line.

After just four days of training, the Browns took the field for their first exhibition game, against the University of Texas Longhorns. The Longhorns might have been a college team, but unlike the Browns' scant few days of training, Texas had been practicing for two months and also had Bibb Falk, who was property of the White Sox.

The Browns only used five players who could be considered regulars—Williams, Tobin and Smith manned the outfield, Jacobson played first base, and backup catcher Josh Billings was behind the plate.

Batting cleanup, Williams surprised everyone by bunting for a hit in the second inning in his first plate appearance. But his next time up, an inning later, he crushed a pitch to deep center field that rolled to the barbed wire fence out there as Williams circled the bases for a home run. The homer "was one of the longest hits ever registered at the park,"[8] claimed the *Globe Democrat.*

He would also single in the fifth and nearly had another extra-base hit in the sixth when "his long drive to right field fell foul by a half foot."[9] He finished 3-for-5 as the Browns won 11–8.

After not playing in a game since the previous August, Williams's effort was clearly the standout performance for St. Louis. *The Sporting News* report of the game included: "Further cause for satisfaction in this game was the way Ken Williams slammed the ball, indicating he's come back as strong as touted."[10]

Williams's finger was causing him some discomfort—it was more of a trouble in the field than at the plate, as he proved in a 19–4 win over the Fort Worth Panthers on March 6. Williams went 2-for-4 with a triple, but dropped a shallow line drive.

"It is noticeable that Ken Williams is swinging from the hip," wrote the *Globe Democrat*, "clouting the ball long and hard with the ability to cross the opposition because of his knack at bunting."[11]

Williams wasn't just hitting the ball, he was hitting with authority. On March 10 against San Antonio he went 4-for-5 with a triple, which would have been a home run if not for an agreed-upon rule that any ball hit into the cotton fields adjacent to the field would count as a three-base hit. The next day, another triple, and on March 14 at Houston he hit a pair of doubles. Williams hit another double in an intrasquad game, and on March 20 against San Antonio he hit a home run over the right-field fence, believed to be the first time that had ever occurred at that park. Sisler, who arrived in camp March 4, would match the feat in the ninth inning.

Williams had a hit in the Browns' first seven games—and multiple-hit games in six of those—before finally going 0-for-3 against San Antonio on March 21, although he did steal a base and score a run. His fielding was coming along as well. He was noted for making three spectacular catches in a win over Houston.

"Williams seems hot for a big year," opined *The Sporting News*. "The story of the Browns in the 1919 race might have been different had he not been out of the game so much with sickness and injuries."[12]

Williams was predicting big things for himself as well, saying he'd hit around .350. There was also some talk that Williams wanted to break Babe Ruth's home run record. "The only way they'll stop me this year is to put me on the hospital list," he said. "They will not do it if I'm in the game every day."[13]

When he wasn't hitting or making big claims about his expected 1920 production, Williams, as well as the rest of the Browns, had to find different ways to entertain himself. All businesses in Taylor were closed on Sundays, so there was a lot of sitting around in the hotel and talking baseball or swapping war stories. A local drugstore invited the players to come by for free malts. Then there was the opportunity that crossed their paths on March 21.

Before the Browns' game against San Antonio, a Lt. Doyle, a St. Louis native stationed at nearby Kelley Field, offered to take up players in his airplane, giving Williams an opportunity to do what very few Americans could claim—fly.

Williams was one of the few to accept the offer (Severeid went up twice). While trainer "Bits" Bierhalter wanted a normal, straight flight, Williams asked Doyle to "go through all the stunts,"[14] which included doing loops. Perhaps not surprisingly, the March 21 spring training game—which was played after this flying stunt—was the only spring training game in which Williams went hitless. In St. Louis's final five spring training games—played against Tulsa, Wichita and Joplin—Williams had seven extra-base hits, including three homers in two games at Wichita.

The Browns returned to St. Louis to play in the city series, which began at Sportsman's Park on April 3. Cold and rainy weather held down the crowds, shortened a couple of games and even caused Browns manager Jimmy Burke to not play his regulars for fear they'd get hurt.

In a sloppily played game—eight errors were committed—on April 7, a 13–11 Browns win, Williams hit a three-run home run off young left-hander Ace Reinhart on a 2–0 pitch. He would go 3-for-5 with the homer and a steal in the win. As in 1919, the Browns would win the city series four games to two. Williams went 5-for-12 with five runs scored.

Browns owner Phil Ball rewarded his team by giving each player $100. This was not unusual for Ball, who took the team out to the theater when he was visiting them in Houston during spring training. He also paid for new uniforms to be worn on Sundays and holidays, as he was tired of the players having extremely dirty uniforms in front of what usually were the largest crowds at Sportsman's Park.

"Clean stands, clean seats, clean players and clean baseball appeal to me.... I dislike a slovenly baseball player," Ball said. "I think all spectators dislike slovenliness, too. So we are going to dress up the Browns as well as we can. I hope the Sunday suits will prove to be winning suits, too."[15]

While the uniforms might have made the Browns look nicer and the team was thought of more highly than usual—syndicated columnist Norman E. Brown wrote "The Browns have graduated from the joke class, as everyone knows"[16]—oddsmakers had them at 10–1 to win the American League. Cleveland and New York were at 3–1, Chicago and Detroit 4–1 and the now Ruth-less Red Sox 8–1. Brooklyn, which would win the National League pennant, were also at 10–1.

The 1920 season presented a few rule changes, but none more notable than the outlawing of "freak" pitches, such as the spitball. Each team could designate two pitchers to be allowed to throw the spitball. The Browns selected Urban Shocker and Bert Gallia.

Allan Sothoron, who also threw the spitball, was not selected and was summarily pounded in the season opener in Cleveland in front of 25,000 fans. He allowed 13 hits as the Browns lost to Stan Coveleski—who was designated to throw the spitter—5–0. Immediately, the Browns realized their mistake and tried to switch designations and have Sothoron allowed to throw the spitball and not Gallia. Rain dampened much of the Browns' early schedule. The team got in only three games before hosting its home opener on April 22.

All the talk of a fixed World Series in the offseason made the issue of gambling at ballparks come to the forefront. This was a regular pastime at many major-league games, especially in Boston. Browns business manager Bob Quinn wanted to put a halt to it in St. Louis. He announced that if anyone was caught exchanging money or gamblers were caught in the stands, his "special police"[17] would arrest them. "It is either the game or the gamblers. One most go," Quinn declared. "Personally I am inclined to think that the gamblers will go."[18]

Those who put money on Coveleski to beat the Browns again would have made a good bet, as Cleveland won handily 11–3 on St. Louis's opening day. The next day brought another postponement—already the Browns' sixth of the season.

The sporadic playing of games didn't affect Williams, who hit in the team's first five games and seven of the first eight (batting .429). However, the team's fortunes weren't going as well, and Williams couldn't keep up his hot pace, either.

After 21 games, the Browns—who were 67–72 in 1919—were just 10–11, tied for fifth place. Williams's average had slipped to .293 and he had yet to hit a home run. His fielding was more than adequate, though, and he'd thrill the crowd with the occasional great catch, like when he dove into the bleachers to snare a drive off the bat of the Tigers' Ty Cobb on May 8 in Detroit.

On May 16, he faced Walter Johnson for the first time since "The Big Train" broke his finger with a fastball the previous August. With the score tied at 2 in the eighth inning, Williams doubled and eventually scored the go-ahead run on a Jacobson single (the Browns won 4–2).

Del Pratt played second base for the Browns from 1912 to 1917 before being dealt to the Yankees. St. Louis would get Urban Shocker, who turned into their ace starter, as part of the trade (George Grantham Bain Collection, Library of Congress).

Two days later, in a 17–8 loss to the Senators, Williams got plugged in the ribs on a throw to first by Washington third baseman Frank Ellerbe. The thought was Williams would be out at least a week, but he was back in the lineup in the Browns' next game in New York on May 20. From center field he saw Sothoron commit three throwing errors, a problem which would haunt him his entire career.

Williams, on the other hand, was making plays in center field bordering on superb. In the ninth inning of a 2–0 game against the Yankees on May 22, New York's Del Pratt hit a rising line drive to center field. Williams had raced in but then needed to make a jumping, one-handed catch. The 25,000 Yankee fans had thought Pratt's shot was going to be a home run (as did the reporters for the *New York Times, St. Louis Globe Democrat* and *St. Louis Post-Dispatch*). As there was a runner on third, it would have tied the game, but instead the play helped St. Louis win 2–1.

On May 25, Williams threw out Mike Menosky and Tim Hendryx at the plate on back-to-back plays in the first inning, both trying to score from second base on singles. On May 28, he threw out Bobby Veach trying to go to third on a Harry Heilmann single. But earlier in the game, he also booted Cobb's single, allowing the Georgia Peach to go to second, so clearly not all was perfect in Williams's outfield play.

Williams finally got his first home run on May 29 in St. Louis against Detroit's Howard Ehmke. The shot went into the right-field bleachers, but the Browns still lost, 5–3. They were defeated again by Detroit on May 30—St. Louis's seventh straight loss, putting them at 13–21 in sixth place, five games behind fifth-place Chicago.

Burke, for reasons not made clear, decided to change his outfield positioning. Williams went from center field to left field, Jacobson from right to center, and Tobin from left to right.

The move didn't affect Williams. In the first game of a May 31 double-header, he smashed the first pitch he saw from Red Faber in the second inning into the right-field bleachers. Williams would score both Browns runs as St. Louis won 2–0 to break its long losing streak. He also homered June 3 off Chicago's Roy Wilkinson.

Williams also showed off his arm in left field in a 7–6 win at Cleveland on June 4 (in a game the Indians began by having the first three batters attempt to bunt against Sothoron). In the seventh inning, he snared Doc Johnston's liner, then threw to Sisler at first to double up Bill Wambsganss.

St. Louis would win three of four games in Cleveland—and also leave with a new coach: Lee Fohl, who earlier in the season had been fired by the Indians, joined the team as a pitching and base coach. While the Browns were starting to turn things around, Williams was down to hitting just .254, although he did lead the team in runs with 25 and was tied for second with four steals.

A return home to St. Louis helped heat up Williams's bat. He hit in 14 of the next 15 games with nine multi-hit games. Some of the highlights:

- 3-for-4 with a home run and steal off Walter Johnson on June 8. This also began three straight games with multiple hits (7-for-13).
- 4-for-5 with two triples and a steal in a 15–4 win over Boston on June 12.
- Three straight two-hit games from June 13 to 15. Including the previous day's four-hit game, he was 10-for-17 over that four-game stretch with a double, two triples and two steals.
- He was also credited with great catches against Washington's Patsy Gharrity and Frank Ellerbe on June 10 and Boston's Harry Hooper on June 14 (the ones on Gharrity and Hooper saving extra-base hits).

In a four-game sweep of the A's from June 16 to 19, Williams went 6-for-15 with a pair of doubles. The Browns had won 10 straight to even their record at 27–27 and Williams had lifted his average 55 points, to .309.

The *St. Louis Globe Democrat* declared "Bring on the Yankees,"[19] referring to New York, which was in second place with a 37–21 record. Everyone was feeling pretty good about the Browns as fans filled Sportsman's Park. The opening game between the two teams was delayed as the overfilled crowd, which was roped off in the outfield, started closing in on the infield and had to be moved back.

However, the Browns weren't in the Yankees' class just yet, losing two of three games (with one rained out). In the lone win, the second of the three, Williams had a pair of RBI singles.

Williams hit his fifth home run of the season in the first game of a double-header off Cleveland's Ray Caldwell on June 29, but his batting average dipped down to .298 by the time St. Louis ended its home stand. However, Williams got hot again once the Browns embarked on a road trip beginning July 1. Well, more specifically, July 2, as he went 1-for-8 in a double-header on July 1.

In a three-game burst from July 2 to 4 in Chicago, Williams was 8-for-13 with two doubles. He also threw out Happy Felsch "by yards"[20] at the plate as Felsch tried to score following a fly out in a July 3 loss to the White Sox.

Then, after going 0-for-4 in the first game of a double-header in Detroit on July 5, Williams put together a five-game hitting streak against the Tigers and Red Sox. He went 10-for-18 with a double and two triples, pushing his average to .321.

St. Louis then moved to New York, where the Browns became the first team to win a series at the Polo Grounds against the Yankees in 1920, taking three of five games. The second game of double-header on July 13 was reportedly the largest crowd ever at the Polo Grounds—World Series included—at 38,823. Williams didn't succumb to the pressure, going 2-for-4 in Game 2; Ruth struck out five times in the two games.

Ruth would hit HR No. 29—tying the record he set the previous season—in the 11th inning to win a slugfest for the Yankees, 13–10. Williams had an interesting game as well, tripling to lead off the second and also walking later in the inning and being part of a triple steal. In the fifth, his deep fly off Hank Thormahlen went over the heads of Ruth and Ping Bodie; it rolled to the fence, and he had his second career inside-the-park home run.

Williams would tail off a bit as the team went to Philadelphia, but as the road trip wrapped up in Washington and Detroit, he was hitting .309, fourth best among Browns regulars.

Despite traveling secretary Willis Johnson's declaring the Browns had a good chance to win the American League, in actuality, St. Louis was below .500 (43–47) as it returned home following an 11–13 road trip and 17 games behind league-leading Cleveland.

Nevertheless, the Browns once again took three of five from the Yankees, who entered St. Louis just 1½ games in back of the Indians. Williams played a part in each win: Throwing out Wally Pipp at third base following a fly ball (with Ruth the next hitter) and robbing Bodie of a home run in the opener; delivering an RBI single in a 4–3 win; and driving in three runs, including two on a triple in a 13–10 victory.

Despite a 10-game hitting streak from July 29 to August 6, Williams was still fighting for respect. In the sixth inning of St. Louis's August 6 game against Washington, the Senators purposely walked Jacobson to load the bases for Williams in a 6–all tie. After fouling off the first pitch against left-hander Harry Courtney, Williams clobbered the next offering over the right-field pavilion and onto Grand Avenue, for the first of his five career grand slams. Soon thereafter, tragedy would hit baseball and the Browns.

St. Louis split a pair of games in Cleveland on August 14–15, with the Indians heading to New York and the Browns traveling to Washington. The next day, Cleveland's Ray Chapman was hit by a pitch from the Yankees' Carl Mays and eventually died.

The Browns already had a history with Mays. Sisler nearly came to blows with the pitcher in 1919 after he felt Mays was going headhunting. Earlier in 1920, Hank Severeid had words with Mays after a similar experience. In the heat of the moment surrounding Chapman's death, Browns players met and came to a unanimous decision: They'd boycott any game in which Mays took the mound.

The *St. Louis Globe Democrat* reported the Browns wanted Mays banned from baseball. "[Browns players] gathered together today following receipt of the news of the death of Ray Chapman and decided that they would write to every player in the American League, asking that they cooperate in stopping the pitcher from performing in the Ban Johnson circuit, resorting to the refusal to play against the twirler if need be,"[21] the paper wrote in its August 17 edition.

The *Globe Democrat* went on to report that Browns players didn't think Mays hit Chapman on purpose, but with his history of brushbacks—of which they knew first-hand—Mays's "record is against him."[22] And just to cement there was no love lost, the paper said "many of the Browns denounce Mays in no uncertain terms and their language would not look well in print."[23]

Business manager Bob Quinn was affected on a more intimate level, having known Chapman from his time running the American Association's team in Columbus when Chapman was a player there.

"His loss is personal to me," Quinn said of Chapman. "I feel as if I have lost a member of my own family. Relative to Carl Mays, I have nothing to comment. Unfortunately, he will feel the blow more than anyone."[24]

The Browns would have another death hit close to home. Otto Stiffel, who bought the Browns with Phil Ball but had sold his shares in 1919, killed himself two days after Chapman's death. Despite getting loans from Ball and Walter Fritsch, another Browns investor, he was in debt due to both his business and affinity for horse racing. He wrote in his suicide note he took his drastic action due to a "financial jam."[25]

The Browns won two of three in Washington, then, after three rainouts there and in Philadelphia plus a Sunday off (Sunday baseball games were outlawed in both Philadelphia and Boston), St. Louis players had plenty of time to mourn and think.

While winning three of four games in both Philadelphia and Boston, Browns players met a couple of times to discuss the Mays situation. A letter from the Indians arrived as well—contents unknown—prompting another meeting.

American League president Ban Johnson warned the Browns, and other teams, to end any talk of a boycott. Quinn, who went from St. Louis to Cleveland to attend Chapman's funeral, joined the road trip to persuade the Browns to play.

St. Louis arrived in New York for an August 29 game. But any decision about Mays seemed late, as he had already pitched (and won) two games for the Yankees since the beaning.

Perhaps also getting the Browns off the hook was the fact that Mays entered in relief of Jack Quinn. When he entered, Yankees fans cheered him and sarcastically called out to Browns players, "Why don't you strike?"[26]

The Browns didn't strike, but they did engage in some nasty bench jockeying, forcing Mays to say something to umpire Bill Dineen, who, according to the *New York Times*, "put a stop to the unsportsmanlike actions."[27]

Mays would get the last laugh on this day, pitching 3⅔ scoreless innings to get the win and also knock in a run with a single. Then, two days later, Mays pitched a four-hit shutout against the Browns, who perhaps would have been better off going on strike.

The Browns would return home going 12–11 on their road trip, although having lost five in a row. Upon arrival in St. Louis, Williams appeared to have picked up a new—and incorrect—nickname as well. Both the *Globe Democrat* and *Post-Dispatch* were calling him "Moose Jaw" Williams.

Williams was often called "Moose" because he was tall for the era (although the nickname probably would have better served Jacobson, who was two inches taller and 20 or 30 pounds heavier than Williams). More than likely, the writers took the extra step of assigning the city to Williams since he had once played in the Western Canada League. Either way, the nickname got plenty of play in the papers in the Browns' first two days back in town.

In the first game of a double-header against Washington on September 9, Williams drove in all five St. Louis runs in a 6–5 12-inning loss. He hit a two-run homer off Eric Erickson in the sixth inning, in the eighth he tripled in a run against Tom Zachary, and in the 12th doubled in a pair off Zachary.

In the second game, he made an unassisted double play in the first inning, making a great play on what looked to be a Sam Rice extra-base hit. He then ran in and touched second base to easily force out Joe Judge, who had rounded third base, thinking the hit would fall.

Williams's defensive brilliance was on display in the first inning of the next game as well, the first game of a double-header on September 11 (the September 10 game was rained out). With the bases loaded and one out, he raced in to grab Clyde Milan's sinking liner before it hit the ground, and while still running threw to Joe Gedeon at second base for an inning-ending double play.

At the plate, "Moose Jaw" connected for a home run in both games of the double-header as well, hitting the only home run Harry Biemiller would allow in 17 innings that season in the first game, and touching lefty Zachary in the second game. However, Williams also crashed into the left-field fence in the second game, causing him to appear only twice as a pinch hitter in the next seven games.

He returned just as the Yankees were back in town, which meant a big crowd. The large attendance was fortunate for Ruth, who brought along a band consisting of youths from his old school, St. Mary's of Baltimore, who were raising money to rebuild buildings destroyed in a fire. The oversized crowd meant spectators on the field, and Williams likely lost a triple in the opener when he hit one into the mass of fans, which by rule resulted in an automatic double.

The Browns won the opener, but the Yankees took the next two. Mays was jeered by the crowd, but nevertheless winning (his 25th game) in extra innings. New York players not only beat the Browns in the series finale, but they also took time to snack on some ice cream during the sixth inning (somehow Ruth had to be behind that).

Williams went 4-for-10 in three games against the Tigers, giving him a 10-game hitting streak when he started. He was hit by a pitch and walked in his two pinch-hit appearances. He had to leave the game on September 24 after colliding with Jacobson while going for a Clyde Manion fly ball. Williams was "bowled over"[28] and was in obvious pain, so the game had to be delayed. Teammates circled around him, but he was eventually able to limp off the field.

But the injury—later described as to his knee—would end Williams's season. He didn't quite get to his preseason goals, but he finished with a .307 batting average, 10 home runs and a .480 slugging percentage, the latter of which was good for 10th in the American League. His 18 stolen bases ranked him eighth, and his 13 triples were ninth best in the AL.

Williams didn't remain out of the news, albeit erroneously. On September 28, newspapers were filled with such headlines as "Eight White Sox Indicted for Fraud"[29] and "White Sox Players Indicted; Cicotte Confesses."[30]

As the stories continued, pictures of the offending players were published. In its September 29 early edition, the *St. Louis Post-Dispatch* accidentally used a picture of Ken Williams for White Sox pitcher Claude Williams. A correction was printed in a later edition on the front page as well as the next day in the sports section. They read in part:

> The group picture was intended to be players connected with the 'throwing' of the last world's series [*sic*], in which Kenneth Williams had no part whatever.
>
> Kenneth Williams has not been mentioned in the variety of report or rumor of betting on baseball games. In fact, he has been one of the strong props of the team. Gossip has connected the name of one St. Louisian with the betting scandal, but it was not Kenneth Williams.[31]

As it turned out, the White Sox—minus the eight who had been suspended by Chicago owner Charles Comiskey—next played in St. Louis, where they were at first greeted with jokes, but later cheers. The Browns, without Williams and against the White Sox's "remains,"[32] won two of three games to finish the season at 76–77, good enough for fourth place, the team's highest finish in the standings since 1908, when it also was fourth. Owner Phil Ball was so pleased with the first-division finish, he gave the players $6,000 to be divvied up among them.

Yet all was certainly not all right in St. Louis. Late in the season, rumors had started that Burke, despite the first-division finish (he was also the only Browns manager not to finish below fifth place), would not be back.

Another rumor turned into reality as it became known that Browns second baseman Gedeon was somehow involved in the White Sox scandal. Gedeon denied being in on the fix, but did admit he won $600 on the 1919 World Series.

Gedeon had to travel to Chicago from Sacramento just weeks after the conclusion of the season to testify before the grand jury. There, he said he had heard the Reds were going to win and, fatefully, said he had been in a room when gamblers were discussing the fix.

Less than a month later, Gedeon found out his penance for telling the truth: He was released by the Browns on November 18 and went unclaimed by every other major-league club.

"That's the end of Joe Gedeon in baseball," *The Sporting News* correctly surmised. "There was too much stain on Gedeon's part in the 1919 World's Series to make anything else possible."[33] Ironically, the eight White Sox players involved and suspended were still reserved by Chicago—just in case.

Gedeon's release had two effects: 1. It cost St. Louis a valuable player just as the team was seemingly starting to turn things around. Gedeon was just 26 and batted .292 with a .355 on-base percentage in 1920 and was known as one of the best hit-and-run batters in the league. His being gone would create a void for the Browns. 2. Any other player who had even dared to think about mentioning anything he knew about the fix certainly was going to keep quiet. What happened to those who spoke up, and were a little too close to things, was clear.

Roughly two years later, Gedeon's fate would gnaw at *The Sporting News*, which wrote in 1922: "There are other players in the big leagues today who knew as much as Gedeon and bet more money—but their club owners failed to take the drastic action that Phil Ball of the Browns took."[34]

Gedeon did last longer than Burke, however. The manager was asked to resign. When he refused, the Browns gave him his "official release."[35] Burke apparently drew the ire of club officials for a few reasons. In the middle of the season, he asked them to open up their wallets and bring in more quality players to shore up some of their holes. Burke was also blamed when infielder Johnny Shovlin decided to leave the team for a Steelton (Pennsylvania) Industrial League team, of all places. There was also some questioning of Burke's strategies, such as how long he kept starting pitchers in when they appeared to be fading.

Whatever the reasons, Quinn and the Browns thought it was time for a change. Quickly the focus turned to Lee Fohl, who had joined the club in midseason. It was reported that not only was Fohl offered the job during the season, but he also was making noise to get Burke fired with him as the replacement.

When Burke was not brought back, Fohl sent a notarized letter to the *Globe Democrat* stating that he was never offered the job, nor "at any time tried to undermine the late manager of the St. Louis Browns."[36]

If not Fohl, then who? Clarence "Pants" Rowland was rumored, but instead he was hired by Columbus of the American Association. There was a call for Sisler to be named manager. Ty Cobb had just been hired to manage the Tigers, so having a player manage the team wasn't out of the question. But Sisler asked not to be considered, as he wanted to concentrate on just playing.

As the 1920 came to a close, the Browns still had no manager. Williams probably wasn't concerned. He wasn't going to be asked, and obviously someone would be at the helm.

As usual, he had yet to send in a signed contract, instead enjoying his time with his wife on the West Coast, driving from Oregon to California and back. He reportedly made the drive from Sacramento to Grants Pass in just 20 hours, despite some difficult conditions. "Out in Oregon they are hailing him as a record breaking motor tourist,"[37] reported *The Sporting News*. It wouldn't be too much longer before Williams was a record-breaking baseball player.

Chapter 8

Changing Style and Becoming a Top Slugger

As usual, Ken Williams was one of the last Browns players to send in his signed contract. He had turned 30 years old in 1920 and in his fifth year in a major-league uniform finally played a full season, appearing in 141 games (compared to 148 games combined with the Reds in 1915–16 and Browns in 1918–19). He had acquitted himself more than reasonably as he found himself in the top 10 of a few offensive categories in the American League. It caught the notice of Louisville Slugger. In what would be a fortuitous move for the company, Williams signed on before the 1921 season to now use the Louisville Slugger model.

Like the other returning players on the Browns, Williams got a bump in salary for 1921 to $4,200, up from $3,300. The $900 raise wasn't the largest, but it was among the better raises. George Sisler signed a multiyear contract and got a bump from $10,000 to $12,500, while Baby Doll Jacobson went from $3,000 to $5,000 after batting .355 with 216 hits and 122 RBI as well as a .501 slugging percentage.

Several other players also got raises to the $4,200 mark, including shortstop Wally Gerber (from $3,500), who hit .279 but was more known for his defense; Earl Smith (from $3,000), who moved to third base from the outfield in part to make room for Williams and batted .306 in 103 games while playing spotty-at-best defense; and inconsistent starting pitcher Dixie Davis (from $3,000), who won 18 games and had an ERA of 3.17 but also led the league in walks.

The team would be playing for a new manager, but a familiar face. After Jimmy Burke had been dismissed and Sisler said he wasn't interested in the job, the Browns turned to Lee Fohl, who had been brought over the previous season as a coach.

Fohl had managed Cleveland from 1915 to 1919, leaving the team midway through the 1919 season, following a July 18 game in which Boston's Babe Ruth hit a grand slam in the top of the ninth inning to give the Red Sox an eventual 8–7 win. The Indians had led 7–2 going into the last inning and Fohl brought in lefty Fritz Coumbe, who hadn't pitched since May 13, to face Ruth. The resulting home run turned the fans against Fohl, who decided to step down despite the team's being in third place and just 5½ games out of first.

Fohl hadn't intended to coach or manage again in the majors. After leaving the Indians, he took a job with the Templar Motors Company of Cleveland, managing their baseball team.

Fohl wasn't your normal manager—as partly evidenced when he sent in a notarized letter to the St. Louis papers to say he had never been offered the Browns' managerial job during the 1920 season. But he also taught things a little differently and perhaps was a little ahead of his time—telling runners they stole off the pitcher, not the catcher, and teaching outfielders to hit a cutoff man instead of throwing it all the way into the infield. In addition, Fohl made a point to have his outfielders communicate, so they wouldn't run into each other, as Williams and Jacobson did at the tail-end of 1920, costing Williams the rest of his season. Fohl also believed that for a pitcher to be effective in relief, he should be in that role exclusively.

Of course, Fohl also had his quirks—when he was managing in Cleveland, he insisted that his first-base coaches be left-handed, and enlisted two pitchers to handle that duty. It was reported in a 1916 story that Fohl "has a long list of things that he wants done just so in order to get the break of luck."[1]

He was also known—despite the Coumbe incident—for his handling of pitchers, and that was one area of need for the Browns. The team finished with the third-worst ERA (4.03) in the American League in 1920 while walking the most batters.

But the Browns returned most of their position players, with Severeid behind the plate, Sisler at first, Gerber at short, and an outfield of Williams, Jacobson and Johnny Tobin. "With the outfield and catching staff there is a lot of strength on the club now," Fohl said. "The infield and pitching give me the most concern."[2]

Of biggest concern to Fohl had to be third base and second base. At third, Smith could hit, but he played the position like an outfielder. Despite his proclamations—he wrote traveling secretary Willis Johnson, "I will have the best season of my life because I love to play there, and where my heart is, there's where my work is"[3]—this was hardly a position without some question marks.

The Browns should have had Joe Gedeon at second base, but after his involvement in the Black Sox scandal and his subsequent release by the Browns (even though he was exonerated by the Chicago grand jury), he wasn't to find a job playing organized baseball again (and in fact would later be banned for life by baseball commissioner Judge Kenesaw Landis). Instead, Fohl would have to rely finding a diamond in the rough—or so he hoped—from a couple of raw recruits: 26-year-old Billy Gleason, who had played sparingly with Pittsburgh from 1916 to 1917; and 21-year-old Marty McManus, who batted .283 with 10 home runs for Tulsa in 1920 and also was 3-for-4 in one appearance with the Browns. Notwithstanding the questions surrounding those infield spots, Cleveland player-manager Tris Speaker regarded the Browns as "trouble makers"[4] in the upcoming season.

Another year meant another spring training home for the Browns. In 1921, the Browns would head to Bogalusa, Louisiana, a city of around 16,000 which just 14 years earlier could have been described as "a tent-pitched camp."[5] A lumber town, Bogalusa was located right off the Great Northern Railroad, making it convenient for traveling to and from the town.

There were two baseball fields in Bogalusa, and the president of the New Orleans Pelicans, who was overseeing their preparation for the Browns' arrival, said the "clubhouses are the finest in the South."[6] And indeed, they were well stocked, with 36 lockers, five showers, toilets, heated water, a rubbing table, a punching bag and various other equipment found in a gym.

"I took the offer of this place as a joke, at first," Browns business manager Bob Quinn said of Bogalusa, "but I changed my mind when I arrived there.... The hotel maintains a nine-hole golf course and there are bungalows for the married men.... It has been arranged that the hotel and the local clubs will give at least two dances weekly to help entertain the players."[7]

As with any small town which hosted a major-league team for spring training, there was excitement. Thousands turned out to the train station to greet the team, which was serenaded by a band and paraded to their hotel before being given a tour by car of the city and its ballparks. While the clubhouses might have been grand, the fields were not in good as shape, with infields of clay.

By the time Williams arrived for his first practice on March 2, roughly a week after most of the other players made their way to Bogalusa, the fields were fixed up as well as could be done. Either way, as usual it didn't affect Williams's hitting. Facing team ace Urban Shocker in his first batting practice session, he hit the ball hard and sent one over the eight-foot-high right-field wall. "He was perfectly happy,"[8] reported Martin Haley of the *St. Louis Post-Dispatch.*

Williams didn't need much time to adjust to hitting in games, either. He was pulled early from the team's first two intrasquad games, getting a hit in each, and went 3-for-4 with a double and a home run (either over the left fielder's head, according to the *St. Louis Globe Democrat,* or over the right-field wall, as per the *St. Louis Post-Dispatch*). He continued to pelt balls over the fence in practice and hit another home run in an intrasquad game, as well as a double against the Milwaukee Brewers.

"Kenneth Williams has arrived at the stage where he should be a terrific clouter … it will not be a surprise to see him hitting them safely this season, not only as often as both Jacobson and Tobin, but harder,"[9] wrote the *St. Louis Globe Democrat.*

But intrasquad games and facing minor leaguers were one thing. Going against major leaguers was another. Williams proved his worth against that competition as well. On March 15, Brooklyn, the 1920 National League champs, came to Bogalusa and were whipped by the Browns 17–3. Williams was 3-for-5 with two home runs, hitting them off lefty Sam Post and Johnny Miljus.

But Williams also was hit in the foot by a pitch, which would cause him to miss a few days. When he came back, just to prove he was healthy, he stole a base in each of two wins over the Pelicans on March 19–20.

However, Williams was out again, this time struck by a high fever (it was being called tonsillitis, which was a catch-all term at the time for many different illnesses). Williams was able to return for the Browns' final exhibition before heading back to St. Louis, a 9–2 loss to Brooklyn in New Orleans on March 27 (Williams went 1-for-3 with a walk).

But the time away also gave Frank Wetzel a chance to play and show he could hit. After he collected seven hits in two games against Mobile and Louisville, *The Sporting News* wrote that Wetzel "is going to make Ken Williams hustle."[10]

The Browns and Cardinals once again hooked up for their preseason city series, although all the games were to be played at Sportsman's Park, as that was now the home of both teams. The Cardinals had left their old ballpark for Sportsman's Park midway through the 1920 season.

Williams started each of the first six games, but with the series tied at three games each, he was on the bench and Wetzel in left field in the seventh and deciding game as the Cardinals had lefty Jakie May on the mound.

Wetzel went 2-for-3, but with the game on the line, it was Williams called in to hit. The Browns were trailing 4–1, but May loaded the bases with none out. He struck out George

Sisler, then walked Jacobson—his third walk issued in the inning—to force in a run. With Wetzel up, Burt Shotton—the Cardinals' Sunday manager, as the religious Branch Rickey would not take the field on what he considered a holy day—brought in right-hander and future Hall of Famer Jesse Haines to pitch, and Fohl countered by sending up Williams to the plate.

On a 2–1 pitch, Williams ripped a single to right field to tie the game. Tobin would follow with a fly ball that scored Jacobson, and the Browns would go on to win 5–4 and once again take the city series, four games to three. An exhibition game before the start of the season might not seem like much, but over 30 years later Cardinals infielder Spec Toporcer, a rookie in 1921, recalled the atmosphere.

"Rickey wanted very much to win [the series], as it would mean a great deal to Cardinal prestige if we took the series [both teams had finished in third place in 1920]," Toporcer told *The Sporting News* in 1952. "These were not ordinary games; the crowds were large and there was a World's Series atmosphere, with rivalry tense and bitter."[11]

The prognosticators saw the 1921 Browns as being a good, but not great, team. George Daley of the *New York Morning World* picked them to finish in fourth place, behind Cleveland, New York and Washington. The *St. Louis Post-Dispatch*'s John Wray thought the team would do no worse than third place.

Fohl was not one to make predictions. But as for the team's style of play, he noted: "Slugging put the Browns into the first division last year, and I'm going to stay with it."[12] He added: "I've got the best outfield in the league in 'Baby Doll' Jacobson, Kenneth Williams and John Tobin."[13]

The Browns would be tested right off the bat. Their first opponent was the defending world champion Cleveland Indians at Sportsman's Park. And in case anyone forgot the Indians won the 1920 World Series, they showed up for the opener wearing jerseys which had World's Champions written across the front, with no mention of Cleveland or Indians to be found, except for the "C" emblazoned on their caps.

There was concern how baseball fans would react in the opener, what with the grand jury in Chicago investigating the Black Sox. Commissioner Landis made sure to address the Cardinals and Cubs, who were opening in Chicago. But his speech was intended for more than just those two teams:

> It is literally true to say that never before in any field of activity has anything been scrutinized as will our activity this season. We must put up with grandstand whispers about little misplays for a while, but characteristic spirit of fair play will soon snuff out that attitude....
>
> The American public always deals with its affairs on the merits of the case. We must play the game as hard as ever; no hanging back when we see a hard chance for fear of that mutter in the stands. Don't be afraid. If you strike out, that has been done before; if a pitcher blows up, that also has been done before. The crowd will have sense enough to understand in the long run. The only thing it won't forgive is being afraid to take a chance. Take chances and fight always.[14]

Landis's fears were not unwarranted, but in St. Louis, they still came out in droves (an estimated 14,000–15,000) despite a cloudy day—and in fact, it rained 10 minutes before the start of the game. As usual, a band played, local luminaries took part in pregame ceremonies, and the games went on.

Williams started the opener; he went 0-for-4 as the Browns beat the Indians 4–2, but surprisingly found himself in what we would call nowadays a platoon situation. With lefty

Duster Mails pitching in the second game of the season, Fohl sat Williams and started Wetzel—although he went back to Williams quickly after Mails couldn't make it out of the first inning and right-hander Guy Morton entered the game. (Cleveland's next two pitchers were both lefties, however.)

He sat again four days later when lefty Dicky Kerr pitched for the White Sox. This time Williams didn't get in the game as Kerr went the distance in a 3–2 St. Louis win. Wetzel went 1-for-4.

On April 26, the Browns faced Kerr again, and not only did Wetzel again start, but he also doubled and homered. That gave him one more extra-base hit than Williams, who had just one double, and that came in the second game of the season.

So it was no surprise when Fohl once again started Wetzel on May 1 against the Tigers and southpaw Red Oldham, but Williams got into the game late when right-hander Howard Ehmke came in to pitch. Williams walked twice, once intentionally. Wetzel was 0-for-3 to lower his batting average to .286 in his limited playing time, but still better than Williams's .262.

In the next game, a 7–6 win in 13 innings on a bitterly cold day in Detroit that saw only around 300 people come out to brave the wind, Williams went 2-for-6. After missing the next game—at St. Louis against the Tigers on May 5—because Oldham started, Williams went on a mini-tear, going 7-for-13 in the next three games against Detroit. That stretch included a 4-for-5 day on May 7 that saw his first home run of the season, a majestic shot which the *Post-Dispatch* called "one of the highest ever seen at Sportsman's Park."[15]

Williams was now hitting .328 on the young season while Wetzel, who went 1-for-4 in that May 5 game, was down to .250. The platoon was over. When Oldham started for Detroit against the Browns on May 9, Williams was in the starting lineup. He'd go 2-for-4 in a game shortened by rain and wouldn't miss another start until mid–July.

Williams continued his hot hitting as the A's came to town. He went 2-for-2 in the opener in a 1–0 win on May 11, then found his power stroke, going 3-for-5 with a double and triple the next day and 1-for-2 with a double on May 13. He also ended the final game—a 7–5 win—with a leaping grab near the left-field fence on a deep fly hit by Philadelphia's Tilly Walker.

With the Red Sox in town next, an event happened that likely changed the course of Williams's career. We don't know the exact date, but both Williams and umpire Billy Evans, who wrote a syndicated column, referred to a game early in the spring of 1921.

Williams was sitting on the bench with teammates when the subject of Babe Ruth came up. Williams wrote about what happened next in a 1922 article:

> My teammates began telling me what a chase they would give Ruth if able to take a healthy swing, as I did.
>
> "This fence here is made to order for you," remarked one of the players.
>
> He had reference to the right field bleachers in St. Louis. Since I am a left-handed hitter he figured that would be an ideal spot for me to shoot at.
>
> "You ought to be able to pull 15 or 20 balls into the right field bleachers every year," remarked another player.
>
> "Any time a pitcher puts a ball on the inside to you he ought to say a prayer. You ought to whale away with a full swing on any of those babies on the inside. If you did, you would have many a pitcher in trouble."
>
> Well, all that dope the boys were slipping me that afternoon got me thinking.
>
> At first I thought maybe they were just kidding me. The more I thought of it, the more I was convinced they were in earnest.

> They all seemed to think I was a much better hitter than I thought I was. I kept thinking it all over and decided I would try to give Ruth a chase.[16]

Evans wrote that he was there that same day and relayed a similar tale in a column from April 1922:

> I was sitting on the bench in St. Louis on the day I believe Williams shifted from the line hitter to the slugger. The day previous Williams had been retired on three towering fly balls that just failed to clear the fence. Sitting on the bench Williams was bemoaning his tough luck.
>
> "If you would start pulling those balls on the inside into the right field, you would hit 15 or 20 home runs on this park every year," said another teammate. Several other St. Louis players offered advice. All of them lauded the ability of Williams to hit.
>
> "Looks as if all these guys think I am a better hitter than I do myself. Starting today I am going to take a healthy cut." That afternoon Williams made a home run.[17]

Signs point to the day in question being May 15, 1921. Williams went 0-for-5 the previous day in an 8–6 win over Boston, and Evans was one of the two umpires in that game. Also, Ruth was on a home run tear, with 11 home runs in his first 22 games, including one on May 14; thus, bringing up his name in the dugout is hardly a far-fetched notion.

And, as Evans noted, Williams hit a home run on May 15—a monstrous shot off Boston's Elmer Meyers in the first inning (his first at-bat with his new approach) that "landed on the east side of Grand Avenue."[18]

Not that a power surge came immediately for Williams, although he did double in his next game, then had singles in each of the next six (including a bunt single and one two-hit game).

But then, suddenly, it did, although ironically his next home run would not be to right field. Against the Yankees on May 23, Williams clubbed a deep line drive off Waite Hoyt (who allowed only three homers in 282⅓ innings in 1921) past center fielder Ping Bodie, where it went all the way to the flagpole in the deepest part of the park. This would be Williams's third and final inside-the-park home run of his career and the only one to occur at Sportsman's Park.

Williams singled the next day to extend his hit streak to 10 games. He made it 11 games on May 25 with a two-out RBI triple in the ninth inning to tie the game at 6, eventually scoring the winning run on a Jack Quinn wild pitch.

The Yankees left Sportsman's Park and Cleveland arrived, but the Indians couldn't cool off Williams. In the opening game May 26—a rain-shortened affair—Williams singled twice and tripled to right center, the ball hitting just below the top of the fence. Williams wouldn't be denied a home run the next day. In fact, he'd hit two.

Jim Bagby had received advice from Mails on how to pitch Williams, but in the end went with his own plan. In the first at-bat in the first inning, Bagby tried a fastball, which Williams hit for a home run onto Grand Avenue. In the sixth, he went with curveballs, which also resulted in a homer, whose distance was "a few short feet from going into the street."[19] Bagby faced Williams one more time, and while he didn't homer, he hit it to the fence, where it was caught by Elmer Smith. "Doggone! That fellow's the most unnaturalist hitter I ever did see—no more judgment than a hawg,"[20] Bagby reportedly said.

To which Mails replied, "You should'a give him low ones on the outside." That didn't sit well with Bagby, who angrily answered, "You should go soak your head. I done give him all my repertory and I hope I never see him again."[21]

Whether those words were actually said is up for debate, but the point of the story is Williams was hitting everything thrown to him, and hitting them a long way. And two days later, Williams hit two more balls over the fence against Cleveland's George Uhle. The first hit the roof of the right-field pavilion, while the second sailed out of the stadium and across Grand Avenue.

That gave Williams seven home runs since May 7. However, all those longballs didn't do the Browns that much good as St. Louis suffered a four-game sweep at the hands of Cleveland, leaving its season record at 14–22 and putting the Browns in sixth place. "It will be a welcome relief to have the Browns go away for a month,"[22] opined *The Sporting News*.

Going on the road didn't affect Williams's power stroke. St. Louis's first stop away from home was in Chicago at cavernous Comiskey Park. Only 20 home runs were hit off White Sox pitchers at Comiskey in 1921, and one of them came in game two of a May 30 double-header when Williams hit a Red Faber pitch that "whistled into the right field stand."[23]

Overall, Williams was 5-for-10 in the double-header to raise his average to .379. He also drove in three runs in each game, giving him 11 RBI in his last three games, 15 in his last five and 16 in his last six. He added another RBI the next day on a triple as the Browns won 8–7 to take two of three from Chicago.

The Browns next traveled to New York, where they were met by third baseman Frank Ellerbe, acquired in a deal with Washington for Earl Smith. Ellerbe was a third baseman by trade, while Smith continued to prove he was not.

In the opening game at the Polo Grounds on June 2, Williams hit what he thought was a home run but was called foul. In 1921, if the ball went over the fence fair, but landed in foul territory, it was considered a foul ball. This would not be the first time Williams would lose a home run in this fashion.

Williams did go 2-for-4 with a double in that game and then 4-for-5 the following day to raise his average to what would be a season high .392. His slugging percentage, which had been below .400 as late as May 8, was now at .633.

On June 4, Williams had another hit that should have been a home run ruled foul. In the first inning with Frank Wetzel on first base, Williams clubbed a Jack Quinn pitch over the double-decked right-field grandstand. It was clearly a fair ball when it went far over the fence, but as it left the ballpark, it started to tail foul. Williams, thinking it was a home run, rounded the bases. Much to his—and the fans'—surprise, as Williams rounded second base he was informed by umpire Dick Nallin that it was a foul ball.

According to *St. Louis Globe Democrat* correspondent Charles A. Lovelt, who was at the game, "Those thousands in position to judge indicated unmistakably it passed out of the park fair by four or five feet."[24]

Back at the plate, Williams hit another long fly into the stands; this time there was no question it was foul. Quinn, perhaps wisely, eventually walked Williams, who would end up hitless, although he did reach on what was ruled an error when his hard liner went off the cheek of Yankees first baseman Wally Pipp.

After going 3-for-7 with four RBI in the next two games against New York, Williams went to Boston with the Browns, where he had two more hits against the Red Sox, including a first-inning home run ("a mighty wallop"[25]) off Bullet Joe Bush.

Williams also collided with shortstop Wally Gerber (not the last time that would ever happen) and the Browns lost (as they did three of five times in New York). They did win the next day, 2–1, although Williams went 0-for-4, ending a streak in which he'd reached base—by hit, walk or error—in 24 straight games. In those 24 games, which stretched from May 15 to June 7, Williams was 39-for-94 (.415) with a .766 slugging percentage (three doubles, three triples, eight home runs) and 34 RBI. Nine of those 24 games, in which he hit .447, came on the road.

Despite the 0-fer, Williams was one of the few steady presences in the lineup. Sisler was hitting .371, but had missed a number of games and just returned. Jacobson was batting over .300 but called out by Fohl for not hitting for enough power. He had yet to hit a home run and was slugging only .405—nearly 100 points lower than his 1920 figure—in his first 50 games.

Beyond Sisler's missing some time, the infield was a mess. Dud Lee was starting at second and batting just .151. Gerber and Ellerbe were known more for their gloves than their bats, and Gerber would be lost for over a month after breaking his wrist when it was hit by a pitch. Young Marty McManus had started some in May both at third and second, but had slumped so badly, down to .230, he was benched. Fohl was desperate; he moved Lee to shortstop for the injured Gerber and put Lyman Lamb, formerly an outfielder who started the year at third base and was benched, at second base. Lamb had played second only once in the majors—on May 31 as a substitute. "Last year we had a terrible infield at times,"[26] Fohl would recall the next spring.

One interesting thing about the Browns was they liked to attempt double steals, which also helps account for many of Williams's inflated caught stealings (he was, for example, thrown out at home against the Yankees on June 6). But it also might have cost him some steals in the record books. On June 9, he and Sisler pulled off a double steal—Sisler scoring. Williams stole second, but overran the base. Boston catcher Muddy Ruel fired down to second base but threw the ball into center field, allowing Williams to score. The box score in all the papers (both in St. Louis and Boston) had Williams with a steal. But the daily account of Williams's season on baseball-reference.com and retrosheet.org credit only Sisler with a steal in that game. (There is at least one more missing steal found for Williams in 1926. The Society for American Baseball Research has located a number of RBI corrections, which should give Williams at least five more in his career.)

When Williams wasn't running on the basepaths or making fine plays in the field (he had a "wonder play"[27] against the A's on June 11 and a "sensational one-handed stab"[28] at Washington on June 15, both on foul flies), he continued to hit the ball hard. Starting June 9, Williams had an extra-base hit in six straight games with six doubles (including two in that first game) and a home run, his 10th of the season, off Philadelphia's Slim Harriss on June 13. It cleared the right-field wall at Shibe Park, which stood 380 feet from home plate. A Philadelphia newspaper described the home run as a "slam over the right field fence, a la Babe Ruth."[29]

The Browns continued to struggle, however. St. Louis lost the first four games of a series in Washington to drop to seventh place with a record of 25–33. The fourth loss was witnessed by former President Woodrow Wilson, who watched the game in his car. He'd witness Williams make a fine running catch "almost to the jury box"[30] to retire Bing Miller, whom he also robbed of hit on a deep fly two days prior.

Williams led St. Louis back to the win column June 19 in the finale against the Senators, going 3-for-5 with two doubles off Hall of Famer Walter Johnson and scoring both runs in the Browns' 10-inning, 2–1 victory over Washington.

St. Louis finished up its road trip by splitting two games in Detroit—Williams homered off Hooks Dauss in the second with two outs in the ninth to tie the game, which the Browns would win 6–4 in 10 innings—and losing three of four to Cleveland.

In the 27-game road trip, which lasted from May 30 to June 28, Williams hit .342 with 10 doubles, a triple and four home runs. He also scored 18 runs and drove in 26.

The Browns returned home to face the White Sox at the same time the Black Sox trial was under way in Chicago. Williams made some news of his own by hitting a home run on four consecutive days.

It started on June 29 with a sixth-inning shot off Red Faber. On June 30, he doubled in the opener of a double-header, and then provided the only run in the second game with a home run into the right-field bleachers in the second inning on Roy Wilkinson's first pitch to him.

On July 1, he broke a 2–all tie with a solo home run in the bottom of the eighth inning off Cy Twombly—father of the famous artist of the same name—the only home run Twombly would allow in his 27⅔ major-league innings (the Browns, though, would lose as Chicago scored twice in the ninth against Emilio Palmero). This game also marked the fifth straight multiple-hit game for Williams. Twice (June 28 and game 2 of a double-header on July 1) he had three hits.

July 2 brought another double-header, but this one was delayed as fans and players—who were lined up on the baselines—listened to updates of the Jack Dempsey-Georges Carpentier fight, being held in Jersey City, New Jersey. Over 9,000 were in attendance at Sportsman's Park (an estimated 7,500 stood outside the *Globe Democrat* office for the latest) to hear the blow-by-blow described by a person bellowing it through a loudspeaker after getting the results given to him by a telegrapher, who transcribed messages via wire on a typewriter.

After the fight, which began at 1 p.m. St. Louis time and ended with a Dempsey fourth-round knockout, the "telemegaphone station"[31] was removed from the field and the games were played.

Williams made it a home run on his fourth consecutive day by hitting one off Shovel Hodge in Game 2, causing the *Globe Democrat* to declare, "There is no one close enough to dispute Ken's runner-up title, prince of the round-abouters."[32] Ruth, of course, was king.

Williams didn't homer in the July 3 finale against the White Sox, but he did hit one to the fence off Faber and defensively robbed Eddie Mulligan—his old Jefferson Barracks teammate—with a leaping, one-handed grab.

The Browns lost that July 3 game, and then proceeded to be swept in a three-game series by the Tigers to drop them to 32–44. The *Globe Democrat* not only felt the season was over for St. Louis—running a story with the headline "Browns Practically Through So Far as 1921 Is Concerned"[33]—but it also lamented that Williams wasn't getting enough credit.

"What does Williams receive for holding the title, prince to King Babe?" the paper asked. "A bare mention in local circles. What would he get if the Browns were up in the race? National publicity at least."[34]

The Sporting News concurred, noting, "Williams is running next to Babe Ruth in homers, and running Ruth enough of a race to show that even if not 'king' of sluggers he's at least of royal blood."[35]

Williams told *The Sporting News*, however, that despite his rash of home runs, he wasn't particularly satisfied with his play. "I'm falling short too often, hitting long flies, and I think maybe a few more triples and two-baggers would be better for the Browns,"[36] he said. True to his word, Williams would hit a double and/or triple in each of the next five games and six of the next seven.

In the Browns' first game after being swept by the Tigers, Williams tripled in a 12–2 win at home over Washington on July 8. He'd also hit his 16th home run, a three-run shot into the right-field bleachers, off lefty Tom Zachary.

The next day, he doubled, tripled and was walked with the bases loaded. The Browns won that game as well, 12–3, and recorded the final out when Jimmy Austin pulled the hidden ball trick on the Senators' Pat Gharrity. Williams would tell his sons how much Austin loved to win and was a fun-loving player—helping the groundskeepers pick up the bases after games and sliding into players in the showers after a win. No doubt Austin gleefully got a little wet after this victory.

Williams doubled in each of the next two games against Washington, then vs. the Yankees, he doubled and tripled—the latter hit bouncing off the head of New York's Chick Fewster. After an 0-for-4 game, he doubled again against New York, which swept a rain-shortened three-game series.

The *St. Louis Globe Democrat* had looked forward to a Ruth-Williams duel, and during the series the *St. Louis Post-Dispatch*'s John Wray used the nickname "Home Run"[37] Williams for the first time to describe Williams in the majors. Williams, though, was playing through a fever and did not hit a home run, while Ruth hit three, including two in one game, to give him 35 on the season.

Doctors finally ordered Williams to stay in bed, which he did briefly, missing a doubleheader on July 17 against the visiting A's. He was on the bench July 18 and was called in to hit for pitcher Elam Vangilder. Adding injury to illness, he was hit by a pitch on the head.

Williams was back in the lineup July 19, as was Johnny Tobin, who missed a few games with a split finger, as the Browns completed a five-game sweep of Philadelphia. Williams, obviously feeling OK after his bout with "tonsillitis" (again, a catch-all phrase, which was also used to describe his condition in spring training) and taking one off the noggin, went 2-for-4.

The Browns were still only 40–48 with the sweep, and there had been rumblings prior to the wins that Lee Fohl wouldn't last the season as manager. Owner Phil Ball quashed any rumors by circulating a letter that stated Fohl would be back in 1922, noting that many injuries and the loss of Gedeon—and the inability to replace him—didn't allow Fohl to "show his true value as a manager."[38]

Ironically, two days after Ball's announcement, the Browns held a day for their former manager, Jimmy Burke, who was now coaching with the Red Sox. Before the St. Louis–Boston game, the St. Louis resident was feted with numerous gifts, including a floral arrangement, a gold watch and a traveling bag.

Williams socked another double in that game as well, a 10–9 Browns win in 12 innings. St. Louis made it seven straight victories the next day with an 8–1 trouncing, Williams going 2-for-4 with three runs, one coming on a double steal with Hank Severeid. He also made a great, leaping catch on Del Pratt's fly, but also allowed a single go through his legs for an error. This problem was thought to have been corrected in spring training, but he'd have difficulties on grounders throughout his career.

Lee Fohl, Browns manager from 1921 until he was let go late in 1923 (George Grantham Bain Collection, Library of Congress).

Williams's single with the bases loaded in the 10th inning scored Tobin with the winning run on July 23, giving the Browns their eighth consecutive victory. However, they'd lose a key part of their offense for a short while as George Sisler punched umpire George Hildebrand—although Sisler said he pulled his punch—after arguing a close play at first base. Amazingly, Sisler would be suspended only through July 29. With travel days and a rainout, he'd miss only three games.

With Sisler out, Williams moved to third in the order and accounted for both of St. Louis's runs—with a sacrifice fly and RBI double—as the winning streak came to an end in a 10–2 loss to the Red Sox.

St. Louis hit the road after the loss. After splitting a pair of games with the Yankees, the Browns took two of three at Boston. On August 2, the same day famed Italian tenor Enrico Caruso died and the Black Sox were acquitted, Williams went 6-for-7 in a double-header sweep.

Williams would go only 3-for-17 in Philadelphia, the teams splitting the four games, but in his final at-bat of the series in the second game of an August 6 double-header, he did hit his first home run in nearly a month, "a vicious drive over the right-field wall"[39] against the A's Dave Keefe. Including that home run, Williams would finish up the road trip on a seven-game hit streak. More ignominiously, he'd make an error in each of five straight games from August 4 to 9.

The Browns would take three of four in Washington as St. Louis closed in on the Senators in the standings, moving into fourth place. Williams went 1-for-3 with two walks against Walter Johnson in the only loss, 16–5 on August 8.

The teams would play an incredible 19-inning game on August 9. St. Louis's Dixie Davis pitched a complete game and did not allow a hit in the final nine innings. (Washington used two pitchers; George Mogridge went 9⅓ and Jose Acosta 9⅔.) Davis appeared to have given the Browns the lead in the 16th inning by tripling and scoring after the ball was thrown away, but he was called out after missing second base. St. Louis eventually won 8–6, with Williams scoring one of the runs in the 19th.

The Browns won twice at Detroit to finish their 15-game road trip with a 10–5 record. St. Louis then returned home and won two of three from the Tigers to reach .500 for the first time since April 23.

Williams didn't have an extra-base hit in 15 games—dating back to August 6—but then homered three times in a week. Home run No. 18 came against the Yankees' Bill Piercy in the second game of a double-header on August 21. No. 19 off Benn Karr won the game in the 10th inning of a 12–11 victory over Boston, and No. 20 occurred on August 26 against Philadelphia's Ed Rommel. All three games were St. Louis wins as the Browns went 10–6 on their home stand to move within one game of Washington for third place.

As August turned into September, the Browns snuck into third place past the Senators by mere percentage points (both teams had 65 wins). The difference between third and fourth place meant one team's players getting World Series money and the other not. Browns business manager Bob Quinn emphatically stated his team would not be putting in untested rookies down the stretch as his team chased some of the postseason loot.

Williams was doing his part to help St. Louis finish in third. When he wasn't hitting home runs or making terrific catches in the outfield, he was flashing his speed on the basepaths. The stories and box scores from the newspapers of the time reveal he stole nine bases in a 12-game stretch from August 22 to September 2 (he is officially only credited with six).

Fohl moved Williams to sixth in the batting order in September whenever the Browns faced a left-handed starter, but he remained in the cleanup spot vs. righties. While five of his first 16 career home runs came off lefties, in 1921 he hit only one HR off a southpaw—Washington's Zachary—and though he would obviously fare better against righties throughout his career, he'd hit at least four HRs off lefties each year from 1922 to 1926.

After batting sixth in the first game of a September 5 double-header at Cleveland against Duster Mails, Williams was back at the four spot in the second game against George Uhle. And in the eighth inning of that second game against Jim Bagby, he clubbed a three-run homer over Dunn Field's 20-foot right-field wall, giving him a home run in seven of the eight American League ballparks. (The exception was Washington's Griffith Stadium, but Senators pitchers only allowed 13 home runs there in all of 1921.)

That game started Williams on a 13-game stretch in which he hit .444 with four home runs while driving in 21 runs. He had six RBI in the September 5 game he homered in, and also had games in which he drove in four and five, accounting for half of the six times he had four or more RBI in a game that season.

Williams socked a home run in both ends of a double-header in front of 30,000 at the Polo Grounds on September 15—hitting them off Carl Mays and Waite Hoyt—but the feat was overshadowed by Ruth, who broke his own single-season record with home run No. 55 in the first game.

Williams hit his final home run of 1921 in Philadelphia on September 19 in a 7–4 win in which he drove in five of the runs. Four days later he hurt his leg in a game in Boston and started only two more games—the first game of a double-header in Boston on September 24 and a 2–0 win in New York on September 27.

Without Williams, the Browns finished off the season by winning their final two games in Detroit—which assured them of third place at 81–73, a scant half-game ahead of Washington. The Senators won eight of their final 12 games, while the Browns held them off, going 8–6 to close the season.

After the Giants beat the Yankees in eight games in the World Series, the Browns reaped their reward for finishing in third place, getting roughly $585 per man from their share of the postseason proceeds.

Williams finished the season on a strong note. In his final 33 games (starting from his four-hit game August 24), he batted .371 with a .463 on-base percentage, .569 slugging percentage, 30 runs and 32 RBI. In the year's final road trip, he batted .378 with a .600 slugging percentage and 17 RBI in his 13 games played.

For the 1921 season, Williams played in 146 games—five more than he did the previous season—and batted .347 with a .429 on-base percentage and .561 slugging percentage. He hit 24 home runs, scored 115 runs and drove in 117, while stealing 20 bases (according to the official records; he likely had closer to 25 in reality), making Williams the first 20–20 player (at least 20 HR and 20 SB) in American League history. The only player previously to do this was the Chicago Cubs' Frank "Wildfire" Schulte in 1911, who had 21 home runs and 23 steals.

"Once upon a time not so many years back the making of 24 home runs in the American League would have made a player a nationally discussed figure," Williams would write in 1922. "Yet last season my home-run record meant nothing to the fans. Only a few really knew I made 24."[40]

Williams would later note that while he came up with a reputation as a home run hitter from his time in the Pacific Coast League, he also earned the rep of someone who liked pitches up high, "between his waist and shoulders."[41]

So Williams had Browns pitchers throw him low in practice over and over again to help him adjust to what was perceived as his weakness. "Then the laugh was on the other foot,"[42] he said.

In addition to his hitting prowess, Williams walked 74 times while striking out on only 42 occasions, the latter actually representing his career high for a season. In fact, his ratio of striking out once every 13 at-bats was also the worst of his career with regular playing time. By comparison, Babe Ruth struck out once every 6.7 at-bats in 1921, and his career best mark was once every 10.5 at-bats in 1931, also the only time that mark ever reached double digits in his career.

Williams's .347 average was good for eighth in the American League—although just fourth-best on the Browns. He was fourth in the AL in slugging percentage, behind just Hall of Famers Ruth, Harry Heilmann and Ty Cobb. In on-base percentage, only those latter three and fellow Hall of Famer Tris Speaker had better marks than Williams's .429.

Williams was also tied for second in home runs (but alone in second in at-bats per HR) in the American League with the Yankees' Bob Meusel, sixth in runs, sixth in RBI, seventh in total bases, seventh in walks, seventh in stolen bases and tied for ninth in hits.

When adding in the National League, only the Cardinals' Rogers Hornsby—another future Hall of Famer—had a better slugging percentage than Williams, and no one in the NL hit more home runs. Ken Williams was coming into his own as a hitter and slugger, and he was just getting started.

Chapter 9

"Who makes fans forget about Babe Ruth?"

Just because the 1921 season was over doesn't mean there wasn't more baseball to be played—or at least attempted to be played. A proposed Browns-Cardinals city series didn't happen, as the National League team decided it could do better at the gate playing other clubs, including a local black club, the National Negro League's St. Louis Giants, and traveling to other cities. (But this doesn't mean the Cards would fare better in the field, *The Sporting News* noting, "The negroes, more power to them, made the Cardinals look pretty minor leagueish."[1])

Williams had been part of a group of players to be managed by Cincinnati infielder Sammy Bohne; they were to travel and play games in Panama and all over South America. However, that trip never came to fruition.

When those plans fell through, for the first time Williams was asked to take part in barnstorming teams. This was a way for the players to stay in shape and make a little money while also bringing Major League Baseball to people in places who would likely never otherwise get an opportunity to see the stars of the game they could only read about.

Williams was supposed to play in games in Ogden, Utah, and Bakersfield, California, but doesn't appear to have done so. He did suit up and play October 25 in Mount Olive, Illinois, in a tribute game for Browns teammate Johnny Tobin, who played in that town in 1911.

Many players barnstormed—but some weren't supposed to. The rule at the time—enacted in 1911—was if you played in the World Series, you couldn't barnstorm. Babe Ruth, who played in the '21 World Series with the Yankees, flouted the rule, telling baseball commissioner Judge Kenesaw Landis he would play regardless. "I see no reason why this rule should be invoked against me when Sisler of St. Louis and others who shared in the Worlds Series money are playing exhibition games unmolested by Judge Landis,"[2] Ruth said.

While Ruth certainly had a point—and the American League would eventually change its policy—going toe-to-toe with Landis was not a good idea. Ruth, as well as Yankees outfielder Bob Meusel and pitcher Bill Piercy, would play in an exhibition against the Polish Nations of Buffalo. Two other teammates, pitcher Carl Mays and catcher Wally Schang, heeded Landis's warning of punishment and pulled out.

Landis showed Ruth who was boss, fining him his World Series share ($3,362.26) and suspending the Yankees slugger for five weeks, until May 20, 1922. Certainly this was not good for the Yankees, but, while Ruth's presence would be missed at the gate, it was a boon

for other American League teams, including the Browns. But the Browns needed more than the absence of Ruth for five weeks to contend for a pennant.

J.C. Kofoed wrote in *The Sporting News*: "The outfield of the St. Louis Browns impressed me last summer as being one of the most powerful in the game.... And defensively, these young men need no lessons, either.... If the Browns infield can be tuned up as high as the outfield combination the team won't be so very far away from the flag next season."[3]

Earlier in the year, *The Sporting News* also noted that Browns business manager Bob Quinn had better trade for pitching so the team "can hold opponents to less than a thousand runs in a season."[4]

Quinn didn't really solve the first problem—the team hoped second baseman Marty McManus would improve as a replacement for Joe Gedeon, now ruled ineligible to play professional baseball. Whether due to lack of a trade partner or confidence in players on the roster, the Browns seemed fine with going with Frank Ellerbe at third base and Billy Mullen providing some spring training competition.

But Quinn knew the Browns needed pitching. St. Louis allowed 844 runs in 1921 and had a 4.61 ERA, tied for second worst in the American League. The team's 556 walks and 3.6 bases on balls per nine innings were the worst in the AL, while the 1.521 WHIP was sixth among the eight teams.

Urban Shocker (27–12, 3.55 ERA) had turned into the team's ace, but Elam Vangilder 11–12, 3.94) was the only other

Top: **Outfielder Johnny "Jack" Tobin batted .300 or over every year from 1919 to 1925, with the exception of 1924, when he hit .299.** ***Bottom:*** **Marty McManus, who played primarily at second base for the Browns, 1921–26 (both photographs, George Grantham Bain Collection, Library of Congress).**

The ever-inconsistent Dixie Davis, who once pitched all 19 innings of a game (George Grantham Bain Collection, Library of Congress).

pitcher on the roster who pitched more than one inning and had an ERA under 4. Dixie Davis (16–16, 4.44) was still inconsistent and wild, although manager Lee Fohl said he expected big things from Vangilder and lefty Bill Bayne (11–5, 4.72).

The rest of the staff was, to put it mildly, rather forgettable.

So Quinn made a drastic move. He dealt eight players—pitchers Grover Lowdermilk, Emelio Palmero, Ray Sanders and Bill Burwell, infielders Dud Lee and Bill Gleason, first baseman Phil Todt and a player to be named later—to Columbus of the American Association for Dave Danforth.

"Yes, and I have 11 more players who I will be willing to give for any other one pitcher who I believe will help my club," responded manager Lee Fohl to the critics of the deal. "If Danforth can win 12 games for me it will have been a good deal. The players I have given for him could not be counted on to deliver that many victories."[5]

The Browns weren't the only club impressed with Danforth, who at 32 had been around the block, including stints in the majors with the Philadelphia A's (1911–12) and Chicago White Sox (1916–19). The Cubs, Indians, Reds and Yankees reportedly also made offers for Danforth, who had a stellar season with Columbus (and had struck out 10 Browns in six innings in a September 29 exhibition game) of the American Association. According to *The Sporting News*, the left-hander pitched 329 innings and had a 2.66 ERA with 204 strikeouts, 114 walks and 35 hit batters. The *St. Louis Globe Democrat* had his record at 27–15 (the Society for American Baseball Research lists it as 25–16), with eight of his losses coming in one-run games.

As noted above, the Browns weren't the only team looking to shore up their pitching. In late December the Yankees obtained the top two starting pitchers from the Red Sox (not the first or last time these two teams would engage in a questionable deal), Bullet Joe Bush and Sam Jones, the latter of whom had been declared unavailable by Boston just a few weeks earlier. To get Bush (16–9, 3.50 in 1921) and Jones (23–16, 3.22) as well as starting shortstop Everett Scott, all the Yankees had to give up was a pair of unproven pitchers in Rip Collins and Piercy, 38-year-old pitcher Jack Quinn, aging shortstop Roger Peckinpaugh (who would be dealt a month later to Washington in a trade for Joe Dugan and later would also be involved in a controversial Yankees-Red Sox trade), and $100,000.

The Sporting News thought the Red Sox would be looking for an outfielder in any deal for pitcher, but wondered, "Who would trade a Tobin or Williams, however, for even Sam Jones?"[6]

One letter-writer to Quinn said the Browns should deal Williams and backup catcher Josh Billings to the Red Sox for outfielders Elmer Smith—acquired from Cleveland in a deal a few days after they traded Bush and Jones—and Shano Collins. "Why, I wouldn't trade Williams alone for both Smith and Collins," Quinn said. "Ken'll play rings around both those lads this coming year, and did so last season."[7]

Quinn was wise not to listen to the fan—Smith quickly became a part-time player in 1922, and Collins, who was 35, enjoyed just one more season as a regular. Quinn did bolster his team's outfield depth, though, acquiring lefty Chick Shorten on waivers and purchasing minor leaguer Cedric Durst.

How these moves would pan out for the Browns remained to be seen, but Ruth thought St. Louis would be a contender. Finding other ways to travel and earn money in the offseason, Ruth was performing in a show in January 1922 called *That's Good* at St. Louis's Orpheum Theater. When asked which team would give the Yankees the biggest challenge, Ruth smartly replied, "This is St. Louis, isn't it? Well, why go further? The Browns look as if they are going to be mighty troublesome."[8]

First, of course, there was the matter of getting Browns players to sign their contracts. As usual, Williams was one of the last to send in his signed contract, with only Bill Jacobson and Dixie Davis, who at one point threatened to quit baseball "to devote all his time to street-paving business,"[9] getting theirs in later among the regular players.

Williams got a boost in salary from $4,200 to $6,000, which was still well behind the $12,500 George Sisler was earning in his multiyear contract, but more than starting catcher Hank Severeid, who signed a two-year deal after the 1920 season calling for $5,750 a year (although he, too, briefly claimed he might quit baseball to tend to his farm in Story Creek, Iowa). Jacobson and shortstop Wally Gerber both also got boosts to $6,000 a year, although Jacobson signed a four-year contract calling for that same salary each season.

Ken Williams with the St. Louis Browns in 1922 (George Grantham Bain Collection, Library of Congress).

With his contract situation out of the way, Williams was ready to head to spring training—in yet another new locale for the Browns. Williams would make his way to Los Angeles, join up with Jimmy Austin, and take a train for three days to Mobile, Alabama, where Quinn had wanted to hold spring training in 1920 before then-manager Jimmy Burke refused.

Monroe Park, where the Browns trained, actually had a grass infield—compared to clay or dirt as in years past—and the team would have access to two of the three clubhouses. The Battle Hotel, where the team was housed, was a roughly 30-minute ride via trolley car to the park. Conveniently, the trolley line passed right by both the hotel and ballpark. And Mobile wasn't some small town in the middle of nowhere with nothing to do other than play ball and sit in the hotel and play cards. There were a number of movie and vaudeville houses as well as a golf course.

Entertainment aside, what Ken Williams wanted to do was play ball—and hit. Williams and Austin arrived in Mobile "in the wee small hours"[10] on February 28, but both were at the park March 1.

As usual, Williams gravitated towards batting practice. Showing no rust from his off-season layoff, he poked a couple of pitches from Urban Shocker over the right-field fence. Players asked for the groundskeeper to remove a couple of boards from the fence so they wouldn't have to climb over it—instead walking on through—every time somebody sailed a ball over it (which Williams did five times in his opening practice).

After a couple of days off due to extreme cold, Williams was back at it again March 4, sending a number of balls over the fence. When the games started, Williams didn't stop.

Williams only played part of the first intrasquad scrimmage March 6, but was in long enough to hit one over the right-field fence off John Overlock. On March 11, in an 11–2 win over the Mobile Bears, he homered off Charles Fulton (and also doubled off lefty Jesse Sigmon, although he was out trying for a triple).

After hitting 12 over the fence in practice on March 14, Williams homered in an intrasquad game on March 17 and again the next day in a win over Mobile. With commissioner Landis in attendance, Williams showed off another part of his game in a 9–1 win over Mobile on March 22, stealing his fifth base of the spring.

He followed that up with a double in four straight games: against Brooklyn (off Dutch Ruether); back-to-back games vs. Louisville in Pensacola (into a stiff wind in the first one, although he did hit five over the fence in batting practice); and in an 11–0 win in New Orleans, where he had three hits (two off lefties) and also stole another base.

While in New Orleans, Browns owner Phil Ball paid a visit. The annual city series between the Browns and Cardinals was not going to be played in 1922. There were different reasons given, but largely it was theorized that both teams expected to be in the pennant race and had more to lose than gain. Still, the two St. Louis contingents were to play two spring training exhibition games in New Orleans on April 1–2 and two back home April 8–9. Ball took his team to dinner and emphasized how much he wanted the Browns to win all four of those games.

The Browns won the first game 6–5, with Williams, batting sixth against left-hander Bill Sherdel, hitting a two-run homer in the bottom of the sixth to tie the game at five. The Browns would win in the bottom of the ninth when Tobin singled in McManus.

Ball was in good spirits early in the second game as the Browns took a 6–1 lead after five innings, but surely his mood changed as the Cardinals came back and were victorious 7–6. As the day before, Williams was 1-for-3, although with just a single in this one.

The Browns played a few games in Mississippi and one in Tennessee before heading back to St. Louis. In a 14–1 win over Jackson on April 5, Williams tripled, homered, stole two bases and got into an argument after a called strike with umpire Lefty Leifeld—who was also the Browns' pitching coach.

Back in St. Louis, the Browns were the home team in their first meeting against the Cardinals. The Cards were displaying their new uniform, which had two birds on a bat across the front of the jersey. "It will be by far the gaudiest bit of baseball heraldry that ever dazzled a fan's eye,"[11] declared the *St. Louis Post-Dispatch*. The Browns, meanwhile, were in their usual cream-colored uniforms with brown socks.

Fashion aside, the Browns won an exciting game in front of 12,000 fans at Sportsman's Park, including American League president Ban Johnson, who sat in a box seat behind the Browns dugout. With one out in the bottom of the ninth of a 2–all game, Williams singled past first baseman Jim Bottomley, sending Jacobson to third. Gerber followed with a single to left field to give the Browns the win.

In the second of the two games, Williams put on something of a show for the estimated 29,000 fans—the largest crowd ever for a game in St. Louis. At the plate, Williams had two hits, both two-run doubles (in the fifth and seventh innings) into the overflow crowd. In the field, he had four assists, including throwing two runners out at the plate—Bottomley, trying to score after a Heine Mueller fly in the first; and Milt Stock, after Williams raced over to snare Austin McHenry's foul fly in the third. In all, eight runners were thrown out at home in the game, including Sisler three times.

Thanks in large part to Williams's play both at bat and in the field, the Browns won 6–3 to win the unofficial city series three games to one. A jubilant Ball once again gave each player a reward, $100 for their efforts.

The Browns headed to Chicago to open the season. Despite winning 81 games and finishing third in 1921 and at least slightly addressing pitching concerns, the Browns were pegged to finish fourth in the American League by the Baseball Writers' Association behind New York, Cleveland and Washington. Even without Babe Ruth and Bob Meusel for a little over a month, the Yankees were a unanimous choice among the writers to capture the American League crown.

AL president Ban Johnson didn't necessarily agree with that prediction. A week into the season at St. Louis's opener he'd claim, "I saw the Browns in their two spring series games with the Cardinals and I cannot see where the Yanks, even with Ruth and Meusel in the lineup, are one whit superior.... While New York may have the individual sluggers who surpass the Browns hitters, I must confess that I believe St. Louis is the better of the two as a team."[12]

Despite its being opening day, a baseball game was likely on the back burner of most people's minds in Chicago. The headlines flashed of Fatty Arbuckle's acquittal in his third trial while the White Sox were contending with the absence of Dickie Kerr. Kerr had won 40 games over the last two seasons while pitching over 550 innings, but was holding out for a reported $8,500 salary—which would be a $4,000 raise. (Kerr wouldn't pitch in the majors again until 1925.) On top of that, it was a typical cold April day in Chicago with winds whipping off Lake Michigan to chill things even further. It was so cold that the White Sox didn't even hold any special pregame opening day ceremony.

St. Louis's bats were frigid as well, collecting just three hits off Red Faber in the opener, but still squeaking out a 3–2 win with Williams scoring the go-ahead run in the seventh inning. The cold remained the next day, and only 2,000 hearty fans turned out to see Danforth pitch a complete game, walking nine and striking out seven, in a 4–2 Browns win. After a postponement, St. Louis made it a three-game sweep April 15 with a 14–0 pasting of the White Sox as the Browns collected 21 hits. Williams's three hits were as many as Chicago had off Vangilder, who went the distance.

In addition to the sweep, White Sox fans learned of the death of Chicago baseball legend "Cap" Anson on April 14. All in all, it was not a good weekend for the hometown fans in the Windy City.

The Browns next traveled to Cleveland. After dropping the first two games 3–0 and 17–2, they won the finale 15–1, with Williams and Sisler both stealing three bases, even in a blowout. Williams walked and swiped second in the eighth and later in the inning scored on a double steal, which increased St. Louis's lead to 10–1. The Browns pulled off another double steal during a five-run ninth with Sisler and Frank Ellerbe, and Sisler pulled off a straight steal at home as well. Williams would be the only American League player other than Sisler in 1922 to steal three bases in a game. Sisler would do it two other times as well.

But Williams's speed wasn't his main drawing card. It was said that Cleveland fans were disappointed in Williams's performance because he didn't "smack one over the fence."[13] Through St. Louis's first eight games—the six on the road at Chicago and Cleveland, and then the first two forays at home—Williams was still homerless. However, in a 10-inning loss to the White Sox on April 21, he did swat two balls down the right-field line and over the pavilion which were both "foul by inches."[14]

April 22, 1922, isn't etched into the minds of baseball fans as a significant date. But it is when Ken Williams finally got his power stroke going and made American League history.

In the first inning, the Browns were already up 1–0 on Jose Acosta, who was making his first and only start of the season for the White Sox. Williams got a belt-high fastball and crushed it onto (or, according to the *St. Louis Post-Dispatch*, completely over) the pavilion roof and onto Grand Avenue for a two-run home run. "For distance it is doubtful if Williams initial drive in the opening inning has ever been excelled,"[15] surmised the *Post-Dispatch*.

In the third, Williams hit a blistering drive to right field, but Harry Hooper was able to make the catch and perhaps rob Williams of extra bases. Despite these two hard-hit balls, Acosta faced Williams again in the sixth inning (and as in the first inning, with Sisler on first base). This time Williams hit a scorching liner into the right-field seats to give the Browns a 5–3 lead.

Williams's turn at bat came up again in the seventh with Sisler on first base, perhaps his lucky sign. Now on the mound for Chicago, though, was a lefty, Joubert Lum Davenport. Lefty, righty, it didn't matter to Williams on this day. With another crash he sent a third ball over the right-field fence, to the great delight of the estimated 9,000 fans in attendance. (Over 80 years later, Jack Williams, the younger of Williams's two sons, said he was in possession of that third home run ball.)

Although the United Press International report thought this might be the first time in major-league history a player hit three homers in a game, in fact it was the 11th overall. But none had done it in 25 years, since Cincinnati's Jake Beckley hit three against St. Louis's Willie Sudhoff on September 26, 1897 (although one was a "bounce" homer). And this was, in fact, the first time it had ever been done in the American League. Not even Babe Ruth, much to his chagrin, could make that claim.

"Once this spring [Ruth] admitted he was yearning to swat three homers in one game," it was reported. "He wanted to be the first man to do it for his circuit. What a pity a holiday crowd couldn't have seen it and how the folks will brag who did see it."[16]

The Sporting News, noting the lack of national attention to the feat, wrote, "Were Ken a member of the New York Yankees all the Gotham sports pages would have pictured his wrists, his hands, his legs, his keen eyes, his 'stance' at bat, and not even have overlooked a glimpse of his Adam's apple."[17]

The publication went on to note that after Williams swatted the three home runs, a photographer was charged to get a picture of the Browns slugger while batting. However, the photos that came back were not of Williams but of Bill "Baby Doll" Jacobson, who not only didn't bear a resemblance to Williams but also batted right-handed. "What [if] Babe Ruth [hit] three home runs in one ball game! Sporting editors would have wired every syndicate in operation to rush story and photographs," opined *The Sporting News*. "But Ken hits three of them and a photographer on the ground doesn't even know which is Ken and which is Bill Jacobson."[18]

St. Louis needed all of Williams's three homers and six RBI to beat the White Sox that day as Dixie Davis walked 11 in 8⅔ innings, leaving after allowing three runs in the ninth inning. But Urban Shocker, after walking in a run, finally got the last out, else Williams might have had the even rarer feat of hitting three home runs in a losing effort.

Attendance spiked the next day to 16,000, but then again it was a Sunday, which usually had a higher fan turnout. The locals certainly went home happy. Johnny Tobin's homer in the 10th won it for the Browns 4–3, while Williams went 3-for-3 with another home run. He also stole a base and made a couple of good catches in left field, including a diving catch to rob Eddie Collins of a hit, doing a somersault in the process while holding onto the ball. "Ken Williams, in his present mood, is going to be a hard boy to stop," wrote the *St. Louis Globe Democrat*. "He is all over that field, plate and bases doing everything now."[19]

A new team came into town on April 24—the Tigers, who started left-hander Red Oldham in the series opener. Despite Williams's hitting four home runs in two games, as well as owning a streak of five consecutive hits, Lee Fohl dropped the left-handed hitting Williams to sixth in the batting order.

No matter. In Williams's first plate appearance, he made it six straight hits and his fifth home run in three days as he deposited Oldham's first offering onto the right-field pavilion roof and on down below to Grand Avenue. "Zowie!" the *Globe Democrat* wrote of the blast. "It was doing a mile in less than nothing."[20]

Williams's consecutive hit streak would end at six, but he'd collect a single later for another multiple-hit game as the Browns won 6–2. Despite all the success, it didn't mean Williams was content. His crabby disposition was on full display April 25 against the Tigers.

It started with the Tigers, specifically Dan Howley and Ty Cobb, who were coaching on the basepaths, yelling at starter Dave Danforth about his delivery. Williams took such exception that he ran in from left field and confronted umpire George Hildebrand to protest. It didn't help, as a rattled Danforth was taken out of the game before retiring a hitter in the second inning, having walked four batters.

An angered Williams took his frustration out on Howard Ehmke in the home half of the first as he hit his sixth home run of the season, all of which had come in the last four games. The national media might not have been paying attention, but the St. Louis papers were. They were quick to note that Ruth didn't hit his sixth home run in 1921 (when he belted a record 59) until May 2.

In the fifth inning, Williams nearly hit another home run, but the ball tailed foul over the roof. Ehmke's next pitch went all the way to the backstop. Williams said something to Hildebrand—presumably about it being an illegal pitch of some kind—as he argued once the ball was returned to the pitcher. As the player and umpire exchanged words around home plate, the Tigers players threw the ball around the infield, and made sure to get the ball dirty. That was enough for Hildebrand to cede to Williams's protest and throw the ball out of the game. Williams would eventually single.

Finally, in the seventh inning Williams was brushed on the foot by an Ehmke pitch, but he refused to take first base, saying the ball didn't hit him. As usual, Williams wanted to hit, not be hit. Hildebrand, weary from all the arguments in this game, let Williams have his way, and after another loud, long foul, Williams singled, perhaps finally happy after getting his way and finishing with three hits.

After winning the first two games, the Browns fell in the finale 2–0, but Williams—again batting sixth as Detroit started a lefty, Bert Cole—rapped out two more hits and stole two bases. This marked Williams's fifth straight multiple-hit game. It was very early, but after an 0-for-7 start to the season, Williams was now hitting .440 with the six home runs and eight stolen bases. In his last five games, Williams was 13-for-18 with six home runs, 11 RBI, seven runs and four stolen bases.

A rainout on April 27 didn't slow down Williams. It had been a while since there had been a sunny day in St. Louis, but April 28 was one such day. The nice weather provided a decent weekday crowd of around 8,000. Like those who turned out the previous week to Sportsman's Park, they were witness to the fine all-around play of Williams.

In the third inning, he made a running, lunging grab of Tris Speaker's fly to near the wall. Then in the fifth, his diving catch of a low liner to left center robbed Cleveland's star center fielder of another hit, and he added a double somersault to further please the crowd.

While the catches drew robust cheers, the fans wanted to see Williams bat. And in the seventh, he delighted them once again. His old pal Duster Mails was on the mound for Cleveland—the same Mails who claimed Williams rode him so much in the minors he had left the team. Williams drilled an offering from the left-hander and lined it into the right-field seats for home run No. 7 on the season (three of which had come against southpaws). It also broke a 2–all tie and lifted the Browns to a 3–2 win.

Next up for Williams and the Browns was Cleveland pitcher Stan Coveleski, a future Hall of Famer who had won at least 22 games in each of the previous four seasons (and surrendered a combined 16 home runs in that span over 1,227 innings). But despite his credentials, Coveleski was wary of Williams and walked him on four pitches in his first at-bat (and Williams would promptly steal his ninth base of the season). Such was the attention on Williams that the headline of the *Post-Dispatch*'s afternoon edition, which included updated information on the game, in part read "WILLIAMS WALKS WITH MAN ON."[21]

In the fifth inning, with two outs and Tobin on third after tripling to lead off the frame, Coveleski this time gave Williams something to hit. And hit it he did. Williams swung at Coveleski's first pitch, "a terrific line drive which scattered the fans halfway up in the dead right-field open-air seats."[22] Home run No. 8 tied the game at 2.

Coveleski was still on the mound in the ninth inning with the Indians clinging to a 5–4 lead and he retired Sisler, who went 0-for-4, on a grounder to short. In this situation, Williams wasn't waiting for a walk. Once again he swung at Coveleski's first offering, and this time hit it even further than the home run back in the fifth as it kept rising over the pavilion and onto Grand Avenue. It was only a question of whether it would remain fair or foul. As in previous seasons, the rule remained that if a ball went over the fence, but curved foul even in flight, it was a foul ball.

The *St. Louis Globe Democrat* captured the scene thusly: "[T]he leather [was] 'going' to great heights to clear the corner of the right-field pavilion by many feet. Ball appeared to be headed foul … when it went fair out of sight; the fans let loose a crescendo of deafening applause that shook the stands to their foundations.… It was a fitting return for this new Sultan of Swat who is making Babe Ruth appear as but a Babe in comparison."[23]

The Ruth comparisons were beginning to take hold. The *Globe Democrat* noted, "Williams differs as completely from Ruth as day and night. 'Babe' is a huge fellow, flashy and totally devoid of the speed that an all-round star should have. Williams is 6-feet, 1 inches tall, 177 pounds and is fast enough to have stolen nine bases in the 15 games played by the Browns so far."[24]

St. Louis would win in 10 innings as starting pitcher Elam Vangilder doubled, moved to third on a grounder, and scored on Frank Ellerbe's single. Vangilder pitched all 10 innings and improved his record to 4–0, but Williams was the story. He had six home runs in his last four games and nine HRs in his last seven games.

In an era when players weren't quoted in game stories, it was nevertheless time to get Williams's feelings on his amazing streak in print. "Confidence is my only explanation,"

Williams is quoted as saying. "I feel that there isn't a pitcher in the league that I cannot hit. That feeling is no doubt due to the fine play of the entire team; but my entire mental attitude has changed. I'm not wondering if I can hit an opposing pitcher. I know I can; I feel that he is perhaps afraid of me and maybe that's the reason I'm hitting on all cylinders this year."[25]

When asked if he changed his batting style, Williams said as in the past (or likely at least since 1921) he stood "with my left foot on the rear line of the batter's box, draw my bat back as the pitcher winds up and then whack away. I attribute all improvement to increased confidence."[26]

Williams was hitting at a blistering rate. He had a seven-game hitting streak (16-for-25, .640) and knocking home runs at a rate previously unseen except for by Ruth, who heretofore was thought to be in a home run league of his own.

Taking note of Williams's play, St. Louis officials decided to honor him before the Browns' game on Sunday, April 30. Since it was Music Week in St. Louis, funds were collected ($148 was raised at the last count given), and in a pregame ceremony in front of an overflow crowd of 26,000, the mayor and the president of the board of police commissioners, among others, presented Williams with a music cabinet (likely a Victrola, or something along those lines).

Having given Williams his "day," the St. Louis fans were primed to see their hero hit a home run. But when Williams stepped to the plate in the first inning, the Indians' Jim Bagby wasn't in the mind to oblige. With a man on first and two out, Bagby walked Williams, causing the hometown faithful to elicit a chorus of jeers. The *Globe Democrat* reported the walk was intentional, but with a runner on first, it was more likely that Bagby just didn't give Williams anything good to hit. Perhaps the memory of Williams's two home run game against him in 1921 was still fresh in his mind.

Williams didn't give the fans the home run they had hoped for, but he did hit a long fly ball to left center, which resulted in a run scoring, and he also took part in a double play after a fly out. But Browns fans found other reasons to cheer. Tied at nine in the bottom of the eighth inning, St. Louis scored twice. During the inning, the excited overflow crowd in the outfield started advancing further inward. Cleveland's Speaker had to call time to get a police officer to herd the fans back to their original place.

The reason for the exuberance was not just that the Browns were going to win a game, and an exciting 11–9 affair at that, but that the victory moved St. Louis into a first-place tie with the Yankees at 11–5. When the final out was recorded, "hats were tossed in the air, cushions heaved about in reckless abandon. The field, that had taken care of an overflow crowd of 5,000 spectators, was a scene of the wildest rejoicing."[27]

When St. Louis romped over Cleveland the next day, May 1, 14–2 and New York lost to Boston, 5–2, the Browns were in first place all by themselves. Williams had just one hit in the win, although he scored twice, was hit by a pitch and stole a base. But he was a large reason why the Browns were off to such a hot start and had St. Louisians feeling good, for a change, about their American League team. The *St. Louis Post-Dispatch*'s L.C. Davis wrote an ode to Williams. It read:

> Ken Williams.
> Whose name is on every tongue?
> Ken Williams.
> Whose praises are daily sung?

Ken Williams.
Who is the roosters' joy and pride?
Who gives the pesky pill a ride
And separates it from its hide?
Ken Williams.
Who is one most admired youth?
Ken Williams.
Who makes fans forget Babe Ruth?
Ken Williams.
Who is the guy so calm and cool?
Who swings his trusty batting tool
And knocks the pellet for a goal?
Ken Williams.[28]

OK, so it wasn't exactly "Casey at the Bat," but it gives an indication the way people were feeling about the Browns' left fielder.

And the attention was starting to get beyond the local papers as well. The May 4 edition of *The Sporting News* featured a Louisville Slugger advertisement with Williams and the headline: "Certainlee [*sic*] Ken Swings a Slugger."

In addition, Williams was commissioned to write 10 articles documenting his thoughts on such things as the reasons for his early home run success, his strategy at the plate and his season goals (of the latter of which he wrote, "My one ambition is to lead the home-run hitters of the American League for this season of 1922"[29]). These were no doubt ghostwritten and there isn't a lot of insight and more than a few clichés, but they do provide a rare glimpse of Williams in his own words (or at least words attributed to him).

St. Louis fans would have to just read about Williams's exploits for a while as the team headed out on a road trip. In Detroit, where the Browns lost two of three, Williams threw out a runner trying to stretch a double into a triple in the opener. He followed up a first-inning triple by hitting a majestic two-run home run off Oldham in the fifth to give St. Louis a 5–3 lead in the second game (only for the Browns to lose in the ninth on Harry Heilmann's three-run homer). Williams caught a long fly to left in the finale off the bat of Fats Fothergill, who had the rare task of being sent in to pinch-hit for Ty Cobb (he is the only player to hit for Cobb after 1906, the Hall of Famer's rookie season).

Then it was on to Washington, where the now well-known Williams was asked to roll out the first ball at a bowling tournament. Williams probably had a better chance of rolling a strike in D.C. than hitting a home run, as Senators pitchers allowed only three home runs in all of 1922 at cavernous Griffith Stadium. But he did manage to double in the first three games (two of which St. Louis won), including knocking in the eventual winning run in the opener and tying the game at 5 in the sixth inning of a 7–5 win on May 9.

"The breaks were against [Williams] in that series," wrote Billy Evans, who was one of the two umpires when the Browns played the Senators. "Two of his drives, which netted only two bases, failed to clear the right field wall at Washington by a scant margin. Either of them would have been home runs in St. Louis or the Polo grounds [*sic*]."[30]

After the Browns took three of four from Washington, the next stop on the trip was Philadelphia, which had a friendlier confines than Griffith Stadium. In the opener, the Browns hit four home runs (although one was a "bounce" home run by Chick Shorten, which supposedly ricocheted off shortstop Chick Galloway's head and bounced past outfielder Tilly Walker before hopping over the fence), including a long drive by Williams over the right-field wall off Slim Harriss in the seventh inning.

For Williams, it was his 50th career home run—with 35 of those coming in his last 159 games. It was also his 11th of the season and the comparison to Ruth's 1921 record year continued, as it was noted Ruth didn't hit *his* 11th home run until May 14, two days *after* Williams notched his 11th. Williams wasn't necessarily shying away from the talk of him and Ruth in the same sentence.

"Ruth is a remarkable batter. He is a superman if there ever was one," Williams wrote in one of his articles from his 10-part series. "It seems almost foolish for anyone to aspire to equal his feats of slugging, yet that is my ambition. In making three home runs in a game I have already done something that the great Ruth has not yet accomplished."[31]

In another article he added: "It is my opinion that any player who can make 40 home runs in the American League this year will lead the organization in that department of play. I am positive that will be too great a number for Ruth to overcome. I want to rank second to Ruth [and his record 59 home runs] if I am unable to top his mark."[32]

The comparisons to Ruth were only beginning, what with a trip to New York on the schedule after the next series at Boston. The teams got the first two games in, but back-to-back rainouts only seemed to fuel the anticipation of the Browns vs. Yankees, or, perhaps more accurately, Williams vs. Ruth.

Reserved seats for the May 20 opener—which was also Ruth's return—went on sale two days before game day. Fans lined up early at the Yankees box office, with an estimated 2,000 people there bright and early, with it "extending from the Yankee offices [on West 42nd Street] to Eighth Avenue, half a block away."[33] The line never dissipated, and when the office closed at 5 p.m., roughly 3,200 tickets had been purchased.

"We had to turn hundreds away," Yankees business manager Ed Barrow told the *New York Times*. "I don't remember anything like the rush of today except that of last fall, when the World's Series seats were put on sale."[34] Barrow was also quick to note there were still plenty of seats to be had—35,000 unreserved tickets, which would go on sale May 20 at noon.

According to Davis J. Walsh, sports editor of the International News Service, the ticket sales were "not only a testimonial to Ruth as Ruth, but recognition of the fact that Williams, as a slugger, is no temporary institution."[35] With the buildup also came the comparisons and, wrote Walsh, "we can think of no types more dissimilar in style and appearance."[36]

"Everyone is familiar with Ruth's man-in-the-moon countenance, his barrel of a chest and pipestem legs," Walsh continued. "He and Williams have about as much in common there as [British socialite] Mrs. Asquith and [vaudeville actress] Eva Tanguay. The St. Louis outfielder is a lean, sun-bitten individual of dour, lugubrious expression and few words, at least as far as the ballfield is concerned. He would make an excellent undertaker."[37]

A wire article that appeared in several papers used some stereotypes and generalizations to describe the pair to the reading public: "Ruth, while tall, is built on much heavier than Williams and weighs perhaps 40 pounds more. Williams is the nervous type, Ruth the solid. Williams worries when in a slump. Ruth accepts such things as a matter of course. Williams' features are sharp; Ruth's are rounded. Williams looks the athlete all over, as he doesn't carry a pound of extra weight. Ruth, with his large waist line, always seems lacking in condition.

In only one respect is there a sameness, both players strike out a great deal. This is true of all batters who are free swingers."[38] (It should be noted that Williams only struck out 31 times in 1922. His high for a season was 42, and three times he had more home runs than strikeouts.)

There was still some question whether Ruth (and fellow outfielder Bob Meusel) would play. While their suspension technically ended May 19, they still had to apply for reinstatement. At one minute past midnight on May 20, the Yankees telegraphed such a letter to the commissioner's office. Judge Landis approved it in the morning and Ruth and Meusel were in that day's lineup in front of a packed Polo Grounds of 40,000 fans.

Before the start of the game, Ruth was given a few presents—from Yankee fans he received a silver baseball bat and a floral arrangement, while "an admirer from Baltimore"[39] gave Ruth a silver cup which contained dirt from around home plate of St. Mary's Industrial School, which Ruth had attended in his youth.

Even from a distance and with no numbers on their uniforms it wouldn't have been hard to spot Ruth and Meusel on this day. While the uniforms of their Yankees teammates showed the wear and tear of playing a month-plus of baseball, Ruth and Meusel sported clean, white apparel.

After all the pregame buildup and hype, the game was, as typically happens, anticlimactic, at least where the two protagonists were concerned. Ruth was given a big ovation in the bottom of the first inning before striking out in his first plate appearance of the season. On the day, Ruth would go 0-for-4 and not get the ball out of the infield against Urban Shocker, who only allowed three hits. Sisler received a similar ovation in the visitor's half; in fact, the *Globe Democrat* observed, "Sisler and Williams got as much applause as Ruth when they advanced to the plate, at least it seemed to us."[40]

Williams wasn't faring much better than Ruth, at least early on, grounding to the pitcher and fouling out to the third baseman in his first two trips to the plate. In the sixth, he hit a long drive to right-center field, but Whitey Witt tracked it down. Williams laced a sharp single to right in the eighth and stole second, but it came with two down and he was stranded there.

The Browns were trailing 2–1 in the ninth, but erupted for seven runs, with Williams bringing home the go-ahead tally. With one run in, two out and runners on second and third, the Yankees elected to walk Sisler intentionally to get to Williams, a move the *Globe Democrat's* Martin Haley labeled "an insult."[41] But Sam Jones then walked Williams—unintentionally—to give the Browns a 3–2 lead. Baby Doll Jacobson followed with the only grand slam of his 11-year career to put the game away.

The win was big news in St. Louis. Forget screen idol Rudolph Valentino's arrest on bigamy charges; the Browns' win rated a front-page headline in the *Post-Dispatch*, and in all capital letters to boot. The paper even ran a separate box to recap "what the home run rivals did,"[42] giving a detailed account of each at-bat for Ruth and Williams.

The second game of the series wasn't much better for the slugging duo. After popping up in the first inning, Ruth threw his "vivid green bat"[43] in disgust. He would eventually double in a run in the fifth inning, although not without controversy. Ruth was tagged out 10 feet from the base trying to go to third while Witt was scoring. Browns catcher Hank Severeid said St. Louis got Ruth out before Witt scored, but umpire Ollie Chill said otherwise. Severeid hotly contested the call and later would say, "Chill knew he was wrong or I would have gotten the gate."[44]

That would be Ruth's only hit while Williams went 0-for-5 as the Yankees won 6–5 in 10 innings. Interestingly, after Aaron Ward singled and went to second on a Jacobson error leading off in the 10th, the Browns elected to pitch to Ruth, who grounded out. Ward went to third on the play and would score on the next play.

It was another 0-fer for Williams on May 22 in yet another extra-inning loss for the Browns. Williams failed to get a hit in five at-bats as St. Louis lost 6–5 in 13 innings. Meusel finally got his first hit of the season to open the 13th and he eventually scored the winning run on an Everett Scott double. Despite being frustrated earlier in the game—once again throwing his bat after making an out—Ruth struck his first home run, connecting off Elam Vangilder in the eighth.

The finale of the series featured another late rally by the Browns as Shocker won his second of the series. Williams also increased his home run lead over Ruth back to 11. With the game tied at 3 in the seventh and two men down, Williams crushed the first pitch he saw from Carl Mays and hit it on a line into the upper deck of the right-field grandstand for his 12th homer of the season.

As Williams rounded the bases, according to the *New York Times*, "Ruth, looking on from left field, was observed to pale slightly as he watched Williams receiving the plaudits of 15,000 fans."[45] He followed that up with a great over-the-shoulder catch to rob Mays of extra bases in the home seventh. St. Louis then poured on five more runs in the eighth to win 11–3 and split the series.

While the Browns left New York in the same spot as they arrived—two games behind the Yankees for first place—the *Post-Dispatch* was impressed with how St. Louis played, noting, in part, that the Browns stole 12 bases while the Yankees were caught in each of their three attempts. "The Browns showed more speed, played faster, cleaner ball and showed that they could come from behind to win,"[46] the paper observed.

Despite his hitting a home run in the May 23 game, perhaps the pressure was getting to Williams a bit. In nine games from May 17 to 28—which followed his 4-for-5 performance at Boston—Williams went into a 3-for-34 tailspin, including going 0-for-13 in a four-game series in Chicago. "Is trying to hit home runs ruining Williams as a batter?"[47] the Associated Press wondered.

"In the games I umpired with the Browns in the east, Ken was cutting a little too hard at the ball, with the result that he was losing some of the accuracy of his stroke,"[48] wrote Evans.

The Browns returned to St. Louis with a 22–17 record, putting them 2½ games behind the Yankees. The Tigers were in town, and Detroit was sending out left-hander Bert Cole in the opener. That meant Williams was back in the sixth spot in the batting order as he tried to snap out of his slump.

"It has always seemed to me that the sixth position in the batting order is the ideal spot for the free swinger, the fellow with the extra base habit," Williams wrote in one of his articles. "It may be purely imagination on my part, but it has always seemed to me that the sixth batter is more often called upon to whale away at the ball rather than pull some so-called inside stuff."[49]

It didn't hurt that Williams was facing Cole. Even though it was a lefty-on-lefty matchup, Williams had gone 2-for-2 in his previous outing vs. the Tigers' starting pitcher, and he singled in the second inning in the May 29 game.

In the third inning, Detroit player-manager Ty Cobb told Cole to intentionally walk Hank Severeid to load the bases for Williams. Cole's first pitch was a slow curveball that Williams hammered into the right-field seats for his second career grand slam (the first was also off a left-hander).

A couple of weeks earlier, Williams, noting four of his first 10 home runs were off lefties, had written, "With a left-hander working there is nothing I like better than a fast ball on the inside about letter high. It is a very easy matter to pull such a pitch with great force to right field. A curve ball that doesn't take much of a break and is on the inside is also an easy ball for a left-handed batsman to take liberties with."[50]

Williams added a double off Cole in front of a Ladies' Day crowd of 10,000 as he went 3-for-4 and saw his average jump 12 points, from .281 to .293, just from this one day.

While he would go just 3-for-13 the rest of the series against the Tigers, each of his hits went for extra bases. He doubled in both ends of a Memorial Day double-header sweep, then knocked in two runs with a triple to the center-field fence in a 7–5 win to finish off a four-game sweep on May 31.

Home run No. 14 came two days later when, to open the fourth inning, he connected off Chicago left-hander Ferdie Schupp, depositing the pitcher's first hurl over the right-field pavilion and onto Grand Avenue (he'd also single in a run in the frame as St. Louis tallied seven times).

Not forgetting his other skills, Williams swiped two bases against White Sox catcher Ray Schalk in their June 4 game—giving him 17 steals on the season—and looked to have hit his 15th home run, only to have it called foul as he ran around the bases. He raised his steal total to 18 as he swiped home on a double steal with Jacobson against the Red Sox, but his home run total was still at 14 (although he had two triples in four games against Boston) as the Yankees came to town.

Ruth had just three home runs in his first three weeks, yet his appearance, of course, drew attention. The Browns sold out of all their reserved seats for the first two games in advance. The Illinois Traction System ran an advertisement in the *Decatur Review* letting people know they had a chance to see Ruth vs. Williams for just $4.30 round trip from Decatur to St. Louis on June 10 and/or 11 (ticket to the game not included).

More than 20,000 fans turned out for the June 10 opener, and they saw a tense game in which Ruth hit a homer off Urban Shocker, Shocker brushed back both Carl Mays and Whitey Witt, each of whom headed towards the mound before being held back, and Browns owner Phil Ball took a foul under his right eye which resulted in his getting four stitches.

The Browns lost the game 14–5 as Shocker lasted only three innings. He was so angry at his performance that he talked Lee Fohl into allowing him to pitch the next day. Shocker went seven innings this time, but St. Louis lost again, 8–4, and Shocker strained his right thigh so badly he had to be hospitalized and wouldn't pitch again until July 4.

Fohl shook the lineup up in the next game on June 12. Chick Shorten replaced Jacobson and other players were moved around in the order, with Marty McManus moving up from eighth to fifth and Hank Severeid and Frank Ellerbe each dropping a spot to seventh and eighth, respectively.

The moves, in part, worked. Shorten (two) and Severeid (three) had five of St. Louis's nine hits. Williams had three, including a two-run homer in the first inning off Bullet Joe Bush and an RBI double in the eighth. The Browns cruised 7–1 behind the pitching of rookie

Hub Pruett, who tossed a complete game and three times struck out Ruth. The Babe "choked up on the bat … gripping it two inches from the handle."[51]

Williams was leading the league with 15 home runs, but conceded that "no one but the Babe himself will be able to repeat his Herculean feat of last season,"[52] when the Bambino connected for 59 homers.

The Browns won the finale 13–4 as St. Louis drew more than 75,000 fans for the four-game series, which "broke all record for attendance at the local park."[53] Washington came to town next, and after an 0-for-3 game in the opener, which saw his average dip to .280, Williams started to come alive. In the second game of the series on June 15, he went 2-for-3 and, despite making a throwing error earlier in the game, "Kenny more than retrieved this boot by hitching his way to a roaming star that oft had him drawing rounds of applause on scintillating catches."[54]

The cheers were louder in the next contest when he chased Tom Zachary from the game with a home run to right-center field. Of Williams's 16 home runs, seven were now off left-handers, including three of his last four. He nearly had home run No. 17 in the eighth inning, but his drive off Albert "Chief" Youngblood, who was making his major-league debut, was just a few inches shy from clearing the right-center field fence and he had to settle for a triple.

The game also marked St. Louis's third straight win over Washington. Coupled with the Yankees' losing three in a row to the Tigers, it meant the Browns were back in first place by a half a game.

The Yankees, as it turned out, were in the middle of an eight-game losing streak. Meanwhile, the Browns welcomed the A's to town. Philadelphia was in the rare spot of not coming to St. Louis in last place, although just barely—the A's were in seventh.

St. Louis took three of the four games against the A's with Williams homering off Eddie Rommel in a 5–3 win on June 18, and then again in a 7–3 win on June 20 off Charlie Eckert, the latter making its way to Grand Avenue. He also nearly had an inside-the-park homer in the fifth inning of the June 18 game, but he was thrown out at home after his deep blast to center field.

Sixty-three games into the season and Williams had shown off all facets of his game. His slump hurt his batting average, but he had it back up to .294. He was showing off his power, with 18 home runs and a .622 slugging percentage, and speed, having stolen 21 bases. And don't forget about his arm, either.

While the A's were at Sportsman's Park, Williams and Tilly Walker, who was known for his arm strength, held a contest. Walker stood at home plate and Williams by the left-field fence. The two then threw the ball back and forth a few times. Walker barely got the ball to Williams, while the Browns outfielder was able to sail his throws over Walker's head. "The Browns' outfielder had the best of it by at least 25 feet in the exchange of throws,"[55] reported *The Sporting News*. It was only June, but it was quite clear already this was the season of Ken Williams.

Chapter 10

Starting the 30–30 Club

At 38–25, the Browns were one of three American League teams above .500, along with the Yankees (37–27) and Tigers (33–29). St. Louis hit the road once again, starting in Detroit, where the teams split four games. The Yankees, meanwhile, were losers of 12 of their last 14.

The series in Detroit wasn't without incident. The June 24 game, a 13–4 Browns win, played in front of a packed house with overflow crowds in both right and center field, was especially eventful.

In the third inning, Williams "exhibited a characteristic Williams wallop"[1] when he hit a three-run homer off Herman Pillette (who allowed only 6 HRs in 274⅔ innings in 1922) into the right-field stands. He perhaps paid the price for that smash in the fifth when Pillette hit him with a pitch.

Then in the sixth, things got out of hand. The Tigers had the bases loaded and two out against Dave Danforth with Ty Cobb at bat. First-base coach Fred Haney had an idea to distract the pitcher. He picked up Detroit first baseman Lu Blue's glove—players left their gloves on the field after each inning back then—and threw it over his head as Danforth was about to pitch. The move didn't work, as Danforth struck out Cobb. After the whiff, Browns coach Jimmy Austin vaulted from the St. Louis dugout and with a swift kick booted Blue's glove into the stands.

Haney and Blue went after Austin, and Tigers players approached the St. Louis dugout with fists flying—"none landed."[2] It was reported that five police officers had to be summoned to restore order. Interestingly, Cobb was not among the combatants. He was too busy inspecting the baseball thrown by Danforth, who was often accused of throwing doctored pitches. Nothing else came of the incident, and another overflow crowd of 25,000 turned out the next day to watch Dixie Davis blank the hometown club on four hits.

St. Louis then played Cleveland for six games—three on the road and three at home. The Browns lost two of three at Dunn Field, but Williams was 6-for-13 with four RBI. He was now hitting .303, and as the team returned to Sportsman's Park for a brief stay, Williams had himself a product endorsement.

Both Williams and Urban Shocker were now spokesmen for Merrell's Penetrating Oil, an arm liniment (which cost 35 cents or 60 cents "at your drug store"[3]) made in St. Louis. Ads appeared in the local papers in which Williams declared, "Tell the fans of St. Louis that I'm a strong booster for Merrell's Penetrating Oil. It puts pep into tired muscles and quietly relieves sprains and bruises."[4]

Merrell's Penetrating Oil was, as it turned out, a modern-day snake oil. In 1933, the U.S.

government would order all remaining product to be destroyed after determining it had no curative ingredients and that it actually contained "volatile oils including turpentine oil and eucalyptol."[5]

Nevertheless, Williams's endorsement couldn't have hurt sales. One of the ads appeared in the June 30 *Globe Democrat*. Williams tripled and had two RBI in a 10–3 win over the Indians that day. He followed that up with an RBI single in a 4–3 win July 1, plus showed off his defensive prowess, which was described the *Post-Dispatch*'s correspondent:

> Williams is fleet of foot. He has the grace, the speed, the courage, the skill.... And yesterday his skill, his speed, his courage were rampant. He dashed in to the edge of the infield and caught flies which were out of the infield's reach. He tore over to the foul line and snared a line drive from [Tris] Speaker's bat which no one thought he had a chance to catch. Speaker was amazed. Tris could not believe that the catch had been made. He stood nonplussed between first and second, and shook his head and finally walked to the dugout. Then Williams started with the crack of the bat and brought down a smash from the bat of [Riggs] Stephenson, the very next batter.[6]

A catch Williams didn't make in the game provided some amusement. As Williams raced in for a shallow pop, shortstop Wally Gerber ran out. The two nearly collided, but Williams did "some clever sidestepping."[7] When he saw Gerber caught the fly, Williams ran over and gave the shortstop a hug.

All the love was for Williams the next day, St. Louis's final home game for 23 days. A crowd of 19,000 endured some rain and found it worthwhile when Williams hit a three-run home run off Duster Mails in the fifth inning to give the Browns the lead for good, 4–1 (St. Louis would win 9–4). Interestingly, in the seventh with St. Louis up 6–1, Williams bunted Baby Doll Jacobson to second base, although he nearly beat the throw to first base from third baseman Stephenson.

The home run for Williams was his 20th of the season, three more than the closest contender in the American League (the A's Walker) and two more than National League leader Rogers Hornsby, of the St. Louis Cardinals. Babe Ruth had 13, but in an article he wrote, "If Commissioner Landis would withdraw his anti-gambling edict long enough to allow me to make one bet, I'd like to wager one good cigar against another that I will deliver my 25th home run of the season before Kenneth Williams of the Browns makes his."[8]

Williams was already the first American League player to have 20 home runs and 20 stolen bases in a season, and now he was the first in major-league history to do it in back-to-back seasons. But his most noteworthy club would come later.

Another kind of club—of the baseball bat kind—was to be delivered to Williams posthaste. His home run swatting was getting him lots of attention, and bat manufacturers were more than happy to be associated with him. Despite his arrangement with Louisville Slugger, the Winchester Company made some bats for Williams based on the player's specific instructions and specifications, weighing in at 44 ounces (it was reported the average bat in the majors was 36 ounces).

After splitting a double-header in Chicago, the Browns made a long journey—a 30-hour train ride—to Boston. Some animus between the Browns and Red Sox and the latter's affinity for the Yankees would emerge, and not for the last time in 1922.

St. Louis and Boston were scheduled to play a double-header on July 6. But the Red Sox and owner Harry Frazee decided it had rained too much—despite its clearing up later in the day—and postponed the games. This would force the Browns to play three straight double-headers in Boston from July 7 to 10, excluding July 9 as there was no baseball in Beantown on Sundays, before heading to New York to play the Yankees.

"Frazee's purpose is too obvious to need pointing out," complained Browns vice president Walter Fritsch to the *St. Louis Post-Dispatch*. "We go to New York after this series and three double-headers in three days, even if there is an open date, will send us to the Polo Grounds with our pitching staff overworked. I am certain Frazee postponed the games today deliberately to aid the Yankees. The deal between these two clubs, financial and as to players, in the past two years, show how closely these two clubs' owners are united."[9]

While the Browns may have been unhappy with the situation, the reception from Red Sox fans was more than cordial. "A mighty welcome was given the St. Louisians as they took their turn at bat," reported the *Globe Dispatch*, "especially so in the case of George Sisler and Ken Williams."[10]

Williams's disposition didn't match the Red Sox faithful as he was kicked out of the opening game of the initial double-header—meaning, by the rules of the day, he also had to miss the second game—but certainly the St. Louis slugger was feeling much better by the time his team left Boston.

In the final two double-headers, Williams went 7-for-15—pushing his average to .305 (it wouldn't dip lower than .301 the rest of the season) with a pair of doubles, a triple, four runs, four RBI and three stolen bases. The Browns, though, split all three double-headers and headed to New York leading the Yankees by 1½ games. But they were low on pitching arms, as two of the six games went 13 innings (Dixie Davis went 12⅔ innings in Game 1 of the third double-header).

Williams continued his hot hitting in the opener against the Yankees with two more hits. But he helped contribute to a 2–1 loss by being picked off, overrunning second base on a steal attempt and being tagged out, and having an Aaron Ward fly ball go off his glove and over the fence for a solo home run that put New York on top by the eventual final score.

Unbowed, Williams homered off Waite Hoyt in the next game and scored twice as the Browns won 7–4, with Hub Pruett, who pitched three times in the Red Sox series, going 5⅔ innings while walking seven and hitting a batter. But he whiffed Ruth three times and even got a big ovation from the Yankees fans after being taken out of the game. After a rainout, Shocker asked to pitch again—he started the opener—and lost 4–0, having now pitched 24 innings in the last eight days.

After losing two of three to the Yankees, the Browns split a pair with the Senators and were fortunate rain wiped out the finale, as they were trailing 5–1 before the game could be made official.

The Browns traveled to Philadelphia, and they weren't the only ones. Adolph Rettig started for the A's in the series opener July 19 just hours after stepping off a train. Rettig played college baseball at Seton Hall with Philadelphia catcher Frank Bruggy, and A's manager Connie Mack relented and used the semipro pitcher against the Browns. Mack figured Philadelphia didn't have much chance to beat Urban Shocker anyway, as the St. Louis starter had owned the A's in recent years, boasting a 12–1 record vs. Mack's team dating back to 1919.

Improbably, Rettig pitched a complete game, baffling the Browns with his "slow ball."[11] Tilly Walker hit two home runs off Shocker—giving him 23 on the season, or two more than Williams—as Philadelphia won 6–3. Williams did have an RBI double in the first inning, beginning a streak of 23 games in which he scored or had an RBI, but was retired by Rettig the next four times he came to the plate.

With the Browns having lost four of their last six games, and the last one to a semipro pitcher, vice president Walter Fritsch "threw a team party," according to the *Post-Dispatch*. "He bought cigarettes, mints (untouched) and a few other things, took the boys to his suite of rooms and told them to sing, talk and yell about anything about baseball."[12]

Perhaps the move by Fritsch loosened the Browns up, as they convincingly won the next three games over the A's by scores of 4–0, 10–2 and 10–1. Williams was 6-for-12 in the three contests with a double, triple, steal, four runs and three RBI.

The Browns lost to the Tigers on July 23, 11–6, but it wasn't the defeat that sent St. Louis management and newspaper writers into an uproar. For on this day, the Yankees swung another one of their deals with the Red Sox, acquiring third baseman Joe Dugan and outfielder Elmer Smith for infielders Chick Fewster and Johnny Mitchell, outfielder Elmer Miller, a pitcher to be named later (to be Lefty O'Doul) and $50,000.

The immediate reaction from the public was outrage. This was considered to be the latest egregious trade between the two teams. New York had obtained Babe Ruth and Carl Mays, among others, in previous deals. "I have no comment to make," Browns owner Phil Ball said. "The deal speaks for itself."[13]

"There is nothing for me to say," said St. Louis business manager Bob Quinn. "I tried to introduce legislation years ago against the Yankee-Red Sox manner of dealing, to no avail."[14]

Others weren't so careful with their words. "It's a crime," bluntly stated Indians player-manager Tris Speaker, who noted when Cleveland inquired about Dugan, the Red Sox asked back for quality major leaguers like Joe Evans and Jim Bagby. "Either Dugan or Smith is worth $10,000 or more, and the entire bunch of New York players is not worth $10,000."[15]

Even American League president Ban Johnson expressed his misgivings. "A point has been reached where the public regards with aversions and apprehension any deal for players between the Boston and New York clubs,"[16] he said.

The hometown *Boston Herald* wasn't pleased with the deal, writing, "Another disgusting trade between the Red Sox and the New York Yankees was made ... [with players] tossed in to Boston for camouflage purposes. The latest deal assures the Hub of still poorer baseball than it has been seeing at Fenway Park, and Frazee has tightened his hold on his hold of the 'Champion Wrecker of the Baseball Age.'"[17]

The Frazee mentioned was Red Sox owner Harry Frazee, who saw no issue with his latest trade with the Yankees, saying he'd bet that Boston would finish in the first division and "if we had a shortstop like Mitchell we'd be in the first division right now."[18]

There wasn't exactly a line of people willing to back Frazee in his claim. "From this viewpoint the deal was one calculated as [an] ... effort by the obliging Boston magnate to strengthen the wobbling Yankees in their desperate effort to retain the pennant," wrote *Sporting News* columnist Francis C. Richter. "It also lends more color to the long-pending suspicion of a 'community of interest' between the two clubs wholly to the advantage of the New York club."[19]

The move didn't go over well with St. Louis fans either, obviously. *Post-Dispatch* columnist John Wray's column on the trade was titled "The Unholy Alliance,"[20] while the *Globe Democrat* noted that Browns fans felt "it is practically an attempt to purchase the American League flag for the Yankees. Rubert [*sic*] ... and Huston practically hold the whip hand over Frazee because of loans to the Boston club in which they are interested."[21]

History, of course, shows us that those who complained in 1922 were correct: the deal was a steal for the Yankees. However, there was nothing anyone could do about it, and the Browns had to make the best of the situation.

Ironically, the Yankees were the first opponent for the Browns when they returned home July 25. The lineup New York sent out that day included five former Red Sox players—Dugan, Ruth, Wally Schang, Everett Scott and Mays—as well as five other players, including starting pitchers Waite Hoyt, Joe Bush and Sam Jones.

The Yankees were booed mercilessly by the crowd of 19,000, and especially so the former Red Sox players. Dugan and Ruth got the biggest jeers of them all. But the Browns fans had a lot to cheer about as well, as the hometown team won 8–0, with Williams hitting a "titanic clout"[22] off Mays in the first—he also threw out Ruth trying to score in the fourth—as Shocker allowed just six hits in pitching a shutout.

But that was just one game. The Yankees came out with more fight the next day—both against the Browns and themselves. Ruth hit a pair of home runs and also exchanged punches with first baseman Wally Pipp on the bench as New York won 11–6. The Yankees won 6–5 in 11 innings in the third game of the series, and the Browns also lost pitcher Dave Danforth for 10 days after he was thrown out for "loading"[23] up the ball. Danforth said he was just rubbing up a new baseball with dirt, which was permissible by the rules.

Williams homered the next day off Sam Jones—ironically, this came one day after Browns VP Fritsch said Williams was no longer trying to establish a home run record—but the Yankees won again, 7–3, allowing them to vault over the Browns and into first place.

Boston invaded Sportsman's Park next, and in a Browns 4–1 win on July 29, Williams connected for a two-run homer off Herb Pennock, tying him with Tilly Walker for the American League lead in home runs with 24. Home run No. 25 came the next day—no word if Ruth sent Williams a cigar—another two-run shot, this time off Benn Karr in another 4–1 victory.

Williams made it four straight games with a home run when Johnny Tobin and he went back-to-back off Jack Quinn in the seventh inning of a 6–2 victory. Williams also was moved to center field in the middle of the game. With George Sisler hurt—he was spiked in the series opener—Baby Doll Jacobson moved to first base and Chick Shorten to center. But Shorten misplayed a ball badly in the fourth inning, which turned into a triple, and Williams was sent to center field in the fifth (and "made three splendid catches"[24] in the fifth, eighth and ninth innings). He'd stay in center field for nearly three weeks.

As July turned to August, Williams still had his power stroke going. In a 5–2 win over the Red Sox on August 1, Williams lined a Rip Collins (4 HR in 210⅔ IP in 1922) offering into the right-field stands. It was his sixth home run of the home stand and No. 27 on the season, tying him with Rogers Hornsby for the major-league lead. The *Post-Dispatch* offered an understated observation: "He's certainly found the range once more."[25]

Williams and the Browns had a new opponent on August 2 in Philadelphia, but the A's couldn't cool off the St. Louis slugger. Williams led off the eighth inning with a titanic blast to right field off Eddie Rommel that "cleared the bleachers by 10 or 12 feet"[26] before landing on Grand Avenue.

It was the sixth consecutive game in which Williams hit a home run—a feat that had never before been accomplished in the majors. The record would be tied by George Kelly (1924), Lou Gehrig (1931), Walker Cooper (1947) and Willie Mays (1955) before being broken by Dale Long, who hit one in eight straight in 1956. Williams held the American League record for 55 years until Don Mattingly also hit a homer in eight consecutive games in 1987. Williams accomplished his feat at a good time—the Browns were without both George Sisler and Hank Severeid, two key hitters in the lineup, during his home run streak.

Williams's streak ended the next day—but just barely. He hit a ball onto the right-field roof in the fourth inning, but it landed four feet foul, before doubling down the right-field line. In the ninth, he cracked another double that hit the fence. Three feet higher and it would have been a home run.

Everything Williams was doing was superb. In a 9–4 win on August 4, he threw out Jimmy Dykes at home trying to score on a fly, had three hits—including a double and triple—and raced around to score from second base on a slow roller hit to A's second baseman Ralph Young.

Sisler returned to the lineup August 5 (and lined into a triple play in his first at-bat), but Williams stayed in center field with Jacobson going to left. No matter; he went 3-for-8 in the next two games with a run and two RBI before making more history.

With left-hander George Mogridge on the mound for Washington on August 7, Williams batted sixth in the lineup. In the sixth inning, with Jacobson on base, Williams smoked Mogridge's first pitch, lining a shot that quickly ended up in the right-field stands.

The Browns had a big inning in the sixth—they'd score nine times—and Williams came up again, this time against right-hander Eric Erickson and again with Jacobson on base. With a 1–1 count, Williams lofted a high fly ball over the pavilion roof and sent it bounding onto the street for his second home run of the inning.

A quick check by reporters found it was the first time in major-league history this had been accomplished, although that wasn't quite true. It had been done in the National League in 1880 and 1894, as well as the Players League twice in 1890. However, this was the first time a player had hit two home runs in the same inning in the American League as well as in the "modern" baseball era. In Williams's lifetime, this feat would be accomplished only seven other times. "For days to come followers of the game will be talking about this big session for the Browns in 1922, when Williams hit two home runs,"[27] wrote the *Post-Dispatch*'s Herman Wecke.

Williams also had an RBI single in that contest. In his last 14 games, he was hitting .420 (21–50) with four doubles, a triple, nine home runs, 17 runs and 22 RBI. He also had raised his average from .296 to .324 in a month's time—and he'd never fall below that mark the rest of the season.

And Williams kept on hitting. He went 4-for-8 in the final two games against Washington; then, starting a long road trip in Chicago, he was 2-for-4 in both games against the White Sox.

Williams went 3-for-8 in a double-header split at Washington on August 15, but saw his streak of scoring a run or producing an RBI end at 23 straight games. That stands as the 11th-best streak of all time, and through 2016 only 31 players in major-league history had streaks of 20 or more games. After that double-header, Williams went on a 10-game run-producing streak, knocking two hits in half those games.

Although manager Lee Fohl had praised Williams's play in center field, in particular his range and throwing arm, a permanent move back to left field was made August 18 (Williams was also put back in the cleanup spot after batting sixth in nine of the previous 10 games).

There was a report that Williams didn't like playing center and he felt it altered his hitting, but if it did, it was in a good way. In 16 games when starting in center, Williams hit .476 (30-for-63) with an .841 slugging percentage (seven doubles, two triples, four home runs).

An incident in the second game of a double-header against the Senators on August 16 might have hastened the move as well. With heavy rain falling, Washington, winning 7–3, tried to speed up the game to make it official. In the bottom of the fourth, Sam Rice barely ran to first base on a double-play grounder. The next batter, Bucky Harris, then hit a grounder up the middle. Williams fielded the ball and Harris went to second—trying to be thrown out to end the inning. But in a scene reminiscent of *The Bad News Bears*, Williams just held the ball. Harris then went to third, and again Williams just cradled the ball. Finally, when Harris tried to score, Williams pegged the ball towards the plate, but too late to nab Harris, who was credited with just his second home run of the season and one of only nine in his 12-year career.

The move back to left field certainly didn't disagree with Williams. He knocked home runs in both ends of an August 19 double-header at Philadelphia. Then, on August 21 in a 7–6 loss to the A's, Williams made history yet again. Although no one realized it or made mention of it in the papers, it would be remembered forever.

In the seventh inning he executed a double steal with Hank Severeid—his 30th stolen base of the season, making him, with his 32 homers, the founding member of the 30–30 club. He'd be the lone member of that club until Willie Mays did it 44 years later in 1956. Being the first to hit 30 HRs and steal 30 in a season was the accomplishment that meant most to Williams in his post-baseball life, and at the time of his death, only he and Mays (who did it again in 1957) had reached that plateau.

Back in the present, there were no headlines or honors bestowed to Williams, although the people of St. Louis had begun inundating the Browns with telegrams as the team kept flip-flopping with the Yankees for first place.

The St. Louis Advertising Club wanted to hold a party for the team upon its return from the road trip, although Fohl quashed that idea, noting the team hadn't won the pennant and were in a tight race, so any celebration would be premature. The Browns also received telegrams of support from the St. Louis Pennant Lover Club, the Optimists Club, the Kiwanis Club, Chevrolet employees, Bell Telephone and more. The St. Louis Rotary Club sent a note praising the Browns' main slugger: "Babe Ruth and his homers don't worry us. Ken Williams has us convinced he can swat rings around the Babe and more than that. You've got team work and spirit that counts."[28]

The Browns were at least playing like champions. They swept a three-game series in Boston, with Williams extending his hitting streak to 28 games. Despite his high batting average—.334 entering the series finale—and hitting streak, Williams twice tried to sacrifice bunt in the third game, a 13–2 win. St. Louis held a half-game lead over New York, which happened to be the next stop on the Browns' road trip.

Thirty-eight thousand fans saw Williams's hit streak end at 28 in the first game of an August 25 double-header, although the Browns won 3–1. The 28 games was the longest hitting streak in the majors up until that point, although Williams's teammate Sisler hit in his 24th straight game and would do so in 17 more. The Browns would drop the second game of the twin bill, but staged a rally in the ninth to pull within 6–5, only to have Marty McManus hit a deep fly to the Eddie Grant monument in center field which Whitey Witt was able to track down.

The Browns lost again August 26 and, after rain postponed the game the next day, on August 28 as well. In the latter, the game went into extra innings, and in the top of the 10th with two runners on base, Browns third baseman Eddie Foster lined a pitch down the right-field line that was called foul. Foster would pop out and the Yankees would win in 11 innings. Sisler, who was the on-deck batter, would always refer to that as the "foul two-bagger."[29] Years later he would say, "I can still see in my mind where the ball hit. It was a fair ball."[30]

Eddie Foster, who was acquired late in the 1922 season to try to solidify the third base position (George Grantham Bain Collection, Library of Congress).

The Browns rebounded to take two of three in both Cleveland and Detroit, but still were two games behind the Yankees. However, the good news was St. Louis would play its final 23 games of the season all at Sportsman's Park.

The Browns would host each of the seven American League teams during this extended home stand, but everyone knew which series was the most important. Earlier in the week while in Cleveland, business manager Bob Quinn was already circling the series against the Yankees from September 16 to 18 on the calendar.

"There's no beating around the bush. If we win the series [against the Yankees] decisively, I do not think there will be any doubt about us winning the pennant," Quinn stated. "If we lose it, we may as well admit the supporting of the other team and be satisfied with second place."[31]

But the Yankees series was still roughly two weeks away. Cleveland was in town first, although not at the time anticipated. A train delay pushed back the start time of a Labor Day double-header.

The wait only got an enthusiastic Browns fan base even more excited. The city hadn't seen a pennant since the American Association's St. Louis Brown Stockings won that league's crown in four consecutive seasons, concluding in 1888. The St. Louis Maroons captured the Union Association's title in 1884 as well, making it five straight years the city celebrated a championship.

The delay also gave the Browns a little more time to take batting practice and for Ken Williams to talk. Williams told reporters before the game he "had the range on the right field fence and expected to add to his home-run total."[32] Williams knew what he was talking about.

In Game 1, he had three hits, including a two-run homer off lefty Jim Joe Edwards—the only home run the rookie would allow in 1922 in his 92⅔ innings. In fact, the entire Browns team was hitting the ball well, as St. Louis rapped out 15 in hits in both ends of the doubleheader and won by the convincing scores of 10–3 and 12–1.

The Yankees were rained out, and thus the Browns moved to within one game of first place. And that night, despite the protestations of Fohl, the second-place Browns were feted at the Missouri Theater.

Lee Fohl led the Browns to a franchise-record 93 wins in 1922. Fohl's record with the Browns was 226–183 (.553 winning percentage) (George Grantham Bain Collection, Library of Congress).

Thousands showed up just to applaud the Browns players, each of whom appeared on stage and took a bow while also receiving a gold watch, which was engraved with "Presented by the citizens of St. Louis to [player's name] 1922."[33] Sisler even made a speech. The *Post-Dispatch* dubbed it "The Greatest Civic Event since the [1903] World's Fair."[34]

The Browns didn't let the ceremony get to their heads; in fact, they may have been more inspired. They again pounded out 15 hits in holding on to beat the Indians 10–9 on September 5 and tallied 14 more the next day in an 11–3 win.

Williams proved himself to be quite the prophet as he hit home run No. 34, a grand slam off Dan Boone, in the September 5 game, and socked No. 35—"a murderous clout"[35]—against lefty John Middleton on September 6. Middleton was making his major-league debut, and this would be the only home run he'd allow in his short career (he'd make one other appearance and pitch a total of 7⅓ innings).

The St. Louis players certainly were having fun. When Baby Doll Jacobson homered off George Uhle in the third inning of the September 6 game, Williams waited for him at third base so the two could jog home together. The entire town was enjoying the ride. St. Louis was half-game in first place over the Yankees and nothing else mattered.

"Baseball in St. Louis has reached a serious stage," wrote the *Post-Dispatch*'s J. Roy Stockton. "Who cares about what happened in the umpteenth annual renewal of the great labor classics, the coal strike or the railroad strike? Who cares what happened to the bonus or the tariff? The Browns are in first place with 20 games still to play."[36]

The Tigers invaded St. Louis next, and although the Browns lost the opener, 8–3, Williams hit a home run for the third straight game, accounting for all his team's runs when he took Syl Johnson deep in the seventh inning.

The home run streak reached four games—and the fifth straight day he'd done so—in a 16–0 plastering of Detroit the next day, although this one was a shot into the left-field bleachers. Williams also scored a season-high four runs and drove in three, giving him 15 RBI over his last four games (and 18 over his last six).

Williams's prodigious power earned him a bit of marketing power. Advertisements starting appearing in newspapers with the quote from Williams: "I wish to announce that I am now connected with The Kirkland Piano Co. dealers in Brunswick Photographers and Records."[37]

There were no ads featuring other Browns players, Sisler included. Williams, who was listed as a vice-president of the Kirkland Piano Co. in the ad, went on to say, "If you are in the market for a musical instrument give me a call."[38]

The sweet music continued for Williams, the Browns and their fans on September 11 as St. Louis scored once in the eighth inning and twice in the ninth to beat Detroit, 6–5. However, a bad chord was struck in the game.

Sisler, who tripled in the tying run and scored the game-winner, injured his shoulder while stretching for an errant Wally Gerber throw. He couldn't even raise his arm without being in substantial pain. The first baseman, who now owned a 39-game hit streak, would be out at least for three games, but, as team physician Dr. Robert Hyland noted, Sisler vowed he "will try to get into the Yankee series, despite all advice."[39]

Without Sisler in the lineup, the Browns put Jacobson at first base and had Chick Shorten in center field and batting third in the lineup right ahead of Williams. That plan worked the first day. In the eighth inning, with Shorten on second base, the Tigers decided to intentionally walk Williams. However, with catcher Johnny Bassler standing up and stepping to the side, Williams was able to reach out at the third pitch and flick it to right field for a hit, with Shorten going to third and Williams taking second as Detroit threw in to home. Jacobson then singled in both runners, and that ended up being the difference in the game as the Browns won 8–6.

Sisler missed the next three games against the Red Sox as well. The Browns used Marty McManus in the opening game at first base and lost 3–1, then had catcher Pat Collins play at that position for the first time in his career—and St. Louis won two straight. At the end of play on September 15, the Browns were just a half-game out of first place behind the Yankees, who were finally coming to town.

The matchup was much-ballyhooed not only in St. Louis, where it was front-page news the day before the start of the series, but also across the nation. It was dubbed the "Little World Series,"[40] and the results from each inning would be posted on bulletin boards all over the country, including Grants Pass, Oregon, which was soundly rooting for hometown hero Ken Williams.

Fans started lining up to get into the ballpark at 5 a.m. for the opening game. The game itself was a tough ticket, even with some temporary box seats installed to hold a larger crowd. A pair of men from Oklahoma City said they paid $45 for $2.50 seats, while box seats were said to be going for up to $30. Depending on the report, there were between 26,000 and 30,000 in attendance, and that included roughly 2,000 fans standing behind a roped-off area in the outfield.

The overflow crowd certainly was happy to see Sisler back in the lineup and Yankee-killer Shocker on the mound. They also saw a rarity in a regular-season game: three umpires instead of the normal two. Three was the number usually reserved for World Series games. So if you weren't sure this was a big series, that was another clue.

The fans had reason to cheer in the top of the first inning as Williams made a running, leaping catch of a liner to left-center field, then nearly doubled Witt off first base with a near-perfect throw despite making the peg while off-balance.

The Yankees took the early lead in the opener on an Everett Scott RBI single in the second inning and Wally Pipp's sacrifice fly in the third, with Joe Dugan just beating Williams's throw home on the latter.

The Browns got one back in the sixth as Eddie Foster, recently returned from injury, singled in a run and put runners on the corners with one out. But Sisler, who earlier doubled to extend his hit streak to 40 games, hit into a double play to kill the rally. Williams would single to open the seventh, but after seeing the next two batters fly out, he tried to get into scoring position and was caught stealing.

Urban Shocker was 126–80 with a 3.19 ERA in seven seasons with the St. Louis Browns and earned the reputation as a Yankees killer (George Grantham Bain Collection, Library of Congress).

It was still 2–1 into the bottom of the ninth inning and the Browns had Foster, Sisler and Williams due up against New York starter Bob Shawkey. Foster opened with a fly ball to right-center field. Right fielder Bob Meusel called off center fielder Witt and made the catch. However, as Witt retreated out of the way, he was struck "square in the forehead"[41] by a pop bottle, which knocked him to the ground. The force was so great that the bottom of the bottle fell off. Players, umpires and even fans rushed out to help Witt, who had to be carried to the locker room. He was found to just have a severe cut, which was then stitched up. In the days following, rewards would be offered to find the bottle-throwing culprit, but none was ever definitively found.

There was still a game to be finished, of course, and Shawkey made quick work of it. Sisler was out trying to bunt, of all things, and Williams lofted a fly ball to right field, where Elmer Smith, who came in for Witt with Meusel moving to center, made the catch. The Yankees won, 2–1, and took a 1½-game lead over the Browns.

St. Louis was still within striking distance and by winning the next two games it would be in first place, but, according to Sisler, Witt's getting hit in the head with the bottle "has taken the heart out of the Browns."[42]

Witt, somewhat surprisingly, was in the Yankees lineup the next day, and he got a hand from the big crowd … in batting practice. Pitcher Bullet Joe Bush provided some comic relief by going out to shag fly balls wearing protective gear on the back of his head, back and legs, which drew some laughs from the fans.

Despite the loss the previous day, it was another party atmosphere at Sportsman's Park. A band played songs such as "Hail, Hail, the Gang's All Here" before the game and between innings. Witt was cheered again when he went to the plate to open the game, while Babe Ruth was of course jeered.

The Browns had Hub Pruett on the mound for the second game—he notably fooled Ruth often with his screwball, striking him out 12 times in 13 at-bats entering the day. But Ruth would account for the game's first run with a high fly that cleared the right-field wall in the sixth inning for a solo home run.

Hub Pruett, the left-handed pitcher who had Babe Ruth's number (George Grantham Bain Collection, Library of Congress).

Williams tied the game in the home half, his single scoring one and putting runners on the corners, prompting fans to throw hats, seat cushions, scorecards and whatever else they could find in the air in jubilation. Williams stole second base and then, with two outs, scored on Hank Severeid's single to give the Browns a 3–1 lead, and once again set off a frenzy in the stands.

In the top of the eighth inning, Williams helped restore some order. Fans in the left-field seats tried to distract Yankees pinch hitter Norm McMillan by waving white handkerchiefs. Umpire Bill Dineen called time and stopped the game and Williams went over to the crowd and urged them to cease, which they did.

Then, in the bottom of the eighth, Williams helped put the game away. He hit his 38th home run, a two-run blast, to provide some padding for Pruett, who ended up going the distance while striking out eight (including Ruth one more time).

There would still be a week and a half of games to be played, but the importance of the series finale between the two teams was evident, and another sold-out, overflow crowd of around 30,000 packed Sportsman's Park.

Dixie Davis took the hill for the Browns against 24-game winner Bush. Davis might have had the best "stuff" on the staff, but was also maddeningly inconsistent. However, after working out of a first-inning jam, Davis settled down.

It was scoreless until the fifth, when Jacobson doubled into the overflow crowd and eventually scored on a sacrifice fly. In the seventh, Williams followed suit, doubling into the crowd. Jacobson bunted him to third and McManus doubled to make it 2–0, although he was left stranded on second base.

After the first inning, Davis allowed only one hit and two walks until Joe Dugan, he of that controversial trade, doubled with one out in the eighth. Davis struck out Ruth for the second out, but Pipp singled to make it 2–1 before Davis ended the inning by also striking out Meusel.

The Browns went down in order in their eighth, but needed just three outs to move back into first place. Wally Schang led off the inning with a liner that went off Davis's glove,

Schang safe at first on a single. Left-hander Elmer Smith then stepped in to hit for Aaron Ward, and the first pitch got past Severeid for a passed ball. Lee Fohl then came out and replaced Davis with Pruett, who had just pitched a complete game the day before. The Yankees countered by bringing in a righty, Mike McNally.

Fohl later claimed he took Davis out and put in the southpaw Pruett in order to get the Yankees to remove Smith, yet he waited until after the passed ball to do so. The manager also said they knew McNally would be bunting, and the play was for Severeid to throw to third base.

It happened exactly as Fohl predicted, only Severeid's throw to Eddie Foster was wide of the base and Schang was safe. The Yankees then filled the bases with none out when Pruett walked Scott.

Out went Pruett without retiring a batter and in came Shocker, who at least had had one day of rest since *he* threw a complete game. He got Bush to hit a grounder to McManus at second base and he threw home for a force. One out, but bases still loaded. And, as it happened, up stepped Witt with a chance to exact revenge on the entire Browns fandom for the bottle that had hit him in the noggin. That's exactly what he did, causing a headache among the St. Louis faithful with a clean single over second base into center field which scored two runs to give the Yankees a 3–2 lead. Dugan would hit into an inning-ending double play, but the damage had been done.

Bush then got Sisler to ground out (ending his hit streak at an American League record 41 games), Williams to pop out and Jacobson to bounce one to short. Making matters worse, Jacobson only went about halfway down the line as he was easily thrown out to end the game. Johnny Tobin would say Jacobson hurt his knee while fielding Witt's hit in the top of the inning and exacerbated it on his swing, but whether that was just a longtime teammate covering up is unknown. Ruth, in his syndicated column, used that incident as proof that the Browns had given up on the pennant.

"Even now the Yankees are claiming nothing and I know the Browns are conceding nothing," read the column, undoubtedly written by a ghostwriter, which also had Ruth wondering why Davis was taken out of the game. "At the same time I honestly believe that the Browns know they are beaten. Else why did Baby Doll Jacobson loaf on his grounder to Everett Scott after two were gone in the ninth inning? To my way of thinking it was pretty good evidence that the day's defeat was a blow from which the Browns will never recover."[43]

The immediate impact certainly was one of utter disappointment. "Yesterday's game was a heart breaker, boys, a heart breaker,"[44] declared the *Globe Democrat*, all while noting the Browns had a favorable schedule in their final nine games and things weren't over yet. But the Browns' own Bob Quinn provided the future mindset of his team weeks earlier when he had uttered his comment about being satisfied with second place if they couldn't beat the Yankees.

Around this time the Grants Pass chamber of commerce sent Williams a telegram. It read: "We are surely proud of the showing you are making. Grants Pass is pulling for you to the last man. Keep up the good work and hit 'em hard. The Grants Pass ball club has brought home the bacon this year and we expect you to do the same. Hurry home as soon as possible. The steelheads are biting."[45] Certainly, Williams would prefer to delay his offseason fishing to participate in some postseason baseball.

The truth was, the season wasn't over and the next two teams St. Louis played were two of the worst in the league. Washington and Philadelphia were games the Browns certainly could win even without Sisler, who was planning to sit out the series against the Senators.

The Browns had to face Walter Johnson in the opener against the Senators, but homers by Williams in the fourth, his 39th, and Collins in the eighth staked Elam Vangilder to a 2–1 lead. But, once again, the Browns couldn't close it out, and Washington scored three times in the eighth of Vangilder.

With two down in the ninth, Severeid singled. Still some hope left for the Browns! Collins was up again, already having proven he could hit Johnson, and he did so again, knocking one of the future Hall of Famer's pitches deep to left-field … and off the screen, about a foot short of a home run. Severeid scored, but Wally Gerber grounded out and the Browns lost 4–3.

The shell-shocked Browns were then routed the next day, 5–0, getting just four hits in being shut out by rookie Ray Francis, who would finish the season with a 4.28 ERA. Supposedly able to make up ground against a weak opponent, St. Louis now found itself 3½ games back of New York.

The Browns won the finale against Washington, barely. They nearly blew a 7–0 lead and held on for a 7–6 victory. Before the game, Sisler was presented with the trophy for being named American League Most Valuable Player—there was no waiting for the end of the season here—by eight writers which covered the teams in each city, who could only put on their ballot one player from a team. The only other player on the Browns who received a vote was Urban Shocker. Amazingly, Eddie Rommel, of the seventh-place A's, finished in second place, and Chicago's Ray Schalk, who hit .281 with four home runs, was third. But baseball's only 30–30 player wasn't on any ballot, thanks to the rules of the day.

St. Louis took two of three from Boston, but were three games out with three to play. The lead went down to two games after the Browns beat the White Sox 3–2 on September 29 while the Yankees lost to the Red Sox 1–0.

However, Boston had one more helping hand to give New York. Instead of starting Herb Pennock on September 30 in his scheduled start, the Red Sox instead thrust rookie Alex Ferguson to the mound. He gave up four straight hits before Pennock was inserted, but it allowed the Yankees to score three runs, and despite Pennock's not allowing a run over the next seven innings (and Benn Karr the final two), it was more than enough, as Waite Hoyt and Joe Bush were touched for only one run. St. Louis also won, beating Chicago 11–7, but it meant nothing except for how far behind the Browns would finish.

That number was, agonizingly, one as the Browns won their finale, 2–1 over Chicago, while the Yankees fell to the Senators in Washington 6–1. Twenty-three years later, Jacobson bemoaned his club's fate in an interview with *The Sporting News*.

"I … blame our club for not hustling more after the Yankees beat us, two out of three, in a September series," said Jacobson, who was ironically accused of not hustling on that last out of the series finale against the Yankees. "After the Yanks left town, we blew our next two games to Washington.… When we eventually lost the pennant only by a game, the importance of those Washington defeats may well be realized.… I don't know whether we could have beaten [John] McGraw's 1922 team, but I'll bet my life we could have made a better Series showing than those Yankees [who were swept]."[46]

The 1922 St. Louis Browns finished with a record of 93–61, the most wins in franchise history. Although the team didn't win the pennant, the 1949 book "Baseball's Greatest Teams" lists the 1922 Browns as the 14th best club of all time. Of the 16 teams presented on the list, the Browns were the only one not to make the World Series.

Browns owner Phil Ball thought highly of his club as well, despite the team's falling short of first place. While the Browns would eventually split a pot of $18,548.23 (or $662.44 a man) for finishing in second, for their fine effort Ball gave the players another $20,000 to divvy up amongst themselves. The players didn't split the money evenly, with shares reported being between $200 and $1,000. Williams likely was included in the latter.

Williams certainly was deserving of a nice bonus. He closed the season getting a hit in 26 of the final 28 games, batting .360 over that stretch with a .416 on-base percentage and .596 slugging percentage. He hit seven home runs, scored 31 runs and drove in 34 in those 28 contests.

He might not have garnered any MVP votes, but he had that kind of season. Williams finished with a .332 batting average, .413 on-base percentage, .627 slugging percentage, 34 doubles, 11 triples, 39 home runs, 128 runs, 155 RBI and 37 stolen bases. As the founder, so to speak, of the 30–30 club, he remains to this day the only member to have more home runs and stolen bases in that season than strikeouts (he had but 31).

Williams led the American League in home runs—breaking Babe Ruth's four-year streak in that category. He also led the major leagues in runs batted in (and he had 29 more than the player with the second-most in the AL, Detroit's Bobby Veach) and total bases (367).

Williams's name was strewn all over the leaderboards: Sixth in the AL in batting average, eighth in on-base percentage, second in slugging percentage, second in stolen bases, third in runs, tied for fifth in hits, tied for eighth in doubles, tied for 10th in triples, and fifth in walks. For those who prefer more modern stats, Williams was second in WAR among position players and second in offensive WAR in the American League and third in both those categories in the majors.

Not surprisingly, Williams found himself littered on a number of postseason All-Star team lists, including those of Yankees manager Miller Huggins, Yankees pitcher Carl Mays and *Baseball Magazine* writer F.C. Lane.

Williams had an offer to play some more baseball after the season but declined to participate in an "expenses only"[47] trip to Japan and did not travel with Sisler on a barnstorming tour toward New England.

Instead, Williams, along with his wife, drove from St. Louis back to Grants Pass, Oregon, in a new Haynes roadster he had just purchased, making several stops along the way, including Kinsley, Kansas; Grand Junction, Colorado; and Pueblo, Colorado, in the latter of which he "received a welcome which might be accorded a conquerer [*sic*] by the old Romans."[48]

In Pueblo, Williams was prodded to attend a local baseball game, throw out the first pitch and make a short speech. He also ran the public scoreboard for the *Pueblo Star-Journal* during the first two games of the World Series.

But the real hero's welcome came when Williams made it back home, to Grants Pass. As far as its residents were concerned, Williams had helped put their town on the map with numerous mentions of Grants Pass in newspapers and magazines around the country over the past six months. His every move that offseason was tracked, from his arrival to the city to being honored by the local men's club, the Cavemen, to when he left town to go visit relatives.

It was also reported that Williams felt good about the Browns team for 1923, as they'd be bringing back a majority of the players. But first, Williams had to sign a contract. And after the season he had, he wanted to be paid more. A lot more.

Chapter 11

Setting Career Highs Amid Team Strife

Ken Williams made $6,000 in 1922 and he felt after the season he had, a raise was in order. Williams had made a name for himself, further evidenced in the offseason as he was included among some of baseball's greats in a national advertisement for Louisville Slugger bats.

He wasn't looking for a treasure of the sort that would be found in the recently opened tomb of King Tutankhamen, but a rumor quickly took hold that Williams wanted more than $20,000. There was another making the rounds that when leaving St. Louis, Williams told friends he didn't think he'd be back.

Browns business manager Bob Quinn claimed not to be concerned, but as contracts from other players started coming in, there had to be a tinge of worry. Finally, Williams made contact with the St. Louis boss and said he wanted to negotiate in person and not by mail. Williams left Oregon with his wife in early February and made the two-week drive to St. Louis, arriving February 23, and quickly had himself an audience with Quinn.

Negotiating as a player couldn't have been easy in 1923. If a player didn't sign, there was little other recourse as teams retained rights through the reserve clause. Also, there were no agents, and players had no idea what other players were making. There was no basis for comparison. And even the information being printed wasn't always accurate. For example, it was reported that the Yankees cut the salaries of outfielder Bob Meusel and pitcher Waite Hoyt by $500. But in reality, both got raises—Meusel got a $1,000 boost to $9,000, while Hoyt signed for $10,000 per annum, a $4,000 raise from his 1922 salary. (If only Williams had known about Meusel, who had a fine season in '22 but whose statistics paled in comparison to Williams.)

The issue with Williams, however, didn't turn out to be salary. He and Quinn actually came to a fairly quick agreement on Saturday, February 24. "Williams surprised me by the reasonable view he took of things,"[1] said Quinn, surely not a good sign for a player when the business manager makes this kind of statement.

What Williams wanted was something not many ballplayers had in the early 20th century: *security.* Williams wanted a three-year contract, and on this he would not budge. What he knew, and the baseball world did not, was he would turn 33 in June. While he wouldn't get a raise over the next three seasons, he would be making $3,500 more than he made in 1922. It was a willing trade-off.

So two days later, on Monday, February 26, Williams and Quinn reached an agreement on a three-year contract worth $9,500 per season. He was one of the last Browns to sign, but he did so with a week to spare before the team left for spring training in Mobile, Alabama.

A big crowd gathered at the Battle Hotel in Mobile to greet Williams, among others, upon arrival into town, but the ballplayers weren't on the train expected. As a result, manager Lee Fohl, the Browns' coaches and fans, all went home without seeing the St. Louis outfielder.

But Williams did arrive later, and his presence at the ballpark on March 7—along with that of Baby Doll Jacobson, who was a popular player and earned his nickname while playing for Mobile in 1912–13—drew larger crowds for practice than had been there in previous days.

Noticeably absent from the workout, though, was George Sisler. He was supposed to come down on the same train as Williams. However, he was ordered to stay behind by his doctor, but not due to a problem with the shoulder he had injured at the tail end of the 1922 season. Sisler suffered what was called "an attack of influenza" by Browns business manager Bob Quinn, who added, "There is no danger that he will be unable to start the season."[2]

When it was reported that Sisler wouldn't arrive to Mobile until later, Williams proclaimed, "If Sisler can't play we're ruined. We can fill other gaps that exist, but there's no other like Sisler."[3]

The situation would be more dire than Quinn let on, with the question of what was ailing Sisler and how long he might be out extended throughout spring training like a soap opera. Early on, Quinn tried to sign Stuffy McInnis, who had been released, for $18,000, but McInnis's wife didn't want to leave Boston—and she never would—where he had played for the Red Sox from 1918 to 1921 before being traded to Cleveland. Instead he signed with the Boston Braves for less money. Quinn didn't try too hard to land a first baseman after that, thinking Sisler would eventually arrive and could get back into form soon enough.

Williams, as usual, needed little time to knock off the rust of an offseason without baseball. He sent the second pitch he faced over the fence in right field and proceeded to knock seven more over as well.

He followed that up the next day with a home run in an intrasquad scrimmage. Then, in the team's first exhibition game against Mobile on March 10, he hit a deep home run to right, which was "sky high and perhaps the longest hit on the local diamond."[4]

The Browns and Bears played three more games—with Williams collecting three hits, including another home run in the second game—before a cold snap hit, causing the postponement of a couple of games.

The layoff only fueled more Sisler speculation and reporting. Sisler himself admitted he didn't give the team the full prognosis originally, but, after likely having to undergo a nasal operation, said he thought he'd be back in time for opening day. Then came a rumor that Sisler would be out for the season, followed the next day by one in which he'd be back by April 2–3.

Meanwhile, with the hope that Sisler would return, the Browns didn't search for a new first baseman. Who would play there? Perhaps rookie Johnny Schulte, catcher Pat Collins or Cedric Durst, who was trying to make the conversion from the outfield.

It certainly wouldn't be Williams, who early in camp was praised by the *St. Louis Post-Dispatch* for his garden play in 1922. The paper mentioned him in the same sentence as Tris Speaker and Ty Cobb when discussing outfield defense, and in one story in early April called him "one of the greatest defensive outfielders in the game."[5]

Sisler or no Sisler, Williams kept doing what he did: hitting. He had three hits, including a triple, in the first game at Shreveport, then hit a towering homer over the right-center field fence on March 23. The next day, it was a new city—Dallas—but the same result, as Williams clubbed a pitch off Eddie Bryan that "crashed against the roof of the building adjoining the field."[6]

While Williams could still use his legs—he bunted for a hit and stole a base at Wichita Falls—he was feasting on the minor-league pitching he was facing on the Browns' spring training trip.

In Fort Worth, he hit home runs in back-to-back games, including a three-run shot on March 30 off Lil Stoner, who pitched for Detroit in 1922 and would make it back to the majors from 1924 to 1931 with the Tigers and Pirates.

In that game in which he homered off Stoner, a 5–1 St. Louis win, Williams also took the field in the ninth inning without his glove. He did have one ball bounce out of his hands, but he caught the final out of the game with his bare hands on a nice running catch in foul territory.

Williams was doing this all with an elastic band around his left knee, which he had hurt back in Mobile. Then in New Orleans—where "gamblers wave their money openly and make bets on every pitched ball, every batter, without any interference"[7]—he injured his other knee while sliding into third base.

As the Browns made their way back to St. Louis through New Orleans and Memphis, Williams would return to health, proving so by hitting a ball into the right-field seats upon the team's return to Sportsman's Park for batting practice. The Browns finished up the exhibition season with a couple of games against the Cardinals.

However, while Williams was set to go, there was still no Sisler, who now supposedly was out until at least June. The Browns tried to extract either Joe "Moon" Harris or George Burns from the Red Sox, but Boston wouldn't budge—this wasn't the Yankees calling, after all.

The Browns, despite playing all minor-league teams in their spring training, beat the Cardinals, who were coming off wins over Detroit, 3–0 and 11–3. "The showing the Browns made set them to thinking furiously and raised that hazy thing known as 'morale' about a million per cent,"[8] opined *The Sporting News.*

Williams went 1-for-3 in the opener and hit a triple and home run in the second game. Durst seemingly cemented his spot as the team's first baseman with a homer as well, although he did strike out three times against lefty Bill Sherdel in the first game.

And indeed, as the Browns got the regular season underway against the Tigers in St. Louis, Durst was at first base. He didn't bat third in the lineup, where in the past Sisler was penciled in each day. Batting in front of Williams, who was in his usual cleanup spot, was rookie third baseman Gene Robertson. Robertson had hit .350 in spring training and would lead off, followed by shortstop Wally Gerber and right fielder Johnny Tobin.

Needless to say, not all were impressed by St. Louis's top of the order. "With Tobin—a good a batter as Johnny is—batting in Sisler's old position, the pitchers will not have to watch the bases so much and he will not be on as frequently as George," theorized a syndicated article. "The Big Train will be missed in more ways than one by Lee Fohl's club."[9]

That theory wasn't accurate, at least for the opener on April 18. The top three hitters all scored a run, thanks in part to Williams. In the fourth, the Browns loaded the bases and Detroit brought in lefty Ray Francis in to face Williams, who ripped the first pitch by the southpaw into center field for a two-run single. In the seventh, Williams took Francis deep into the right-center field bleachers (just one of two home runs Francis would surrender in 79⅔ innings that season; the other was to White Sox pitcher Ted Blankenship on October 4). Williams finished with three hits, two runs and the three RBI—but the Browns still lost 9–6. Urban Shocker couldn't get out of the second inning, allowing six runs, and the last four spots in the order went a combined 1-for-12, with the only hit a pinch-hit single by pitcher Elam Vangilder. In his debut at first base, Durst went 0-for-2 and was hit for by Bill Whaley.

Indicative of the lineup concerns was the second game of the season, an 8–3 loss to the Tigers. Williams had four hits—but didn't score and drove in just a lone run as his teammates combined had just one more hit than the Browns left fielder (Tobin, batting third again, was 0-for-5).

Sisler showed up for St. Louis's third game of the season, though only as a spectator. But it was the first time he had been with the team since the end of the 1922 season—he had been advised by a doctor to not attend a preseason dinner held by owner Phil Ball at the Missouri Athletic Association. Perhaps his presence buoyed the troops, as the Browns won their first game, 5–3, with Sisler's replacement, Durst, hitting a go-ahead two-run homer.

But that was a rare good moment for Durst, and for the Browns, who struggled out of the gate. Durst lost his job at first by April 24 due to poor fielding as well as a .160 batting average.

Durst was hardly the only one who wasn't performing up to par. Tobin was hitting .244 with just two extra-base hits, both doubles, after an 0-for-4 game April 29. Hank Severeid also only had two doubles though April 29—he wouldn't collect his third extra-base hit until he doubled on May 11—and was batting .268 (which quickly momentarily slipped to .250). Like Tobin, Baby Doll Jacobson started out hitting .244 and had only one extra-base hit—a triple.

Williams, on the other hand, was excelling both in the field, where he already had a couple of assists, and at the plate. He had a hit in nine of St. Louis's 10 games and was batting .415. He hit a "tremendous"[10] home run off Chicago's Red Faber in a 7–7 tie April 23, then went deep in back-to-back games against the Tigers in Detroit. On April 26, Detroit's home opener, he tied the game in the 6th with a shot off Rip Collins, who would allow only three home runs all season, in a game St. Louis would win 4–3. The next day he hit one off Syl Johnson in a 5–2 Detroit victory.

The four home runs quickly put Williams out in front in the American League. No. 5 would come a few days later on May 1, a two-run shot off the White Sox's Dixie Leverette. But it was once again in a loss as St. Louis was 4–8–1 after 13 games.

That home run started Williams on a nine-game hit streak. He finished up the Chicago series with a double in the second game and a 3-for-5 performance in the finale. Up next was Cleveland and Williams hit a two-out, three-run homer off Stan Coveleski in the seventh inning to put the Browns on top for good. Durst, getting some rare playing time due to Marty McManus's being ejected, would hit two homers in his two times at bat.

On May 5 came home run No. 7, a "tremendous drive"[11] off the Indians' Jim Joe Edwards, which "cleared the high screen (in right field), sailed across the street and landed on the roof of a house."[12] It was such a wallop that *St. Louis Post-Dispatch* columnist J. Roy Stockton claimed, "It was one of the longest hits the Brownie slugger ever made."[13]

But, as usual, it wasn't just Williams's bat making noise. In Cleveland he made several great catches to rob Indians players of extra-base hits in the opening two games and also made a "wonderful throw from deep center"[14] to nail Rube Lutzke at third base as he tried to turn a double into a triple. In the finale, "he only had two chances, but each one of them would have been for an extra base hit had any other gardener been cavorting in the left pasture."[15]

Williams offered a bit of a hint as to his fielding prowess. In a syndicated article from the Associated Editors, Williams answered the question: "Is it important that the outfielders should get signals telling what is to be pitched to a batter?"[16] His answer:

> The distance traveled by a fly ball and the way it curves in the air depend a great deal on what kind of a curve the pitcher has pitched. It is therefore important that the catcher's signals be relayed to the outfield so that the fielders may know in advance what is to be pitched and regulate their position accordingly. Usually the second baseman or the shortstop is the man who relays the signals. It must be done in a way that the opposing coaches cannot detect it.[17]

Williams could also do the surprising. In a 14–3 win at Philadelphia on May 11, with the count 3–0, he bunted for a hit. He also could benefit from some now-outdated rules. In a 3–0 win over Boston at Sportsman's Park on May 13, Williams hit a "skipping grounder through first base territory"[18] that headed down the line, hit a pole, "climbed [the fence] like a squirrel in a tree,"[19] and went over. These "bounce home runs" were indeed home runs back in 1923. It would be the only one he'd ever be credited with. (And to be fair, as previously noted, he also lost a number of home runs to the rule that if the ball curved foul after going over the fence, it was a foul ball and not a homer.)

That home run was Williams's eighth, which represented 16.3 percent of all the home runs hit in the American League. Through May 13, Junior Circuit batters had hit just 49 home runs (compared to 103 in the National League, including 13 by Cy Williams).

With rainouts the next two days, players had plenty of time to play cards—and discuss the situation with Sisler. Since spring training, Sisler's teammates had no idea if and when he'd show up, with the hope of his arrival ebbing and flowing each day. Browns players saw Sisler come to Sportsman's Park, although he'd take his spot not on the bench but in the upper deck of the grandstand while wearing dark eyeglasses. He wore shades not to hide his identity but to protect himself from the sun's glare, which bothered him even more in his current condition.

"Some of the Brownies are inclined to believe that Sisler will be back in the game before the campaign ends,"[20] reported the *St. Louis Globe Democrat*. But that belief was really more blind faith. It was hard to imagine Sisler being out for the season—after all, the team *had* to know about his condition, but as yet no first baseman had been added to the roster as manager Lee Fohl held an in-season audition for the position. (Still, even a month later, team VP Walter Fristch would tell the *Post-Dispatch*, "I would not be greatly surprised to see Sisler in uniform in August."[21])

That all changed May 17 when the Browns put in a waiver claim for Brooklyn's Dutch Schliebner, eventually sending pitcher Dutch Henry (who had irked Browns management by asking for a substantial raise in the offseason) and $2,500 to the Dodgers for the first baseman.

Picking up Schliebner (pronounced "Scheebner," according to the *Post-Dispatch*) was not the same as getting a McInnis, Burns or Harris. While he did hit .354 with Little Rock in 1922, he was known more as a glove man than a hitter. The New York writers who were in St. Louis for the ongoing Browns-Yankees series "do not praise Schliebner very highly"[22] and noted his lack of batting prowess.

In fact, Schliebner had started the season in Brooklyn only because regular first baseman Jack Fournier had been holding out. Once Fournier signed, which he did, Schliebner was expendable. Schliebner, who would turn 32 on May 19 (also his debut with the Browns), had no major-league experience beyond his 19 games with Brooklyn, where he was 19-for-76 (.250) with four doubles (.303 slugging percentage), and would not play in the majors after his sojourn with the Browns in 1923.

About the only thing Schliebner shared with Sisler was the first letter of their surname. The Browns had already lost three games to the Yankees at home—Williams was robbed of a homer in the second by Whitey Witt—before Schliebner's arrival. While the stability at first base helped, he was placed eighth in the order, not exactly a boon for the top of the order or any protection for Williams.

Nevertheless, Williams went 3-for-4 with a double and a home run in Schliebner's debut as the Yankees finished off a four-game sweep. Williams's homer came in the 10th inning, but it wasn't enough as New York starting pitcher Carl Mays had tripled in a pair in the top half of the inning. The game might not have gone to extras if Schliebner had come through with the bases loaded and two out in the eighth, but instead he hit a soft liner to Mays.

Williams boosted his average to .331 in a 10-inning win over Washington on May 20, one of those being a double that raised his slugging percentage to .636. But there was another trend as well: Williams was being walked more often. He drew three walks in the game mentioned above and two more the next day, giving him seven bases on balls in his past four games and nine in his last six.

But there were times when Williams couldn't be walked, in the ninth inning of a 0–0 game on May 26 against Cleveland, for example. With Baby Doll Jacobson on first base after walking against George Uhle, Williams, the AL's leading home run hitter, laid down a bunt. Catcher Steve O'Neill threw to first base—but no one was covering. The ball went into right field and Jacobson raced home with the game-winning—and lone—run.

Winning moments were rare for these Browns, who, with the win, were now 14–19 and in sixth place. A brief reprieve occurred May 29–June 2 as St. Louis won five of six games in Detroit and Chicago and Williams had an extra-base hit (four doubles and two triples) in five straight.

But reality returned when the Browns visited Philadelphia, as they lost three of four. In the finale, a 6–5 loss, St. Louis had a runner thrown out at home in the ninth and Williams fanned against Rube Walberg to end the game, prompting A's fans to rush the field in celebration.

In Washington, Williams continued to bat fourth in the lineup even when facing left-handers, such as Tom Zachary, whom Williams had two doubles against in the second of the three-game set. St. Louis took two of three from the Senators, with Williams walking twice in the finale against Walter Johnson, one of which was intentional.

The next stop for the Browns was in New York and their first appearance in the new Yankee Stadium, which opened in April. Williams rapped out two hits in his debut there—two of the four against Joe Bush, who threw a shutout. But he slumped in the final three games, going a combined 1-for-11 with the lone hit a triple in the finale. While the Browns did collect their first win against the Yankees all season (they won just one of the four games), the series is better remembered for the first major-league appearance of Lou Gehrig, who came in as a fielding replacement in the third game and recorded the final out on a grounder by Tobin.

After the series against the Yankees, Williams's average was at a season-low .299, prompting Fohl to move the St. Louis left fielder to seventh in the batting order. He did this for all five games in Boston despite the fact each Red Sox starting pitcher threw right-handed.

Williams had never batted lower than sixth with the Browns and hadn't batted seventh since his rookie season with the Reds in 1915, when he did so 28 times. He responded to this demotion in the lineup by going 8-for-14 as St. Louis won four of five. In the only game the Browns lost, Williams was 0-for-2 with a walk.

That raised his average to .316, and with it also came a bump in the lineup to the three spot. Williams wouldn't bat lower than fourth the rest of the year.

While his average was back over .300 (it had been below for only two days) and his on-base percentage was at .405, despite being featured in a couple of national Louisville Slugger ads (which appeared in *The Sporting News*, among others), Williams's slugging percentage had dipped to .546. This was still very respectable, but nearly 100 points lower than what it had been a month earlier.

Williams's last home run had been back on May 19. Finally, on June 26, the finale of a four-game series in Cleveland, he ended that 32-game drought by connecting off George Uhle in the ninth inning to spoil the Indians starter's shutout. It was only the third home run hit over the fence at Dunn Field in 1923 (Chicago and Detroit would not hit any homers in Cleveland that season).

Two days later and back in St. Louis, Williams made it back-to-back games with a homer as he celebrated his 33rd birthday by depositing a pitch from Detroit's Syl Johnson onto Grand Avenue.

Batting third seemed to agree with Williams. Those home runs came in the early part of a 12-game stretch in which Williams, batting third for all but one of those games when he was in the cleanup spot, went 18-for-46 (.391). He had a .462 on-base percentage and .761 slugging percentage thanks to half of his hits going for extra bases (five doubles, four home runs). He also struck out just one time while reaching base via a walk on six occasions.

As was the case all season, though, the Yankees put a damper on things. New York won three of four games in Sportsman's Park, with Ruth hitting three home runs, including one that broke the front window of a car dealership across the street from the stadium (although two of his homers, including the one mentioned here, came in the only Browns victory). When the Yankees left town after the July 9 game, the Browns were in sixth place, 16 games behind New York, which was running away with the American League. The closest contender was Cleveland, 12 games back.

Williams was hitting the ball better, and maybe it had something to do with his bat. It was reported that Williams ordered heavier bats for 1923—six ounces heavier—with a bigger barrel in an attempt to put more thump in his swing and compete with Ruth for the home run title. But, so says the story, instead it caused him to be late on his swing and hit more balls to left field. His teammates, again according to the report, tried to get him to switch to his older bats and even broke some of the new ones to accomplish that feat.

Whether that it is true or not, Williams was seemingly out of his slump. It helped that Washington, where Williams bashed his way out of the seven-hole, came to town next. In the four-game series with the Senators, Williams was a blistering 10-for-17 with a double, triple and three home runs. He was now hitting .333 with a .606 slugging percentage.

However, in the final game of the series he was hit in the ankle on a pitch from Henry

Sedgewick. Williams would finish the game—his 1-for-4 effort was his worst in the series, and also the only time St. Louis fell to Washington—but he was limited to two pinch-hitting appearances over the next six games.

When Williams was ready to return, he came back with a bang. On July 20, in his first start since being sidelined, he doubled and homered off the A's Eddie Rommel. The next day he lined a three-run homer on a 3–2 pitch against Philadelphia's Slim Harriss, and two games later, against Cleveland, he once again got to the Indians' Uhle, this time a two-run shot. In his first four games back from the injury, Williams was 7-for-18 with three home runs as well as a beautiful over-the-shoulder catch to rob Philly's Bing Miller of extra bases.

That was part of a five-game mini-hitting streak for Williams, who, after two hitless games against Cleveland, went on another five-game run. In this one he went 13-for-21, including a double against Washington in the first game of an August 2 double-header after the Browns batted out of order and Williams, who had walked, was sent up to hit again.

Later that night, Williams and everyone else in the Browns' hotel were likely awakened by noise from the streets, as people flooded outside in Washington, D.C., upon the news of the death of President Warren Harding.

With the nation in mourning, no games were played August 3, but they resumed August 4 with the Browns and Senators scheduled for a double-header. Game 2 would be rained out, but the opener was played with "President Harding's box ... draped in black."[23] Williams went 2-for-5 in that game as he'd begin a 12-game hitting streak.

Williams followed up his two-hit game with a three-hit performance in the opening game against the Yankees in New York. He tripled off Sam Jones in the first, homered against "Sad Sam" in the third, then knocked the Yankees starter out of the game in the fifth with his second triple. The Browns led 8–4, but allowed four in the bottom of the fifth and eventually lost in 13 innings to their nemesis.

Williams made it three straight multiple-hit games with a 2-for-4 game the next day, but it was a play in the field that caused one of the stranger scoring decisions in major-league history.

In the fifth inning, Aaron Ward was on first base with two down. Fred Hofman then singled to left, sending Ward scampering to third base. However, Williams just held the ball after picking it up, seemingly daring Ward to try to score. Ward raced for home and beat Williams's throw, with Hofman taking second. Strangely, both Ward and Hofman were credited with a stolen base by the official scorer, and they've remained credited with that for over 90 years (it would be just one of six steals for Hofman in 378 career games).

On August 7, Williams hit his 99th career home run to lead the Browns to a 12–10 win over the Yankees. Any victory over New York these days was notable, but the big news came after the game: Browns owner Phil Ball announced he had fired Lee Fohl. This was not a rash decision made overnight. Fohl had been losing the team's confidence all season.

It started back in late April when promising rookie pitcher Hollis Thurston refused to pitch batting practice because it was too cold in Detroit. Pitchers on the roster throwing BP was not unheard of, but Thurston, despite having pitched only two major-league games, decided to take a stand. He was subsequently suspended by Fohl, sent home and eventually claimed on waivers by the White Sox, where he would post an above-average 3.05 ERA in 1923 and enjoy a solid nine-year career with Chicago, Washington and Brooklyn.

In May, it was Pat Collins's turn to be insubordinate, complaining about his lack of playing time. He said if he wasn't going to catch (his usual position), Fohl should put him at first base, a spot he had manned for five games in 1922 and where Fohl had been trying the untested Cedric Durst. Fohl told Collins he was in charge and the team would do things his way, and to prove it, he suspended Collins without pay. The suspension would last only two days, but Collins would never play first base in 1923, or ever again in the majors, for that matter.

Then there was the matter of Johnny Tobin, whom we'd now call a character. It was reported that one of his favorite pastimes was standing on his head. So he wasn't exactly your run-of-the-mill ballplayer, nor someone necessarily easy on a manager.

Much to Fohl's chagrin and objection, Tobin purchased a monkey while in New York, reportedly for $25 from an out-of-work actor. Tobin took the monkey—"Tut"—on a road trip, where his antics only continued to further infuriate Fohl. The matter ended when someone, supposedly traveling secretary Willis Johnson, fed the monkey sugared tobacco, causing "Tut" to die.

Fohl also lost an ally at the end of June in Bob Quinn, who resigned from his position as Browns business manager to purchase a controlling interest in the Boston Red Sox. Rumors quickly spread that Fohl would follow Quinn to Boston, and eventually that would indeed be the case. But at the time Fohl said he had no intention of quitting the Browns. However, the decision to leave the Browns would not be his, and the final straw would come a month after Quinn left.

Ball wasn't shy about expressing his displeasure with Fohl, and there was talk of a firing in early July. When the Browns lost to the Yankees 6–4 on July 8, Ball second-guessed Fohl on a number of managerial moves, including leaving Hub Pruett in the game too long (he was lifted with one out in the third inning, but had allowed three hits and six walks), taking Dave Danforth out too early, and even his choice of a pinch hitter in the ninth inning.

"You bet there's truth to it," Ball responded after the game when asked if a managerial change could be in order. "I'm tired of looking at ball games like this afternoon's. I don't mind the Browns losing when the other fellow is better, but I hate a game dropped by poor management."[24]

The Browns had fallen to 34–38 with the loss, but would rally and after a double-header sweep of the A's on August 1 were seven games over .500 at 51–44. But Fohl's fate was sealed after the first game of the twin bill.

The Browns—and thus, Ball—had paid a stiff price for Dave Danforth before the 1922 season, giving up eight players. But Fohl never seemed to be on board with using the pitcher and even sent him to the minors in 1922, much to the displeasure of the St. Louis owner. (Fohl had said at the time the big trade for Danforth would be worth it if the pitcher won 12 games; he only won five in 1922.)

In that August 1 game, Danforth was into the ninth inning, pitching a two-hit shutout when umpire George Moriarty inspected a baseball after a Danforth pitch and immediately ejected him for "persistently and willfully discoloring the ball."

Danforth, as usual, decried his innocence. But his teammates also came to his defense. The ejection meant an automatic 10-game suspension unless overturned on appeal. All of Danforth's teammates, and reportedly new business manager Bill Friel as well (not to mention Ball), supported the pitcher and asked Fohl to step up and protest the ruling. But Fohl did not, and whatever part of the clubhouse he hadn't already lost was gone, too. (American League president Ban Johnson would eventually say, "There is not a shadow of a doubt as to the guilt of Danforth."[25])

Then on August 2, in the first game of a double-header against Washington, Fohl had the embarrassment of seeing his team called for batting out of order—twice. It took a week—perhaps because Ball was out of town—before Fohl was let go. In a telegram sent to newspapers, Ball indicated Fohl was fired "for the good of the game and the morale of the players."[26]

For his part, Fohl was angered by Ball's statement, saying it was the same thing said about the Chicago White Sox players who were suspended from baseball for their part in fixing the 1919 World Series. As to the latter, he blamed Browns VP Walter Fritsch, "the greatest second guesser in the business."[27]

Fohl would protest to Johnson about Ball's remark. Everyone would eventually meet and smooth things over as best as possible, but the bottom line was Fohl was still out, taking with him a more-than respectable (especially for the Browns) 226–183 record with St. Louis.

"I always felt that Lee Fohl was an excellent manager, knew baseball thoroughly, but was often second-guessed by his players because there was never much rapport between him and his men," *St. Louis Star* writer Ray Gillespie would say years later. "He had an odd personality, seemingly hard to understand and not easy to get along with."[28]

Jimmy Austin, longtime Browns player, coach, previous managerial fill-in (in 1913 and 1918) and a one-time Williams traveling partner to spring training, was named interim manager. Williams helped out his old buddy in his 1923 managerial debut by driving in three runs, including two on his 100th career home run, in helping the Browns beat the Yankees 4–3.

St. Louis lost its next two games in Boston, Williams going 3-for-4 in both games to raise his average to .345, but Austin was in a positive mood. "We're going to stage a great battle for second place," he said as the Browns returned to St. Louis for a home stand. "The team has its eyes on second money and I believe it will finish in this position if it gets it share of breaks."[29]

Alas, Austin's positive outlook did not extend to the play of his ballclub. The Browns lost two of three to the Yankees. Danforth received a standing ovation in his return, but, despite pitching a complete game and allowing only three hits, he lost 3–1. Then St. Louis was swept by Washington to drop under .500 and into fourth place.

Williams, who homered in the opener against the Senators, saw his 12-game hit streak come to an end in the series finale against Washington. He also saw his bat taken away.

Williams had started using a handmade bat. He said it had been too heavy—one report had it at 58 ounces—so he bored a hole in the middle to lighten it, then plugged it. Washington happened across the bat accidentally, and after the teams' August 20 game, manager Donie Bush presented the bat to umpire George Hildebrand and protested any game in which Williams used the bat and St. Louis won.

Williams wasn't the first slugger to try a homemade bat. For over a month Babe Ruth had been using a bat made for him by future Hall of Famer Sam Crawford, who had taken sections of four bats and glued them together. Crawford aimed to sell the bats for $8 ($6 more than the average bat a player used), but finally after six weeks American League president Ban Johnson put the kibosh on Ruth's using it. It was reported Ruth started using his new bat, named "Betty Bingle," on July 2 when he was hitting .352. At the time of the banishment, Ruth was hitting .402. This was not a new practice, even on the Browns. George Sisler had once hammered nails into his bat, but had to give it up as the rules stated bats must be all-wood.

Johnson ruled no more trick bats could be used (he also claimed up to a dozen players were using them), but also no protests would be upheld. Moreover, any future use would result in a five-game suspension.

Fans of the time appeared to react with a yawn rather than a gasp. "Fans only showed mild interest in this new 'scandal,'" wrote *The Sporting News*. "Fact is, they have grown used to Ken Williams' eccentricities and he'll have to do something more sensational than tear buttons off his shirt or plug his bat to excite the populace. Ken is a wonderful ball player, and there is none more popular—also Ken is a showman whose dramatics are taken about as seriously as one would take [noted Clown Prince of Baseball] Nick Altrock playing Romeo."[30]

If anyone thought Williams needed a plugged bat to hit the ball well, he quickly discounted that theory. The day after Johnson made his ruling on trick bats and having his bat ruled "ineligible"[31] by umpire Brick Owens, Williams went 3-for-7 with a double and a home run in a double-header sweep of the Red Sox.

St. Louis would win six straight, with Williams collecting at least one hit in each. In the sixth game, a 4–1 win over Philadelphia, Williams socked his third home run since the bat incident. His shot off left-hander Fred Heimach was declared "one of the hardest hit balls ever credited to Ken's powerful swing"[32] by the *Globe Democrat*. It was Williams's 25th home run, placing him in second place in the American League, seven behind Ruth and eight ahead of Detroit's Harry Heilmann.

A bout of food poisoning sidelined Williams for a few days but he returned September 1 and proceeded to put together a 12-game hitting streak. He batted .449 during that streak and hit three home runs, including one off Chicago's Claude Gillenwater in the first game of a September 8 double-header in which Williams fell a single short of the cycle. Gillenwater was sent to the minors after the game and never again appeared in a major-league uniform.

Williams's homer in the second game of a double-header on September 15 in Philadelphia off Bob Hasty "bounced so high from the hard surface on the street that it landed on a second story bay window."[33]

The hitting streak came to end the next day when Williams went 0-for-1 with four walks, one of those being intentional. He hit in the next three games, meaning Williams had a hit in 34 of the previous 37 games, batting .439 with a .519 on-base percentage and .773 slugging percentage (thanks in part to 10 home runs). So, of course, he then followed that performance up with his first three-game hitless streak in over a year.

The final out in that hitless streak was a pop out with two on and two out in the ninth inning, which gave the Yankees a 4–3 win and also clinched the American League pennant for New York.

Despite the three-game anomaly, Williams was still hitting .349 and had 28 home runs. On September 21, with still a couple of weeks left in the season, the tally for the AL Most Valuable Player Award was announced. Ruth was the easy winner with 64 votes, 27 more than anyone else. Williams, one of four Browns to be placed on the ballots, had four votes. Shortstop Wally Gerber, who would end up hitting .282 with one home run and four stolen bases, had the most on the club with 20 votes. Urban Shocker received five votes and Marty McManus four.

Williams would hit only one more home run the rest of the season—September 29 against Chicago's Ted Blankenship. He would, however, partake in three double steals in two days in late September, all against the Red Sox. In the first game of a September 24 double-header, he pulled one with Tobin, heading to third after the ball was thrown into center field. Then after McManus walked, he pulled the stunt again, scoring when Howie Shanks's relay home went over the catcher's head (although Williams is only credited with one steal in the official box score). The next day, he and McManus pulled the trick once more, and Williams also stole another base, showing off his versatility as a player once again.

But the Browns would limp to the finish. Urban Shocker was fined and suspended after refusing to go on a road trip because his wife wasn't allowed to travel with the team. He wouldn't pitch for the Browns after September 7, when he won his 20th game.

Meanwhile, the Browns couldn't get themselves into position in the standings to be awarded any postseason money, cemented in fourth place throughout September. The Browns lost three of four to Cleveland in their final home series of the season. In the finale on October 4, with 19,000 people attending an Army-Navy airfield show, only a few hundred showed up at Sportsman's Park, but those who did lustily booed the hometown club, which lost 9–1 despite outhitting the Indians 13–12.

St. Louis finished out the season by being swept in Detroit, allowing the Tigers to leap over Cleveland for second place and eventually causing some scrutiny. The Browns ended the year in fifth place with a 74–78 record. After his three-game hitless streak, Williams finished the season getting a hit in 14 of the final 15 games (424/485/610), knocking in 12 runs.

Overall, Williams set career highs with a .357 batting average (5th in the AL, 7th in MLB), .439 on-base percentage (6th in the AL), 198 hits (6th in the AL), 37 doubles (tied for 8th in the AL) and 79 walks (tied for 7th in the AL). His .623 slugging percentage (3rd in the AL, 4th in MLB) was just four points off his best mark, set a season before. He obviously missed Sisler's getting on base in front of him as his RBI went from 117 and 155 the two previous seasons to 91 (tied for 9th in the AL) in 1923. However, he did score 106 runs (8th in the AL), the third straight year he topped 100, and is officially credited with 18 stolen bases (tied for 5th in the AL). His 78 extra-base hits and 346 total bases were both third in the American League and the majors, while his 29 home runs placed him second behind Ruth and the Phillies' Cy Williams, who each had 41.

The season might have been over for Williams and the Browns, but there was more baseball to be played. A deal was struck between the Browns and the Negro National League's Detroit Stars to play three games from October 8 to 10 at Mack Park in Detroit.

The Stars boasted many good players, including future Hall of Famers Turkey Stearnes and Andy Cooper. The team was boosted for this series with the addition of two other players—Chicago's John Beckwith and Indianapolis's Oscar Charleston, the latter also a future Hall of Famer.

The Browns didn't have the services of Tobin or McManus and instead started Bill Whaley, who played 23 games for St. Louis in 1923, in the outfield. The team recruited Cleveland's Bill Wambsganss to man second base. The series was not sanctioned by the Browns and some of the media took exception.

"A fairly pathetic story came from Detroit that a bunch of Browns had hung over there after closing the season to play a series with 'a bunch of niggers, and that the black and tan engagements would be resumed in St. Louis.' They did not help their standing locally, in this semi–Southern city,"[34] wrote *The Sporting News* in its "Caught on the Fly" column. "The St. Louis club had nothing to say about it, as the season had closed and the players been paid off. The Browns ... seemed all pepped up at the chance to make a few dollars by playing the negro team."[35]

The Browns stormed out to a 6–0 lead after three innings in the opener against Bill Force, arguably Detroit's best pitcher. But the Stars chiseled back and tied the game thanks to an Edgar Wesley solo homer in the fifth and a five-run sixth, which included a Beckwith home run. While Buck Alexander and Cooper pitched well in relief, Dave Danforth, who struck out nine, was left in to go the distance, and Wesley hit his second home run in the ninth to win the game for the Stars. Williams batted fourth, had a single (he was either 1-for-2 or 1-for-3, depending on the source), and scored on a home run by, of all people, Dutch Schliebner, who hit four all season for the Browns. The *Detroit Free-Press* declared, "Although five errors were made, the fielding by both teams was of approved major league variety."[36]

Ray Kolp pitched for the Browns from 1921 to 1924 and was one of those who played with the St. Louis contingent against the Detroit Negro National League team after the 1923 season (George Grantham Bain Collection, Library of Congress).

The next day provided the same result. Detroit repeated with a 7–6 victory and won in the ninth inning when Force hit a three-run homer, one of four home runs off Browns pitcher Elam Vangilder. Charleston had two and Stearnes had the other. Williams had two of St. Louis's nine hits.

In the finale, the Browns finally pulled one out. Ray Kolp made it three straight complete games for St. Louis pitchers—there were only three in town—and also had three hits, including a home run as the Browns won 11–6. St. Louis hit two other homers and Charleston once again went deep for Detroit. Williams contributed with a double.

This was not the only series between a major-league team and a Negro league team, and it wasn't the only time the MLBers lost a series (the Philadelphia A's did as well). But the series and result gained enough notoriety, along with the others, that commissioner Judge Landis outlawed such exhibitions starting in 1924.

Of course, the Browns were under no such restriction in 1923, but there would be no return series with the Stars in St. Louis. The Browns would barnstorm some more, with games in Ypsilanti, Michigan, and Oshkosh, Wisconsin.

What was a tumultuous season ended with bit of extra money and goodwill, as players would provide the opposition with souvenirs and autographs, likely giving people memories for a lifetime, since this might have been their only opportunity to see a major-leaguer in person.

As the Browns finished up their playing, the direction of the team quickly came into focus. On October 20, as had been rumored during the season, George Sisler was named manager.

Chapter 12

Powered Off and Back On

It was a mostly new regime in charge of the St. Louis Browns in 1924. Phil Ball was still the owner—which had to be good news to Dave Danforth—but the pairing of business manager Bob Quinn and manager Lee Fohl, who were now both with the Boston Red Sox, was replaced by Bill Friel and George Sisler.

Sisler quickly tempered the situation with Urban Shocker, still angry over the treatment of his wife, and who had applied to commissioner Judge Landis to become a free agent. Less than two months after Sisler took the manager's job, Ball and Friel announced Shocker would not be dealt. Thanks to some added intervention from Quinn, Shocker would eventually withdraw his petition and agree to once again pitch for the Browns.

Shocker's return would no doubt be a boon. But Friel was out to remake the roster, especially following the disappointing fifth-place finish in 1923. "What the Browns need most," he said, "is another outfielder, a pitcher and a third baseman."[1]

The latter two positions weren't a revelation. The Browns' weakness had always been lack of consistently good pitching. Meanwhile, third base had been something of a black hole in 1923. Homer Ezzell hit just .244 with six doubles in 88 games and would eventually be traded in April 1924. Eddie Foster batted only .180 with two doubles in 27 games and was released in November, his playing days over. And Gene Robertson couldn't follow up on his good play in his brief time with the team in 1922, batting .247, although he did have the highest slugging percentage of the three—although even that was a moribund .295.

Then there was the outfield. Ken Williams, Baby Doll Jacobson and Johnny Tobin were all getting older, of course, but each of the trio had hit .300 or better in every season since 1919. However, while Williams was coming off two of the finest back-to-back seasons in all of baseball and was dubbed "one of the best sluggers in the game"[2] by syndicated sportswriter Henry L. Farrell, Jacobson's .309 average, .343 on-base percentage and .419 slugging percentage were his worst in those past five seasons. Tobin's .317 average was his worst in the past five years as well, and his .363 on-base percentage second worst, but his .476 slugging percentage was the second-highest of his career and he'd knocked 13 home runs in both 1922 and '23.

Nevertheless, in mid–December 1923 the Browns recalled Herschel Bennett from Tulsa. Bennett appeared in five games with St. Louis early in '23, going 0-for-4, but perhaps more importantly the team had paid $25,000 for him. Bennett, who like Williams and Tobin was left-handed, had hit .330 with 13 home runs with Tulsa in 1923 and .370 with 24 home runs the year prior.

Sisler, though, would waylay any concerns early in spring training as to who his outfield trio would be. He quickly announced he'd keep Williams in left, Jacobson in center and Tobin in right.

The big question with the Browns, of course, was would Sisler play? Early on, the player-manager said he'd pitch if he couldn't play first base. But once spring training began in Mobile, it was plain Sisler would reoccupy his old spot at first.

But in the offseason, the Browns weren't so sure, so Friel was on the lookout for a replacement yet again. Schliebner, as the New York writers had predicted, wasn't the answer.

In September, Friel had tried to buy Bill Terry from Toledo for $50,000, only to be told he was already property of the New York Giants. Then Friel set his eyes on a New York Yankees prospect, Lou Gehrig.

Gehrig had made his major-league debut against the Browns in 1923 and wound up playing 13 games, batting .423 with a .769 slugging percentage. But he wasn't in New York's plans for 1924, and manager Miller Huggins wanted him to get more experience in the minors. In order to send Gehrig back down, the Yankees would have to pass him through waivers.

The first time they did this, the Browns and one other unreported team put in a claim, so the Yankees revoked the waivers. New York tried it again, and once again the Browns put in a claim. It was thought a trade could be in the works—perhaps Shocker could have been involved if Sisler hadn't already said he wanted the pitcher on his staff.

Friel was being coy about the situation. At first he said he didn't put in a claim and that Gehrig seemed like a nice enough prospect, but he really didn't know anything about him. Then it was reported Friel would pay the waiver price, but not make any deal for Gehrig. Finally, once Sisler was shown to be in playing condition, the Browns gave up their cat-and-mouse game and Gehrig passed through waivers and back to Hartford of the Eastern League. He would return to the Yankees in 1924 for a cup of coffee before tormenting American League pitchers—and especially Browns pitchers—during his Hall of Fame career.

Sisler was one of the first 10 players to arrive at spring training in Mobile. Williams would arrive four days later claiming to be a little overweight, which likely meant a pound or two, as he maintained the same weight not only during his playing days but also in his post-baseball life as well.

As usual, it didn't take long for Williams to shake the rust off his bat. He went 2-for-2 with a walk in the team's first practice game, then homered off Shocker in the next. However, a couple of days later, while training with a medicine ball, Williams injured his elbow. It was an ominous start before the real spring training games even began, and it set the tone for Williams's season.

On March 13, three days after the above incident occurred, Williams re-aggravated the injury during a bunting drill. Trainer Martin Lawler, in his first year with the team after coming over from Philadelphia to replace longtime trainer Bits Bierholder, who had joined Fohl in Boston, gave Williams's arm an "electric baking treatment."[3]

While Williams said his arm was not at full health, he nevertheless played. On March 15 he had a single and made a great catch in the field during an intrasquad game. But in St. Louis's first two exhibition games against Mobile he went 0-for-8, although he did steal two bases in the second game.

By March 23, the arm and elbow were apparently feeling better. He doubled, had another hard-hit ball caught, and made three spectacular catches in a 6–2 win over Mobile. He then hit three home runs in three days, March 25–27, two in intrasquad games and another versus Mobile. But he still wasn't 100 percent, as evidenced by his practice throws from the outfield, where he could only reach the pitcher's mound from left field, hardly the usual distance for someone with one of the best, if not the best, arms in the league.

With the arm better but still not perfect, Williams suddenly had another problem to worry about. In a March 29 game against Mobile, he fouled a ball off his foot, and specifically his right big toe. It was bad enough that Joe Evans, a backup outfielder signed by the Browns in March and who was also a doctor, "'drilled' the mashed digit for bad blood."[4]

Williams would only pinch-hit three times over the next seven games. As usual, he'd return with gusto. Williams singled in his return to the field and scored the go-ahead run in the 14th inning of a win at Fort Worth on April 7, doubled and stole a base against the Panthers the next day, went 2-for-3 with a home run at Tulsa on April 9, and finished off the exhibition season against minor-league teams by going 3-for-4 with a double, triple, steal, two runs and two RBI. Just an hour and a half after that game against Tulsa ended, the Browns were on a train headed to St. Louis.

Sisler, of course, was the story for the Browns as they played the Cardinals twice at Sportsman's Park. The overflow crowds gave Sisler a big hand at the games and even larger applause when he tripled in a run in the opener, a 4–1 Browns win.

Perhaps the fans also breathed a sigh of relief, not only seeing Sisler back on the field but also Williams showing no signs of his injury issues. In the first game, he robbed Cardinals outfielder Taylor Douthit of a home run in the third inning, reaching into the crowd to snare the ball. He then homered in the sixth inning on a 3–2 pitch from fellow left-hander Bill Sherdel. Williams finished off his exhibition season by rapping out three hits, including a triple, in a 6–4 loss to the Cardinals (Sisler was 0-for-4).

American League president Ban Johnson was impressed by what he saw, saying "The Browns again appear to be the strong, well-balanced club it was in 1922.... It will be a hard club to beat."[5]

St. Louis opened the season in Chicago and Sisler wrote down a familiar lineup, with Tobin leading off, Gerber second, himself third, Williams fourth, Marty McManus fifth, Baby Doll Jacobson sixth, Hank Severeid seventh, Frank Ellerbe—the third baseman du jour—eighth, and Urban Shocker pitching and batting ninth. The Browns won Sisler's managerial debut 7–3, Williams going 1-for-4 with an RBI. But things quickly took a downturn.

St. Louis lost the next three games. In one, Williams was intentionally walked in the third inning to load the bases for McManus, who hit into a double play. In that same game, both Williams and McManus were ejected, following on the heels of Gerber, who had been tossed in the previous game. And in the finale, not only were they beaten 5–1 by Hollis Thornton, the pitcher exiled by Lee Fohl tossed a complete game seven-hitter, but also Williams strained a muscle in his back and had to leave the game.

The next day, "Williams was out of the lineup on order of a physician"[6] and was eventually sent back to St. Louis to be under the care of team doctor Dr. Robert Hyland. Williams tried to get back onto the field in St. Louis's home opener on April 23, but Hyland wouldn't allow it.

After missing a week, Williams was back in the cleanup spot on April 25, going 1-for-4 with a walk as the Browns once again fell to Thurston and the White Sox. He got his first extra-base hit the next day, a double, one of his three hits as the Browns beat visiting Cleveland.

He then was 3-for-4 with a homer, three runs and two RBI in a crushing 10–9 loss the following day. The Browns had battled back from down 7–0 to take a 9–8 lead into the ninth inning, only to allow two runs.

The Browns were in last place at 3–9, but Williams's return was expected to buoy the club. They had won just once—9–5 over Chicago in the home opener—without Williams in the lineup.

"The return of Williams to the game … promises to have an invigorating effect," surmised *The Sporting News*. "Kenny smacked one [home run] Sunday which showed that he can still put a lot of steam behind his swing."[7] Right on cue, the Browns reeled off five consecutive victories. Williams went 11-for-19 (.579) with three home runs and 12 RBI in those five games.

"Riding along the crest of Kenny Williams' inspirational hitting, the Browns during the last week began to look like the imposing first division team that it should be,"[8] wrote *The Sporting News*, in an appropriate follow-up to its comment the previous week.

He blasted a three-run homer off Earl Whitehill in an 8–7 win over Detroit on May 1, the first of four straight wins over the Tigers, who entered St. Louis in first place. The next day Williams drove in three runs, including two on a triple, then followed that up with a 5-for-5 performance, including a homer off Ken Holloway in the first inning and a single through the box to score the game-winning run against Whitehill in the ninth.

In the final game of the sweep over Detroit, Williams tied the game in the ninth with a home run off Hooks Dauss, who two batters later served up another one to Severeid. But it was Williams who was drawing the attention, being called "the most dangerous hitter in the American League."[9]

"His work in the last series with the Tigers indicates the murderous manner in which he treats pitchers and baseballs,"[10] wrote national syndicated columnist Norman E. Brown.

St. Louis moved on to Cleveland, and Williams pushed his hitting streak since returning from his injury to 10 games, barely missing a home run in each of the first two games. The Browns took three of four games and suddenly were 11–10 and in fourth place, but just three games behind the league-leading Yankees.

A series of rainouts caused St. Louis to play just once in Boston against former manager Fohl. The Browns won that one, 5–3, as Dave Danforth—his handling one of the reasons Fohl was let go by the Browns—pitching a complete game while Williams was 2-for-3 with a triple, scoring twice and driving in another.

Then it was off to New York. Williams had often been in the shadow of Babe Ruth, and the opening game on May 14 appeared to be more of the same as it was declared Babe Ruth day, with commissioner Landis attending and the Yankees raising their 1923 pennant flag. But it was Williams who owned the day.

Williams paced a 16-hit St. Louis attack as he went 4-for-4 with a double and a walk while scoring twice and driving in three. For good measure, he also stole his first base of the season.

Ruth would homer the next day, but so did Williams—"a torrid smack"[11] off Herb Pennock "which went high and long"[12]—and Sisler as the Browns won again, 2–1, moving St. Louis just one-half game behind the Yankees in the standings.

After a rainout, the Yankees would salvage the series finale, 7–2, but Williams had two more hits, including a double, to raise his average to .452, which topped the American League.

Rain again played havoc with the Browns' road trip as the middle two games of their four-game set in Washington were washed away, but St. Louis won the two that were played, meaning they had won 13 of its last 15 games. Williams had a hit in each and made an incredible running catch in the sixth inning of a 3–1 win on May 22 to prevent the Senators from tying the score at 2.

Williams closed the month of May by having an extra-base hit in six of seven games, including three home runs. On May 27 in Detroit against Bert Cole, a left-hander, he hammered a pitch over the right-field wall and out of the stadium, "a trick seldom accomplished at Navin Field. The ball cleared the wall a good 15 feet and landed in a lumber yard on the opposite side of the street."[13]

In a Memorial Day double-header in St. Louis against the White Sox, he homered in both games, the fourth time he had accomplished that feat in his career. But despite his prodigious power—his slugging percentage was over .700 as late as May 30—Williams couldn't carry the team to wins all by himself. Injuries began stacking up. McManus, who hadn't missed a game in the previous two years, was out with a broken thumb. Gene Robertson, who was establishing himself as the team's third baseman, was nursing a sore hand. Backup catcher Pat Collins had boils all over a hand. Pitcher Elam Vangilder bruised three fingers on his pitching hand when he lost his grip while cranking a phonograph.

Meanwhile, Tobin was struggling at the plate and would hurt his back. Sisler was playing every day, but had trouble maintaining a .300 average. And so more losses than wins started to pile up. St. Louis dropped to .500 (17–17) and to fourth place on May 29. Williams went in a mini-slump, going hitless for three straight games to open June, as the Browns lost four straight and fell to sixth place. Meanwhile, former manager Lee Fohl had the Red Sox in first after winning the first two of four games in St. Louis.

The Browns would rebound with five consecutive wins, including three in a row over the Yankees. Williams had a hit in each of the wins and played a big part in the fifth victory, a 5–3 win over the Yankees on June 9. He homered off New York's Sam Jones in the fifth inning for St. Louis's first run. After knocking in the go-ahead run with a fielder's choice in the fifth, Williams then stole second and went to third on an overthrow. On the next pitch, he stole home for the fifth and final run.

Alas, prosperity didn't last long in St. Louis in 1924. After that winning streak the Browns lost four straight, prompting Sisler to shake up the lineup, moving Gerber to eighth and bumping everyone else up one spot. This meant Sisler was batting second and Williams, for the first time all season, hit third. The move agreed with Williams and, to a lesser extent, the Browns.

Sisler stuck with that lineup for 14 games. During that stretch, Williams was 19-for-45 (.422) with five home runs (and an .822 slugging percentage)—one of which tore right through a spectator's umbrella before landing on Grand Avenue—20 runs, 16 RBI and six steals. He also walked 17 times *without striking out once*. Williams now had 14 home runs, second to Ruth's 17. And with Williams leading the way, the Browns posted an 8–6 record in that span.

But St. Louis had a long road trip to deal with—the team left St. Louis after a June 26 rainout and wouldn't return to Sportsman's Park until July 26, with 33 games scheduled in that month away.

When the Browns opened by losing two of three to the White Sox (with former Brown

Thurston beating St. Louis for the fifth time to no defeats in 1924), Sisler readjusted the lineup again, putting Norm McMillan, who was filling in at second base for McManus, in the second spot in the order and sliding himself back to third and Williams fourth. Williams would bat cleanup the rest of the season. His return to fourth did not provide an immediate boon: he went 0-for-7 as the Browns were swept in a double-header in Cleveland and dropped to seventh place in the standings.

It was certainly a small sample size for Williams in the three-hole and he was used to batting fourth, but he was hitting .347 with a .463 on-base percentage and .633 slugging percentage when the brief experiment ended. Just over two weeks later, after St. Louis's July 15 game, those numbers were down to .317, .430 and .571.

Not that there weren't moments of productivity. He had three hits and three RBI in a game in Cleveland, tripled in a run, then scored when catcher Johnny Bassler dropped the throw in Detroit. He also had a couple of home runs and a triple in New York.

And, of course, Williams was still regarded as one of the game's top hitters, as evidenced by his inclusion of one of 12 players in the latest autograph baseball bat line advertisement from Louisville Slugger.

But it was also in New York where Williams' season would take a turn for the worse. After suffering injuries early in the year, Williams had been mostly healthy. But in the series finale against the Yankees on July 15, Williams broke two bones in his left foot while sliding into a base.

With the Browns still on their elongated road trip, Williams was sent back to St. Louis. A cast was placed on his foot, and Williams would need the aid of crutches. It was announced by the Browns that Williams wouldn't be ready to return to the field for at least two weeks, but even that was a bit premature.

Williams had a week as he awaited the return of his teammates. He perhaps read up on the Leopold and Loeb trial, which began in Chicago a few days after Williams set foot back in St. Louis. Listening to the Gene Tunney–Georges Carpentier fight, which Tunney won in a 15-round TKO, was a likely option to help pass time. With the Cardinals in town, a visit to Sportsman's Park wasn't out of the question, either.

On August 3, roughly 2½ weeks after he broke his foot, Williams had his cast removed. He rejoined the Browns on August 5, although only to sit on the bench. He was able to do a little pregame warmup and was dressed in uniform, but he wasn't ready to play just yet.

That opportunity came two days later. Williams had missed 22 games (which included three double-headers) when he was called upon to hit for pitcher George Lyons in the sixth inning with two outs and Wally Gerber on base. He promptly singled to right-center field, but it was clear his foot was not fully healed as he struggled to run to first base. He'd have to run no further as Syl Simon was called upon to run for Williams.

Williams was called upon to pinch-hit in each of the next four games. He would go 0-for-4 (although he did knock in a run with a grounder) and it was obvious he had been rushed back too quickly, even for one at-bat a game.

The team was getting back to full health—other than Williams—and the bats—also other than Williams's—were starting to come alive. As St. Louis ended its home stand on August 10, Tobin, who had been as low as 254/321/352 on May 24, was up to 322/380/421. Robertson (321/362/419) and McManus (312/394/452) were back in the lineup as well, with the latter raising his average nearly 30 points in three weeks, while Baby Doll Jacobson was having a bounce-back year and batting 329/371/551. Even with Sisler still struggling to hit .300 (he was at .299), the Browns had managed to claw their way into fourth place with a 57–51 record. That prompted longtime New York sportswriter Joe Vila to state that "if Sisler had Kenny Williams back in the good playing condition, Sisler could lay claim to the [American League] flag right now."[14]

Vila might have been overstating things, but St. Louis certainly could have used Williams in the lineup. His replacement in left field was Joe Evans, who technically took over after Herschel Bennett, the original sub for Williams, broke his arm after being hit by a pitch just a few days following Williams's injury. In the time Williams was sidelined, Evans appeared in 33 games with 32 starts and batted just .242 with a .326 on-base percentage and .297 slugging percentage. He also struck out 10 times—nearly matching Williams's entire total for the season. Certainly, Williams would have produced at the plate much better than Evans. Williams hadn't hit that poorly since he came up with Cincinnati in the Deadball Era—and even then his rookie season was on par with Evans's stretch as a starter.

But Williams, still not healthy enough to play, had to leave the team briefly to tend to his ill wife back in St. Louis. He'd return to the team, but his return to the lineup didn't come until August 24 in Cleveland.

It had been 38 games between starts for Williams and he had only had those five pinch-hit appearances. In his return, Williams went 2-for-3 with a double and a walk against Indians left-hander Sherry Smith, who allowed just five hits overall in pitching a complete game.

St. Louis was no-hit by Walter Johnson in a seven-inning game the next day (Williams was 0-for-2 with a walk), but Williams would get a hit in seven of the next eight games, including a trio of three-hit performances.

On September 1, in the first game of a double-header at home against Cleveland, Williams had one of his best games of the season. He went 3-for-4 and broke an 8–all tie in the eighth with a two-run homer off Bob Kuhn (in the only inning of his major-league career). He also doubled and, despite still being noticeably hobbled, took part in a double steal with McManus.

If it wasn't his foot that was bothering him then it was his back—he had aggravated the strain he suffered in spring training—and it was affecting his swing and power. After that home run off Kuhn, Williams went 11 games without an extra-base hit, nearly unheard of for him in his time with the Browns.

He broke that streak with a double against Boston in the second game of a double-header on September 13. However, in his first 26 games back from injury, he had only one home run and just that one extra-base hit in a 16-game stretch.

Nevertheless, he was still a popular figure in St. Louis. During this power outage, the Liberty Music Hall used Williams to help promote an upcoming show, *Hit and Run*, which Williams is quoted as saying "is as good as any homer with the bases full."[15]

Williams wouldn't know that feeling again in 1924, although he did hit one more home run, a three-run shot in the first inning of a wild 15–14 10-inning win over Washington on September 20.

There was only a week left in the season and Sisler would use a lot of substitutes in the remaining games, but Williams, who perhaps could have used a break, was kept in the lineup.

He surely wouldn't have wanted to miss a charity exhibition game held September 26. Former Browns pitcher and later coach and scout Carl Weilman, who spent his entire career with the Browns organization, had died unexpectedly earlier in the year at the age of 34. Weilman had been ill, although he had returned to the team to once again scout players, and the cost of previous surgeries left his widow and family in dire need of money.

The Browns held a day for Weilman. There were contests and a band, and to cap it off the Browns played a team made up of major-league scouts. The game itself was "a farcical event,"[16] but a good time was had by all. At one point, the Browns moved their outfielders to the infield—for the first time since his minor-league days, Williams played third base—and vice-versa. Sisler played every position on the diamond. Theodore Breitenstein, who had pitched for the 19th century St. Louis Browns of the American Association and National League, pitched three innings despite being 65 years old. The game lasted eight innings before the megaphoned announcer declared it was being called "on account of weakness."[17] It was no laughing matter that the game raised $5,000 for the Weilmans, who it was reported could now pay the mortgage that was due.

St. Louis traveled to Cleveland to finish their season with their hearts obviously not in the game as they fell 12–1 in the opener. Rain prevented the finale from being played, and certainly no one on the Browns was complaining. After a brief run, St. Louis finished in fourth place with a 74–78 record. Sisler barely squeaked over the .300 mark, ending at .305.

Despite playing in only 114 games, Williams still finished second on the team in batting average (.324 to McManus's .333) and home runs (18, one behind Jacobson). He did lead the Browns with a .425 on-base percentage, .533 slugging percentage, 20 steals and 69 walks. He also was third on the team in runs (78) and second in RBI (84). He struck out only 17 times in 483 plate appearances, thus making it the second time in three years he had more home runs than strikeouts. In the American League, Williams finished tied for second in slugging percentage, fourth in home runs, tied for sixth in steals and seventh in on-base percentage.

It was by almost anyone's standards a very successful season at the plate, and it was enough to garner Williams one vote on the MVP ballots. But Williams, as he had shown, was capable of much more. The midseason injuries just took too much of a toll. From the time he was moved back to fourth in the lineup to the end of the season, he lost nearly 100 points in slugging percentage. Clearly, Williams had not been playing at 100 percent.

Rest was a good antidote. But there was still more baseball for him to play—and to be paid for playing. Williams was enlisted to manage a team of Browns players on a three-week barnstorming tour. They started out in Fremont, Ohio, against a team of local all-stars, then played in front of a "record crowd"[18] in Lima against another local conglomerate. Williams renewed acquaintances there with Chuck Reynolds, who played for Calgary of the Western Canada League in 1914, and was coaxed by the local paper to say he thought Washington would beat the Giants in the World Series.

Williams pleased the fans by hitting a home run against a legion team in Sterling, Illinois, then led the Browns against a team of Cleveland Indians in a three-game set played at the Columbus Country Fair in Portage, Wisconsin. The tour concluded in Centralia, Illinois, on October 19 with players from the Browns, White Sox, Cubs and Red Sox joining together to defeat the hometown team.

Williams headed back west to Oregon, but there was one more pit stop to be made. A new ballpark had been built in southeast Los Angeles at 38th and Compton Avenue for the California Winter League. The field was supposed to be inaugurated with a matchup between two Negro League clubs—the winter league was integrated in terms of all-black teams playing all-white teams—but their travel was delayed. So an exhibition was arranged, which included several major leaguers, Williams among them.

On October 25, the $16,000 Pirrone Park (later to be known as Los Angeles White Sox Park) held its first game with teams managed by Joe Pirrone, who had footed the bill for the park, and Carl Sawyer, a former player who performed comedy routines at baseball games along the lines of Al Schacht and Nick Altrock.

Williams played center field for Pirrone's team and in his first plate appearance hit the first home run at the new ballfield. The *Los Angeles Times* described the ball as being "hit nine miles over the right-field fence for the circuit. Williams's clout was one of the longest ever hit in Los Angeles, the ball clearing Ascot avenue while it was still rising."[19]

Another game was staged the next day and Williams played in that, as well as one more game before the November 1 barnstorming deadline. An exhibition was organized in Brea, California, a town of 1,500, on October 31 to benefit the Elks Club Christmas fund. Williams, a member of the Elks, would play for the Anaheim Elks team. The big draw, though, was the pitching matchup. Walter Johnson, who lived in nearby Olinda, California, as a teenager, pitched for Anaheim, and Babe Ruth took the mound for a major-league all-star team, which included the retired Sam Crawford at first base. An estimated 15,000 people turned out to the Brea Bowl for the game. Ruth pitched all nine innings and hit two home runs as his team won 11–1 in what the *Los Angeles Times* dubbed "the greatest deluxe sand lot game Southern California has ever seen."[20]

With no more baseball exhibitions allowed, Williams made his annual pilgrimage back to Grants Pass, where he'd finally have time to spend with his wife and 1-year-old son, Ken

Ken Williams (right), time and place unknown. The player to the left of Williams is believed to be Hall of Famer Sam Crawford (courtesy Larry LaBeck).

Jr., as well as prepare for the upcoming season. However, where Williams would be doing that playing was coming into question.

Sisler was looking to remake the Browns and there were reports of several players being made available for trade, including Williams, catcher Hank Severeid and pitcher Urban Shocker.

The Yankees were reportedly interested in Williams, but would not give up pitcher Waite Hoyt in a deal. *The Sporting News* surmised that Williams would be a great fit in Detroit, that "Williams is the dashing, fighting type, a player that [Ty] Cobb likes and which adds fuel to the rumor."[21] Of course, Tigers second baseman Charlie Gehringer would later say Williams was among the players Cobb hated the most.

"I remember one time, in St. Louis, he [Cobb] kept me after school, like a teacher would," recalled Gehringer, who began his career in 1924 but wouldn't play against Williams in St. Louis until 1926. "Just kept me sitting in the clubhouse for an hour after everybody had left the ball park. This was because I'd let Ken Williams, who Cobb disliked very much, beat out a bunt. Now Ken Williams was a very powerful hitter. How are you going to play him up on the grass so he can't beat out a bunt? He'll knock your teeth out. I thought that was ridiculous. But he kept me sitting there for an hour."[22]

Sisler, though, halted any trade talk of Williams in early December. "I am willing to sell or trade Shocker," he said during the winter meetings, "as I am willing to trade or sell most any member of the team with the exception of Ken Williams."[23]

Indeed, Shocker was very much in play and the Browns received many offers, but none to their liking. However, the Yankees finally were able to get back the pitcher whom they had unwisely dealt to St. Louis back in 1918, and they didn't have to give up Hoyt, whom the Browns kept insisting would need to be in any deal.

Instead, St. Louis received three other pitchers for Shocker, who went 126–80 in seven seasons with the team. Most notable was veteran Bullet Joe Bush, who had just turned 32 and had a 171–152 record and 3.25 ERA for the A's, Red Sox and Yankees. Also acquired was 29-year-old Milt Gaston, who had made his major-league debut in 1924, and 26-year-old rookie Joe Giard, who was coming off a 20-win season with Toledo.

"As to Shocker, he is a great pitcher," Bush said, "but I cannot see where the Yanks got the best of the deal."[24] History would prove Bush wrong. While Shocker would only pitch three seasons for New York before tragically dying during the 1928 season, he was effective for the Yankees during that time, while the three pitchers obtained by the Browns would not amount to much.

While Williams wasn't going anywhere, Sisler was far from done retooling the roster before the team headed to spring training. He had the Browns pay $7,500 to recall Cedric Durst from Los Angeles of the PCL then deal him and three others—catcher Pat Collins, infielder Norm McMillan and pitcher Ray Kolp—to Toledo for 30-year-old catcher Leo Dixon, known for his defense and throwing arm, not his bat. Dixon had hit .272 for St. Paul in 1924, but with Indianapolis in the previous three seasons he batted .238, .213 and .202.

Sisler also released Hub Pruett to Oakland, had previously sent Bill Bayne to Tulsa on an option, and had to give George Lyons to Toledo in order to get Giard. That meant only five pitchers were left from St. Louis's 1924 staff—Elam Vangilder, Dixie Davis, Ernie Wingard, George Grant and Dave Danforth, the latter of whom was holding out.

The offense hadn't been tinkered with much and Sisler indicated he was fine with that part of the roster, although right field was in some question as "Johnny Tobin had an all-around bad season last year."[25] Tobin had finished at 299/357/390, his lowest numbers since 1918. The outfielder blamed it on aching teeth, "which, he says, poisoned his entire system."[26] As a result, in the offseason Tobin had five teeth pulled.

Sisler and the Browns had more problems: along with Danforth, Jacobson, McManus and Dixon were all holding out with no resolution on the horizon. Those players were all missing as the Browns opened camp in their new spring training home in Tarpon Springs, Florida. That new locale had to please Williams. Despite the longer drive, there were plenty of places to go fishing. During a March 22 deep sea fishing outing on the Gulf of Mexico it was reported Williams, the noted angler, "landed two 10-pound fish at the same time."[27]

However, Williams was in Florida to hit, not fish (or at least that was the priority). But it didn't take long for an old problem to flare up, as Williams's back, which he hurt in spring training in 1924 and again later in the season, was strained once more.

Williams took a couple of days off and practiced a new swing to help prevent further injury. With the Browns, Williams had held his bat out front before a pitch, waving it menacingly at the pitcher. But to ease his back, Williams went to his stance from his minor-league days, when he would stand with his bat loaded and ready behind the plate. Whatever he was doing, it was working.

After hitting a home run in an intrasquad game and sending several balls over the fence in practice, Williams doubled in a 7–3 win over the Dodgers on March 11. He homered twice, drove in seven and stole a base in a 15–5 victory over Brooklyn in Clearwater on March 14.

By the time St. Louis and Brooklyn met again on March 19, Danforth and Dixon (who had wanted part of his purchase price, which he did not get) had signed and arrived in camp.

But neither of those players was going to help the offense. McManus was still holding out for $10,000, a $2,500 bump from the previous season. Jacobson also wanted $10,000, which was a $4,000 increase.

Williams kept hitting away, swatting three doubles in the next two-game set with the Dodgers. But as the team left Tarpon Springs on March 29 and headed on a 10-day trip back to St. Louis, the pair of holdouts remained away from the team.

Perhaps it was related to Jacobson's absence and potentially some overuse, but as the team headed north, both Williams and Tobin started complaining of sore arms. Neither was sure how it occurred, but opponents were well aware of the ailments. In an April 1 game in Jacksonville against Cincinnati, Reds baserunners kept trying to take an extra base on Williams. He did throw a runner out at the plate, but it was on a shallow hit to left, normally a spot a runner would never test the strong arm of St. Louis's left fielder.

McManus would sign and join the team April 2—he received a $500 raise after all of that, but noted he hadn't even picked up a baseball since last season. Jacobson was at least practicing with Milwaukee of the American Association. While McManus would undoubtedly help the offense, he was an infielder, meaning Williams kept playing despite his sore arm.

The arm might have affected Williams's throwing, but his hitting was undisturbed. In a 13–2 win at Nashville on April 5 he hit his first home run since March 14 and also doubled. The next day against Nashville he had four hits, including another home run, and in the final two games on the road in Memphis he had three hits, including a double.

There were two more games to be played against the Cardinals at Sportsman's Park. The teams split, with Williams having three hits and scoring three runs in a 7–6 win and going hitless but making a fantastic running catch on a foul fly in a 6–5 loss.

With the season upon the Browns, the team went into full attack on its lone holdout. Business manager Bill Friel said Jacobson was not a "winning ballplayer"[28] and no other team in the majors wanted him in a deal. He added that Jacobson had been "just getting by"[29] for a few years. Owner Phil Ball took his aim at *St. Louis Globe Democrat* writer Martin Haley, calling him a "press agent"[30] for Jacobson. He added that the outfielder no longer had a job with the team and St. Louis was in search of a new player to take his place.

With that backdrop, St. Louis opened its season in St. Louis with Sisler saying he'd platoon Herschel Bennett and Joe Evans in center field. The Browns proved for one game, at least, that Jacobson wasn't needed—at least on offense.

There were the usual ceremonies before the opener—the mayor threw out the first pitch, floral arrangements were given to several players, including managers Sisler and Tris Speaker—and also the unusual—McManus was married earlier that morning. When it came time to get down to business, St. Louis's hitters did just that.

The Browns pounded out 20 hits against Cleveland pitchers. Williams went 3-for-6. He had an RBI double in the first, a three-run homer in the fourth—which chased starting pitcher Sherry Smith—and later added another double.

However, Browns pitching did little better, and the St. Louis fielding, or at least that of three players, was abysmal. The Browns lost 21–14 as the Indians rapped out 19 hits of their own and were aided by 10 St. Louis errors, all committed by Sisler (4), McManus (3) and Bennett (3), who had come into the game after Evans left with an illness. Bennett dropped two flies during a 12-run eighth inning.

The mood of St. Louis fans certainly wasn't lifted with Joe Bush knocked out in the third inning. Meanwhile, in the Yankees' opener Urban Shocker pitched a complete game in a 5–1 win, allowing seven hits, or two fewer than Bush. It was an ignominious start to the season, to say the least.

The Browns lost the next two games to the Indians 2–1 and 1–0—Williams had three of St. Louis's nine hits in those games—and then 14–5 to the White Sox. As the game against Chicago neared its conclusion, St. Louis fans closed in on Ball and yelled at him for not having signed Jacobson. The outfielder's offense might have helped, but seeing big offseason acquisition Bush get shelled again—this time allowing 12 hits and 10 runs in 6⅔ innings—surely didn't help matters.

St. Louis didn't need Jacobson the next day. Williams homered off Charlie Robertson and Jacobson sub Bennett added another off Ken Ash as the Browns won their first game, 11–4 over the White Sox.

The Browns won two of their next three games and Jacobson finally came into the fold. American League president Ban Johnson interceded and came to agreeing terms with Jacobson on behalf of St. Louis. The outfielder didn't get the $4,000 bump he was looking for, instead signing a two-year contract worth $7,500 per season, a $1,500 raise from 1924. Despite the previous words from Ball and Friel, Jacobson served as a pinch hitter for two games before taking his place in center field on April 25 in Cleveland.

It wasn't quite like old times, with Tobin headed to the bench upon Jacobson's return and Bennett sliding over to right field. But some things did remain the same, namely Williams's hitting prowess. He had three hits in Jacobson's starting debut, a 6–5 Browns win, and was batting .391 with a .652 slugging percentage 11 games into the season.

Williams went through another of his mini-slumps, as every ballplayer is prone to do, with just two hits in his next 23 at-bats. But on May 3 he went 2-for-4 and once again homered off Robertson. Two days later against the Tigers, in a game famed for Ty Cobb's saying he tried to hit home runs (and he did, three of them, as he lofted fly balls into a stiff wind over the right-field fence), Williams went 4-for-5. He went 4-for-9 in the next two games against Detroit, and in the second game drove in the game-winner in the bottom of the ninth. With the score tied at 5 and runners on first and third, he clubbed a ball over Cobb's head. There was nothing the Tigers center fielder could do, so he watched it fly, then made a beeline to the locker room.

Williams started picking up the pace as the Yankees came to town. After going hitless in the opener—Shocker tossing a five-hit shutout while Bush, again, was rocked early—Williams went 5-for-12 in the next three games, including hitting a home run off Bob Shawkey in the finale.

But for the Browns it didn't matter how well Williams was hitting. The pitching was just atrocious—and that description still might be kind. Even without Babe Ruth—who wouldn't play until June thanks to "The Bellyache Heard 'Round the World"—the Yankees topped 10 runs in three of the four games (the other was a 1–1 tie). Fortunately for St. Louis, it scored 19 in the finale to salvage one win. In the Browns' first 26 games, the pitching staff had surrendered 10 or more runs an incredible 10 times, including five of the last seven.

Williams, though, was in a groove. In the opening game against Washington he drove in four runs as he homered twice—both coming off lefties, Tom Zachary and Vean Gregg. Neither homer was a cheapie; the shot of Zachary bounced off the right-field pavilion roof. "They would have registered for homers in any park,"[31] claimed *The Sporting News*. That gave Williams six home runs, tying him for the AL lead with Philadelphia's Al Simmons. Number seven came two days later off Stan Coveleski.

The Browns hadn't allowed 10+ runs in three games, but that came to an end as Bush was hammered again in a 12–7 loss to the Senators. In five starts at Sportsman's Park, Bush had lasted only 13 innings while allowing 37 hits—20 for extra bases—and 33 runs. The next three games also featured a team scoring 10 or more runs—the Browns beat the Red Sox 10–7 and 11–6, then lost to Boston 12–7. The streak ended on May 18 as Bush—yes, Bush—tossed a nine-hit complete game in an 8–2 win over the Red Sox as George Sisler extended his hitting streak to 34 games.

Sisler's streak would end the next day. Williams might not have had a hitting streak, but on that day he made it 13 out of 16 games with a hit as he blasted his first grand slam in nearly three years off Slim Harriss. In that 16-game span, Williams raised his slash line from 289/333/526 to 324/361/606.

St. Louis lost three of four to the A's, including a 20–4 game, the second time a team had scored 20 or more off the Browns. In the series finale, Williams went 0-for-4 off a lefty, Rube Walberg.

Despite Williams's two homers off lefties just 12 days earlier, the more recent performance against Walberg likely was the reason why Sisler moved Williams to fifth in the lineup—McManus moved from fifth to fourth—the next day in both games of a double-header against Cleveland, which started a southpaw in each.

The ploy worked. In his first at-bat of the first game, Williams hit a two-run home run off Joe Shaute. He now had nine home runs, with four of them off left-handers. Williams would add two singles in the game and drove in three runs overall as St. Louis won 8–4.

In the second game, he had an RBI single in the fourth inning; then, in a 4–all game, he led off the ninth with a single. After being bunted to second and following an intentional walk to Hank Severeid, Williams stole third base. He got such a jump on pitcher Jim Joe Edwards he made it to the base standing up. Edwards then walked Wally Gerber to load the bases for pitcher Dave Danforth. Bush, who would have a lifetime .250 batting average and batted .339 for the Yankees in 1924, was brought in to bat for Danforth. He singled to right field and Williams trotted home with the winning run, his single and steal the keys to victory.

After going 3-for-16 over the next five games, Williams went on a hitting tear on the road. It started in a 15–11 win at Chicago on May 31—starter Ernie Wingard going the distance for the Browns, allowing 19 hits—in which Williams went 3-for-4 with two runs. The next day in Cleveland, he had three more hits, including a triple and a home run, and drove in six runs.

Two days later he was 2-for-3, but his biggest accomplishment might have been being intentionally walked twice by lefty Joe Shaute. Neither instance worked, as Baby Doll Jacobson would follow with an RBI single and two-run double in a 7–6 win, which got St. Louis to .500.

As well as Williams hit in Cleveland, he was scorching hot when St. Louis visited New York. He went 7-for-19 in the four games and homered in the first three. In the opener he hit two out of the park against Urban Shocker and also tripled off the former Browns hurler. However, the Browns lost three of four as they allowed two more games of 10+ runs (including the last game in Cleveland, it was three straight), marking 17 times the St. Louis pitching staff had allowed double-digit runs.

Williams's hitting streak reached 11 with a pair of four-hit, four RBI games in Boston, narrowly missing the cycle both times (he needed a home run in the first and the triple in the second). After a hitless game, he went 5-for-8 against Boston and Washington. "[Williams] murdered the ball in the series in Boston, and all but carried the team to victory in the first two games himself,"[32] declared *The Sporting News*.

In 14 games—which included an 0-for-4 in Boston—Williams hit .516 and drove in 24 runs while scoring 20. He also had four doubles, three triples and six home runs as he raised his slash line from May 30 of 318/368/570 to 369/411/672 two weeks later after a loss in Washington. The Browns went 8–6 in those games, but that still left them at 28–30 in fifth place.

Of course, hitting was far from the only thing Williams was known for. He was still supplying the Browns with great defense—his one-handed sliding catch of a Denny Williams liner in the eighth inning against the Red Sox on June 11 helped preserve a 9–7 win. The next day he "robbed [Ira] Flagstead of a triple by a spectacular one-handed catch."[33]

In addition, there was still that famed Williams temper. On June 4 in Cleveland, he argued after being thrown out at first and was ejected, although at first he failed to leave the field and Sisler had to intervene. In Detroit on June 27, Williams hit a grounder to first, and instead of running to the base, he turned and complained to umpire George Hildebrand that catcher Johnny Bassler kept him from running to first by stepping on his foot. Williams was ejected from the game for his use of "strenuous language."[34] It wasn't reported what Williams said, but it was bad enough that he was suspended indefinitely.

When the Browns returned to St. Louis on June 29 to face Detroit, Williams was still out of the lineup. Also gone was catcher Hank Severeid, traded to Washington for catcher Bill "Pinky" Hargrave and pitcher George Mogridge, who was expected to boost the starting staff. Of course, in typical Browns fashion, Mogridge developed a sore elbow after beating the Tigers 5–2 in that June 29 game and didn't pitch for St. Louis again.

Williams would miss three games, returning July 1 against the White Sox, but the time off didn't have much of an effect. In his first at-bat upon his return, he homered off Ted Lyons; then, in the second inning, he threw out Harry Hooper trying to go to second base after a fly out.

Longtime Browns catcher Hank Severeid played in the minors until he was 46 (George Grantham Bain Collection, Library of Congress).

This wasn't just a one-game comeback. Williams homered in each of the next three days as well, the final one coming in game 2 of a July 4 double-header. The four home runs in five games gave Williams 19 on the season, propelling him into the American League lead.

Williams wouldn't hit home run No. 20 until July 12, in which time New York's Bob Meusel passed him for tops in the AL with 21. However, two days later Williams celebrated the 10th anniversary of his major-league debut by tying Meusel, hitting a three-run shot onto Grand Avenue off Curly Ogden—the only home run the Washington pitcher would allow in 1925 in 42 innings. Williams then made it back-to-back games with homers when he took Boston's Ted Wingfield deep.

The homers came in the middle of a five-game win streak which vaulted St. Louis to third place. Williams's bat was a big reason, but the *St. Louis Globe Democrat* also noted, "Kenny Williams is making a lot of sensational catches these days."[35] Specifically, Williams made two great catches on Washington's Earl McNeely on July 14, and Boston's Flagstead once again fell victim to the left fielder's glove, this time in St. Louis's fifth straight victory on July 17.

Despite turning 35 on June 28, Williams still had some speed left in his legs as well. On July 19 he stole two bases against the A's—the second time in a week he had two steals in a game (also doing it against Boston on July 14). He was credited for one in the 10th inning when first baseman Bing Miller held the ball too long after a tapper back to the mound, tying the game. The Browns would lose in 12–8 in 15 innings, the 21st time they allowed 10+ runs.

But it was his power that got Williams the most attention, and perhaps what he did best. On July 19 he hit No. 23 off Philadelphia's Rube Walberg. No. 24—and the 150th of his career—came off the A's Jack Quinn.

St. Louis was in third place as it departed for another road trip. But then the Browns were swept in a three-game series in Cleveland, with the Indians scoring 10, 12 and 11 runs in their wins. The losses dropped the Browns to fourth place. It also meant that they allowed 10+ runs in 25.2 percent of their games thus far.

It was hard enough for any hitting to make up for that kind of pitching, and scoring runs got even more difficult for the Browns as Williams was sidelined with a sore arm. He'd miss six games, during which the Browns were swept by the seventh-place Yankees. But St. Louis took three games in Boston against the last-place Red Sox, who at 29–72 had trouble beating any team, healthy or otherwise. Williams returned for a double-header in Washington and doubled in each game. He put together an eight-game hitting streak as St. Louis headed to Cleveland.

He was having an MVP-type year. Williams had rebounded from, for him, an off season, mashing the ball as he had in 1922–23, and on pace to lead the league in home runs for the second time in four years. But all of that would change with one pitch.

Chapter 13

One Pitch Changes Everything

The August 14 game between the Browns and Indians at Dunn Field was turning into a showcase of Ken Williams's skills. In the first inning, he displayed his speed by beating out a hit back to pitcher Sherry Smith, who then became so concerned with Williams on base that he threw a pickoff attempt away. Williams would reach second base and eventually score.

In the sixth, Williams showed off his power no matter who was on the mound as he blasted a pitch from the left-handed Smith over the right-field wall for a three-run home run. It was American League–leading home run No. 25 for Williams, two more than Bob Meusel of the Yankees. Williams flashed his defensive prowess in the seventh, making a "sensational one-handed catch of Joe Sewell's liner."[1]

By the eighth inning, Cleveland had a new pitcher. Smith was taken out after six innings, and his replacement, Bert Cole, was removed for a pinch hitter in the seventh. On the hill in the eighth inning for the Indians was right-hander Byron Speece, who used an extreme submarine motion and was described as having an "underhand"[2] delivery. With two outs in the inning, George Sisler tripled, bringing up Williams, although Sisler would steal home during the at-bat.

Speece was having trouble locating his pitches against Williams, pitching three straight balls nowhere near the strike zone. The fourth pitch quickly sailed up and in. Instinctively, Williams flinched his head to the right. *WHACK!*

The ball hit Williams squarely in the head, near his right ear. He immediately crumpled to the ground. There were reports that Williams was unconscious, albeit briefly, before getting back up. As his teammates rushed to his side, Williams tried to walk to first base. Instead, he staggered and lost his balance, nearly falling forward. Williams had to be helped to the clubhouse. The magnitude of the injury wasn't known, and he was given a bag of cracked ice to put on his head.

"Ice is generally pretty cold but it didn't feel that way to me. In fact, I didn't feel a thing," Williams would recall a year later. "My head felt numb. Besides, it seemed rather foolish to lie there with a sack around my bean."[3]

Williams decided he was well enough to take a shower and head back to the team hotel. As it happened, right around that time Chick Fewster entered the Browns' clubhouse. Fewster was a utility player for Cleveland (and who would hit for Speece in the ninth inning) who just happened to have had his skull fractured by a beaning during a spring training game in 1920 and nearly died. Ever since then, Fewster had empathy whenever he saw a player hit in the head and would try to comfort and help out the hit batter.

When he heard Williams say he was going to shower, Fewster spoke up, telling him not to do that. "It's the worst thing you can possibly think of," Fewster told Williams. "It might put you out for good."[4]

Williams would always tell this story and add that he would later read about a minor-league player who was hit in the head, took a shower, and then died. He was indebted to Fewster for his advice.

The next day, Williams reported that he was dizzy and was kept out of the lineup. The Browns played one more game in Cleveland and then the team took a train back to St. Louis. That couldn't have been a comfortable trip for Williams.

Back in St. Louis, Williams, still experiencing dizzy spells, was sent to a hospital where team doctor Robert Hyland took X-rays and discovered there was no skull fracture, but Williams did have a "slight"[5] concussion.

Hyland's prognosis was that rest would solve the issue. He had Williams remain in the hospital but required absolute quiet around the Browns outfielder. Williams's hospital stay was expected to be for a few days, but it turned into two weeks.

Eventually, Williams, who was also suffering from blurred vision, asked about playing baseball again this season. "They reminded me 1926 was another year and that I played about all the baseball I was likely to play in 1925,"[6] Williams recalled.

Hyland decided to let Williams head home to Oregon to convalesce and recover. So, on September 8 the Williams family headed back to Grants Pass, and the Browns announced the outfielder was done for the season.

"It was a new experience for me and one that I don't want to repeat," Williams would later say. "Of course, I've been hit before, and on the head at that, but a glancing blow. That was a direct bull's eye."[7]

Williams finished the 1925 season having played in 102 games while hitting .331 with a .390 on-base percentage and .613 slugging percentage, the latter of which would lead the American League (only one other player in the majors was over .600, the Cardinals' Rogers Hornsby).

Bob Meusel would pass Williams for the home run lead and end with 33. Williams averaged 16.4 at-bats per home run, best in the AL, so with a full season there's little doubt he would have won the HR crown.

Despite playing in only two-thirds of the season, Williams was sixth in the AL with 61 extra-base hits. His 105 RBI not only tied for 6th in the American League, but also allowed Williams to join rare company with two seasons of more RBI than games played, having also accomplished this in 1922.

In addition, Williams struck out just 14 times (the rate of a strikeout every 29.4 at-bats was 9th in the AL), meaning this was the third time in four seasons he had more home runs than strikeouts. Williams was the first to accomplish this feat in 1922. After 1925, he had done it three times, matching the total number it had been achieved by anyone else (Tris Speaker in 1923 and Irish Meusel in 1923 and 1925). Only six other players in the history of the game would have more HRs than strikeouts three times. Only three players would accomplish this at a more advanced age than Williams was in 1925: Lefty O'Doul (1932) and Johnny Mize (1948) were also both 35, but a few months older; while Barry Bonds (39) had a cloud of suspicion in the performance-enhancing drugs era. Only 19 times has a player had more homers than strikeouts at age 32 or greater, and Williams did it on three of those occasions.

"It was a pretty sad day, that August 14th, for me," Williams said. "I believe it would have been my best season if I hadn't been injured."[8]

Without Williams, the Browns actually finished in third place—but surprisingly not because of their hitting. Joe Evans and Herschel Bennett split the time in left field after Williams's injury, and neither hit a home run. Harry Rice, who was getting most of the playing time in right field, injured his knee in early September and only returned for the final three games (in which he went hitless). George Sisler ended with a .345 batting average, but endured an 0-for-26 slump late in the season.

Instead, it was the pitching that spurred St. Louis's move up the standings. Having thrown just two shutouts and allowed 10 or more runs 25 times before Williams's injury, Browns pitchers tossed five shutouts and gave up 10+ runs just four times (and two of those were in a season-finale double-header) in the final month and a half.

The poster boy for the pitching staff was Joe Giard, whose final numbers were a 10–5 record with a 5.04 ERA, but he was 7–3 with a 3.57 ERA in that span. Even Joe Bush won three of his last four starts, two of which where shutouts—including a one-hitter against Washington at, of all places, Sportsman's Park.

The third-place finish meant Williams received playoff money, which amounted to around $650 (*The Sporting News* reported the figure as $642 in its October 22 edition and $658.17 in its October 29 edition). The extra money helped Williams's wallet, but not his head.

Back in Oregon trying to get healthy and in shape for the 1926 season, Williams had occasion to go hunting with buddies Jud Pernoll and Buck Seeman. While out on one of these trips, Williams grew tired and sat down on a tree stump. Then he started hearing a strange buzz. He looked every which way to find out what kind of bird could be making such a noise, but nothing was spotted. "For a time I couldn't make out what was happening," he recalled. "Then the thought occurred to me that the buzzing was really inside my own head. It was."[9]

Symptoms persisted throughout the fall, but in late December Williams mailed a letter to Browns business manager Bill Friel stating he was "feeling fine and will be as good as ever next season."

Perhaps this was Williams just playing things safe to ensure he had a job with the Browns in 1926. But it also hinted to St. Louis management of a much-needed offensive weapon. As *The Sporting News* noted, of active players currently in the American League, Williams was eighth in career batting average (minimum 700 at-bats) at .331 (they used only his numbers with the Browns, discounting his time with Cincinnati). The seven players ahead of Williams would all someday be elected to the Hall of Fame: Ty Cobb, George Sisler, Tris Speaker, Al Simmons, Babe Ruth, Harry Heilmann and Eddie Collins.

But with the way his 1925 season ended, Williams would have to re-prove himself. For their part, the Browns saw his worth. Coming off his three-year contract in which he earned $9,500 per season, Williams would re-up with St. Louis for one year at the same amount.

George Sisler was clearly in charge of the Browns' roster. He sent owner Phil Ball favorite Dave Danforth to Milwaukee in exchange in part for second baseman Oscar Mellilo, signed football star Ernie Nevers to a lucrative contract—Ball didn't even know for how much, although it was reported St. Louis gave him $8,500 ($3,500 more than reported offers from the New York Giants and Cincinnati Reds) plus a stipulation Nevers couldn't be sent to the minors without his agreement—dealt pitcher George Mogridge to the Yankees for 36-year-old catcher Wally Schang, and traded longtime outfielder and St. Louis native Johnny Tobin to Washington, along with Joe Bush, who couldn't wait to get back east, for pitchers Tom Zachary and Win Ballou.

Coming off his injury, Williams might not have had much trade value to begin with, but Sisler made sure to know he knew who his left fielder was going to be in 1926. Upon arrival at spring training at Tarpon Springs, Sisler declared "the outfield with Williams, [Baby Doll] Jacobson and [Harry] Rice performing up to their standard could hardly be improved upon."[10]

Williams wanted to get to camp a little early. He left Grants Pass on February 22 and made the five-day drive to Florida. Upon arrival, Williams declared himself to be in fine shape, and to prove it he joined his teammates in bunting drills, batting practice and shagging fly balls. His mood was very positive. "I don't see how they can stop us if some of the pitchers come through," he proclaimed. "Look at the spirit out there. Never saw so much hustle since I joined the ballclub."[11]

There might have been some concern when Williams joined Sisler, Dixie Davis and Gene Robertson on the golf course on an off day but didn't play—Williams said he went to watch and give Davis a hard time—but those fears were alleviated quickly once the Browns started playing.

In the team's first intrasquad game on March 5, Williams hit a pitch from left-hander Stewart Bolen over the right-field fence. He followed that up by going 2-for-5 with a stolen base the next day, while his double in the ninth inning of the March 9 scrimmage tied the game.

His success continued as competition against other teams began, with St. Louis taking on Brooklyn in three games, two of which were held in Tarpon Springs. In the first game vs. the Dodgers he was part of a double steal with Marty McManus and was robbed of a home run by right fielder Dick Cox, then in the second game—three days later in Clearwater, Florida—he was 3-for-4 and "turned in several outstanding fielding plays in left field."[12] Finally, on March 15 in a 10-inning game he went 2-for-5.

In St. Louis's next two games—against Buffalo and Brooklyn—Williams was used as a pinch hitter. While he was feeling well at the start of camp, he suddenly was feeling dizzy again and developed a bad headache.

Williams missed the next two games, staying back at the hotel in bed. He went 1-for-3 in a win over the Phillies on March 24, sat out St. Louis's next game the following day, but played all 18 innings of a 3–3 tie against Buffalo in Bradenton on March 26, going 3-for-7 with two doubles and a steal. Williams also played in the final two games before St. Louis broke camp, doubling against the Browns and producing two hits in a scrimmage.

As the team played its way north to St. Louis, Williams hit fourth each game and he rewarded Sisler with that decision. In Quitman, Georgia, against the Columbus Senators, Williams homered and doubled. The Browns played two games in Chattanooga in which Williams had two hits while also making a nice catch on a deep fly ball in the opener and stealing a base in the second game. In Nashville, he had a three-hit game, including a home run that "was a real wallop,"[13] while in Memphis he was 3-for-10 in two games. While he was hitting well, it was noted that Williams "has what seems to be unavoidable in such cases, a tendency to back away from the ball."[14]

The Browns left Memphis at 11:20 p.m. for St. Louis, where they were to play the

Cardinals in the revamped Sportsman's Park. Phil Ball, hoping for a packed house when his team finally won the pennant, had spent $229,000 to reconstruct the pavilions and bleachers. Seating would increase to nearly 30,000 with double-deck stands built in both left and right field.

Of more concern to Williams, perhaps, was the right-field foul line was moved back to 320 feet (left field was pushed to 355 feet), although dead center field was now closer at *only* 430 feet. There was also now a 12-foot outfield wall. As it turns out, the new dimensions and features wouldn't stop Williams.

Nearly 23,000 turned out for the first game in the annual Browns-Cardinals series on April 10. The Browns won 4–3 when Rogers Hornsby fouled out with the bases loaded to end the contest.

Two days later the teams met again, although only around 6,000 showed up as the temperatures dipped. The smaller crowd witnessed Williams hit a ball off the right-field pavilion roof and into the street below. While it was not an official home run in the record books, it gave an air of confidence to the health—both physical and mental—of Williams.

In its season preview, the *St. Louis Globe Democrat* wrote, "Williams, whose mighty club is expected to win many a game for the Sisler-men this year, gave no signs of being 'ball shy' as the result of being hit on the head by a pitched ball last season."[15]

Oddsmakers couldn't quite pin the Browns down. The Senators and A's were listed as 2–1 favorites to win the American League. The Tigers were at 3–1 while the Browns, along with three other teams—Indians, White Sox and Yankees—were at 6–1. Not much was thought of the Red Sox, who were 30–1 long shots. The optimism for the Browns, even slight, was not well placed.

St. Louis opened on the road and returned home with a 1–6 record after trips to Chicago and Detroit. The pitching certainly wasn't helping once again—St. Louis allowed first-inning runs in each of the first four games (including newcomer Zachary, allowing eight in his Browns debut)—but the offense wasn't exactly in form, either, with the four runs being the most scored in those first seven games. Williams was batting just .250 and had only one extra-base hit—a double in the opener that fell into the overflow crowd at Comiskey Park.

The Browns hoped things would change once they got to their new-look ballpark. Although the Cardinals had played at Sportsman's Park to open the season, the dedication for the renovated park occurred in the Browns' initial home game. A band played and the mayor threw out the first pitch—something he decided against doing at the Cardinals' opener.

Despite the increased capacity, only 11,000 turned out to see the expanded seating. The park wasn't the only thing that had changed, as American League umpires were now dressed in white, pinstriped suits—they had worn brown suits previously—with blue caps. They also saw something different—a Browns win. Williams knocked in the first runs for St. Louis in the renovated digs with a two-run single in the third inning of a 5–1 victory over Chicago.

The Browns won two of four from the White Sox and Williams still had just that lone extra-base hit from the season opener. He also was making mistakes on the basepaths, overrunning third base after a bunt and being tagged out in one game and caught stealing in another, causing the *Globe Democrat* to dub him "Wild Moose of the Runways."[16]

On April 25, Williams finally got untracked, as did several other Browns, thanks in part to a stiff wind. Williams hit his first home run of the season off the same pitcher who had tossed him his final home run in 1925, Cleveland's Sherry Smith. He added a second home run, one of five for St. Louis on the day, in the sixth off Benn Karr.

Just like in the last game he played against Cleveland, which had ended his 1925 season prematurely, in the eighth inning he faced Byron Speece. This time, it was insult instead of injury as Williams tapped back to the pitcher, who started a double play.

The Browns won that game, 11–5, but then dropped the next three to Cleveland. The local newspapers were getting critical of Sisler, calling for changes in the lineup beyond his propensity to swap out catchers. Particularly painful was the fact that in eight home games, the Browns committed 26 errors—including five in a game on two occasions. "The Browns have been a rank failure," the *Globe Democrat* said of the 4–11 cellar-dwelling American League club, "so why not snap out of it with some radical changes."[17]

Finally, Sisler took heed. As the Browns opened a series against Detroit, the manager made a number of moves. He benched right fielder Harry Rice and inserted Herschel Bennett, moved Ski Melillo from third base to second base and bumped him up from eighth in the order to second, while sliding McManus from second base to third and jumping him from fifth to cleanup in the lineup. Wally Gerber, who had been losing playing time to Bobby LaMotte at shortstop, was back in, and Williams slid to sixth in the order in the next two games as St. Louis faced left-handed starters.

The moves worked, at least for one day, as Bennett had three hits and the Browns defeated the Tigers 3–2. Sisler trotted out the same lineup the next day. This time it didn't work—St. Louis lost 7–6—but Williams drove in four of the runs. He walked with the bases loaded in the first inning and hit a three-run homer in the fifth off lefty Augie Johns that bounced off the roof and onto the street below.

Two days later he repeated the feat but in more dramatic fashion. In the ninth inning of a 6–all tie with one out and one on, Tigers manager Ty Cobb had lefty Ed Wells walk George Sisler to get to Williams, who was back in the cleanup spot. Williams then crushed a Wells pitch onto the roof in right-center field, the ball once again rolling down to the street below.

But moments like that for the Browns—and Williams—were rare. Following that game, the team headed to Cleveland, where it lost two of three games to the Indians. Williams went 4-for-10 with a pair of doubles, including one that nearly went over the fence but hit off the wall with about a foot to spare.

Then it was on to Philadelphia, where the Browns lost the May 6 opener 5–4 as well as two players. Bennett crashed into the wall chasing a Mickey Cochrane fly ball and fractured his skull while Gerber was hit by a pitch and broke a finger.

This game also represented the first time a "Williams shift" was written about. In the third with the bases full, Williams was credited with an RBI single on a grounder to short because A's second baseman Max Bishop "had been laying so far over toward the foul line that Sisler was ahead of him on the rush to second base."[18]

St. Louis dropped the next two as well by scores of 5–1 and 14–0, and after the Sunday day off due to Philadelphia's blue laws, Sisler shook up the lineup once again. This time Cedric Durst was starting in left field over Williams, who had gone 1-for-8 in the previous two defeats. It didn't help that a lefty, Joe Pate, started for the A's, either.

It made no difference as Philadelphia finished off a four-game sweep with a 3–2 victory. The next day Williams was back in the lineup and batting sixth vs. Washington left-hander Dutch Ruether. Williams tripled, but St. Louis lost its fifth straight.

The Browns' skid reached six the next day against Walter Johnson—Williams was back to his fourth spot—and then seven when former teammate Joe Bush tossed a four-hitter in a 6–2 win.

Griffith Stadium in Washington, D.C., was not an easy place to hit a home run, especially over a fence. In 1926, only one Senators player would hit a ball out of the park. Overall, there were just 19 homers hit at Griffith Stadium that season (in 1924 there were only eight!).

On May 14, Ken Williams hit one of those 19—his only home run ever at Griffith Stadium. (His triple two days earlier likewise was his only three-base hit. Needless to say, this was not his favorite ballpark.) It came in the sixth inning off Curly Ogden—it was also the only home run over the fence at home he allowed in his three seasons as a Senator. It was dubbed a "husky homer"[19] and helped the Browns break their losing streak with a 10–7 win.

St. Louis won its second straight in Boston, 6–3, and Williams contributed with an RBI triple. But prosperity never lasted long for this Browns team, which proceeded to lose four straight to the Yankees in New York and a singular game in Detroit. Williams accounted for the only run against the Tigers in a 2–1 loss, but as luck would have it, his long fly ball hit off the top of the fence and went back onto the field for a double. If it had gone in the other direction, he would have had a home run and tied the game.

The Browns finished up a road trip by splitting two games in Cleveland (Williams went 3-for-8), but that still meant they had only nine wins, the only club in the majors without double-digit victories on the season.

With a 4–22 record away from home, Sportsman's Park was a sight for sore eyes. But there weren't many eyes on this Browns team. While St. Louis somehow managed to sweep a four-game series from Cleveland, one game featured just 3,500 fans—28,000 short of capacity—while nearby at Fairmount Park a crowd of 15,000 showed up for the opening of horse racing season.

A better crowd—but still one-third full—of 11,000 turned out May 30 for the final win. American League president Ban Johnson was in attendance as well, and all saw Sisler and Williams hit back-to-back homers in the first inning off Emil Levsen—Williams's coming on a curve—to score all the St. Louis runs in a 3–1 victory.

A May 31 Memorial Day double-header vs. Detroit drew 22,000 to Sportsman's Park, and any cheers Williams might have heard the day before were quickly forgotten. Williams went 0-for-5 in the opening game, a 10–7 loss, failing to advance or score runners on three occasions, including a "half-hearted effort"[20] in the eighth inning on a pop out to the first baseman. In the second game, he had a rough second inning. In the top half, he allowed a ball to go through his legs, leading to two Tigers runs. This prompted owner Phil Ball to leave his box for an inning. In the bottom half, with Detroit leading 5–4 and Sisler on third with two out, he fanned on "bad pitches."[21] He'd finish 1-for-4 and St. Louis would win the second game, but throughout the day he was "booed … unmercifully."[22]

Williams responded with two hits the next day, but went 1-for-8 (with two RBI) in the next two games, dropping his average to .268. The next game, Williams wasn't in the starting lineup, with Bennett taking his place. Yes, Philadelphia ace Lefty Grove was on the mound, but this time it was not a one-game instance. Williams was benched. It was widely believed that Williams hadn't recovered from being hit in the head 10 months earlier.

"It [is] evident then that bean ball had left its marks … this season he hasn't displayed the same confidence at the plate," claimed a nationally syndicated wire service article.

"Approaching the plate Ken has been seen to grit his teeth, but face to face with the pitcher he has changed. Pop-ups and cheap grounders have been offered where in the past Williams rattled many outfield fences."[23]

Williams would sit for five straight games, with Bennett starting in left field each time. His return to action came June 10, when he replaced Rice mid-game (Bennett moving to Rice's spot in right field, Williams playing left). Williams went 1-for-2 with an RBI single in the seventh inning.

Rice wasn't ready to return to the lineup, so Williams got the start the next day. He did not exactly make a case for himself to remain a starter. In the seventh, he ran in on a ball which went over his head for a double. In the ninth, he let a line drive get past him for an error, which eventually led to Boston's taking a 2–1 lead. In the 10th, the Red Sox intentionally walked Sisler to load the bases for Williams, who finished off an 0-for-4 day by fouling out to the catcher on a weak pop fly. Fortunately for the Browns, Marty McManus ripped a two-run single and St. Louis was victorious. When Rice returned the following day, Williams headed back to the bench.

The American League trading deadline was June 15, and on this day the Browns made a move, sending Baby Doll Jacobson to Boston in a three-team deal and receiving in return outfielder Bing Miller from the Athletics. Jacobson had hit 34 home runs over the previous two seasons and batted .341 in 1925, but he was hitting only .286 with two home runs in 50 games in 1926 for St. Louis and was losing playing time on occasion to Cedric Durst.

Thus, one of the greatest outfield trios in baseball history was officially broken up. From 1919 to 1925, Williams, Jacobson and Tobin had each hit .300 or better save one—when Tobin hit .299 in 1924. With Jacobson off to Boston, now only Williams remained. Tobin had been dealt to Washington in the offseason. He was struggling there and would be released in a couple of weeks and eventually sign with the Red Sox, joining his old Browns outfield mate Jacobson.

Miller entered the season a career .317 hitter and was four years younger than Jacobson. While still productive with the A's, he had slipped slightly to .291 in 38 games with two home runs.

At the time of the trade, Miller was with the A's in Cleveland. Instead of leaving for St. Louis, where the Browns were playing, he headed to Philadelphia to get his affairs in order and arrange for his belongings to be shipped to his new home.

This meant St. Louis was playing one outfielder short. Sisler admitted later that his plan was to have Miller start in left field. Durst was set in center and Rice in right. That left Bennett or Williams as the replacement for the yet-to-arrive Miller.

Bennett had started in Williams's place June 5–10 and then again June 15. He also went 3-for-26 in that span with five strikeouts. With that recent history at the forefront, Sisler penciled in Williams in left field, batting fourth, against Washington's Bullet Joe Bush on June 17, the Browns' first game since the Jacobson trade.

Williams had missed four straight games, and this was only his second start in 12 contests. In the second inning he came to the plate with the bases full, and like the Williams of old, he sent a Bush pitch out onto Grand Avenue for the last of his five career grand slams. However, Miller joined the club two days later and Williams was back to being mostly a spectator.

He did have his moments, though. On June 20 against Washington—Miller's second game with the Browns—Williams entered in the seventh inning as a pinch hitter for Wally

Gerber and socked a three-run home run off Walter Johnson to tie the game at 4. In the ninth, he was intentionally walked by Firpo Marberry to load the bases, and the next batter, Bobby LaMotte, singled to win the game. Then, in the first game of a June 26 double-header, his pinch-hit single in the top of the ninth in Chicago tied the game at 3, with St. Louis eventually winning 5–4.

But once Miller had arrived, Williams's starts were limited to exhibition games. On June 23, Williams went 1-for-3 with a double, steal and hit by pitch in a 3–2 win over the Massillon (Ohio) Agathons. Attendance was high at this game, with an estimated 4,000 showing up to Central Steel Field, no doubt not only to see a major-league team, but also Sisler, who grew up roughly 10 miles north in Manchester.

The crowd was much smaller in Canton, Ohio, on July 7 when the Browns beat the Canton Hooper Coals, 8–4, but Williams provided the 1,500 or so who turned out quite the memory by hitting two home runs. After the exhibition in Massillon, Sisler offered up his take on the Browns, who were in seventh place at 25–39 in his third year as manager.

"I had hopes of keeping this club well up in the race," he told the *Massillon Evening Independent*. "And we hope to finish much higher than we are now. The team is playing better ball now than at any time this season. When the campaign opened we were not getting any consistent hitting and the pitching was not good. And on top of this we ran into a bunch of injuries that forced our regulars out of the game. For a long time we never started two ball games with the same lineup. Better hitting will go a long way to pulling us up in the race."[24]

It took a couple of weeks after Sisler made that statement, but he finally made a move to bolster St. Louis's hitting. From June 17, when Jacobson was traded, to July 17, Cedric Durst, who had taken over as the starting center fielder, was hitting just .234 with a higher on-base percentage (.328) than slugging percentage (.327). His only home run during that span was in the game after Jacobson was traded.

On July 18 in New York against the Yankees, Durst was in Williams's place on the bench, his time as a starter all but over. Williams batted fourth and played left field, with Miller sliding over to center, where he hadn't played in over two years, his last appearance there coming on May 31, 1924.

Despite making his first start in a month and having only 10 plate appearances during that time, Williams cracked a two-run homer in the third inning off Sam Jones in a 4–0 win which "landed … in front of the exit gate."[25] That was the last batter Jones would face, but hardly the last chance for Williams.

He started the next two games as well, marking the first time Williams had started three consecutive games since May 11–June 4. He also had a hit in each game and stole his first base since May 21.

A trip to Boston was up next, and Sisler kept Williams in the lineup. In an opening-series double-header on July 21, Williams went 5-for-9. He doubled and tripled in the opener and had three hits in the second game, driving in two runs in each.

He had a hit the next day as well, but it was his glove that drew the most attention. In left field, Boston had a steep incline. With the score 5–4 in the bottom of the 11th inning and the tying run on second, Williams ended the game by running up the hill to catch a fly hit by Sy Rosenthal, then fell backwards and slid back downwards, all the while clinging onto the ball. In its headline for the win, the *St. Louis Globe Democrat* proclaimed, "Remarkable Catch Saves Game."[26]

In a 10-inning win the next day, Williams went 2-for-5 with a double and two runs scored as St. Louis won again. The Browns were 6–1 since Williams re-entered the lineup. "The failure of the Boston pitchers to stop this slugger was one of the reasons why the Browns have made a clean sweep of the series thus far," the *Globe Democrat* wrote. "Williams has also been playing a fine game in the field."[27]

The winning for St. Louis wouldn't keep up, but Williams's play would. In the final game of a fairly successful road trip (the team played .500 ball), he homered in Cleveland off Sherry Smith.

Back at home in St. Louis, the Yankees made amends for losing three of four in New York by sweeping the Browns, winning by a combined seven runs in four games. Williams, though, made a stellar catch in the opener, and later in the series added an RBI triple, which barely missed going over the fence, and a two-run home run.

On August 1, he drove in the eventual game-winning run with a single in the bottom of the eighth against Washington. Also in that game he hit a ball off the top of the right-field wall for a double. That was his second near-home run in a week (and he also hit one); Williams was finding his power stroke.

In the 58 games he played prior to his July 18 start, Williams had 16 extra-base hits—five doubles, three triples and eight home runs—for a .439 slugging percentage. In his 16 games since becoming a starter again, Williams already had 10 extra-base hits—five doubles, two triples and three home runs—for a .613 slugging percentage. He also was hitting .323 and had a .408 on-base percentage along with three stolen bases, 15 runs and 16 RBI.

Any confidence issues he might have had after being hit in the skull with a pitch the previous August appeared to be over. And to prove it, Williams would hit a home run in each of the next four games.

It started August 2 with a solo shot off Washington's Dutch Ruether. He followed that up with a two-run homer against General Crowder, the first four-bagger Crowder gave up in the big leagues. Philadelphia came to town next, and Williams took Jack Quinn deep with a two-run homer in the opener, and did the same against Rube Walberg the following day. The streak ended, as many did, against Lefty Grove.

Williams's power surge wasn't helping attendance, however (at least not for the Browns; the Cardinals, on their way to the National League pennant, were drawing record crowds). On August 10, for a game between the teams with the two worst records—the Browns and Red Sox—only 1,000 fans were in Sportsman's Park seats.

According to the *Globe Democrat*, Williams "drew the only cheer from the small crowd"[28] when he went back to the wall to catch a long fly off the bat of Wally Shaner. But he provided some other moments worthy of a holler, as well.

In the fourth inning, he ripped an RBI double. In the seventh, it as a "pretty catch of a long drive by Jacobson,"[29] and in the eighth he broke a 4–all tie with a two-run homer off Fred Heimach onto the right-field roof. The home run off Heimach meant three of his last five home runs and four of the last seven had been hit off left-handers.

St. Louis won the game 6–4, but would finish up at Sportsman's Park two days later with a 7–10 home stand, yet another reason for the poor crowds. There was no such problem in Cleveland, where the Indians were in second place. Over 25,000 turned out for a doubleheader on August 15.

In the opening game, the throng saw Williams throw out Garland Buckeye at home, trying to score from third on a pop single to shallow left field. Then in the eighth, Williams hurt Buckeye with his bat, hitting a solo home run. It was just one of three homers Buckeye—another left-hander—would allow in 1926 in 165⅔ innings (the other two were hit by future Hall of Famers Babe Ruth and Al Simmons).

Just a month and a half earlier Williams had been benched, with no indication whatsoever of ever returning to the lineup. Now he had 17 home runs on the season, which improbably were the second-most of anyone in the major leagues, behind just Ruth, who was well ahead of the pack with 39. And then, just as improbably, Williams was out of the lineup.

After the double-header in Cleveland (he had tripled in the second game), St. Louis headed to Boston for five games, including two double-headers, before going to New York. Williams went 2-for-7 in the first double-header, 0-for-7 in the next, and 1-for-4 in the series finale. Following an exhibition game against the Portland Eskimos, he started the opener in New York on August 20 and was 1-for-4 with a walk and a run. St. Louis made five errors in the 10–4 loss, but Williams didn't account for any.

Inexplicably, he would make just three starts the rest of the season. Perhaps the reason for benching Williams was his recent slump in Boston and, for one game, New York. The *Globe Democrat* even noted after Williams wasn't used as a substitute for an injured player in an August 24 game because he "played such a poor game in the preceding New York series that Sisler has benched him for a while."[30] He was, however, used as a pinch hitter later in that game.

Nonetheless, even with that six-game skid, from the time he regained his spot in the starting lineup Williams had raised his slash line from 263/327/439 to 278/347/511. In those 35 games, he had hit 301/376/617 with nine home runs, four steals, 27 runs and 34 RBI.

Another possibility for his benching was that Sisler didn't take too kindly to a comment Williams reportedly made in a game at Boston on August 17. Williams had a tough day, fouling out three times. On the final one, he threw his bat towards the bench—located right in front of Fenway Park's box seats. Umpire Bill McGowan warned Williams that such continued behavior could get him thrown out of the game. Williams felt the umpire was getting confrontational.

As reported by umpire Billy Evans in his syndicated column, McGowan said, "Nothing of the sort. I am just trying to explain to you an American League ruling."[31] To which Williams responded, "Well, can you imagine anything funnier than that. He insists on playing American League rules but we are not even in the league."[32]

Sisler could have heard these comments or, more likely, read them later in Evans's story, since he started Williams a couple of more games. But one can imagine the leader of the Browns wouldn't be too keen on one of his players insulting the team Sisler had guided to such a poor record.

Whatever the reasoning, even Williams's time as a pinch hitter was becoming more infrequent. He was used in back-to-back games August 23–24, then again in the second game of a double-header August 26. His fourth appearance came August 28, and while he didn't play August 30, he did manage to get thrown out of that game along with Sisler.

Once September hit, Williams mostly sat. He pinch-hit on September 2 but didn't play again until September 12, when he drew his first start in 21 days, batting fourth and going 0-for-1 with two walks. Even then, he started the second game of the double-header, but watched the first as Sisler used 37-year-old catcher Wally Schang in left field.

Williams would start only two more games: September 17 in Philadelphia, when he went 0-for-2 with two walks, a run and an RBI; and game 2 of a double-header in St. Louis against New York, going 3-for-5 with a triple.

The Browns closed the season with a double-header at home against the Yankees. Williams did not play in the opener and did not start the finale. However, late in the game, the few fans left at the park started hollering at Sisler to mix things up. They wanted the player/manager to pitch, and they wanted to see some of their favorites play. Sisler acquiesced.

One of the first things he did was put 46-year-old coach Jimmy Austin in at third base—and he went 1-for-2, doubling in a run, stealing a base and scoring. Sisler put himself on the mound for the final two innings—he pitched two scoreless innings, walking two and striking out three.

Finally, he had center fielder Harry Rice and shortstop Wally Gerber swap positions and called Williams off the bench to play second base, a position he hadn't played since his Western Canada League days. Williams didn't field a ball, and the circumstances almost had a farewell kind of feeling.

The season certainly didn't turn out the way the Browns or Williams thought it would. St. Louis finished in seventh place with a record of 62–92 and saw the Cardinals capture the city's attention by winning the pennant and the World Series.

Williams, of course, had his ups and downs in 1926. He had, for him, a down year. For most anyone else, hitting .280 with a .354 on-base percentage and .510 slugging percentage would be a call for a raise in salary.

Williams started out slow, undoubtedly in part trying to regain his confidence from being hit in the head. The numbers after he became a starter again in mid–July bear out that he did just that.

A Ken Williams 1926 Spalding Champions baseball card (courtesy Larry LaBeck).

Despite playing in just 108 games with 401 plate appearances, Williams was the only member of the Browns to reach double digits in home runs, and his slugging percentage was only topped by Schang (.516), who had fewer plate appearances (332) than Williams.

Williams finished tied for fourth in the AL in home runs and seventh in slugging percentage, although he was second behind only Ruth in at-bats per home run. In fact he was closer to Ruth than the third-place finisher was to him (Ruth was at 10.5 AB/HR, Williams 20.4 and Al Simmons was third at 30.7).

One publication that recognized Williams's hitting prowess as among the game's best was *Baseball Magazine*. In its June 1927 edition in which the monthly looked back at the 1926 season, it ranked hitters in order of average bases per hit. Ruth was first at 1.98 but Williams came in second at 1.82. The next four behind Williams were Lou Gehrig (1.75),

Jim Bottomley (1.69), Hack Wilson (1.67) and Tony Lazzeri (1.65), all of whom are Hall of Famers.

"It was generally thought Williams would suffer after being the victim of a bean ball," author William Lindsey wrote. "Although not a regular the past season, Williams remains a powerful slugger."[33] In its September 1927 edition, *Baseball Magazine* took its statistical look even further.

Writer C.H. Dorey came up with a stat he called run-making average (RBI+R—HR/AB) and provided results combining the 1925 and '26 seasons. Williams came in fifth in this stat at .363. The top four would all be future Hall of Famers—Ty Cobb (.452), Ruth (.409), Rogers Hornsby (.403) and Harry Heilmann (.373).

Colleague J. Newton Colver set out to determine both the greatest hitter and hardest hitter to that point in baseball history, with a minimum of 10 years' experience. Williams ended up ranked high on both lists.

To determine the hardest hitter, Colver used an interesting mix of three criteria: total bases to games played, average total bases per each hit, and all-time batting records held (these "records" could be anything Colver deemed relevant).

In Colver's rankings, Williams finished tied for second with Hornsby. Ruth, to no one's surprise, was first. Ed Delahanty was fourth and Shoeless Joe Jackson fifth. Hornsby, Ruth and Delahanty are all in the Hall of Fame, and Jackson no doubt would be if eligible.

In the opinion of Amos Rusie, a future Hall of Famer who won 246 games pitching mainly in the 19th century, Williams was not out of place in that grouping. "Not much surprise will be occasioned, probably, by the presence of Kenneth Williams and Hornsby's name up there," Colver wrote. "Rusie had no idea what a tabulation like this would show but he freely declares Ruth, Williams and Hornsby could hit the ball every bit as hard—and probably a bit harder—than any other great hitters that ever lived."[34]

For naming the greatest batter of all time, Colver had nine categories: batting average, points over league average (he was way ahead of his time on this one), percent of years hitting above .300, percent of years hitting above .400, percent of years leading the league, total bases to each hit, total bases to games played and records in slugging and batting.

Colver's figures showed Williams with a .320 batting average, 48 points above league average, batting over .300 70 percent of the time, 1.710 total bases/hit, 1.98 total bases/game and six records owned.

Williams didn't place as high on the all-time greatest hitter list, but he did finish 13th with the names above him a veritable who's who of Hall of Famers: Hornsby, Cobb, Ruth, Jackson, Dan Brouthers, Delahanty, Cap Anson, Tris Speaker, George Sisler, Pete Browning, Honus Wagner and Sam Thompson.

The accolades certainly show that Williams ranked among the game's all-time greats through the 1926 season. But now it was time to turn the page to 1927. The upcoming off-season would be full of rumors, and not just about where Williams would be playing. But first, if he indeed was going to remain in St. Louis, Williams would once again be playing for a new manager.

Chapter 14

Battling for Playing Time

The St. Louis Browns' 1926 season ended September 26. George Sisler's tenure as manager would last just two more weeks. There were whispers, as usual, of a change. Donie Bush, Roger Peckinpaugh and others were mentioned as a possible Browns skipper a week and half before Sisler was officially let go.

Things couldn't have gone much worse for Sisler as manager. Two out of his three years the team finished under .500, including winning only 62 games in '26. Not helping his cause was his own scouting ability. The players Sisler brought in were of little or no help. Second baseman Oscar Melillo hit just .255. Leo Dixon was a failure at catcher, hitting even worse than expected at .191 with a .247 slugging percentage in 33 games. The pitching was worse still. Joe Giard regressed to 3–10 with a 7.00 ERA. Win Ballou, who Sisler insisted St. Louis get in a trade with Washington, did win 11 games, but had an ERA of 4.79. Ernie Nevers (2–4, 4.46) and Chet Falk (4–4, 5.35) were no better, while waiver claim Charlie Robertson (1–2, 8.36) was at the end of the line.

On top of all that, he didn't have the respect of the players in terms of his managerial ability. Sisler and Marty McManus reportedly clashed, and he was chastised for his treatment of Williams as well as his lack of help when hitters, including Williams, had difficulties or slumps.

On October 11, the day after the St. Louis Cardinals won the World Series, the inevitable became official as the Browns announced Sisler would not return as manager. The Browns reportedly had 10 candidates, but focused on Dan Howley, who had never managed in the majors but who led the Toronto Maple Leafs to the International League pennant in 1926.

Howley had other suitors. The Red Sox, who dumped Lee Fohl after three ignominious years, were one. The Tigers saw Ty Cobb leave after resigning due to a gambling scandal (although that part was kept under wraps from the public) and were purported to be another possible landing spot, as Howley had once coached in Detroit. But as it turned out, the news of Cobb's resignation was made public on the same day the Browns announced they had hired Howley, giving him a three-year contract.

With a new manager, especially one from outside the organization, comes new thinking. Browns owner Phil Ball gave Howley free reign to set the roster as he liked—although Ball did note he had veto power. It was quickly reported that "the Browns are planning a wholesale shakeup."[1]

For Ken Williams, this had to be a time of uncertainty. Before Howley had been hired, there was a report that regardless of who was managing the Browns, Williams was going to be ticketed for the minors.

Returning from the minor-league meetings in Asheville, North Carolina, in early December, Howley sent notice of his intentions with the Browns. "I've got to shake up the club, I believe, to get it going on the right foot the team needs new blood,"[2] he proclaimed.

The Browns had some outfield depth and had acquired Fred Schulte (who was listed at 22, but, like Williams, was actually three years older than his accepted age) from Milwaukee of the American Association the previous August, so it didn't take long after Howley's statement for Williams's name to make it into the rumor mill.

Like Cobb in Detroit, Tris Speaker resigned from his post with Cleveland. The Indians were in the market for an outfielder. "Williams would be a logical successor to Speaker," theorized the *St. Louis Globe Democrat*, "as the Moose is a good outfielder, has a strong arm and possesses, when in a mood, a left-hand punch."[3]

The Browns, as always, were in the search of pitching. In fact, Howley had stated directly that was the club's biggest weakness. No one would argue that point, as St. Louis had a 4.66 ERA in 1926, second-worst in the American League, and walked 654 batters, nearly 100 more than any other club in the majors.

It was thought that the Browns might be interested in Emil Levsen, Jake Miller or Joe Shaute, but Howley zeroed in on Levsen, who was 16–13 with a 3.41 in his first full season in the majors in 1926, at the age of 28.

However, new manager Jack McAllister was hesitant to tinker too much with a Cleveland roster that was coming off a second-place finish. McAllister said the Indians would be happy to purchase Williams, but as far as trading one of his pitchers, that wasn't going to happen.

"No, I am going to stand pat on my regulars," McAllister said in mid–December while traveling through Chicago. "Williams might do us some good, but I do not want to alter the team that all but won the pennant this year. Guess you understand my position. I think we have a pretty good ball club as it is."[4]

Cleveland would end up winning just 66 games and finishing in sixth place. The Indians' outfielders all were average or worse in 1927, while Levsen could not repeat his previous year's success either, going 3–7 with a 5.49 ERA. He'd pitch in just 11 games in 1928, failing to win a game in three decisions and posting a 5.44 ERA, and wouldn't appear in the major leagues again.

While the rumor mill kept spinning, Howley finally made a trade on January 15, 1927, sending Marty McManus to Detroit. Catcher Bill Hargrave and shortstop Bobby LaMotte were also included in the deal, but they were to report to Toronto. In return, the Browns got a few of Howley's former Maple Leaf players—third baseman Billy Mullen (a St. Louis native who had a cup of coffee with the Browns in 1920 and 1921), shortstop Otis Miller and pitcher Walter "Lefty" Stewart, along with Tigers third baseman Frank O'Rourke.

One club Howley and the Browns had been talking to for some time was the Yankees, and once again Williams' name was being brought up. The discussions began before the winter meetings, then lasted through the gathering and beyond. The parameters of the deal seemed to be the Browns acquiring three pitchers—likely Walter Beall, Sam Jones and Myles Thomas—while giving up Williams, Cedric Durst and Joe Giard.

However, with the talks still going on in late January, Howley changed his tune. "I cannot afford to let loose of Williams before I find out how Schulte stacks up,"[5] the new Browns skipper said. "We need all the batting punch we can get, and if Williams returns to his form of a couple of seasons back he will supply much of that punch." But then Ty Cobb changed all of that in a hurry.

◆ ◆ ◆

Ty Cobb had been a thorn in the Browns' side at the beginning of 1927, but by the end of January, St. Louis was hoping Cobb would be wearing its uniform in the upcoming season.

It started when Cobb—and Tris Speaker—resigned from their posts as managers after a gambling scandal was brought to light. Gambling had been a problem in baseball since the beginning of the game, and the 1919 World Series shed the brightest light on the issue. In this instance, the pair of the game's greats had been accused by pitcher Dutch Leonard of betting and fixing a game late in the 1919 season.

Perhaps to deflect from the accusations against him (as Johnny Tobin would theorize), in early January 1927, Cobb told Bert Walker of the *Detroit Times* that the Browns helped the Tigers win games at the end of the 1923 season and thus secure Detroit second place over Cleveland. This would give Tigers players a larger cut of the playoff money than if they had finished in third. In those games, the Browns lost 9–1, 12–3 and 7–6, the last of which the Tigers won in the bottom of the ninth inning.

Among the players Cobb listed as being complicit was Williams, who was 6-for-11 in the three-game series. When contacted by wire by the *St. Louis Globe Democrat* about the accusation, Williams replied, "Your wire a complete surprise to me. I know absolutely nothing regarding the games mentioned."[6]

Other players also came out and said they had no idea what Cobb was talking about. McManus said the Browns were still angry with the Tigers for losing three straight one-run games to the Yankees after New York won two of three in St. Louis at the tail end of the 1922 season.

"As far as I know, the Browns have always fought to win," said the recently traded McManus. "I say that Cobb lies. The Browns always battled hardest against the Detroit club, because if there is one thing the Browns liked to do it was beat the team managed by Cobb."[7]

Cobb would eventually deny making those comments to Walker, while the reporter continued to reaffirm the opposite, saying they were spoken when the pair drove together from Chicago to Augusta, Georgia. Amazingly, the controversy just drifted away and was quickly forgotten—especially in St. Louis when the Browns had a chance to sign Cobb.

Just days after Howley said he wouldn't trade Williams, Commissioner Judge Kenesaw Landis ruled that Cobb and Speaker were exonerated of the gambling fix charges, but were placed on the reserve list of their teams—yet could negotiate with other teams, without the signing team having to give the Tigers or Indians compensation. Basically, the pair were free agents. It didn't take long for Speaker to find a job, signing on January 31 with the Washington Senators.

The Browns also moved quickly in their pursuit of Cobb. The team originally had thought it might have a clean shot at Cobb. Before Landis's ruling, it was believed the players would have to pass through waivers. The American League would have first bidding and Boston, which had the first option of a claim, already said it would pass on Cobb. The Browns would be next after the Red Sox and planned to put in a claim. Landis's ruling foiled that.

Nevertheless, the Browns were believed to be the frontrunner for Cobb. Howley was purported to be good friends with the outfielder. Also, not only had Howley coached the Tigers, but also when he managed in Toronto, he and Cobb arranged for exhibitions between their two clubs each season.

"Cobb has done more for me in baseball than any one man in the game," Howley said. "He is one of the best friends I have and I believe the Browns will sign him to a contract if suitable arrangements are made."[8] The addition of Cobb would necessitate the subtraction of a Browns outfielder, namely Williams.

It was reported if and when the Browns signed Cobb, St. Louis would likely ship Williams to the Yankees. A trade of Williams and Ernie Nevers for Jones and Beall was mentioned. Yankees manager Miller Huggins claimed a trade had nearly been consummated, a charge the Browns heavily denied.

"As far as Williams and Nevers are concerned, we have never mentioned their names in connection with a deal with the Yankees and under no consideration will we consider this fellow pitcher Beall in any trade we possibly make with the American League champions,"[9] Browns business manager Bill Friel said.

Of course, first the Browns had to actually convince Cobb to sign with them. They set out to do that right from the start. The day after Landis's ruling, owner Phil Ball wired Cobb. Howley did not hide the fact he wanted Cobb on his team. He postponed a trip to check out the Browns' spring training site at Tarpon Springs, Florida, to visit—and negotiate—with Cobb, who was on a hunting trip.

Despite saying the Browns were one of five teams vying for Cobb, Howley was confident enough in his bid that he went to New York to negotiate a trade with the Yankees. However, in the end, money talked (as it does now as well), and Cobb chose to sign with the Philadelphia A's, who offered a more lucrative contract than the Browns.

After Cobb signed, Friel admitted Williams would have been on the block and likely traded to the Yankees. St. Louis did end up making a trade with New York, sending Durst and Giard for Jones. Williams was staying put, albeit at a pay cut. He'd make $7,500 in 1927, $2,000 less than his previous contract.

◆ ◆ ◆

Williams was one of the last few players to arrive at spring training camp—word was he had missed a train connection along the way—but when he stepped foot in Tarpon Springs, he, as usual, looked to be in the same playing condition as he was in the final game of the 1926 season—or, really, any year.

He was also one of the final connections to the pennant-chasing team of just five years earlier. Only Williams, George Sisler—who re-signed with the team despite losing his job as manager—and pitcher Elam Vangilder remained from that 1922 season.

Williams's outfield mates had already been shipped away, as had catcher Hank Severeid. Marty McManus was dealt in the offseason, and Dixie Davis became the latest pitcher to depart when he was sold to the Kansas City Blues of the American Association.

One thing is clear—St. Louis wasn't replacing those former players with much power. Some members of the Browns had been in camp for nearly two weeks before Williams's arrival. Yet it was Williams who was the first to hit a ball over the fence. That still wasn't enough to impress his new manager, it appears.

As exhibition games got underway, Williams was not finding his name in the lineup card. In St. Louis's first seven games against major- and minor-league teams, Williams was used only as a pinch hitter, and that occurred in only two games.

On March 21, Williams got his first start, but was replaced in the fifth inning by Bing Miller on a double switch. It went like this for the rest of spring training, with Williams usually starting and Miller taking over sometime in midgame (Miller did make one start with Williams subbing in), with the exception of the March 25 and March 30 games, when Williams played the entire nine innings.

It was unclear who would start in left field when the season began—Williams or Miller. Howley was impressed with newcomer Fred Schulte and was going to start him in center field with Harry Rice in right. The two-game series at Sportsman's Park against the Cardinals didn't offer much enlightenment, as Williams played one game and Miller the other.

It would be a few days before either outfielder would find out. Rain doused St. Louis, causing the postponement of three attempts at opening day. On April 15, the Browns finally met the Tigers in the first game of the season (although it would be stopped short after five innings with the score tied at 2 due to another deluge of rain) and Miller was starting in left field against Detroit left-hander Earl Whitehill.

Williams started the next day, going 1-for-2 with an RBI in helping Howley to his first-major league victory, a 3–1 win over Chicago. But the manager brought in Miller to hit for Williams after the White Sox put lefty Bert Cole on the mound late in the game.

On Easter Sunday, April 17, Williams was back in left field, where he made one of eight Browns errors against the White Sox, dropping a fly ball in the second inning. He also threw out a runner trying to go to third base on a single in the fifth. But he made his biggest mark in the eighth, breaking a 3–all tie with a home run off Tommy Thomas. Unfortunately for the Browns, they made four of their errors in the ninth and allowed nine runs, losing 12–5.

If it appeared Howley was going with a platoon system in left field—Chicago's Thomas was right-handed—but that notion was quickly halted the next day. Despite having hit what was at the time a pivotal home run in the previous game, Williams was out of the lineup and Miller in against the White Sox's Ted Blankenship—a righty—on April 18.

St. Louis's next two games were against left-handers in Detroit, Whitehill and Cole, so Miller got the nod. But Miller also started in the following two games against the Tigers' Sam Gibson and Cleveland's Emil Levsen, both right-handers.

Williams would get back into the starting lineup on April 26 and the lefty-righty platoon was back in vogue, as he played in 13 of the next 15 games, including 10 starts. Williams wasn't really making a case for himself to be in the lineup, though. He'd make the occasional fantastic catch, but he was hitting just 234/308/319 with only two extra-base hits. Along with his earlier home run, he had doubled in two runs in a 16–9 loss in Washington on May 7.

But then came an unexpected opportunity. Schulte injured his right leg, which had been bothering him for a few days, trying to run out a grounder on May 14 against Philadelphia in the first game of a home stand. St. Louis was carrying two backup outfielders—Williams and Herschel Bennett, both of whom batted left-handed. While Williams might have been stuck wanting more starts, Bennett was still looking for his first. He had played in only 10 games to date, all in a reserve role. It wasn't a difficult decision for Howley. Williams was the choice to replace Shulte in the lineup. Bennett would have to wait until June 30 to get his first start.

Williams batted sixth, the spot Schulte had been occupying, against lefty Rube Walberg of Philadelphia on May 15. While he went 0-for-1, Williams did walk three times, including one to load the bases one batter before Wally Schang hit a grand slam. Williams had now appeared in back-to-back games for the Browns with four plate appearances in each. That was the tune-up he apparently needed for regular play.

Williams would put together a 10-game hitting streak, with multiple hits in seven of those contests, including the first six. By the end of the streak, his average would be up to .376, along with a .465 on-base percentage and .659 slugging percentage.

When he started the streak, Williams had just the two extra-base hits. On May 16, he started his hitting tear with four hits, including two doubles off Jack Quinn and a home run against Sam Gray in a 10–8 loss to Philadelphia.

Williams drove in three runs that game and repeated the feat the next day when he went 2-for-3. Boston came into town next, and Williams kept it going, tripling and hitting a home run off Red Ruffing. The next day it was two more hits, including a home run onto the right-field roof off Slim Harriss to win the game in the bottom of the 10th inning.

Schulte's misfortune was turning into a boon for Williams—and the Browns. In the last four games, Williams was 10-for-16 with two doubles, a triple, three home runs, seven runs and nine RBI. Bing Miller was hitting .446 on May 18 to lead the American League (an 0-for-4 on May 19 brought him down to .423), thus the chances of Williams' getting into the lineup without Schulte's injury would have been unlikely. The Browns had also won three of the four and moved into a tie for third place in the American League.

After being idle for a day, the Browns won their fourth straight game on May 21, 7–4 over Boston. The entire St. Louis outfield—as well as former Brown Johnny Tobin, now patrolling right field for the Red Sox—had three hits. Williams also scored twice and drove in two.

However, the biggest cheer of the game came after the top of the fourth inning, when St. Louis's megaphone announcer told all at Sportsman's Park that Charles Lindbergh had landed in Paris after 33½ hours of flight in his plane, *Spirit of St. Louis*. That news garnered the first four pages of the *St. Louis Globe Democrat*, as well as page six and parts of page 10. The Browns back in third place (they had dropped to fourth on their day off) was the lead sports story—on page 11.

While Lindbergh was the toast of the town and nation, Williams and the Browns kept making their less significant news. In St. Louis's May 22 6–5 win over the Red Sox, its fifth straight victory, while Miller and Rice went hitless, Williams had his sixth straight multi-hit game, including a two-run homer onto Grand Avenue off Danny MacFayden in the fourth inning. He also "made two fine catches in left, on Tobin's low liner in the first and Flagstead's long liner in the ninth."[10] St. Louis's winning streak came to an end the following day as the Browns were three-hit by Tommy Thomas, but Williams had a hit and two walks, and scored the lone run in the 4–1 loss.

Chicago had St. Louis's number and took a double-header from the Browns on May 25, although Williams went 3-for-4 with a home run over the right-field roof in the opener and had one of five St. Louis hits in the second game.

The Browns lost both games of a double-header to Cleveland the following day and

Williams's hit streak ended at 10 in the second game, although he did score a run and steal a base. In those 10 games, Williams was 21-for-37 (.568) with 12 runs, 15 RBI and nine extra-base hits, including five home runs. Only one other Browns player would hit more than five home runs *all season*.

St. Louis ended its home stand by losing two of three with Cleveland, including splitting another double-header (Williams had two hits in both games). The Browns were struggling, finishing the home stand with a 12–13 record and dropping to sixth place, but Williams was not. His place in the lineup seemed secure, especially after he went 4-for-8 in Chicago in a double-header split against the White Sox on Memorial Day. Williams was now batting .370.

However, he went 0-for-2 the next day in Chicago and hitless in three at-bats in St. Louis's next game, June 2 at Washington. Schulte, who had appeared in just nine games—all as a pinch hitter—since he reinjured his leg was back in the lineup June 3.

Since Miller was still hitting over .400, and Howley apparently wanted Schulte in center and Rice (batting .293, 60 points lower than Williams) in right, Williams was the odd man out once again.

For the next three weeks, there wasn't much excitement on the field for Williams. The most notable occurrences would have been watching teammate Milt Gaston run into the stands in Philadelphia and punch a fan on June 7. This was also the next game Williams "appeared" in; he was called into pinch hit, but then was replaced when the A's changed pitchers. Also, there was a 25-minute delay in New York on June 16 for the arrival of Lindbergh, who would eventually see Williams stride to the plate to pinch-hit in the ninth inning when he grounded out to end the game.

While Williams was flourishing as an everyday starter, pinch hitting was not agreeing with him. He failed in his first five pinch-hit appearances before singling for Oscar Melillo in the second game of a double-header in Chicago on June 22.

On June 23, after 14 straight games on the bench, Williams replaced Miller in the lineup and even batted fourth—Miller's regular spot—for the first time since May 13. Despite a 2-for-2 game with a walk in the shortened six-inning game, Williams didn't get back-to-back starts until June 30–July 1, his first consecutive starts in a month.

In the July 1 game he went 4-for-5 with two doubles, three runs and three RBI, which perhaps earned Williams a third consecutive start. He had an RBI double in a loss to the White Sox, but got a fourth straight start and hammered out four hits including two home runs off the White Sox's Ted Blankenship in front of a smaller-than-usual Saturday crowd at Sportsman's Park. And then ... back to the bench.

Howley had been using Williams along with Rice in center and Herschel Bennett in right. Rice was not a natural center fielder, so Howley put Schulte back in the lineup, moved Rice over to his normal right field spot, and kept Bennett in the lineup in left.

That threesome didn't last long. On July 6, Schulte ran into the concrete left-field wall in Sportsman's Park face first while chasing a long fly ball off the bat of Detroit's Jack Warner in the eighth inning. Schulte was knocked unconscious and wouldn't wake up until later in the Detroit clubhouse. It was reported that he had a concussion, a fractured rib, a fractured wrist and a broken forearm. Needless to say, he was done for the season (although amazingly—and inexplicably—he would appear in one game, on August 17).

Schulte's injury didn't rush Williams into the lineup this time. But after two more games—and six in total after starting those four straight—Williams was back in the lineup once again on July 9, although in center field, where he hadn't played since coming in as a late replacement in a September 19, 1926, game. Williams hadn't started in center field in nearly five years, since a stretch back in August 1922.

The experiment only lasted three games—it didn't have to do with his hitting, as in Williams's third game he hit a two-run home run—but that didn't mean his time as a starter was done, either.

In fact, while he was moved back to left field, he also was bumped up in the order to the cleanup spot. Williams would remain batting fourth for the rest of the season, with a few exceptions: he batted third once when Sisler was out and fifth against left-hander Tom Zachary. The latter was a rare case, as Howley had taken to sitting Williams against some southpaws, no matter how he had been hitting.

In a late July series against the Senators at Sportsman's Park, Williams went 8-for-18 in the first five games, which included two double-headers. In one, he notched the first hit for St. Louis with a home run off Bump Hadley (who allowed only two homers in 198⅔ innings in 1927). But with Zachary on the mound in the finale of the home stand, Williams sat. The Browns went just 11–15–1 in their long stay at Sportsman's Park, then followed that up with a putrid 3–11 road trip, dropping to seventh place.

St. Louis returned home and found itself playing in front of sparse crowds. A Saturday game on August 20 against Boston had fewer than 2,000 fans. A series against Philadelphia included estimated attendances of 1,200 and 500.

The Yankees were coming to town with their "Murderer's Row" led by Babe Ruth and Lou Gehrig, both of whom entered St. Louis with 40 home runs, and the Browns saw an uptick of 5,000 fans for a Saturday game and 14,000 on Sunday. An increased attendance, but it still made Sportsman's Park seem empty thanks to the additional seating installed the previous year.

While the St. Louis crowd saw both Ruth and Gehrig homer in the series, they also witnessed Williams begin a bit of a hot streak. Against the Yankees, Williams went 4-for-12, including a home run—his first since August 6 in Philadelphia—out onto the street off left-hander Dutch Ruether, although the Browns were once against swept by New York, whose winning streak against St. Louis reached 12 games.

He also took part in two double plays in the August 28 game. On his first, he raced to catch a Ruether foul ball, then whipped the ball home to nail Benny Bengough. "Ken's throw was so perfect that Bengough was out [by] 15 feet,"[11] reported the *Globe Democrat.*

Detroit came to town next and Williams hit the ball all over the park. He was 8-for-21 (.381) with a double, triple and three home runs (a .952 slugging percentage). "Ken Williams' home run bat of the past week has stirred up memories of half a decade ago when the Moose was breaking bull's eye records at the North Grand shooting gallery,"[12] observed the *Globe Democrat.*

In the first game of a double-header in Cleveland the next day, he had his fourth straight two-hit game, and also homered for the fifth time in nine games. It would be the first home run Willis Hudlin allowed all season, and the only one at home (overall, he would allow three in 264⅔ innings). Dunn Field was not an easy place to hit one over the fence. Only 21 homers would be hit there all season, 11 by the opposition.

He'd double in the next two games, missing his second home run at Dunn Field on one of those by a foot. In the first game of a series at Yankee Stadium he made it eight consecutive games with an extra-base hit (and nine of 10, and 10 of 12) by accounting for the Browns' only run with a "lofty clout into the right-field bleachers."[13]

Perhaps it was because New York kept on beating the Browns, but on two occasions Yankee fans took to cheering Williams on plays that resulted in the home team's being retired. On September 9, the same day his extra-base hit streak ended, he "earned a great hand from the crowd by disposing of Benny Bengough in the third inning through a brilliant running one-handed catch in deep left."[14]

Then on September 11, Williams "brought down the house"[15] with a running, outstretched, one-handed catch of a Ruth long fly. The Browns actually won, 6–2, to end New York's 21-game winning streak over them (a major-league record against one team).

The Browns left New York 40 games out of first place, buried in seventh place, five games behind sixth-place Cleveland with the season dwindling down.

Williams would play all four games in Boston, where the only team with a worse record than St. Louis would win three of four, and all five games in Philadelphia, with the Browns earning just one victory.

Washington was next, and Williams would start the first two games—he'd witness Walter Johnson's final major-league home run in the second contest, as well as inexplicably switch positions with center fielder Herschel Bennett midway through the game.

Bennett would start the next two games in Washington, and it looked as though Williams's time might have been done. Howley said he was going to start some younger players in St. Louis's final home stand to end the season.

While Howley did use players such as first baseman Guy Sturdy, second baseman Buster Adams and shortstop Red Kress, he put Williams back in left field for the final five games.

Williams closed out the season with a hit in each game, including three in the finale. He tripled in that game—his only extra-base hit in those five contests—but when he tried to take advantage of Chicago starting pitcher Frank Stewart, who was making his only major-league appearance, by trying to steal home, he was cut down.

Nevertheless, that final burst—he went 8-for-18—raised his average six points to .322 and his on-base percentage to over .400 at .403. Despite not homering in the final three weeks (his last was September 8 in New York), Williams finished with 17 home runs, or nearly one-third of the 55 the entire Browns team hit for the season (Harry Rice was second on the team with seven), which was good enough for fourth in the American League.

Williams was also third in home runs per at-bat, behind just Ruth and Gehrig, fifth in slugging percentage (.525) and 10th in on-base percentage. Not bad for someone who in June had turned 37, in an era when the majority of players that age were out of baseball or finishing up their careers in the minor leagues.

Williams did a little barnstorming with a team organized by teammate Herschel Bennett—although Williams might have managed the club as well, according to one newspaper report. Among the players on the team were Detroit's Charlie Gehringer and Marty McManus, the former an ex-Brown, Cleveland's Homer Summa and Browns teammates Bennett, Ernie Wingard and Elam Vangilder.

The group was working its way west, playing in towns in Iowa (including a stop at the Iowa state penitentiary) and Kansas, but Williams had to leave the squad earlier than expected due to what was dubbed "an illness in his family."[16]

Back at Grants Pass, no doubt the conversation turned to his future with the Browns, as it didn't take long for St. Louis to start turning over its ballclub. On October 19, St. Louis added outfielder Earl McNeely, who had hit over .300 in two of his four seasons with Washington. A few weeks later, Bennett and Wingard were sold to Milwaukee of the American Association, ending their days as major leaguers.

The rumor mill was heating up as well. Owner Phil Ball was putting out "feelers"[17] on longtime first baseman George Sisler. In Philadelphia, it was reported that a trade of Bing Miller or Ken Williams to the A's was likely to be consummated shortly, with infielder Chick Galloway and a pitcher, either Ed Rommel or Sammy Gray, headed to St. Louis.

Browns business manager Bill Friel quickly discounted the report, saying, "I haven't heard a thing about any such deal. There may be a swap engineered, but I am not familiar with it or any of its details."[18]

Williams's name had come up over the years in trade rumors, but this time it appeared as though his time with the Browns was coming to an end. That was solidified by comments from manager Dan Howley prior to the winter meetings.

When asked if the Browns were going to make a lot of trades, Howley responded, "We must do it. We're going to bat with a young club next spring and we're going to get the makings this winter."[19]

Regardless of using his true age or the lie he perpetuated during his baseball career, Williams did not fit into any kind of youth movement. Howley's early thought of an outfield was McNeely, who turned 30 in May, Fred Schulte, thought to be 24 but really 27, and Harry Rice, 26.

At the winter meetings in New York, Yankees manager Miller Huggins said he wanted to strengthen his team's outfield, and Williams's name came up, although Huggins denied he was after the Browns left fielder.

The dominoes for the Browns started falling December 13. Bing Miller—and not Williams—was indeed dealt to Philadelphia for Sam Gray. The same day, St. Louis also sent Rice and Elam Vangilder to Detroit for outfielder Heine Manush and first baseman Lu Blue. The arrival of Blue meant one thing—Sisler was on the way out, and indeed he was sold to Washington the following day for $25,000.

There was only one member of the 1922 Browns team left on the St. Louis roster, but not for long. On December 15, the phone rang at Ken Williams's home at North 5th Street in Grants Pass. It was someone from the local paper, the *Courier*. Had he heard the news? He had been traded.

Chapter 15

Goodbye St. Louis, Hello ... Boston?

The fact the St. Louis Browns traded Ken Williams on December 15, 1927, came as little surprise. The team had been making a number of deals in an effort to shake up the team and get younger. No, it was where Williams was sent that was the shock.

Over the years, several teams had shown an interest in Williams, including the Yankees and Indians. With Williams on the block, the demand was again high. The Browns received numerous offers, but one team decided to pony up cash—$10,000, to be exact—and not players. That, in the end, was the biggest factor in St. Louis sending Williams to, of all teams, the Boston Red Sox, the only team which had a worse record than the Browns in 1927.

Since Williams started playing for St. Louis on a regular basis in 1919, Boston had never finished higher than fifth place and posted a losing record each year (the Red Sox's best mark in that span was 75–79 in 1921). "Being sent from the Browns to the Redsox [*sic*] is like being compelled to do a high dive from the frying pan into the fire,"[1] wrote the *Pittsburgh Press*.

Red Sox magnate Bob Quinn was more than familiar with Williams and, like other teams, had been trying to pry the outfielder loose from the Browns for years. But Quinn had also been spouting a mantra of "build with youth."[2] Even with his disguised age of 34 (35 in June), Williams did not fit that bill.

The *Chester Times* noted the Red Sox outfield, as currently constructed, consisted of graybeards Williams, Ira Flagstead (35 in September) and Johnny Tobin (36 in May, although he would be released before spring training).

Nevertheless, Flagstead and Tobin were the top-two hitters from the previous Boston team, albeit one which was on the winning side of the ledger just 51 times. Flagstead's four home runs were second on the team (Phil Todt had six). As a club, the Red Sox were last in the American League in 1927 in batting average (.259), on-base percentage (.320) and slugging percentage (.357) and second-to-last in home runs (28).

"Williams will give the Red Sox an added punch which they sadly need," wrote the *Boston Globe*, "to say nothing of what a big improvement he will make in the outfield."[3] It was an assertion the paper would continue to make.

Williams, at age 37, was certainly on the downside of his career, but he definitely made his mark in St. Louis. In 10 seasons with the Browns (including the two games he played in 1918), Williams had a .326 average, which is the second-highest in St. Louis Browns/Baltimore Orioles franchise history among players with at least 2,000 plate appearances. His .403 on-base percentage is tops in franchise history (minimum 2,000 plate appearances). Hall of Famer Goose Goslin, who only played three seasons with the Browns, had a .404 OBP in

1,798 PA. Next on the list behind Williams are two more Hall of Famers, Frank Robinson (.401 in 3,492 PA) and Heinie Manush (.399/1,542).

Williams's .548 slugging percentage and .961 OPS (on base + slugging) are 10 points higher than anyone else in franchise history (Goslin is second at .548 and .951, Robinson third at .543 and .944).

Through the 2015 season, Williams ranked 6th in franchise history RBI (811) and 10th in runs (757) and total bases (2,239) despite having more than 1,000 fewer plate appearances than anyone else in the top 10.

One record Williams will never relinquish is being the all-time leader in home runs in Browns history. His 185 homers with St. Louis are 15 more than Harlond Clift (who also had roughly 1,300 more plate appearances) and also 9th all-time on the franchise list through 2016. "Williams was one of the most popular outfielders the Browns have had in recent years,"[4] wrote Alan W. Price of the *St. Louis Globe Democrat*.

Informed of the trade by the *Grants Pass Courier*, Williams wasn't quoted, but the paper mentioned that he "asserted today that he knows he has several years left in the main show and that the change which has been affected probably will be to his benefit."[5]

That thinking was echoed elsewhere. The *New York Sun*'s John B. Foster, who had a syndicated column, was especially bullish on Boston's addition of Williams:

> Boston lost between 10 and 20 games in 1927—perhaps even 20 is too small a number—because the outfield could not bat well with men on bases. If Williams can bat as well as he did for St. Louis, he will be dynamite for Boston, which has had previous little explosive[ness] in the outfield.
>
> If the presence of Williams can win 20 more games for Boston in 1928, the team will have about 70 victories. That will mean its rise to the top of the second division or close to it. To expect 20 victories by the ascension of a hard hitting outfielder may be expecting too much but the change of one player frequently will tip the baseball scales in a most unaccountable manner.[6]

The Sporting News saw many reasons why Williams should be happy going to his new locale. "For one thing, Ken will find the Boston climate more conducive to hustling all the time than the heat and humidity of St. Louis during the height of the season," reasoned the weekly.

"In the second place, he will not be bothered by the background of many disputes and differences of opinion. Thirdly, he will find the Boston crowd friendly to him and patient with him whatever shortcomings he may show."[7]

American League publicity directory Henry Edwards, recalling the contract controversy between Williams, Boston and Sacramento in 1911, would remark, "Finally after those 17 years he landed with the Red Sox."[8]

Quinn reconnected with Williams in late January with a letter to his Grants Pass home, likely offering similar platitudes. He also included a contract with a salary calling for Williams to make $9,500, a $2,000 raise from 1927 and the same amount he earned in his more prodigious days in St. Louis.

Williams took very little time in returning a letter to Quinn—as well as the signed contract. The *Boston Globe* reprinted a portion of Williams's reply:

> Received the contract four or five minutes ago, and surely appreciate the way you spoke. I gave the Browns all I had but I still think there is more than one good year left in me and it will suit me to give them to you.
>
> I sure will do my best, and I only hope that it will be enough to help the club up several notches. In the last few days I have read of a few changes in the Red Sox, and it looks to me as if we should not finish at the bottom again.

> Sent my boy to his first school this morning, so he will be able to pinch hit for someone this year, but not for me, because I am going to do my own hitting. Hope I can do there as good as you expect. I surely will try.[9]

Contract out of the way, Williams spent the next few weeks relaxing in Oregon at his house on North 5th Street before making his way to Red Sox spring training in Bradenton, Florida. And he made the trek via automobile, which was quite the feat in 1928. The Associated Press reported the ride was over 3,800 miles (using modern-day highways it is around 3,100–3,200 miles). Making the drive with his wife and 4-year-old son, Ken Jr., Williams completed the trip in 10 days—two fewer than was anticipated.

While Ken Jr. was with his mother back at the hotel—and asking anyone who would listen if they would take him fishing—his father went to the ballpark armed with three bats, including one he called "Old Ironsides," and just like his spring training time with the Browns, he started putting balls over the fence on Day 1.

Whether it was being back on the field, the 70-degree warmth or the feeling of starting fresh with a new ballclub, Williams was in a good mood after his first practice. "It is great to be with a team of spirit and I am mighty glad to be back working for Bob Quinn," Williams said. "I also consider it a privilege to be playing under [Bill] Carrigan's management and I think my work this year will very much warrant the Boston club's taking me over."[10]

Williams' pep and vigor were being noted daily by the Boston papers and the outfielder couldn't help but keep professing his excitement. After a March 1 workout, he told reporters, "Boys, I never enjoyed a day's practice more than today's. There's a lot of 'kick' out there with this outfit."[11]

Manager Bill Carrigan managed the Red Sox to World Series titles in 1915 and 1916 before abruptly retiring, and was hired before the 1927 season to try to revert Boston back to its glory days—or at least a winning record. He was pleased with what he saw from Williams early in spring training, and the *Boston Globe* reported that "if there is any one position which is nailed down as the campaigning starts it is left field, with the ex–St. Louis slugger as the occupant."[12]

Williams, in turn, was highly complimentary of Carrigan. He told *The Sporting News* that the Boston skipper was regarded as one of the best and brightest, according to players from around the American League.

"That may sound like a sweet boost for the teacher by the new student," Williams is quoted as saying. "But it's the truth, as you can find by asking almost any of the older players in the league."[13]

After a couple of instrasquad games, the Red Sox set out against major-league competition. They played the Cardinals in Bradenton and the Phillies in Winter Haven. Williams batted cleanup both games, going 3-for-6 over the two contests.

Next up were the Boston Braves back in Bradenton. While the Red Sox supposedly had "their jaws set for business,"[14] the National Leaguers brought over a brass band to play before the game. This wasn't exactly the Browns-Cardinals rivalry. Nevertheless, Williams endeared himself to the Red Sox faithful by going 3-for-5 with a triple. "The old boy's eyes are 100 percent right,"[15] stated the *Boston Globe*.

When Williams played, he hit. In two games against Buffalo and one vs. the Dodgers he went 4-for-7 with a triple and a steal. On March 20, he had two more hits against the Cardinals, but he also suffered an injury which was dubbed a strained left groin.

That sidelined him for roughly a week, and even when he returned he clearly wasn't in full health. Playing on a bad surface in Augusta, Georgia—it was described as a "high school ballpark"[16]—as the Red Sox wound down their spring training probably didn't help.

After declaring him a cinch for the left-field job, the *Boston Globe* now speculated, "Ken Williams has no great inside track over [Arlie] Tarbert for left field."[17] However, Williams was the second-leading hitter on the team during spring training behind just young infielder Buddy Myer. The position was his. But what exactly was he getting into?

Early in spring training, when asked if his sale to the Red Sox was a fortunate move, Williams replied, "I know I believe in Santa Claus now."[18] He might have wanted to check for coal in his stocking, however.

Any thoughts of Boston's being a pennant-winning club were dispelled as the team broke camp in Bradenton—by none other than the team's highest-ranking executives. When asked about the American League pennant, Carrigan replied, "I don't think we can win it ourselves and we may not make the first division this season, but we will have a hustling, fighting ball club and we certainly do not expect to be last."[19] Now those are words that surely motivated a team and excited a fan base.

Carrigan did praise Williams, though, saying he would "strengthen our outfield,"[20] but he was sparse in high compliments elsewhere. His catcher, Fred Hofmann was "steady"[21] and had "plenty of experience"[22] (in fact, Hofmann had never played more than 87 games in a season, which had occurred in 1927). And the Red Sox's infield "may not be the best infield in the world, but they certainly are not the worst in the league."[23]

Owner Quinn also tempered any enthusiasm, saying, "Of course we do not expect to win the pennant, but we do expect to make a much better showing than we did last year, a much better showing than we have made for the last several years."[24] Quinn wasn't exactly shooting for the moon. In the past three seasons, the Red Sox had won 51, 46 and 47 games.

The nation's writers didn't provide much more hope, picking Boston to finish last in the eight-team league. The highest any writer thought the Red Sox would finish was sixth—Boston got one vote for that position in the standings. The others who voted (some only turned in their top-four teams) had Boston seventh (18) or eighth (25).

There were complications for Williams playing in Boston—specifically Fenway Park—as well. Fenway Park in 1928 looked much different from how it does in modern times. The right-field fence was 358 feet (by contrast, Yankee Stadium's right-field fence was only 294 feet away), as the bullpens still were in foul territory. They wouldn't be moved to right field until years later, shortening the distance to the fence by some 50 feet, which would help another Williams—Ted. As a result, Ken Williams had hit only two home runs in 291 career at-bats at the American League park (June 7, 1921, against Joe Bush, and June 11, 1925, against Jack Quinn). He had, however, hit seven of his 70 American League triples at Fenway.

Also, there was no Green Monster yet at Fenway. Instead, left field had a steep 10-foot incline known as Duffy's Cliff, so named after Duffy Lewis, who patrolled left for the Red Sox from 1910 to 1917 (Fenway opened in 1912). Left field was a challenge for any player, never mind a soon-to-be 38-year-old.

Boston, though, opened the 1928 season not at home but in Washington, D.C., on April 10. The Red Sox–Senators game was the only game on the docket in all the majors. President Calvin Coolidge was there, exhibiting a "rare smile"[25] after throwing out the first pitch to umpire Brick Owens, as well as Vice-President Charles Dawes, British General Frederick McCracken and new American League president Ernest Barnard.

While the weather was "bitterly cold,"[26] Carrigan's outlook had warmed some as his team prepared for its first game. The manager, who had received a wire from Boston's mayor wishing the Red Sox a "successful season,"[27] had backed off earlier predictions of doom and gloom.

"The Red Sox are considerably stronger today than a year ago," he told the *Boston Herald.* "I am not making any predictions, but I hope I can help give the Boston fans that good brand of baseball to which, as the best fans in the land, they certainly are entitled."[28]

The *Boston Globe* wrote that this year's Red Sox "appear to be the best club which has all sported the red hose at Fenway since those dark days following the breakup of Boston's last championship club."[29]

Williams was not quoted anywhere—as players rarely were—before that first game. It had to be strange putting on the gray uniform of Boston—a new road look for the Red Sox—after wearing St. Louis's colors for the previous decade.

Making things perhaps a bit more odd were a couple of the faces on the opposite bench. George Sisler was with Washington, although he was relegated to pinch-hitting duty with Joe Judge at first base. On the mound for the Senators was Milt Gaston, his teammate with the Browns from 1924 to 1927, who was dealt to Washington weeks after the 1927 season ended.

A big crowd turned out to watch the game despite the horrible weather. Although it never rained, gray skies were predominant, a biting wind blew, and it was so cold that those in attendance wore "overcoats, sweaters and mufflers,"[30] while Boston players sported their brand-new sweater jackets with black, leather sleeves to keep warm.

Williams batted fourth, but his first time taking swings for Boston didn't come until the second inning—by which time Coolidge had already bid a hasty retreat out of the stadium and to warmer lodgings. He started off his Red Sox career with a single, eventually scoring on a triple. In the third inning, he singled again, this time his hit to center field driving in a run to give Boston a 4–3 lead, although he was thrown out trying to take second base.

While the *Boston Globe* would say Williams "was not quite home in the field,"[31] he did make an impact play. In the eighth inning Washington already had one run in to cut Boston's lead to 7–5 when Muddy Ruel singled to left field. But Williams fired to second base to catch Babe Ganzel, who had overrun the base, for the final out. The Red Sox won by that 7–5 score, with Williams finishing 2-for-3 with a walk. There wasn't much time to celebrate the win. This was just a one-off game in Washington and both teams had to head to the train station to play the next day at 3 p.m. in Boston.

As in Washington, it was cold in Boston, with temperatures in the low to mid–30s for the Red Sox's opening day. It was cold enough that Mayor Malcolm Nichols didn't attend, even though he was scheduled to catch the first pitch from Massachusetts Gov. Alvan Nichols (the president of City Council, Tom Greene, took his place).

Fenway Park sported a fresh coat of paint on its fences as well as a new picket fence in front of the left-field bleachers, replacing a worn-out wooden barrier. On the field, as instructed by the new AL president, there was the outline for on-deck batters to stand, which, according to the *Boston Globe*, "looks like a hammer thrower's circle."[32] The on-deck batter rule was still confusing, as evidenced in the opener, when the umpiring crew had to admonish both teams on multiple occasions to have only one hitter in the circle.

The win in Washington didn't set the fan base into a tizzy—of course, the near-freezing temperatures and stiff winds didn't help, either. Only around 8,000 turned out for Boston's opener. Those who did attend were bundled up, as were the players. Boston's outfield of Williams, Ira Flagstead and Doug Taitt all wore their Horace Partridge-made sweater jackets in the field. The fans weren't getting warm from cheering, either, as the Red Sox fell behind 7–0 after five innings. Finally, Williams gave them reason to hoot and holler.

In the sixth, after Phil Todt had singled, Williams hit one "into the teeth of the gale"[33] off Firpo Marberry and over the right-field fence for a home run. The Senators immediately protested, saying the ball had curved foul. Umpire Willie Giesel noted the ball turned foul *after* clearing the fence. In the past, this would have been determined a foul ball—and Williams had lost several home runs over the years because of this—but the rule was changed in 1928, so that once the ball went over the fence it was considered a home run "provided it disappears from view in fair territory,"[34] no matter where it landed. Williams's first home run as a member of the Red Sox was deemed a "colossal clout"[35] by the *Boston Herald.*

In the eighth, Washington player-manager Bucky Harris talked with Marberry before Williams's next turn at the plate, with two out and two on. Marberry then pitched a "slow ball on the outside."[36]

Weeks later, when asked the toughest pitch to hit, Williams said: "The hardest ball for any batter, good or poor, to hit is a low ball on the outside. It is the farthest from the direct line of vision between the pitcher and batter, hence harder to judge. It's farther away from you than any other ball and hence harder to hit effectively and get your swing behind it, well timed. There are mighty few batters in the game that have any success hitting such a ball."[37] Fortunately for Williams, he was one such a hitter. He reached out and sent the ball down the left-field line for a double that scored both runners.

Boston would lose 8–4, with Williams accounting for all of the Red Sox's runs and three of their eight hits (he also had doubled previously). The early reviews of Williams were, of course, glowing. "If it hadn't been for Kennie [*sic*] Williams and his stout stick of ash, the day would have been really dismal for Boston and the Sox,"[38] wrote the *Boston Post.*

In a column entitled Live Tips and Topics, "Sportsman" opined, "If yesterday's performance was a sample of the way Ken Williams is going to click 'em this year, he is slated to be mighty popular in this man's town."[39]

In his Sports Comment, which appeared in the *Boston Post,* the *New York Times'* Arthur Daley gushed, "Ken Williams … is well on his way to being a hero in Boston."[40] Daley noted Williams droved in four runs "and at the same time won the former St. Louis star a warm place in the heart of fans."[41]

A rainout the next day didn't dull the Red Sox faithful's appreciation for Williams. The first two times he came to the plate in Boston's next game he was greeting by a rousing ovation—and both times he responded with singles. Williams also made a fine play, racing into left-center field to rob Grant Gillis of a sure double with a one-handed catch. "Kenneth Williams looks very much different in left field from anybody the Red Sox had had in that territory in recent years,"[42] observed the *Boston Globe.*

Not all was perfect—he stranded a number of runners in a 6–5 loss to Washington on April 15—but his time in Boston was starting out more than well. Williams reached base in his first 30 games in a Red Sox uniform, his longest on-base streak since 1923, when he had a run that reached 51 games. In those 30 games with Boston, he had a hit in 27 of them (and one of the hitless was an 0-for-1 five-inning shortened game), including nine multiple-hit games.

The Yankees came to town in mid–April. New York had dominated Boston in recent years, going 37–18 in Fenway Park from 1923 to 1927, and Babe Ruth, who began his career with the Red Sox, was still deified.

Williams did his best to make the fans forget about the Yankees slugger, as he homered twice in the four-game series; however, Boston lost three of those contests. He swatted a three-run homer off Waite Hoyt in the ninth inning of a 10–7 loss on April 18.

The next day was also the running of the Boston Marathon, and the Red Sox played a traditional double-header, with the opener at 10:30 a.m. and the second game at 3:30 p.m. A small crowd saw the Red Sox win the first game, 7–6, with Williams scoring the tying run in the eighth. With the marathon over, more than 35,000 packed Fenway for the afternoon affair, and Williams treated them to a home run off Herb Pennock in the fourth inning as the "big crowd had a chance to cut loose"[43] with cheers. But Ruth homered in the fifth, and the noise emanating afterwards was even louder.

Shortstop Wally Gerber played for the St. Louis Browns from 1917 to 1928, then joined Ken Williams with the Boston Red Sox for the final years of both their careers (George Grantham Bain Collection, Library of Congress).

"It is quite the style to glorify the Babe's homers," wrote the *Boston Herald*. "But it is almost a shame to have the crowd lose sight of the fact that the Red Sox have in Ken Williams, lanky left fielder, a most robust home run hitter."[44]

After two weeks, Williams was leading the American League in total bases, but things weren't going well for the Red Sox as a team. Boston traded for Williams's old St. Louis teammate, shortstop Wally Gerber, in an effort to solidify the infield. As April neared a close with Boston 4–9 and in the AL cellar, Carrigan bluntly stated, "Things have been going just about as I expected."[45]

Boston finished the month with another loss, 4–1 to Philadelphia, although Williams made a "remarkable"[46] catch on a long foul by Ty Cobb and also rapped out two more hits, boosting his average to .373, fifth in the American League.

Williams kept on hitting, although he was robbed of two home runs by the elements. Twice in the first week of May, a long fly ball off his bat was knocked down by the wind, once resulting in a double and the other time an out.

By May 11, the Red Sox had worked their way out of the cellar and into seventh place at 8–15–1, averaging fewer than four runs per game. Despite the record and lack of overall offensive production, Williams was one of four newcomers credited for the Red Sox's putting up a "better showing"[47] compared to 1927. And now it was time to face his former teammates.

Chapter 16

Winding Down a Career

Having played in the National League to begin his career, Williams had never opposed the St. Louis Browns previously. The first game against his old team—occurring on May 12 at Fenway—couldn't have gone more swimmingly.

The score was knotted at 1 early, but Boston erupted for 11 runs in the third inning. Williams accounted for three of those. He had a sacrifice fly early in the inning, and then, as the first batter to face Walter Beck—who was the third pitcher of the inning—he hit a "lengthy wallop into the right field stands"[1] for a two-run home run. The Red Sox would win 15–2 with the governor of Massachusetts in attendance, although surely Williams was feeling like royalty after this one.

"We'll bet that Ken Williams just hated to hit that home run against his old pals,"[2] wrote the *Boston Herald*'s Bob Dunbar, the sarcasm dripping from each word. While Williams was undoubtedly feeling sky-high, that would be the final home run he'd ever hit at Fenway Park.

Williams followed up with a two-hit game the next day in a 3–2 Red Sox win over the Browns, and then chipped in a surprising bunt single in a 3–1 victory. In Williams's first series against his former team, his Boston squad came away with a three-game sweep. The Red Sox had won four straight and were now tied for fifth place.

It was very early in the season and it wasn't as though Boston was showing itself to be a pennant contender, but the Red Sox were proving themselves something to behold. The *Harvard Crimson* tried to sum up the feeling around town in an article titled "Not in the Best Cellar Class":

> Laila Hanoun, Hindu Fakir, has just prophesied that New York will be inundated by a great flood twenty years from now, that the Romanoffs will be restored to the throne of Russia, and much more. It must be true, for the miracles have already begun to occur. The lowly Red Sox, nobody's toast, have left the cellar. Not only have they left the cellar but are tied for fifth place with the Senators, and are what the sporting pages choose to call "perilously close to fourth place."
>
> The Red Sox have won four games in a row, and five of the last six they have played. To the baseball world this is a miracle quite the equal of the restoration of a fallen dynasty, considerably more of one, in fact. At the start of every baseball season for the past ten years or more the cry has gone forth that the Red Sox have come to life again, but all in vain. September found them at the bottom of the column.
>
> Up in the dizzy heights of fourth or fifth place the Carriganites may well smile, for they are achieving the unheard of, and are bringing joy to the hearts of all Boston fandom. But perhaps the Hindu seer is slightly astigmatic, and just as Stalin and his conferes intend to have no more of the Romanoffs, Washington, Detroit and Chicago may soon tire of this prank of the Red Sox.[3]

Boston made it five straight wins with an 11-inning, 5–4 victory over Detroit. Williams had three hits, a run and an RBI, and was walked in the 11th to load the bases, setting up the game-winning sacrifice fly. The victory was considered big enough news to garner a front-page headline in the *Boston Globe* right below "Five Held in 'Rum Graft' One Names 15 Policeman."[4]

The following day, the Red Sox earned that top headline. "Sox Run Victory String Up to Six"[5] was considered bigger news than the anticipated arrival of the pilots—so named the Bremen flyers—who flew the first East-West trans-Atlantic flight, from Ireland to Newfoundland.

Again Williams had three hits, and his two-run single in the second inning broke a 2–all tie in an eventual 5–3 win. He also showed off some of his younger daring on the basepaths. In the sixth, after beating out an infield hit, he advanced to second base after a foul out to the catcher and one batter later scored on a single. "Ken Williams is playing the smartest baseball of his career right now,"[6] noted the *Boston Herald*. Williams also made a great play in the fifth, robbing Fats Fothergill of a hit with the bases loaded on a running catch to end the inning.

Flags hung at Fenway Park, extending from the first-base side to the left-field bleachers, displaying the league's standings. For the first time in a long four years, the Red Sox would be fourth in that order.

"They certainly have given everybody a big surprise," Tigers manager George Moriarty said. "If anyone had said six weeks ago that the Red Sox would do as well as they have done he would have been laughed at."[7]

Wrote the *Boston Post*'s Bill Cunningham: "The local Red Stockings, after playing dummy so long, have suddenly busted loose and begun to play baseball.... Downtown, on the trains, in the restaurants—everywhere—folks were talking baseball and the Red Sox for the first time in years."[8]

A big part of those conversations had to be Ken Williams, who was Boston's leading hitter at .355. The *Boston Post* ran a cartoon of the Red Sox outfielder, claiming, "Ken Williams has more than made good on his promise to give his all for Bob Quinn."[9]

The Red Sox left Boston for New York, and even a double-header split with the Yankees was big news, garnering front-page headlines in both the *Boston Post* and the *Boston Herald*. After winning the opener 8–4 to end New York's winning streak at eight, the Red Sox saw their seven-game victory march end in the second game. It was not a good game for Williams, as well.

His 30-game on-base streak came to a halt—Williams batted 355/408/536 in that span with 17 runs and 20 RBI—but that wasn't the worst thing that happened that game for Williams. In the sixth inning, he chased a long fly ball hit by Bob Meusel. Williams crashed into the concrete left-field fence and ended up, along with the ball, in the stands. Meusel had a home run while Williams came away with a sore leg.

He was able to finish the game, but he woke up "stiff and sore"[10] the next day, and Carrigan opted to leave him out of the lineup. It would be reported that Williams's leg was "severely bruised"[11] and he also had "several muscle sprains."[12] In place of Williams in left field, Carrigan used Jack Rothrock, who had appeared in the outfield just once (as a late substitute in right field on May 7) in his previous 169 major-league games. The Red Sox lost 14–4 and the *Boston Post*'s Jack Mahoney put his finger on the problem: "The effect of the loss of Williams knocked the gimp completely out of the box and they reverted back to their old-time form and got slaughtered by the Yankees," wrote Mahoney of Boston's performance in the loss. "Taking the heaviest hitter on the team out of the lineup and substituting him for a weak hitter as is Jack Rothrock … was like taking the bullet out of a gun."[13]

Williams wasn't ready to start the series finale in New York either, although he was brought in as a pinch hitter for Freddy Hofmann in the eighth, striking out. The Red Sox lost that one as well, 2–1. It wasn't just the reporters who thought Boston needed Williams in the lineup; the players and his manager were saying the same thing.

"We might as well have won three of those four games against the Yankees," Carrigan said. "Our boys feel that way.… They spoke several times about us lacking Ken Williams in that last game.… They felt that if Ken were in there we'd have won."[14]

Carrigan added that Williams had a "severe muscle bruise"[15] and he wasn't sure when the outfielder would return to the lineup, even though Williams had expressed his desire to play in the next game. "If there is any possibility of [Williams] playing the veteran will be right in there, as he shares the fighting and winning spirit of the Red Sox and is crazy to play,"[16] declared the *Boston Post*.

Despite having a noticeable limp, Williams indeed did play in the Red Sox's next game, May 25 against Washington in Boston, a 5–0 win. He went 3-for-3 with a walk and drove in the game's first run with an RBI single. In the seventh inning after his third single, Rothrock was brought in to run for Williams, who left to a rousing ovation from the 4,500 or so at Fenway Park.

Williams's return was also greeted favorably by the local press. The *Boston Herald* noted, "The Sox need Kenneth in their midst, as a working brother."[17] Melvin Webb, Jr., of the *Boston Globe* wrote, "Makes some difference when Ken Williams gets back in the ball game." He added, "Ken Williams' leg may be sore, but there is, apparently, nothing wrong with his batting eye."[18]

The Red Sox were 15–18 and in fourth place. During a three-game stretch in which Boston wasn't scheduled for a game, the *Boston Post* ran a picture of several Red Sox players, including Williams, with wide grins on their faces. "They're all smiling, for these Red Sox, and not without reason—the whole town's smiling,"[19] read the photo caption.

His old St. Louis teammate George Sisler was back in the same town after being bought by the National League Braves on May 27 from Washington, but it was Williams who was the king of the Boston baseball scene.

However, things took a turn on Memorial Day, May 30. In the second game of a doubleheader in Boston, Philadelphia's Mule Haas hit a blooper out into shallow left field. Shortstop Wally Gerber drifted back to make a play while Williams sped in from his spot in left field looking to corral the ball as well. Instead, the two players—as had happened a couple of times when they were teammates in St. Louis—collided at full speed. Both were knocked backwards, flat on their backs.

Gerber got the worst of it. He suffered a gash on his face and had to be carried off the field by two teammates. An hour later, he was reported to still be woozy, clearly concussed as he talked as though he were in New York City. Williams was dazed as well, but was able to walk off the field under his own power.

Gerber wouldn't play again until June 12. Amazingly, Williams was starting in left field in Boston's next game, which wasn't until June 2 in Cleveland. Perhaps not so surprising, he was hitless in three at-bats with a walk.

He did follow that up with a two-hit game against the Indians the next day, and then, after several rainouts, had a two-run single on June 7 in Detroit and hit a two-run homer off the Tigers' Lil Stoner in the first game of a June 9 double-header.

The series Williams was undoubtedly looking forward to came next as Boston traveled to St. Louis for four games, June 10–13. The *St. Louis Globe Democrat* even played up the return of former Browns Williams and Gerber, although the latter would miss the first two games of the series.

A crowd of 10,000 was on hand for the opener and they gave Williams a "great ovation"[20] when he strode to the plate in the first inning. He would, however, go hitless in his four at-bats with a walk, and would misplay a ball into a triple in the 10th inning (although the runner would not score) as the Red Sox lost 2–1 in 12 innings.

In the second game, he flashed his defensive skills with a couple of fine running catches. He struggled with the bat again, though, and resorted to bunting down the third-base line in the ninth inning to pick up his first hit of the series in yet another 2–1 defeat. He went 1-for-5 in the third game, but he did make "two brilliant catches,"[21] albeit in front of only 500 or so paying customers as Boston finally won one, 5–2.

Williams saved his best for last in the series. In the fourth inning, he blasted a solo home run off Jack Ogden, brother of Curly, whom Williams had taken deep back in 1926 in Washington. This was also to be his final home run at Sportsman's Park.

In the seventh inning, with two runners on base, reliever Ed Strelecki threw two balls to Williams, then was taken out in favor of Hooks Wiltse, a lefty, who threw a wild pitch. Williams then hit a sacrifice fly to center field, narrowing the Red Sox's deficit to 8–7. Boston would tie the game, but lose 9–8 in 10 innings.

Despite the home run, Williams was not in full health. His arm had been bothering him, and then on June 15 in Chicago he injured his knee while sliding into second base. Williams didn't start the next day, although he hit for Doug Taitt in the sixth inning and stayed in the game.

Williams had slumped down to a .305 batting average, but that was still tops on the club. No regular player on Boston was batting over .300. And now Williams was out of the lineup once again.

His arm was hurting bad enough that the Red Sox sent him to Rochester, New York, to get treatment on it from Dr. Harry Knight, who, as it turned out, had no diagnosis for the injury. Williams trusted it would work itself out and stayed in Rochester, where he practiced with the International League team there hoping his arm would improve. But he returned to Boston in the same shape as when he left.

Injured or not, he was back in the lineup—"It is futile to say that Ken's absence does not hurt the Red Sox,"[22] surmised *The Sporting News*—as the Red Sox began a string of five double-headers in five days in three cities.

Williams went hitless in the opener against Washington on June 27, but in the next nine games—from the second game vs. the Senators through the final double-header July 2 in Philadelphia—he had a hit in each of the nine contests, going 16-for-36 (.444) with 10 runs and 13 RBI. He even hit a home run off the Athletics' Lefty Grove out of Shibe Park and onto 20th Avenue below. Williams's average bottomed out at .298 after that first game against Washington, but by July 2 he was back up to .322.

The Red Sox were hardly done with double-headers. After a single game July 3, there was another double-header July 4. Then after one game July 5, the Red Sox played double-headers in Boston on July 7 and on July 9 against Detroit (with a day off in between on Sunday due to Boston's laws prohibiting baseball games that day). At 38, Williams had slowed down and was described by the *Boston Herald* as being "not particularly fast,"[23] but he did steal a base in both ends of the July 9 double-header, including a double steal in the second game with Williams swiping home.

Williams had also slowed down at the plate. After going 2-for-11 in a three-game series at home against the Browns, his batting average was down to .297. Carrigan would move Williams temporarily to the fifth spot in the order (ironically after Williams went 4-for-7 in a double-header against Chicago). Whether or not the lineup switch was the reason, Williams went on a 10-game hitting streak, including a 4-for-4 effort against Cleveland.

After another run of double-headers—three straight on July 25, 26 and 28 (the Red Sox played 15 double-headers in a 32-day stretch, June 27–July 28)—Williams was back up to .325 (thanks in part to going 6-for-9 in the two games on July 28 against the Tigers). He also doubled in each game and had six doubles in his last 10 games, but his power certainly wasn't as it was earlier in the season. Since June 9, Williams's slugging percentage was below .500, with a low of .428 after a July 16 double-header.

Was it age or injury? Clearly Williams wasn't the same hitter he had been in his halcyon days with the Browns, but at the same point he was slugging over .500 for the first two months of the season. His various ailments—arm, leg, the collision with Gerber—were obviously taking their toll.

He still had his moments—Williams had eight multi-hit games in August, but he also was hitless in nine of his starts that month. He drove in just three runs and had four extra-base hits in all of August, numbers which he'd often put up in a game during his heyday. He hit just .280 in the month with a .341 on-base percentage and .333 slugging percentage. By the middle of the month he had been dropped to sixth in the batting order, and not only against lefties, as had happened in years past.

On September 3, he broke a 60-game homerless streak after hitting one out at Yankee Stadium off New York's Henry Johnson to lead off the ninth inning to give Boston a 4–1 lead (the run would prove to be important as New York scored twice in the home ninth). The streak should have ended at 59, but in the opening game of that day's double-header, Yankees center fielder Earle Combs reached over the fence to rob Williams of a grand slam.

Wins had become rare for Boston as well. Williams had helped carry the team early, and even then the team had a losing record. With his bat having gone cold, Boston was now cemented in last place, 11 games behind seventh-place Cleveland. It would normally be a time to take a look at some younger players, but Carrigan said he'd put out his normal lineup against teams involved in the pennant race or first-division money. Of course, except for the Red Sox and Browns, who had third place pretty well locked up, something was on the line for every other team. The Yankees and A's were battling for the pennant while the Senators, White Sox, Tigers and Indians were all within 3½ games of each other for fourth place. "[A]ll those clubs out there are fighting and we intend to be at our best against all of them, so 'no lads,'"[24] Carrigan told reporters.

Thus Williams remained in the lineup when the Red Sox played a double-header—of course—in Boston on September 7. In Game 1, Philadelphia's Grove struck out 11, including Williams twice. Williams struck out only 15 times all season and those would be his last in 1928.

Boston had double-headers each of the next two days against Philadelphia and at Washington, and Williams played in three of the four games as well as a September 10 game against the Senators.

On September 11, Boston played an exhibition game in Pittsburgh against the National League's Pirates. There was no reason given why this game was held in-season—the *Pittsburgh Press* openly questioned the notion—but it was the 25th anniversary of the first World Series and this was Boston's first appearance in Pittsburgh since the two teams met in 1903. The Red Sox won the game, 5–1, and Williams, batting fourth, hit a home run in the eighth inning off Elmer Tutwiler, who had been called up to Pittsburgh just a couple of weeks earlier.

That would be his last extra-base hit of the season, even though this one didn't count in the official statistics. Taking away this exhibition, in his last 14 games—all coming right after his home run in New York—Williams did not have an extra-base hit.

As the season wound down, Williams was used more as a substitute. He started only one of the final eight games—the second game of a double-header in Cleveland in which he was 3-for-4 with two runs, two RBI and a stolen base. That would be his final game of 1928 as he sat out the final three contests. Boston would finish in last place with just 57 wins—although that was six-game improvement from 1927.

Williams ended the 1928 season with a .303 batting average, .356 on-base percentage and .413 slugging percentage, numbers respectable for many players, and especially considering he was the seventh-oldest position player in the majors. (Among those, only two others, Max Carey and Sam Rice, played in at least 100 games.) He was second on the Red Sox in each of those categories, as well as home runs (8), while his 67 RBI were third best. But those numbers were not vintage Williams, who turned more into a contact hitter (he struck out just once every 30.8 at-bats, the sixth-best ratio in the American League).

The turning point in Williams's season was May 30, when he and Gerber collided chasing a Texas leaguer. At the time of that incident, Williams's slash line was 338/394/500. In the 96 games played after May 30, his slash line was 290/342/381. Perhaps not coincidentally, Boston was 15–22 (.406) on May 30 and 42–74 (.362) after.

When a team wins just 57 games, changes are certainly going to occur. First, Boston sent pitcher Slim Harriss and infielder Billy Rogell to St. Paul of the American Association for catcher Alex Gaston and outfielder Russ Scarritt, the latter of whom batted left and hit .356 in 1928. Neither of those facts boded well for Williams.

Ten days later the Red Sox traded Buddy Myer to Washington for five players: pitchers Hod Lisenbee and Milt Gaston, infielders Grant Gillis and Bobby Reeves, and outfielder Elliot Bigelow, another lefty. The *Boston Herald* would dub this "undoubtedly one of the best deals which the Red Sox have made in the last decade."[25]

Based on some of the players Boston was swindled out of in the past, perhaps this was accurate, but Myer would turn into a star player in Washington while the haul for the Red Sox would produce just middling results.

One change for the 1929 season would be that the Red Sox would finally play games in Boston on Sundays. After much legal wrangling—and accusations of bribery and blackmail—the Boston city council approved play on Sunday. The Red Sox, though, would play their Sunday home games at Braves Field, since there a church within 1,000 feet of Fenway and the new Sunday Sports Act had a 1,000-foot restriction. This news likely delighted Williams. During the offseason in Grants Pass, he had complained to friends about how it was harder to hit home runs at Fenway Park. Meanwhile, Braves Field had been turned into a much cozier ballpark after years of deep fences.

There was one potential change in the offseason that could have been a boon to Williams and perhaps extended his career. National League president John Heydler had an idea which he thought would "speed up the game"[26] and "make it more interesting [and] more colorful."[27]

Heydler proposed that instead of pitchers batting, a rule would be instituted in which one player would be designated to pinch-hit for the pitcher throughout the game. Longtime New York Giants manager John McGraw, for one, liked and backed the idea. It, however, did not go over as well in the American League.

"The manager would not have a chance to do any managing,"[28] protested Cleveland manager Roger Peckinpaugh. Said Chicago White Sox manager Lena Blackburne: "My pitchers would assassinate me if they could not take their regular turns at bat. A pitcher lends a doubtful but interesting angle to the game."[29]

Perhaps spurred on by their managers, the AL owners decided to vote down the plan. In a time of conformity, the National League also would reject the proposal. "All I wanted to do was present the idea," Heydler would say after the votes were cast, "no matter if it were tabled.... I still contend the idea has merits."[30]

The designated hitter, of course, would be enacted by the AL in 1973, far too late for Ken Williams. But if such a rule were used in 1929, perhaps he could have stuck around just a little longer. Hitting would never be a problem for someone like Williams, no matter his age.

As in the previous offseason, Williams drove from Grants Pass to Bradenton with his wife and son, Ken Jr. He arrived at a camp not exactly littered with youngsters. Bart Whitman of the *Boston Herald* calculated the average age of the 27 Red Sox in camp was 27 years old, although that wasn't considering the fact that Williams and the Gaston brothers, Alex and Milt, were listed three years younger than their actual age. Turning 39 in June, Williams was the third-oldest regular position player in the American League (behind catcher Wally Schang, who would play in 94 games for St. Louis, and longtime Washington outfielder Sam Rice, who was four months Williams's senior).

There was also a glut of outfielders in Bradenton. Jack Rothrock had been moved there from the infield. Ira Flagstead and Doug Taitt returned from the 1928 team as well. They were joined by offseason acquisitions Scarritt and Bigelow along with George Loepp, who had played in 15 games for Boston in '28, and youngsters Otto Dumas and Charlie Small.

Williams still had the name recognition among the group. After all, no one else on the team had a fielder's glove with his name on it sold by Montgomery Ward. But when they divvied up the teams for the first intrasquad scrimmage game between the Regulars and Yannigans, for the first time since he was brought up by the Browns, Williams was put on the Yannigans. Scarritt, Rothrock and Bigelow were on the Regulars while Loepp and Taitt joined Williams (Flagstead had yet to report to camp).

Williams went 0-for-2 in his first two games with the Yannigans, playing only part of each before being replaced by Dumas and Small. When the games began, Williams was a sub, entering late in left field in a 13–3 loss to the Cardinals in Bradenton. He went 1-for-2 in a 13–4 victory over the Cincinnati Reds, but then didn't play against Indianapolis in Sarasota. "I can't say now that there is any one sure to be in that [starting] lineup,"[31] Carrigan declared.

Over the next few games, Williams continued to either be a late substitute or did not play at all. Rothrock or Scarritt were getting the playing time in his old position of left field, while Flagstead—finally having arrived—was in center and Bigelow and Taitt splitting time in right.

That didn't mean Williams wasn't having fun, though. When light-hitting shortstop Wally Gerber ripped a triple, Williams playfully fell off the bench in mock surprise and wondered if "the millennium had been reached."[32]

Given a chance to play in an intrasquad game on March 26, he launched a three-run home run deep into a grove of palmetto trees out in right field. "I'd like to get 28 hits like that this season," Williams remarked after the scrimmage. "And I wouldn't care in what part in the American League circuit I hit them, as most of them would be out of the orchard anyway. It certainly felt good."[33]

Those feelings were few and far between. Over the next five games—three against other teams and two scrimmages—Williams played just once, getting one at-bat as a substitute for Scarritt in a benefit game for the local American Legion post. He did win a prize in the postgame raffle—an embroidered piece with the inscription "When shall we meet again?" That was an appropriate expression for Williams to receive, especially in regards to his place in the starting lineup.

Williams started to get a bit more playing time and was hitting the ball well, but it all came in the role of a replacement for Flagstead or Rothrock. In a four-game stretch against minor-league clubs, Williams went 8-for-10 in a reserve role. But as the team finished its sojourn north, Williams never was given a starting nod.

The Red Sox were to finish up their training schedule with two games against the Boston Braves. The first was canceled due to rain, snow and wind. The second was played at Braves Field on April 14—the first Sunday baseball game ever in Boston. Flagstead (left), Rothrock (center) and Scarritt (right) were the starting outfield, although Williams came in as a late sub and was hitless in one at-bat while fielding two fly balls.

Carrigan insisted he had not come to any conclusions about the starting lineup and added, "The outfield situation is such that there may be a brand-new combination out there in a month."[34]

Nevertheless, when the season finally opened—the first two days were rained out—in New York on April 18, Williams was not in the starting lineup. He, along with other Red Sox players, however, took part in the parade to the center-field flagpole for the raising of the Yankees' 1928 American League championship and World Series banners. That might have been awkward for Boston players, except for the fact the team insisted on taking part in the ceremony.

For the first time, Red Sox road games were being broadcast over the radio. The broadcast crew would have an easier time recognizing players on the Yankees, who, in another first, wore numbers on their uniforms.

Setting the tone for early in the season, Williams would enter midway through the game for Flagstead and go 0-for-2. He would finish out the month with three pinch-hitting appearances, failing to record a hit or reach base.

A 24–6 romp by the A's on May 1 allowed Carrigan to substitute freely—he brought in reserves at every position other than catcher, including Williams for Rothrock in center—and Williams finally reached base with a walk, although he was now 0-for-6 on the season.

Hit No. 1 came in his next appearance, as a pinch hitter for shortstop Hal Ryhne. It was the ninth inning and Boston trailed Detroit 2–1 when Williams led off with a single against Tigers starter Vic Sorrell. He was removed for a pinch runner, but it didn't matter as two fielder's choices and a strikeout ended the game.

Williams was used as a pinch hitter in each of the next four games as well, but his best result was a sacrifice bunt. After being used in the field the next day (Scarritt had been hit for by Jerry Standaert, a first baseman), he walked as a pinch hitter against the Browns on May 10. However, with the Red Sox down one, Williams, "always trying the unexpected,"[35] attempted to steal second base and was cut down by St. Louis catcher Rick Ferrell.

Williams continued to get sporadic opportunities the rest of May. A trade of left-handed–hitting Doug Taitt on May 23 didn't yield more playing time as Boston received another outfielder, Bill Barrett, a right-hander, in return from the Chicago White Sox. Williams did collect a hit in three consecutive pinch-hitting appearances from May 26 to 28, but as the month came to a close he was batting just .211 (4-for-19).

Unlike in his first year in Boston, there wasn't a big uproar of getting Williams into the lineup. The Red Sox finished May with a paltry 11–27 record, the worst in the major leagues. Inserting a veteran outfielder, whether he was his actual 38 or thought-of 35, didn't make sense in the current climate, as Boston was starting three players in their 20s in their outfield (Rothrock, Scarritt and Barrett).

As June began, nothing changed. Williams was a ninth-inning substitute in left field on June 1 after Scarritt was hit for, the first time he needed his fielding glove since May 22 and his first time in left since May 14.

After three more unsuccessful pinch-hitting appearances on June 4, 6 and 8, Williams was hitting just .182 (4-for-22) with two walks. He had scored just one run and had yet to drive in a run.

And then on June 9, for the first time all season, Boston manager Bill Carrigan wrote in Williams's name in the starting lineup. Jack Rothrock sat on the bench (Rothrock was batting a respectable 288/389/399, but that paled in comparison to Barrett [372/481/512] and Scarritt [311/359/459]). Williams, two and half weeks shy of his 39th birthday, took his place in center field, of all places.

Williams, who had batted two times in a game twice all season—April 18 and May 1—would have to face Detroit's George Uhle, who entered with a 9–1 record and 1.73 ERA, at Fenway Park.

Modern pundits would likely call someone like Williams a professional hitter, someone who could roll out of bed and smack a couple of hits on any given day. And even with as little experience at the plate as he had in 1929, that's exactly what Williams did. In the fifth inning, Williams hit a rocket to left field off Uhle for a double, his first extra-base hit of the season. Two singles later, he scored.

The game was tied at 3 heading into the ninth inning and Detroit tallied three times in its half. When Williams stepped up during Boston's turn at bat, there was already one run in, and Red Sox had runners at first and third and nobody out. Williams hit one "right on the nose"[36] to center field for another double, scoring one to make it 7–5. Pinch hitter Red Ruffing's fly out scored another as Williams raced to third. Charlie Berry, batting for pitcher Ed Morris, then singled past third base with Williams trotting in from third base with the tying run, "and great was the rejoicing and thunderous the noise"[37] as he crossed the plate. Berry would eventually come around with the winning run. It might not have been the Ken Williams effect of 1928, but it was something.

Williams got another start the next day. Facing Detroit's Sorrell, he went 2-for-4 with a double to left field in the fifth inning. His bat was rounding into prime shape, but his legs weren't. Two batters later he tried to score on a single to left field by pitcher Ruffing but was easily thrown out (surely much to the chagrin of Ruffing, who lost 1–0, his 11th defeat in as many starts).

Despite getting four hits in two games, Williams was back on the bench June 11 with Bill Barrett moving from right to center and Ernest Bigelow taking Williams's place in the lineup and in right field.

Williams didn't play in that game or the following one, but was used as a pinch hitter in the next five games, compiling three hits, including a double. His single on June 16 when he hit for Wally Gerber against the Browns at Braves Field lifted his average to .303. It took him half a month to get his average above .300 and it would never dip below that mark the rest of the season.

After sitting out the first game of a June 18 double-header in New York against lefty Fred Heimach, Williams was back in the starting lineup for game two, with right-hander George Pipgras on the mound. Instead of batting seventh, though, Carrigan had Williams hitting third in the lineup. The move paid off, and quickly.

In the first inning, Williams hit a two-run homer off Pipgras—his first home run since September 3, 1928, which was also in the second game of a Yankee Stadium double-header—giving Boston a lead it would never relinquish. Williams finished 2-for-4 with three RBI, making him 6-for-11 in his three starts.

Given a chance to play, Williams had worked his way into a platoon. Carrigan would start rotating Williams and Rothrock in center field, with the switch-hitting Rothrock sitting against right-handed starting pitchers.

Williams's first string of three straight starts in the 1929 season began June 26 in Philadelphia. He had two hits, including a first-inning solo home run off eventual 24-game winner George Earnshaw (who allowed just eight homers in 252⅔ innings in 1929), but also lined into a double play to end the game.

Boston had lost eight straight with that defeat and no one could blame Carrigan if he wanted to shake things up or go with younger players. But he kept Williams in the lineup, and on his last day as a 38-year-old, Williams had three hits, including a double to left-center and an RBI triple up against the center-field Fenway Park bleachers to help the Red Sox end their long skid with a 4–1 win over Washington.

On his 39th birthday, also the first time he started in three consecutive games all season, Williams aided Boston to a second straight victory as he blasted another double to center and made a "monumental catch"[38] on a long Goose Goslin fly ball in the seventh inning.

The Red Sox finished off a sweep of Washington on June 29 as Williams went 2-for-3 with a pair of doubles in making his fourth straight start. Over that span he was 8-for-13. It was hard to ignore that Williams should be in the starting lineup, and the next day, against the Yankees at Braves Field, Carrigan had Williams in center field despite left-hander Ed Wells pitching for New York.

Boston fell, 6–4, but Williams was 2-for-3 with two walks. He blooped a double to left field in the first inning to give him an extra-base hit in each of his last five games (five doubles, a triple and a home run).

Williams entered June batting just .211 with two walks and no extra-base hits. In 23 games that month, which included 11 starts (all of which came in the final three weeks), Williams was 22-for-51 (.431) with 10 doubles, a triple and two home runs (.784 slugging percentage). His batting average was now a team-high .371 (he also had a .629 slugging percentage). If there were doubts whether Williams could still play, he answered any questions in June.

His starting streak reached nine games before he finally sat back-to-back games with southpaws Tom Zachary of New York and Philadelphia's Lefty Grove pitching. Williams then put together a modest six-game hitting streak—which included one pinch-hitting performance—in which he was 7-for-18 (.389) with four walks and two doubles.

After failing to get a hit as a pinch hitter on July 15, the next day Williams went 2-for-4 with a two-run double in an 11–2 win over the Browns in St. Louis. He started again July 17 and singled and walked in his first two plate appearances against Sam Gray.

But in the fifth inning, after catching a deep fly ball off the bat of Ed Roetz in right-center field, Williams crashed into the concrete wall at his former home ballpark. He held onto the ball, but was clearly injured and dazed. The Browns' Heine Manush was able to score from second base on the play.

Williams sat out the next game, in Chicago, and was on the bench the following day as well, although he was called upon to hit for Berry in the seventh inning, delivering a single to center. Back in the lineup on July 20, Williams went 2-for-4. He had now hit in 18 of his last 20 games dating back to June 25, with a slash line of 410/478/623 in that span.

Yet, he was playing at less than 100 percent. While he made a couple of nice plays in a 10–0 loss to the White Sox on July 21—ranging deep and making a "wild leap"[39] to catch a Ted Lyons fly, and later throwing out Willie Kamm at the plate—that crash into the fence in St. Louis had taken its toll. He had a pain in his side that wouldn't go away, no doubt exacerbated by swinging the bat and making throws from the outfield like the one that nailed Kamm.

The fact their hottest hitter was hurt was just all part of another lowly season in Boston. The Red Sox headed home from Chicago having gone 4–15 on their recent road trip—with nine of the defeats coming by just one tantalizing run. Boston was 26–63, easily the worst record in the majors and eight games behind seventh-place Chicago—which had just swept a three-game series from the Red Sox.

When the Red Sox returned to Boston, Williams went to see a doctor. No bones were broken, but Williams did have bruises and a likely strained muscle.

Williams was reduced to pinch-hitting duty the rest of the month, although he did finally get a start in the second game of a double-header on July 31, batting cleanup for the final time in his major-league career. While Williams may never bat fourth again, even at this late stage of his career there was time for something new.

On August 1, Cleveland scored in each of the first four innings to take a 9–1 lead. Carrigan had seen enough, at least from a few players. He made some early substitutions. Bigelow replaced Bill Barrett in right field, Bob Barrett (no relation to Bill) came in at third for Bill Regan, Johnny Heving took over at catcher for Berry, and Williams was inserted for Phil Todt—at first base.

Not only had Williams never played first base in the major leagues, but he also had only played a position other than outfield just once—in the final game of the 1926 season, when on a lark he played second base. But in that game he never touched the ball. That wouldn't be the case at first. "[Carrigan] might as well experiment when all is lost for that day,"[40] opined the *Boston Herald*.

Williams appeared to acquit himself at the position, recording seven putouts without an error, although perhaps there were some hard-hit balls he didn't come up with. After doing what the *Boston Herald* called "some artful dodging"[41] at first base, as he approached the batter's box in the ninth inning one of the Indians players yelled at Williams, "Hey Mistah Chase"—referring to Hal Chase, a former teammate of Williams's in Cincinnati in 1916 and regarded as one of the finest fielding first basemen of all time—"you better get yourself a bird cage, or you-all will lose your schoolgirl complexion."[42]

The next day, Williams got another chance to play first base. He had hit for Berry in the ninth inning and was intentionally walked—he then proceeded to steal the 154th (official) and final stolen base of his career—and Todt had been taken out for a pinch runner. In the top of the 10th, he did record one putout, but also Moe Berg hit a slow roller in Williams's direction, which squeezed past both him and second baseman Wally Gerber. A run would score on the play to give Chicago the lead. Boston would rally for two runs to win, but the experiment of Williams at first base was over.

Williams's career was inevitably winding down. But he still had one momentous game left in him. He got the start in center field against the White Sox on August 4, a Sunday game played at Braves Field. Defensively, he was noted for "making some nice running catches."[43] But, as usual, it was with the bat that he would serve the greatest notice.

In the first inning, he crushed a pitch from Chicago's Ed Walsh—son of the Hall of Famer—sending it off a cigarette sign in right-center field for a triple. In the third, he hit a shot into the right-field bleachers, barely foul. He then hit the next pitch over the first-base bag—but that, too, was called foul. He'd pop out, but he had Walsh's number. And in the fifth, he walloped a Walsh offering into the "far corner"[44] of the right-field pavilion for the final home run of his career, No. 196. He also scored three of Boston's eight runs, the first time he had touched home plate that many times in a game since April 18, 1928.

Williams started the next two games as well, the final ones of the home stand, including on August 8 against Washington left-hander Lloyd Brown, although Carrigan used Ruffing to hit for him in the ninth inning of the 3–2 loss.

Boston traveled to Chicago next to play the White Sox on August 10. Even though he had started three straight games, there was no doubt he'd be in the lineup, as Walsh was on the mound for the White Sox.

Batting third, Williams began the day in center field and later moved to left when Rothrock replaced Scarritt. Williams's day against Walsh wasn't as successful as his last outing against the Chicago right-hander. He went 0-for-2 with a sacrifice and two walks while scoring a run.

At some point in the game, Williams fouled a ball off his foot. He played the entire game, but the injury was serious enough that he sat out the next couple of contests and eventually was sent back to Boston by Carrigan "for repairs."[45] Williams would never play another game in the major leagues.

In September, the *Syracuse Herald* ran an article on pinch hitters. At the end, it remarked that Williams is "old and slowed up and he wouldn't do for regular duty in the outfield, but he is staying in the majors because he can hit."[46] If only there were that permanent pinch hitter for the pitcher.

That hypothesis was inaccurate, however. Williams showed early on in the season that pinch hitting might not be his forte. He needed regular work. In the 28 games he started for Boston in 1929, Williams batted .344 with a .417 on-base percentage and .604 slugging percentage. Overall on the season in limited duty (74 games, 161 plate appearances), he hit .345 with a .409 on-base percentage and .540 slugging percentage, all easily team highs (the next best slugger was Ruffing, a pitcher, at .439).

Changes, once again, would be afoot in Boston in the offseason. Carrigan, who liked old-school players like Williams, went back into retirement. He led Boston to more wins each year he was manager, but that still amounted to just 166 over three seasons. Heinie Wagner, another from the heyday championship years in the teens, was hired as his replacement.

The offseason was a quiet one for Williams back in Oregon. The stock market had crashed in October, but this was not something that would immediately impact Williams and his family. He was preparing to be one of the 38 Red Sox players to be training in Sarasota, Florida, in the spring. But the seeds for his departure were planted in mid–January and it wasn't too long thereafter he was no longer property of the Red Sox.

Chapter 17

Back to the Minors

Heinie Wagner was a friend and cohort of Bill Carrigan. The two played together for years on good Red Sox teams in the 1910s, were briefly partners in a minor-league team, and when Carrigan came back to manage Boston in 1927, he hired Wagner as one of his coaches.

Carrigan was fed up with the game and players—the usual next-generation problems of "they don't do the things we used to do"—but he didn't dissuade Wagner from succeeding him, or at least failed to do so.

Boston won just 59 games in 1929 and wasn't poised to be any better in 1930. Only one starting position player was 25 or under—Jack Rothrock, who would turn 25 in March.

On January 18, Wagner came into Boston for a luncheon. There, he and Bob Quinn talked shop. The Red Sox had made no moves all offseason, save for the drafting of a few Rule 5 players back in October—infielder Otis Miller, 29, a teammate of Ken Williams on the Browns in 1927; first baseman Bill Sweeney, 25; and pitcher George Smith, 28.

Boston didn't have a lot of wherewithal to get better. The talent on the team was marginal as it was, and Quinn didn't have the money to go out and make big splashes for young minor-league superstars. But during that lunch the two decided to get younger in the outfield.

On January 29, the team sold Williams to the New York Yankees for the $1,500 waiver price, then turned around and gave that money to the A's for outfielder Tom Oliver, a 27-year-old who had never played in the majors and who batted .338 for Little Rock in 1929.

Quinn had a history with Williams and wanted to get him to somewhere he might be able to fit in. He thought the Yankees would be that place. "Kenneth had not exactly outlived his usefulness here, but Quinn felt the veteran left-handed slugger will have one of those well-known new leases on life with the Yanks,"[1] wrote the *Boston Herald*.

In the many years since this transaction, it has been falsely reported as fact that the Yankees made this move to pressure Babe Ruth into signing. Ruth had been holding out, balking at the Yankees' offer of $75,000.

The Yankees had already gotten rid of Bob Meusel, sold to Cincinnati in October, and backup outfielder/pinch hitter Ben Paschal, who was traded to St. Paul of the American Association, as part of a deal to acquire catcher Bubbles Hargrave.

There was an opening in New York for Williams in a limited role—and not as some stalking horse to get Ruth back in camp. In its story on the transaction, the Associated Press reported Williams "can not be expected to make a place for himself in the Yankees outfield, but probably will be used as a pinch hitter."[2]

As late as February 23, Richard Vidmer of the *New York Daily News* in his season preview included Williams in his list of Yankees outfielders, but noted he "probably will be used principally as a pinch hitter."[3]

When he found out Williams was available, manager Bob Shawkey urged team president Ed Barrow to get the outfielder, as he imagined Williams getting a few shots at the short right-field fence at Yankee Stadium.

Barrow had his own reasoning for picking up someone like Williams. "We've traded Meusel and Ruth won't sign. We've got some fine-looking youngsters like [Sam] Byrd and [Dusty] Cooke, but you can't be too sure about inexperienced players," Barrow told the *New York Herald Tribune*. "They may be great and then again they may not. Williams knows what it's all about and he will be a handy man to have around in case—well, in case."[4]

In a line fed to newspapermen, Williams seemed overjoyed to be with New York, although the statement is fraught with questions as to whether Williams actually said any of it.

"I've wanted to be a Yank since I first broke into major-league ball with Cincinnati in 1915," Williams was purported to say. "Now that I've made the grade I'm going to make good. They say I'm through but I'm only six months older than Babe Ruth and he's still worth $80,000 per year."[5] The quote, however, reeks of public relations.

First, when Williams broke in with the Reds, the Yankees finished in fifth place with a 69–83 record. The previous four years, the Yankees placed sixth, seventh, eighth and sixth, never finishing above .500 and totaling wins in the 50s twice. This was hardly a model franchise one dreamed to be a part of. Second, Williams never called attention to his fake age. This was something always brought up by others.

Regardless of the reason or feelings, Williams had a chance to once again play for a good team. The Yankees had won 88 games in 1929 and finished in second place, although the death of manager Miller Huggins put a shroud on the season. Shawkey, who pitched for the team from 1915 to 1927, was brought in to manage. (Ironically, 1930 would be the only season both he and Boston's Wagner would ever manage in the majors.)

Williams was labeled one of four Yankees holdouts in mid–February, but that more had to do with the timing of New York's acquiring him and getting a contract sent out to Grants Pass. Despite the claim from Yankees management that owner Jacob Ruppert "made no salary cuts this season,"[6] Williams was offered $8,000, down from the $9,500 he had earned in each of his years with Boston. That offer was more than fair for a player looked at as a reserve, and Williams sent back the contract with his signature in short order.

Williams made the trip to St. Petersburg for spring training, but this time by himself and by train. His wife had been pregnant, but there were complications. Ethel Williams had been "having problems"[7] during the pregnancy and went to Eugene, Oregon, to see Dr. Merle Howard, a cousin. Ethel went into labor and gave birth to a second son, Jack, on December 31, 1929, but she nearly didn't survive.

"My mother, supposedly, died on the table as she was giving birth," Jack said years later, relaying the tale told to him, "and Dr. Merle just kept working on her for 10 or 15 minutes beyond what was normal to bring her back, and he did, so everything was great from then on."[8] The Williamses were so indebted, they gave Jack the middle name of Merle.

A little over a month later, Williams had moved from the Red Sox to the Yankees and a month after that, he entered a Pullman car to make his trek to Florida. Needless to say, his life had been something of a whirlwind.

Williams arrived in St. Petersburg the morning of March 3 with many of the other veterans, save second baseman Tony Lazzeri, who was still on his way from California. It was unseasonably cold—temperatures dipping below freezing at night—and local legend and former mayor Al Lang was seen wearing a heavy jacket.

Ruth had been mulling around camp for days, watching practice, and he took part in stretching exercises with Williams, Lou Gehrig, Herb Pennock, Ed Wells and Tom Zachary, in an effort to warm up. The group also took plenty of pictures, but did nothing else strenuous on the cold day.

The next day was just as cold, and Shawkey pushed practice back so the players could have additional time to warm up. It was on this day that Williams's major-league career would really come to an end as he hurt his back during practice, the cold weather likely not helping.

Ruth was again in camp, although in a white sweatshirt as young outfielder Cooke wore the No. 3 uniform. However, despite being unsigned, Ruth did participate in a scrimmage on March 6, playing first base and hitting a single and a triple. As the team practiced on March 7, Williams "spent most of the day in the club house"[9] due to his "lame back."[10]

The *New York Times* reported, "Manager Shawkey is anxiously awaiting the addition of Williams to his working forces."[11] A few days passed and Williams was still out, while Ruth had signed on May 10 and New York had played its first two spring training games against the Boston Braves.

There was a ray of hope, however, as the *Times* noted Williams was back at practice on May 12 and had a chance to play when the Yankees renewed action against the Braves in a few days.

Alas, when the game came, Williams was still unable to play. A week went by with the Yankees playing the Braves, Reds and Cardinals over that stretch and Williams not seeing any action. Finally, the Yankees had no choice but to release him.

The move likely was unsurprising to Williams and perhaps a relief. His wife was still recovering back home, and before he even left for training camp, "it was rumored on the streets of Grants Pass … that he would attempt to get transferred to the Pacific Coast [League],"[12] according to the *Grants Pass Daily Courier*. The *Courier* also noted that Williams "had told intimate friends that he could save more money on a smaller salary in the Pacific Coast League than he could by playing in the majors."[13]

Williams told reporters that he was headed back home, "where his wife was ill."[14] It didn't take long to figure out where Williams wanted to play. Upon his release from the Yankees, Williams sent a telegram to Tom Turner, president of the Portland Beavers, asking for a meeting at the San Jose train depot.

Finishing out a pro career in the minors was hardly the exception in those days. The difference was Williams was doing it at a much later age than most of his contemporaries. Williams was still a productive hitter in the majors at age 39 when many of those he played with or against were done in baseball. The fact he played in the majors at that advanced age in that era was indeed rare.

Looking back at his teammates with the 1922 Browns, George Sisler played his last season in the majors in 1930 at age 37 with the Braves, but he never topped a .327 batting average or .430 slugging percentage in his final four seasons. He then played two more years in the minors. The slugging second baseman of that team, Marty McManus, played until 1934—

but at 34 he was done, before he too went off to play in the minor leagues. Shortstop Wally Gerber hadn't had a slugging percentage over .300 since 1925, but he hung around thanks to his reputation with the glove. Like Williams, his final season was with the Red Sox in 1929—although he batted just .165 in 61 games. Gerber then played one year in St. Paul, turning 39 in August. Catcher Hank Severeid was done in the majors at age 35, but amazingly played in the minors until he was 46.

Williams's longtime outfield mates in St. Louis, Baby Doll Jacobson and Johnny Tobin, both played their final major-league seasons in 1927 at the ages of 36 and 35. Jacobson would play two more years in the minors—appearing on four teams in 1928—while Tobin would play sporadically over the next three years, playing in only 83 games.

Even Bob Meusel, who battled Williams for a couple of home run crowns and whom the Yankees sold to the Reds the previous October, would play only one season in Cincinnati and then two years in the minors. He was done at 35 (Williams was having one of his best major-league seasons at age 35, in 1925, before being hit in the head).

The *Portland Oregonian* noted the Beavers "must have more batting power,"[15] but if Williams asked for a "big league salary plus a sweetener for signing, 'tis hardly likely they will come to terms."[16]

The meeting did not go well. The two ended up talking nearly all day at the Beavers training camp in San Jose. When asked about how things went, a gruff Williams told reporters he had turned down Turner's offer and there's no way he'd sign unless the Portland president "revises his figures."[17]

When reporters pressed for more details, Williams snapped back, "Get the rest from Turner. I don't care to go into details. So far as I am concerned, my mind is made up."[18] Turner didn't give many more details, other than he thought he had made a "very liberal"[19] offer to Williams, who reportedly wanted a $5,000 signing bonus on top of his contract.

A stewing Williams headed home to Grants Pass, but it didn't take him long to realize that Portland indeed was where he wanted to play. There were overtures from other teams in other leagues, but Williams had hoped to play out west and near his hometown, limiting his options. San Francisco, the next closest team to Grants Pass in the PCL, had said it wasn't interested in signing Williams.

A few days after turning down Turner's offer, Williams called the Portland boss and told him he'd accept terms. He would make $5,000 for the season and also be paid a $2,500 bonus, overall just $500 less than if he had made the Yankees (although the Beavers played a longer schedule and thus more games in the PCL).

"I could have gone back east if I wanted to," Williams told the Associated Press after agreeing to terms with the Beavers, "but with my wife sick I didn't want to. Portland will please me much better. It means that I will be closer to home, for one thing."[20]

Portland was finishing up its spring training, but Williams would leave to join the team as it ventured back to Oregon. He was a bit concerned that the squad had gone through most of its training, but assured that he was "in pretty good shape, and I don't think it will take me long to be at the top of my form."[21]

Williams arrived at camp in San Jose—which had been "electrified"[22] with the news of his signing—on April 3 and would see many familiar faces, including his former teammate from the last time he played in Portland back in 1917, the eccentric Duster Mails. Former major leaguers on the team included Walter French, Carl Mays, ex–Browns teammates Tony

Rego (who would be released at the end of the month) and Gene Robertson, and player-manager Larry Woodall.

Williams had yet to play in a spring game, even with New York, but the next day he was in the starting lineup for Portland batting fourth and playing right field—a position he had played exactly once in the majors—July 2, 1929 (and only for part of the game). Nevertheless, he went 1-for-3 with a double and a run. And just like that, Williams was part of Portland's starting lineup with the season set to begin just four days later.

Williams would admit he wasn't in shape yet and might need a couple of weeks before his legs felt right—and the *Oregonian* would note that he was "quite plainly out of shape"[23]—yet he opened the season with eight hits in his first 18 at-bats.

Having this particular former major leaguer on the team—someone who was from and lived in Oregon and previously played for the Beavers, albeit 13 years earlier—was an attraction for Portland. The Beavers' home opener on April 22 drew roughly 4,000 more fans than any other PCL opening game.

By all accounts, being back in Portland agreed with Williams. Despite the fact he would soon turn 40, Williams could still hit. There was—not counting a 4½-inning rained-out game—a 15-game hit streak early in the season in which he went a blistering 31-for-57 (.544). There was another 17-game hit streak which ended on June 7 in which he was 25-for-65 (.385) with three doubles, four home runs, 18 RBI and 11 runs. In late June–early July there would be a tremendous 12-game streak (20-for-36, .556). Right around the midpoint of the season, July 19, Williams was leading Portland in batting and 15th in the league with a .346 average. He also had 17 doubles, three triples and nine home runs in his 321 at-bats.

There were some other smaller hit streaks along the way—five games here, six games there—and Williams maintained consistency throughout the season. He would finish leading the team with a .350 average (good for ninth in the league), .500 slugging percentage, 110 RBI and, believe it or not, 23 stolen bases. His 14 home runs were second on the Beavers only to future major leaguer Bob Johnson, who had 21. "There were times when it was just impossible for an opposing pitcher to keep Williams from hitting,"[24] the *Oregonian*'s L.H. Gregory would later write.

Williams was also having a good time out in the field. He would occasionally banter with fans in the left-field bleachers. Often he would talk to himself, much to the delight of the paying customers.

Once while chasing after a ball he exclaimed to himself, "I'm a goner, I'm a goner,"[25] only to then say to himself, "I got a break on that one"[26] when it hit foul. After one particularly splendid running grab, Williams said to himself for all to hear, "That was a great catch, Ken!"[27]

Not all was peachy, of course. There was still the "crabby" side of Williams that would go on display. In particular was a game in Oakland on September 11, a 7–1 Portland loss. When outfield mate Roger Cramer dove for a line drive and it was called a hit, Williams protested. So did pitcher Mails, who was ejected. Williams came in from the outfield to issue his protests to umpire Louie Kolis and decided not to return to his position. Instead, Williams took his place "around shortstop."[28] Kolis told Williams to get back to the outfield, which, of course, Williams refused to do, especially after being so ordered. Kolis then ejected Williams. "Kolis may have been wrong in trying to tell Williams where he should play for a batter," wrote the *Oakland Tribune*, "but at the same time the fans approved of his stand."[29]

That was one of Williams's last games. He'd appear in a few more—even serving as acting manager in one after Larry Woodall was ejected—before missing the final 33 games. Injuries took their toll throughout the season—no surprise, perhaps, for a 40-year-old ballplayer—and Williams would miss 50 games overall, playing in 148 of Portland's 198 (which was also his most games since 1922, when he appeared in 153).

While Williams no doubt relished playing in Portland, close to home, and he enjoyed a solid season at the plate, it was yet another poor team on which he played. Portland went 39–61 in the first half of the season and 42–56 in the second half. The 81–117 overall record was the worst in the PCL.

That Portland team had several future and former major leaguers, as did the other teams around the Pacific Coast League. But Williams would get one more chance to show he was a major-league caliber hitter.

A traveling team of star major leaguers was to make a stop in Portland for a game October 19 after winding their way through Montana and Washington. This team was made up of a number of players in their prime, not to mention future Hall of Famers, including Detroit second baseman Charlie Gehringer, who hit .330 with a .534 slugging percentage in 1930, and outfielder Harry Heilmann (.337, 19 home runs, .577 slugging percentage). Other players included former teammates of Williams, catcher Wally Schang and outfielder Bing Miller. On the mound for this all-star conglomeration would be Lefty Grove, who was coming off a season in which he went 28–5 with a 2.54 ERA in leading the Philadelphia Athletics to their second consecutive World Series championship.

Williams hadn't played since September 14, but he was not going to miss this ballgame. He would play on a team of "locals," an intermixing of Portland teammates such as Bob Johnson and Gene Robertson, along with Brooklyn's Johnny Frederick, who lived in Oregon, and area semi-pro players. Williams would bat his customary fourth in the lineup and play his usual left field.

If Grove wasn't giving it his all, it didn't show up in the box score. The Athletics ace pitched all nine innings of a 4–3 victory. He also struck out every batter at least once (including the final three)—11 in total—except for one: Williams.

In perhaps his last hurrah, and against a Hall of Fame hurler no less, Williams, who had his troubles at times against lefties, socked two doubles—the Portland locals only had seven hits—and scored twice.

But while the major leaguers would move on to play in Yakima, Washington (Grove would start again, pitching one inning and striking out all three batters he faced before moving to left field), Williams's days of facing major leaguers was indeed over.

While Williams's career in the big leagues was done, he wasn't quite ready to end his professional playing days. Despite approaching his 41st birthday, Williams was back with Portland in 1931 and in the offseason was listed as a likely starting outfielder by *The Sporting News*, along with former Red Sox teammate Ira Flagstead and Homer Summa, who was done in the majors after a 10-year career, but who was just 32.

However, in Portland's first spring training game on March 11, new Beavers manager Spencer Abbott fielded an outfield of Summa, Flagstead and Ed Coleman, who played for San Francisco in 1930. Two days later, Summa was gone, dealt to Mission for Fred Berger. Unlike Summa, Coleman and Williams, Berger was a right-handed hitter. Williams and Berger would split time in left field in spring training.

Portland represented a homecoming for Williams, of course, but it wasn't the only familiar haunt he'd visit. The Beavers played two spring training games in 1931 against Seattle in Woodland, California, where Williams had appeared briefly before embarking on his pro career with Regina of the Western Canada League in 1913.

It was noted that some in the crowd remembered Williams, who was described as a "tall lanky youth"[30] when he played for Woodland. Only the youth part had changed about his appearance. The man they called "Home Run" back in 1913 put a charge into the ball some 18 years later as well, tripling in one of the two Portland wins.

It was another dose of his previous playing days when Portland opened the season in San Francisco, the first to play in the Seals' new $1.25 million stadium. Taking the ceremonial first swing was certainly someone Williams knew, but likely didn't approach, Ty Cobb. It wasn't noted in the story whether the two spoke, but since Cobb never liked Williams and at one time accused Williams and other St. Louis Browns of throwing games, if they did meet, one can imagine a short, curt exchange.

Williams started that game (going 1-for-5) and was seeing the majority of the playing time. He was just 3-for-16 in the first four games, but with three walks and a hit by pitch, he had an on-base percentage of .350. The next day, April 11, he had four hits and five RBI in a 17–0 Portland win over the Seals.

But the times were changing all around Williams. Youth surrounded him. Berger was just 22 and Portland received 25-year-old Bob Johnson back from the A's. The game itself wasn't necessarily changing, but other facets of it were.

In 1930, several PCL teams installed floodlights to allow for baseball to be played at night, preceding such action in the major leagues by five years. Portland played its first night game on July 22, 1930—Williams had a single his first time at-bat and went 4-for-5.

"You can't stop progress and I believe night baseball games are a step forward in the national pastime, so let there be light at Wrigley Field,"[31] Los Angeles Angels owner Williams Wrigley, Jr., had stated.

Not everyone had the foresight of Wrigley, however. After the Beavers' initial game under the lights, the *Oregonian*'s L.H. Gregory wrote, "I wasn't sure before, but after seeing my first night baseball game, it is the belief of your correspondent that night baseball will not replace the daylight kind. Not permanently, now or ever. It's a great novelty.... I am convinced the night game is a freak of the baseball fashion parade. Class it for permanency with blue shoes for men and picture hats for women."[32]

Williams was more pragmatic in his approach to night baseball. Less than a week after Portland's foray into the new world of lights, Williams was visiting a cousin in Eugene, Oregon, and remarked he was "not especially enthusiastic over night baseball and says many of the players have not become accustomed to night playing. He says it certainly has helped the box office, however."[33]

Lights weren't the only change to Portland's Stadium on Vaughn Street. A grandstand was to be built by May 1, or else the mayor was threatening to tear down a fence and run a street right through the stadium, behind first base. An expensive speaker system was installed, said to cost around $12,000 and provided by the Standard Oil company, so announcements of players, music before the game and during the "seventh inning intermission,"[34] as well as other information could be heard throughout the stadium (and supposedly up to a mile away as well).

But before Portland opened its home season, it still had to finish up a long opening road trip in Oakland. The game on April 14 provided another rarity for Williams—the game was being broadcast on radio, with KLX sports announcer Otto Egenberger providing the details.

In the fifth inning, Egenberger told listeners of Williams's stepping to the plate and socking a two-run home run over the right-field wall off Oakland's Frank Tubbs. What neither Egenberger nor Williams nor anyone knew was that would be Williams's final home run as a professional baseball player.

Williams was cemented as one of Portland's starting outfielders, along with Berger and Coleman. The Beavers beat the Oaks in the game Williams homered, and then hammered Oakland the next day 19–6, putting them at 6–3 and in first place. Williams was 12-for-25 in his last five games—which included one time in which he was hitless in three at-bats—with the home run, two triples and 11 RBI.

Williams started the first 12 games for Portland—which upped its record to 8–4 after a 5–0 win over Oakland on April 18—batting .340 (18-for-53) in that span. But he wasn't able to complete that 12th start.

With Portland leading 2–0 in the fifth inning, Williams drove a ball deep to center field, the hit easily scoring Berger, who was on third after tripling. Williams looked to duplicate Berger's feat, but when he slid into third, he came up writhing in pain. He left the field carried away by some of his teammates.

Williams's ankle was severely sprained and there was no clear timetable for his return. Portland immediately went into a funk, losing six of its next seven games. However, there was a bright spot for the Beavers.

With Williams hurt, Portland started playing Bob Johnson, who had been sent to the Beavers from the Philadelphia A's on April 10. Johnson would play left field on occasion and rotate in at second base as well when Ira Flagstead was used in the outfield.

The 25-year-old Johnson, who would eventually hit 288 home runs in the majors, quickly showed he belonged in the lineup. He hit in eight of his first nine games, going 18-for-31 with a couple of home runs.

The world around Williams was once again changing. It was a young man's sport and slowly turning into a power game. And not just in baseball. On May 1, the Empire State Building, representing America's desire to get bigger and better, was opened, reaching 1,200 feet into the sky.

Williams, who helped usher in the power era, was finally able to get off the bench and onto the field the previous day. He wasn't fully healthy, but was called upon to hit against Herman Pillette with two out in the ninth inning with a man on first base and Portland down by one. After not playing for two weeks, Williams didn't wait around. He smacked the first pitch he saw for a "roaring single"[35] to set the Beavers up with runners at the corners, but Larry Woodall then bounced to second to end the game.

Two days later he entered the game after Berger was taken out for a pinch runner. Williams played left field for two innings and in the ninth raced home—as much as one can on a hobbled ankle—from second base to score the winning run on a single up the middle by Jack Fenton.

Abbott decided Williams was healthy enough to be back in the starting lineup. Williams played left field in both ends of a double-header against Mission, but he was hitless in seven at-bats (but still second the PCL in batting average, minimum 40 at-bats).

On May 5, Williams had an RBI single, but two days later he looked his age against Seattle's Johnny Miljus and Dick Bonelly, weakly popping up twice, hitting a slow bouncer on another and waving on a Bonelly curveball for strike three.

Williams responded to the poor outing with a 1-for-3 game, along with an RBI the next game, but on May 9 he wasn't in the starting lineup. Flagstead was in left and Coleman in right with Johnson in center, the latter hitting another home run.

On May 10, exactly 16 years to the day when his major-league career looked to be over after the Cincinnati Reds waived him out of the National League and back to Spokane, Ken Williams was released from the Portland Beavers.

The main reason given was Williams's legs just couldn't get back in shape. But Portland also had a lot of emerging young players—players who could possibly be sold or traded to the majors—in Berger, Johnson and Coleman. Flagstead would also eventually be traded to Seattle to give the trio more playing time. (And it was rewarded, as Berger hit .275 with nine home runs, Johnson .337 with 22 home runs, and Coleman .358 with 57 doubles, 14 triples, 37 HR and 183 RBI.)

A late slump brought Williams's average down to .276 (21-for-76) and he had just four extra-base hits (a double, two triples and a homer), but he did finish with 15 RBI and 12 runs in his 20 games with Portland in 1931.

Every team in the Pacific Coast League passed on Williams in waivers. There would later be a rumor that Williams was headed to Kansas City to sign with the American Association Blues, but that never came to pass. Ken Williams's professional baseball career was over.

"Well, they all walk down the long baseball trail to retirement in time," Gregory wrote, "and it's legs that fail them more often than eyes or arms."[36] A United Press story summed up the end of Williams's days with, "He passed on with the regrets of many admirers."[37]

Williams had plenty of boosters back in his hometown of Grants Pass, where he headed once Portland released him. "He came back to Grants Pass and he just decided to put [professional baseball] out of his mind," Ken Williams, Jr., said. "As I understand it, he had a chance at a coaching job back east with one of the teams—which one, I have no idea of course—and he wouldn't take it. He wanted to come home to Grants Pass. I think he just wanted to get away from it."[38]

Coming full circle on his career, Williams signed up with the local team, the Cavemen, which eventually would be financially sponsored by the Elks Lodge, of which Williams was a member.

He played several games, batting cleanup, of course, but playing first base, likely to help save his legs. Williams was even joined at times by 43-year-old Jud Pernoll, who preceded Williams on the old Grants Pass semipro team. But Williams's baseball career ended much like it started—with little fanfare.

Chapter 18

The Hometown Boy Returns to Grants Pass—and St. Louis

When the Grants Pass baseball team opened its 1932 season at Jacksonville, Ken Williams was there and in the batter's box. However, unlike in previous years when he took his place at the plate, this time Williams was there for purely ceremonial reasons.

Mayor George Fox was there to throw out the first pitch and Williams to take the opening swing. With a good-natured flail, Williams missed Fox's offering and the season was underway—a baseball season that would no longer include Ken Williams as a participant.

Now that Ken Williams was retired, he had to find something else to bide his time and provide for his family, which included a now 8-year-old Ken Jr. and 2-year-old Jack. This was no easy task. He had little education and played baseball all of his adult life. On top of that, the United States was in the early years of the Great Depression, which would last until the end of the decade.

The Williamses were fortunate that Ken made enough money during his baseball career to provide them with some comfort. They owned their own house—estimated worth of $5,000 in 1930—which was built when they lived in St. Louis and Ken played for the Browns.

The one-story house on 5th Street had an expansive attic, where the boys slept. There were two bedrooms on the main floor along with a family room, dining room and a small kitchen. The house also featured a rarity in Grants Pass for that time period—a large basement, although it regularly flooded during the winter months.

Still, there was the task of trying to feed the family. Yes, Williams had some money left over from his playing days, but with no other income that would only last so long. For a quick fix, Ken Jr. and his cousins, who had a house adjacent to the Williams's backyard, would husk the walnut trees that formed a barrier between their two homes. They would eat whatever nuts they could and give away the remainder to whomever was in need.

And, of course, Williams could always get out his rod and reel. "Later on, my brother told me, there were times when dad and mom went kind of hungry to feed us kids," Jack Williams recalled. "I don't think very hungry because dad would just go fishing. He could outfish anyone for 100 miles around."[1]

To make money, at one point Ken and Ethel got a double broiler and set it up in the basement. There, they cooked up what would be known as Kenny's Crackers. They would set wire racks up around some of the local restaurants and bars to sell the product and Ken Jr. would help stock them as he rode around town on his newspaper route.

"And that's the way they got through some of the time during the depression, was making Kenny's Crackers," Jack Williams said. "These were great. I can just vaguely remember them. They were like potato chips, only they were this kind of puffy stuff. Only they were chocolate and cheese and tomato and several other flavors, and they were great."[2]

Thanks to his time in the major leagues, Ken Williams was somewhat of a local celebrity—he'd referee an occasional boxing or wrestling match and help out with the high school baseball team. In 1934, he sent one youngster out to his old stomping ground in Woodland, California, to the training camp of the Pacific Coast League's Mission Reds, with instructions to give manager Gabby Street a note from Williams introducing this player, Art La Von. Street noted that La Von had no baseball cleats, so the player said he'd go get some. Street never saw him again.

Baseball would remain part of Williams's life in some capacity. He'd occasionally venture to the high school and lend a hand when needed, offering advice gleaned from his years as a professional.

Not that his kids had any inkling of his career. Ken and Ethel Williams rarely if ever talked about his past. "He wasn't the sort of fellow to talk about 'back in the old days,'" Jack Williams said. "He wouldn't even play ball with us kids much. He'd play a little catch, and that was about it, because he claimed that by then things had changed, and things were all different."[3]

Ken Williams, Jr., said his parents never kept a scrapbook of Ken Williams's baseball days, which they seemed to regret later in life. "The only thing I knew was the home run thing in '22," remembered Ken Jr. "They just never talked about it. It was in the past. Whether it hurt or not, I just don't know."[4]

As far as the Williams boys knew, the baseballs their dad had were just ordinary balls for their use to play catch. Of course, those baseballs had signatures, including from his former St. Louis Browns teammates. At least, they included them until the boys got through playing.

"I bet they were thrilled to death with me," Ken Jr. wryly related. "They had whole team signatures on the ball, and things like that. And I know I ruined two or three of them and threw them out."[5]

This certainly didn't go over well with Ken Williams, who was a stern father. "He had me scared to death, but he never touched me. Never got a whipping from him or anything like that,"[6] said Jack Williams, who noted his friends wouldn't come over if his dad was home.

But, like any dad, there were times he'd play catch with his sons. Ken Jr. would play for his high school team and local clubs. Once when he was in high school he asked his dad for some advice. "How do you see a curveball, Dad?" Ken Jr. wondered. To which Ken Williams replied, "I watch the stitches."[7]

"And I said, wait a minute, wait a minute," Ken Jr. recalled over 60 years later. "I'm having trouble seeing the ball and you're seeing the stitches? And he said, 'Well, yeah, you can tell which way the ball is going.' He had around 20–15 [eyesight] I think."[8] Needless to say, Ken Jr.'s baseball career ended in Grants Pass. The elder Williams's baseball career wasn't forgotten, though.

In 1936, in "recognition of long and meritorious service to baseball,"[9] Williams was issued a lifetime pass to any Major League Baseball game. Of course, living in Oregon and the West Coast—and not one to travel out of that area—there was little use for such a card in 1936. But that would change in 1937.

By that time, Williams would have himself a full-time job (Ethel Williams would later also get a job, in the office of a local dairy during World War II). Grants Pass was forming a complete police force and needed officers. Williams was given a uniform, a badge and a portable siren that he'd use in the family car. The job paid well enough. According to the 1940 census, he worked 48 hours a week and made $1,320 in 1939, which was just slightly below the average yearly income in the United States ($1,368).

In mid–July of 1937, Williams would take some vacation time. He and his family were headed to St. Louis to celebrate the 15th anniversary of the 1922 Browns. Like the many times he traveled to spring training, on July 13 Williams boarded himself, his wife and kids into the family car and made the 2,000-mile, three-day trek from Grants Pass to St. Louis. Upon arrival at their hotel, young Jack Williams was amazed by the height of the buildings and made notice of the elevator, the first time he had ever encountered one.

The entire 1922 Browns team sojourned in St. Louis, including manager Lee Fohl and coach Lefty Leifeld, with four exceptions. Pitcher Urban Shocker had died in 1928 due to a congenital heart condition, while third baseman Eddie Foster was killed just six months before the event in a mysterious car accident where he was found dead half a mile down the road from his automobile. At age 46, Hank Severeid was still doing a little catching as well as managing for the Galveston team in the Texas League, so he couldn't attend. Third baseman Gene Robertson, meanwhile, couldn't be located.

The occupations of the former players were quite varied. While Williams was now a policeman, Elam Vangilder farmed—when he wasn't pitching for a semi-pro team in Cape Girardeau. Dave Danforth was a dentist, Chick Shorten a grocer, Pat Collins ran a bowling alley, while Wally Gerber remained in baseball as an umpire in the Mid-Atlantic League.

The group was greeted by a welcoming committee of Marty McManus, Johnny Tobin and Heinie Meine (who pitched in just one game for the '22 Browns before resurfacing with Pittsburgh from 1929 to 1934), all of whom lived in St. Louis. Their first order of business came the day before the official ceremony.

On July 16, the reassembled team made their way to Bellefontaine and Calvary cemeteries to pay their respects and lay floral wreaths at the graves of owner Phil Ball, who died in 1933, and Shocker.

The public reunion took place July 17 before the Browns played Philadelphia. The 1922 team would play a three-inning game against the current St. Louis squad. The majority of the former players were out of shape and hadn't played baseball in years. Williams's hair was now on the silver side and he had a few more wrinkles in his face, but thanks to his great genetics he was still at his playing weight (which couldn't be said of many of his cohorts).

The present-day Browns would play against the latter-day team with the same lineup they'd use against the A's, except for the pitcher-catcher battery. Williams jogged out to his usual place in left field and made two plays, including racing back to catch a deep fly off the bat of Beau Bell. At the plate, he'd only bat once, grounding out to second base.

The '22 team would record three hits—although on the final one, Chick Shorten was thrown out trying for a double after hitting the ball to the fence—and lost 2–0. Perhaps the pregame affair did the '37 Browns some good, though, as they scored seven runs in the first two innings in beating Philadelphia 10–2, one of their only 46 wins on the season.

There was still time for some reminiscing and plenty was done. Williams recalled the time he went back for a Bob Meusel fly ball and Baby Doll Jacobson told him he had plenty of room—right before Williams ran into the wall while the ball sailed over, 15 rows deep.

Writer Martin J. Haley recounted how the Red Sox, for whatever reason, didn't start Herb Pennock on the final day of the season against the Yankees but went with rookie Alex Ferguson instead, New York earning its clinching victory. "It appeared as if the Browns were not supposed to win that season,"[10] Haley said.

Referred to as a meeting of the "almost champions,"[11] that 1937 event would serve as the one and only true reunion of that 1922 team, perhaps the greatest in Browns history. Ken Williams would head back to Grants Pass and wouldn't set foot back in St. Louis, home of all those memories, for another two decades. Williams returned to his job as a policeman and rarely left his hometown. "He was a hometown boy, he really was. He came back there and just lived, that's all,"[12] Ken Williams, Jr., said.

In February 1944, his friend and fellow ex–major leaguer Jud Pernoll died. Pernoll had owned the Owl Billiard Parlor, a bar that housed billiard and snooker tables. On August 1, it was announced that Williams, along with his business partner Whitey Fleming, purchased the pool hall from R.E. Jewell, who had been Pernoll's partner.

Williams resigned as a police officer, and the Owl Billiard Parlor is where he would spend the majority of the remainder of his life. He'd help tend bar, watch over things, talk to friends who still called him "Dink," and once in a while regale customers with stories from his baseball past. "If you knew baseball, Ken would talk to you about it but only if you brought it up,"[13] employee Russell Blacksmith would say years later. "They made a good living out of it,"[14] said Ken Williams, Jr.

The Williams family. Ken is in the back row at the right; to his left are brothers Henry, Charlie and Edward. Carrie Williams is in front, with one unidentified family member (courtesy Larry LaBeck).

Ken Williams with Babe Ruth in Grants Pass, Oregon, circa 1932 (courtesy Larry LaBeck).

Baseball remained a part of Williams's life as well, although only intermittently. Williams was still something of a celebrity when his career ended—and his prestige was surely enhanced when American icons Babe Ruth and Jack Dempsey came for a visit to the small Oregon town. Williams and Ruth are shown in a photo holding fish, perhaps caught by the former home run rivals that day, although the long coat Williams is wearing, as well as the suit and tie adorning Ruth, might counterbalance that argument.

After suiting up in the reunion game in 1937, Williams donned the garb of the Oregon Cavemen—a team made up of former Grants Pass, Portland and Salem players—in an old-timers' game in Salem in June of 1940. Williams wouldn't play again after that, but he'd be invited to old-timers' games and attend as a spectator, including one in 1951 in Eugene with Ty Cobb also in attendance.

It wasn't just games, though. Williams started being recognized for how he played as well. In 1944, the *Portland Oregonian*'s Joe Gibbs placed Williams in his outfield on an all-star team, noting, "Williams was more than a long-distance hitter."[15] In 1953, the Portland Beavers had fans select an all-time team for the franchise's 50th anniversary and Williams was voted in as the left fielder. In 1954, Branch Rickey wrote an article for *Life* magazine and ranked the best hitters in baseball since 1920 using his own created formula. Williams was 16th on Rickey's list.

The biggest honor, though, came via a telegram near the end of 1957. Bob Burnes, the sports editor of the *St. Louis Globe Democrat*, wired Williams to let him know of his selection on the all-time all–St. Louis baseball team. Williams was invited to St. Louis in January 1958 for a dinner hosted by the local chapter of the Baseball Writers Association of America (BBWAA), which was celebrating its 50th year. There was no doubt that Williams would attend.

To be named to this team was an amazing accomplishment. First, because the Browns were no longer in St. Louis, having moved to Baltimore for the 1954 season. Second, due to the other names on the team, which was dotted with current and future Hall of Fame players.

The infield consisted of George Sisler, Rogers Hornsby, Frankie Frisch and Marty Marion. Bob O'Farrell and Hank Severeid were the catchers. Joining Williams in the outfield were Terry Moore and Stan Musial. Red Schoendienst (utility infield) and Tobin (utility outfield) rounded out the position players. Only four pitchers were named, but three are in the Hall of Fame and the other is arguably the greatest pitcher in Browns history: Grover Cleveland Alexander, Dizzy Dean, Jesse Haines and Urban Shocker.

This time, the nearly 68-year-old Williams avoided the nation's roads and flew to St. Louis from Medford, Oregon. Upon his arrival, he immediately caught up with Tobin and spent many hours talking to his former outfield mate. The two likely shared a story involving Ken Jr.

Williams's older son was stationed at Jefferson Barracks during World War II, just like his dad nearly 30 years prior during the First World War. Williams told his son to look up an old teammate, who happened to be the captain of the fire department.

"[I] found where that was, one of the sheds, and stepped in there and two guys sitting there and I walked up and said I'm looking for so-and-so," recalled Ken Jr., "and the guy said well, if you spit, you'll spit right on him. Oh, geez. I just told him hello for dad. That's the last I saw of him, too."[16] One can imagine the two old ballplayers sharing a laugh over that story.

Williams and Tobin joined the other players—everyone on the all-star team was in attendance other than Dean, whose father-in-law had died, and Alexander and Shocker, who had passed away—for a tour of Busch Stadium, formerly known as Sportsman's Park.

The stadium itself was similar in dimensions to what they had been when Williams played—although the fence in right field was actually closer by nearly 6 feet than in the 1920s when Williams was cranking out homers. "We still can remember that terrific swing and seeing him pump balls out of the park in the twenties,"[17] Burnes had written in the lead-up to the event.

One thing that had changed significantly was the clubhouse. Williams was wide-eyed impressed when he saw the whirlpool, television sets and even a record player for the players' use. Hornsby, obviously not as dazzled as Williams, curtly remarked, "Well, all this doesn't make a player. He still has to get out and show he knows how to play."[18]

The ceremony took place on January 21, 1958—coinciding with the NBA All-Star Game, which was to be played in St. Louis the following day—at the Hotel Sheraton–Jefferson with a $10-a-plate dinner, which sold out. It was a big enough deal that local radio station KMOX broadcast the ceremony.

The NBA players were there, including such notables as Boston's Bill Russell and Bob Cousy, Cincinnati's Maurice Stokes and St. Louis's own Bob Pettit, and Irish tenor Morton Downey served as a warmup act. The coaches in the All-Star Game, Alex Hannum of St. Louis and Boston's Red Auerbach, as well as NBA president Maurice Podoloff, all said a few words before the baseball festivities got underway.

Buddy Blattner, a St. Louis native who broadcast the *Game of the Week* (sponsored by St. Louis brewer Falstaff) with Dizzy Dean, emceed the event. The players were called up individually, given a nice plaque to commemorate the occasion and their placement on the all–St. Louis team and allowed to say a few words. Severeid, for example, proclaimed, "[L]et me assure you that while the Browns are no longer on the baseball scene, their memory will never die."[19]

The applause was great for all the players, which was no surprise for someone like Musial, who was still playing for the Cardinals and was coming off a season in which he led the National League with a .351 batting average. But the ovation saved for Williams was quite unexpected, at least by the former Brown.

Hours before even receiving his plaque, Williams was uneasy with the ceremony. He wasn't sure what he'd say and figured his reception would be tepid at best, especially compared to some of the other players.

But then Williams was announced. And then like a wave came the great applause. Williams's eyes welled with tears, and the applause grew even louder. As his son, Jack, would later say, "He couldn't talk that night. He never thought that people paid that much attention to him. He didn't realize how well known he really was."[20]

There are varying accounts as to the few words Williams was able to utter, but they displayed the great weight they carried. According to the *St. Louis Post-Dispatch*, Williams was able to get out, "This is the greatest honor I've ever had. It's wonderful to be back in St. Louis, a great privilege. Thanks to the fans, the owners, all of you."[21] Other accounts have Williams saying, "This is the most wonderful thing that has ever happened to me. All I can say is 'thank you.'"[22]

As the dinner and ceremony ended, people left the hotel, some straggling around to say goodbyes or reminisce one final time. The last to leave was Williams, because, he said, "I'm afraid this will be my last business."[23]

Williams was going to turn 68 in June; certainly he didn't see a lot of travel in his future. But he had had health issues as well. Despite all the fish he ate and his incredible metabolism, Williams wasn't a picture of health. He enjoyed a drink every now and again, especially when he went to play cards with friends, and everywhere he went he had a pack of cigarettes in his shirt pocket.

In 1945, Williams had suffered a heart attack. He became the first person in Josephine

County to be placed in an oxygen tank. Because Williams was something of a celebrity, this was news, and a picture appeared in the paper—complete with the mayor and a few others smoking cigars nearby.

"The whole thing could have blown sky-high. And they didn't know back then," Jack Williams remembered. "The mayor has a great big old stogie in mouth and he's probably not two feet from the oxygen tent."[24]

Beyond the lucky absence of an explosion, Williams was also fortunate to have survived the ordeal. "They thought, at that time, that he lived through it because his heart broke through and created another way to get blood around to get wherever it had to go in the heart, because they couldn't do anything about it at the time,"[25] Ken Jr. said.

Williams lost some weight, got tired of eating fish—Ethel would insist he eat it because it was good for him—and started getting nervous or fidgety right after the heart attack, but Jack noted, "I wouldn't say he changed a great deal as far as anything else is concerned."[26]

Williams went back to running the Owl Billiard Parlor and would continue to do so until around 1957. One report said he was told to quit by his doctor. However, Ken Williams, Jr., said new laws required the pool hall to install a restaurant, which didn't sit well with his father.

"I can remember dad was a little upset about it because they had to build a kitchen in the back of it and throw a couple of tables out to serve food," Ken Jr. said. "And I have no idea what they served, not too much I imagine. He sold it right after that."[27]

Williams was now retired, playing cards when he could and maybe hitting a fishing hole once in a while. He found out in July 1958 that the St. Louis Browns Fan Club had him as a part of their all-time Browns team (joining him in the outfield were, fittingly, Tobin and Jacobson). Other than these recent honors, he'd just turn on the *Game of the Week* during the season, and that was his total involvement in baseball. He hadn't been to a major-league game since that Browns reunion in St. Louis back in 1937.

But then, suddenly, there was one more chance. Bing Devine, the general manager of the Cardinals, invited the 13 living players from the all–St. Louis team back to town in August, for a game at Busch Stadium, so that more people than the 1,000 who happened to turn up at the BBWAA dinner could celebrate them.

Despite his declaration that he wouldn't return, Williams indeed made it back to St. Louis for this event. And it was quite the affair. Before the game between the Cardinals and Cincinnati Reds, St. Louis owner August A. Busch entertained the players—12 of the 13 living players were there, all but Schoendienst, who was still active, playing for the Milwaukee Braves—in his penthouse at the stadium.

"I wish I had all you fellows on my team. Then I wouldn't have a worry in the world,"[28] Busch told the players. Haines responded, "Mr. Busch, every one of us would give our right arm to be back here playing, even if for just one night."[29]

Perhaps a few would have liked to have seen Williams take a few swings. Burnes would write before the event, "A lot of fellows will be making book, Ken Williams, that you could still smash one onto Grand Avenue."[30]

The ceremony took place before the game, with players entering the stadium in left field in cars, two to a vehicle. The catchers, O'Farrell and Severeid, were in the first car. Williams and Tobin—"the old Brownie buddies,"[31] as emcee Joe Garagiola called them—followed.

Each player was wearing a uniform made by Rawlings to replicate the ones they wore

The original St. Louis Browns fan club based in Chicago (which went defunct sometime in the 1970s) came up with this promotion to get Ken Williams into the Hall of Fame by stumping for him on matchbook covers.

then they played (or in Musial's case, his actual uniform), although a little bigger than the ones they wore back in the day. It was noted that Williams was an exception, slim as usual (that metabolism and all), while Dizzy Dean wore a size 48.

The players circled the field in the cars. They eventually were called on individually by Garagiola and handed a silver money clip which was engraved with every all–St. Louis team member's name. In addition, pictures of each player were dedicated and would hang on display in the right-field concourse.

Williams and the others then retreated to the press box to watch the game, a 5–4 Cardinals victory. The game featured five home runs, which would cause Williams, Tobin and O'Farrell to grumble about the propensity of longballs. The former players said they were being cheapened due to the shortening of fences.

"They've pulled in the fences and livened the ball," Williams told *The Sporting News* was his main complaint about modern-day baseball:

> Do I think the present-day home-run sluggers will break Babe Ruth's record of 60 in one season? Well, they'll hit more than 60 homers, but it'll be a synthetic record, because Ruth hit genuine wallops far out of sight, not pop-fly cheap homers like they're getting today.
>
> Batters today are using 31- or 32-ounce bats, whereas my bat used to weigh 48 ounces. I have one at home that I weighed the other day. Still straight as a rifle barrel, but it's lost some of its weight—now down to 44. If the Babe were swinging these little lively bats at those close-in fences, he'd whack 100 or more homers in a season today, without any trouble.[32]

Tobin had coached for the Browns from 1949 to 1951, but found the job frustrating. He was the master of the bunt—and specifically the drag bunt—during his playing days, but bemoaned "nobody wanted to work too hard at bunting and if you're going to be good at it, you really have to work. And another thing, everybody wanted to swing for the fences."[33]

After the game, the troupe moved to Musial's restaurant—Stan Musial and Biggie's—

for dinner, drinks and a lot of conversation. Williams didn't shy away from speaking his mind. The Giants and Dodgers were playing their first season in California. Williams offered some perspective.

"Look at all the confusion they're having out there because their ballparks are not ready," he said. "Of course, that's a sore subject with me because I hated to see our Browns moved out of St. Louis. When I played here, back in the '20s, the Browns were the favored team here and I simply can't believe our St. Louis fans turned their backs on our old club."[34]

Williams also talked about the money players were making. He was specifically not happy with the bonus baby phenomenon, in which young players got big salaries right away and then stayed with the major-league team all year but rarely played.

He said:

> I wish I were young again. You don't have to play a game these days to get those big bonuses. It's reached a point where the clubs are outbidding each other for the kids' services. But I guess it's like buying an untried yearling race horse; you have to take a chance that he'll be a winner for you later on.
>
> But when you analyze the thing, it doesn't seem right for a seasoned player to work every day to earn his salary of say, $10,000, when along comes an untried kid, who actually sits on the bench all season and receives perhaps $70,000 or $100,000 for going for the ride.[35]

The night wasn't just about complaining—those are easy topics to discuss with old-timers; the game was always better back in their day. Memories were shared, and perhaps a few tall tales, and baseballs were handed out so each player could get autographs from the other members of the all–St. Louis team.

Once again, just like back in January, the night wound down and people started to leave. And once again, it was Ken Williams who turned off the lights, finally leaving at 3 a.m. This time it *would* be Williams's last venture to St. Louis. Five months later, he was dead.

On January 22, 1959, Ken Williams had a heart attack in his sleep and died. He had not been ill, so this wasn't expected. But with his history, it was known this could happen at any time. The official cause of death was coronary occlusion due to coronary sclerosis.

"He had a rather massive heart attack several years before he passed away. He had a massive heart attack several years before he died and, like now, somebody that's had a bad heart attack you know can do something that's going to do you in. And he lived his life that way," Jack Williams said. "He didn't really take good care of himself, as far as babying himself or anything like that, but everybody knew he had a heart attack and it could come at any minute that he could be gone. So it didn't come as totally unexpected. He did die in his sleep, so there was no … he had a heart attack while he was sleeping. And that was unexpected. It wasn't like he was ill for quite a while or anything like that, so in that sense it was unexpected."[36]

Williams's death made the front page of the *Grants Pass Daily Courier*, and two days later, his funeral was held and his body cremated. *The Sporting News* ran a big article in its January 28 edition on Williams's death, calling him "one of the American League's top sluggers during the roaring '20s."[37] Williams, who was 68 at the time of his death, was said to be 65 in the obit. That long-ago lie he'd told about his age was still fooling people to the end.

Chapter 19

Ken Williams's Legacy

"Another of baseball's greats has passed on. He is Ken Williams, who should move into the game's Hall of Fame in the not too distant future. It is regretable [sic] *that he hasn't done so during his lifetime."*—Jack Fulp[1]

If baseball's Hall of Fame had been created earlier, perhaps by 10 or 20 years, Ken Williams would have had a legitimate chance to be a member of that exclusive club. Williams finished his career with 196 home runs, which were the fourth-most in major-league history at the time he played his final game. He had entered the top-10 list in homers as far back as 1923, when he passed a trio of players for 10th place. After the 1924 season Williams had vaulted to sixth, and in 1925 cemented his place in fourth, where he would stay through the 1930 season, despite no longer being a major-league player.

Williams remained in the top 10 (tied for eighth) through the 1933 season and wasn't knocked out for good until future Hall of Famer Chuck Klein passed him on May 2, 1934. By that time, Williams would have been out of the game for five years—which, by the current rules (enacted in 1954), would have put him on the Hall of Fame ballot that year.

The home runs might have kept Williams in the public forefront, but his play would have as well. It wouldn't have been that far along since he had been tearing the cover off the baseball with regularity.

In the 1920s, Williams was fourth in home runs, fifth in slugging percentage, fifth in OPS (on-base + slugging), fifth in total average, seventh in runs batted in, seventh in on-base percentage, eighth in runs created, ninth in total bases and 11th in batting average. Every player who appears above Williams in these categories is in the Hall of Fame with one exception (Lu Blue, who was sixth in on-base percentage at .405, but is not in the top 10 of any of the other listed categories. The only categories in which Blue finished in the top 10 in the '20s were walks (second) and runs (sixth); Williams was 13th in runs.).

Would that have been enough to get him in the Hall? Well, consider that the five-year waiting period after retirement rule was not enacted for nearly 20 years. In fact, from 1936 to 1945, there was no waiting period. Players could technically have been admitted while still active (and many active players did indeed receive votes). That changed in 1946, but the waiting period was all of just one year.

If the Hall had been conceived of years earlier—and there was very little if any waiting period, as in the actual early stages—that would have only increased the odds of Williams's being elected.

But, of course, the first voting for the Hall of Fame didn't occur until 1936, and by 1942, only 13 players had been elected by the Baseball Writers Association of America—and none would be elected again until 1947. The Old Timers committee did induct many players who spent all or part of their career in the 19th century during that span and in fact had admitted 22 players through 1946. Lou Gehrig, admitted via a special election shortly after being diagnosed with amyotrophic lateral sclerosis, and other game pioneers and managers had also been inducted.

With so few players having been elected, it meant there were many deserving candidates who had to get in. We'd probably consider Jimmie Foxx a shoo-in nowadays, yet even with the lax eligibility requirements, it took Foxx, who last played in 1945, until 1951 to get into the Hall.

Foxx amazingly received only 6.2 percent of the vote in 1947 (incredibly, less than the 9.3 percent he got in 1936, when he was active). In 1948, that was boosted to 41.3 percent then to 55.6 percent and 61.3 percent before he finally made it in 1951, although still with just 79.2 percent of the vote (75 percent needed for induction).

This was hardly the only case. Even with just the one-year waiting period, it took years for such "no doubters" as Mel Ott (last played in 1947, elected in 1951), Paul Waner (1945, 1952) Lefty Grove (1941, 1947) and Charlie Gehringer (1941, 1949) to be inducted.

The more the years passed and the more the game changed, fewer and fewer people remembered Ken Williams and his accomplishments, especially when comparing him to the truly all-time greats.

Williams did receive one vote in both 1956 and 1958 (there was no voting in 1957 and '59 as the BBWAA temporarily voted every other year), perhaps a token vote to keep his name out there. In 1960, Williams was no longer eligible for the ballot.

According to his sons, Williams didn't get votes because of differences with a baseball writer. "I guess he had some sort of a tiff with one of the sportswriters there in St. Louis," Jack Williams explained. "And I think he always thought that guy kept him out."[2]

Ken Williams, Jr., relayed this story:

> There was some guy that blackballed him. Somebody had said that. I went back east a few years back, and I went to the St. Louis Cardinals [stadium] and downstairs they have a thing down there about some of the St. Louis Browns and he's in that. I talked to a guy who was a fan of his, and he told me this guy had simply blackballed dad and would not change his mind no matter what they did. He explained it to me that one guy could stop everything and that's all there was to it. The way he talked it was personal, and the guy just wouldn't change his mind.[3]

Jack O'Connell the secretary/treasurer of the BBWAA dismissed this notion. "BBWAA voting for the Hall of Fame is confidential," he wrote in an email correspondence for this book.

> A player must be named on 75 percent of ballots cast for election. Even if one voter 'black-balled' Mr. Williams, it would not have been sufficient to ensure he was not elected. This is not a process whereby a handful of people in a room debate cases. It is an election of scores or hundreds of writers (now approximately 575, then between 300–400) with three-quarters plurality needed for election. Despite what Mr. Williams' sons may have been told, it is impossible for one writer no matter how biased against a candidate could sway the vote in that manner.[4]

As noted previously, Williams's statistics compare favorably to those who played in the same era. Eventually, people once again started taking notice. The Veterans' Committee began inducting a great number of players in the 1960s, 18 in total, plus three managers and an executive. That kind of admittance continued into the early 1970s. In 1970, Earle Combs was among the two elected, and in 1971 the committee admitted seven, including six players, among them Chick Hafey. Six more players made it via that route from 1972 to 1974, including George Kelly and Jim Bottomley.

The election of Kelly was one that came under great scrutiny. Bob Burnes of *The Sporting News* and *St. Louis Globe Democrat* listed the statistics of several other players, including Williams, Billy Herman, Ernie Lombardi and Hack Wilson, as more deserving candidates. All but Williams eventually would make it to the Hall.

Burnes wrote of Kelly's Hall of Fame election in 1973:

> At best his qualifications are marginal. Without question, he was a popular figure on a convivial team, well liked by teammates, opponents and the media.
>
> ...[C]ronyism had to exist among some members of the committee who knew him, played with him, or against him or wrote the stories of his day. This does not add up to the stature of the Hall of Fame, which only wants the very best.
>
> Perhaps this was evident in the words of some of the members who, in explaining their selection, talked about his powerful arm. For a first baseman, who seldom has to use his arm that much, it is scarcely a recommendation.
>
> This is not a criticism of Kelly himself. It is more the fact that so many others were more deserving which makes us question his selection.[5]

After seeing the elections through the Veterans' Committee of Kelly (1973), Bottomley (1974), Earl Averill (1975), Herman (1975), Fred Lindstrom (1976) and Joe Sewell (1977), noted author (and eventually Hall of Famer himself) Leonard Koppett spoke out in the defense of Ken Williams, as well as Babe Herman, Chuck Klein, Lefty O'Doul, Arky Vaughan and Cy Williams. He even compared the statistics of Kelly to both Williamses (Ken batted 22 points higher than Kelly and had 48 more home runs and 89 more steals).

"The decisions of the Veterans Committee for Hall of Fame selection defy rationality," Koppett wrote. "...[A] Hall of Fame that has Averill in and Klein out, or Kelly in and Ken Williams out, or Herman in and [Joe] Gordon and [Bobby] Doerr out, is a joke."[6]

Williams's cause was again struck up in the 1980s in *The Baseball Digest*. In a 1981 article titled "These Greats Belong in the Hall of Fame," George Vass listed Williams in his starting lineup—all of whom have since made the Hall of Fame except for Williams and Joe Jackson, who is ineligible. (The other starters in Vass's lineup were Ernie Lombardi, Johnny Mize, Bill Mazeroski, Luis Aparacio, George Kell, Enos Slaugher and pitchers Juan Marichal, Hal Newhouser and Hoyt Wilhelm.)

Vass explained his inclusion of Williams: "Ken Williams belongs in a category of neglected standouts of the distant past, his cause not helped by the fact that he played for the extinct and generally unsuccessful St. Louis Browns. But Williams' lifetime .319 average was built on season figures such as .357, .347 and .346, and he hit over .300 in ten seasons, seven of those consecutive. In 1922 he broke through the middle of the Babe Ruth rampage to lead the A.L. with 39 homers and 155 RBI."[7]

Williams himself would have agreed with part of Vass's reasoning, as he once told his son Jack, "I didn't play on a pennant winner, so I don't have a chance." That comment was all his son needed to hear. "That's the only thing he said and I let it stick," Jack Williams said. "I never asked him about it again."[8]

Burnes issued another salvo for Williams in the April 1982 *Baseball Digest*, including him in his article of "Ten Players Who Belong in the Hall of Fame!"

"To old St. Louis Browns fans, his lack of recognition is a miscarriage of justice," he wrote of Williams. "An emotional man who never sought recognition, his credentials scream for acceptance now."[9]

Burnes continued to carry the flag for Williams years later. In a 1987 article on Williams in the *Grants Pass Daily Courier*, Burnes noted he was "pushing ... very hard"[10] for Williams's inclusion into the Hall of Fame.

In that same article, *The Sporting News* historian Paul McFarland also was blunt about his assessment of Williams and the Hall. "Ken Williams was a tremendous outfielder and a helluva power hitter with a great arm," McFarland is quoted as saying. "There are guys in the Hall of Fame now who couldn't carry his jockstrap."[11]

Nevertheless, despite the praise, and even campaigning, Williams remains out of the Hall of Fame. Since those 1970s elections he did have one more chance, being included on the 2003 Veterans' Committee ballot. However, he received just eight votes (9.9 percent), which was fewer than such players as Curt Flood, Marty Marion, Roger Maris and Carl Mays.

As the home run became more prevalent, his accomplishments appeared to be diminishing. A career with 196 home runs certainly pales in comparison to the numbers even middle-of-the-road players put up in the era of performance-enhancing drugs.

Just how do Williams's career numbers stack up? His official statistics in his 1,397 career games: 1,552 hits, 916 RBI, 860 runs, 285 doubles, 77 triples, 196 home runs, 154 stolen bases, .319 batting average, .393 on-base percentage, .530 slugging percentage and .924 OPS. He also walked nearly twice as much as he struck out (566 to 287). Defensively, his 35 double plays as a left fielder are third-most all-time according to baseball-reference.com. (Note: The Society for American Baseball Research, Retrosheet and this author have found many discrepancies, and Williams's RBI and steals totals are in actuality higher.)

Through the 2016 season, Williams's .319 batting average is 53rd all-time. Of those 52 ranked ahead of him, only Lefty O'Doul (11 seasons, but only six as a full-time position player), Joe Jackson (ineligible/banned), Dave Orr (played eight seasons, thus ineligible for Hall of Fame), Jake Stenzel (nine seasons thus ineligible), Riggs Stevenson (only four seasons with 400 or more plate appearances and a notoriously bad fielder), Mike Donlin (only five seasons with 400+ plate appearances), Bill Lange (seven seasons), Tip O'Neill (10 seasons, 19th century player), Bob Fothergill (two seasons with 400+ plate appearances), Babe Herman (another notoriously poor fielder) and Miguel Cabrera (active player) are not in the Hall of Fame.

In addition, Williams is 48th all-time in slugging percentage, although of those who are ranked higher, 24 played in what has become known as the Steroid Era. Of the other 23, all but three (Dick Allen, Herman and O'Doul) are in the Hall of Fame. Williams's career slugging percentage is better than such Hall of Famers as Ty Cobb, Harmon Killebrew, Eddie Mathews, Chick Hafey, Harry Heilmann, Willie McCovey, Mike Schmidt and Willie Stargell, among many others.

Williams also ranks 46th in career OPS, with 21 of those ahead of him having played in the steroid era. Only three others ahead of him are not in the Hall of Fame—Jackson, O'Doul and Charlie Keller.

Despite hitting "only" 196 home runs, Williams does rank among the all-time leaders as well. In 2003, writing for the website Baseball Analysts, Rich Lederer computed that Ken Williams ranked as the fifth-best home run hitter of all time by using the methodology of home runs hit divided by the league average based on outs (he also did the same based on plate appearances). In both computations, Williams finished fifth. Here are Lederer's top-10 lists for each:

HR/League Average Based on Outs (min. 5,000 PA)

Player	*Rate*	*Actual HR*	*League*
Babe Ruth	777	714	92
Lou Gehrig	426	493	116
Jimmie Foxx	407	534	131
Cy Williams	390	251	64
Ken Williams	378	196	52
Mel Ott	372	511	137
Rogers Hornsby	365	301	82
Hank Greenberg	362	331	91
Ted Williams	359	521	145
Hack Wilson	351	244	69

HR/League Average Based on Plate Appearances (min. 5,000 PA)

Player	*Rate*	*Actual HR*	*League*
Babe Ruth	635	714	112
Cy Williams	370	251	68
Lou Gehrig	369	493	134
Jimmie Foxx	363	534	147
Ken Williams	361	196	54
Tilly Walker	346	118	34
Home Run Baker	339	96	28
Mel Ott	327	511	156
Hank Greenberg	329	331	101
Hack Wilson	326	244	75

"It is unfortunate that the memory of Ken Williams has faded into the distant past along with baggy flannel uniforms, doubleheaders, and the game of 'pepper,'" wrote Lederer. "As an indication of the lack of respect for his contributions, Ken Williams received only one vote for the HOF in 1956 and 1958."[12]

Williams is best known for being the inaugural member of the 30-30 club—30 home runs and 30 steals in the same season (he also was just the second player to be in the 20-20 club). It is a club he was the only member of for over 30 years. In fact, at the time of his death, only Williams and Willie Mays had accomplished the feat, the latter doing it in both 1956 and '57. Williams was the lone American League player in the 30-30 club for nearly 50 years, with Tommy Harper joining him in 1970.

In addition, until the outbreak of 30-30 players beginning in 1987 (not-so-coincidentally a juiced-ball year, as well as the beginning of the so-called Steroid Era), only Williams, Mays, Hank Aaron and Dale Murphy hit .300 in their 30-30 seasons. Williams is *still* the only player to have more home runs and steals than strikeouts in his 30–30 season (in his case, 39 HR, 37 SB and 31 K).

This was hardly a fluke. Despite being a power hitter, Williams was not prone to strike out. For his career, his strikeout percentage was just 5.1 percent. In the 1920s, when he played the crux of his time, it was only 4.7 percent—and his home run percentage was 3.7 percent. For comparison's sake, Babe Ruth had a 12.5 percent strikeout percentage in his career and 12.8 percent in the '20s (his HR percent for his career was 6.7 percent).

Since 1920, only 62 times has a player had more home runs than strikeouts (the criteria being qualifying for the batting title). Williams did it three of those occasions and was the first to do so, in 1922. He also did it in 1924 (18 HR, 17 K) and 1925 (25 HR, 14 K). After the 1925 season, Williams had accomplished the feat three times—as many as every other player in baseball combined (Irish Meusel did it in 1923 and '25, Tris Speaker in 1923).

Williams is also known as the player who broke Babe Ruth's streak of leading the league in home runs, which Ruth did in the American League from 1918 to 1921, then again in 1923–24, with Williams taking the crown in 1922. In that 1922 season, Williams hit nine of his 39 home runs in April, a record that stood until Frank Robinson duplicated the feat 47 years later with Baltimore.

Also that season, Williams set a major-league record by homering in six consecutive games, a mark which wasn't topped until 1956, when Pittsburgh's Dale Long did it in eight straight. No American League player bested Williams's record for 65 years, when the Yankees' Don Mattingly matched Long's streak.

On August 7 of that year, Williams also became the first major-league player in the modern era (post–19th century) to homer twice in the same inning. Only six other AL players accomplished that same feat before the start of the Steroid Era (it was done 18 times in the American League and 16 in the National League from 1990 to 2015).

Williams put himself in more rarified company by twice having more runs batted in than games played—in 1922 he had 155 RBI in 153 games and in 1925 had 105 RBI in 102 games. Only nine other players in major-league history have had more RBI than games played two or more times. Seven of those are in the Hall of Fame (Joe DiMaggio, Jimmie Foxx, Lou Gehrig, Hank Greenberg, Babe Ruth, Al Simmons, Ted Williams and Hack Wilson). The other two were aided by performance-enhancing drugs (Juan Gonzalez and Manny Ramirez).

There are, of course, critics, who claim Williams's totals were enhanced by playing many games at Sportsman's Park, whose right field fence was between 315 feet (1921–25) and 320 feet (1926–28) during his time playing for the Browns. And Williams did hit the majority of his home runs in St. Louis (138 of his 196).

However, Sportsman's Park was hardly the only stadium with a short right-field fence. The Polo Grounds, home of the Giants and Yankees, didn't even reach 260 feet down the right-field line. When it was built in 1923, Yankee Stadium was under 300 feet down both the left- and right-field line. Left field was pushed back to 301 feet in 1928, while right field remained under 300 until 1976.

Present-day Fenway Park has the shortest distance to right field, 302 feet—yes, less than the Williams-era Sportsman's Park—and it was 320 feet when Williams played there in 1928 and '29. Oriole Park at Camden Yards, home of the Baltimore Orioles (formerly the Browns) is only 318 feet to right field. (Note: all previous figures via ballparks.com.)

Yes, Williams took advantage of the park he played in—as did many players, including Hall of Famers. One notorious example from around Williams's era is Chuck Klein, who for several years played in a band box known as the Baker Bowl in Philadelphia. The right-field fence was just 280 feet away and it expanded to right-center by only 20 feet. Even straightaway center field was "only" 408 feet, a short distance for that time period. And did the left-handed Klein ever take advantage.

In 1930, Klein batted .439—over 100 points higher than his road average—with a .794 slugging percentage at the Baker Bowl. In 1931, he was at .401 and .740, while his road numbers were a paltry .269 and .421. In '32, Klein hit an incredible .423 with a .799 slugging percentage at home. On the road, he was just .266 and .481. In his Triple Crown year of 1933, Klein batted a nearly unthinkable .467 at the Baker Bowl along with a .789 slugging percentage. On the road? Just .280 and .436.

Klein was dealt to the Cubs and his average dipped to .301 for the season in 1934, then .293 with a .488 slugging percentage in '35. After 29 games in 1936, he was dealt back to the Phillies, where he got his season average to .309 and slugging to .520. In 1937, he finished at .325, thanks in part to batting .383 at home with a .657 slugging percentage.

Klein's career line is very similar to Williams's: .320 batting average, .379 on-base percentage and .543 slugging percentage. Chuck Klein was inducted into the Hall of Fame in 1980.

And it isn't just stars of a long-ago age who benefited in this way. Jim Rice took full advantage of playing in Fenway Park over the course of his career. Rice's career line at home: .320 average, .546 slugging. On the road: .277 average, .489 slugging. And according to a SABR email in 2008, Rice's home park adjusted number is 106 (100 being average, anything over favors the hitter) and Williams's home-field advantage was 104. Jim Rice, of course, is also in the Hall of Fame. Yet, Williams's chances of ever making the Hall of Fame are likely very remote, especially as each passing year goes by.

"I think through the years I have received calls from people that were interested in starting a campaign or something to get dad into the Hall, oh, at least four or five times," Jack Williams said, "and nothing ever comes of it. All I can do is wish them the best; there's nothing I can do."[13]

While he compares well—if not better—to contemporaries like Jim Bottomley, Earl Combs, Fred Lindstrom, George Kelly and Chuck Klein, all of whom are in the Hall of Fame, and stood out among the all-time greats in the 1920s, a player is often judged not in a group, but by his own merits.

Williams certainly set his mark with the records mentioned earlier, but he hit fewer than 200 home runs. Had fewer than 1,000 runs and RBI. Accumulated just over 1,500 hits. That can be a tough sell despite all the other accomplishments.

Ken Williams, Jr., was always hopeful about the notion, but also realistic. "From what I heard, I thought he should be [in the Hall of Fame] because he had so many records. He was the first to make them," he said. "But, you know, I don't think about it. It's not going to do him any good. So I just kind of put that on the burner, too."[14]

Ken Williams's Hall of Fame case might be best summed up with "What if?" What if he had made it to the majors at a younger age? What if Buck Herzog hadn't tried to change his style of swing? What if he had become a regular before the age of 30 (186 of his 196 homers came while Williams was in his 30s)? What if the Browns had won the 1922 pennant or World Series? What if he hadn't been beaned in 1925, likely costing him a home run title and finishing with more than 200 career HRs? What if he had been traded to the Yankees? What if he played for a winner? What if he played for a team that still existed? What if? What if? What if?

In the end, perhaps Williams's place in history will come down to that age-old trivia question, which will be repeated for as long as there is baseball being played: Who was the major leagues' first 30–30 player?

He, of course, was much more than a trivia answer. Maybe that's enough, but possibly the words preceding these helped provide a little more depth, a little more knowledge and a little more understanding of what kind of player he was.

Regardless, Ken Williams has his place in history. "I like the idea that somebody is thinking about him,"[15] Ken Williams, Jr., remarked when asked about a potential book on his dad. Ken Williams might be a forgotten star, but he'll always be remembered.

Appendix A: Career Statistics

Year	*Team*	*G*	*AB*	*R*	*H*	*2b*	*3b*	*HR*	*RBI*	*SB*	*BA*	*OBP*	*SLG*
1911	Sacramento	4	8	1	3	0	1	0	0	0	.375	.444	.625
1913	Regina	101	359	n/a	105	9	13	5	n/a	12	.292	n/a	.432
1914	Regina/Edm.*	119	445	78	140	12	10	12	n/a	42	.315	n/a	.467
1915	Spokane	79	309	54	105	18	5	6	n/a	36	.340	n/a	.489
	Cincinnati	71	219	22	53	10	4	0	16	4	.242	.297	.324
1916	Cincinnati	10	27	1	3	0	0	0	1	1	.111	.172	.111
	Spokane	76	292	n/a	86	15	4	5	n/a	n/a	.295	n/a	.425
	Portland	53	183	21	52	11	1	4	n/a	14	.284	n/a	.421
1917	Portland	192	737	117	231	43	8	24	n/a	61	.313	n/a	.491
1918	St. Louis (AL)	2	1	0	0	0	0	0	1	0	.000	.500	.000
1919	St. Louis (AL)	65	227	32	68	10	5	6	35	7	.300	.376	.476
1920	St. Louis (AL)	141	521	90	160	34	13	10	72	18	.307	.362	.480
1921	St. Louis (AL)	146	547	115	190	31	7	24	117	20	.347	.429	.561
1922	St. Louis (AL)	153	585	128	194	34	11	39	155	37	.332	.413	.627
1923	St. Louis (AL)	147	555	106	198	37	12	29	91	18	.357	.439	.623
1924	St. Louis (AL)	114	398	78	129	21	4	18	84	20	.324	.425	.533
1925	St. Louis (AL)	102	411	83	136	31	5	25	105	10	.331	.390	.613
1926	St. Louis (AL)	108	347	55	97	15	7	17	77	5	.280	.354	.510
1927	St. Louis (AL)	131	423	79	136	23	6	17	74	9	.322	.403	.525
1928	Boston (AL)	133	462	59	140	25	1	8	67	4	.303	.356	.413
1929	Boston (AL)	74	139	21	48	14	2	3	21	1	.345	.409	.540
1930	Portland	148	546	93	191	32	4	14	110	23	.350	n/a	.500
1931	Portland	20	76	12	21	1	2	1	15	0	.276	n/a	.382
MLB TOTALS		**1,397**	**5,624**	**860**	**1,552**	**285**	**77**	**196**	**916**	**154**	**.319**	**.393**	**.530**

*Williams played for both Regina and Edmonton in 1914. His exact statistics for each team are unknown; however, he was hitting .299 for Regina when released.

Appendix B: Home Run Log

Number	*Date*	*Opponent*	*Park/Stadium*	*Pitcher*
1	7/7/19	Indians	Sportsman's Park	Guy Morton
2	7/15/19	A's	Sportsman's Park	Scott Perry
3	7/17/19	Yankees	Sportsman's Park	Jack Quinn
4*%	7/25/19	White Sox	Comiskey Park	Lefty Williams
5*	8/17/19 (G2)	Red Sox	Sportsman's Park	Herb Pennock
6	8/25/19	Senators	Sportsman's Park	Jim Shaw
7	5/29/20	Tigers	Sportsman's Park	Howard Ehmke
8	5/31/20	White Sox	Sportsman's Park	Red Faber
9	6/3/20	White Sox	Sportsman's Park	Roy Wilkinson
10	6/8/20	Senators	Sportsman's Park	Walter Johnson
11	6/29/20 (G1)	Indians	Sportsman's Park	Ray Caldwell
12*%	7/15/20	Yankees	Polo Grounds	Hank Thormahlen
13*#	8/6/20	Senators	Sportsman's Park	Harry Courtney
14	9/9/20 (G1)	Senators	Sportsman's Park	Eric Erickson
15	9/11/20 (G1)	Senators	Sportsman's Park	Harry Biemiller
16*	9/11/20 (G2)	Senators	Sportsman's Park	Tom Zachary
17	5/8/21	Tigers	Sportsman's Park	Hooks Dauss
18	5/15/21	Red Sox	Sportsman's Park	Elmer Myers
19%	5/22/21	Yankees	Sportsman's Park	Waite Hoyt
20	5/27/21	Indians	Sportsman's Park	Jim Bagby
21	5/27/21	Indians	Sportsman's Park	Jim Bagby
22	5/29/21	Indians	Sportsman's Park	George Uhle
23	5/29/21	Indians	Sportsman's Park	George Uhle
24	5/30/21 (G2)	White Sox	Comiskey Park	Red Faber
25	6/7/21	Red Sox	Fenway Park	Joe Bush
26	6/11/21	A's	Shibe Park	Slim Harriss
27	6/22/21	Tigers	Navin Field	Hooks Dauss
28	6/29/21	White Sox	Sportsman's Park	Red Faber
29	6/30/21 (G2)	White Sox	Sportsman's Park	Roy Wilkinson
30	7/1/21	White Sox	Sportsman's Park	Cy Twombly
31	7/2/21 (G2)	White Sox	Sportsman's Park	Shovel Hodge
32*	7/8/21	Senators	Sportsman's Park	Tom Zachary
33	8/6/21	A's	Shibe Park	Dave Keefe
34	8/21/21	Yankees	Sportsman's Park	Bill Piercy
35	8/24/21	Red Sox	Sportsman's Park	Ben Karr
36	8/27/21	A's	Sportsman's Park	Eddie Rommel
37	9/5/21	Indians	Dunn Field	Jim Bagby
38	9/15/21 (G1)	Yankees	Polo Grounds	Carl Mays
39	9/15/21 (G2)	Yankees	Polo Grounds	Bill Piercy

Number	*Date*	*Opponent*	*Park/Stadium*	*Pitcher*
40	9/19/21	A's	Shibe Park	Harvey Freeman
41	4/22/22	White Sox	Sportsman's Park	Jose Acosta
42	4/22/22	White Sox	Sportsman's Park	Jose Acosta
43*	4/22/22	White Sox	Sportsman's Park	Lum Davenport
44	4/23/22	White Sox	Sportsman's Park	Shovel Hodge
45*	4/24/22	Tigers	Sportsman's Park	Red Oldham
46	4/25/22	Tigers	Sportsman's Park	Howard Ehmke
47*	4/28/22	Indians	Sportsman's Park	Duster Mails
48	4/29/22	Indians	Sportsman's Park	Stan Coveleski
49	4/29/22	Indians	Sportsman's Park	Stan Coveleski
50*	5/4/22	Tigers	Navin Field	Red Oldham
51	5/12/22	A's	Shibe Park	Slim Harriss
52	5/23/22	Yankees	Polo Grounds	Carl Mays
53*#	5/29/22	Tigers	Sportsman's Park	Bert Cole
54*	6/2/22	White Sox	Sportsman's Park	Ferdie Schupp
55	6/12/22	Yankees	Sportsman's Park	Joe Bush
56*	6/16/22	Senators	Sportsman's Park	Tom Zachary
57	6/18/22	A's	Sportsman's Park	Eddie Rommel
58	6/20/22	A's	Sportsman's Park	Charlie Eckert
59	6/22/22	Tigers	Navin Field	Herman Pillette
60*	7/2/22	Indians	Sportsman's Park	Duster Mails
61	7/12/22	Yankees	Polo Grounds	Waite Hoyt
62	7/25/22	Yankees	Sportsman's Park	Carl Mays
63	7/28/22	Yankees	Sportsman's Park	Sam Jones
64*	7/29/22	Red Sox	Sportsman's Park	Herb Pennock
65	7/30/22	Red Sox	Sportsman's Park	Benn Karr
66	7/31/22	Red Sox	Sportsman's Park	Jack Quinn
67	8/1/22	Red Sox	Sportsman's Park	Rip Collins
68	8/2/22	A's	Sportsman's Park	Eddie Rommel
69*	8/7/22	Senators	Sportsman's Park	George Mogridge
70	8/7/22	Senators	Sportsman's Park	Eric Erickson
71	8/19/22 (G1)	A's	Shibe Park	Gus Ketchum
72	8/19/22 (G2)	A's	Shibe Park	Eddie Rommel
73*	9/4/22 (G1)	Indians	Sportsman's Park	Jim Joe Edwards
74#	9/5/22	Indians	Sportsman's Park	Dan Boone
75*	9/6/22	Indians	Sportsman's Park	John "Lefty" Middleton
76	9/8/22	Tigers	Sportsman's Park	Syl Johnson
77	9/9/22	Tigers	Sportsman's Park	Carl Holling
78	9/17/22	Yankees	Sportsman's Park	Sam Jones
79	9/19/22	Senators	Sportsman's Park	Walter Johnson
80	4/18/23	Tigers	Sportsman's Park	Ray Francis
81	4/23/23	White Sox	Sportsman's Park	Red Faber
82	4/26/23	Tigers	Navin Field	Rip Collins
83	4/27/23	Tigers	Navin Field	Syl Johnson
84	5/1/23	White Sox	Comiskey Park	Dixie Leverette
85	5/4/23	Indians	Dunn Field	Stan Coveleski
86*	5/5/23	Indians	Dunn Field	Jim Joe Edwards
87^	5/13/23	Red Sox	Sportsman's Park	Bill Piercy
88	5/19/23	Yankees	Sportsman's Park	Carl Mays
89	6/26/23	Indians	Dunn Field	George Uhle
90	6/28/23	Tigers	Sportsman's Park	Syl Johnson
91	7/4/23 (G2)	White Sox	Sportsman's Park	Ted Blankenship
92	7/6/23	Yankees	Sportsman's Park	Waite Hoyt
93	7/10/23	Senators	Sportsman's Park	Paul Zahniser

Number	*Date*	*Opponent*	*Park/Stadium*	*Pitcher*
94*	7/11/23	Senators	Sportsman's Park	George Mogridge
95	7/20/23	A's	Sportsman's Park	Eddie Rommel
96	7/21/23	A's	Sportsman's Park	Slim Harriss
97	7/23/23	Indians	Sportsman's Park	George Uhle
98	8/5/23	Yankees	Yankee Stadium	Sam Jones
99	8/6/23	Yankees	Yankee Stadium	Bob Shawkey
100*	8/7/23	Yankees	Yankee Stadium	Herb Pennock
101	8/18/23	Senators	Sportsman's Park	Paul Zahniser
102	8/22/23 (G2)	Red Sox	Sportsman's Park	Jack Quinn
103	8/23/23	Red Sox	Sportsman's Park	Alex Ferguson
104*	8/26/23	A's	Sportsman's Park	Fred Heimach
105	9/2/23	Tigers	Sportsman's Park	Syl Johnson
106	9/8/23 (G1)	White Sox	Comiskey Park	Claral Gillenwater
107	9/15/23 (G2)	A's	Shibe Park	Bob Hasty
108	9/29/23 (G1)	White Sox	Sportsman's Park	Ted Blankenship
109	4/27/24	Indians	Sportsman's Park	George Uhle
110*	5/1/24	Tigers	Sportsman's Park	Earl Whitehill
111	5/3/24	Tigers	Sportsman's Park	Ken Holloway
112	5/4/24	Tigers	Sportsman's Park	Hooks Dauss
113	5/15/24	Yankees	Yankee Stadium	Herb Pennock
114*	5/27/24	Tigers	Navin Field	Bert Cole
115	5/30/24 (G1)	White Sox	Sportsman's Park	Doug McWeeny
116	5/30/24 (G2)	White Sox	Sportsman's Park	Sloppy Thurston
117	6/9/24	Yankees	Sportsman's Park	Sam Jones
118*	6/14/24	Senators	Sportsman's Park	George Mogridge
119	6/15/24	A's	Sportsman's Park	Sam Gray
120*	6/18/24	A's	Sportsman's Park	Roy Meeker
121	6/19/24	White Sox	Sportsman's Park	Ted Blankenship
122	6/21/24 (G1)	White Sox	Sportsman's Park	Sloppy Thurston
123	7/12/24	Yankees	Yankee Stadium	Waite Hoyt
124	7/14/24 (G1)	Yankees	Yankee Stadium	Herb Pennock
125	9/1/24 (G1)	Indians	Sportsman's Park	Bob Kuhn
126	9/20/24	Senators	Sportsman's Park	Joe Martina
127*	4/14/25	Indians	Sportsman's Park	Sherrod Smith
128	4/19/25	White Sox	Sportsman's Park	Charlie Robertson
129	5/3/25	White Sox	Comiskey Park	Charlie Robertson
130	5/11/25	Yankees	Sportsman's Park	Bob Shawkey
131*	5/12/25	Senators	Sportsman's Park	Tom Zachary
132*	5/12/25	Senators	Sportsman's Park	Vean Gregg
133	5/14/25	Senators	Sportsman's Park	Stan Coveleski
134#	5/20/25	A's	Sportsman's Park	Slim Harriss
135*	5/26/25 (G1)	Indians	Sportsman's Park	Joe Shaute
136	6/1/25	Indians	Dunn Field	Benn Karr
137	6/5/25	Yankees	Yankee Stadium	Urban Shocker
138	6/5/25	Yankees	Yankee Stadium	Urban Shocker
139	6/6/25	Yankees	Yankee Stadium	Sam Jones
140	6/7/25	Yankees	Yankee Stadium	Urban Shocker
141	6/11/25	Red Sox	Fenway Park	Jack Quinn
142	7/1/25	White Sox	Sportsman's Park	Ted Lyons
143	7/2/25	White Sox	Sportsman's Park	Charlie Robertson
144	7/3/25	Tigers	Sportsman's Park	Hooks Dauss
145	7/4/25 (G2)	Tigers	Sportsman's Park	Rip Collins
146	7/12/25	Senators	Sportsman's Park	Stan Coveleski
147	7/14/25	Senators	Sportsman's Park	Curly Ogden

Number	*Date*	*Opponent*	*Park/Stadium*	*Pitcher*
148	7/15/25	Red Sox	Sportsman's Park	Ted Wingfield
149*	7/20/25	A's	Sportsman's Park	Rube Walberg
150	7/21/25	A's	Sportsman's Park	Jack Quinn
151*	8/14/25	Indians	Dunn Field	Sherrod Smith
152*	4/25/26	Indians	Sportsman's Park	Sherrod Smith
153	4/25/26	Indians	Sportsman's Park	Ben Karr
154*	4/30/26	Tigers	Sportsman's Park	Augie Johns
155*	5/2/26	Tigers	Sportsman's Park	Ed Wells
156	5/14/26	Senators	Griffith Stadium	Curly Ogden
157	5/30/26	Indians	Sportsman's Park	Emil Levsen
158#	6/17/26	Senators	Sportsman's Park	Joe Bush
159	6/20/26	Senators	Sportsman's Park	Walter Johnson
160	7/18/26	Yankees	Yankee Stadium	Sam Jones
161*	7/25/26	Indians	Dunn Field	Sherry Smith
162	7/30/26	Yankees	Sportsman's Park	Herb McQuaid
163*	8/2/26	Senators	Sportsman's Park	Dutch Ruether
164	8/3/26	Senators	Sportsman's Park	General Crowder
165	8/4/26	A's	Sportsman's Park	Jack Quinn
166*	8/5/26	A's	Sportsman's Park	Rube Walberg
167*	8/10/26	Red Sox	Sportsman's Park	Fred Heimach
168*	8/15/26 (G1)	Indians	Dunn Field	Garland Buckeye
169	4/17/27	White Sox	Sportsman's Park	Tommy Thomas
170	5/14/27	A's	Sportsman's Park	Sam Gray
171	5/18/27	Red Sox	Sportsman's Park	Red Ruffing
172	5/19/27	Red Sox	Sportsman's Park	Slim Harriss
173	5/22/27	Red Sox	Sportsman's Park	Danny MacFayden
174	5/25/27 (G1)	White Sox	Sportsman's Park	Ted Blankenship
175	7/3/27	White Sox	Sportsman's Park	Ted Blankenship
176	7/3/27	White Sox	Sportsman's Park	Ted Blankenship
177	7/11/27	A's	Sportsman's Park	Jack Quinn
178	7/21/27 (G2)	Senators	Sportsman's Park	Bump Hadley
179	8/6/27 (G2)	A's	Shibe Park	Jack Quinn
180*	8/27/27	Yankees	Sportsman's Park	Dutch Ruether
181	8/31/27	Tigers	Sportsman's Park	Lil Stoner
182	9/1/27	Tigers	Sportsman's Park	Sam Gibson
183	9/3/27	Tigers	Sportsman's Park	Rip Collins
184	9/5/27 (G1)	Indians	Dunn Field	Willis Hudlin
185	9/8/27	Yankees	Yankee Stadium	Waite Hoyt
186	4/11/28	Senators	Fenway Park	Firpo Marberry
187	4/18/28	Yankees	Fenway Park	Waite Hoyt
188	4/19/28 (G2)	Yankees	Fenway Park	Herb Pennock
189	5/12/28	Browns	Fenway Park	Boom-Boom Beck
190	6/9/28	Tigers	Navin Field	Lil Stoner
191	6/13/28	Browns	Sportsman's Park	Jack Ogden
192*	7/2/28	A's	Shibe Park	Lefty Grove
193	9/3/28 (G2)	Yankees	Yankee Stadium	Henry Johnson
194	6/18/29 (G2)	Yankees	Yankee Stadium	George Pipgras
195	6/26/29	A's	Shibe Park	George Earnshaw
196	8/4/29	White Sox	Braves Field	Ed Walsh

* - vs. left-handed pitcher
\# - grand slam
% - inside the park
^ - bounce home run

Appendix C: Articles Appearing Under Williams's Byline

After going on an early home run tear, Ken was commissioned to write 10 articles chronicling the 1922 season. From May to July 1922, the syndicated articles appeared in such papers as the *Appleton (Wis.) Post, Fort Wayne (Ind.) Journal-Gazette, Iowa Press-Citizen, Lima (Ohio) News, Modesto (Calif.) Evening News, Olean (N.Y.) Times* and *Wichita (Texas) Daily Times,* among many others.

The articles are presented in their entirety below, in roughly the order they were published.

Kenneth Williams Aims to Be Leading Home Run Hitter of 1922

My one ambition is to lead the home-run hitters of the American League for the season of 1922.

I am positive I will accomplish that feat. I am already out in front with a comfortable margin.

Last year with Bob Meusel I shared second honors to Ruth in the matter of home runs. This season I hope to show the way to all the American League sluggers.

When the season opened I made up my mind to go after these honors. With Ruth and Meusel under suspension I felt I was offered a great opportunity to break into the home-run spotlight.

Thus far I have succeeded very well in my efforts to show the way. Getting three home runs in one game, something no American League batsman has ever been able to do, gave me a great start. I am now on the way, hitting on all six.

Ruth's suspension is a very unfortunate thing for Ruth and mighty lucky for me. If Ruth was in the game there is a chance that he would be out in front, and the 10 home runs that I have already made wouldn't be getting any consideration.

Ruth is a remarkable batter. He is a superman if ever there was one. It seems almost foolish for anyone to aspire to equal his feats of slugging, yet that is my ambition. In making three home runs in one game I have already done something that the great Ruth has not yet accomplished.

In order to hit home runs a batsman must get the breaks. Team play is the big thing in baseball. No individual should sacrifice team play for a personal record.

In making my present home-run record I have always played for my team rather than myself. Conditions of the game have always justified my taking a healthy swing, which is the only way you can make a home run.

That is lesson number one in the art of making home runs.

Williams's Goal Forty Home Runs

Since I have broken into the home run spotlight a great many people have asked me what chance I believe I have to beat Babe Ruth's record of 59 home runs.

Frankly, I am not aiming to top Ruth's record. Of course, I would be delighted to turn the trick, but honestly I am not shooting quite that high.

Ruth is getting a very late start. In all probability, after getting back into the game, it will be a couple of weeks before he hits his stride.

That means that Ruth will be spotting me a start of about seven weeks. Great as Ruth is, I don't believe he can overcome the handicap which the suspension by Judge Landis has imposed.

It is my opinion that any player who can make 40 home runs in the American League this year will lead the organization in that department of play. I am positive that will be too great a number for Ruth to overcome.

I want to rank second to Ruth if I am unable to top his mark. I feel that 40 home runs will give me such an honor. Ruth and Meusel are the two outstanding sluggers in the American League. They are really the only batters I have to fear. And with the big handicap imposed by Judge Landis they don't loom up dangerously.

I don't believe any batsman in the history of modern baseball will equal the deeds of Ruth. Batters of his type happen about every 100 years.

My goal is to lead the American League in home runs in 1922.

In accomplishing that feat I hope to make at least 40 home runs, which will rank next to Ruth in the annals of swat.

Right Handers Preferred, but Southpaws Will Do

Unlike a great many left handers, southpaw pitching is far from poison to me.

Frankly, I prefer hitting against right handers, but I take them as they come.

In the first 10 home runs I made this year four were off southpaw pitching.

Regardless of the style of pitching a batter faces the ball will travel if it is hit on the nose.

With a left hander working there is nothing I like better than a fast ball on the inside about letter high. It is a very easy matter to pull such a pitch with great force to right field.

A curve ball that doesn't take much of a break and is on the inside is also an easy ball for a left-handed batsman to take liberties with.

Ordinarily spitball pitching is not the ideal style for the making of home runs. When a pitcher has his spitter breaking well and keeps it low the batter almost invariably tops the ball, thereby hitting it on the ground.

When a spitball pitcher [is] working the batter must try to pick on the fast one, or whale away at a high spitball. A spitball breaking at the waist line is not nearly so hard to hit as one that shoots across the plate at the knee.

A left hander who has a good curve and control makes it difficult for a left-handed batter to get a good crack at the ball by keeping his curve low and on the outside.

However, if I were to select the pitching to suit my fancy I would call for right handers, and the more speed the better.

Ken Just Emerging from Shadow

One man can be so big in baseball, do such remarkable things that he completely overshadows the feats of other players.

That is what the American League batters have been up against for three or four years in the person of Babe Ruth.

With Ruth the hitting of home runs was such an easy task that he took away some of the premium that fandom has always placed on a swat for the circuit.

Ruth hit so many home runs during the past three years that when some other player made a home run it received little more than passing mention.

Last season I hit .347 in the American League. I made 31 two-base hits, seven three-base hits and 24 home runs. Ordinarily that would be considered a mighty good season at the bat.

Ruth, however, with 44 two-baggers, 16 three-baggers and 59 home runs, had all the rest of us stopped cold.

Once upon a time not so many years back the making of 24 home runs in the American League would have made a player a nationally discussed figure.

Yet last season my home-run record meant nothing to the fans. Only a few really knew I made 24.

Ruth was the dominating figure of the American League. When players are keenly interested in the doings of some star it gives you some idea of his importance.

Ball players as a rule look on any great feat as all in the day's work.

For the last two years, however, every big league player would on turning the sport sheet look at the New York score the very first thing to see if Ruth had hit any homers.

That is one reason why my showing has created such a stir in the early weeks of the season. I am sure a lot of people wondered how I ever started making home runs. Few of the fans knew I was the runner-up in 1921, simply because Ruth had so far eclipsed the rest of us and we were in the also ran class.

How Ken Got Flying Start on Home Runs

I have already been asked a great number of times to what I attributed my flying start in the matter of home runs.

It would be impossible to answer that query without bringing into the discussion any number of things.

In the first place, it has always seemed to me that sixth position in the batting order is the ideal spot for the free swinger, the fellow with the extra base habit.

It may be purely imagination on my part, but it has always seemed to me that the sixth batter is more often called upon to whale away at the ball rather than pull some so-called inside stuff.

In a great many of the games in which I made home runs thus far this year, the healthy wallop was the play. Conditions of the game, the score, men on bases, and the number of outs invariably called upon me to take a healthy swing.

That, of course, gave me a slight edge over the pitcher. He was forced to pitch me in the pinch, with the result that I have profiled considerably in the matter of home runs.

Another thing that has greatly aided me has been picking the proper ball. The pitcher is always trying to outguess the batter. Likewise the batsman is constantly matching his wits against the pitcher.

Pitchers use a change of pace in delivering the ball and I have adopted that system at the bat.

Several times with the count two balls and no strikes I have hopped the cripple.

In baseball when a pitcher is in the hole and almost forced to get the next one over it is known as the cripple and regarded as a ball fairly easy to hit.

Perhaps my next time up I hit at the very first ball pitched, feeling that possibly the pitcher would try to get me in the hole. In that way I have kept opposing pitchers in hot water. That is half the battle in hitting, getting the edge on the pitcher.

Why Ken Changed His Style

One of the things that has helped considerably in my home run making is the fact that I have altered my style at the plate.

Up to last year I always tried to hit to all fields. Last season I would go for a stretch of games always taking a free swing, and if unable to make home runs, I would shift back to my style of trying to hit to all fields.

Ty Cobb, Tris Speaker, George Sisler and Eddie Collins are left-handed hitters. None of them can be claimed as sluggers. They hit the ball hard, usually on the line, but never get the distance that Ruth put into his swats.

Yes, I seriously doubt if it would be possible to get four more scientific hitters than the quartet I have mentioned. Cobb, Speaker, Sisler and Collins hit to all fields.

The general impression among the fans is that left-handed hitters are dead right-field hitters. That may be true with the slugger type, but it certainly doesn't hold good for the scientific hitter.

Batters like Collins, Cobb, Sisler and Speaker hit balls on the outside harder than do a majority of the right-handed batters. This, of course, is due to a keen eye and the proper timing of the ball. When a ball is pitched inside to they them [*sic*] can pull it equally hard to right field.

Until the season of 1921 I tried to follow along the lines I have mentioned, hitting to all fields, according to the style of pitching that I was called upon to race.

That style of hitting, however, does not make for home runs. Hitting home runs is not a scientific feat. It is good judgment and proper timing of pitching, plus brute strength.

To make home runs you must take a healthy cut at the ball. That is what I am doing this year and it is why I am getting home runs. My purpose is not to try to hit in certain fields; rather to hit it out of the field.

Healthy Swing Is Home Run Recipe

When a fellow in any business suddenly achieves success, right away every one wants to know the formula.

For me to try to tell the sporting world how I hit home runs would be nothing more than a huge joke. It just can't be done.

Every batter has his own peculiar style. The style of a great many batters is in no way fitted for the making of home runs. It would be foolish to try to change the style of any player in an effort to make him a home-run hitter.

Batting is to a great extent a natural gift. True, it is often possible to correct certain faults, but hitting the ball hard is largely a gift. Nature must endow you with a free swing, the style that produces long drives.

"Hit 'em where they ain't," is the formula I understand a great hitter of year ago gave when interviewed on how to make base hits.

I might go that one better, and say that to hit home runs the surest is to hit the old pill over the fence or into the stands. And in order to turn that trick you must take a healthy swing.

Then it would seem that the most necessary thing for a batsman to do, who aspires to be a home-run hitter, is to take a healthy swing. You can take it from me that is one thing I do. I like nothing better than taking a healthy cut at the ball.

I don't mind striking out if I have my cuts, but I do hate to have the umpire call them. All of which proves the old theory that you can't make base hits with your bat on your shoulder.

Picking the proper ball to whale away at is most important. Get the pitcher in the hole, rather than let him get the edge on you. Mix up your style at the plate. Have confidence in your ability. Don't worry when the breaks are against you. Rather smile when they are with you. On the season, it's a 50–50 proposition.

What Makes a Man Shine as a Batter?

What makes a great batter?

My ability to make home runs has caused that question to be put up to me a great many times.

Right off the reel, let me impress on the readers of this article the fact I am not posing as a great batter.

Lovers of baseball unquestionably have been much interested in my home run batting spree. That interest on the part of fandom has caused me temporarily to take the place of Ruth in the eyes of the sport world as the premier slugger of the major leagues.

Of course I have certain definite ideas about batting. It also has been my good fortune to have seen a great many of the best hitters in the two major leagues in action.

Take our own club for instance. We have some mighty sweet hitters in Sisler, Jacobson, Severeid and Tobin. I have profited much by watching these players and exchanging ideas with them.

Here are some pointers I feel safe in offering, relative to hitting the ball:

Concentrate at all times. Keep your eye on the ball.

Have absolute confidence in your ability. Feel free that you have the edge on the pitcher.

Don't hit at bad balls. If a player gets a reputation as a hitter, opposing pitchers constantly try to make him bite on bad balls. Don't fall for it.

Don't let the pitcher outguess you. Try to turn that very trick on him. Make him pitch.

Instead of letting the pitcher get you in the hole, look over his offering carefully and try to get the edge on him.

When you get the opposing pitcher in the hole, take advantage of such a condition. Profit by the situation you have created.

Williams Gives Due Credit to Mates

My teammates on the St. Louis American League club deserve the credit for any honors I may hang up as a home-run hitter.

The confidence of my teammates in my ability to hit home runs inspired me to go out and try to do the things they insisted I could.

Early in the spring of 1921 I was seated on the Browns' bench at St. Louis with a number of other players. We were discussing Babe Ruth and the things he was doing at the bat.

Suddenly the conversation switched from Ruth to yours truly. My teammates began telling me what a chase they would give Ruth if able to take a healthy swing, as I did.

"This fence here is made to order for you," remarked one of the players. He had reference to the right field bleachers in St. Louis. Since I am a left-handed hitter he figured that would be an ideal spot for me to shoot at.

"You ought to be able to pull 15 or 20 balls into the right field bleachers every year," remarked another player.

"Any time a pitcher puts a ball on the inside to you he ought to say a prayer. You ought to whale away with a full swing on any of those babies on the inside. If you did, you would have many a pitcher in trouble."

Well, all that the dope the boys were slipping me that afternoon got me thinking.

At first I thought maybe they were just kidding me. The more I thought of it, the more I was convinced they were in earnest.

They all seemed to think I was a much better hitter than I thought I was. I kept thinking it all over and decided I would try to give Ruth a chase.

While I never made him very uncomfortable, still I was runner-up practically all last season.

Most Kicks Kick Kicker Not Kickee

Observation will show you that the leading hitters of the game invariably pick up on the cripple.

That is, with the count two balls and no strikes, and the pitcher really forced to try to get the next one over, whale away at it if it looks good.

At other times it is good policy to make up your mind to hit the first ball pitched, if it is over.

Such tactics keep the pitcher on edge and greatly aid the batter.

If a batter has a habit of taking the first ball, wise pitchers soon get hip to it and make it a point to get that ball over for a strike.

With a strike on the batter the pitcher has the upper hand. It enables him to work on the batter and thereby make much trouble for him. Have the proper temperament. Don't crab at the umpire. Kicking fails to change a decision and in turn throws the batter off stride.

I know this to be the case because I have often kicked over a strike and became so peeved that while I was still crabbing I would see another strike whiz by and I would be in no position to swing at it.

While I still find it impossible to accept every ruling of the umpire without dissenting I have made it a point never to kick unless I feel justified in so doing.

My kicks this year are honest ones, and I am going to make them in such a way that the umpire will respect my opinion rather than make him feel like giving me the [heave] ho.

However, I still maintain the only certain formula for making home runs is to hit them into the stands and over the fence.

Chapter Notes

Chapter 1

1. Greg Hanberg, "Quiet slugger lets his bat talk for him," *Grants Pass Daily Courier*, Aug. 28, 1987.
2. *The Sporting News*, Jan. 29, 1958.
3. Josephine County Historical Highlights I compiled by Edna May Hill (Josephine County Library System, Josephine County Historical Society, Klucker Printery, Medford, Ore., 1980).
4. Jack Sutton, 110 Years with Josephine: The History of Josephine County, Oregon (Josephine County Historical Society, Medford, Ore., 1966).
5. *Oregon Observer*, 1892.
6. *Rogue River Courier*, April 15, 1907.
7. *Rogue River Courier*, July 3, 1908.
8. *Rogue River Courier*, June 12, 1906.
9. *Rogue River Courier*, May 4, 1907.
10. *Umpqua Valley News*, circa May 4, 1908.
11. *Rogue River Courier*, March 26, 1909.
12. Ibid.
13. *Rogue River Courier*, April 2, 1909.
14. *Siskiyou News*, May 2, 1909.
15. *Siskiyou News*, June 3, 1909.
16. *Siskiyou News*, May 30, 1909.
17. *Siskiyou News*, June 17, 1909.
18. *Siskiyou News*, Sept. 30, 1909.
19. *Central Point Herald*, Jan. 6, 1910.
20. *Rogue River Courier*, June 10, 1910.
21. *The Sporting News*, March 1, 1923.
22. *Medford Daily Tribune*, circa May 1, 1911.
23. *Medford Daily Tribune*, circa May 8, 1911.
24. *Medford Daily Tribune*, circa May 29, 1911.
25. *Boston Herald*, May 18, 1929.
26. *Medford Daily Tribune*, circa June 19, 1911.
27. Ibid.
28. Ibid.
29. Ibid.
30. *Rogue River Courier*, June 30, 1911.
31. *Sacramento Bee*, Aug. 21, 1911.
32. *Sacramento Bee*, Aug. 23, 1911.
33. *Rogue River Courier*, Aug. 11, 1911.
34. *St. Louis Globe Democrat*, April 5, 1918.
35. *Sacramento Bee*, Aug. 24, 1911.
36. *The Oregonian*, Aug. 24, 1911.
37. *Sacramento Bee*, Aug. 28, 1911.
38. Ken Williams, Jr., interview, Feb. 22, 2008.
39. *The Oregonian*, Aug. 26, 1911.
40. *The Oregonian*, Aug. 27, 1911.
41. *Sacramento Bee*, Aug. 29, 1911.
42. *The Sporting Life*, Nov. 25, 1911.
43. Ibid.

Chapter 2

1. *Rogue River Courier*, June 3, 1912.
2. *Siskiyou News*, May 5, 1910.
3. Jack Williams interview, Feb. 20, 2008.
4. *Siskiyou News*, Aug. 1, 1912.
5. *Rogue River Courier*, Aug. 5, 1912.
6. *Siskiyou News*, Aug. 22, 1912.
7. *The Sporting News*, Feb. 6, 1912.
8. *Regina Leader*, unknown.
9. *Regina Leader*, March 8, 1913.
10. *Woodland Daily Democrat*, April 27, 1922.
11. *Regina Leader*, April 4, 1913.
12. *Rogue River Courier*, April 11, 1913.
13. *Regina Leader*, April 17, 1913.
14. *Regina Leader*, April 28, 1913.
15. *Regina Leader*, May 5, 1913.
16. Ibid.
17. *Regina Leader*, May 6, 1913.
18. *Regina Leader*, May 9, 1913.
19. Ibid.
20. Ibid.
21. *Regina Leader*, May 10, 1913.
22. *Regina Leader*, May 27, 1913.
23. *Regina Leader*, May 28, 1913.
24. Ibid.
25. *Regina Leader*, June 8, 1913.
26. *Regina Leader*, July 9, 1913.
27. *Regina Leader*, July 11, 1913.
28. *The Sporting News*, Aug. 7, 1913.
29. *Edmonton Journal*, Aug. 7, 1913.
30. *Regina Leader*, Aug. 24, 1913.
31. *Edmonton Journal*, Aug. 23, 1913.
32. *Regina Leader*, Aug. 30, 1913.
33. Ibid.
34. *Regina Leader*, Sept. 1, 1913.
35. *The Sporting News*, Sept. 18, 1913.
36. *Regina Morning Leader Post*, unknown.
37. *Regina Morning Leader Post*, Feb. 17, 1914.

38. *Regina Morning Leader Post*, March 11, 1914.
39. *Woodland Daily Democrat*, April 6, 1914.
40. *Regina Leader*, May 21, 1914.
41. *Regina Leader*, May 31, 1914.
42. *Regina Leader*, June 6, 1914.
43. *Edmonton Journal*, April 28, 1914.
44. *Edmonton Journal*, March 21, 1914.
45. *Regina Morning Leader Post*, June 13, 1914.
46. *Edmonton Journal*, June 13, 1914.
47. *Edmonton Journal*, June 17, 1914.
48. *Edmonton Journal*, Aug. 8, 1914.
49. *Edmonton Journal*, Aug. 12, 1914.
50. *Edmonton Journal*, Aug. 15, 1914.
51. *Edmonton Bulletin*, Aug. 22, 1914.
52. *Edmonton Journal*, Sept. 22, 1914.

Chapter 3

1. *The Sporting News*, Oct. 19, 1914.
2. *Spokesman-Review*, Jan. 15, 1915.
3. *Spokane Daily Chronicle*, April 12, 1915.
4. *Spokesman-Review*, April 18, 1915.
5. Ibid.
6. Ibid.
7. Ibid.
8. *Spokesman-Review*, April 24, 1915.
9. *Spokesman-Review*, May 4, 1914.
10. *Spokesman-Review*, May 9, 1915.
11. *Spokesman-Review*, May 17, 1915.
12. *Spokane Daily Chronicle*, May 28, 1915.
13. *Spokesman-Review*, June 12, 1915.
14. *Spokesman-Review*, June 20, 1915.
15. Ibid.
16. Ibid.
17. *Spokesman-Review*, June 21, 1915.
18. *Spokesman-Review*, June 28, 1915.
19. *Spokesman-Review*, July 3, 1915.
20. Ibid.
21. *Spokesman-Review*, July 5, 1915.
22. Letter from L.E. Ragsdale to August Hermann (sic), June 18, 1915, Ken Williams Baseball Hall of Fame clip file.
23. *Spokesman-Review*, July 10, 1915.
24. *Spokane Daily Chronicle*, July 9, 1915.
25. *The Sporting News*, Sept. 30, 1915.

Chapter 4

1. *Spokesman-Review*, July 10, 1915.
2. *Sporting Life*, July 31, 1915.
3. Ibid.
4. *Cincinnati Enquirer*, July 15, 1915.
5. Ibid.
6. *Cincinnati Enquirer*, July 16, 1915.
7. Ibid.
8. *Cincinnati Enquirer*, July 21, 1915.
9. *Cincinnati Enquirer*, July 18, 1915.
10. *Cincinnati Enquirer*, July 22, 1915.
11. *Olean Evening Herald*, May 22, 1924.
12. *The Sporting News*, July 29, 1915.
13. *Cincinnati Enquirer*, July 23, 1915.
14. Ibid.
15. *The Sporting News*, July 29, 1915.
16. *Sporting Life*, Aug. 14, 1915.
17. *Cincinnati Enquirer*, Aug. 2, 1915.
18. *Cincinnati Enquirer*, Aug. 7, 1915.
19. *The Sporting News*, Nov. 14, 1914.
20. *Cincinnati Enquirer*, Aug. 13, 1915.
21. *Cincinnati Enquirer*, Jan. 28, 1935.
22. *Cincinnati Enquirer*, Aug. 20, 1915.
23. *The Sporting News*, Oct. 7, 1915.
24. *Spokesman-Review*, Oct. 29, 1915.
25. *Spokesman-Review*, Nov. 14, 1915.
26. *The Sporting News*, Nov. 18, 1915.
27. *The Oregonian*, June 10, 1917.
28. *Spokesman-Review*, Oct. 29, 1915.
29. *Cincinnati Enquirer*, April 21, 1916.
30. *The Sporting News*, Oct. 15, 1942.
31. Ibid.
32. *Sporting Life*, May 13, 1916.
33. *Spokesman-Review*, May 7, 1916.
34. *The Sporting News*, Oct. 15, 1942.
35. *Janesville Gazette*, May 15, 1916.
36. *Spokesman-Review*, May 7, 1916.
37. Ibid.

Chapter 5

1. *Spokesman-Review*, May 7, 1916.
2. Ibid.
3. Ibid.
4. *Sporting Life*, July 22, 1916.
5. *Spokesman-Review*, Aug. 2, 1916.
6. *Spokesman-Review*, Aug. 10, 1916.
7. *The Oregonian*, Aug. 10, 1916.
8. *Spokane Daily Chronicle*, Aug. 10, 1916.
9. *Spokesman-Review*, Aug. 23, 1916.
10. *Spokesman-Review*, Aug. 24, 1916.
11. *Tacoma Times*, Aug. 24, 1916.
12. *Morning Oregonian*, Aug. 24, 1916.
13. Ibid.
14. *The Oregonian*, Sept. 2, 1916.
15. *Salt Lake City Tribune*, Sept. 11, 1916.
16. *Portland Journal*, Sept. 10, 1916.
17. *Spokesman-Review*, Sept. 30, 1916.
18. *The Oregonian*, Jan. 14, 1917.
19. *The Oregonian*, Jan. 17, 1917.
20. *The Oregonian*, Jan. 14, 1917.
21. Ibid.
22. *The Oregonian*, Jan. 20, 1917.
23. *The Sporting News*, Feb. 8, 1917.
24. *Oakland Tribune*, Feb. 9, 1917.
25. *The Oregonian*, Jan. 20, 1917.
26. *The Oregonian*, March 2, 1917.
27. *The Oregonian*, March 4, 1917.
28. *The Sporting News*, Feb. 4, 1917.
29. *The Oregonian*, Feb. 22, 1917.
30. *The Oregonian*, Feb. 23, 1917.
31. *Honolulu Star-Bulletin*, March 2, 1917.
32. *Honolulu Star-Bulletin*, March 5, 1917.
33. *The Oregonian*, March 11, 1917.
34. *Honolulu Star-Bulletin*, March 15, 1917.
35. Ibid.
36. *The Oregonian*, March 21, 1917.

37. Ibid.
38. *The Oregonian*, April 2, 1917.
39. *The Oregonian*, May 5, 1917.
40. *The Oregonian*, May 9, 1917.
41. *The Oregonian*, June 4, 1917.
42. *The Oregonian*, June 5, 1917.
43. *The Oregonian*, Jan. 19, 1917.
44. *The Oregonian*, June 14, 1917.
45. *The Evening News*, June 23, 1917.
46. *The Oregonian*, June 11, 1917.
47. Ibid.
48. *St. Louis Post-Dispatch*, June 13, 1917.
49. *The Oregonian*, June 15, 1917.
50. Ibid.
51. *The Oregonian*, June 17, 1917.
52. *Oakland Tribune*, June 21, 1917.
53. *The Oregonian*, Aug. 11, 1917.
54. *The Oregonian*, Sept. 27, 1917.
55. *Oakland Tribune*, Oct. 30, 1917.
56. *The Sporting News*, Nov. 15, 1917.

Chapter 6

1. *Spokesman-Review*, March 19, 1914.
2. *The Morning Leader*, Jan. 25, 1918.
3. *Ogden Standard*, Jan. 24, 1918.
4. *St. Louis Post-Dispatch*, Jan. 31, 1918.
5. *St. Louis Post-Dispatch*, Feb. 16, 1918.
6. *St. Louis Post-Dispatch*, Feb. 26, 1918.
7. Roger. A Godin, "The 1922 St. Louis Browns: Best of the American League's Worst" (Jefferson, NC: McFarland, 1991).
8. *St. Louis Post-Dispatch*, March 10, 1918.
9. *St. Louis Post-Dispatch*, March, 15, 1918.
10. *St. Louis Post-Dispatch*, March, 22, 1918.
11. *St. Louis Post-Dispatch*, March 25, 1918.
12. *The Morning Leader*, March 31, 1918.
13. Ibid.
14. *St. Louis Globe Democrat*, April 6, 1918.
15. *St. Louis Post-Dispatch*, April 25, 1918.
16. *St. Louis Post-Dispatch*, May 3, 1918.
17. *Rogue River Courier*, May 15, 1918.
18. *St. Louis Post-Dispatch*, Aug. 22, 1918.
19. *Alton Evening Telegraph*, Aug. 10, 1918.
20. *Alton Evening Telegraph*, Sept. 3, 1918.
21. Ibid.
22. *The Sporting News*, Sept. 26, 1918.
23. *Spokane Daily Chronicle*, Oct. 30, 1918.
24. Ibid.
25. Interview with Jack Williams, Sept. 15, 2006.
26. *Grants Pass Daily Courier*, March 10, 1919.
27. *St. Louis Post-Dispatch*, July 14, 1919.
28. *St. Louis Post-Dispatch*, March 18, 1919.
29. *St. Louis Post-Dispatch*, March 21, 1919.
30. *St. Louis Post-Dispatch*, March 31, 1919.
31. *St. Louis Globe Democrat*, March 30, 1919.
32. *St. Louis Globe Democrat*, April 21, 1919.
33. *St. Louis Globe Democrat*, April 24, 1919.
34. *St. Louis Post-Dispatch*, May 3, 1919.
35. *St. Louis Post-Dispatch*, May 7, 1919.
36. *St. Louis Globe Democrat*, May 7, 1919.
37. *St. Louis Post-Dispatch*, May 7, 1919.
38. *St. Louis Globe Democrat*, May 8, 1919.
39. *St. Louis Globe Democrat*, May 29, 1919.
40. Interview with Jack Williams, Sept. 15, 2006.
41. *St. Louis Globe Democrat*, July 8, 1919.
42. *St. Louis Globe Democrat*, July 14, 1919.
43. *St. Louis Globe Democrat*, July 16, 1919.
44. *St. Louis Post-Dispatch*, July 18, 1919.
45. *St. Louis Globe Democrat*, July 18, 1919.
46. *St. Louis Post-Dispatch*, July 28, 1919.
47. *St. Louis Post-Dispatch*, Aug. 10, 1919.
48. Ibid.
49. *St. Louis Globe Democrat*, Aug. 18, 1919.
50. Ibid.

Chapter 7

1. *St. Louis Globe Democrat*, March 9, 1920.
2. *The Sporting News*, Jan. 19, 1922.
3. *St. Louis Globe Democrat*, Jan. 18, 1920.
4. *The Sporting News*, Feb. 5, 1920.
5. *St. Louis Globe Democrat*, Feb. 28, 1920.
6. *St. Louis Globe Democrat*, Feb. 29, 1920.
7. Ibid.
8. *St. Louis Globe Democrat*, March 3, 1920.
9. Ibid.
10. *The Sporting News*, March 11, 1920.
11. *St. Louis Globe Democrat*, March 6, 1920.
12. *The Sporting News*, March 18, 1920.
13. *St. Louis Globe Democrat*, March 22, 1920.
14. *St. Louis Post-Dispatch*, March 22, 1920.
15. *The Sporting News*, March 18, 1920.
16. *Capital Times*, April 13, 1920.
17. *St. Louis Globe Democrat*, April 20, 1920.
18. Ibid.
19. *St. Louis Globe Democrat*, June 20, 1920.
20. *St. Louis Globe Democrat*, July 5, 1920.
21. *St. Louis Globe Democrat*, Aug. 17, 1920.
22. *St. Louis Globe Democrat*, Aug. 18, 1920.
23. Ibid.
24. Ibid.
25. *St. Louis Globe Democrat*, Aug. 19, 1920.
26. *St. Louis Post-Dispatch*, Aug. 30, 1920.
27. *New York Times*, Aug. 30, 1920.
28. *St. Louis Post-Dispatch*, Sept. 25, 1920.
29. *St. Louis Globe Democrat*, Sept. 29, 1920.
30. *St. Louis Post-Dispatch*, Sept. 29, 1920.
31. *St. Louis Post-Dispatch*, Sept. 30, 1920.
32. *The Sporting News*, Oct. 7, 1920.
33. *The Sporting News*, Nov. 25, 1920.
34. *The Sporting News*, Sept. 1, 1922.
35. *St. Louis Globe Democrat*, Nov. 5, 1920.
36. *St. Louis Globe Democrat*, Nov. 26, 1920.
37. *The Sporting News*, Dec. 9, 1920.

Chapter 8

1. *Spokane Daily Chronicle*, July 6, 1916.
2. *St. Louis Globe Democrat*, Jan. 10, 1921.
3. *St. Louis Post-Dispatch*, Jan. 16, 1921.
4. *St. Louis Globe Democrat*, Jan. 24, 1921.
5. *St. Louis Globe Democrat*, March 18, 1921.

6. *St. Louis Globe Democrat*, Jan. 25, 1921.
7. *St. Louis Post-Dispatch*, Jan. 9, 1921.
8. *St. Louis Post-Dispatch*, March 3, 1921.
9. *St. Louis Globe Democrat*, March 10, 1921.
10. *The Sporting News*, March 24, 1921.
11. *The Sporting News*, March 5, 1952.
12. *Fort Wayne Journal Gazette*, March 20, 1921.
13. Ibid.
14. *St. Louis Post-Dispatch*, April 14, 1921.
15. *St. Louis Post-Dispatch*, May 8, 1921.
16. *Lima News*, May 17, 1921.
17. *The Evening Independent*, May 3, 1922.
18. *St. Louis Globe Democrat*, May 16, 1921.
19. *St. Louis Globe Democrat*, May 28, 1921.
20. *Oakland Tribune*, June 24, 1921.
21. Ibid.
22. *The Sporting News*, June 2, 1921.
23. *St. Louis Globe Democrat*, May 31, 1921.
24. *St. Louis Globe Democrat*, June 5, 1921.
25. *St. Louis Globe Democrat*, June 8, 1921.
26. *St. Louis Post-Dispatch*, March 25, 1922.
27. *St. Louis Globe Democrat*, June 12, 1921.
28. *St. Louis Globe Democrat*, June 16, 1921.
29. *Evening Public Ledger*, June 14, 1921.
30. *St. Louis Globe Democrat*, June 19, 1921.
31. *St. Louis Globe Democrat*, July 3, 1921.
32. Ibid.
33. *St. Louis Globe Democrat*, July 8, 1921.
34. Ibid.
35. *The Sporting News*, July 7, 1921.
36. Ibid.
37. *St. Louis Post-Dispatch*, July 15, 1921.
38. *St. Louis Globe Democrat* and *St. Louis Post-Dispatch*, July 19, 1921.
39. *St. Louis Globe Democrat*, Aug. 7, 1921.
40. *Modesto Evening News*, May 19, 1922.
41. *Olean Evening Herald*, May 22, 1924.
42. Ibid.

Chapter 9

1. *The Sporting News*, Oct. 13, 1921.
2. *St. Louis Globe Democrat*, Oct. 12, 1921.
3. *The Sporting News*, Dec. 8, 1921.
4. *The Sporting News*, Sept. 8, 1921.
5. *The Evening News*, Dec. 27, 1921.
6. *The Sporting News*, Dec. 1, 1921.
7. *St. Louis Globe Democrat*, Feb. 16, 1922.
8. *St. Louis Globe Democrat*, Jan. 10, 1922.
9. *St. Louis Globe Democrat*, March 3, 1922.
10. *St. Louis Globe Democrat*, March 1, 1922.
11. *St. Louis Post-Dispatch*, April 9, 1922.
12. *St. Louis Post-Dispatch*, April 21, 1922.
13. *St. Louis Globe Democrat*, April 17, 1922.
14. *St. Louis Globe Democrat*, April 22, 1922.
15. *St. Louis Post-Dispatch*, April 23, 1922.
16. *Syracuse Herald*, April 27, 1922.
17. *The Sporting News*, April 27, 1922.
18. Ibid.
19. *St. Louis Globe Democrat*, April 24, 1922.
20. *St. Louis Globe Democrat*, April 25, 1922.
21. *St. Louis Post-Dispatch*, April 29, 1922.
22. *St. Louis Globe Democrat*, April 30, 1922.
23. Ibid.
24. Ibid.
25. Ibid.
26. Ibid.
27. *St. Louis Globe Democrat*, May 1, 1922.
28. *St. Louis Post-Dispatch*, May 2, 1922.
29. *Iowa Press-Citizen*, May 13, 1922.
30. *Charleston Daily Mail*, June 4, 1922.
31. *Iowa Press-Citizen*, May 13, 1922.
32. *Olean Times*, May 15, 1922.
33. *New York Times*, May 19, 1922.
34. Ibid.
35. *Coshocton Tribune*, May 11, 1922.
36. Ibid.
37. Ibid.
38. *Olean Evening Times*, May 20, 1922.
39. *New York Times*, May 21, 1922.
40. *St. Louis Globe Democrat*, May 21, 1922.
41. Ibid.
42. *St. Louis Post-Dispatch*, May 21, 1922.
43. *New York Times*, May 22, 1922.
44. *St. Louis Globe Democrat*, May 22, 1922.
45. *New York Times*, May 24, 1922.
46. *St. Louis Post-Dispatch*, May 24, 1922.
47. *Nebraska State Journal*, June 10, 1922.
48. *Charleston Daily Mail*, June 4, 1922.
49. *Olean Evening Times*, May 20, 1922.
50. *Olean Evening Times*, May 19, 1922.
51. *St. Louis Globe Democrat*, June 13, 1922.
52. *St. Louis Globe Democrat*, June 14, 1922.
53. *Wisconsin Daily Rapids*, June 27, 1922.
54. *St. Louis Globe Democrat*, June 16, 1922.
55. *The Sporting News*, June 29, 1922.

Chapter 10

1. *St. Louis Globe Democrat*, June 25, 1922.
2. Ibid.
3. *St. Louis Globe Democrat*, June 30, 1922, and St. Louis Post-Dispatch, July 5, 1922.
4. Ibid.
5. http://archive.nlm.nih.gov/fdanj/bitstream/123456789/68243/3/FDNJ21205.pdf
6. *St. Louis Post-Dispatch*, July 2, 1922.
7. Ibid.
8. *Syracuse Herald*, July 6, 1922.
9. *St. Louis Post-Dispatch*, July 7, 1922.
10. *St. Louis Globe Democrat*, July 8, 1922.
11. *Ironwood Daily Globe*, Aug. 5, 1922.
12. *St. Louis Post-Dispatch*, July 20, 1922.
13. *St. Louis Globe Democrat*, July 25, 1922.
14. Ibid.
15. *St. Louis Globe Democrat*, July 24, 1922.
16. *St. Louis Globe Democrat*, July 25, 1922.
17. *New York Times*, July 25, 1922.
18. Ibid.
19. *The Sporting News*, Aug. 10, 1922.
20. *St. Louis Post-Dispatch*, July 24, 1922.
21. *St. Louis Globe Democrat*, July 24, 1922.
22. *St. Louis Post-Dispatch*, July 26, 1922.
23. *St. Louis Post-Dispatch*, July 28, 1922.

24. *St. Louis Globe Democrat*, Aug. 1, 1922.
25. *St. Louis Post-Dispatch*, Aug. 2, 1922.
26. *St. Louis Globe Democrat*, Aug. 3, 1922.
27. *St. Louis Post-Dispatch*, Aug. 8, 1922.
28. *St. Louis Globe Democract*, Aug. 23, 1922.
29. Tom Meany, Baseball's Greatest Teams (A.S. Barnes, 1949).
30. Ibid.
31. *St. Louis Globe Democrat*, Aug. 31, 1922.
32. *St. Louis Post-Dispatch*, Sept. 5, 1922.
33. *St. Louis Globe Democrat*, Sept. 6, 1922.
34. *St. Louis Post-Dispatch*, Sept. 5, 1922.
35. *St. Louis Globe Democrat*, Sept. 7, 1922.
36. *St. Louis Post-Dispatch*, Sept. 7, 1922.
37. *St. Louis Globe Democrat*, Sept. 11, 1922.
38. Ibid.
39. *St. Louis Post-Dispatch*, Sept. 13, 1922.
40. *St. Louis Globe Democrat*, Sept. 16, 1922.
41. *St. Louis Post-Dispatch*, Sept. 17, 1922.
42. Ibid.
43. *St. Louis Post-Dispatch*, Sept. 19, 1922.
44. *St. Louis Globe Democrat*, Sept. 19, 1922.
45. *Evening Independent*, Sept. 30, 1922.
46. *The Sporting News*, Jan. 11, 1945.
47. Roger A. Godin, "The 1922 St. Louis Browns: Best of the American League's Worst" (Jefferson, NC: McFarland, 1991).
48. *Grants Pass Daily Courier*, Oct. 14, 1922.

Chapter 11

1. *St. Louis Globe Democrat*, Feb. 24, 1923.
2. *St. Louis Post-Dispatch*, March 11, 1923.
3. *St. Louis Post-Dispatch*, March 10, 1923.
4. *St. Louis Globe Democrat*, March 11, 1923.
5. *St. Louis Post-Dispatch*, April 6, 1923.
6. *St. Louis Post-Dispatch*, March 25, 1923.
7. *Decatur Daily Review*, April 10, 1923.
8. *The Sporting News*, April 19, 1923.
9. *Hornell* (N.Y.) *Evening Tribune-Times*, April 26, 1923.
10. *St. Louis Post-Dispatch*, April 24, 1923.
11. *St. Louis Post-Dispatch*, May 6, 1923.
12. Ibid.
13. Ibid.
14. *St. Louis Globe Democrat*, May 6, 1923.
15. *St. Louis Globe Democrat*, May 8, 1923.
16. *Syracuse Herald*, May 3, 1923.
17. Ibid.
18. *The Sporting News*, May 17, 1923.
19. Ibid.
20. *St. Louis Globe Democrat*, May 15, 1923.
21. *St. Louis Post-Dispatch*, June 13, 1923.
22. *St. Louis Post-Dispatch*, May 19, 1923.
23. *St. Louis Globe Democrat*, Aug. 5, 1923.
24. *St. Louis Globe Democrat*, July 9, 1923.
25. *St. Louis Globe Democrat*, Aug. 12, 1923.
26. *St. Louis Globe Democrat*, Aug. 8, 1923.
27. *St. Louis Globe Democrat*, Aug. 10, 1923.
28. Roger A. Godin, "The 1922 St. Louis Browns: Best of the American League's Worst" (Jefferson, NC: McFarland, 1991).
29. *St. Louis Globe Democrat*, Aug. 14, 1923.
30. *The Sporting News*, Aug. 30, 1923.
31. Ibid.
32. *St. Louis Globe Democrat*, Aug. 27, 1923.
33. *St. Louis Globe Democrat*, Sept. 16, 1923.
34. *The Sporting News*, Oct. 18, 1923.
35. Ibid.
36. *Detroit Free-Press*, Oct. 9, 1923.

Chapter 12

1. *St. Louis Globe Democrat*, Dec. 15, 1923.
2. *Lincoln Daily State Journal*, April 11, 1924.
3. *St. Louis Globe Democrat*, March 14, 1924.
4. *St. Louis Globe Democrat*, March 30, 1924.
5. *St. Louis Globe Democrat*, April 13, 1924.
6. *St. Louis Globe Democrat*, April 20, 1924.
7. *The Sporting News*, May 1, 1924.
8. *The Sporting News*, May 8, 1924.
9. *St. Louis Globe Democrat*, May 5, 1924.
10. *Olean Evening Herald*, May 22, 1924.
11. *St. Louis Globe Democrat*, May 16, 1924.
12. Ibid.
13. *St. Louis Globe Democrat*, May 28, 1924.
14. *St. Louis Globe Democrat*, Aug. 13, 1924.
15. *St. Louis Globe Democrat*, Sept. 18, 1924.
16. *St. Louis Globe Democrat*, Sept. 27, 1924.
17. Ibid.
18. *Lima News*, Oct. 1.
19. *Los Angeles Times*, Oct. 26.
20. http://cwcfamily.org/articles/family/breabow-l.htm.
21. *The Sporting News*, Nov. 6, 1924.
22. Donald Honig, "Baseball When the Grass Was Real: Baseball from the Twenties to the Forties Told by the Men Who Played It" (Coward, McCann & Geoghegan, 1975).
23. *Washington Post*, Dec. 3, 1924.
24. *St. Louis Globe Democrat*, Dec. 17, 1924.
25. *St. Louis Globe Democrat*, Feb. 23, 1925.
26. *St. Louis Globe Democrat*, March 4, 1925.
27. *St. Petersburg Times*, March 23, 1925.
28. *St. Louis Globe Democrat*, April 10, 1925.
29. Ibid.
30. *St. Louis Globe Democrat*, April 12, 1925.
31. *The Sporting News*, May 21, 1925.
32. *The Sporting News*, June 18, 1925.
33. *St. Louis Globe Democrat*, June 13, 1925.
34. *St. Louis Globe Democrat*, June 28, 1925.
35. *St. Louis Globe Democrat*, July 18, 1925.

Chapter 13

1. *St. Louis Globe Democrat*, April 15, 1925.
2. Ibid.
3. *Baseball Magazine*, "A Black Day for the St. Louis Browns" (August 1926, vol. 37, Issue 3).
4. Ibid.
5. *The Sporting News*, Aug. 27, 1925.
6. *Baseball Magazine*, "A Black Day for the St. Louis Browns" (August 1926, vol. 37, Issue 3).

7. Ibid.
8. Ibid.
9. Ibid.
10. *St. Louis Globe Democrat*, Feb. 24, 1926.
11. *St. Louis Globe Democrat*, Feb. 28, 1926.
12. *St. Louis Globe Democrat*, March 14, 1926.
13. *St. Louis Globe Democrat*, April 8, 1926.
14. *Baseball Magazine*, "A Black Day for the St. Louis Browns" (August 1926, vol. 37, Issue 3).
15. *St. Louis Globe Democrat*, April 13, 1926.
16. *St. Louis Globe Democrat*, April 25, 1926.
17. *St. Louis Globe Democrat*, April 29, 1926.
18. *St. Louis Globe Democrat*, May 7, 1926.
19. *St. Louis Globe Democrat*, May 15, 1926.
20. *St. Louis Globe Democrat*, June 1, 1926.
21. Ibid.
22. Ibid.
23. *Zanesville* (Ohio) *Times Recorder*, June 26, 1926.
24. *Massillon Evening Independent*, June 24, 1926.
25. *St. Louis Globe Democrat*, July 19, 1926.
26. *St. Louis Globe Democrat*, July 23, 1926.
27. *St. Louis Globe Democrat*, July 24, 1926.
28. *St. Louis Globe Democrat*, Aug. 11, 1926.
29. Ibid.
30. *St. Louis Globe Democrat*, Aug. 25, 1926.
31. *Ironwood Daily Globe*, Aug. 31, 1926.
32. Ibid.
33. *Baseball Magazine*, "The Slugging Stars of 1926" (June 1927, vol. 39, Issue 1).
34. *Baseball Magazine*, "Who Was the Greatest Batter of All Time?" (September 1927, vol. 39, Issue 4).

Chapter 14

1. *St. Louis Globe Democrat*, Nov. 27, 1926.
2. *St. Louis Globe Democrat*, Dec. 10, 1926.
3. *St. Louis Globe Democrat*, Dec. 13, 1926.
4. *Evening Independent*, Dec. 15, 1926.
5. *St. Louis Globe Democrat*, Jan. 24, 1927.
6. *St. Louis Globe Democrat*, Jan. 4, 1927.
7. *St. Louis Globe Democrat*, Jan. 3, 1927.
8. *St. Louis Globe Democrat*, Jan. 28, 1927.
9. *St. Louis Globe Democrat*, Feb. 1, 1927.
10. *St. Louis Globe Democrat*, May 22, 1927.
11. *St. Louis Globe Democrat*, Aug. 29, 1927.
12. *St. Louis Globe Democrat*, Sept. 4, 1927.
13. *St. Louis Globe Democrat*, Sept. 9, 1927.
14. *St. Louis Globe Democrat*, Sept. 10, 1927.
15. *St. Louis Globe Democrat*, Sept. 12, 1927.
16. *Iola Daily Register*, Oct. 15, 1927.
17. *St. Louis Globe Democrat*, Nov. 14, 1927.
18. *St. Louis Globe Democrat*, Nov. 11, 1927.
19. *St. Louis Globe Democrat*, Nov. 27, 1927.

Chapter 15

1. *Pittsburgh Press*, Dec. 30, 1927.
2. *Chester Times*, Dec. 31, 1927.
3. *Boston Globe*, Dec. 16, 1927.
4. *St. Louis Globe Democrat*, Dec. 16, 1927.
5. *Grants Pass Daily Courier*, Dec. 16, 1927.
6. *Syracuse Herald*, Jan. 1, 1928.
7. *The Sporting News*, Feb. 2, 1928.
8. *Constitution Tribune*, Aug. 10, 1929.
9. *Boston Globe*, Feb. 1, 1928.
10. *Boston Globe*, Feb. 28, 1928.
11. *Boston Globe*, March 2, 1928.
12. *Boston Globe*, March 5, 1928.
13. *The Sporting News*, March 8, 1928.
14. *Boston Globe*, March 10, 1928.
15. Ibid.
16. *Boston Globe*, April 6, 1928.
17. *Boston Globe*, April 5, 1928.
18. *Boston Globe*, Feb. 29, 1928.
19. *Decatur Evening Herald*, March 26, 1928.
20. Ibid.
21. Ibid.
22. Ibid.
23. Ibid.
24. UPI, March 2.
25. *Boston Herald*, April 11, 1928.
26. Ibid.
27. *Boston Globe*, April 11, 1928.
28. *Boston Herald*, April 10, 1928.
29. *Boston Globe*, April 9, 1928.
30. *The Evening Independent*, April 11, 1928.
31. *Boston Globe*, April 11, 1928.
32. *Boston Globe*, April 12, 1928.
33. *Boston Post*, April 12, 1928.
34. *Boston Herald*, April 12, 1928.
35. Ibid.
36. Ibid.
37. *Youngstown Vindicator*, April 22, 1928.
38. *Boston Post*, April 12, 1928.
39. Ibid.
40. Ibid.
41. Ibid.
42. *Boston Globe*, April 14, 1928.
43. *Boston Globe*, April 20, 1928.
44. *Boston Herald*, April 20, 1928.
45. *Boston Globe*, April 30, 1928.
46. *Boston Globe*, April 31, 1928.
47. *Boston Globe*, May 1, 1928.

Chapter 16

1. *Boston Post*, May 13, 1928.
2. *Boston Herald*, May 13, 1928.
3. *Harvard Crimson*, May 17, 1928.
4. *Boston Herald*, May 17, 1928.
5. *Boston Herald*, May 18, 1928.
6. *Boston Herald*, May 18, 1928.
7. *Boston Herald*, May 19, 1928.
8. *Boston Post*, May 20, 1928.
9. *Boston Post*, May 21, 1928.
10. *Boston Herald*, May 23, 1928.
11. *Boston Herald*, May 24, 1928.
12. Ibid.
13. *Boston Post*, May 23, 1928.
14. *Boston Herald*, May 25, 1928.
15. *Boston Herald*, May 25, 1928.
16. *Boston Post*, May 25, 1928.
17. *Boston Herald*, May 26, 1928.

18. *Boston Herald*, May 26, 1928.
19. *Boston Post*, May 28, 1928.
20. *Boston Herald*, June 11, 1928.
21. *Boston Herald*, June 13, 1928.
22. *The Sporting News*, June 28, 1928.
23. *Boston Herald*, July 10, 1928.
24. *Boston Herald*, Sept. 7, 1928.
25. *Boston Herald*, Dec. 16, 1928.
26. *Boston Post*, Dec. 12, 1928.
27. *Boston Herald*, Dec. 12, 1928.
28. *Boston Post*, Dec. 12, 1928.
29. Ibid.
30. *Boston Post*, Dec. 14, 1928.
31. *Boston Herald*, March 17, 1929.
32. *Boston Herald*, March 26, 1929.
33. *Boston Herald*, March 27, 1929.
34. *Boston Herald*, April 14, 1929.
35. *Boston Herald*, May 11, 1929.
36. *Boston Herald*, June 10, 1929.
37. Ibid.
38. *Boston Herald*, June 29, 1929.
39. *Boston Herald*, July 22, 1929.
40. *Boston Herald*, Aug. 2, 1929.
41. Ibid.
42. Ibid.
43. *Boston Herald*, Aug. 5, 1929.
44. Ibid.
45. *Boston Herald*, Aug. 15, 1929.
46. *Syracuse Herald*, Sept. 8, 1929.

Chapter 17

1. *Boston Herald*, Jan. 30, 1930.
2. *Galveston Daily News*, Jan. 30, 1930.
3. *New York Herald Tribune*, Feb. 23, 1930.
4. *New York Herald Tribune*, Jan. 30, 1930.
5. *Charleston Daily Mail*, March 23, 1930.
6. *Pittsburgh Press*, Feb. 11, 1930.
7. Interview with Jack Williams, Feb. 20, 2008.
8. Ibid.
9. *Appleton Post-Crescent*, March 8, 1930.
10. Ibid.
11. *New York Times*, March 9, 1930.
12. *Grants Pass Daily Courier*, March 23, 1930.
13. Ibid.
14. *Charleston Daily Mail*, March 23, 1930.
15. *The Oregonian*, March 27, 1930.
16. Ibid.
17. *The Oregonian*, March 28, 1930.
18. Ibid.
19. Ibid.
20. *Grants Pass Daily Courier*, April 1, 1930.
21. Ibid.
22. *The Oregonian*, March 31, 1930.
23. *The Oregonian*, April 13, 1930.
24. *The Oregonian*, May 11, 1931.
25. *The Oregonian*, Sept. 3, 1931.
26. Ibid.
27. Ibid.
28. *Oakland Tribune*, Sept. 12.
29. Ibid.
30. *The Oregonian*, April 1, 1931.
31. *The Oregonian*, June 22, 1930.
32. *The Oregonian*, July 24, 1930.
33. *Eugene Register-Guard*, July 29, 1930.
34. *The Oregonian*, April 19, 1931.
35. *The Oregonian*, May 1, 1931.
36. *The Oregonian*, May 12, 1931.
37. *Charleston Gazette*, June 20, 1931.
38. Interview with Ken Williams, Jr., Dec. 7, 2006.

Chapter 18

1. Interview with Jack Williams, May 30, 2007.
2. Ibid.
3. Interview with Jack Williams, Sept. 15, 2006.
4. Interview with Ken Williams, Jr., Dec. 7, 2006.
5. Ibid.
6. Interview with Jack Williams, Sept. 15, 2006.
7. Interview with Ken Williams, Jr., Feb. 22, 2008.
8. Ibid.
9. *Grants Pass Daily Courier*, Sept. 20, 1936.
10. *St. Louis Globe Democrat*, July 18, 1937.
11. *Pampa Daily News*, July 18, 1937.
12. Interview with Ken Williams, Jr., Dec. 7, 2006.
13. Greg Hanberg, "Quiet slugger let his bat talk for him," *Grants Pass Daily Courier*, Aug. 28, 1987.
14. Interview with Ken Williams, Jr., Dec. 7, 2006.
15. *Grants Pass Daily Courier*, March 15, 1944.
16. Interview with Ken Williams, Jr., Dec. 7, 2006.
17. *St. Louis Globe Democrat*, Jan. 20, 1958.
18. *The Sporting News*, Jan. 29, 1958.
19. Ibid.
20. Greg Hanberg, "Quiet slugger let his bat talk for him," *Grants Pass Daily Courier*, Aug. 28, 1987.
21. Roger A. Godin, "The 1922 St. Louis Browns: Best of the American League's Worst" (Jefferson, NC: McFarland, 1991).
22. *The Sporting News*, Jan. 29, 1958.
23. *St. Louis Globe Democrat*, Jan. 22, 1958.
24. Interview with Jack Williams, Sept. 15, 2006.
25. Interview with Ken Williams, Jr., Dec. 7, 2006.
26. Interview with Jack Williams, Sept. 15, 2006.
27. Interview with Ken Williams, Jr., Dec. 7, 2006.
28. *St. Louis Globe Democrat*, Aug. 20, 1958.
29. Ibid.
30. *St. Louis Globe Democrat*, Aug. 19, 1958.
31. *St. Louis Globe Democrat*, Aug. 20, 1958.
32. *The Sporting News*, Aug. 27, 1958.
33. *The Sporting News*, Dec. 27, 1969.
34. *The Sporting News*, Aug. 27, 1958.
35. Ibid.
36. Interview with Jack Williams, Sept. 15, 2006.
37. *The Sporting News*, Jan. 28, 1959.

Chapter 19

1. *The Progress-Index* (Petersburg, Va.), Jan. 23, 1959.
2. Interview with Jack Williams, Oct. 6, 2006.
3. Interview with Ken Williams, Jr., Dec. 7, 2006.
4. Email correspondence with Jack O'Connell, Dec. 19, 2006.

5. *The Sporting News*, Feb. 17, 1973.
6. *The Sporting News*, Feb. 19, 1977.
7. George Vass, "These Greats Belong in the Hall of Fame," *Baseball Digest* (January 1981, vol. 4, Issue 1).
8. Greg Hanberg, "Quiet slugger let his bat talk for him," *Grants Pass Daily Courier*, Aug. 28, 1987.
9. Robert Burnes, "Ten Players Who Belong in the Hall of Fame!," *Baseball Digest* (April 1982, vol. 41, No. 4).
10. Greg Hanberg, "Fame eludes Williams," *Grants Pass Daily Courier*, Aug. 28, 1987.
11. Ibid.
12. http://baseballanalysts.com/archives/2003/08/the_greatest_an.php
13. Interview with Jack Williams, Oct. 6, 2006.
14. Interview with Ken Williams, Jr., Dec. 7, 2006.
15. Ibid.

Bibliography

Books

Burk, Robert F. *Much More Than a Game: Players, Owners & American Baseball Since 1921*. Chapel Hill: University of North Carolina Press, 2001.

Carter, Craig, ed. *Daguerrotypes*. 8th edition. St. Louis: *The Sporting News*, 1990.

Curran, William. *Big Sticks: The Batting Revolution of the Twenties*. New York: William Morrow, 1990.

Finch, Robert, L.H. Addington and Ben M. Morgan, eds. *The Story of Minor League Baseball*. Columbus, OH: Stoneman, 1953.

Godin, Roger A. *The 1922 St. Louis Browns: Best of the American League's Worst*. Jefferson, NC: McFarland, 1991.

Hill, Edna May. *Josephine County Historical Highlights I*. Medford, OR: Josephine County Library System and Josephine County Historical Society, 1980.

A History of Josephine County Oregon. Grants Pass, OR: The Josephine County Historical Society, 1988.

Honig, Donald. *Baseball When the Grass Was Real: Baseball from the Twenties to the Forties Told by the Men Who Played It*. New York: Coward, McCann & Geoghegan, 1975.

James, Bill. *The New Bill James Historical Baseball Abstract; The Classic—Completely Revised*. New York: Free Press, 2001.

Meaney, Tom. *Baseball's Greatest Hitters*. New York: A.S. Barnes, 1950.

______. *Baseball's Greatest Teams*. New York: A.S. Barnes, 1949.

Montville, Leigh. *The Big Bam: The Life and Times of Babe Ruth*. New York: Doubleday, 2006.

Seymour, Harold, and Dorothy Seymour Mills. *Baseball: The Golden Age*. New York: Oxford University Press, 1971.

Sutton, Jack. *110 Years with Josephine: The History of Josephine County, Oregon*. Medford, OR: Josephine County Historical Society, 1966.

Articles

"A Black Day for the St. Louis Browns." *Baseball Magazine*, August 1926.

Burnes, Robert. "Ten Players Who Belong in the Hall of Fame!" *Baseball Digest*, April 1982.

Colver, Newton. "Who Was the Greatest Batter of All Time?" *Baseball Magazine*, September 1927.

Dorey, C.H. "The Slugging Stars of 1926." *Baseball Magazine*, June 1927.

Grants Pass and Josephine County: Northern Gateway to the Redwood Empire. Grants Pass Chamber of Commerce leaflet, 1940.

Hanberg, Greg. "Fame Eludes Williams." *Grants Pass Daily Courier*, Aug. 28, 1987.

______. "Quiet Slugger Let His Bat Talk for Him." *Grants Pass Daily Courier*, Aug. 28, 1987.

Vass, George. "These Greats Belong in the Hall of Fame." *Baseball Digest*, January 1981.

Newspapers

Boston Globe
Boston Herald
Boston Post
Central Point (OR) *Herald*
Cincinnati Enquirer
Detroit Free-Press
Edmonton Bulletin
Edmonton Journal
Grants Pass (OR) *Daily Courier*

Medford (OR) *Daily Tribune*
New York Herald Tribune
Oregon (WI) *Observer*
The Oregonian (Portland, OR)
Regina (SK) *Leader*
Regina (SK) *Morning Leader Post*
Rogue River (OR) *Courier*
Sacramento Bee
St. Louis Globe Democrat
St. Louis Post-Dispatch
Siskiyou (CA) *News*
Spokane Daily Chronicle
Spokane Spokesman-Review
Umpqua (OR) *Valley News*
Woodland (CA) *Daily Democrat*

Collections

Ken Williams clippings file, Josephine County Historical Society.
Ken Williams clippings file, National Baseball Hall of Fame.

Interviews

Jack Williams
Ken Williams Jr.

Online Resources

archive.nlm.nih.gov/fdanj/bitstream/123456789/68243/3/FDNJ21205.pdf
attheplate.com/wcbl
baseballalmanac.com
baseballanalysts.com/archives/2003/08/the_greatest_an.php
baseball-reference.com
censusrecords.com
chatterfromthedugout.com
chroniclingamerica.loc.gov
cwcfamily.org/articles/family/breabowl.htm
Google News Archive
historylink.org
LA84 foundation digital library
mlb.com
newspapers.com
nytimes.com/ref/membercenter/nytarchive.html
paperofrecord.com
retrosheet.org
SABR Bio Project
webtrail.com/history/grantspass.shtml

Index

Numbers in ***bold italics*** refer to pages with photographs.

Stop Faking It!

Finally Understanding Science So You Can Teach It

More Chemistry Basics

More Chemistry Basics

By William C. Robertson, PhD
In consultation with Michael S. Kralik, PhD,
and Ann Cutler, PhD
Illustrated by Brian Diskin

Arlington, Virginia

Claire Reinburg, Director
Jennifer Horak, Managing Editor
Andrew Cocke, Senior Editor
Judy Cusick, Senior Editor
Wendy Rubin, Associate Editor
Amy America, Book Acquisition Coordinator

Art and Design
Will Thomas Jr., Director

Printing and Production
Catherine Lorrain, Director
Jack Parker, Electronic Prepress Technician

SciLinks
Tyson Brown, Director
Virginie Chokouanga, Customer Service and Database Coordinator

National Science Teachers Association
Francis Q. Eberle, PhD, Executive Director
David Beacom, Publisher

13 12 11 10 4 3 2 1

Library of Congress Cataloging-in-Publication Data
Robertson, William C.
More chemistry basics / William C. Robertson ; in consultation with Michael S. Kralik and Ann Cutler; illustrated by Brian Diskin.
p. cm. -- (Stop faking it!)
Includes index.
ISBN 978-1-933531-47-2
1. Chemistry--Popular works. I. Title. II. Title: Chemistry basics.
QD37.R534 2010
540--dc22
2009052866
e-ISBN 978-1-936137-74-9

NSTA is committed to publishing material that promotes the best in inquiry-based science education. However, conditions of actual use may vary, and the safety procedures and practices described in this book are intended to serve only as a guide. Additional precautionary measures may be required. NSTA and the authors do not warrant or represent that the procedures and practices in this book meet any safety code or standard of federal, state, or local regulations. NSTA and the authors disclaim any liability for personal injury or damage to property arising out of or relating to the use of this book, including any of the recommendations, instructions, or materials contained therein.

Featuring sciLINKS®—a new way of connecting text and the Internet. Up-to-the-minute online content, classroom ideas, and other materials are just a click away.

Contents

Preface

Prior to the publication of this book, teachers often asked me whether the book would be more advanced than the first book, *Chemistry Basics*. The answer to that question is yes and no. First, this book builds on concepts discussed in the first book. Although the first chapter of this book is a review of the concepts covered in the first book, the review will not suffice if you are not somewhat familiar with those concepts. So, you need to know a few things about basic chemistry before tackling this book. Second, there are a number of topics in this book that might be considered advanced chemistry, such as the uncertainty principle in quantum mechanics, the formation of different kinds of bonds, and oxidation-reduction reactions. Many of the reviewers of the book said things such as, "The teachers in your audience will never teach some of these concepts to their students. The students won't see some of these concepts until high school or even college." That might be true, but I believe that your understanding of the so-called higher-level concepts will enhance your teaching. When little Susie says, "These orbits of electrons aren't correct; my mom says we can't really know what electrons are doing," what will be your response? It could be, "We don't discuss that in sixth grade—you'll learn that in high school." But if you actually know what Susie is talking about, you have a choice. You can discuss it with her individually, or you might even decide that the subject will be great for a class discussion. If you don't know what Susie is talking about, you have no choice and no control over the situation. You need to ask yourself whether you want the content of your curriculum to be in charge of what happens, or if you want your knowledge of the subject matter to be in charge of what happens. I prefer the latter. Also, it is empowering to know more than you will ever need to teach the students. It gives you a comfort level and just might affect how you address certain topics. Teaching is more fun when you are secure in the depth of your understanding.

One more thing on this topic. There is a lot of tradition in the teaching of science. You simply don't address certain concepts until you get to a particular grade level. This implies that some ideas are much more difficult to understand than others. I strongly believe, however, that anyone can understand, say, the basics of quantum mechanics. Yes, a complete mathematical treatment of the subject requires a sophistication with math, but the basic concepts are not that difficult to understand. You can avoid the math complexities (as I do, for the most part, in this book) and still grasp the major concepts. As someone (I forget who) said, you can teach anyone of any age just about any concept, as long as you do so in an intellectually honest manner. This means that anyone can learn any concept, but you must take care not to alter the concept in the process to the point that you are teaching lies, which unfortunately happens too often when we try to "dumb down" certain material. Suffice to say that I try to remain intellectually honest in everything I write.

Content aside, this book is arranged the same as all the other books in the *Stop Faking It!* series. I ask you to do a few simple activities prior to the explanation of any concepts. We understand concepts better when we can anchor them to concrete experiences, and that's the purpose of these sections. It might be tempting to just read through the Things To Do sections, but I strongly encourage you to do the activities. They could make the difference between memorizing concepts and truly understanding them. Memorization fades, but understanding lasts.

Finally, I want to be clear that this is not a comprehensive chemistry book, even when combined with the first chemistry book in the series. For example, I do not deal with equilibrium in chemical equations or solubility of solids immersed in solutions, both traditional chemistry concepts. I also do not do justice to the vast field of organic chemistry. This book is not a textbook, and none of the books in the *SFI* series are intended to be comprehensive textbooks. My goal is to help you obtain a deep understanding of a number of basic chemistry concepts. I hope that with this understanding, you will know what those short descriptions of content in activity books are all about and will have the basis for knowing what's going on in a textbook. Also, although there are activities in this book, the activities are there to help you understand concepts and are not necessarily intended as classroom activities. That's not to say that you can't use some of these activities in the classroom, but rather that you should consider safety and appropriateness before using the activities with your students.

Safety Note

Though the activities in this volume don't require anything more volatile than household vinegar, safety should always be in the forefront of the mind of every teacher. (This is not intended as a book of classroom activities, by the way. Rather, the activities are designed to enhance your understanding of the subject before you get into the classroom.) Your individual school, or possibly the school system of which your school is a part, likely has rules and procedures for classroom and laboratory safety.

You can also find specific guidelines for the safe storage, use, and disposal of thousands of types of chemical products in the Material Safety Data Sheets (MSDS). Start with *http://www.ilpi.com/msds/#Internet.* This site links to dozens of free searchable databases, including those of top American and European universities.

NSTA has also published several award-winning titles covering the safety theme at all school levels. For the elementary level, there's *Exploring Safely: A Guide for Elementary Teachers* and the *Safety in the Elementary Science Classroom* flipchart. Middle school-level offerings are *Inquiring Safely: A Guide for Middle School Teachers* and the *Safety in the Middle School Science Classroom* flipchart. Finally, there's *Investigating Safely: A Guide for High School Teachers.*

How to Get Special Materials

You can visit the following websites to get supplies for chemistry activities.

Arbor Scientific. *www.arborsci.com/SearchResult.aspx?CategoryID=4*

Carolina. *www.carolina.com*

Edmund Scientific. *http://scientificsonline.com*

Educational Innovations. *www.teachersource.com/Chemistry.aspx*

Hi-Valley Chemical. *www.hvchemical.com*
(*Note:* Although other suppliers require that you are affiliated with a school or other institution, Hi-Valley will sell supplies to private individuals—which is important for home schoolers or others who are not affiliated with an institution.)

Sargent-Welch. *http://sargentwelch.com/chemicals/c/4749*

Science Kit. *http://sciencekit.com*

Ward's Natural Science. *http://wardsci.com/category.asp_Q_c_E_1251*

About the Author

As the author of NSTA Press's *Stop Faking It!* series, Bill Robertson believes science can be both accessible and fun—if it's presented so that people can readily understand it. Robertson is a science education writer, reviews and edits science materials, and frequently conducts inservice teacher workshops as well as seminars at NSTA conferences. Bill has published research in cognitive science that addresses the difference between memorizing and understanding and how that affects learning. He has also taught college-level physics and math and developed K–12 science curricula, teacher materials, and award-winning science kits. He earned a master's degree in physics from the University of Illinois and a PhD in science education from the University of Colorado.

About the Illustrator

The recently-out-of-debt, soon-to-be-famous, humorous illustrator Brian Diskin grew up outside of Chicago. He graduated from Northern Illinois University with a degree in commercial illustration, after which he taught himself cartooning. His art has appeared in many books, including *The Beerbellie Diet* and *How a Real Locomotive Works*. You can also find his art in newspapers, on greeting cards, on T-shirts, and on refrigerators. At any given time he can be found teaching watercolors and cartooning, and hopefully working on his ever-expanding series of *Stop Faking It!* books. You can view his work at *www.briandiskin.com.*

About the Consultants

Michael Kralik received his PhD in chemistry from the University of Utah with postdoctorate studies in chemistry, pharmacology, and toxicology. He has been faculty at the university and has conducted many faculty and staff development seminars. Kralik has established product development and manufacturing operations domestically and internationally, and has directed the development of hundreds of products for major corporations in chemical, medical, pharmaceutical, and electronics industries. He has developed K–12 science curricula, teacher inservice workshops, and many award-winning educational toys, games, and science kits.

Ann Cutler is the field editor for the *Journal of College Science Teaching,* a position she has held since 2006. She is an associate professor of chemistry at the University of Indianapolis in Indiana and has a doctorate in inorganic chemistry from Purdue University.

Acknowledgments

The *Stop Faking It!* series of books is produced by the NSTA Press: Claire Reinburg, director; Jennifer Horak, managing editor; Wendy Rubin, associate editor; Will Thomas Jr., art director; Catherine Lorrain, printing and production director; and Jack Parker, electronic prepress technician. Will Thomas Jr. designed the cover from an illustration provided by artist Brian Diskin, who also created the inside illustrations.

This book was reviewed by Dennis Huffman (Lanier Middle School, Texas), Sue Vogel (Thomas Jefferson High School, Iowa), and Peggy Carlisle (Pecan Park Elementary School, Mississippi).

Dedication

I dedicate this book to two people. The first is Michael Kralik, a good friend and valuable colleague for many years who has served as a consultant on both chemistry books. There's a saying in science education that all activities are recycled—there really isn't anything new. People who say that have never met Michael, who consistently comes up with inventive ways to introduce concepts. The second person is Ann Cutler, who was a reviewer for both chemistry books. I can honestly say that Ann has fundamentally changed the content of both books and, with this second book, saved me from embarrassing myself with hastily written, wrong explanations.

Déjà Review

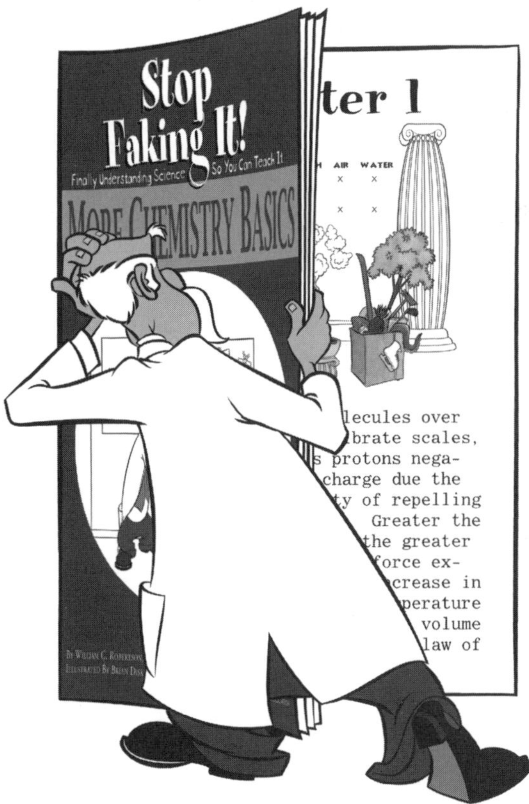

This is the second chemistry book in the *Stop Faking It!* series; the first one is called *Chemistry Basics*. This second book introduces new concepts and expands on many of the concepts presented in the first book, so it would help if you knew the contents of the first book before picking up this one. Now, I can't assume that you have already worked your way through the first book. It's also possible that you worked your way through that book but need a refresher on the contents. Hence, I'm beginning this book with a chapter that reviews the content of *Chemistry Basics*. In no way should you consider this chapter a substitute for going through the first book, though. If your knowledge of chemistry concepts is at all shaky, I strongly advise you to work through *Chemistry Basics* first.

Because this is a review chapter, it does not follow my usual format. Normally, I have you, the reader, perform a few simple activities before reading explanations of concepts. The explanations use the results of the activities to help you anchor the concepts to experiences, thus leading to a deeper understanding than would otherwise be possible. If I did the activity thing in this chapter, then this chapter would be as long as the first book, and that wouldn't make much sense. So, what follows here are explanations of concepts *sans* activities.

As such, this first chapter represents what you normally expect from a textbook or other science resource, which is a set of straightforward explanations. If you do own *Chemistry Basics,* comparing this chapter to that book will provide a clear example of what it's like to learn science concepts with and without use of the Learning Cycle.

And yes, I realize that *déjà review* is the same as saying *re-review.* Makes sense to me, though, because there is a summary section at the end of each chapter in *Chemistry Basics*. You can consider a summary section a review, so this chapter counts as the second review of the material. And yes, I realize that most of you don't care whether or not I justify the chapter title!

Using models to explain observations

Topic: Atomic Theory
Go to: *www.scilinks.org*
Code: MCB001

The primary building block of chemistry is **atomic theory**–our model of what tiny little things called atoms look like and how they behave, both alone and in interactions with other atoms. Using atoms to explain observations is typical of what scientists do–develop **models**. For example, two magnets exert forces on each other. These forces can be attractive or repulsive. To describe and explain such interactions, physicists invented things called **magnetic fields**. With rules for the magnetic field lines that magnets generate and for how magnets and other objects react when in the presence of magnetic field lines, you can understand all sorts of things magnetic in nature. Figure 1.1 shows the magnetic field lines associated with a bar magnet.[1]

Figure 1.1

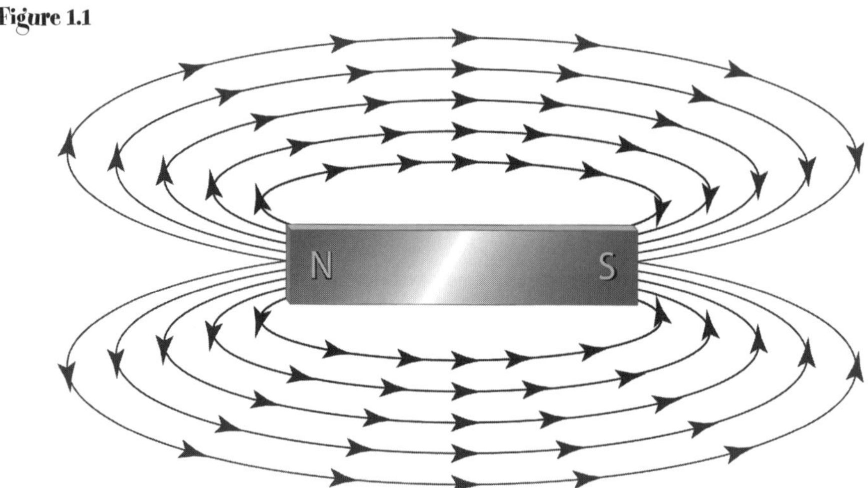

[1] The magnetic field lines shown in Figure 1.1 are just an example of the models that scientists use. I'm not expecting you to know what these field lines represent with respect to magnetic interactions.

The process of creating scientific models began long ago. One of the earliest models to explain the workings of the universe came from the early Greeks, who proposed that there are four main elements in the universe: earth, air, water, and fire. All things in the universe are composed of these elements in different proportions, and these four elements strive to attain their "proper" places in the universe, illustrated in Figure 1.2. You can explain the properties of objects and what happens when different substances interact simply by determining how much of each of the four basic elements the substances contain.

Figure 1.2

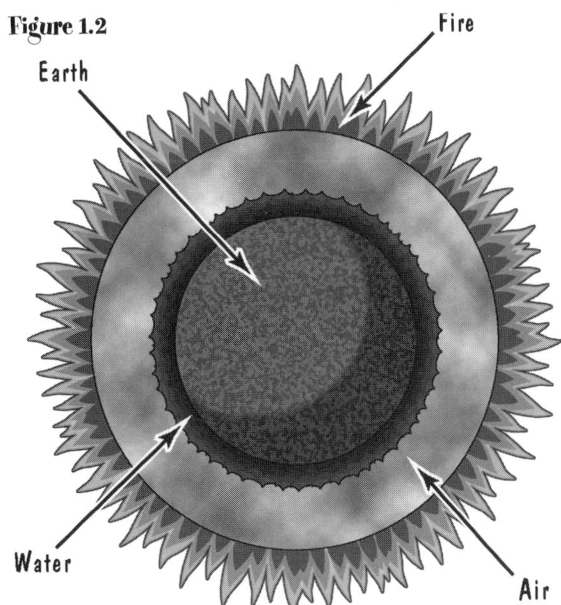

It turns out you can use the model of earth, water, air, and fire to explain many occurrences. This model was so effective, in fact, that it's a wonder that the theory that atoms (tiny, indivisible, marblelike objects that make up everything in the universe) exist ever got a foothold in the scientific and philosophic communities. The theory of atoms was established, though, and over the span of hundreds of years the model of the atom underwent lots of changes and currently is a pretty sophisticated model. The next section explains our current model of the atom. I use the word *current* because it's a pretty good bet that our model of the atom a hundred years from now will look quite a bit different from our model of the atom today. Personally, I'm expecting a similar result when I look into a mirror a hundred years from now, assuming that living to be 160 years old will soon be commonplace.

Topic: Atomic Models
Go to: *www.scilinks.org*
Code: MCB002

Atomic fashions, or what not to wear if you want to keep up with the halogens

The rather obscure title of this section means that I intend to explain scientists' currently accepted model of what your typical atom looks like. Atoms are all different, but they have many characteristics in common. Most books address the model of the atom as it developed historically, and my first chemistry book in this series takes that approach. Here, though, it's probably best to just cut to the chase and present a modern picture of the atom.

Atomic fashions

Atoms are composed of a positively charged, concentrated center called the **nucleus**, surrounded by negatively charged **electrons**. The nucleus contains positively charged **protons** and zero-charged **neutrons**. In electrically neutral atoms, there are equal numbers of protons and electrons. The number of neutrons in a nucleus varies. Hydrogen has no neutrons, and many of the lighter atoms have equal numbers of protons and neutrons. Even within one type of atom, the number of neutrons can vary. Atoms that have the same number of protons but different numbers of neutrons are called **isotopes**.

Before moving on, I want to show you a drawing of an atom that one often finds in elementary school textbooks and reference books for laypeople. Figure 1.3 shows protons and neutrons in the nucleus, surrounded by electrons moving in orbits not unlike the orbits of planets around the Sun.

Note the circle and slash through this drawing, indicating that it's wrong. Electrons do *not* orbit the nucleus like this. If they did, they would radiate energy away rapidly, resulting in a quick collapse of the universe. No collapsing universe that I notice, so why do books still use this outdated drawing? I've had people tell me it's useful for early grades because it's easier to understand than a more accurate drawing (which we'll get to later), but I'm not buying that. My position is that you can explain just about any concept to any age group in an intellectually honest way, which means you might need to

Figure 1.3

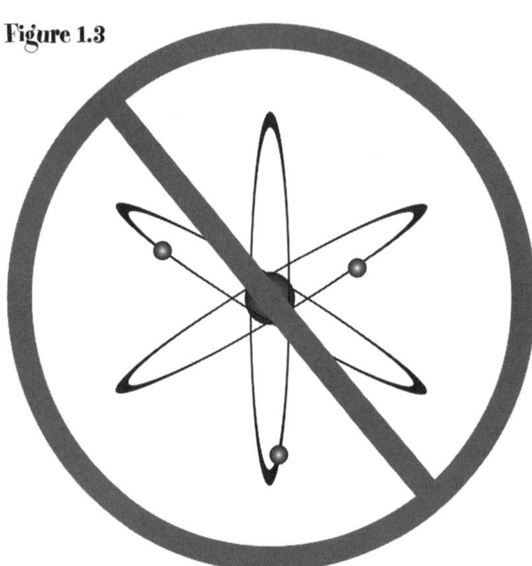

simplify things a bit, but you can stay true to the correct model. Orbits aren't true to the correct model, so I think an adjustment is in order. Unfortunately, the textbook companies don't ask for my advice much!

Anyway, let's move on. Protons and neutrons have approximately the same mass (we'll usually assume that the masses are equal), and both are much more massive than electrons. The mass of an electron is so small, in fact (over 1,000 times smaller than the mass of a proton), that it's common to ignore the electron mass when determining the mass of an atom. Electrons also are physically smaller than protons and neutrons—so small, in fact, that they don't have a measurable size.[2] Even though electrons are that tiny, they do help determine the overall size of an atom because they move around in a "cloud" that extends beyond the confines of the nucleus. The farther out the electron cloud extends, the larger the atom.

More details

We do know more about an atom than what makes it up. We have some idea of what the protons, neutrons, and electrons are doing. The protons and neutrons in the nucleus (Remember, the nucleus by far makes up most of the mass in an atom.) pretty much stay put in relation to the atom as a whole, even though all atoms in the universe are themselves moving at all times.[3] The electrons are a different story. As I mentioned, they don't move in circular orbits. So, what are the electrons doing? We know that they have only certain energies, with those energies being dictated by the type of atom you have. We speak of atoms as having **energy levels** or **energy shells** in which the electrons can reside. It's sort of like the electrons can sit in a football stadium but only in rows 2, 7, 15, and so on. The in-between rows (in-between energies in an atom) aren't available to the electrons. It's not that those energies don't exist but rather that they're off-limits for electrons in different atoms. This fits with the notion that electrons behave as bundles of waves (a premise of the mathematics of quantum mechanics) that are confined, in this case confined because of the electric attraction between the electrons

SCiLINKS®
THE WORLD'S A CLICK AWAY
Topic: Energy Levels
Go to: *www.scilinks.org*
Code: MCB003

[2] It might seem strange to you that something doesn't have a measurable size, but that's the case with electrons as well as with other subatomic objects in the universe. Scientists consider such objects to be point objects. And if the existence of point objects troubles you greatly, keep in mind one of my favorite phrases: All of science is made up. Mathematically, electrons act like they have zero size, so that's what we have to deal with, even if it doesn't seem to make sense.

[3] Here I refer to a random jiggling motion that characterizes all atoms, even those that make up solids. Even at the lowest temperatures possible, atoms still jiggle just a bit.

Figure 1.4

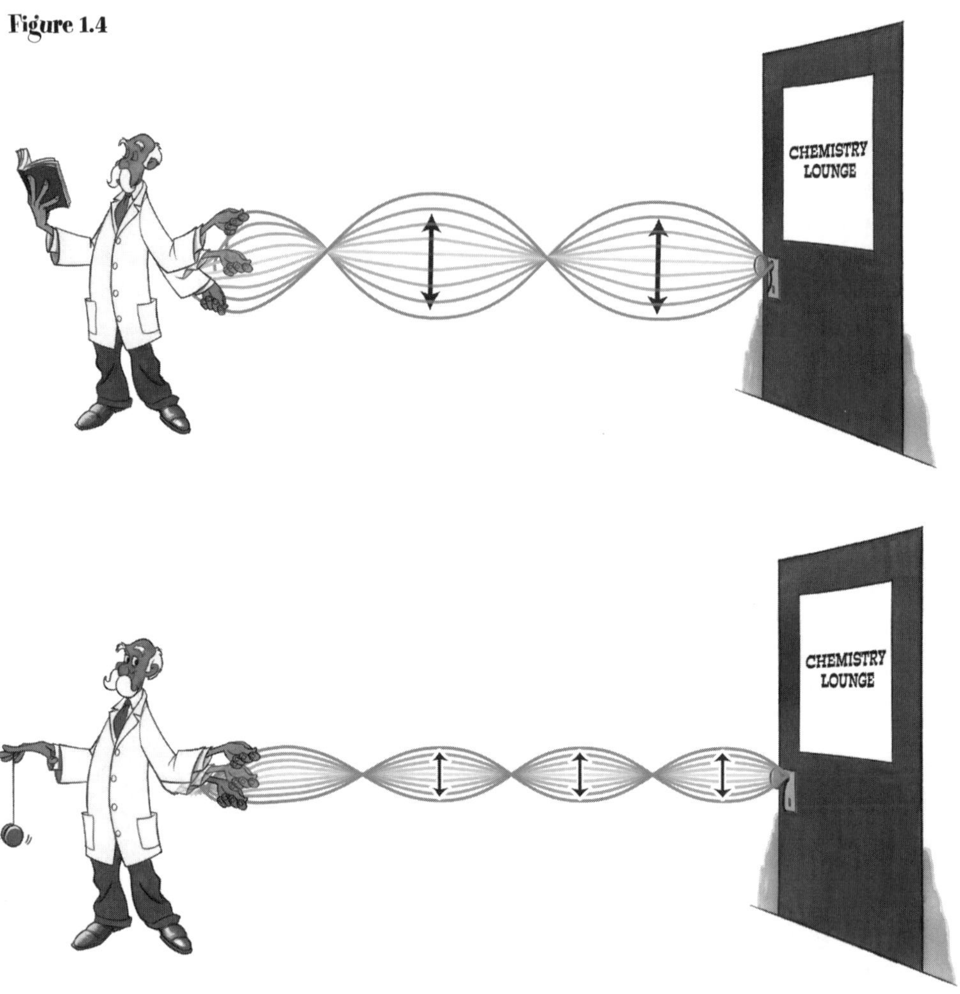

and the nucleus. When you confine waves, only certain "resonant" energies are allowed, as demonstrated using waves on a string shown in Figure 1.4.[4]

The electrons can only have certain energies, but they can jump from one energy level to the next. In the process, the atom either gives off or absorbs electromagnetic waves, some of which we know as light. Figure 1.5 shows an electron jumping between two energy levels in an atom. This drawing is a cross-section of the two lowest energy levels in an atom. These energy levels (orbitals) are spherical in shape and are known as the 1*s* and 2*s* orbitals.

[4] Keep in mind that this is a review chapter. If this is your first introduction to the fact that electrons reside in distinct energy levels and why that is, then you really should pick up a more basic resource on this (say, my first chemistry book in the series ... hint, hint) to understand the topic better.

Okay, so we know that the electrons can have certain energies and jump from one energy level to another. What are they *doing* in the meantime? Well, we don't know for sure. The best we can come up with is a **probability distribution** for each electron, which is a mathematical description of the probability of finding the electron in any given place at any given time. Pictorially, we show this as shaded regions. Figure 1.6 shows a cross-section of the probability distribution for the lowest energy level in any atom (the entire lowest-energy probability distribution is spherical). The darker the shading, the more likely the electron is to be found at that location.[5]

Figure 1.5

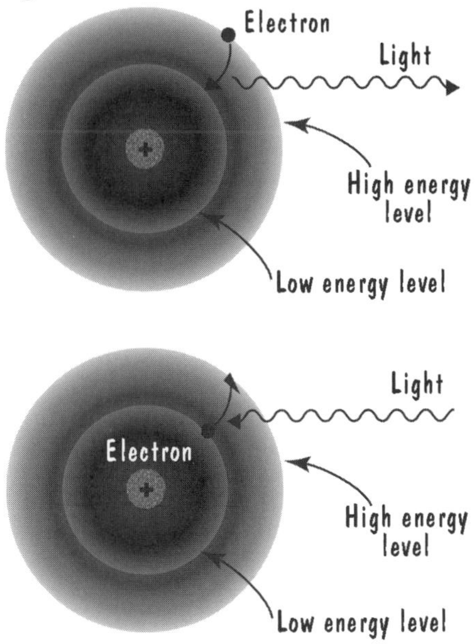

Figure 1.6

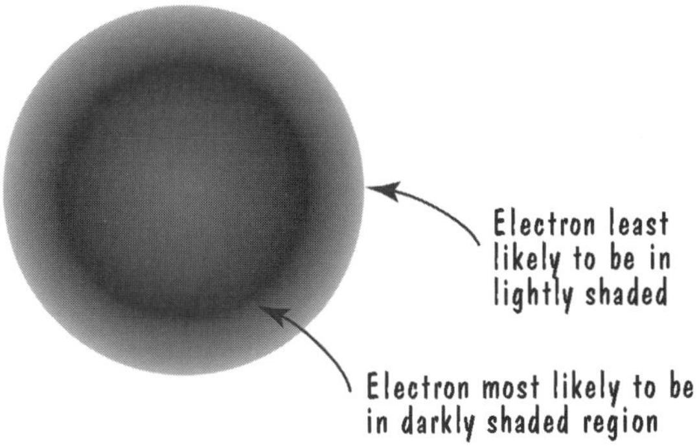

As you go from lower to higher energy levels in an atom, the shapes of the probability distributions change. Figure 1.7 (p. 8) shows the shapes of the distributions for three different energies of a major energy level within an atom. We call each of these distributions and parts of distributions **orbitals**, so it is common to refer to an electron as residing in "such and such an orbital" rather than give its precise energy. For example, we might talk about a 3*s* electron (3 referring to the main energy level and *s* to its sub-energy level, or orbital) or a 4*d* electron (again, the 4 is the main energy level and *d* is its sub-energy level or orbital).

[5] When I discuss orbitals later in the book, I'll explain why we can't know an electron's exact location.

Figure 1.7

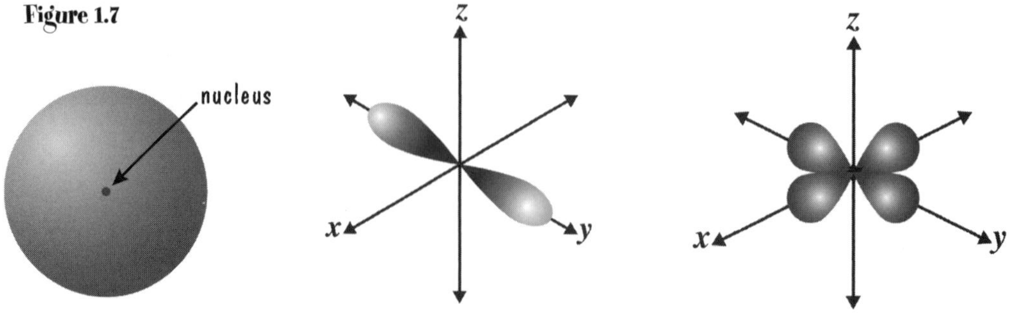

The 1*s* energy level probability distribution

The 2*p* energy level probability distribution

The 3*d* energy level probability distribution

Low energy is best

One major principle that governs the universe is that systems (any specific object or collection of objects) tend toward configurations that have the lowest energy.[6] What that means is that objects in a system tend to spontaneously rearrange themselves to achieve a lower energy. For example, a rock on a cliff has more energy at the top of the cliff (farther from the Earth) than at the bottom (closer to the Earth), so its natural tendency is to fall to the bottom, where the energy is lower. Similarly, because negative electrons are attracted to the positive nucleus in an atom, the atom can have lower energy when the electrons are closer to the nucleus. Closer to the nucleus generally means lower energy levels for the electrons.[7] We could also say that electrons tend to drop to the lowest energy orbitals possible. Now, the lowest energy *possible* in a system of objects might not be the lowest energy *imaginable*. With our rock falling off a cliff, the rock might get stuck on a ledge halfway down the cliff; then the rock is at the lowest energy possible (the ledge stopped it) but not the lowest energy imaginable (the bottom of the cliff).

From rocks to electrons in atoms. The lowest energy level available to an electron might not be the lowest energy level imaginable of the atom. You see, each orbital in an atom can hold only so many electrons. The 1*s* orbital in an atom can only hold two electrons, so if you add an electron to an atom that already has two electrons, the new electron has to reside in the next highest energy level,

---

[6] This principle is not anything magical but rather just a convenient way to figure out what will happen in different situations. Systems tend toward lowest energy as a direct consequence of definitions of energy. Not gonna show you that right now.

[7] Don't let Figure 1.7 confuse you about this idea. The drawings there reflect the shapes of the different orbitals but not necessarily their relative sizes. So, even though it looks like an electron in the *d* orbital (far-right drawing) might spend more time near the nucleus than an electron in the *s* orbital (far-left drawing), that's not the case.

which happens to be the 2*s* orbital. A good analogy is the game of Stadium Checkers (shown in Figure 1.8; search the internet for a description of the game) with the bottom holes plugged. You can drop marbles down toward the center by moving the rings. Once the lowest ring is full, new marbles have to reside in the next ring up. When that one's full, new marbles have to reside in the next ring up from that one.

Figure 1.8

So, here's our picture of what electrons are doing in an atom. We can draw orbitals, or probability distributions, that tell us where the electrons are *likely* to be. Electrons in different orbitals have different energies, and electrons tend to reside in the lowest energy orbital possible. We think of energy levels in an atom as existing even when they don't contain electrons, just as there are spaces available for marbles in Stadium Checkers even if the spaces don't contain a marble. This whole situation lets us draw energy level diagrams for atoms. The energy level diagram for oxygen is shown in Figure 1.9. Note that the electrons occupy the lowest energy levels possible, even though slots in higher energy

Figure 1.9

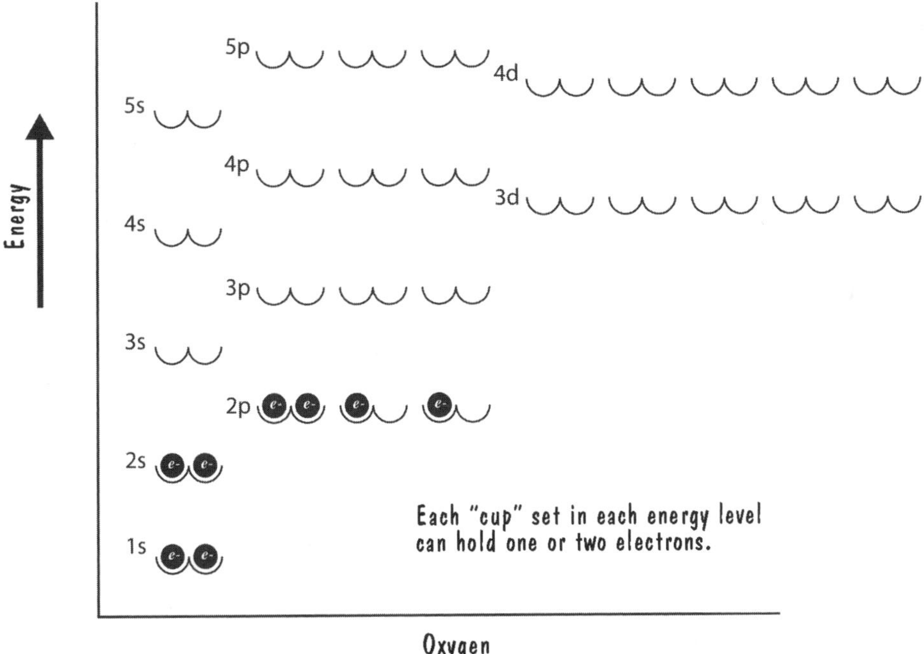

levels are available. Also note that in energy level diagrams the horizontal axis has no meaning other than to show different orbitals distinctly. The only direction to worry about is the vertical direction, which separates the electron positions by energy.

If you add energy to an atom (by heating it up, maybe), you can send electrons into higher energy slots. The electrons then spontaneously head back to the lower energy slots and emit electromagnetic waves, which might be in the visible part of the spectrum (light). Remember that we refer to different main energy levels as *shells*. It turns out that filled shells have lower energies than unfilled shells or orbitals. This is important when two or more atoms get together. For example, our oxygen atom would just love to grab a couple of electrons from another atom to fill up its *2p* orbital, thus filling up its outer shell. The *way* in which atoms grab or give up electrons is the subject of bonds between atoms, covered later in this chapter.

The concept of filled and unfilled electron shells in atoms is extremely important for understanding how atoms behave around other atoms. Filled shells are usually quite stable and generally correspond to lower energies than unfilled shells. So in a sense, atoms "like" to have filled electron shells.[8] Different orbitals can accommodate different numbers of electrons, so what constitutes a filled shell depends on the orbitals involved. Filled *s* orbitals contain two electrons, filled *p* orbitals contain six electrons, and filled *d* orbitals contain ten electrons. See Table 1.1.

Table 1.1

Orbital	Maximum number of electrons
s	2
p	6
d	10
f	14

More on this as we discuss ...

[8] Some people get all apoplectic over anthropomorphism (assigning human characteristics such as likes and dislikes to nonhuman animals or objects) in science. I don't. I say if it helps you understand, go for it. If anyone really thinks atoms think like humans, science might not be that person's thing.

"No, Professor. I said 'Periodic Table,' not 'periodical table.'"

The Periodic Table

And so we come to the one thing that causes an increase in blood pressure if one had a bad experience in chemistry–the Periodic Table (Figure 1.10, p. 12). Most likely that's because many of us were required to memorize some or most of this table in school. If you look at the table as an organizational chart or map, however, it's not very scary but actually quite useful. Each place in the table is reserved for a particular atom or element. An element is something composed of only one kind of atom, so for the purposes of studying the Periodic Table, we'll use the terms *element* and *atom* interchangeably. Thus, I might refer to an atom of carbon or the element carbon when talking about what occupies the sixth place in the Periodic Table.

Let's run through what all the numbers and such on this table mean. The letters stand for different elements (or atoms): H for hydrogen, He for helium, O for oxygen, Be for beryllium, Ag for silver, and on and on and on.[9]

[9] You might be troubled by the fact that element symbols sometimes don't seem to represent the element names, such as Ag for silver and W for tungsten. This is because contributions to the positions of elements on the Periodic Table have come from all over the world. The original German name for tungsten, for example, is *wolfram*. Hence, W represents tungsten in the table. The Latin name for silver is *argentum*, leading to the symbol Ag for silver. Further trivia: The Latin name for mercury is *hydroargentum* (leading to a symbol of Hg), which means liquid silver, which is what mercury looks like.

Figure 1.10

Periodic Table of Elements

1 H Hydrogen 1.00794																	2 He Helium 4.00260
3 Li Lithium 6.941	4 Be Berylium 9.01218											5 B Boron 10.81	6 C Carbon 12.011	7 N Nitrogen 14.0067	8 O Oxygen 15.9994	9 F Flourine 18.998403	10 Ne Neon 20.179
11 Na Sodium 22.98977	12 Mg Magnesium 24.305											13 Al Aluminum 26.98154	14 Si Silicon 28.0855	15 P Phosphorus 30.97376	16 S Sulfur 32.06	17 Cl Chlorine 35.453	18 Ar Argon 39.948
19 K Potassium 39.0983	20 Ca Calcium 40.08	21 Sc Scandium 44.9559	22 Ti Titanium 47.88	23 V Vanadium 50.9415	24 Cr Chromium 51.996	25 Mn Manganese 54.9380	26 Fe Iron 55.847	27 Co Cobalt 58.9332	28 Ni Nickel 58.69	29 Cu Copper 63.546	30 Zn Zinc 65.38	31 Ga Gallium 69.72	32 Ge Germanium 72.59	33 As Arsenic 74.9216	34 Se Selenium 78.96	35 Br Bromine 79.904	36 Kr Krypton 83.80
37 Rb Rubidium 85.467	38 Sr Strontium 87.62	39 Y Yttrium 88.9059	40 Zr Zirconium 91.22	41 Nb Niobium 92.9064	42 Mo Molybdenum 95.94	43 Tc Technetium (98)	44 Ru Ruthenium 101.07	45 Rh Rhodium 102.9055	46 Pd Palladium 106.42	47 Ag Silver 107.8682	48 Cd Cadmium 112.41	49 In Indium 114.82	50 Sn Tin 118.69	51 Sb Antimony 121.75	52 Te Tellurium 127.60	53 I Iodine 126.9045	54 Xe Xenon 131.29
55 Cs Cesium 132.9054	56 Ba Barium 137.33	57 La Lanthanum 138.9055	72 Hf Hafnium 178.49	73 Ta Tantalum 180.9479	74 W Tungsten 183.85	75 Re Rhenium 186.207	76 Os Osmium 190.2	77 Ir Iridium 192.2	78 Pt Platinum 195.08	79 Au Gold 196.9665	80 Hg Mercury 200.59	81 Tl Thallium 204.383	82 Pb Lead 207.2	83 Bi Bismuth 208.9804	84 Po Polonium (209)	85 At Astantine (210)	86 Rn Radon (222)
87 Fr Francium (223)	88 Ra Radium (226)	89 Ac Actinium (227)	104 Rf Rutherfordium (261)	105 Db Dubnium (262)	106 Sg Seaborgium (266)	107 Bh Bohrium (264)	108 Hs Hassium (269)	109 Mt Meitnerium (268)	110 Uun Ununnium	111 Uuu Unununium (285)	112 Uub Ununbium (284)	113 Uut Ununtrium (289)	114 Uuq Ununquadium (288)	115 Uup Ununpentium (292)	116 Uuh Ununhexium	117 Uus Ununseptium	118 Uuo Ununoctium

58 Ce Cerium 140.12	59 Pr Praseodymium 140.9077	60 Nd Neodymium 144.24	61 Pm Promethium (145)	62 Sm Samarium 150.36	63 Eu Europium 151.96	64 Gd Gadolinium 157.25	65 Tb Terbium 158.9254	66 Dy Dysprosium 162.50	67 Ho Holmium 164.9304	68 Er Erbium 167.26	69 Tm Thulium 168.9342	70 Yb Ytterbium 173.04	71 Lu Lutetium 174.967
90 Th Thorium 232.0381	91 Pa Protactinium 231.0359	92 U Uranium 238.0289	93 Np Neptunium 237.0482	94 Pu Plutonium (244)	95 Am Americium (243)	96 Cm Curium (247)	97 Bk Berkelium (247)	98 Cf Californium (251)	99 Es Einsteinium (252)	100 Fm Fermium (257)	101 Md Mendelevium (258)	102 No Nobelium (259)	103 Lr Lawrencium (260)

Topic: Periodic Table
Go to: *www.scilinks.org*
Code: MCB004

The main number on each element (1 for hydrogen, 2 for helium, 20 for calcium) is called the **atomic number**, which tells you how many protons are in the atom. The number of protons in an atom is the atom's main distinguishing characteristic. If you change the number of protons (which is not an easy thing to do), you have a different atom that corresponds to a different element. For a neutral atom, the atomic number also tells you the number of electrons in the atom. A neutral atom has no net charge because there is an equal number of positive charges (protons) and negative charges (electrons). **Ions**—atoms that have extra electrons or lack electrons—are still the same element because they have the same number of protons. The atomic number is always an integer—you can't have a fraction of a proton or an electron

The second number, at the bottom of each listed element in the Periodic Table, is called the **atomic mass**.[10] Atomic masses are not nice, round numbers but rather numbers such as 28.086 and 65.37. If you round off the atomic mass, the number you end up with tells you the total number of protons and neutrons in the most commonly occurring form of the atom. The atomic mass is measured in what are called **atomic mass units**. In this system, the mass of a proton is equal to exactly 1 and the mass of a neutron is equal to exactly 1.[11] The mass of an electron is really small compared to the masses of protons and neutrons, so we can ignore the electron's mass for most purposes in chemistry. So the electrons are still there in our atoms—we just don't count their mass.

An important thing to remember: Atoms with different numbers of protons are different elements. Different numbers of electrons or neutrons, however, do not necessarily indicate different elements.

Now take a look at hydrogen in the Periodic Table. Hydrogen contains 1 proton and 1 electron, with zero neutrons. Why, then, isn't the atomic mass of hydrogen equal to exactly 1? The reason is that in nature each element can have isotopes. For example, most of the time hydrogen has 1 proton and zero neutrons, but hydrogen can also have 1 neutron (this is called deuterium) or 2 neutrons (this is called tritium) and still be hydrogen. The atomic masses of elements are not integers because of the existence of isotopes. Atomic masses

---

[10] Older texts and even recent publications use the term *atomic weight* instead of *atomic mass*. The proper term is *atomic mass,* but for years the convention was to use *atomic weight,* and old habits die hard.

[11] We use atomic mass units instead of actual masses for simplicity. Also, the mass of a proton is different from the mass of a neutron, but the difference is small enough that we don't have to worry about it here.

are *averages* of the atomic masses that naturally occur in nature, and virtually all atoms can exist in isotope form.

As we move from left to right across the table, and as we form new rows, we encounter atoms that have one more proton than the previous atom. With neutral atoms, that also means that each successive atom has one more electron than the previous atom (that statement is not necessarily true for ions!). So, while protons determine an atom's identity, we sometimes focus just on what's happening to the electrons as we go from element to element.

Recall that as you add electrons to energy levels, the electrons fill the lowest energy levels first. Once lower energy levels are filled (remember that energy levels can hold only so many electrons), electrons fill the higher energy levels, just as in Stadium Checkers. So, as you move from left to right across the Periodic Table, you are adding protons and electrons[12] to atoms. As this happens, the electrons–in cooperation with the nuclei of atoms–obey the simple principle that systems naturally tend to be in their lowest energy.

Let's look at this pattern in more detail. In hydrogen, as in other atoms, the lowest energy level is 1*s*. Two electrons can reside in that energy level. When you add a proton and two neutrons to hydrogen, you get helium. You also get another electron, which fills the 1*s* energy level. I mentioned before that atoms with nothing but filled energy levels are extremely stable and represent low-energy situations. If you want to add an electron to a filled energy level, clearly that's a difficult thing to do. It is also difficult to remove an electron from an entirely filled energy level.

Noble gas

Well, we have helium with a filled 1*s* energy level. Helium is a **noble gas**. Noble gases are also called **inert gases**. The word *inert* means unresponsive or inactive, and that describes helium. Helium just plain doesn't interact much with other atoms.

Topic: Inert Gases
Go to: *www.scilinks.org*
Code: MCB005

Before continuing, recall that scientists refer to the energy levels in atoms as **shells**. Outer shells are higher energy levels and inner shells are lower energy levels. This terminology no doubt dates back to when people thought of electrons as moving in circular orbits around the nucleus, which of course we now know they don't. Electrons in an outermost shell are known as **valence electrons**. We only consider *s* and *p* electrons when counting valence electrons.[13] We

[12] Keep in mind that we're not physically adding protons and electrons but describing a pattern in the table.

[13] Electrons in *d* and *f* orbitals generally aren't considered valence electrons because, as explained in a few pages, adding electrons to *d* and *f* orbitals occurs in inner shells.

would say, then, that hydrogen has one valence electron and helium has two valence electrons.[14]

Noble Gas

Back to the Periodic Table. In the second row, we start with lithium. It has a completely filled 1*s* energy level, plus an extra electron that hangs out in the 2*s* energy level. With an open slot in that energy level, lithium readily interacts with other atoms. The next atom in the second row is beryllium, which has a filled 2*s* energy level and, thus, two valence electrons. Shouldn't be a surprise that beryllium isn't quite as anxious as lithium to interact with other atoms because it has a filled 2*s* energy level, which is more stable than a half-filled 2*s* energy level.

Next we jump across a gap to the element boron. The reason we jump a gap will be clear later. After you jump the gap, you will notice that there are five elements before you get to the final atom on the right, which is neon. What's happening as you move through those five atoms is that electrons are filling the 2*p* energy level. By the time you get to neon, the 2*p* energy level is filled. Neon has a filled "shell" of eight electrons (recall that the *s* energy level holds up to two electrons and the *p* energy level can hold up to six electrons), and so, like helium, neon is an inert gas. Filled shells with eight valence electrons don't interact much with other atoms, so neon doesn't take part in many chemical reactions. You might expect that those five atoms before you get to argon—boron, carbon, nitrogen, oxygen, and fluorine—*do* interact with other atoms, and that expectation is correct.

The third row, beginning with sodium and ending with argon, follows the same pattern. It's all about electrons filling the lowest possible energy levels in an atom.[15] The fourth row, which begins with potassium and ends with krypton,

---

[14] The two electrons in helium make up a filled shell, so they don't interact readily with electrons in other atoms. I mention this because we commonly think of valence electrons as interactive. Not so with the noble gases.

[15] We're focusing on what happens to electrons in neutral atoms, but don't forget that as you go from element to element, the identifying change in the atoms is the change in the number of protons.

all of a sudden has atoms in the gap. Why? Because at this point we begin filling the energy level 3*d*. The 3*d* energy level can hold ten electrons, which is why there are ten atoms filling the gap until you get to gallium. At that point, adding protons and their corresponding electrons involves the 4*p* energy level. Because each *p* level holds six electrons, we traverse six atoms in getting to the atom of krypton. Krypton has a filled 1*s* level, a filled 2*s* level, a filled 2*p* level, a filled 3*s* level, a filled 3*p* level, a filled 4*s* level, a filled 3*d* level, and a filled 4*p* level.

I should say something about the two rows at the very bottom that are separated from the rest of the Periodic Table. These represent a progression of elements in which electrons are filling *f* energy levels. If we included them in the main portion of the Periodic Table, there would be another huge gap that would stretch the table from side to side; then we wouldn't be able to fit a readable Periodic Table on a page. It's sort of like how Alaska and Hawaii are portrayed on a map of the United States. They're not shown in their actual locations because if they were, the rest of the map would not be readable on a normal-size page.

All atoms in a particular column of the Periodic Table have similar properties because they have the same number of valence electrons (electrons in the outermost *s* and *p* energy levels). This general rule is the same for all columns of the Periodic Table. Magnesium, calcium, and strontium have similar properties—they're all shiny, soft metals that react with water to produce hydrogen. Copper, silver, and gold have similar properties—they're also shiny, soft metals that are excellent conductors of heat and electricity. Fluorine, chlorine, bromine, and iodine have similar properties—all react strongly with other elements and exist as diatomic molecules in their pure states. For elements in columns 3 through 12, the number of valence electrons (the *s* and *p* electrons) is not changing because you're adding *d* electrons. Even so, the atoms in these rows have similar properties because they have similar electron arrangements.

Bonding and such

We've all known since maybe third or fourth grade that atoms get together and form larger things called *molecules*. This is what most of chemistry is about. When atoms hold onto one another, we say they form **bonds**. You can understand bond formation by focusing on atoms' desire to have filled outer shells and considering the energy involved.

One kind of bond is the **ionic bond**.[16] This is where one atom steals an electron from another atom. This makes one a positive ion and the other a nega-

[16] There are chemists who prefer not to consider ionic bonds as true chemical bonds, but because opinions are mixed on that issue and ionic bonds seem to fall into the category of chemical bonds for me, we'll stick with that convention.

tive ion, with an electric attraction between the two (opposite charges attract). The result is that the two atoms bond together. Of course, ionic bonds usually involve many more than just two atoms. They usually involve many atoms linked together, as in the salt lattice represented in Figure 1.11.

Figure 1.11

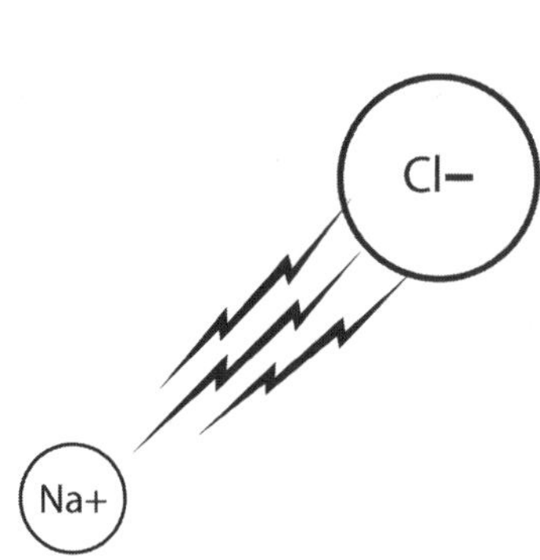

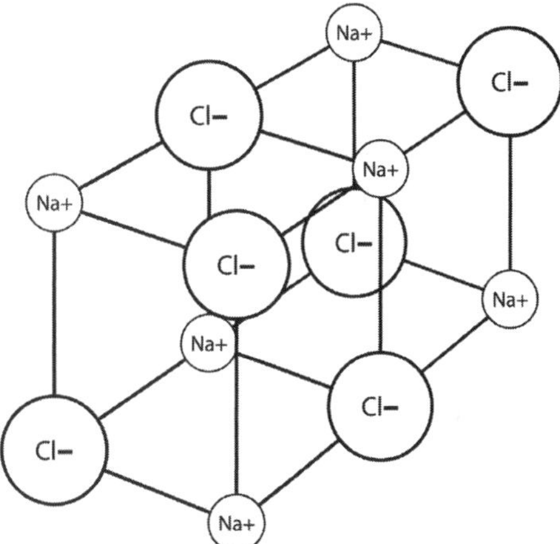

When atoms form ionic bonds, the new bond has a lower energy than the two atoms do separately. This follows the general principle that systems tend toward lower energies. You can predict which atoms will get together and form ionic bonds. For example, atoms in the first column of the periodic table have one valence electron and would love to get another one to fill their *s* shells. Atoms in the next to last column of the Periodic Table need just one electron to fill their outer shells. Remember that filled shells are energetically favorable. So anyway, this means that when you bring together atoms from the first column and atoms from the next to last column, you are likely to get an ionic bond. By the way, there's a number known as an atom's **electronegativity** that lets you know how readily an atom will grab or give up an electron. For details on electronegativity, check a more thorough resource than this chapter, like maybe the first chemistry book in this series.

Topic: Electronegativity
Go to: *www.scilinks.org*
Code: MCB006

The second kind of bond, which has two subclassifications, is a **covalent bond**. Sometimes when atoms get together, it's possible for them to share one or more electrons rather than steal an electron from each other, and that's a covalent bond. By sharing electrons, each atom can satisfy its need for a complete outer shell even though neither atom has a strong enough attraction to or repulsion from electrons for an electron to jump from one atom to another. This sharing of electrons, which forms a bond between the atoms, gives each atom a configuration almost as good as a filled outer shell and is thus more favorable energetically than the atoms staying apart.[17] A few examples of covalent bonds are two hydrogen atoms getting together to share their single electrons and form a hydrogen molecule (H_2), two oxygen atoms getting together to share four electrons (two each) and form an oxygen molecule (O_2), and two hydrogen atoms getting together with one oxygen atom to share a total of four electrons and form a water molecule (H_2O). Figure 1.12 shows the electron-sharing for oxygen and water. I should, of course, be shot for providing the drawing in Figure 1.12. I already told you that electrons don't occupy specific positions in atoms, but the drawing seems to imply that. All I can ask is that you use the drawing as an indication of shared electrons (the ones in the overlapping region) without making the leap that this is what atoms in a covalent bond *actually* look like. Also, keep in mind that the drawing only shows the valence electrons; there are others in each atom not shown.

Figure 1.12

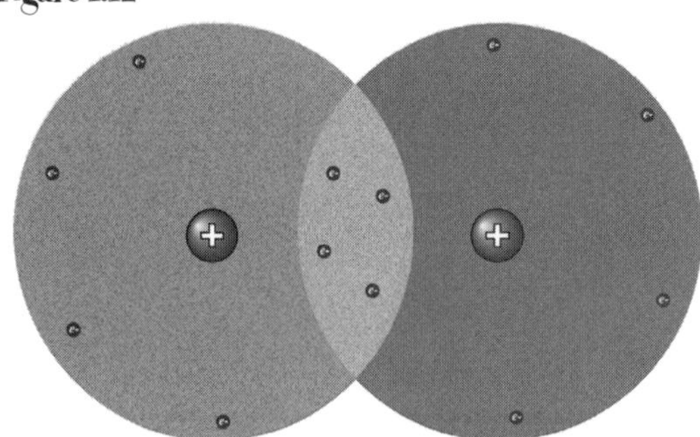

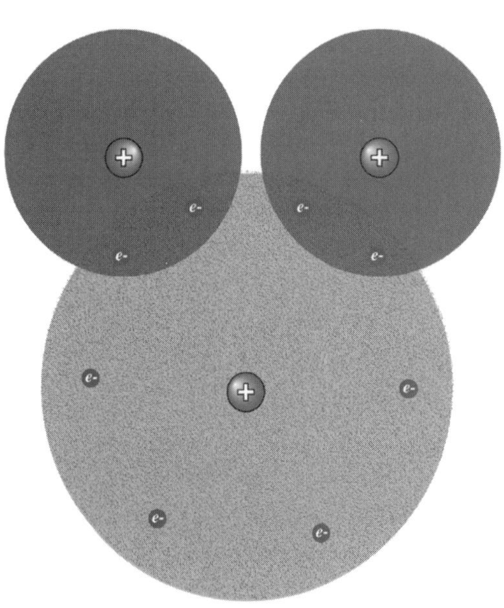

Now for the subclassifications. Sometimes atoms share electrons even though one atom likes electrons (attracts them) more than the other atom does. In this case, you still have the sharing of electrons and a covalent bond, but the electrons spend more time around one of the atoms than they do around the other. Such a bond is called a **polar covalent bond**, with the word *polar* meaning that one part of the molecule is more positive and the other side is more negative. Covalent bonds in which the atoms share the electrons more or less equally are called **nonpolar covalent bonds**. O_2 is a nonpolar covalent bond (the shared electrons hang around each oxygen molecule for about equal amounts of time), and

[17] Remember that filled shells generally represent lower energies than unfilled shells, and systems tend toward lower energies.

H_2O is a polar covalent bond (the shared electrons spend more time around the one oxygen atom than they do around the two hydrogen atoms).

Institute for the Study of Nonpolar Covalent Bonds
Bali Campus

Finally, metals have their own unique kind of bond. Each atom in a metal shares one or more electrons with *all* of the other atoms of that same piece of metal in what's called a **sea of electrons**. So, metals have a whole bunch of free-roaming electrons that can move all over the place. Again, this sharing of the electrons by all of the metal atoms is more favorable energetically than some other configuration.

When chemical structures collide

Chemistry is more than atoms getting together to form molecules. Most often we think of **chemical reactions**, in which one or more chemical compounds get together, atoms switch places, and something observable happens. For example, when you mix baking soda and vinegar, you end up with a new substance called sodium acetate, along with carbon dioxide gas and water. We represent such reactions with a **chemical equation**, which shows how a certain amount of one substance reacts with a certain amount of some other substance(s) to produce a certain amount of new substance(s). For example, our baking soda and vinegar reaction can be represented, first in words and then in chemical formulas, as

vinegar + sodium bicarbonate → sodium acetate + carbon dioxide + water

$$HC_2H_3O_2\ (aq) + NaHCO_3\ (s) \rightarrow NaC_2H_3O_2\ (s) + CO_2\ (g) + H_2O\ (l)$$

In this reaction, we refer to the molecules on the left as **reactants** and the molecules on the right as **products**. The equation shows what happens to single

"No! We don't need collision insurance."

molecules of baking soda (sodium bicarbonate) and vinegar and thus is only *representative* of the thousands or millions of such reactions taking place at once.

If you count up the number of each kind of atom on the left and right sides of the previous equation, you'll find out that the numbers are equal. This is consistent with what is known as the **law of conservation of mass**, which basically states that atoms are not created or destroyed during a chemical reaction. You have to end up with the same number of each kind of atom as you started with. The equation for baking soda and vinegar reflects this fact, but sometimes when you write down the chemical formulas for the reactants and products, the number of atoms doesn't balance. Then you have to go through a process of "balancing" the equation—multiplying each chemical compound on the left and right by various numbers to get the number of atoms on the left and right to come out the same. This process can be easy or take quite a bit of trial and error. The more you practice, the better you get at it, which is how most things in life work.

Why, you might ask, do chemical compounds engage in a chemical reaction? Why don't they just keep to themselves when you mix them together? The answer lies again with energy. Sometimes when you mix two substances together, nothing happens. Sometimes a lot happens, but we huge humans can't see what's going on. Sometimes the substances spontaneously react, and sometimes they even explode. When they do react, it's partially because the products have a lower energy than the reactants. The new bonds that form in the products have an overall lower energy than the original bonds between the reactants. Putting energy aside, you can also understand reactions as taking place because different atoms have different affinities for other atoms. It's like a bunch of hormonal teenagers getting together at a dance. During the dance, some people find they like someone else better than the person they came with, so they switch over and form new partners.

Sometimes you have to add energy to get a chemical reaction to occur. For example, a stick of dynamite will sit around forever doing nothing until you light a fuse (add energy). It's like giving a ball a push (adding energy) over a hump in order for it to get to a lower place, as in Figure 1.13.

Figure 1.13

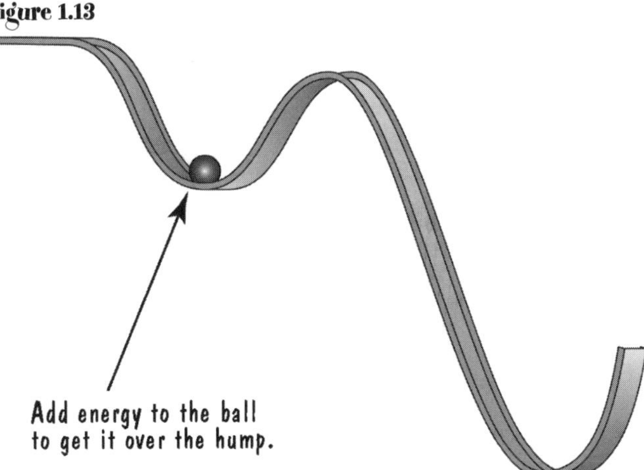

For example, many chemical reactions will occur once you heat up the reactants. Cooking an egg involves chemical reactions that take place only after you add heat. The energy you add to get a reaction going is known as the **activation energy**.

Organic stuff

In the first book, I briefly touched on **organic chemistry**, which is the study of chemical reactions involving carbon. Carbon is special in that its valence electrons are in just the right orientation to allow carbon to form many kinds of bonds with itself and other atoms. This leads to long, chainlike molecules (called **polymers**) that have many useful properties. Here I'm talking about things like polyester, vinyl, and different kinds of volatile substances, such as octane and methane (natural gas). Silicon, being similar to carbon (it's right below carbon in the Periodic Table), also fits into the study of organic chemistry.

Okay, that's my quick summary of the first chemistry book in the *Stop Faking It!* series, *Chemistry Basics*. If this wasn't a summary of concepts for you but rather an introduction, then you really should grab that first book. Doing the activities that precede the thorough explanations there will do much more for your understanding than this single chapter possibly could.

Dynamic Atoms

This chapter is about states of matter and a section of chemistry called **thermodynamics**, which is the inspiration (or lack thereof) for the chapter title. Some of what is in this chapter might seem just a bit disconnected from the content in the rest of the book, but it's an important part of chemistry and helps introduce the equally important concepts of moles and molarity. The best way to introduce those concepts is to start with how gases behave. You also need a basic understanding of the states of matter. If you have read the *Stop Faking It!* book *Air, Water, and Weather*, you will recognize some of the activities in this chapter. Before skipping over those, you should know that the explanations that follow will not be identical to those in the other book.

"'Dynamic atoms'? Is that the best title you two could think of?"

In this chapter, I will assume you have a solid grasp of the following concepts: mass, speed, kinetic energy, and force. If my assumption isn't correct in your case, you might want to learn a bit about those concepts before continuing. The following text box contains a set of brief definitions for those concepts in case you just need a review.

mass—a numerical measure of an object's inertia. Inertia and mass give you an idea of how difficult it is to change the motion of an object. An object with a greater mass is harder to get moving and stop, and hits other objects harder for a given speed. Throughout this book, we will refer primarily to the masses of atoms and molecules and collections of atoms and molecules. The units of mass in the metric system are kilograms.

speed—how fast something is moving in miles per hour, meters per second, etc. The formal definition of speed is (distance traveled)/(time to travel that distance). The direction in which something is moving is irrelevant when calculating speed. It is usually relatively easy to calculate average speed over a given time period, but instantaneous speed (how fast something is moving at a particular instant) tends to be more difficult to determine.

velocity—speed with a specification of direction added. The magnitude of an object's velocity is just its instantaneous speed.

kinetic energy—the energy something has as a result of its motion. The formula for kinetic energy is $\frac{1}{2}mv^2$, where m is the mass of the object and v is the magnitude of the object's velocity. The units of kinetic energy are joules, the units for all forms of energy.

force—any push, pull, nudge, whack, or shove. The units of force in the metric system are newtons.

Things to do before you read the science stuff

To start things off, I'm going to have you think about experiences you already have with water changing from one state to another.[1] By **state,** I mean the categories of solid, liquid, and gas. First, think about water changing from its liquid state (which we call water!) to its solid state, otherwise known as ice. In changing from liquid water to solid ice, does the water molecule change at all? If you don't know the answer to that question, then leave an ice cube out to melt. What do you get when it melts? If you said water, give yourself a good grade. Next, either boil some water or think about the last time you boiled water. What happens? Yep, you get steam. Is the steam still composed of water molecules, or something different? When answering that question, think about what happens to steam when it comes in contact with a cool surface, such as when the steam from your shower comes in contact with the bathroom mirror or when droplets form on the outside of a glass of iced tea on a warm day.

The science stuff

Hopefully the activities described above help convince you that when a substance goes from solid to liquid to gas and back, the basic unit of our substance–the water molecule–doesn't change. If the molecules changed when you froze water, then you wouldn't expect to get water back when ice melts. Similarly, if steam,

[1] If you haven't had the experiences described, by all means do them now.

otherwise known as water vapor, were not composed of water molecules, then you wouldn't expect to get water back when the steam encounters a cool surface.

What happens with water also happens with many other substances. Changing states does not alter the chemical composition of the substance. For example, when you cool oxygen gas (O_2) to very low temperatures, it becomes liquid oxygen that is composed of O_2 molecules. The only difference between liquid and gaseous oxygen is how strongly the molecules are held together.

So, for all substances, they can be solids, liquids, or gases and still be the same basic substance. In a solid, the atoms or molecules are held together so strongly that their positions with respect to one another don't change much. The atoms or molecules in a solid move in a jiggling sort of way, as do all atoms and molecules, but they essentially stay put. The atoms and molecules in liquids move more, rolling around one another without losing touch with the liquid as a whole. The atoms and molecules in a gas are free to bounce around all over the place and don't latch onto one another at all. (When they do latch on, they become liquids!)

More things to do before you read more science stuff

For this section, get yourself to a computer and head to the following link: *http://intro.chem.okstate.edu/1314F00/Laboratory/GLP.htm.* Be sure to read the instructions before starting.

> **Note:** If you don't have a computer handy, imagine a bunch of marbles bouncing around inside a container and following the rules I've described. Ball bearings in a closed petri dish also work well. If you're doing this with a classroom full of kids, you can have the kids pretend to be molecules in an enclosure. I describe such an activity in the *Stop Faking It!* books *Energy* and *Air, Water, and Weather.* Of course, the best way to visualize a gas is with the computer simulation, so do your best to use that.

This is a simulation of how gas molecules behave. To be more precise, this is a simulation of how an *ideal* gas behaves. In an ideal gas, the individual atoms or molecules don't interact with one another unless they collide.[2] When the atoms or molecules collide, they bounce off one another as if they were billiard balls. They also bounce off the walls of the container just as billiard balls do.

[2] An ideal gas is a good first approximation for how all gases behave, and it is a good enough model for us right now. When considering how actual gases behave, you have to allow for the rotation of molecules and the motion of atoms within a molecule, in addition to the fact that real gases do interact in ways beyond just bouncing off one another. For most applications, the ideal gas model works pretty well.

During a collision, it's possible for an individual atom or molecule to speed up or slow down. An atom or molecule also maintains a constant speed in between collisions. Figure 2.1 shows a still drawing of the simulation.

Figure 2.1

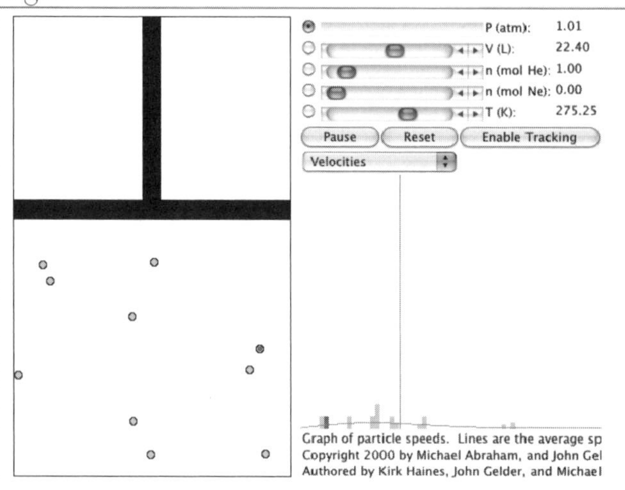

© Michael R. Abraham and John Gelder. Used with permission.

Once you have the simulation running or are actively imagining gas molecules moving around in a closed container, I want you to notice a few things. First, click on the enable tracking button so you can follow easily the motion of a single molecule. Verify that this molecule follows the rules of an ideal gas that I already mentioned. Kinda fun watching the little fella bounce around, huh?

Second, notice that all of the quantities listed in the control bar region—pressure, volume, temperature, etc.—are ones that apply to the gas as a whole. In an actual gas, there are way too many atoms or molecules to track individually. Yes, the graphing region shows the velocities of individual molecules, but that's because there are a limited number of those in this simulation. In practice, you cannot keep track of individual velocities because you are dealing with billions of molecules. Instead, we deal with averages. For example, we register the pressure of the gas (the force per unit area exerted on the walls of the container) instead of the forces that individual molecules exert. We can't keep track of the forces exerted by individual molecules, but we can keep track of the average force they exert on a given area.

Pressure is defined as the force exerted on a given area divided by that area. If you push on your hand with the sharp end of a nail, the area over which that force is exerted is small, and the force per unit area, the pressure, is large—it hurts! If you push with the same force using the flat end of the nail, however, that force is spread out over a larger area, and the resulting pressure is low—it doesn't hurt as much. When considering a gas, you can think about the pressure the gas exerts as being a measure of how hard, overall, the gas pushes on its surroundings and the molecules push on one another.

Third, I want you to take a look at the units of the quantities shown in the control bar. The pressure is measured in the unit **atm**. This is not a reference to quick cash, but rather an abbreviation for *atmospheres*. One atmosphere is a pressure roughly equal to the air pressure at sea level. Volume is measured in liters, a unit with which you should be familiar. The third and fourth control bars indicate the number of atoms of helium and neon that are present. The unit is mol, which stands for the word *mole*. For now, just think of this number as an indicator—not an exact count—of the number of atoms, in either the simulation or the real gas the simulation represents. For example, the default value of the number of moles of helium is 1.0. Clearly, there's more than one atom of helium in the simulation. Later on, you'll find out how many atoms of a real gas this 1.0 represents (a *lot*!). The temperature is measured in degrees Kelvin, or K. Water freezes at 273.16 degrees Kelvin, which is 0 degrees Celsius or about 32 degrees Fahrenheit.

Finally, make sure you understand how the sliding controls work. If you click on what the authors call a radio button (the circle to the left of each control), then that quantity is free to change in response to changing the other quantities. All the other quantities remain fixed unless you move the slider associated with the quantity. So, in the default settings, you can change the volume, the number of each kind of atom, and the temperature. The pressure will change in response to the changes you make.

Okay, on to investigating the behavior of your ideal gas. You can learn quite a bit about gases by simply playing around with the various controls. I encourage you to do that, but I definitely want you to be sure to try the following and see what happens in each case:

- As you change the temperature, what happens to the velocities of the atoms in the gas? Note that the average velocity of each kind of gas (helium or neon) is indicated by a vertical line on the graph.
- What happens to the pressure exerted by the gas as you increase the temperature? What happens to the pressure exerted by the gas as you decrease the temperature?
- What happens to the pressure exerted by the gas as you increase or decrease the number of atoms?
- What happens to the pressure exerted by the gas as you increase or decrease the volume occupied by the gas? Remember that with the pressure radio button checked, the temperature and number of atoms remain constant as you change the volume.

Before moving on to other tasks, think about the results you have obtained so far, and see if they make sense to you in terms of what the atoms are doing.

You've been monitoring changes in pressure as you change other quantities. Should the pressure go up when you increase the number of atoms? Why? Should the pressure decrease when you increase the volume? Why? Go ahead and answer these and other *why* questions. As you do this, keep the following concept in mind: The pressure the gas exerts will be affected by how fast and how often the atoms hit the container walls.

More tasks to try with the simulation:

- Click on the radio button for volume. Find out what happens to the volume as you change the pressure, number of atoms, and temperature. As you do this, be sure to note which quantities are constant and which are changing. For example, with the volume radio button checked, you can find out what happens to the volume when you change the pressure while keeping the number of atoms and the temperature constant. To investigate this in the real world, you would have to set up your apparatus to ensure that these latter quantities remained constant. That can be difficult (how would you ensure that the temperature of the gas didn't change?), which is why a simulation like this one is a valuable tool.
- Click on the radio button for temperature. Find out what happens to the temperature as you change the pressure, volume, and number of atoms. Again, note which quantities are constant and which are changing.
- Click on the radio button for the number of atoms of helium and set the number of atoms of neon at zero. Find out what happens to the number of helium atoms when you change the pressure, volume, and temperature. As you're doing this, realize that you're answering the following question: What must happen to the number of atoms when I change one quantity while requiring that the other quantities remain constant? This would be quite difficult to do in the real world. You would have to have some mechanism for introducing and removing gas molecules from your container. I just want to make sure you don't get the notion that in a real situation atoms would just appear and disappear, which is what happens in the simulation.

As before, take a look at these results and try to make sense of them in terms of the motion and quantity of atoms in the gas. Then do one more thing: Arrange the simulation so that you have both helium and neon atoms present. At any given temperature, find out which atoms, on average, move faster and which on average move slower. Easy task, no?

More science stuff

Lots to explain here. I'll start with the first thing I asked you to do, which was to notice what happens to the speeds[3] of the atoms as you change the temperature. Higher temperatures mean higher speeds, and lower temperatures mean lower speeds. Given that relationship, you might think that the temperature of the gas is a measure of the average speed of the particles in the gas. Not quite true. Imagine you have a thermometer stuck inside the gas to measure the gas's temperature. The hotter the liquid in the thermometer gets, the more it expands and moves up a column on which different temperatures are stamped. The faster the gas particles are going when they hit the thermometer, the more energy they give to the thermometer, and the more the liquid expands. But speed isn't everything. The more massive the particles are, the more energy they give the thermometer in a collision. It's just like getting hit with a pebble going 2 meters per second compared to getting hit with a large rock going 2 meters per second. The rock imparts more energy and hurts more. If we wanted to attain the same "hurt" with the pebble and the large rock, the pebble would have to be moving much faster than the rock.

So our definition of what temperature is should somehow contain both the speed of the particles and their mass, and it does. The temperature of a gas is directly related to the average **kinetic energy** of the gas particles. An object's kinetic energy, or motion energy, is given by the formula $\frac{1}{2}mv^2$, where m is the object's mass and v is the magnitude of the object's velocity. So the greater the mass, the greater the temperature, and the greater the speed, the greater the temperature. Now think back to the last thing I had you do in the previous section. I had you notice that at a given temperature, the neon particles moved slower than the helium particles. This makes sense in terms of our definition of temperature as a measure of the average kinetic energy of the particles. The helium and neon particles, as a whole, have the same temperature and, thus, the same average kinetic energy. Neon is more massive than helium, though; thus, the neon particles will have a smaller velocity because their mass is larger. See Figure 2.2 (p. 30).

Topic: Kinetic Energy
Go to: *www.scilinks.org*
Code: MCB007

[3] There is a difference between speed and velocity. Speed is only concerned with magnitude (how big the quantity is), and velocity includes both magnitude and direction. The authors of the simulation use the word *velocity,* but because we're not recording direction, the correct term to use would be *speed.* Scientists often use the two terms interchangeably when it is clear that we are only considering the magnitude of the velocities, and that's what's happening here. In the text, I will refer to speeds; be aware that the corresponding term in the simulation is *velocities*.

Figure 2.2

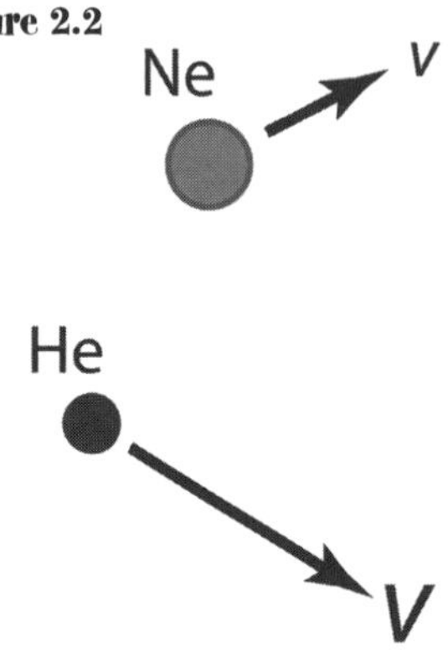

Ne v

Neon kinetic energy = ½ mv^2

He

Helium kinetic energy = ½ mV^2

V

The neon particles have a smaller velocity (indicated by a small v), but they have the same average kinetic energy as the helium particles because they have a larger mass.

On to the other things you did with the simulation. Here are the results you no doubt found.[4]

- With all other quantities held constant, increasing the temperature of the gas increases the pressure the gas exerts on the container. This should make sense to you. Increasing temperature increases the speed of the gas particles. This increased speed makes the particles hit the wall harder, thus increasing the pressure. Conversely, decreasing the temperature decreases the pressure the gas exerts. Take a look at Figure 2.3.

Figure 2.3

The particles on the right move faster and hit the container harder.

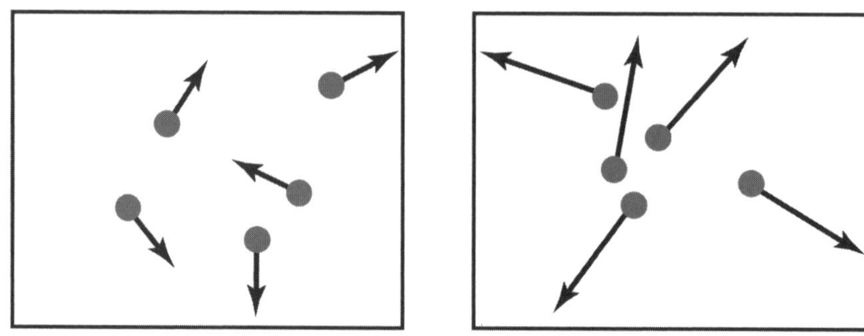

Higher temperature → Greater speed
Higher temperature → Greater pressure

[4] As with all of my books, it's possible for you to find out what should have happened in the activities I ask you to do by reading the section that follows. You will have a better grasp of concepts, though, if you actually do the activities when I tell you to do them. In other words, you understand better when you do activities rather than just read about them.

- With all other quantities held constant, increasing the number of gas particles increases the pressure. These added particles are at the same temperature as the other particles, so they don't hit the container any harder. Because there are more particles, though, they hit the walls of the container more often. More collisions with the container mean a higher pressure. Removing gas particles decreases the pressure because there are fewer collisions with the walls of the container.
- With all other quantities held constant, increasing the volume of the gas decreases the pressure. Because there is now more distance between the walls, the gas particles now hit the walls of the container less often. Fewer collisions mean a lower pressure. Conversely, decreasing the volume increases the pressure, because now the particles hit the walls more often. See Figure 2.4.

Figure 2.4

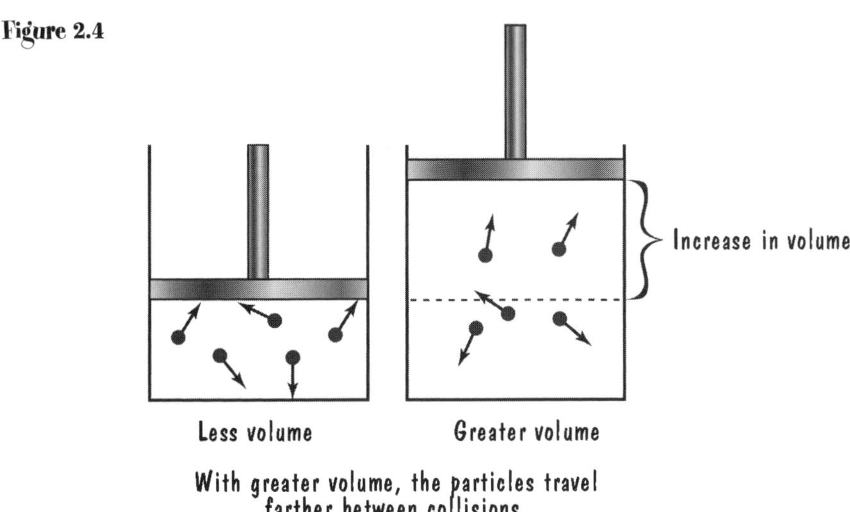

- With all other quantities held constant, increasing the pressure decreases the volume, and decreasing the pressure increases the volume. You have to think a bit to interpret this result. Remember that when you allow the volume to change and then change the pressure, you are requiring that the other quantities stay where they are. You don't change the number of particles or the temperature. With those restrictions, the only way to increase the pressure is by decreasing the volume, and the only way to decrease the pressure is by increasing the volume. See Figure 2.5 (p. 32). Basically, the simulation is doing what it can, given the restrictions you give it. When dealing with an actual gas, it would be really difficult to increase the pressure without changing the temperature.

Figure 2.5

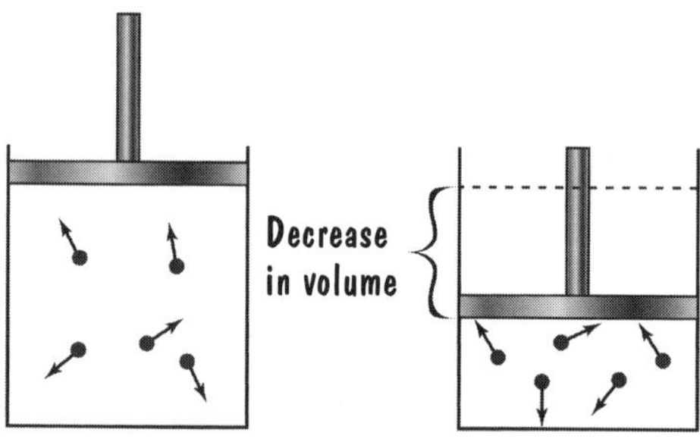

With temperature and number of molecules constant, the only way to increase collisions is to increase pressure. The only way to increase pressure is by decreasing volume.

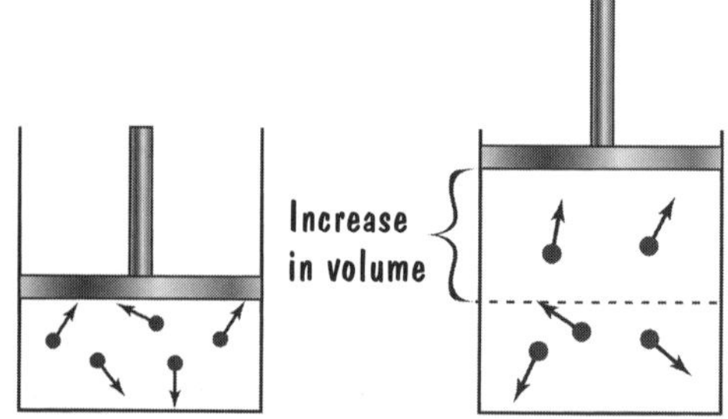

With temperature and number of molecules constant, the only way to decrease collisions is to decrease pressure. The only way to decrease pressure is by increasing volume.

I haven't addressed everything I had you do in the previous section because I think you can figure the rest out for yourself. Just remember how the different quantities are related, that pressure depends on how often and how fast the particles hit the container, and that temperature is a measure of the average kinetic energy of the gas particles.

Even without addressing everything you did, we have enough information to talk about a few laws that scientists came up with many years ago. Chemists who worked on the behavior of gases in the old days didn't have computer simulations to study, primarily because they didn't have computers. They did, however, perform experiments using real gases under controlled conditions.

In the 1700s, Joseph-Louis Gay-Lussac discovered that there was a direct relationship between the pressure and temperature of a gas. He expressed it as

$$\frac{\text{pressure}}{\text{temperature}} = \text{constant}$$

or

$$\frac{P}{T} = \text{constant}$$

This fits with your experience with the simulation. If the pressure divided by the temperature is a constant number, then when you increase the pressure, the temperature also must increase to have P/T equal to the same number. Remember that this is only true if you keep the number of molecules and the volume constant, which is what Gay-Lussac did in his experiments.

Earlier than that, in 1660, Robert Boyle discovered a relationship between the pressure and volume of a gas that's true when holding the temperature and number of molecules constant, which is

$$(\text{pressure})(\text{volume}) = \text{constant}$$

or

$$PV = \text{constant}$$

This is an *inverse relationship,* meaning that as pressure increases, the volume decreases, and as pressure decreases, volume increases. These relationships are true when the temperature and number of molecules are held constant. Again, this fits with what you observed in the simulation.

Still another scientist, Jacques Charles, discovered in 1787 a direct relationship between volume and temperature (number of molecules and pressure held constant), which is

$$\frac{\text{volume}}{\text{temperature}} = \text{constant}$$

or

$$\frac{V}{T} = \text{constant}$$

This is just like the relationship between pressure and temperature. As the pressure increases, the volume must also increase so the ratio V/T remains a constant number.

Finally, Amedeo Avogadro[5] proposed in the 1800s that the number of molecules in a gas was directly proportional to the volume of the gas. This relationship is expressed as

$$\frac{\text{number of molecules}}{\text{volume}} = \text{constant}$$

or

$$\frac{N}{V} = \text{constant}$$

Once again, this fits with what you observed in the simulation. As the number of molecules increases or decreases, the volume of the gas increases or decreases accordingly.

The above relationships are labeled according to the person who discovered them and are thus known as Gay-Lussac's law, Boyle's law, Charles' law, and

[5] As we all know, this famous scientist was immortalized in the song "Rock Me, Amedeo." As you should know if you've read any of my other books, this is just a bad joke with an obscure reference.

Avogadro's principle. As you go over these relationships, it's really important to remember that each law assumes that all other variables associated with the gas are held constant. Now, I suppose for historical reasons all chemistry books make a point of naming all of these laws separately. Fortunately for you, we can tie all of them together in one law known as the **ideal gas law**. Here it is:

(pressure)(volume) = (number of moles)(a constant)(temperature)

or

$$PV = nRT$$

The letter R is the constant number, known as the universal gas constant or the ideal gas constant. The value of this constant is 0.0821 $\frac{L-atm}{mol-K}$. You read the units on this as *liter atmospheres per moles degrees Kelvin.* Liters are units of volume, atmospheres are units of pressure, moles are units related to the number of atoms or molecules, and degrees Kelvin are units of temperature. As with most of my other books, I'm not going to focus on units very much, but I want to be complete and use the proper units. One important thing to remember if you study thermodynamics further is that the ideal gas constant can be expressed in a variety of units, as can other constants in chemistry and physics. If you ever need to use this form of the equation to solve a problem or do an example, be sure to write out all the units and be sure that they all "fit together" before you do the math.

I'm going to give you an example of how to use the ideal gas law in the Applications section. To end this section, though, I want to expand on Avogadro's principle. The basis of the principle is the hypothesis that gases that have the same pressure, volume, and temperature have the same number of molecules. But how could different gases, with different masses for their atoms or molecules, have the same number of atoms or molecules at the same temperature? I mean, wouldn't the heavier gases at the same temperature exert a greater pressure because of the added mass? And wouldn't this mean that there should be *fewer* of the heavier gases in order to have the same pressure, volume, and temperature? If this is what's going through your mind, then possibly you're thinking of temperature in terms of speed only and not as a measure of kinetic energy, which includes the mass of the particles. Think back to the simulation, where more massive particles at the same temperature as less massive particles moved more slowly. So, the same number of massive and not-so-massive particles could be at the same temperature (a measure of kinetic energy and not just speed) and still exert the same pressure at a given volume. See Figure 2.6.

Figure 2.6

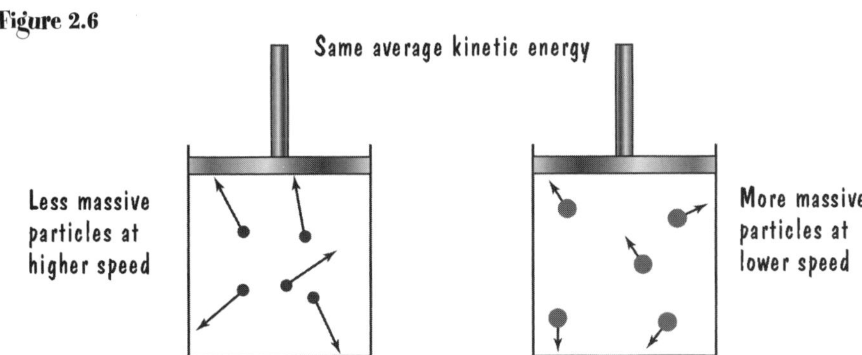

Even more things to do before you read even more science stuff

Gather together 30 pennies or other small objects, such as marbles. Remembering your higher math, you know that there are 12 objects in a dozen, such as for eggs and donuts. How many dozen pennies do you have? Easy.

Now I'm going to define a new quantity called a *grik*. A grik of something contains three objects. So, if you have 12 eggs, that's 4 griks of eggs. How many griks of pennies do you have? Now let's use a new quantity called a *foom*. A foom of something contains 8 objects. How many fooms of pennies do you have?

Even more science stuff

What I had you do in the previous section probably seemed trivial. If so, that's good. It's common for us to specify a certain quantity of things with a special name, such as a dozen, gross, or bushel. If you had 30 pennies, you had 2.5 dozen pennies, 10 griks of pennies, and 3.75 fooms of pennies. There's a quantity often used in chemistry to specify how many atoms or molecules of a substance you have, and it's called a **mole**. One mole contains 6.02214×10^{23} atoms or molecules, and this number is known as **Avogadro's number**. One mole of hydrogen molecules contains 6.02214×10^{23} hydrogen molecules. One mole of xenon atoms contains 6.02214×10^{23} xenon atoms. For that matter, one mole of pennies contains 6.02214×10^{23} pennies, but there aren't that many pennies in existence.

SCILINKS. THE WORLD'S A CLICK AWAY

Topic: Avogadro's Constant

Go to: *www.scilinks.org*

Code: MCB008

I already explained the reasoning that makes Avogadro's principle a good hypothesis, and of course it's been verified many times that gases at a given pressure, volume, and temperature have the same number of atoms or molecules. We can define one mole as the number of molecules in a gas at an agreed-upon pressure, temperature, and volume, known as Standard Temperature and Pressure (STP). The values of these quantities at STP are a pressure of one atmosphere (roughly the atmospheric pressure at sea level), a temperature of 273.16 degrees Kelvin (the freezing temperature of water at a pressure of one atmosphere), and a volume of 22.4 liters. Turns out that Avogadro never knew exactly how many molecules were in a gas at various conditions, so the definition of a mole came after his demise. Poor soul didn't even know the number that has his name.

You might be wondering how in the world chemists chose the values for STP. Well, it has to do with the fact that measuring things in moles goes beyond talking about gases. It also applies to solids and liquids. Let's say you have a mole of helium gas confined in a chamber. Now cool this gas down to very low temperatures so that you now have liquid helium (yes, that's entirely possible, and it's common for laboratories to use liquid helium to cool other things). If you had a mole of helium gas, then you now have a mole of liquid helium. We know this because of the reasoning I gave you in the very first explanation in this chapter: When you change states from solid to liquid to gas and back, the number of atoms or molecules you have remains the same. Check out Figure 2.7. Although the whole idea of measuring quantities in moles originated with gases, it applies to all states of matter and is a convenient way to figure out how much of a substance you have.

Figure 2.7

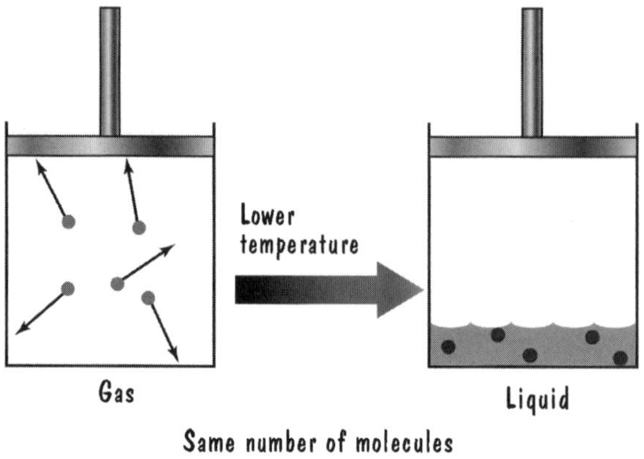

We know that a mole (6.02214×10^{23} atoms or molecules) of any gas takes up 22.4 liters at standard temperature and pressure. There's another, often more useful, way to define a mole using the element carbon. The carbon atom has an atomic mass of exactly 12 if you ignore the other isotopes of carbon.[6] In 12 grams of carbon-12 there is exactly one mole of carbon-12 atoms, which defines what a mole is. Because all atomic masses in the Periodic Table are based on the

[6] The atomic mass is that number at the bottom of an element's box in the Periodic Table. The number tells you how many protons plus neutrons are in the atom. Because the mass of electrons is so small compared to the masses of protons and neutrons, we ignore the electrons' mass when determining the mass of an atom. Isotopes of elements are atoms that contain different numbers of neutrons. For example, carbon comes in the forms carbon-12, carbon-13, and carbon-14. Carbon-14 has two more neutrons in its nucleus than carbon-12.

atomic mass of carbon-12, you can similarly figure out how many moles of other substances you have by determining their masses. Let's look at another element, sulfur. Sulfur's atomic mass is 32.06 (not a whole number because of the existence of isotopes). If you have 32.06 grams of sulfur (this is called a **gram molecular mass** of sulfur), then you have exactly one mole of sulfur, or 6.02214×10^{23} sulfur atoms. If you have 96.18 grams of sulfur, you have three moles of sulfur atoms. Finally, let's consider a molecule such as water. The molecular mass of water is 18.01528 (add the atomic mass of oxygen to two atomic masses of hydrogen). If you have 18.01528 grams of water, you have a gram molecular mass of water and therefore have one mole of water molecules. If you have 18 grams of water, that's a bit more than half an ounce of water, so if you pour out slightly more than half an ounce of water in a dish, the dish contains slightly more than 6.02214×10^{23} molecules of water.

When using moles as a measure of how much stuff you have, you sometimes have to be careful. For example, I just told you that 18.01528 grams of water contains one mole of water molecules, but that amount of water does *not* contain one mole of hydrogen atoms. There are two hydrogen atoms in each water molecule, so a mole of water contains two moles of hydrogen atoms.

To end this chapter, I'm going to introduce a chemistry measurement that is based on moles. If you look at the concentrations of various liquids, you will find the terms **molar** and **molarity**, as in a 0.5 molar solution of sodium hydroxide.[7] Before explaining this term, I should point out that a *solution* is something dissolved in a liquid (often water), and if you specify the *concentration* of a solution, you are saying how much of a particular something you have dissolved in a liquid. Anyway, here is the definition of molarity:

$$\text{molarity} = \frac{\text{number of moles of a substance}}{\text{number of liters of solution}}$$

Molarity is specified with a capital M.

I lied. I have one more thing to tell you. There are two commonly used forms of the ideal gas law. One is the form I already introduced, namely $PV = nRT$. The second, used more by physicists than chemists, is below.

$$PV = NkT$$

[7] I'm only using this as an example, not asking you to actually mess around with sodium hydroxide, but for safety's sake I should go ahead and mention that this chemical can be pretty caustic, especially in the solid pellet form. Take all necessary precautions (gloves, goggles) when handling this stuff.

The only difference is the substitution of *Nk* for *nR*. The upper-case *N* represents the number of molecules of a gas, while the lower-case *n* represents the number of moles of a gas. *k* is known as **Boltzmann's constant** and has a value of 1.381×10^{-23} J/K, with the units reading "joules per degree Kelvin." As with the universal gas constant, Boltzmann's constant has different values depending on the units you use.

Chapter summary

- When the state of a substance—solid, liquid, or gas—changes, the identity of its component molecules does not change
- An ideal gas is one in which we treat the molecules as independent things that act like billiard balls that do not rotate or vibrate. In collisions these molecules can exchange energy, but no energy is lost to the environment.
- The temperature of a gas is directly related to the average kinetic energy of the molecules in the gas. The faster the molecules move, and the more massive they are, the greater the temperature.
- The pressure of a gas is how much force per unit area the molecules exert.
- With volume held constant, the pressure of a gas is directly proportional to the temperature of the gas. Higher temperatures mean higher pressure and lower temperatures mean lower pressure.
- With temperature held constant, the pressure of a gas is inversely proportional to the volume of the gas. Smaller volumes mean higher pressures and larger volumes mean lower pressures.
- With pressure held constant, volume is directly proportional to temperature. Higher temperatures mean larger volumes and lower temperatures mean smaller volumes.
- With volume and temperature held constant, pressure is directly proportional to the number of molecules in a gas. More molecules means higher pressure and fewer molecules means lower pressure.

Applications

1. In the ideal gas simulation I had you mess around with, the lowest temperature possible is 25 degrees Kelvin. Why doesn't the simulation go all the way to 0 degrees Kelvin? The answer is that 0 degrees Kelvin is theoretically impossible to attain. At 0 degrees Kelvin, otherwise known as **absolute zero**, all motion would stop. If all motion in a substance stopped, though, then we would know *exactly* where the molecules are and what they're doing (noth-

ing!). This is a violation of a principle I'm going to introduce in Chapter 3. So, although scientists are able to bring substances to temperatures extremely close to absolute zero, it's theoretically impossible to actually reach absolute zero. Of course, the theory (quantum mechanics) that prevents that might one day be shown to be incorrect, but until that time we're sticking with zero chance of absolute zero temperature for anything.

2. I told you that you can use the ideal gas law instead of remembering all of the separate laws that apply to gases, so I guess I'd better give you an example of that.[8] You can use either form of the ideal gas law, so I'll use the one that's more common in chemistry textbooks, which is $PV = nRT$. Let's suppose you have a gas that's at a temperature of 293 degrees Kelvin and you raise the temperature to 323 degrees Kelvin. You keep the volume constant and the number of moles (also the number of molecules) constant. How does this rise in temperature affect the pressure the gas exerts on its surroundings? Let's call the lower temperature of the gas Situation 1 and the higher temperature of the gas Situation 2. The ideal gas law holds true no matter what temperature and pressure we use, so we can write the following:

$$P_1V_1 = n_1RT_1 \text{ and } P_2V_2 = n_2RT_2$$

The subscripts refer to the different situations. There is no subscript on the R because it's a constant that has the same value in all situations. What I'm going to do is divide the first equation by the second equation,[9] as in

$$\frac{P_1V_1}{P_2V_2} = \frac{n_1RT_1}{n_2RT_2}$$

In our situation, we know that the volume and the number of moles are constant, meaning that $V_1 = V_2$ and $n_1 = n_2$. And of course, $R = R$. Therefore we can cancel the terms that are equal, as in

$$\frac{P_1\cancel{V_1}}{P_2\cancel{V_2}} = \frac{\cancel{n_1}RT_1}{\cancel{n_2}RT_2}$$

That leaves us with

$$\frac{P_1}{P_2} = \frac{T_1}{T_2}$$

[8] Remember that the ideal gas law only applies to an "ideal" gas rather than real gases. It's a good approximation, however, for what will happen with most gases.

[9] Dividing one equation by another equation always results in a new equation that's valid. If this step, or any other step I do here, makes you grind your teeth, it wouldn't be a bad idea to brush up on your basic algebra. I happen to know of a great book for this purpose, the *Stop Faking It!* book on math.

We know the initial and final temperatures and let's assume we know the initial pressure; therefore, all we have to do is solve the above equation for P_2, our final pressure. You can do this algebraic manipulation with a shortcut or two, or you can take it slow so you understand the process. I'll describe the process and then give the result. What you need to do is multiply both sides of this equation by P_2 and then multiply the resulting equation by $\frac{T_1}{T_2}$. That gives you

$$P_2 = \frac{T_2}{T_1} P_1 = \frac{(323\text{ K})}{(293\text{ K})} P_1 = 1.1 P_1$$

So, by increasing the temperature slightly, you have increased the pressure by a factor of 1.1. As with all science calculations, you should stop and make sure the result makes sense. Should increasing the temperature while holding other variables constant increase the pressure? Sure. If I had given you an exact value for the initial pressure (pressure is measured in a variety of units, common ones being Pascals or atmospheres), you could compute an exact value for the final pressure.

3. It might seem that which ideal gas law you use, $PV = NkT$ or $PV = nRT$, is just a matter of taste. There is an important distinction, though. In one case, you are relating the actual number of molecules in a gas to the easily measurable quantities of pressure, volume, and temperature. In the second case, you are relating the number of moles of a gas (an easily measurable quantity—just determine the mass of the gas and use the gram molecular mass of the gas to figure out the number of moles) to the quantities of pressure, volume, and temperature. So the two forms of the gas law make a connection between what we can observe directly, known as extrinsic properties of the gas, and what we cannot observe directly (the actual number of molecules), known as the intrinsic properties of the gas. Not terribly important for everyday calculations, but philosophically important in that we are connecting the observable with the unobservable.

4. Suppose you have 1,000 grams (one kilogram) of methane gas. How many moles of gas do you have, and how many molecules of gas do you have? To find out how many moles of gas you have, you need the gram molecular mass of methane. To figure that out, you need the chemical formula of methane, which is CH_4. One carbon atom has an atomic mass of 12 (I'm going to round off the atomic masses here to simplify things) and one hydrogen atom has an atomic mass of 1. Therefore, CH_4 has a molecular mass of 16 (one carbon and four hydrogens). This means that 16 grams of methane contain one mole of methane molecules. We have 1,000 grams of methane gas, so we have $\frac{1000\text{ grams}}{16\text{ grams per mole}} = 62.5$ moles.

When doing math in a science calculation, people often rely on memorized procedures that don't necessarily make sense to them. For example, why did I just divide 1,000 grams by the number of grams per mole to get the number of moles? It's comparable to figuring out how many cookies you have if each cookie weighs 2 pounds (big cookies!) and you have 40 pounds of cookies. You divide 40 pounds by 2 pounds per cookie to get 20 cookies.

Once we know how many moles of methane we have, it's easy to figure out how many molecules there are. Each mole contains 6.02×10^{23} molecules, so there are (62.5 moles)(6.02×10^{23} molecules per mole) = 376×10^{23} or 3.76×10^{25} molecules.

5. The concept of moles is extremely useful for determining how much of one substance you need to complete a chemical reaction with another substance. For example, the balanced equation for the reaction of zinc with hydrochloric acid is given below. *Note:* I'm not suggesting you actually try this reaction. It's a bit violent, and it's always a risk doing such a reaction with a strong acid.

$$\text{zinc} + \text{hydrochloric acid} \rightarrow \text{zinc chloride} + \text{hydrogen gas}$$

$$Zn\ (s) + 2HCl\ (aq) \rightarrow ZnCl_2\ (s) + H_2\ (g)$$

According to this balanced equation, you need two molecules of hydrochloric acid for every atom of zinc. Of course, we can't measure out individual atoms, so it's more convenient to think in terms of moles. The equation says that for every mole of zinc, you need two moles of hydrochloric acid. Now, let's suppose your sample of zinc has a mass of 130.76 grams, and you have 148.00 grams of HCl.[10] At first glance, it looks like there's not enough HCl to react with and completely use up all of the zinc because they have to be in the ratio of 2 to 1. But we shouldn't compare masses; we should compare the number of *moles*. We need two moles of hydrochloric acid for each mole of zinc, so we better figure out how many moles of each substance we have. The atomic mass of zinc is 65.38 (look it up in the Periodic Table), so if you have 65.38 grams of zinc, you have one mole of zinc atoms (refer back to the discussion of gram molecular mass on page 37 if that doesn't make sense). We have twice that much (130.76 grams), so we have two moles of zinc. Hydrochloric acid is composed of two atoms, so to find the *molecular* mass of HCl, we need to add the atomic masses of hydrogen and chlorine. Again referring to the Periodic Table, we find that the atomic mass of hydrogen is

[10] I'm using numbers that are fairly large by chemical standards for the amounts of each substance we have, just so the math is relatively easy. In practice, these are huge amounts of zinc and hydrochloric acid, and not amounts your average nonindustrial chemist is likely to use.

1.008 and the atomic mass of chlorine is 35.45. Adding these together gives a molecular mass of 36.46 for HCl. So one mole of HCl has a mass of 36.46 grams. Because we have two moles of zinc, we would need four moles of HCl (a 2 to 1 ratio) to use up all of the zinc: $4 \times 36.46 = 145.8$, meaning four moles of HCl has a mass of 145.8 grams. I told you at the beginning that we had 148 grams of HCl, so we have more than enough HCl to react with all of the zinc.

6. Let's create another problem from the previous one. When you obtain hydrochloric acid, it's usually dissolved in water. Suppose the writing on the side of the container says 0.5 M. This means the *molarity* of the solution is 0.5, which means you have 0.5 moles of HCl per liter of solution. How many liters of this solution do you need to complete the above reaction? Well, we have two moles of zinc, so we need four moles of HCl; there's half a mole in each liter of solution, so we would need eight liters (!) of 0.5 M hydrochloric acid solution to complete the reaction. I told you in footnote #10 that the amounts stated in the problem were rather large!

7. In this chapter, we've dealt with ideal gases. The molecules in an ideal gas take up no space and don't have any energy due to vibration or rotation. Of course, real atoms and molecules *do* take up space and most have rotational and vibrational energy. The kinds of energy that we ignore in saying that a gas is an ideal gas affect the temperature of the gas, and the fact that real atoms and molecules take up space affects our calculations of the volume available to the gas. The corrections for a real gas are important if you're doing scientific experiments, and they can be mathematically complex. For purposes of understanding gases in general, the ideal gas is a pretty good approximation.

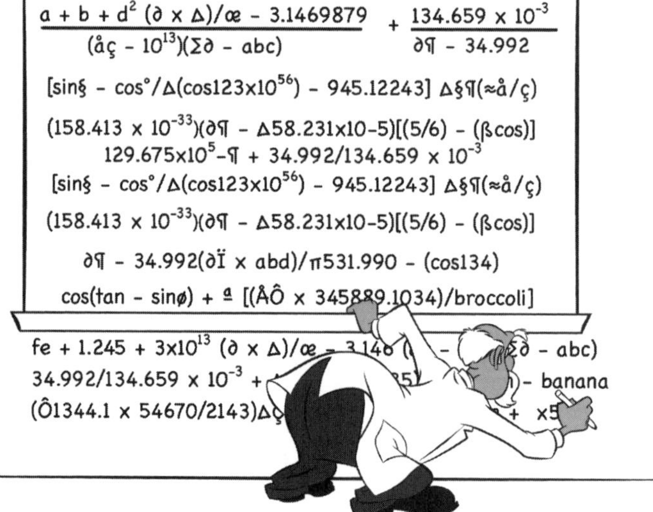

The Name's Bond ... Pi Bond

You'll understand the title of this chapter once you've finished it. By the way, *pi* is pronounced *pie* and represents the Greek letter π. In the meantime, I want you to recall that we picture electrons in atoms as residing in **orbitals**—those fuzzy things that can be spherical, dumbbell-shaped, or even ring-shaped. I'm first going to address orbitals and why they're fuzzy. Then I'm going to deal with how the shapes of orbitals determine the kinds of bonds that form between atoms. Finally, we'll see how the location of orbitals and the electrons in them determine the shapes of molecules.

Topic: Atomic Orbitals

Go to: *www.scilinks.org*

Code: MCB009

"The name's Bond ... Pi Bond."

In discussing and drawing pictures of orbitals, there's potential for confusion in that you might think that if you were small enough to look at an atom directly, you would actually see these fuzzy shapes. Not so. Orbitals represent possible locations of electrons, not a physical thing. This idea is similar to drawing the orbits of the planets around the Sun. We draw those lines to represent the paths of planets, but those lines don't really exist in space. In the same way, atomic orbitals don't exist as physical things but rather are mathematical representations of where we are likely to find electrons.

Things to do before you read the science stuff

Grab something that is unlikely to move when you hit it with a marble, such as a roll of masking tape or a paperweight. Any heavy object will do, but I'll assume from here on out that you're using a roll of masking tape. Also, grab a couple of marbles and find a smooth surface.

Place the masking tape on the surface, and take a trip to imaginationland, in which this roll of masking tape is invisible. Your task is to figure out exactly where this roll of masking tape is by rolling marbles at it and seeing what happens to them after they hit the masking tape. See Figure 3.1. Question: If you rolled a marble at this roll of masking tape more than a hundred times, from all different angles, could you be reasonably certain where the tape is and how big it is? (Remember, it's invisible.)

Figure 3.1

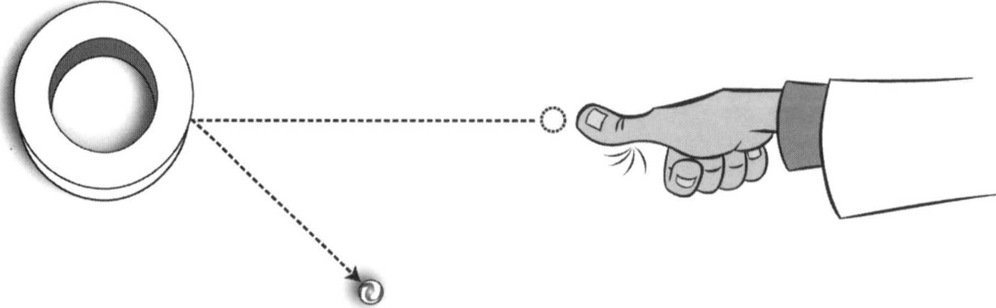

Replace the masking tape with another marble. Again, pretend this second marble is invisible. And again, roll your other marble at this "invisible" marble and see what happens to the marble you rolled. See Figure 3.2. Question: If you roll marbles at this "invisible" marble a hundred times, could you figure out how big this marble is and where exactly it is?

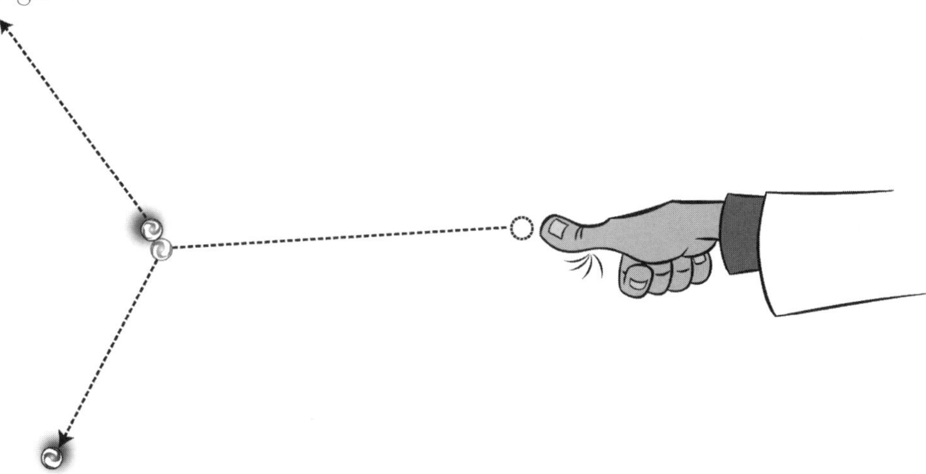

The science stuff

Unless you throw marbles really hard or have a wimpy roll of masking tape, I'm betting the roll of masking tape (or whatever object you used) didn't move when you rolled marbles at it. And I'm betting you reached the conclusion that if the tape was invisible and you rolled enough marbles, you would be able to determine the size and location of the tape fairly accurately.

Firing a marble at a marble, of course, is a different story. The "invisible" marble moves away when you hit it with another marble. So, while you might have known where the invisible marble *was* when you hit it, you do not know where it *is* (after the collision) or how fast it's moving. Therefore, you can't accurately determine a marble's location by hitting it with another marble. This leads us to a conclusion:

When you try to determine an object's location by hitting it with a similar-size object, you disturb the original object's location and lose information about where it is.

What's this got to do with electrons? Be patient, and I'll get there. In the meantime, imagine you're in a room with no light and you want to know where the walls are without moving around and bumping into them. One way to determine where the walls are is to throw tennis balls at the walls. By estimating the speed at which the balls move and listening for when they hit the walls, you can eventually get a good idea about where the walls are, even though you can't see. You figure out where the walls are by hitting the walls with something. Now let's turn the lights on. You can see where the walls are. To do this, you are still hitting the walls with something. One of the scientific models for light is that it's composed of tiny particles called **photons**. According to this model, the way we see objects is by bouncing photons off of them.[1]

Because these photons are insignificantly small compared with the walls in your room or other ordinary objects, all this bouncing by millions of photons doesn't affect the shape or position of your average wall or object. This is like hitting the roll of masking tape with a marble—the marble is small enough that it doesn't significantly disturb the position of the masking tape. We can extend this notion not just to where things are but also to what they're doing; for example, how fast they're moving. The way we know where things are and what they're doing is by bouncing other things off of them. For everyday objects, we're talking about bouncing tiny little photons off them. This process is not unlike bats finding insects by bouncing sound waves (which can be thought of as tiny particles called **phonons**!) off the insects and listening for the reflected sounds. Those phonons are still quite small compared with the insects, so a bat hitting the insects with phonons doesn't disturb them very much. If the insects were of atomic size, however, a bat's sonar would be useless. The phonons hitting the insects[2] would change the position and motion of the insects so much that the bat couldn't locate the insects. Of course, if you're a bat hunting for atom-size insects, you're going to starve to death anyway.

Okay, let's move on to figuring out where electrons are and what they're doing. How are we going to do that? Well, we're going to fire things at them. Let's suppose we reflect a bunch of photons off the electrons.[3] The photons are large enough compared to electrons that when the photons run into the electrons, they disturb both the electrons' positions and their motion. So, you can't get an accurate picture of where electrons are and what they're doing because the very act of observing the electrons disturbs them. Hitting electrons with photons to find out where the electrons are is like hitting a wall with a wrecking ball to find out where the wall is. See Figure 3.3, and please realize that this is supposed to be a humorous depiction of what's going on rather than an accurate model of photons interacting with objects.

---

[1] The exception to this is when the objects around you emit their own light.

[2] Remember we're talking about sound rather than light here. So the bats are hitting the insects with sound particles (phonons) rather than light particles (photons). No, you don't need a full understanding of phonons to get this idea. You can just trust me that it's possible to think of sound as being composed of tiny particles, just as it's possible to think of light as being composed of tiny particles.

[3] We can also investigate electrons by firing particles other than photons at them, but that doesn't change the situation.

Figure 3.3

This is a general principle that applies when investigating all tiny systems such as atoms and things smaller than atoms:

> When dealing with small-scale systems, the very act of observing the systems disturbs them so you can't know precisely where the systems are or what they're doing.

In other words, there is an *uncertainty* in what we know about the position and motion of very small objects such as electrons. In fact, you've probably heard of this principle, known as **Heisenberg's uncertainty principle**, named for the physicist Werner Heisenberg. The uncertainty principle is an integral part of the mathematics of quantum mechanics, and there is more to it than the analogy of hitting masking tape and marbles with marbles, so I don't want to give the impression that the principle is simpler than it actually is. On the other hand, our analogy is appropriate enough that you should now have some idea of why we speak of the location of electrons in terms of probability distributions[4]

[4] For those of you who didn't read the first chapter in this book or the first chemistry book in this series, or if you just plain forgot, fuzzy orbitals represent probability distributions, which are representations of the probability of finding an electron in any given portion of space. The darker the shading in a probability distribution, the more likely you'll find an electron in that place.

(those fuzzy orbitals) rather than specific paths or motions. We can't see the little guys, and we're hitting them with objects that are comparable in energy and size to the electrons themselves. Just as a reminder, Figure 3.4 shows a few of these electron orbitals that are probability distributions.

Figure 3.4

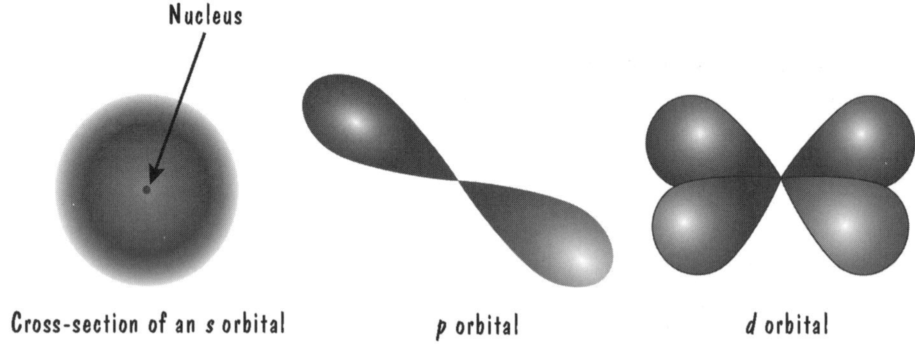

Examples of electron orbitals in atoms

It's important to note that the uncertainty in measurement I'm talking about is not due to scientists just not having sensitive enough equipment. No matter how sensitive the equipment, it is a fundamental fact of nature that we cannot get exact information about what small-scale systems are doing and where they are. In other words, nature will always keep us somewhat in the dark about these measurements. This limitation has bothered many scientists for many years. Even Albert Einstein didn't accept it at first. In referring to the probabilistic nature of the atomic world, in a letter to fellow physicist Max Born, Einstein stated, "I, at any rate, am convinced that He [meaning God] does not throw dice."[5]

I've been using marbles and atom-size insects as an analogy for electrons, but I don't want to leave you with the misconception that electrons can only be thought of as solid objects. In the introduction to this book and in the first chemistry book, I discussed how we can think of electrons (and all particles, for that matter) as collections of waves. It is this wave nature of electrons that is the basis for quantum mechanics, which is the math we use to come up with the uncertainty principle. So, while it is often convenient to consider electrons to be tiny, solid objects, you should always be aware of the model of electrons as waves.

---

[5] Letter to Max Born (4 December 1926); *The Born-Einstein Letters* (translated by Irene Born). Walker and Company, New York, 1971.

I'm going to get just a bit mathematical now, so this is my official warning to those of you with math phobia. I'm not going to use this math in the rest of the book (with the exception of one application at the end of this chapter), so if you really want to skip this text box, that's okay. Anyway, we can express Heisenberg's uncertainty principle mathematically. Two inequalities cover it, and they are

$$p\Delta x \geq \hbar \text{ and } \Delta E \Delta t \geq \hbar$$

where Δp is the uncertainty[6] in measurement of momentum (the momentum of an object is its mass multiplied by its velocity), Δx is the uncertainty in measurement of position, ΔE is the uncertainty in measurement of energy, and Δt is the uncertainty in measurement of time. h is a number known as Planck's constant.

When you add the slash across the h, you read it as *h-bar,* and its value[7] is h divided by 2π. So, what do these inequalities mean? We'll focus on $\Delta p \Delta x \geq \hbar$. This inequality says that the more we know about a particle's position (meaning we get Δx to be very small), the less we know about its momentum (Δp must be correspondingly large to satisfy the inequality). Conversely, the more we know about the momentum of a particle (Δp is very small), the less we know about its position (Δx is very large). To restate that, the more accurately we know a particle's momentum, the less we know about the particle's position, and vice versa. To state it in even one more way, if we know almost exactly what a particle is doing, we know almost nothing about where it is; if we know almost exactly where a particle is, we know almost nothing about what it's doing.[8] Enough math reasoning. I'll address the relationship $\Delta E \Delta t \geq \hbar$ in the Applications section.

What this book is about. It might be important at this point to remind you of the purpose of this book. Reviewers of the first drafts of this book wondered why I cover things such as the uncertainty principle when the vast majority of my intended audience will never teach this material. My view is that you become a better teacher when you know more than you have to teach, so when that bright student asks a difficult question, you have some idea of how to proceed. Plus, the more complete the picture you have of what's going on at an atomic level, the better you understand the more basic stuff. Also, just because certain concepts have traditionally been considered more advanced does not mean that the average person cannot understand them. Between the discussion of probability distributions in my first chemistry book and the discussion here, I think you can get a good grasp of what electrons are doing in atoms.

---

[6] The symbol Δ means *change in* or *uncertainty in*. It is not a separate variable or constant.

[7] You will see many different versions of the uncertainty principle, each having something slightly different on the right side of the inequality. Each version has either h or $\hbar$ divided by 2 or multiplied by 2 or some such thing. The reason for the different versions is that scientists use a variety of ways to define the uncertainty in a quantity. The basic principle remains the same, regardless of the value of the constant on the right side of the inequality.

[8] In Chapter 2, I mentioned that it was impossible for any substance to reach absolute zero. The reason for this is that at absolute zero, particles are motionless, meaning we would know exactly how much momentum they have (zero) while simultaneously knowing exactly where they are. This violates the uncertainty principle, so nothing can be at absolute zero.

More things to do before you read more science stuff

Time for a couple of real activities, which will get us into the subject of atoms and their electrons in orbitals getting together. Get a sheet of wax paper and put a few water drops on the paper. Then pick up an edge of the paper so as to make separate water drops collide. What happens when they collide? Does the new shape look like a regular water drop, or is it somewhat different?

Figure 3.5

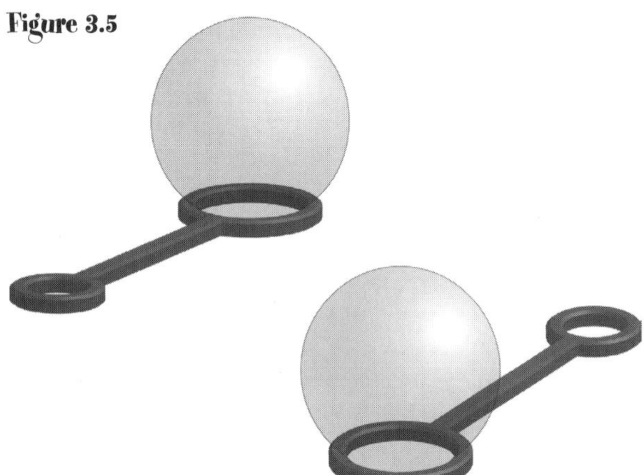

Now get yourself three small bottles of bubble solution with little plastic bubble wands. Also get yourself a friend who likes bubbles. You can do this first part by yourself if you're semicoordinated. Get a plastic wand in each hand and then blow a bunch of bubbles. Catch a bubble on each wand, as shown in Figure 3.5.

Note the shape of each bubble. Now slam the bubbles together. Do this hard enough that the bubbles join together, but not so hard that you break one or both of the bubbles. After a bit of practice, you should end up with something that looks like Figure 3.6.

Figure 3.6

Here's where the friend comes in. Have your friend blow and catch a third bubble on a third wand. Then slam this third bubble into the two joined bubbles, so you get something like Figure 3.7.

Figure 3.7

Now answer a question. Why did the bubbles change shape when you slammed them together? Think energy.

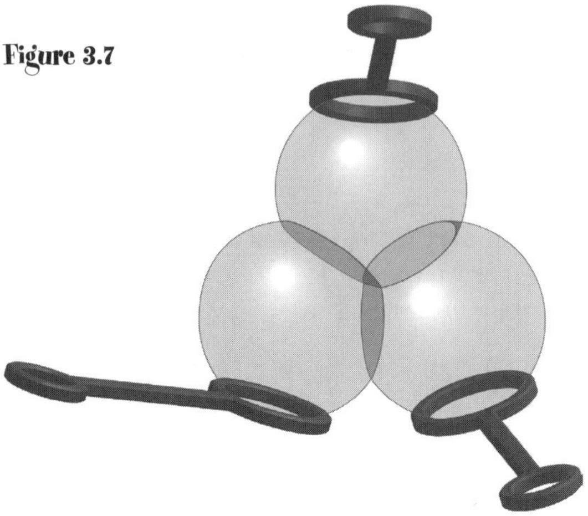

More science stuff

First let's talk about your water drops. When you bring two drops together, they join into a larger shape. This larger shape is elongated, at least at first, and is a reasonable picture of what happens when two *s* orbitals share electrons. This happens when two hydrogen atoms get together to form a hydrogen gas molecule. See Figure 3.8.

Figure 3.8

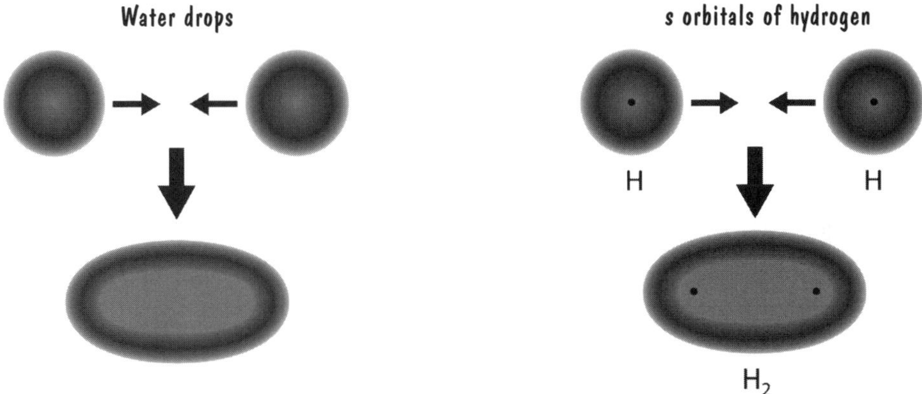

The type of covalent bond illustrated in Figure 3.8 is called a **sigma bond**. Chemists often just use the Greek letter sigma (σ) to indicate this type of bond, as in σ-bond. In sigma bonds, the orbitals connect along the axis between the two atoms. It's important to realize what's going on here. Just as the two water drops formed a new drop, the two *s* orbitals, one from each hydrogen atom, formed a brand-new orbital. This orbital is shared by the two hydrogen nuclei (which are simply protons) and contains the two shared electrons. This new orbital is known as a **hybrid orbital**.

Now, on to the bubbles and why they do what they do. This might seem like a diversion, but it will connect with what I just explained about hydrogen atoms getting together. For starters, let's figure out why bubbles are spherical in the first place. Why not a square or some other shape? The answer is that a sphere is the configuration that has the lowest energy for the bubble. Each molecule in the bubble exerts an attractive force on the molecules around it (you have undoubtedly heard of this as *surface tension*). All of these forces are equal in strength, and therefore can only be accommodated with a spherical shape. For example, if the bubble were a cube, then the forces between molecules along the sides of the square would be different from the forces between molecules at the corners. This would also be a higher energy situation overall for the bubble. See Figure 3.9 (p. 52).

Figure 3.9

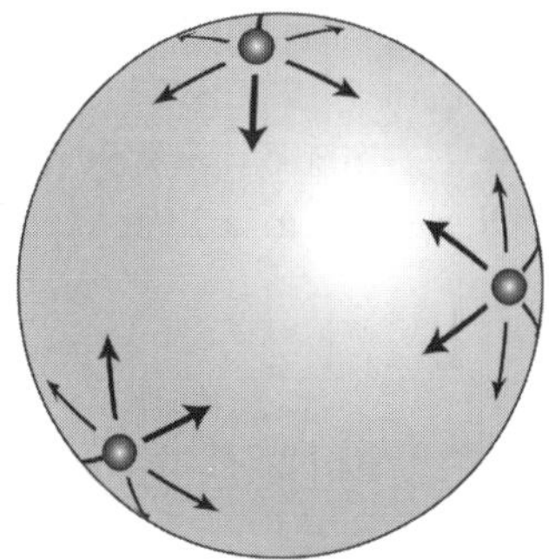

In a sphere, each molecule exerts an equal force on each other molecule. This is the lowest energy possible.

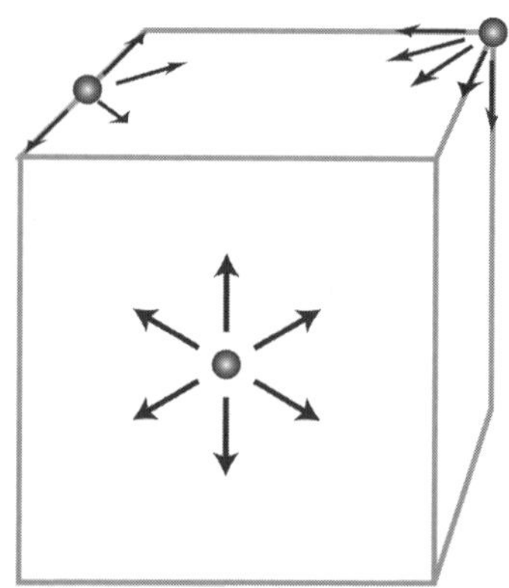

In a cube, the focus on molecules at the corners and on the edges are different from the forces on the faces. This is a high energy shape.

Now let's look at slamming the bubbles together. What you have are two things (the bubbles) that are somewhat flexible vying for the same space. The bubbles are also made of the same kind of molecules, so they can potentially interact. In other words, the molecules in one soap bubble won't differentiate between molecules that are part of their own bubble and those that are part of a different bubble. The result is the bubbles combine into a new shape that has a lower energy than, say, a couple of distorted bubbles occupying the same space. Figure 3.10 shows this distinction.

Notice that this new shape wouldn't happen if the bubbles were made of a solid substance such as rubber. If you had rubber bubbles, they would just collide and not form a new shape. The reason? It would require a great deal of extra energy to get the solids to intermingle—you would have to supply enough heat for them to melt, and then they could join together. So, it's not energetically favorable for rubber bubbles to join together to form a new shape, but it *is* energetically favorable for soap bubbles to join together to form a new shape. If we want, we could call this new shape, shown in Figures 3.6 and 3.7, a **hybrid bubble**. The hybrid bubble is not simply the overlap of the two original bubbles but an entirely new shape.

Figure 3.10

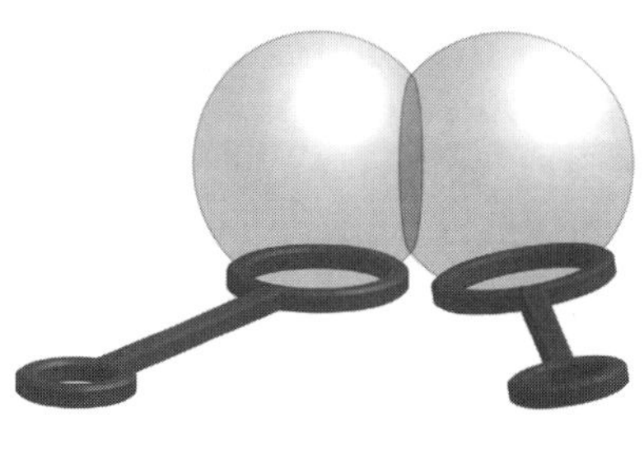

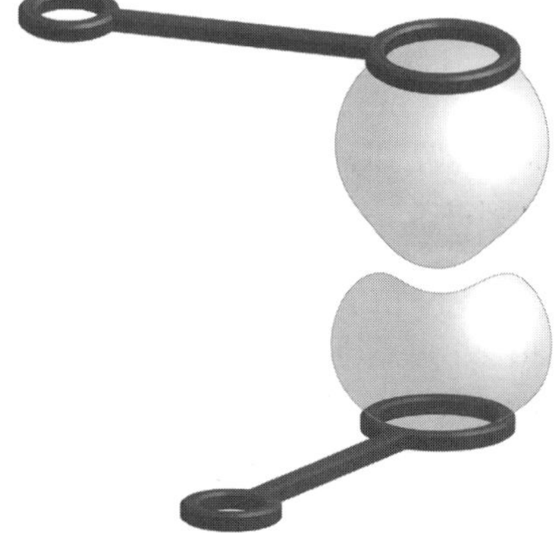

Now, what in the world does this have to do with two hydrogen atoms getting together? Well, the orbitals in these atoms are kind of like soap bubbles. In their original spherical shapes, *s* orbitals represent low energy for an electron in a hydrogen atom. In the process of overlapping and vying for the same space, these orbitals, just as soap bubbles, form into new shapes. The new shape is a lower energy than a simple overlap of the two original orbitals. There is one really important difference between bubbles and orbitals: The bubbles are real, tangible objects. Orbitals are mathematical representations.

A bit more about this new orbital (or any orbital, for that matter) being a mathematical representation. The orbital isn't real in the sense that atom-size people could see it, but rather it's a description of the mathematical probability of finding the two electrons in the space around the two hydrogen nuclei. These electrons clearly are more likely, after the joining of the two atoms, to be found in the region between the nuclei. So, the water drop and bubble analogies are just that—analogies. Orbitals are not real in the same sense that water drops and bubbles are real.

This formation of a new, hybrid orbital obviously happens when you have two atoms with partially filled *s* orbitals, but it can also happen between an *s* orbital and a *p* orbital or between two *p* orbitals. Check out Figure 3.11. Both of the bonds represented there are sigma bonds because they form on the axis between the two atoms. They also represent the sharing of electrons between the two atoms in the newly formed hybrid orbital.

Notice in Figure 3.11 that the original orbitals change shape in a couple of ways. First, much of the space between the nuclei is taken up with orbitals, and

Figure 3.11

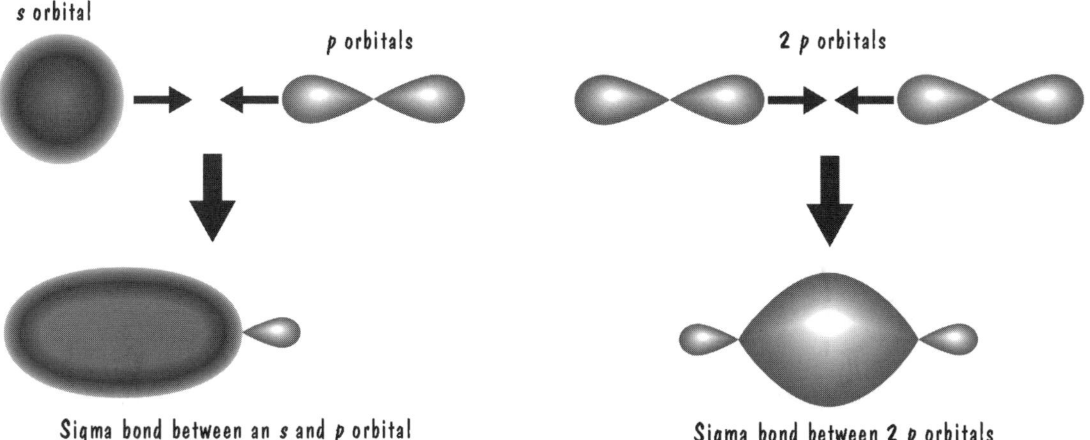

the outside part of the original orbitals (for example, the lobes on the far right and left in the *p-p* combination) gets smaller. What that means is that after the bond is formed, the electrons shared by the atoms spend more of their time between the nuclei than in the spaces not between the nuclei. Makes sense if those electrons are shared electrons. See Figure 3.12.

Before moving on, take a moment and ask yourself why two atoms get together in a covalent bond in the first place. Don't negative charges repel one another? When two partially filled orbitals get near each other, shouldn't they push apart, as in Figure 3.13?

Figure 3.12

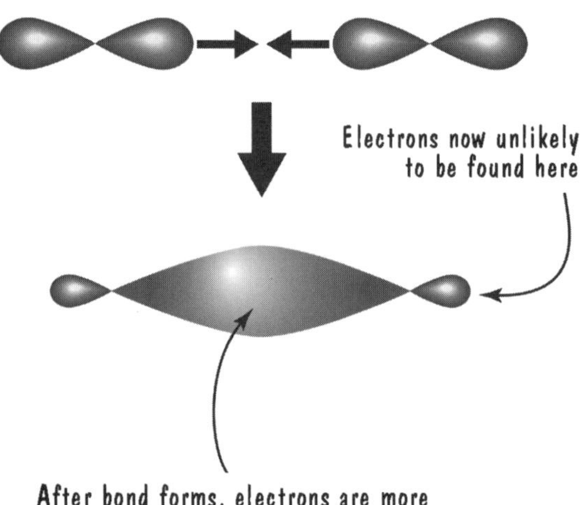

Figure 3.13

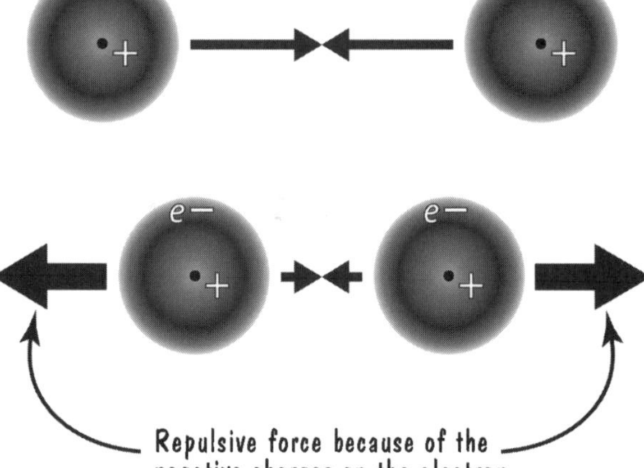

Well, electrons have a property I haven't yet discussed. This property is known as the **electron spin**. The spin of an electron can be up or down. Electron spin is just one more quantum number that one assigns to electrons, which I've discussed earlier. When two electrons with the same spin (both up or both down) come together, they repel each other. When two electrons with opposite spins (one up and one down) come together, there is an attractive force. This attractive force is stronger than the electric repulsion between the electrons, so opposite-spin electrons get together and share the same orbital (in the case of electrons within a single atom) or share a combined hybrid orbital (in the case of electrons from separate atoms sharing a combined orbital). See Figure 3.14.

Topic: Electrons in an Atom
Go to: *www.scilinks.org*
Code: MCB010

So, electrons tend to repel one another because they are both negatively charged. Electrons with opposite spins have an attractive force that overcomes the electric repulsion. Thus, opposite-spin electrons from different atoms will form a bond, but electrons that are already paired up by spin, as happens in a filled orbital, will repel other pairs of electrons. This means that filled orbitals repel one another, which will come into play in just a bit.

Figure 3.14

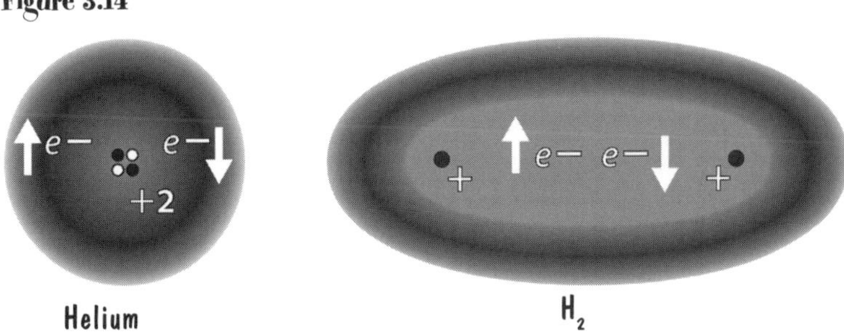

Electrons with opposite spins (indicated by arrows) have an attraction that keeps them in the same orbital despite electric repulsion.

Even more things to do before you read even more science stuff

Now get a bunch of toothpicks and some modeling clay. What you're going to create are a few atoms that have electrons in a filled *s* orbital and partially filled *p* orbitals. (Refer back to Chapter 1 if you need to review what I mean by *filled* and *partially filled* orbitals. Full *s* orbitals contain two electrons, and full *p* orbitals contain two electrons, leading to six total electrons in three filled *p* orbitals.) Using toothpicks and modeling clay, build three of the structures shown in Figure 3.15.

Figure 3.15

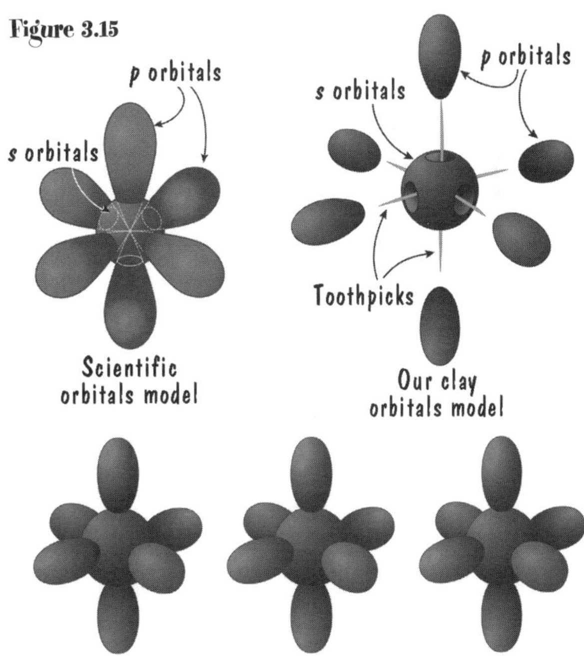

These structures represent the *s* and *p* orbitals in the outer shell of an atom.[9] This atom could be nitrogen, as that's an atom that

[9] The sizes of the *p* orbitals in these drawings are greatly exaggerated, but that exaggeration is necessary for you to visualize things in this activity.

has a filled outer *s* orbital and partially filled outer *p* orbitals. In other words, each dumbbell-shaped *p* orbital has one electron in it, so each *p* orbital is half full. See Figure 3.16.

Figure 3.16

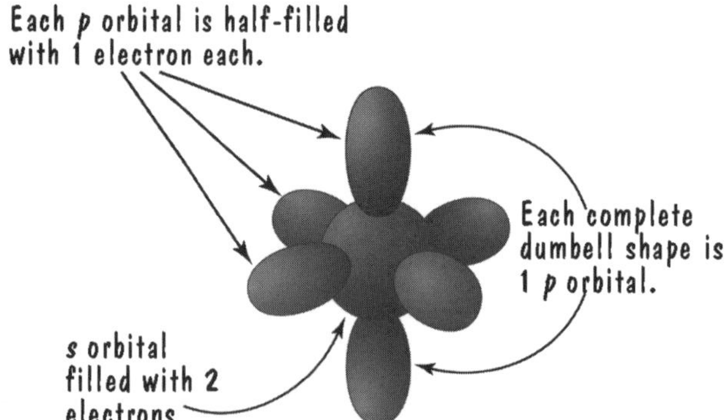

Figure 3.17

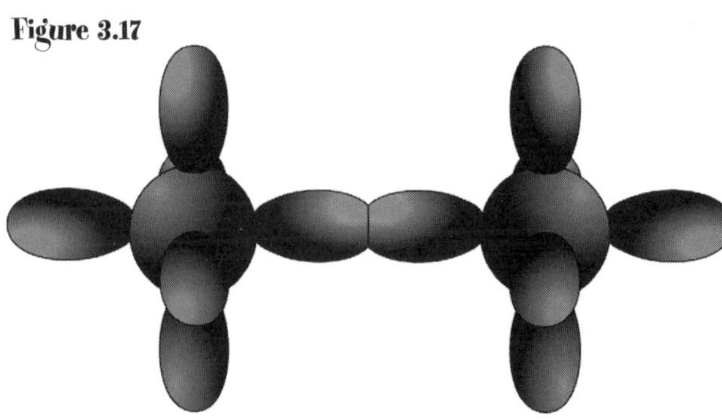

Figure 3.18

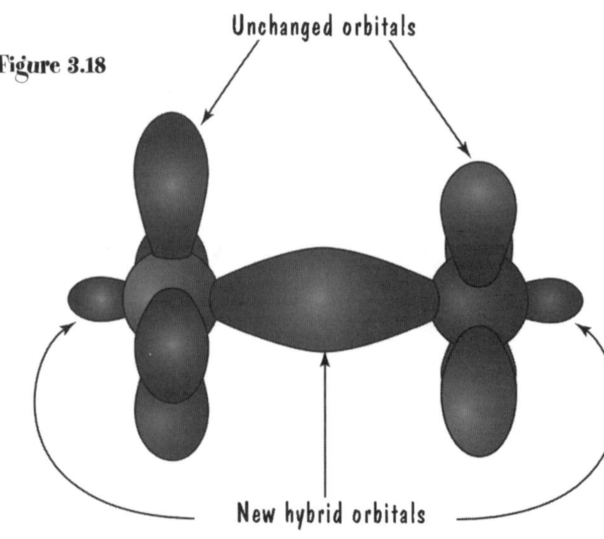

Bring two of these atom models next to each other. As you move the models closer together, ask yourself which orbitals will come in contact first, second, and which third. Assume that when orbitals from different atoms touch, then the orbitals begin sharing electrons in a covalent bond. Also, remember that our *s* orbitals are filled in this example, so there is no sharing of electrons between the *s* orbitals. To get you started, Figure 3.17 shows the two orbitals that will get together first, at least in our model. There's nothing special about the particular *p* orbitals shown connecting with each other. The point is that the "extremities" of the atom will come in contact first, as people with outstretched arms are likely to touch other people first with their hands rather than their bodies.

Once that covalent bond forms, those two connecting *p* orbitals are going to change into a new hybrid orbital. That means, to have a more accurate model of what might actually happen with orbitals, we have to alter our clay to look like Figure 3.18.

Given that the hybrid orbital you just formed stays

put, try to figure out how the other *p* orbitals might get together. This will obviously form two more covalent bonds, or what we call a **triple bond** between the atoms. The next explanation section will clarify this idea further.

Now go back to your three original clay models. If you altered your models to resemble Figure 3.18, change them back. Using these three models, and assuming they connect together in only sigma bonds, try to figure out what shape molecules these atoms can form—spheres, cubes, pyramids, or something else.

Even more science stuff

Now let's see how you did with your clay structures. I already showed you the first orbitals to meet, which are *p* orbitals meeting head on. This is a sigma bond. Once these orbitals are sharing electrons in a covalent bond, you can rotate one or both of your atoms so the other *p* orbitals are lined up, as shown in Figure 3.19.

Figure 3.19

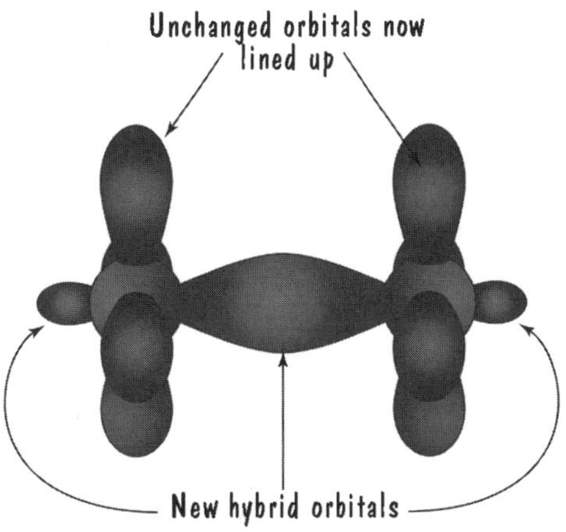

Then you can see how the other *p* orbitals can form sort of a "sideways" bond, pictured in Figure 3.20.

The "sideways" bonds shown in Figure 3.20 are called **pi** (pronounced like *pie*) **bonds**. Sigma bonds are stronger than pi bonds, which leads us to the following rule:

When atoms get together, the first bond is always a sigma bond.

Figure 3.20

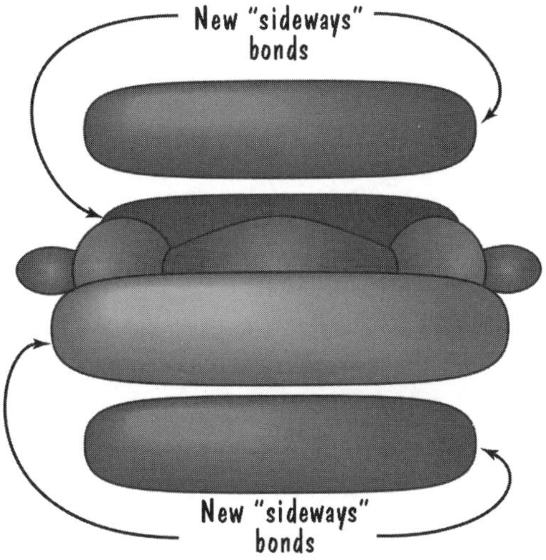

Once that bond is formed, then pi bonds can form. Figure 3.20 shows a triple bond between two atoms. For example, when two nitrogen atoms get together to form N_2, there is a triple bond (a total of six shared electrons) between the two atoms—one sigma bond and two pi bonds. When atoms get together and form a double bond, there's one sigma bond (the one that forms first) and one pi bond.

That's all well and good, but what happens when multiple atoms get together? I had you simulate this event in the second part of the previous section. If you allow only sigma bonds to form between your clay atoms, then you likely came up with a formation like the one in Figure 3.21.

Figure 3.21

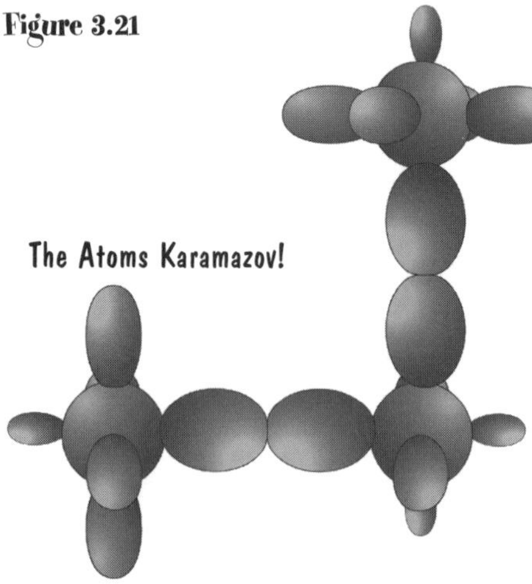

The Atoms Karamazov!

Now imagine adding more and more clay atoms to this structure. Because of the 90-degree angles in the structure, what you're going to form is a cube. If this holds true for all atoms, then that would mean that all molecules (collections of bonded atoms) will have 90-degree angles between atoms, so that the only possible shapes for molecules would be cubes or rectangular prisms. In nature, however, we find all sorts of molecular shapes. That must mean that we don't have a complete picture of bond formation.

The answer to our dilemma lies in the formation of more hybrid orbitals. This time, though, the hybrid orbitals form within a single atom rather than between two atoms. Up to this point, I've had you consider the *s* and *p* orbitals of an atom as if they simply overlap one another. But really, we have the same situation as we did with water drops, soap bubbles, and orbitals from separate atoms coming together. The *s* and *p* orbitals within an atom are competing for the same space. So, often, instead of remaining as separate overlapping orbitals, the orbitals combine into new hybrid orbitals. Figure 3.22 shows a common form of hybridization, in which the one *s* orbital combines with the three *p* orbitals to form four equivalent orbitals that are in the shape of a tetrahedron. This is known as an sp^3 hybridization. The name results from the fact that one *s* orbital combines with three *p* orbitals.

Figure 3.22

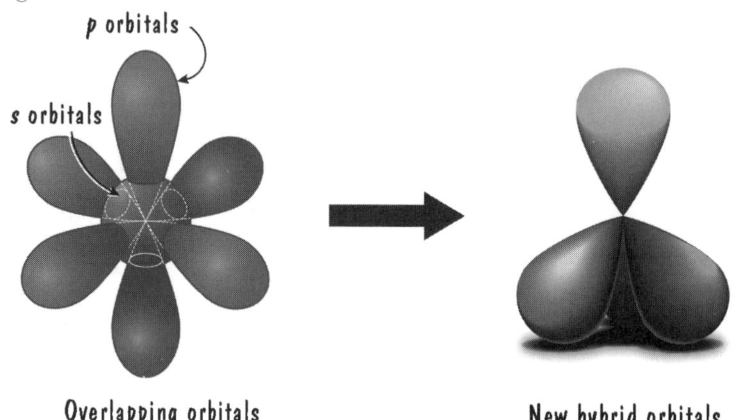

Let's see how this kind of hybridization works for the element carbon. By looking at the Periodic Table, you can see that carbon has four valence electrons—two in the *s* orbital and two in the *p* orbitals. Because the two electrons in the *s* orbital are already paired up, you would expect carbon to share only the two *p* electrons with other atoms, as shown in Figure 3.23.

Figure 3.23

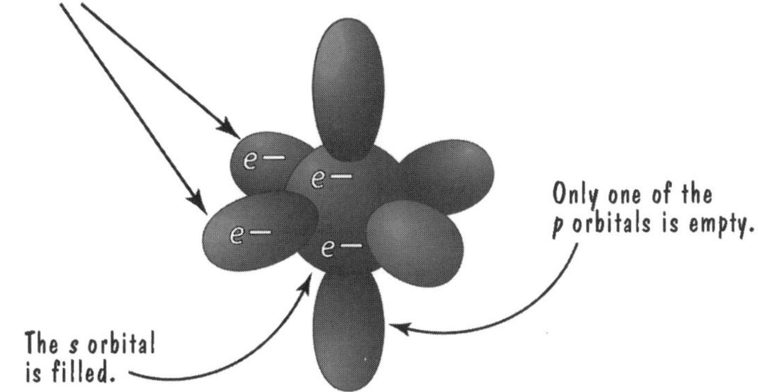

Figure 3.24

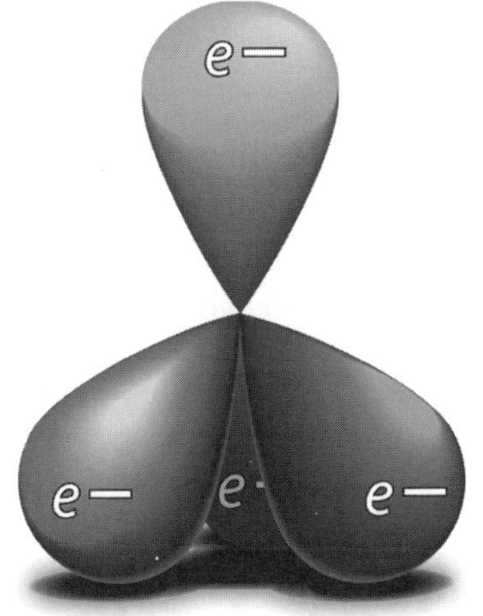

Each hybrid orbital has one electron, and those electrons are as far from one another as possible.

But the outer *s* and *p* orbitals in carbon form four equivalent hybridized orbitals (sp^3), as shown in Figure 3.24. In this arrangement, there are now four unpaired electrons that can bond with other atoms. This leads to carbon being a special atom that can form all kinds of long chain molecules. You might also notice that with this hybridization, the valence electrons in carbon are as far from one another as possible. With the electrons as far away as possible from one another, this is clearly a lower energy situation than the one shown in Figure 3.23.

Another way to look at what's happening with hybrid orbitals is to study energy level diagrams. We'll stick with what happens with carbon. In the outer shell, there are two paired electrons in the *s* orbital and two unpaired electrons in the *p* orbitals. See Figure 3.25 (p. 60).

Figure 3.25

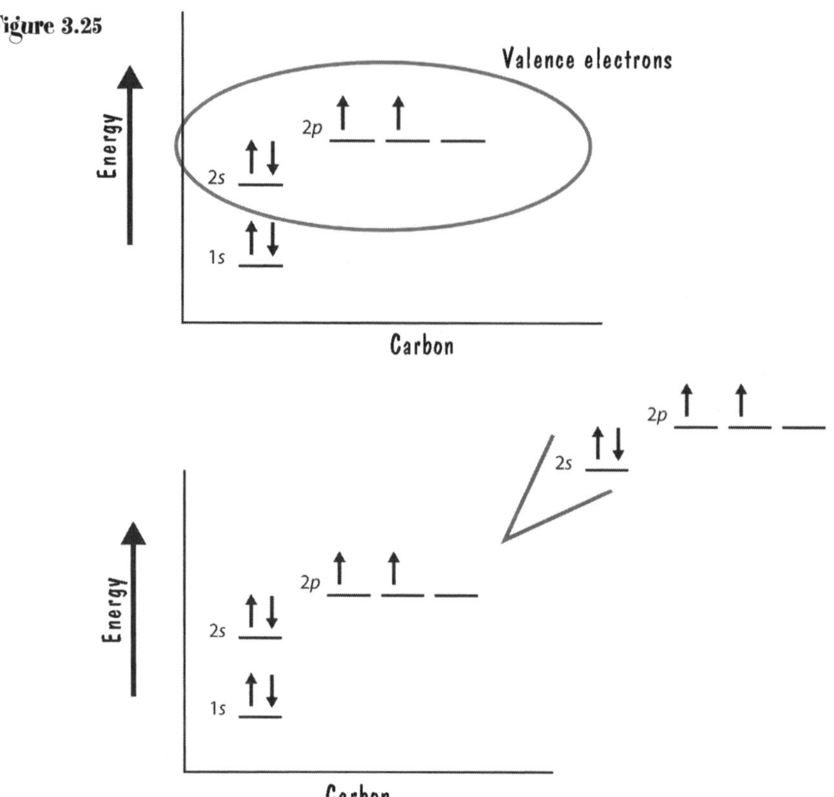

Important note. I'm using a new notation (different from the first chemistry book and the first chapter in this book) to show electrons in different energy levels. Instead of solid circles, I'm now using up and down arrows. The arrows represent the electron spin, which is either up or down. This is the conventional way of doing things, as it shows the pairing of electrons with up and down spins in a given orbital.

These orbitals tend to combine into four hybridized orbitals—the sp^3 orbitals. These new orbitals all have the same energy, as shown in Figure 3.26.

Figure 3.26

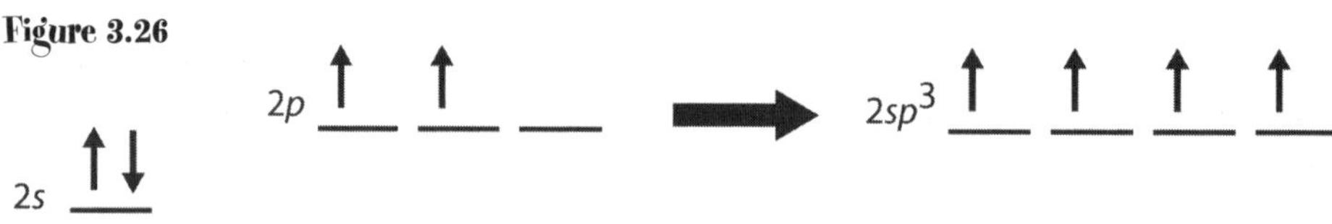

So, instead of one *s* orbital and three *p* orbitals, we have four equivalent sp^3 orbitals.

Hybridization of the orbitals has therefore caused two things to happen. First, the orientation of the outermost orbitals has changed from the shape of a cube, which would lead to 90-degree bonds with other atoms, to the shape of a tetrahedron, which leads to approximately 110-degree bonds with other atoms. Second, hybridization has also changed carbon from an atom that has three orbitals willing to share electrons to an atom that has four equivalent orbitals willing to share electrons. In that process, carbon changes from an atom with limited options for molecule shapes to one that has many options for molecule shapes. In other words, carbon is a special atom primarily because of its hybrid orbitals.

The sp^3 hybrid orbitals aren't the only ones possible. Often the *s* orbital will interact with only one or two of the *p* orbitals and leave the remaining ones alone. Then you get hybrid orbitals labeled sp^2 or *sp*. Figure 3.27 shows the change in energy levels for these two hybrids.

Figure 3.27

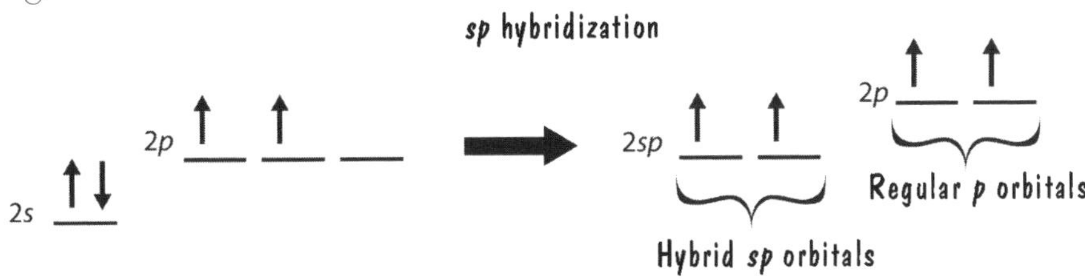

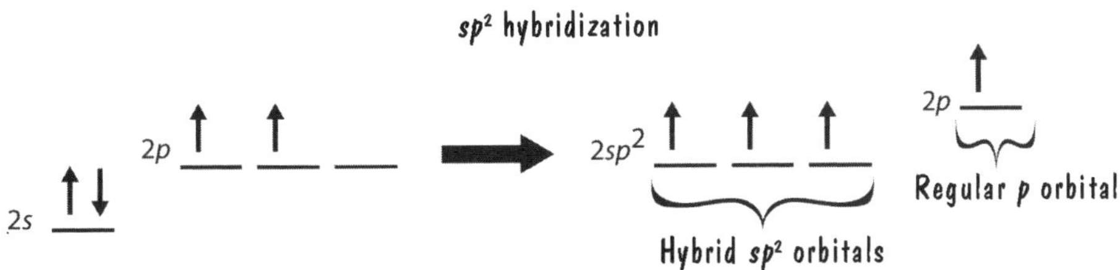

The *d* orbitals in an atom also take part in hybridization, leading to hybrid orbitals such as dsp^3 or d^2sp^3. There is a definite relationship between the structure of molecules and the hybridization of orbitals. Table 3.1 (p. 62) lists various hybrid orbitals and the resulting structures.[10]

---

[10] You can use this table as a general guideline, but the molecular shapes that result in any molecule will not always correspond exactly to these shapes. And no, I don't expect it to be obvious why these hybridizations lead to the shapes given. The table is here for completeness more than anything else.

Table 3.1

Hybridization	Structure
sp	linear
sp^2	planar triangle
sp^3	tetrahedron
dsp^3	trigonal bipyramid
d^2sp^3	octahedron

And even more things to do before you read even more science stuff

This is a short section in which I want you to just think about something. I mentioned in footnote #10 (p. 61) that there isn't always a direct correlation between hybridization and molecular shape. For example, oxygen atoms form sp^3 hybrid orbitals. You would expect, then, that oxygen atoms combining with other atoms as molecules would have an overall shape of a tetrahedron. The angles between bonds in a tetrahedron are about 110 degrees (actually 109.5 degrees). Yet, in a water molecule in which oxygen combines with two hydrogen atoms, the angle between the bonds is only 105 degrees. What do you suppose leads to this nontetrahedral shape? Think about electrons repelling one another.

And even more science stuff

To be honest, I didn't expect you to figure out that dilemma on your own, but I thought I'd give you a try. To see what's happening, let's look at the tetrahedral shape that results from sp^3 hybridization. Oxygen has six valence electrons rather than the four that carbon has. In distributing these six valence electrons among the four hybrid orbitals, you end up with two filled orbitals (two electrons each) and two half-filled orbitals (one electron each). The half-filled orbitals are the ones that bond with hydrogen atoms. See Figure 3.28.

Figure 3.28

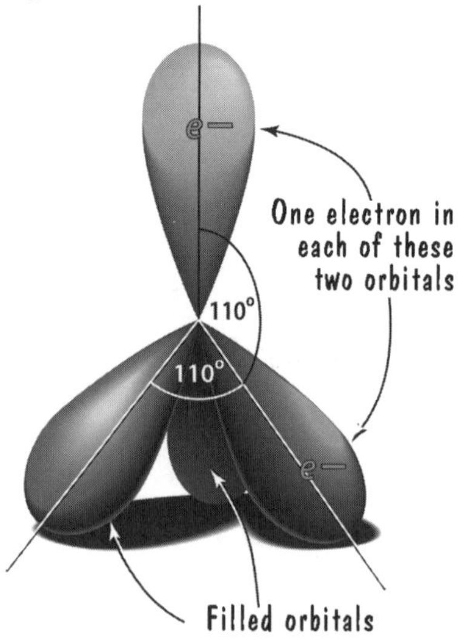

Those negatively charged filled orbitals (remember, they have electrons in them) repel each other and the other orbitals. Because the filled orbitals are larger, in general, than the bonding orbitals, and because they contain two electrons instead of one, their electric repulsion is larger. This bends the tetrahedral shape, as shown in Figure 3.29. That results in the bond angle in a water molecule being less than the expected 110 degrees.

Figure 3.29

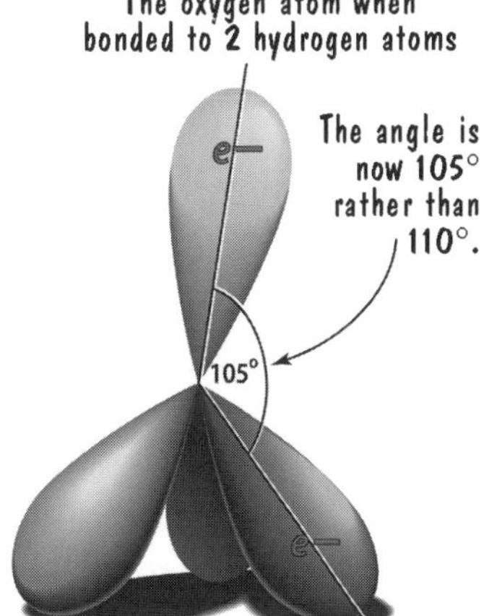

The electric repulsion between the filled orbitals pushes the partially filled orbitals together, making a smaller angle than expected.

The stronger repulsion of filled orbitals affects the shape of many molecules. That means that Table 3.1 seldom gives you the proper shape of a molecule. In addition to knowing what hybridization occurs, you have to factor in the alteration of that shape due to repulsion of filled orbitals. The water molecule is a relatively simple example, but the same principle applies in more complicated situations.

Chapter summary

- The very act of observing what's going on at the scale of atoms and smaller things disturbs what you are observing. This leads to an inherent uncertainty in our understanding of where electrons are and what they're doing. The name given to this concept is Heisenberg's uncertainty principle.
- The shape and orientation of electron orbitals determine how atoms connect in covalent bonds and the overall structure of molecules.
- When two atoms form a covalent bond, the orbitals can connect via a head-on bond, known as a sigma bond, or a sideways bond, known as a pi bond. The first bond to form between atoms is always a sigma bond. After a sigma bond forms, then pi bonds can form. Sigma bonds are stronger than pi bonds.
- Different orbitals will combine into a hybrid orbital when that process is energetically favorable. The hybrid orbital has a different orientation and shape from the original orbitals. The simplest form of hybrid orbital is the combination of two *s* orbitals from different atoms. The existence of hybrid orbitals leads to bond angles other than 90 degrees and allows for a wide variety of molecular structures.
- Hybrid orbitals within a single atom are labeled according to which orbitals are involved. For example, an sp^2 orbital is the combination of one *s* orbital with two *p* orbitals to make three sp^2 orbitals that all have the same energy.

- Filled orbitals (containing two electrons each) tend to distort the shape of a molecule because of the stronger electric repulsion caused by these filled orbitals.

Applications

1. **Note:** You can ignore this application if you didn't read the text box dealing with the mathematics of the uncertainty principle (p. 49). I told you I would address $\Delta E \Delta t \geq \hbar$, one of the inequalities associated with the uncertainty principle, in this section. Guess I'd better do that. Some atoms are radioactive, meaning that they decay into a different form of the atom or a different atom altogether. In the process, the atoms release various subatomic particles. For example, carbon-14 spontaneously decays into carbon-12 with the release of neutrons. The relationship $\Delta E \Delta t \geq \hbar$ tells us that the more we know about the energy of the escaping neutrons, the less we know about when the decay happened. Conversely, the more we know about when the decay happens, the less we know about the energy involved. Just as with electron orbitals, this makes us speak in terms of probabilities. We can state the probability that a given atom of carbon-14 will decay in a given period of time, but we can't know exactly when it will happen. For an interesting paradox that uses this form of the uncertainty principle, search the internet for "Schrödinger's cat."
2. One thing that makes carbon such a versatile atom is its ability to form three different kinds of hybrid orbitals—sp^3, sp^2, and sp. When carbon atoms are connected in a tetrahedron, as happens with sp^3 hybridization, you get diamond. Using sp^2 hybridization, carbon forms into graphite, which has a different shape from diamond and certainly has different properties. When bonded with two oxygen atoms, carbon uses sp hybridization to form a linear carbon dioxide (CO_2) molecule.
3. Here's another example of figuring out the shape of a molecule from knowing what kind of hybrid orbitals it has. We'll look at the molecule NH_3. Nitrogen,

Figure 3.30

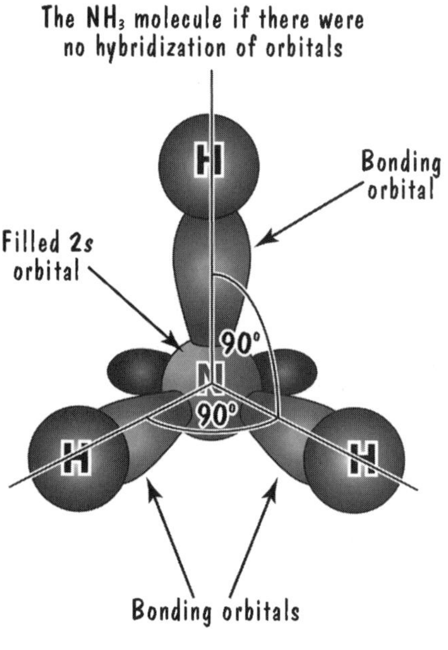

as you can tell from looking at the Periodic Table, has five valence electrons—two electrons in the 2*s* orbital and three electrons in the three 2*p* orbitals. Given this, you might think that the two 2*s* electrons would be perfectly happy to keep to themselves and let the 2*p* electrons bond with other atoms. If that were the case, then the NH_3 molecule would look like Figure 3.30, with a 90-degree angle between the bonds.

But the NH_3 molecule doesn't have 90-degree angles between the bonds, and here's what is happening. Just as with carbon, the valence *s* and *p* orbitals form four equal hybrid orbitals, as shown in Figure 3.31.

Figure 3.31

sp^3 hybrid orbitals

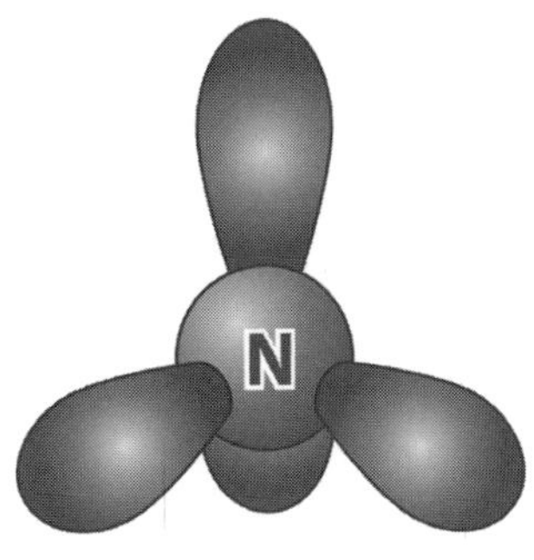

Unlike carbon, which has four valence electrons to be distributed among the four equal hybrid orbitals, nitrogen has five electrons to fill those orbitals. That means one of the orbitals has a complete pair of electrons. The extra repulsion that results from that complete pair of electrons pushes the other bonds slightly away. If there were no such extra repulsion, the angle between the hybrid orbitals would be 109.5 degrees (refer back to the discussion of water molecules in this chapter). With the repulsion, the angle between orbitals is more like 107.3 degrees. See Figure 3.32. Now, you might be wondering what the big deal is. Why worry about 2 degrees of angle? Well, those angles are extremely important for figuring out how and why molecules interact. Often there has to be a certain "fit" between molecules, and the proper angle can be crucial for the right fit.

Figure 3.32

Actual shape of NH_3 molecule due to hybridization and due to repulsion of filled orbital

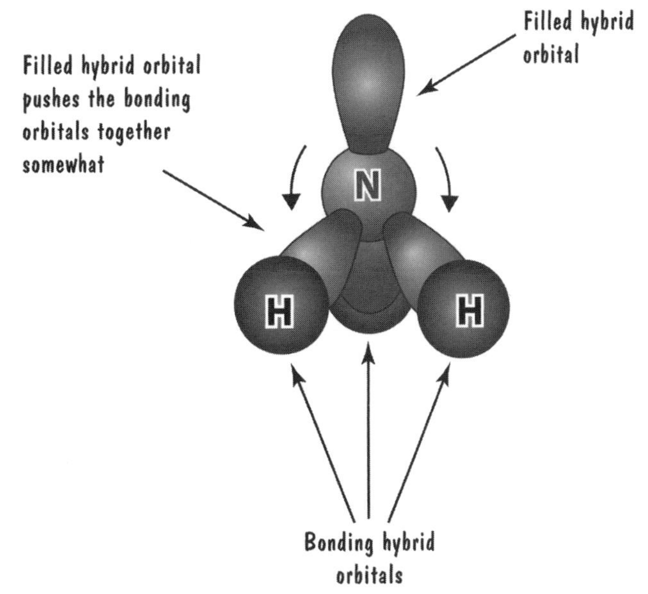

4. In this chapter, I mentioned that atoms such as oxygen

and nitrogen can form double and triple bonds. The first bond that forms is a sigma bond. Once this is formed, other orbitals can overlap "sideways" in a pi bond. Once you get to the fourth row, however, the atoms there tend not to form double or triple bonds with other atoms. Why? The answer is that in this row, beginning with the element zinc, atoms have electrons in filled *d* orbitals. These electrons in the filled (two electrons each) *d* orbitals tend to get in the way of *p* electrons that would otherwise form pi bonds. No pi bonds, no double or triple bonds. Of course, unfilled d orbitals can easily form double and triple bonds, and if the filled *d* orbitals become involved with *s* and *p* orbitals in hybrid orbitals, those hybrid orbitals can then form pi bonds and thus have double and triple bonds. And no, this last application isn't high on the list of things you absolutely have to know to understand bonding. Just something extra for you.

Special Reactions

I covered the basics of chemical reactions in the first chemistry book, including how to write and balance chemical equations that represent those reactions. There is also a quick review of chemical reactions in Chapter 1 of this book. We're going to delve a bit deeper into certain kinds of reactions—ones that occur often enough that it's useful for them to have their own special categories. As you go through this chapter, try to avoid seeing these separate categories as conceptually different from other reactions. The same basic principles govern all chemical reactions, regardless of the category.

Things to do before you read the science stuff

Here's a neat trick to amaze friends and family members. Challenge someone to make a sugar cube catch on fire. For safety's sake, hold the sugar cube with tongs and place a lit match or a candle under it. See Figure 4.1.

Although your chosen person might get the sugar cube to melt or caramelize, he or she will be out of luck when it comes to the cube going up in flames. You come to the rescue with a new sugar cube. Before you place the cube in the tongs, dust it on all sides with cigarette ashes.[1] When you place your dusted cube over a flame, it should catch fire easily. Neat.

Figure 4.1

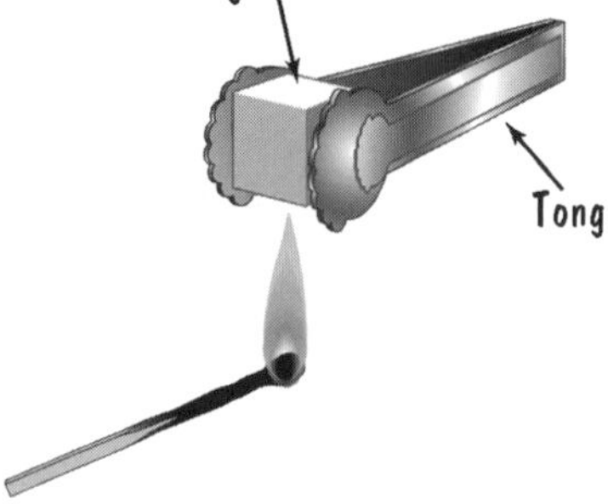

The science stuff

What you just did is an example of a **catalyzed reaction**. A **catalyst** is something that helps a reaction occur or increases the rate of the reaction. Although catalysts affect a reaction, they themselves are not affected by the reaction as a whole. The particular kind of reaction you catalyzed when getting the sugar cube to burn is known as **combustion**, which is just a fancy name for something burning. When a substance burns, oxygen combines with carbon and hydrogen atoms to form carbon dioxide and water. The products—carbon dioxide and water—are always the same in combustion. Therefore, we have a classification known as combustion reactions. All of them are of the form

$$\text{organic molecule} + \text{oxygen} \rightarrow \text{carbon dioxide} + \text{water}$$

The term **organic molecule** refers to molecules that contain primarily carbon and hydrogen.

The above reaction doesn't include the fact that you often have to add energy (via the flame) to get the reaction to go forward. For our sugar cube (composed of sucrose), we can write this as

$$\text{sucrose} + \text{oxygen} + \text{energy} \rightarrow \text{carbon dioxide} + \text{water}$$

or using chemical formulas (and balancing the equation):[2]

[1] For the record, we here at the Stop Faking It! Institute of Higher Learning do not promote smoking. I have to admit, though, that I love the smell of a good cigar.

[2] Those letters in parentheses—(s), (g), and (aq)—refer to the state of the chemical involved in the reaction. These symbols refer to solid, gas, and aqueous, respectively.

$$C_{12}H_{22}O_{11}\ (s) + 12O_2\ (g) + \text{energy} \rightarrow 12CO_2\ (g) + 11H_2O\ (g)$$

Whenever you have to add energy to get a reaction to occur, that energy is referred to as the **activation energy**. We can represent the activation energy with a graph of the energy involved in the reaction versus time, as shown in Figure 4.2.[3]

You can think of the activation energy shown in Figure 4.2 as an "energy hump" you have to get over for the reaction to proceed. Imagine the graph is a track on which you can place a bowling ball. For the bowling ball to go from the energy level on the left side to the lower energy on the right side (you eventually get energy *out* of this process because the ball is now rolling faster on the right side), you have to push the ball (add energy) up to the top of the hump. See Figure 4.3.

Figure 4.2

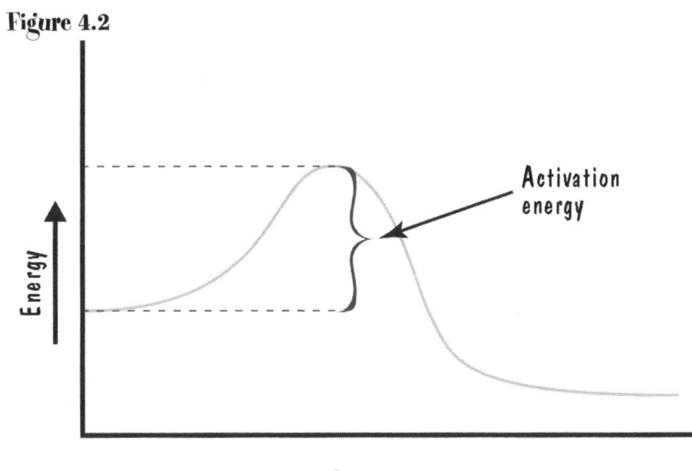

Figure 4.3

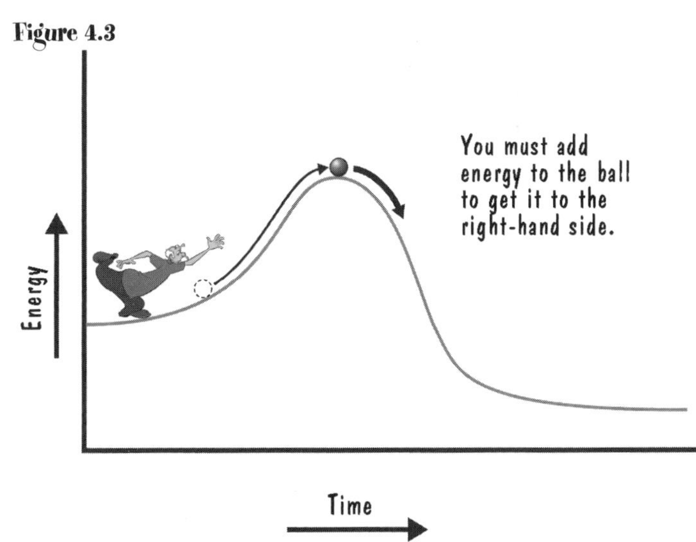

Now let's apply this idea to the sugar cube. For the cube to burn, you have to get over the energy hump to the right side of the graph. A match simply can't provide enough energy to do this. You can solve the problem by

[3] There's potential for confusion in this graph because it looks similar to energy level diagrams for individual atoms, such as Figure 1.9 (p. 9) in Chapter 1. The vertical axis is energy in both cases, but the horizontal axis in Figure 4.2 is time, while the horizontal axis in Figure 1.9 has no meaning. In Figure 4.2, we are tracking the energy of the molecules involved in a chemical reaction as the reaction proceeds, and in Figure 1.9 we are illustrating the energy levels available to electrons in an atom.

adding more energy than a match can provide.[4] Alternatively, you can *lower* the activation energy, which is where the cigarette ash comes in. The ash contains a substance called cerium oxide. The cerium oxide acts as a go-between for the oxygen molecules in the air to combine with the sucrose molecules. With cerium oxide as the mediary, the energy required for the combustion of sucrose is lower than without the cerium oxide, low enough that the energy provided by a lit match is enough for the reaction to proceed. See Figure 4.4.

Figure 4.4

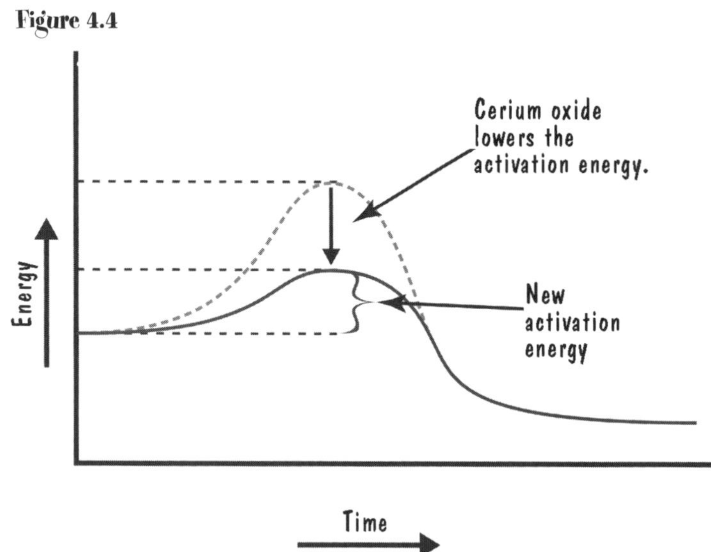

All catalyzed reactions use this same principle. By adding a catalyst to a reaction, you lower the activation energy necessary for the reaction to occur. You might think of the catalyst as a facilitator. You have two molecules that have trouble getting together on issues. In comes the catalyst as mediator, helping the two sides get together. As catalysts often say, "Can't we all just get along?"

More things to do before you read more science stuff

In this section and the next one, I'm not going to deal with reactions, but rather with chemicals that we classify as acids and bases. This little aside is necessary because following these two sections I'm going to deal with acid-base reactions. Seems silly to cover that before you know what acids and bases are! Anyway, for this section you'll need a supply of litmus paper (both red and blue) and a supply of pH paper. You can get these from a science materials supplier or possibly at a place that sells products for swimming pools or spas. You'll also need various liquids to test. Good ones that you can find around the house are vinegar, bleach, black coffee, ammonia, water, baking soda (dissolved in water), and lemon juice. Chemicals that are available from a science supply outfit or maybe already lying around your school include sodium hydroxide, calcium hydroxide, hydrochloric

---

[4] For example, you might get a sugar cube to go up in flames if you trained a blowtorch on it.

acid, and sulfuric acid. If you have these chemicals in different concentrations (different molarities)[5], that would be good.

> **Caution:** Commercial chemicals such as hydrochloric acid and sodium hydroxide can come in concentrations that are downright dangerous. When using these chemicals and somewhat noxious household chemicals such as ammonia, always wear goggles and gloves and have a plan for washing out your eyes if they come in contact with the chemicals. Also, **take care not to mix any of the liquids you have**. Mixing ammonia and bleach, for example, will generate a dangerous gas. Not good (I inadvertently did this once and it's scary!). See Safety Note (p. ix).

Okay. First, dip strips of blue litmus paper in the various liquids you have. Use a new strip for each liquid. The paper will either stay blue or turn red. Then dip strips of red litmus paper in the various liquids. The paper will either stay red or turn blue. Keep track of what liquids cause what reactions in the litmus paper.

Table 4.1

x value	*y* value
1.0	0.00000002
2.0	0.00006
3.0	0.004
4.0	0.8
5.0	25.0
6.0	3200
7.0	2900000
8.0	1400000000

Next get your pH paper and dip those strips (a new one for each liquid) into each liquid. You can compare the color of the strip with a color code that comes with the pH paper to determine a number for the pH—something between 0 and 14.

Now for something completely different. Listed in Table 4.1 are a bunch of ordered pairs of numbers. You're going to try to graph these ordered pairs, with the *x* value going on the *x*-axis and the *y* value going on the *y*-axis. Figure 4.5 shows a sample graph with the first ordered pair plotted on the graph. Use the sample graph or draw one of your own to try to get all of the ordered pairs on one graph. Hint: It's pretty much impossible. You can give up once you know *why* it's impossible.

Figure 4.5

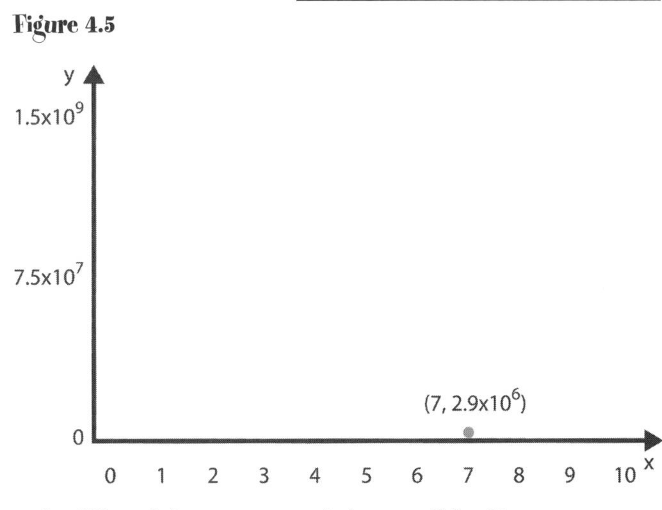

[5] Refer to Chapter 2 of this book for a definition of molarity. We use a capital M for molarity, so a label of 0.5 M means a chemical has a molarity of 0.5 moles per liter. Also, try to keep to low molarities of these substances.

Now use a calculator to take the logarithm of each of the *y* values and create a new table. I've done the first few and the last one for you below in Table 4.2.

Try graphing this second set of ordered pairs. Shouldn't be too difficult as long as you allow for negative *y* values.

Table 4.2

x value	Logarithm of *y* value
1.0	–7.7
2.0	–4.2
3.0	–2.4
4.0	?
5.0	?
6.0	?
7.0	?
8.0	9.1

More science stuff

You no doubt have used the terms *acid* and *acidic* in your everyday life. Many fruits contain citric acid, and we often refer to things we eat as being acidic or non-acidic. Movies let us know that acids can burn you (think *RoboCop*), especially the famous acids hydrochloric acid and sulfuric acid. People can have an acid tongue, but that's something different. Less common in everyday language are the words *base* and *basic*, at least as they apply to chemicals. The term *pH* is also common. We buy pH-balanced shampoos and check the pH of hot tubs and pools.

You probably knew before you even did the previous section that litmus paper helps determine whether a substance is an **acid** or a **base**. If blue litmus paper turns red when dipped in a liquid, the liquid is an acid. If red litmus paper turns blue in a liquid, the liquid is a base. If neither the red nor the blue litmus paper changes color, the liquid is neutral. pH paper takes this a step further and shows *how* acidic or basic a substance is.

Topic: Acids and Bases
Go to: *www.scilinks.org*
Code: MCB011

Great. Now if we only knew what acids and bases *are*! There are a number of ways to define acids and bases, and I'll give you two of them here. Before doing that, I need to remind you of how water interacts with other chemicals. Water molecules are **polar**, with one end being positive and the other negative. See Figure 4.6.

> Figure 4.6 depicts the atoms hydrogen and oxygen. Be careful you don't confuse this drawing with the drawings in Chapter 3 that showed electron orbitals and how they interact. Of course, we can use the orbital drawings to explain exactly why oxygen is a polar molecule. Figure 3.29 is shown again on the next page. Notice that the two orbitals that do not bond with hydrogen atoms are filled with two electrons each. This makes the side of the molecule away from the hydrogen atoms more negative. Thus, a polar molecule.

Figure 3.29

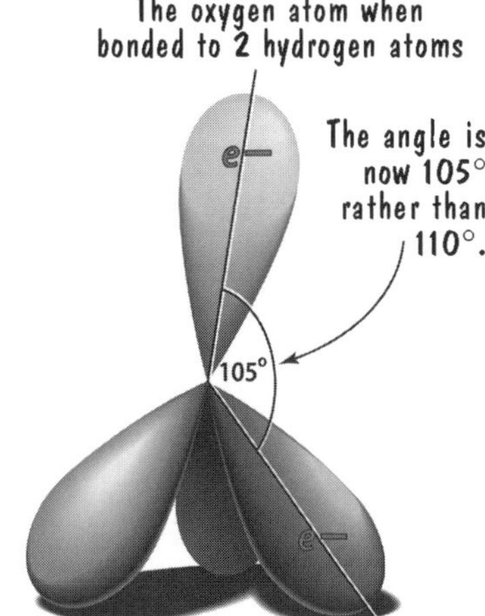

Because water molecules are polar, they interact electrically (you know, like charges repel and unlike charges attract) with other molecules. For example, when you put sodium chloride (table salt) in water, the attraction between different parts of the water molecule and the ions that make up sodium chloride are strong enough that water molecules separate the sodium chloride into positive sodium ions and negative chloride ions, as in Figure 4.7. Notice in this figure that the plus side of the water molecule (the hydrogen side) is attracted to the negatively charged chloride ion, and the negative side of the water molecule (the oxygen side) is attracted to the positively charged sodium ion.[6]

Figure 4.6

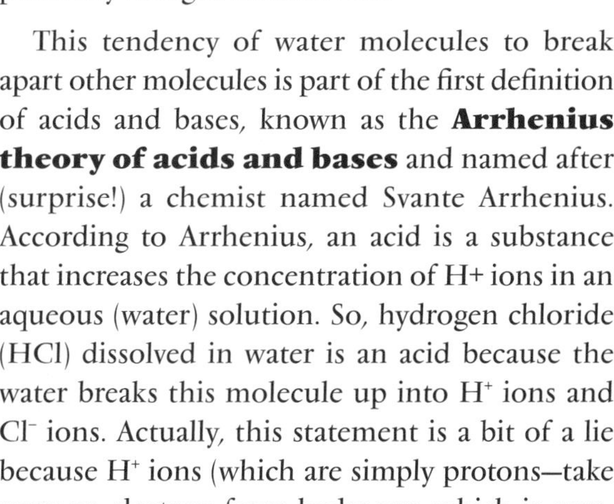

This tendency of water molecules to break apart other molecules is part of the first definition of acids and bases, known as the **Arrhenius theory of acids and bases** and named after (surprise!) a chemist named Svante Arrhenius. According to Arrhenius, an acid is a substance that increases the concentration of H+ ions in an aqueous (water) solution. So, hydrogen chloride (HCl) dissolved in water is an acid because the water breaks this molecule up into H^+ ions and Cl^- ions. Actually, this statement is a bit of a lie because H^+ ions (which are simply protons–take away an electron from hydrogen, which is com-

Figure 4.7

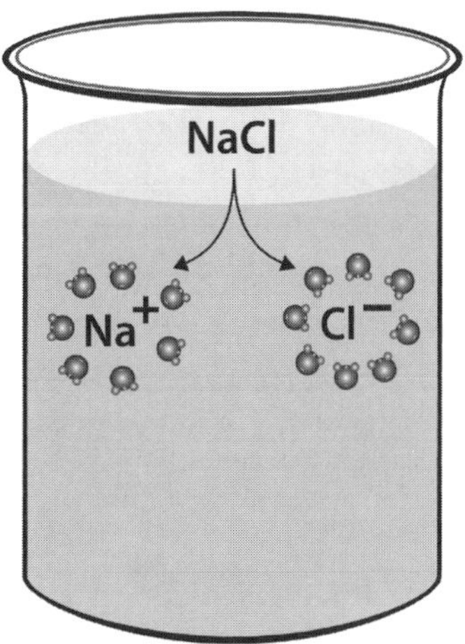

[6] When we break apart molecules with ionic bonds, we say they have been **dissociated**. From experience, you know that the salt disappears in this process because it has dissolved into the water. While molecules with covalent bonds can dissolve in liquid (such as sugar in water), covalent bonds don't dissociate in the process. They retain their molecular identity.

posed of one proton and one electron in its most common state, and all you're left with is a proton) don't exist by themselves in water. Instead, they latch onto water molecules to form what are known as hydronium ions, or H_3O^+. So really, an acid is anything that increases the hydronium ion concentration in an aqueous solution. Check out Figure 4.8.

Figure 4.8

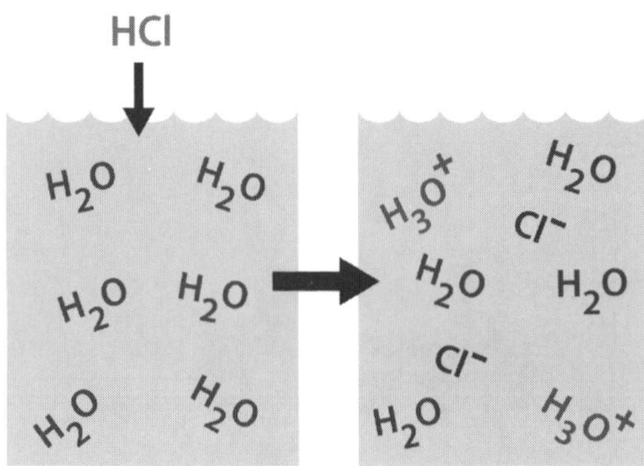

Arrhenius defines a base as anything that increases the concentration of hydroxide ions (OH^-) in an aqueous solution. For example, sodium hydroxide (NaOH) is a base because when you put it in water, the polar water molecules separate it into sodium ions (Na^+) and hydroxide ions (OH^-). Figure 4.9 shows this.

Figure 4.9

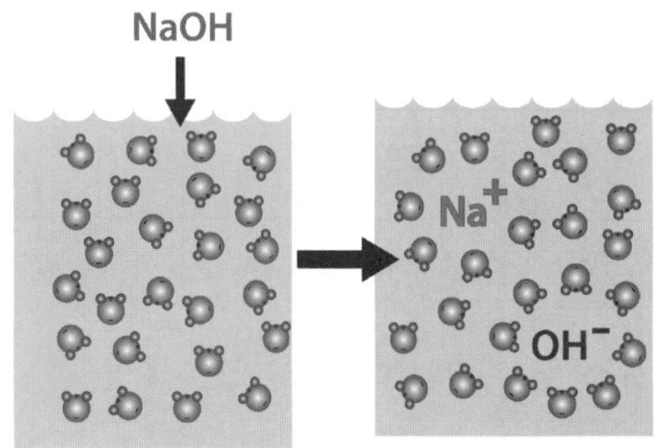

Okay, so what? What's so special about substances that form hydronium ions or hydroxide ions in water? Well, it has to do with what those substances do when they encounter other substances. If a substance produces lots of positively charged hydronium ions, then those ions have a tendency to interact with negatively charged ions. And if a substance produces lots of negatively charged hydroxide ions, then those ions tend to interact with positively charged ions. In other words, we define substances as acids and bases because that helps us figure out how they'll interact in chemical reactions, which is what most of chemistry is about.

I said I would give you two definitions of acids and bases, so I guess I'd better provide the second one. It turns out that molecules containing the hydroxide ion aren't the only ones that increase the concentration of hydroxide ions when dissolved in water. For example, here's what happens when ammonia (NH_3) dissolves in water:

$$NH_3\ (aq) + H_2O\ (l) \rightarrow NH_4^+\ (aq) + OH^-\ (aq)$$ [7]

[7] In case you forgot, (g) means the substance is a gas, (s) means the substance is a solid, and (aq) means the substance is in a solution. One classification that isn't represented here is (l), which indicates a substance that is itself a liquid.

NH_3 contains no hydroxide ions, yet when you put it in water it increases the hydroxide ion concentration. To account for examples such as this, we have what is known as the **Brönsted-Lowry** (Johannes Brönsted and Thomas Lowry) **theory of acids and bases**. In this definition, an acid is any substance that donates protons in a reaction, and a base is any substance that accepts protons in a reaction. This is basically (no pun intended) the same as the Arrhenius definition of acids because if a substance readily donates protons in a reaction, it will also increase the hydronium ion concentration when placed in water. The definition of a base, though, is expanded to include any substance that readily accepts protons in a reaction, and that substance doesn't have to contain hydroxide ions. Let's continue with our above example. There, NH_3 contributed to the OH^- concentration when dissolved in water. But NH_3 is also a proton acceptor (which we have defined as a base) because it picks up a proton to become NH_4^+, as in

$$NH_3\ (aq) + H_3O^+\ (aq) \rightarrow NH_4^+\ (aq) + H_2O\ (l)$$

Topic: pH Scale
Go to: *www.scilinks.org*
Code: MCB012

Let's head back to your use of pH paper and why I had you attempt to graph those sets of numbers. You probably know that pH is a measure of how acidic something is, but you might not completely understand the pH scale, which is what I'm going to explain. First, let's talk about the two graphs I had you attempt to create. The *y* values in the first table (Table 4.1) have a wide range, from really small (0.00000002) to really large (1,400,000,000). If you make the graph so you can distinguish the small values, then the larger ones are on top of one another, and vice versa. Logarithms to the rescue. If you plot the logarithms of the *y* values instead of the original *y* values, then you can graph them easily.

The concentrations of hydronium ions in aqueous solutions are like the numbers in Table 4.1 in that they cover a wide range of values. For example, a strong acid might have a concentration of hydronium ions of 0.01 M, and a weak acid might have a hydronium concentration of 0.000001 M.[8] We use logarithms to compare these numbers and graph them side by side. This leads us to the definition of pH, which is expressed in terms of hydrogen ion concentration, even though we realize that in the real world we're dealing with hydronium ions rather than hydrogen ions.[9] Here's the definition:

pH = negative of the log of the hydrogen ion concentration

---

[8] Remember that M stands for molarity, which is the number of moles of a substance per liter of solution.

[9] Many things in science are done in the name of tradition. The definition of pH was developed before chemists realized that hydrogen ions don't exist when in water. You will sometimes see the expression p(Hydronium) instead of pH, but for the most part, the term pH persists.

Chemists use brackets to indicate concentrations, so we rewrite the hydrogen ion concentration as $[H^+]$, and we have

$$pH = -\log [H^+]$$

The reason for the negative sign is that most concentrations are less than 1.0, and as you saw previously, taking the log of these numbers gives you a negative number. So, the negative sign is just to make most pH values positive.

The nature of logarithms. How do logarithms (or logs) reduce a wide range of values to a small range of values? To understand that, you simply need to know the definition of a logarithm. To take the logarithm of a number, you ask, "10 raised to what power (exponent) will give me this number?" For example, log 100 is equal to 2 because 10 raised to the second power (10 squared) equals 100. Similarly, log 10,000 is equal to 4 because 10 raised to the fourth power equals 10,000. For numbers less than 1, negative exponents come into play. Log 0.01 is equal to –2 because 10 raised to the –2 power equals 0.01. So, just using the numbers I've mentioned here, the numbers 0.01, 100, and 10,000 become, after taking the logarithms of them, –2, 2, and 4. Voilà! A wide range of numbers reduced to a small range of numbers that are a bit easier to work with.

Assuming you used pH paper when I asked you to, you discovered the pH values of a few common liquids. The pH of lemon juice is about 2.3, the pH of vinegar is about 3.0, the pH of orange juice is about 3.5, and the pH of ammonia is about 11.0. Keep in mind that the higher the pH, the smaller the hydronium ion concentration and the greater the hydroxide ion concentration. The usual range of pH values chemists use is from 0.0 (highly acidic) to 14.0 (highly basic), even though values lower (and even negative) and higher are possible. A pH of 7.0 is considered neutral. And remember that pH is a logarithmic scale. That means that a pH of 5 is 10 times more acidic than a pH of 6 and 100 times more acidic than a pH of 7.

Before going on, I want to make a distinction between *strong* acids and bases and *concentrated* acids and bases. Hydrochloric acid is a strong acid because when it's placed in water, its separation into H_3O^+ ions and Cl^- ions is pretty much complete. Substances that readily donate protons are strong acids. However, you could have a solution of hydrochloric acid that has very little HCl dissolved in water or a lot of HCl dissolved in water. In other words, you could have a low *concentration* of a *strong* acid that isn't all that dangerous. If you'll recall, we measure concentration in molarity, so a 0.001 M solution of hydrochloric acid (0.001 moles of HCl per liter of solution) is much weaker overall (and would have a higher pH) than a 0.1 M solution of hydrochloric acid (0.1 moles of HCl per liter of solution), even though you would consider them both to be "strong" acids. And what I just said about acids applies to bases. The moral is to pay just as much attention to the molarity of an acid or base as you do to whether the acid or base is considered to be strong or weak.

Let's try an analogy to illustrate the difference between strong and weak on one hand and concentrated or not concentrated on the other hand. Suppose someone is going to set off firecrackers in your vicinity, and you want to be as safe as possible so as not to incur physical damage. There are tiny firecrackers and really big firecrackers. All other things being equal, you might choose to be in the vicinity of tiny firecrackers. That would be analogous to choosing a weak acid over a strong acid. But let's say this person is going to set off 100 fireworks, and there are two options—they'll be set off in a 3 × 3 meter closed room or in a 10 × 10 kilometer field. The different locations correspond to different concentrations. 100 firecrackers in a small room versus 100 firecrackers in a huge open field. The first option is a high concentration of firecrackers and the second is a low concentration of firecrackers. The difference in concentration is big enough that you could choose the large firecrackers (strong acid) in the large field (low concentration) and be safer than if you chose the small firecrackers (weak acid) in the small room (high concentration). So, the strength of an acid or base is important, but so is the concentration.

"That's correct!! You want to be near the **small** firecrackers. But you're going to have to move faster, Professor, if you want to make it to the next round."

"Our contestant is signaling he wants to be enclosed in the 3 m by 3 m case and **not** the 10 km by 10 km field. My, he certainly is intrepid, isn't he."

Even more things to do before you read even more science stuff

We covered what acids and bases are, so it's time for reactions. For this activity, you'll need some calcium hydroxide (about 0.1 M concentration) dissolved in distilled water (get the powder from a science chemical supplier)[10], a straw, a small amount of *clear* carbonated soda (club soda or lemon-lime soda), a pair of safety goggles, and your breath. Pour a small amount of the calcium hydroxide solution (the liquid you made, not the powder) in a clear glass and notice what color it is (clear, yes?). Use the straw to blow bubbles into the liquid (possible splashback is why you have goggles). Notice any change in the calcium hydroxide (there *should* be a change). Rinse out the glass and pour a small amount of clear carbonated soda into it. By definition, this is clear. Then pour a small amount of calcium hydroxide into the glass and notice any change.

Even more science stuff

If all went well, cloudiness happened. When you blow bubbles into clear calcium hydroxide, it turns cloudy. When you pour clear calcium hydroxide into clear carbonated soda, the solution turns cloudy. The explanation for both of these is that you observed an acid-base reaction. In each case, the cloudiness came from the interaction of an acid—carbonic acid (H_2CO_3)—and a base—calcium hydroxide. A carbonated soda already has carbonic acid in it. When you blow bubbles into calcium hydroxide, the carbon dioxide (CO_2) from your breath interacts with the water in the calcium hydroxide solution to form H_2CO_3. Here's the balanced equation for the interaction of carbonic acid and calcium hydroxide:

$$\text{carbonic acid} + \text{calcium hydroxide} \rightarrow \text{calcium carbonate} + \text{water}$$

$$H_2CO_3\ (aq) + Ca(OH)_2\ (aq) \rightarrow CaCO_3\ (s) + 2H_2O\ (l)$$

Quick review. How did I know the formulas for carbonic acid, calcium hydroxide, and calcium carbonate? Yeah, I could have looked them up, but I didn't. I simply used the Periodic Table along with the knowledge that OH^- has a negative charge (an extra electron) and that CO_3^{2-} has a −2 charge (two extra electrons). Also, if you don't know how I balanced the equation by using two waters, it might be worth reviewing how to balance equations.

Calcium carbonate is an insoluble salt (doesn't dissolve in water), which is why things turned cloudy. In fact, all acid-base reactions have the same result.

[10] The concentration of your dissolved calcium hydroxide isn't critical. About a teaspoon of powder in a cup of distilled water will do the trick. You can also buy solutions of calcium hydroxide so you don't have to bother dissolving any powder into distilled water.

You add the acid and base together, and you get a salt (there are many kinds of salt that can be produced) plus water. The production of salt isn't always easy to see, though. For example, if you mix vinegar (an acid) and ammonia (a base), you won't see any cloudiness. The salt produced in this case (ammonium acetate) stays dissolved in the solution.

Now, you might be thinking that we could figure out this reaction without the whole notion of acids, bases, and acid-base reactions. You would be right. You could simply look at the relative attractions for electrons of the atoms and compounds involved and know that certain bonds are going to be stronger than others.[11] You could also know that carbonic acid is very likely to give up a proton and calcium hydroxide is very likely to accept a proton in this reaction, without classifying them as acids and bases. The bottom line, though, is that there are so many acid-base reactions that it's useful for them to have a category all by themselves. Simply knowing that you are starting with acids and bases tells you what will happen in the reaction without going through all that other stuff.

And even more things to do before you read even more science stuff

You'll need a few special chemicals for this one. The first is methylene blue, which is an acid-base indicator. You just need a tiny amount (maybe 10 drops) of this. The second is glucose (also known as dextrose anhydride), which you can get as a powder in small amounts from a science supply outlet. The third is potassium hydroxide, which you can get as a powder or solution. You'll also need a large glass container with a tight-fitting lid. To make it look all chemistry-like, people traditionally use a 500 ml Erlenmeyer flask with a rubber stopper (see Figure 4.10), but that's not absolutely necessary. Just make sure there's no danger of spilling what you end up with because it can irritate your skin.

Figure 4.10

Now, if I wanted to be mean, I'd give you the molarities of the solutions you need and have you use what you learned in Chapter 2 to make up the solutions. Because I'm a nice guy, though, here's what to do.

---

[11] How we do this is discussed in the first *Stop Faking It!* chemistry book. It involves the concept of electronegativity (a measure of affinity of atoms for electrons) and comparison of the numbers associated with electronegativity.

- Do the following preparations within ten or fifteen minutes of doing the activity. Leave things around for a day, and it won't work.
- Add about 8 grams of potassium hydroxide (KOH) to about 300 ml (that's milliliters) of distilled water in the flask and swirl it to mix thoroughly.
- Add about 10 grams of glucose (dextrose) to this solution and allow it to dissolve.
- Add 6 to 8 drops of methylene blue to the flask and swirl things around again.
- Let everything rest until the solution becomes clear.

Now for the fun part. Stopper the flask and shake up the solution inside. It should turn blue. Let it sit for a bit and it should clear up. Shake it again, and it should turn blue again. You can repeat quite a few times before there's no longer a color change.

And even more science stuff

First, the quick and dirty explanation of what happened. When you shake up the solution, you dissolve oxygen from the air in the container into the solution. The oxygen combines with the molecules in the solution, resulting in a change to the blue color. Then there's a spontaneous reaction in which oxygen is released back into the air, and the solution changes to clear.

Now, that's a pretty general explanation, so obviously we need more detail. There are a fair number of chemicals involved, so I'll just focus on the important ones. When you first mix things together, a couple of things happen. The first is listed below.

$$\text{glucose} + \text{hydroxide ions} \rightarrow \text{gluconic acid} + \text{water} + \text{electrons}$$

Using chemical formulas, this equation looks like

$$HOCH_2(CHOH)_4CHO\ (aq) + 3OH^-\ (aq) \rightarrow HOCH_2(CHOH)_4CO_2\ (aq) + 2H_2O\ (l) + 2e^-$$

Don't get flustered by how complicated the molecules are. We're just going to look at certain parts of the equation to understand what happens to those parts. The hydroxide ions in this equation come from the potassium hydroxide you added to the solution. Also, note that e^- is just the symbol for an electron. Let's look at just the glucose and the gluconic acid molecules. I'll write them to emphasize what's happening at the far right side of each.

$$\underset{\text{glucose}}{HOCH_2(CHOH)_4C\text{-}OH} \quad \text{and} \quad \underset{\text{gluconic acid}}{HOCH_2(CHOH)_4C\text{-}O_2}$$

The only difference between these two molecules is that glucose has an OH on the end and gluconic acid has an O_2 on the end. We know that OH^- ions have an overall charge of −1, so, because the entire molecule is neutral, we can think of the rest of the molecule as having a +1 charge. For gluconic acid, we need to look at the O_2. Oxygen atoms need two electrons to fill their outer shells (refer to the Periodic Table), so when oxygen combines with other molecules, they share two electrons and those shared electrons spend more time near the oxygen.[12] Because there are two oxygen atoms (O_2) instead of one, there are four electrons (two per oxygen atom) spending more time near the O_2. *In a sense,* then, the O_2 at the end of gluconic acid has a −4 charge. Because this molecule is neutral, that means that *in a sense,* the rest of the molecule has a +4 charge. I emphasize the words *in a sense* because we're not talking about an ionic bond, in which electrons have jumped from one atom to another. We're just focusing on where the electrons spend more of their time and assigning plus and minus charges based on this observation.[13] Anyway, what's happened is our glucose molecule, in becoming a gluconic acid molecule, has gone from a +1 "charge" to a +4 "charge." Because the molecule has become more positive, it's as if the molecule has *lost electrons* (losing negative electrons increases the positive charge). When a molecule loses electrons, we say it has undergone **oxidation**. So we would say that the glucose has been oxidized. In this case, the molecule actually added an oxygen molecule, and that's what historically led to this kind of reaction being called an oxidation, but oxidation can take place without oxygen being involved.

Now on to the next equation, and remember that we're just looking at what happens when you first mix the chemicals.

methylene blue (blue form) + glucose → methylene blue (clear form)
+ a bunch of other chemicals

Now let's just focus on what happens to the methylene blue and represent it as the molecular structure rather than just formulas. Again, don't get disturbed by the complexity of the molecule. We'll only focus on small parts of it.

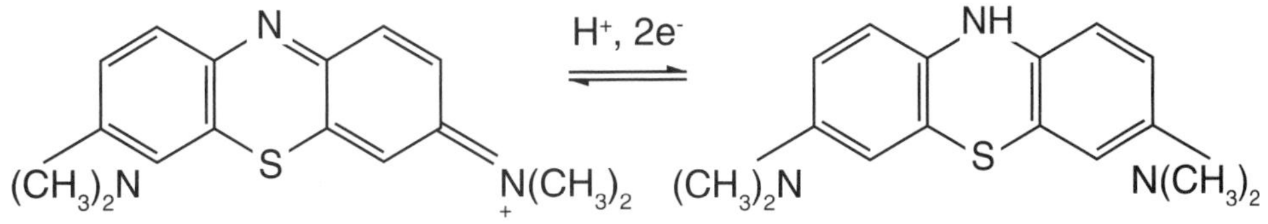

N
$(CH_3)_2N$ S $\overset{+}{N}(CH_3)_2$ $\underset{}{\overset{H^+,\ 2e^-}{\rightleftharpoons}}$ NH
$(CH_3)_2N$ S $N(CH_3)_2$

---

[12] Recall that this happens in water (H_2O) molecules. The shared electrons spend more time around the oxygen atom, making the molecule polar.

[13] The "charges" I'm talking about here are referred to in chemistry circles as **oxidation states**. Just thought I'd mention it in case you come across the term somewhere.

That two-way arrow simply means that this reaction is reversible—it can occur in either direction. In comparing the two molecules, you can see that the one on the left has an N at the top center, while the one on the right has an NH. Also, the plus sign on the lower right of the left molecule has disappeared on the right molecule. The symbols above the arrows indicate how this happened. We have added an H^+ ion and also added two electrons to the molecule on the left. These come from the glucose molecule in the word equation I wrote first. One of the added electrons makes the NH at the top neutral (remember, we added an H^+ ion), and the other gets rid of the plus sign at the lower right. Because we added two negatively charged electrons and only one positively charged H^+ ion, the molecule has gained one electron overall. When a molecule gains an electron, we refer to that as a **reduction**.

Topic: Redox Reactions
Go to: *www.scilinks.org*
Code: MCB013

The reaction I have just described is an example of a special class of chemical reactions known as **oxidation-reduction** reactions, or **redox** reactions for short. When an atom or molecule *loses* electrons in a reaction, we say the substance is oxidized. When an atom or molecule *gains* electrons in a reaction, we say the substance is reduced.[14] In a redox reaction, at least one atom or molecule gains electrons, and at least one atom or molecule loses electrons.

> What happens when a substance is reduced or oxidized can be confusing, but there's an easy way to remember it. Just think of a lion, and remember that **LEO** says **GER**. This stands for **L**oss of **E**lectrons is **O**xidation and **G**ain of **E**lectrons is **R**eduction. And no, I didn't come up with that. I'm not that clever.

As with our previous classifications of reactions, classifying reactions as oxidation-reduction is simply a tool to help our understanding. In that sense, there's nothing new at all in this chapter. Chemicals get together and do their thing. If we can place groups of reactions in separate classifications, however, we can better predict what might happen in other circumstances. That said, I should let you know that there are still many other classifications of reactions that chemists use. The three reactions in this chapter aren't the only ones, but they are major ones and illustrate the classification process. And if you think I've done something wrong by not including all the different types of reactions, I ask you to remember the purpose of this book, which is to help you develop a deep understanding of basic concepts. Don't think of this as a comprehensive resource for all your chemistry needs.

---

[14] As I stated earlier, the reason for the term oxidation-reduction has to do with the fact that these kinds of reactions were at first thought to involve only the combining of oxygen with other molecules, as happens in this reaction. But this class of reactions is much more general and doesn't necessarily include oxygen.

Chapter summary

- A combustion reaction is one in which oxygen combines with a hydrocarbon to produce carbon dioxide and water.
- A catalyst is a substance that speeds up or improves the efficiency of a chemical reaction. The catalyst itself is unchanged as a result of the reaction.
- Activation energy is the energy input required to get a chemical reaction to proceed in a certain direction. A catalyst effectively lowers the activation energy for a reaction.
- An acid is any chemical that, when dissolved in water, increases the concentration of hydronium ions. Alternatively, an acid is anything that donates protons in a reaction.
- A base is any chemical that, when dissolved in water, increases the concentration of hydroxide ions. Alternatively, a base is anything that accepts protons in a reaction.
- pH is a logarithmic scale that measures the concentration of hydronium ions in a solution. The scale ranges from 0 (highly acidic) to 14 (highly basic).
- There is a difference between the strength of an acid or base and the concentration of an acid or base. The strength describes how completely the acid or base donates or accepts protons. The concentration tells how much of an acid or base a solution contains.
- Combining acids and bases always results in the production of a salt and water.
- When an atom or molecule loses electrons during a reaction, we say it is oxidized. When an atom or molecule gains electrons during a reaction, we say it is reduced.
- Oxidation-reduction (redox) reactions involve at least one substance being oxidized and at least one substance being reduced. Keeping track of the oxidation and reduction is a useful way to analyze what happens in a chemical reaction.

Applications

1. Most of us use a catalyst reaction almost every day. Cars have **catalytic converters** that help remove harmful substances before they escape out the exhaust pipe. The reason engines produce harmful substances is that the combustion, or burning, in the engine is never complete. After the engine does its thing, the following harmful substances remain: nitrogen oxide,

nitric oxide, carbon monoxide, and unburned hydrocarbons.[15] To get rid of these bad substances, we'd like the following reactions to occur:

nitrogen oxide → nitrogen + oxygen

nitric oxide → nitrogen + oxygen

carbon monoxide + oxygen → carbon dioxide

hydrocarbons + oxygen → carbon dioxide + water

The balanced chemical equations for these reactions are below. Note that C_xH_y is the generic term for hydrocarbons that can contain any number of carbon and hydrogen atoms (hence the *x* and *y* subscripts rather than numbers). Because we don't have exact numbers for *x* and *y*, the last equation isn't balanced.

$$2NO_2\ (g) \rightarrow N_2\ (g) + 2O_2\ (g)$$
$$2NO\ (g) \rightarrow N_2\ (g) + O_2\ (g)$$
$$2CO\ (g) + O_2\ (g) \rightarrow 2CO_2\ (g)$$
$$C_xH_y\ (s) + O_2\ (g) \rightarrow CO_2\ (g) + H_2O\ (g)$$

Okay. These are the reactions we want to happen, and they do happen somewhat as the byproducts of the engine leave the exhaust. The problem is that they don't happen all that quickly, leaving bad stuff heading out into the atmosphere. That's why we use catalysts that lower the activation energies for these reactions and help them proceed at a rapid rate. A catalytic converter is inserted in the exhaust system of a car so that it receives the bad stuff after it's left the engine. The catalytic converter contains a ceramic core coated with very expensive metals—platinum, rhodium, and palladium—and has two sections. The first section deals with nitrogen oxide and nitric oxide. This first part has platinum and rhodium covering the ceramic. These metals rip nitrogen atoms off the nitrogen oxide and nitric oxide. The leftover oxygen atoms form oxygen molecules, and the nitrogen atoms held by the metals combine to form harmless nitrogen. Figure 4.11 illustrates the process.

Figure 4.11

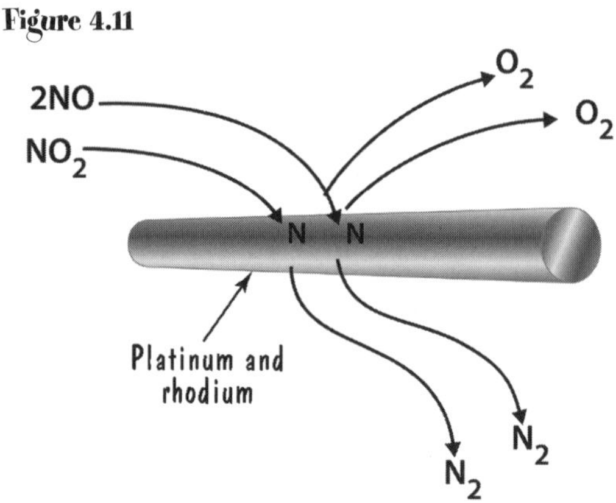

[15] Hydrocarbons are any molecules that contain carbon and hydrogen.

The second part of the catalytic converter deals with the carbon monoxide and the unburned hydrocarbons. Here the ceramic is coated with platinum and palladium. These metals attract carbon monoxide, hydrocarbons, and oxygen. By trapping these molecules, the metals make it easier for them to get together in a chemical reaction. Figure 4.12 illustrates this.

Figure 4.12

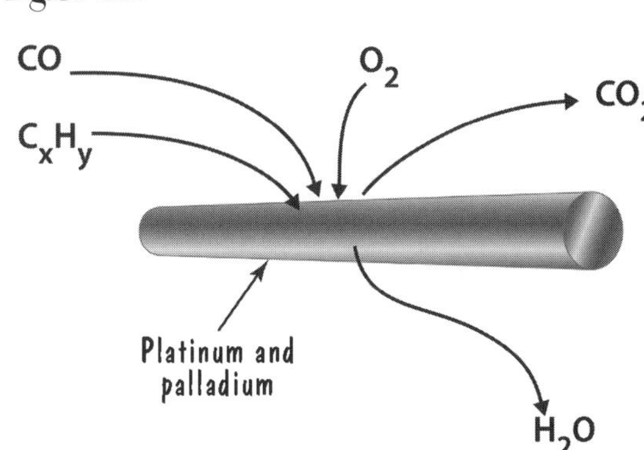

As with all catalyst reactions, the catalysts (the expensive metals) help make it easier for a chemical reaction to take place while not changing themselves in the process. The metals get the other atoms together, or rip molecules apart, while staying on the ceramic. This is a good thing because you want a catalytic converter to last a while.

2. The reactions that take place in the two parts of a catalytic converter are referred to as the *reduction* reaction and the *oxidation* reaction. Can you figure out which is which? Aside from the fact that carbon atoms latch onto oxygen atoms, which indicates an oxidation, you can figure this out by looking at the "charge" (which we call an oxidation state) on the nitrogen atoms and the carbon atoms in each reaction. First, consider the NO molecule. There is a double bond between the atoms, and the electrons in those bonds spend more time around the oxygen than they do around the nitrogen. This is because oxygen has a greater affinity for electrons than nitrogen. This means that we can think of the nitrogen in NO as having a slightly positive charge or oxidation state. As with our earlier examples of oxidation and reduction, it's not that the nitrogen is positively charged and the oxygen negatively charged, but in the molecule they sort of act that way. One product of the reaction is N_2. In this molecule, each nitrogen atom is bonded to another nitrogen atom, so the electrons in the bonds don't prefer one atom over another. Thus, in N_2, the "charge" on each nitrogen is zero. So, nitrogen has effectively *gained* electrons in the reaction (going from a plus charge to zero charge). This means that nitrogen is *reduced,* and the reactions that take place in the first part of a catalytic converter are known as *reduction reactions.* Note, though, that in labeling these as reduction reactions, we're only focusing on what happens to the nitrogen atoms. While the nitrogen is being reduced, the oxygen is being oxidized–you can't have a reduction of one substance without a corresponding oxidation of another substance.

Okay, what about the second part of the catalytic converter? Once again, we just have to look at one of the reactions, such as hydrocarbons adding to oxygen to produce carbon dioxide and water. Let's just look at the carbon atoms. In a hydrocarbon, the carbon atoms are bonded to one another or to hydrogen atoms. When carbon and hydrogen atoms get together, the different affinities for electrons dictate that the electrons will be more attracted to the carbon atoms, so the carbon atoms will have a negative "charge" in hydrocarbons. After the reaction, carbon atoms are bound to oxygen atoms (in CO_2). Again, affinities for electrons tell us what will happen. Electrons spend more time around the oxygen atoms, so the carbon atoms in CO_2 have a positive "charge." Carbon goes from a negative "charge" to a positive "charge."[16] This process involves a loss of electrons, so carbon is *oxidized* in this process. Therefore, the reactions that take place in the second part of the catalytic converter are called *oxidation reactions*.

3. Molecular formulas for acids and bases often are written so it's obvious that they are acids or bases. For acids, the hydrogen ion (proton) that the molecule readily loses is placed at the beginning of the formula rather than lumped with the rest of the hydrogen atoms in the molecule. For example, acetic acid (vinegar) is $HC_2H_3O_2$, with that first H (or sometimes more than one H) being the one that jumps off easily. Lactic acid is $HC_3H_5O_3$, and citric acid is $H_3C_6H_5O_7$. Two structures that easily accept protons, and thus make certain molecules bases, are NH and NH_2. For easy identification, many bases are written with these structures tacked onto the end of the molecular formula. For example, we write the bases dimethylamine, methylamine, and aniline as $(CH_3)_2NH$, CH_3NH_2, and $C_6H_5NH_2$.

4. Acids, bases, and acid-base reactions play a big part in the functioning of the human body. For one thing, your body is pretty sensitive to changes in pH. Anything too acidic or too basic will generally be a problem. Even though your stomach relies on acids to break down foods, too much acid in your stomach can hurt. To counteract this, you take a base called an antacid (duh!). Because bases snarf up hydronium ions, antacids make your stomach less acidic (higher pH). Of course, you have to be careful about what bases you put in your stomach. Ammonia is a pretty strong household base, but it's much too strong to put in your body. When my father had an upset stomach, he always swallowed baking soda and water—a base that is quite a bit stronger than your usual antacid. That usually solved his problem quickly but violently. I don't recommend it!

---

[16] Throughout this application, I have put the word *charge* in quotation marks. To be absolutely correct, I should use the term *oxidation state*. I just want to say once again that these atoms and molecules carry a charge only *in a sense* because while the atoms and molecules are connected, the shared electrons spend more time around one than the other.

5. Sometimes chemical equations are difficult to balance just by trying to balance the number of each kind of atom on both sides of the equation. If the equation is an oxidation-reduction reaction, there's a surefire method for balancing the equation. I won't give a detailed example, but I can tell you that the method involves looking at the oxidation states (that "charge" that atoms and molecules have, sort of, when combined) of the atoms and molecules and balancing the electrons lost with the electrons gained. It's a nifty trick that works every time, so if you find yourself with chemical equations that you just can't balance by inspection, you might want to look up the method and learn it.

Electro-Luminescence

The title of this chapter is a compact way of saying that I'm going to cover two separate branches of chemistry. The first is electrochemistry and the second is the interaction of light with matter. I suppose I could spend an entire chapter on each of these areas, but that would work against the purpose of these books. I want to increase your understanding so that you can tackle regular textbooks, not create a new textbook.

Things to do before you read the science stuff

The first thing I'm going to have you do is a repeat of an activity in the first *Stop Faking It!* book on chemistry, so if you've already done it, rely on that great memory of yours. You need a flashlight bulb, a 1.5-volt battery, three wires about 30 centimeters in length each (stripped at the ends if they're insulated), masking tape, a cup of water, and table salt. You can substitute a threaded bulb and base (get this at an electronics store and make sure its rating is around 1.5 to 3 volts) and wires with alligator clips on the end to make the whole thing a bit easier. Set everything up as shown in Figure 5.1. No salt is involved yet, and make sure the wire ends in the water don't touch each other.

Figure 5.1

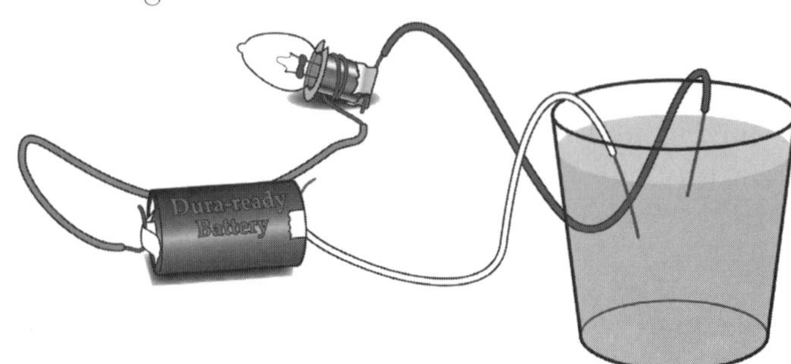

If you've done everything correctly, nothing should happen. Now add a whole bunch of salt to the water and stir it up. With everything in place as in Figure 5.1, the lightbulb should now light. If not, check to make sure all your connections are secure and that the battery isn't dead.

Figure 5.2

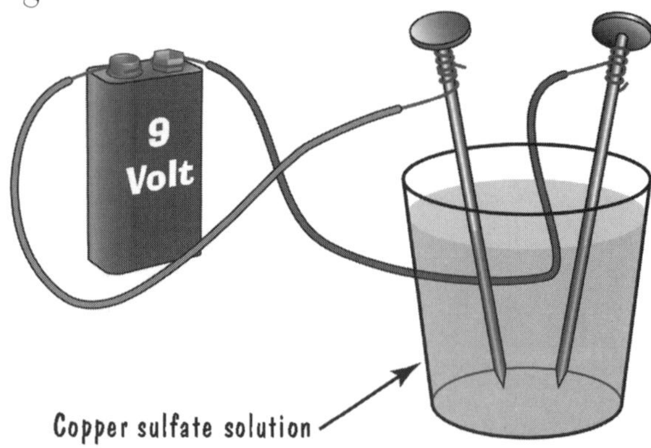

Keep the battery,[1] wires, masking tape, and cup handy. Add to this list a couple of nails and a small amount (about a spoonful) of copper sulfate crystals (a special chemical—check out science supply stores). You can keep the light bulb in the circuit if you want, but it's not necessary. Strip more insulation off each of your wires so you can wrap a fair amount of this bare wire around the nails. Dissolve the copper sulfate crystals in a cup of water (stir until dissolved) and then set things up as in Figure 5.2.[2]

---

[1] What you're about to do will go a lot faster if you use a 9-volt battery instead of a 1.5-volt battery. The former also has the advantage that alligator clips hook easily on its terminals. Of course, if you're patient, then a 1.5-volt battery will do just fine.

[2] This will work better with distilled (not de-ionized) water, but that's not absolutely necessary.

Make sure the nails in the solution do not touch. When setting this up, connect all the components *before* placing the nails in the solution.

Wait a while, at least five or ten minutes. After this time, pull the nails out of the solution and notice any change. There should be a change. The longer you keep the nails in the solution, the greater the change.

One final electrical thing to do is create your own battery. This takes patience, but stick with it. It's rewarding once things work. Here's what you need:

- three galvanized nails (galvanized is important)
- three short (3–4 cm) strips of copper wire (thicker is better—about 16–18 gauge)
- four wires with insulation stripped from the ends (alligator clips are a big plus here)
- an LED (light-emitting diode—check RadioShack or other electronics store)[3]
- three cups or empty 35 mm film canisters with lids (You can get them free at most photo finishing places—the folks at Wally World [Walmart] are especially kind to teachers.)
- vinegar (about a cup)

Figure 5.3 shows how to set up the activity using film canisters. The lids on the film canisters are nice for securing the nails and copper wires so they don't

Figure 5.3

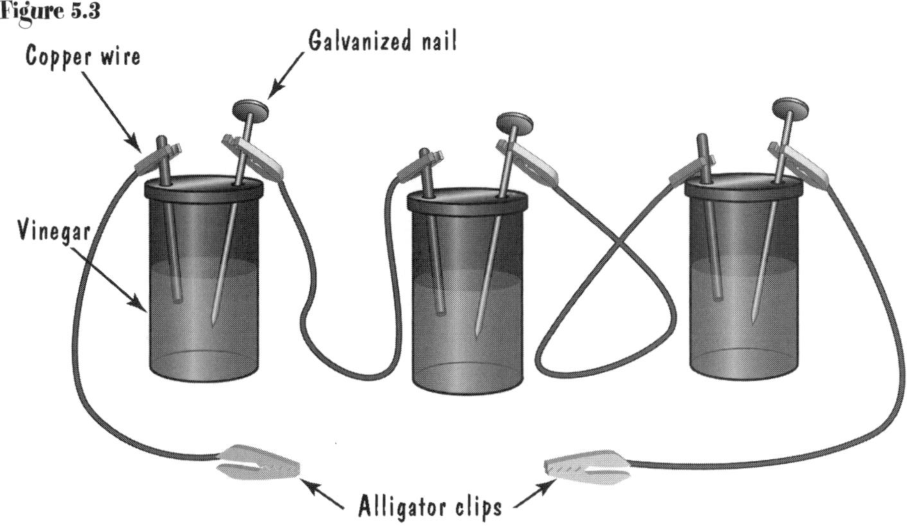

[3] For large quantities of LEDs, snoop around the internet for low prices. I was able to find them cheapest at *www.ledsupply.com,* but there's no guarantee that this site will be up and running by the time this book is in print.

touch. Make sure you put enough vinegar in each canister so both the nail and the copper wire are submerged.

Before you hook up the LED, you need to know which connection is positive and which is negative. The shortest wire leading from the LED is the negative connection, and it's also the wire that's closest to the flat side of the plastic part of the LED. Once you have the positive-negative thing figured out, connect the free wire leading from the copper wire to the positive lead on the LED (the long wire) and connect the free wire leading from the zinc-covered nail to the negative lead on the LED (the short wire). You should see the LED light up. If not, check all the connections and try again. If you still don't get a lit bulb, keep connecting and reconnecting wires and make sure the nails and the copper are scraped clean where they connect to the wires or alligator clips. If you just can't get it to work, hook your LED up to the 1.5-volt battery (positive terminal of battery to long wire on the LED and negative terminal of battery to short wire on the LED) to make sure the LED is working. If so, then it's back to fiddling around with the connections. Before giving up completely, use the tried-and-true method of having a child work on it. They're better at this than we are.

The science stuff

Most people associate the word *electricity* with wires and the motion of electrons through those wires. Makes sense, because that's the kind of electricity we encounter on a day-to-day basis. In the previous section, though, all of your electrical circuits involved liquids—saltwater, copper sulfate dissolved in water, and vinegar. In each case, ions (charged atoms or molecules) in the liquids moved around instead of electrons. An electric current is defined as any movement of charges, not just the movement of electrons. Because we're dealing with ions in addition to electrons, we call the process **electrochemistry**.

Figure 5.4

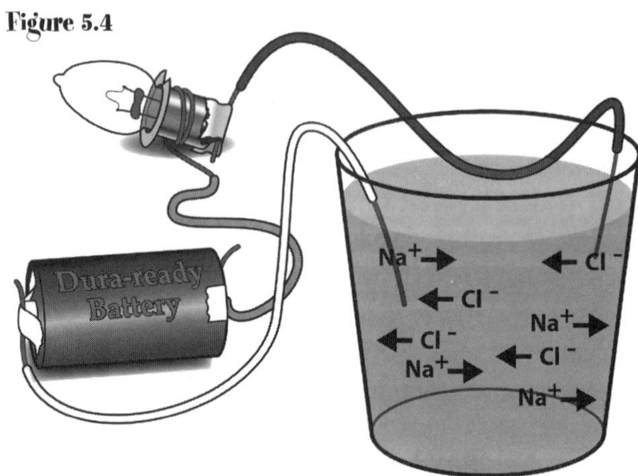

We've discussed before how salt (NaCl) separates into positive sodium ions (Na^+) and negative chloride ions (Cl^-) when you put it in water. When you hook up a battery to wires submerged in saltwater, the positive sodium ions are attracted to the negative terminal of the battery, and the negative chloride ions are attracted to the positive terminal of the battery. This movement of positive and negative ions in the water constitutes an electric current, and you have a complete circuit that lights the lightbulb. Check out Figure 5.4.

Switching to copper sulfate ($CuSO_4$) solution, you have a similar situation. When you dissolve copper sulfate crystals in water, the water molecules separate them into positive copper ions (Cu^{2+}) and negative sulfate ions (SO_4^{2-}). Even though the water molecules tend to isolate these ions, the ions are still free to move toward things that have the opposite charge. So, the Cu^{2+} ions gather around the wire that's connected to the negative terminal of the battery, and the SO_4^{2-} ions gather around the wire that's connected to the positive terminal of the battery. See Figure 5.5.

Figure 5.5

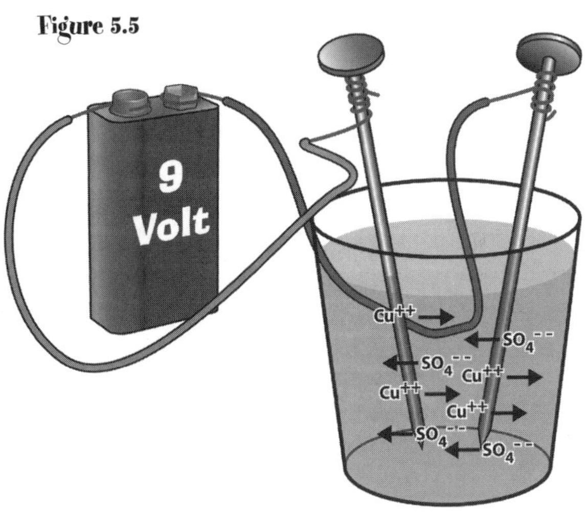

The interesting thing is what happens at the negative terminal. Cu^{2+} ions grab onto free electrons and become regular copper. Whatever metal you have at the negative terminal becomes coated with copper.[4] And yes, that sludge that forms around the negative terminal is also copper. See Figure 5.6.

Figure 5.6

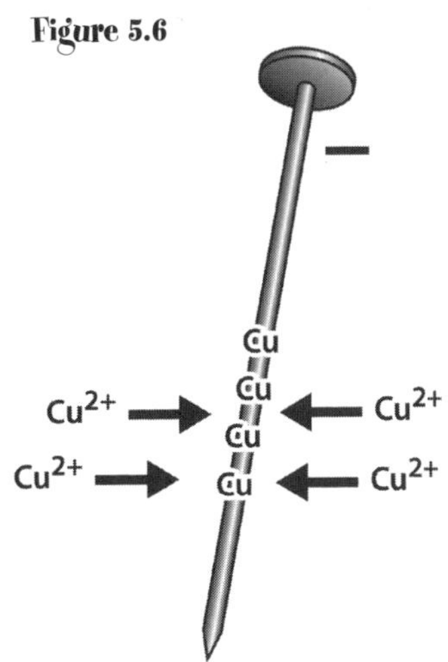

The official name for this process is **electroplating**. Wonder no longer how people can create a ring plated with gold or a piece of coated silverware or a piece of silver-plated jewelry. It's all about creating ions of the plating material and using electric attraction to seduce those ions from one place to another. Of course, this doesn't always have to take place in a liquid. Often it's done within a vacuum (not much air), with molecules of one substance getting charged up and then being attracted to an object that has the opposite charge.

[4] If you ignored my directions and put the nails in the solution before the rest of the circuit was hooked up, you probably ended up with both nails being coated with copper. This is because simply placing a nail in copper sulfate solution will result in some copper ions attaching to the nail. If you don't submerge the nails until the circuit is ready, then copper ions are immediately repelled from the positive terminal when you place it in the water. Then few copper ions will attach to that terminal.

The vacuum process is actually much more efficient than the liquid process because there are fewer other molecules (such as deposited minerals in the liquid) to get in the way of the transfer of metal from one place to another.

The final thing you did in the previous section was make a battery. One film canister with vinegar isn't sufficient to light the LED, which is why I had you connect three of them together. One alone will produce enough voltage (about 1 volt) to light the bulb, but it won't produce enough electric current to light the bulb.[5] Three of these batteries together do the trick.

Now, to understand why our battery causes electrons to move in the outer circuit (the wires and the bulb), we have to look at the chemical reactions taking place with the zinc (this is the metal coating on galvanized nails), copper, and vinegar. Each metal reacts with the vinegar, which is acetic acid dissolved in water. Knowing what we know about what happens to acids in water, we can figure out that acetic acid ($HC_2H_3O_2$) will separate into ions, giving up a proton (a hydrogen nucleus). That free proton readily combines with water to form a hydronium ion (H_3O^+), leaving a negatively charged ion that we call acetate ($C_2H_3O_2^-$). Now we can look at what happens when these ions come in contact with the zinc that covers the galvanized nail.

zinc + vinegar → ???

zinc + hydronium ions + acetate ions → ???

In symbols, this is

$$Zn\ (s) + H_3O^+\ (aq) + C_2H_3O_2^-\ (aq) \rightarrow ???$$

So what goes on the right-hand side of this equation? Well, the extra H^+ in the hydronium ion isn't held to that ion strongly, so it can be fickle and hook up with other atoms or ions. Enter zinc, which would love to get rid of a couple of electrons to get a filled outer shell. The loosely held zinc electrons leave the zinc atom and combine with the H^+ from the hydronium ions. The remaining positively charged zinc ions remain in solution, as do the acetate ions. This leads to the following equation.

[5] I'm not going to get into electric circuits here, but I can maybe help just a bit with why one canister doesn't do the trick, but three canisters do. All batteries, including your vinegar batteries, have what is known as *internal resistance*. This internal resistance impedes the flow of electric current. The less internal resistance a battery has, the more current it can deliver to a device such as an LED. Your vinegar battery has a relatively large internal resistance, so even though one or two canisters have enough voltage to light the LED, they can't produce enough current to light it. You need three of them. A regular 1.5-volt battery has a small internal resistance, so just one will light the LED.

$$\text{zinc + hydronium ions} \rightarrow \text{zinc ions + hydrogen gas + water}$$

$$Zn\ (s) + 2H_3O^+\ (aq) \rightarrow Zn^{2+}\ (aq) + H_2\ (g) + 2H_2O\ (l)$$

As far as our battery is concerned, the only thing to focus on is the fact that neutral zinc becomes a positively charged zinc ion while giving up a couple of electrons. That's easy to write as what's known as a **half-reaction**, and it looks like this:

$$Zn \rightarrow Zn^{2+} + 2e^-$$

where e^- represents an electron.

At the copper wire, a similar reaction takes place. In fact, all you have to do is replace Zn (zinc) with Cu (copper) in the previous equations, and you have what happens at the copper wire. Here's the chemical equation:

$$Cu\ (s) + 2H_3O^+\ (aq) \rightarrow Cu^{2+}\ (aq) + H_2\ (g) + 2H_2O\ (l)$$

And just focusing on the copper, we have

$$Cu \rightarrow Cu^{2+} + 2e^-$$

So, we're producing electrons at the zinc-covered nail and we're producing electrons at the copper wire. How in the world does that make a battery? Well, let's hook up an outside circuit to this setup, as in Figure 5.7.

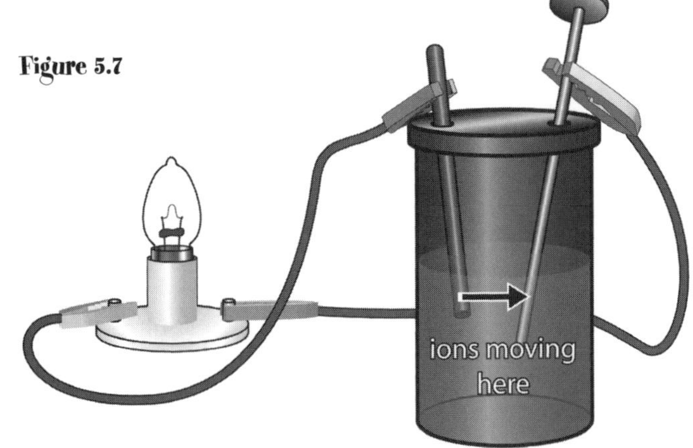

Figure 5.7

Now we have a complete circuit. Electrons can carry electric current in the wire, and ions (zinc and acetate) can carry electric current in the liquid. With everything connected, there is communication between what's happening at the nail and what's happening at the copper wire. Any change at one place will transmit electrically to the other place. And here is where, as is often the case in chemistry, we use energy considerations to figure out what will happen. It turns out that the reaction Zn → Zn^{2+} + $2e^-$ is much more energetically favorable than the reaction Cu → Cu^{2+} + $2e^-$. Both reactions produce electrons, but the reaction with the zinc is stronger—it's like you have a push on the electrons from the nail and a push on the electrons from the copper, but the push from the nail is stronger. The push from the nail wins out, and in fact causes the reaction at the copper to proceed in the reverse direction. Instead of Cu → Cu^{2+} + $2e^-$, what happens is Cu^{2+} + $2e^-$ → Cu. See Figure 5.8. It's kind of like two downhill slopes competing for the direction a ball will roll. The slope leading from the nail is steeper, so the ball (or in this case, electrons in the outer circuit) rolls toward the copper. And when you push electrons from one place to another, you have a battery.

Figure 5.8

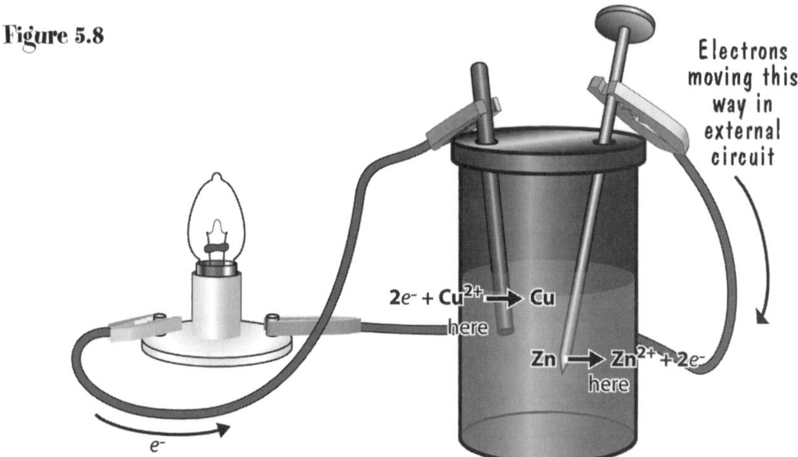

Most batteries work on this same principle. You have two elements (carbon-zinc, nickel-cadmium, and so on) connected by an electrolyte (a substance, usually a liquid, that contains ions that can move freely). There's one point of potential confusion when dealing with chemical batteries. For example, in our vinegar battery, chemists refer to the zinc terminal as being the **cathode**, or positive terminal, and the copper terminal as the **anode**, or negative terminal. These are proper labels when considering what happens to the ions in solution that connect the terminals, but when considering the external circuit (the wires and the bulb), you would properly consider the zinc terminal to be the anode (negative) and the copper terminal to be the cathode (positive) This is because electrons flow in the external circuit *from* the zinc terminal *to* the copper terminal. Figure 5.9 explains it all.

Figure 5.9

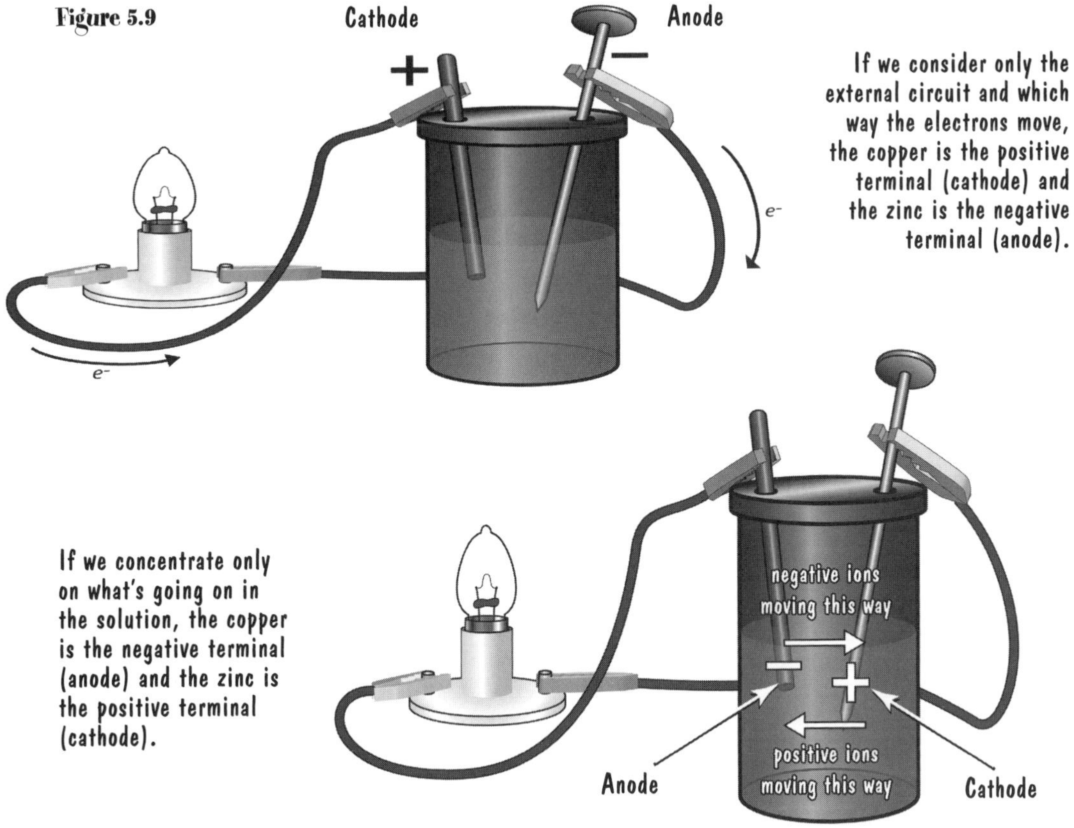

Cathode

Anode

+

−

e^-

e^-

If we consider only the external circuit and which way the electrons move, the copper is the positive terminal (cathode) and the zinc is the negative terminal (anode).

negative ions moving this way

positive ions moving this way

−

+

Anode

Cathode

If we concentrate only on what's going on in the solution, the copper is the negative terminal (anode) and the zinc is the positive terminal (cathode).

More things to do before you read more science stuff

Time to move on from electrochemistry to how light interacts with matter. I'm going to use acid-base indicators for this purpose, but first I'll start with a couple of simple questions. What makes any object the color it is? Yes, the object reflects certain colors of light, but what is going on with the atoms and molecules of that object to make it reflect only certain colors? How can you change the color of an object? Sure, you can dye a shirt a different color, but what's going on with the atoms and molecules of the shirt to make it change color? Answers in the next section, but try to construct your own answers before reading mine.

Topic: Light and Color
Go to: *www.scilinks.org*
Code: MCB014

Next, you will need one or more of the following: phenolphthalein solution (less than an ounce of 1% solution), bromothymol blue solution (about an ounce of 1% solution is enough, and this can be diluted with water in a 1 to 4 ratio and it will work fine), or cabbage juice (just boil a small amount of red cabbage for a few minutes in a cup of water, remove the cabbage, and use the liquid that remains). You will also need sodium hydroxide solution (0.1M to 0.5M)[6], vinegar, and two pipettes (plastic or glass—see Figure 5.10) or eye droppers.

Figure 5.10

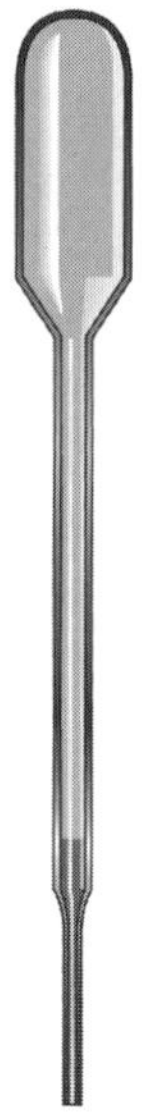

> **CAUTION:** Sodium hydroxide in any concentration is a bit caustic and definitely a skin irritant. Wear goggles and gloves.

For what follows, I'll assume you're using phenolphthalein. The procedure works basically the same way for the other two solutions. Pour a small amount of phenolphthalein solution into a clear cup. Add a bit of water. Use one of your pipettes or eye droppers to add sodium hydroxide to the solution, one drop at a time. You should notice a color change to pink that fades to clear. Keep adding sodium hydroxide until the solution remains pink. Once you get a permanent change in color, begin putting vinegar in the solution one drop at a time. Keep doing this until the color of the solution changes back to clear. You can keep alternating sodium hydroxide and vinegar through many color changes.

> **Using bromothymol blue (BTB) or cabbage juice.** If you use these liquids instead of, or in addition to, phenolphthalein, expect to see two or more color changes. Also, with BTB you should add vinegar to start and then use sodium hydroxide to reverse the color changes.

More science stuff

The simple answer to why objects are the color they are is that they reflect certain colors of light and absorb others when white light shines on them. But how do the different colors of light "know" whether they're supposed to be absorbed or reflected? The answer is that reflection of light is more complicated than many people think. Reflected light doesn't just bounce off objects like a ball bouncing off a wall. Reflected light is actually absorbed by the molecules in the object and then radiated back out. The molecules in the object are an integral part of the process, so it should be no surprise that the *structure* of those molecules determines what colors of light are absorbed and what colors are reflected. See Figure 5.11.

[6] Recall that 0.5 M refers to the molarity of the solution, so 0.5 M means you have 0.5 moles per liter of solution. You will need this info when ordering the chemical. Often sodium hydroxide comes in tablet form. Follow the product instructions for creating the proper solution, and do be careful. Solid sodium hydroxide might look harmless, but it is caustic.

As with chemical reactions in general, the interaction of light with molecules is really the interaction of light with the *electrons* in those molecules. If you change the structure of a molecule, such as by adding or removing certain atoms or changing how the atoms connect, then you can possibly change the colors absorbed and reflected because you are changing where the electrons in the atoms reside.[7]

Figure 5.11

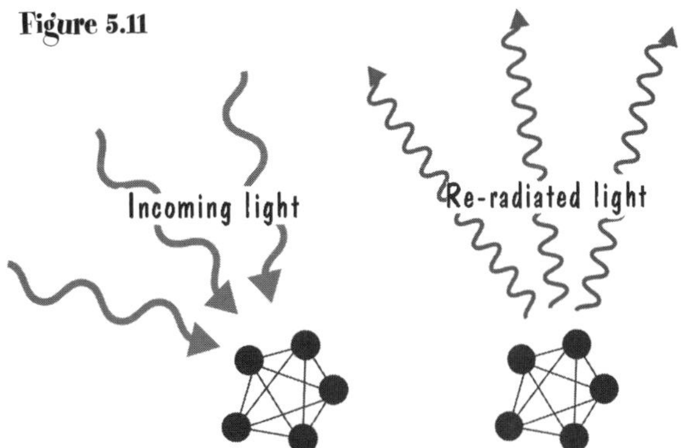

The molecule absorbs the light, then re-radiates none, some, or all of it.

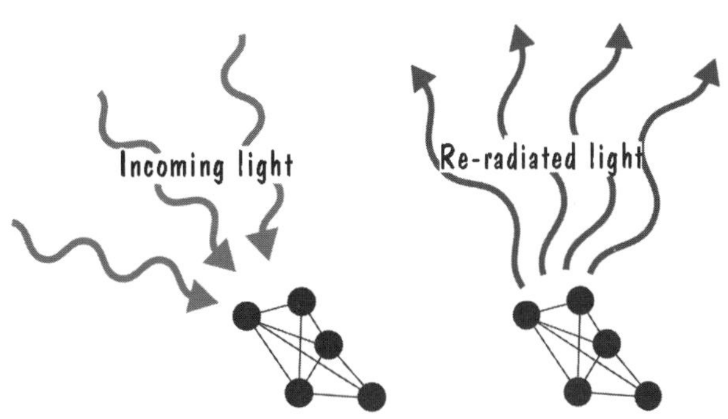

If you change the molecular structure, you can change the colors of light the molecule re-radiates.

Now let's turn our attention to acid-base indicators, and phenolphthalein in particular. If you've taken a chemistry course in either high school or college, you have probably used phenolphthalein. It's used to indicate when a solution changes from a pH of below 8.2 to a pH of above 10.0. If the solution in which you have phenolphthalein is acidic or slightly basic, the phenolphthalein is clear. If the solution in which you have phenolphthalein is basic, with a pH greater than 10.0, the phenolphthalein is pink.[8] Ah, but *why* does the phenolphthalein change colors? Must have something to do with change in the molecular structure. Phenolphthalein is actually a weak acid, meaning that it tends to be a proton donor[9] in chemical reactions. When phenolphthalein is in an acidic or slightly

---

[7] When you change the connections between atoms, you change the distribution of electron energy levels within the atoms, thus changing the "allowed" energies of the electrons. This changes the energy differences between energy levels, which determine the colors of light emitted by an atom. For a review of this process, refer back to Chapter 1.

[8] In really strong, concentrated acids, phenolphthalein is red, and in really strong, concentrated bases, phenolphthalein is again clear. We can safely ignore those situations, because I'm not going to have you mess around with acids and bases that are that strong and concentrated. Not a fan of lawsuits.

[9] Refer to the previous chapter, where I define acids and bases. Acids are proton donors and bases are proton accepters.

basic solution, the molecule looks like Figure 5.12 and is clear in color.[10] And please don't be intimidated by how complex this molecule is. We're only going to focus on specific parts of the molecule.

Figure 5.12

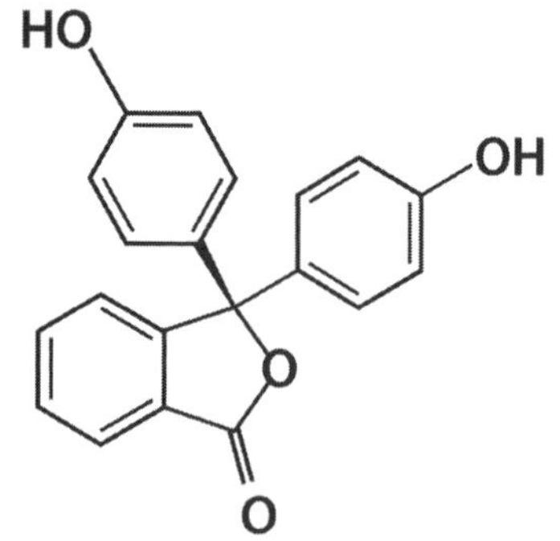

Notice the two OH combinations that are on one side of the molecule. The bond between the oxygen and hydrogen atoms here is not all that strong, so if some other molecule comes along to entice the H^+ ion to leave this combination, it doesn't take much convincing. Well, sodium hydroxide breaks up into Na^+ and OH^- in solution. The free OH^- ions are just the thing to lure the two H^+ ions away from the phenolphthalein molecule. After the protons leave, and after a bit of reorganization, the phenolphthalein now looks like the drawing in Figure 5.13. This new structure re-radiates the color pink.

Figure 5.13

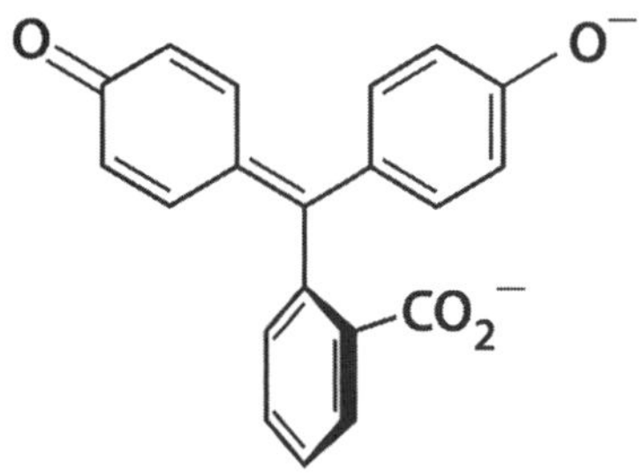

Let's review the concepts I just explained. Whenever a molecule changes shape or structure, as happens in a chemical reaction, the electron energy levels in the atoms contained in the molecules change. Because light is produced when electrons jump from a higher energy level to a lower energy level, and the energy of the light produced is equal to the difference in energy between the two energy levels, a change in energy levels can possibly change the color emitted in the electron jumps. I used acid-base indicators as an example, but I could have used any chemical reaction in which there is a color change. Chemical reactions involve rearrangement of atoms and new structures, and this often leads to changes in re-radiated light. In fact, a color change is one of the first things students learn to look for as evidence that a chemical reaction has taken place. The reason I used acid-base indicators as an example is that it gives us an opportunity to review acids and bases, and you learned that the indicators themselves are either acids or bases.

Topic: Molecular Shapes
Go to: *www.scilinks.org*
Code: MCB015

Bromothymol blue and cabbage juice work in much the same way as phenolphthalein. As the acidity of the solution they're in changes, their molecular structure changes as well. These different structures, three kinds in each case, re-radiate different colors of light. Of course, there are many more kinds of acid-base indicators, and each one is either a weak, low-concentration acid or a weak, low-concentration base. That's why they interact with the acids and bases

[10] Those hexagons in the phenolphthalein molecule might not be familiar to you. They're "rings" of carbon atoms called *benzene rings,* with a carbon atom at each corner. Such rings are common enough in chemistry that you'll see this shorthand notation a lot.

in various solutions. What makes a substance a good acid-base indicator is its ability to change color in a small range of pH values.

One last thing in this section. Why are acid-base indicators *weak* and in *low concentrations*? Wouldn't a strong, concentrated acid or base react even better with the acids and bases in the solution you're dealing with? Yes, it would, and that would be a problem. You want your indicator to indicate through a color change what the pH is of *other* solutions. If your indicator is strong and concentrated, then the pH of the indicator governs the pH of the entire solution.

Even more things to do before you read even more science stuff

Most of the activities I'll have you do in this section represent fairly common experiences, so if you have a good memory for these experiences, you don't absolutely have to get the things I ask. These are cool activities, though, so you might not want to pass up a chance for playtime. First, get a few glow-sticks and a few glow-in-the-dark stickers. Both can be found at your local dollar store. Follow the instructions for using these. How do the instructions differ? Which requires an external source of light? How long does each of these glow? Which is rechargeable?

If you're a baby boomer pack rat, pull out your old "day-glo" posters and your "black" light. If you have no such relic, head to your nearest laser tag facility. This is day-glo heaven. Notice that black lights (which emit primarily ultraviolet light) bring out all sorts of interesting colors, on a poster or your clothes, that weren't there in normal incandescent light or sunshine. What created the new colors and the extra brightness? Was it a change in molecular structure?

Topic: Ultraviolet Light
Go to: *www.scilinks.org*
Code: MCB016

Even more science stuff

Let's start with the last thing I asked you to do (look at things that glow under black light) because that's actually the easiest to understand. Recall that atoms emit light by electrons jumping from a higher energy level to a lower energy level and can absorb light with the result of their electrons jumping from a lower energy level to a higher energy level.[11] This is also true of the electrons in molecules. The only main difference is that the electron energy levels in molecules tend to be a bit more complicated than those in single atoms.[12] The principle is the same.

[11] Check out the brief review of this in Chapter 1 of this book or a fuller explanation in Chapter 2 of the first chemistry book in this series.

[12] Keep in mind that when atoms get together to form molecules, that alters what the electrons are doing. Hybrid orbitals form between the separate atoms, and this leads to different energy levels than you would expect from single atoms.

Electrons in molecules can absorb energy, in the form of light or some other source, and move to higher energy levels. Then those electrons can jump down to lower energy levels, with the emission of energy that is sometimes visible light. When you expose certain molecules to ultraviolet light, which is more energetic than visible light, you can excite the electrons in those molecules to energy levels they don't ordinarily attain (with exposure to everyday visible light, that is). Once the electrons reach these high energy levels, you might expect them to just jump back down to lower levels, emitting ultraviolet light, but something a bit different happens. The molecules and the electrons in them lose energy as the molecules go from a situation in which they're vibrating to a situation in which they're not vibrating as much. See Figure 5.14.

Once they've gone through this "vibrational relaxation," the electrons in the molecules now jump down to a lower energy state and emit light. See Figure 5.15.

These new electron transitions often are in the visible light range and also are highly efficient, resulting in bright colors. Because the energy levels available to electrons in molecules act as a fingerprint of the molecules, the colors you see are unique to particular kinds of molecules. To summarize, you shine ultraviolet light on something, causing its electrons to jump to higher energy levels. After the molecules containing those electrons lose vibrational energy, those electrons then jump back down to lower energy levels, emitting visible light. This leads to way-

Figure 5.14

Molecular energy levels

Electron jumps to a higher energy level.

Molecule loses energy through "vibrational relaxation."

Molecular energy levels

Incoming ultraviolet light

Molecular energy levels

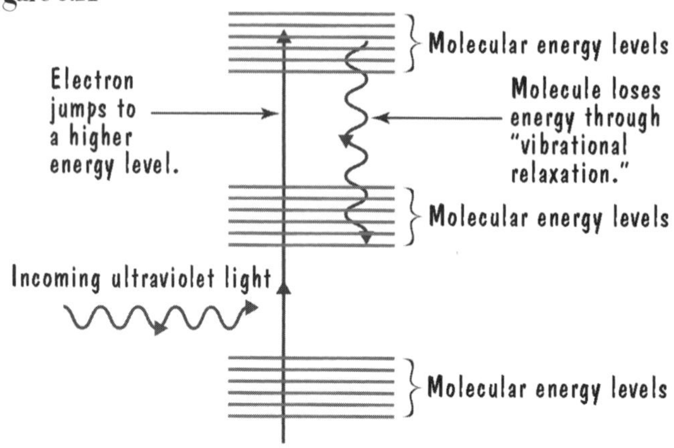

Figure 5.15

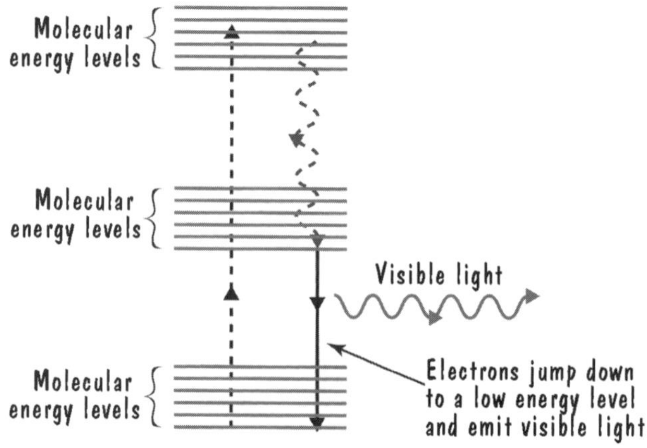

The energy jump here is smaller than the energy jump from the input of ultraviolet light shown in Fig. 5.14. This smaller energy transition results in visible rather than ultraviolet light.

cool day-glo effects and also helps identify elements (see the Applications section, p. 105). There's a special name for this effect—**fluorescence**.

When you stop shining ultraviolet light on a day-glo poster, the poster stops glowing. Not so when you shine visible light on glow-in-the-dark stickers or glow-in-the-dark paint. These things keep emitting light for a long time. Clearly, this is something different from fluorescence. Instead of undergoing "vibrational relaxation" as in fluorescence, the electrons in the molecules undergo a transition to special energy levels in which they're trapped. Transitions from these special energy levels to lower energy levels, with the emission of visible light, are actually "forbidden," meaning they shouldn't happen. But as often happens in the world of quantum mechanics, things that are forbidden actually do happen. I won't go into the math of quantum mechanics that describes all this (As Stuart[13] would say in his demonic voice, "It's ugly!"), but I'll tell you that it has to do with the math telling us that it's impossible for atoms to go from one set of quantum numbers to another set of quantum numbers in a direct transition. Anyway, these so-called forbidden transitions have a low probability of happening. (By now you should realize that probabilities are at the heart of quantum mechanics.) This means that those energy transitions, with the emission of visible light, don't happen very often. The result is that the emission of visible light takes a long time as the electrons stuck in those special energy levels eventually move down to lower energy levels, meaning objects glow for a long time after they've been exposed to the initial energy that excited the electrons in the first place. This process has a special name—**phosphorescence**. Glow-in-the-dark objects undergo phosphorescence.

On to glow sticks, which, once you snap them, glow all by themselves for hours. When you snap a glow stick, you break a glass tube and mix different chemicals. Inside the glass tube is hydrogen peroxide, the stuff you use to clean wounds. In the plastic tube, separate from the hydrogen peroxide, is a chemical called **cyalume** along with a fluorescent dye.[14] The cyalume and hydrogen peroxide mix and produce a molecule known as phenol (active ingredient in a popular throat spray) and another known as peroxyacid ester. The peroxyacid ester spontaneously transforms into carbon dioxide while giving off energy. The fluorescent dye then absorbs this energy and gives off the light you see. This process, shown in Figure 5.16 (p. 104), continues as long as there is hydrogen peroxide and cyalume left in the tube. This might seem like a complicated process, but conceptually it's simple. Chemical reactions produce energy, and this energy causes a dye to undergo fluorescence.

---

[13] Someone familiar with *MADtv* can tell you about this obscure reference.

[14] You can cause this dye to glow before you ever snap the stick by shining ultraviolet light on the stick.

Figure 5.16

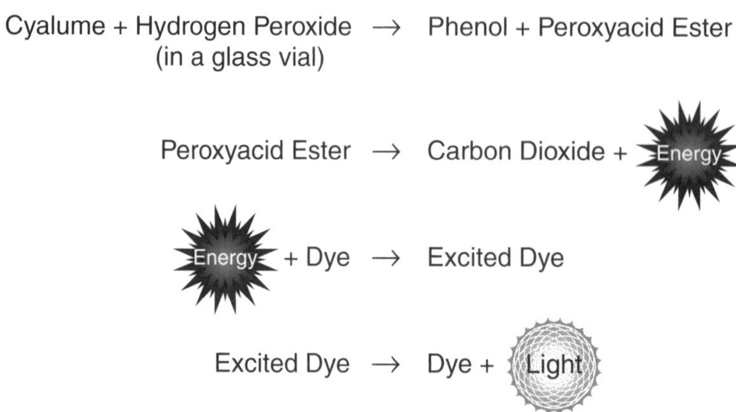

I know that Figure 5.16 looks a bit complicated. Just think of it this way. The top two chemical reactions result in excess energy. That energy then acts like the ultraviolet light in our day-glo example, exciting the electrons in the dye to higher energy levels (that's the third equation). Then, after undergoing vibrational relaxation, the electrons in the dye jump down to a lower energy level and emit the light you see.

To summarize this section, light interacts with matter by interacting with the electrons in atoms. It's all about electrons being excited to higher energy levels and then dropping down to lower energy levels with the emission of light. This is true even with reflected light, which is really the absorption and re-emission of incoming light. You can alter the light that a substance emits by changing molecular structure (which changes the available energy levels) or by hitting atoms or molecules with energy that puts electrons in energy levels in which they don't normally reside when hit with visible light.

Chapter summary

- Liquids containing ions, referred to as electrolytes, can conduct electric current. Electrochemistry is the study of electric current by ions and of the associated chemical reactions.
- The polar nature of water molecules separates many ionic compounds into ions.
- The flow of ions in an electrolyte can be used to electroplate many metals.
- Chemical reactions between various substances and electrolytes can serve as a battery, causing electrons to flow in an external circuit.
- Two half-reactions take place in batteries, with the stronger reaction driving the direction of flow of electrons in an external circuit.
- Objects and substances absorb some colors of light and reflect others. Changes in the molecular structure of substances often change the colors absorbed and the colors reflected.

- Acid-base indicators are either weak acids or weak bases. Because they interact with stronger acids and bases and change color in a limited pH range, they are useful as pH indicators.
- Fluorescence is the process in which molecules absorb ultraviolet light or absorb energy in some other way and quickly emit visible light.
- Phosphorescence is the process in which molecules absorb visible or ultraviolet light and then emit visible light over a long period of time.

Applications

1. Most applications of electrochemistry involve redox reactions, which we went over in the previous chapter. The reactions in a battery are redox reactions. Another common application is the corrosion of metals, as with the rusting of iron. I'm not going to provide all the equations here that go into the rusting of iron because the process is relatively complicated. I do encourage you, though, to look up rusting on the internet. Although there are quite a few equations, each individual equation is relatively straightforward. There are gains and losses of electrons, plus the role of an electrolyte (in this case, water or saltwater) in helping the transfer of electrons. In this way, rusting is not so different from the operation of the battery you created in this chapter.
2. The following website gives you a chance to see what fluorescence in minerals looks like without having to buy an ultraviolet light. Simply move your cursor over the samples to see what they look like under UV light. *http://mineral.galleries.com/minerals/property/fluoresc.htm*.[15]

   Fluorescence isn't the only light-related way to identify rocks and minerals. If you heat some minerals, that can cause electrons trapped in high energy levels to jump down to lower energy levels and emit light, in a process known as **thermoluminescence**. As with all light emitted from atoms, the colors are different for different atoms, leading to identification. A third, less reliable method for identifying rocks and minerals is called **triboluminescence**. Some minerals will emit light when crushed, for the same reason they emit light when heated. Of course, you might want to know why we want to identify rocks and minerals in the first place. Well, oil and gas companies like to know what kind of rocks they might be drilling through, as do hydrologists who might be looking for water supplies. Construction engineers are interested in rock and soil types because rock and soil types

[15] There's always a danger that web links expire over time. If this link doesn't work for you, just put "fluorescence minerals" into a search engine and you'll probably find a site where you can see examples of mineral fluorescence.

affect the design of various projects. And people looking to mine minerals have an obvious interest in where the minerals are.

3. Go into the bathroom, turn off the lights, and look in the mirror as you chew on a wintergreen Life Saver with your mouth open. Triboluminescence in action.

4. We used acid-base indicators to talk about how light interacts with matter, so maybe we should discuss how we use acid-base indicators. One primary use is in a process called titration. Suppose you have one liquid that has a known concentration, or molarity, and another liquid of unknown concentration. If these happen to be an acid and a base, then what we do is add, say, a bit of phenolphthalein to the liquid of known concentration. Then we slowly add the liquid of unknown concentration until the phenolphthalein turns either pink or clear. At that point, we know the pH (or rather the range of pH, because phenolphthalein changes color in a pH range) of the combined liquids and can figure out the concentration of the unknown liquid.

5. Many organisms exhibit bioluminescence, meaning they emit their own light. Contrary to popular opinion, this is not an example of fluorescence or phosphorescence. You already knew that, though, because organisms emit their own light in dark conditions, and fluorescence and phosphorescence require the input of light. Bioluminescence does, however, depend on chemical reactions, and of course the light comes from transitions from high to low energies. Here's how it works in fireflies, which are actually beetles. The reaction depends on adenine triphosphate (ATP), which, as anyone who has studied any biology knows, is involved in carrying energy from one place to another. In a firefly, ATP combines with magnesium ions and a substance called luciferin[16] to form a very high-energy, unstable molecule. This molecule readily combines with oxygen and transforms to a lower energy state, with the emission of light.

[16] Besides its other meaning, *lucifer* is Latin for *light-bringer.* Makes sense.

Half a Life Is Better Than None

Most of chemistry deals with chemical reactions and, hence, with how electrons in atoms behave either in single atoms or when those atoms get together with other atoms. There is a branch, though, that deals with the nuclei of atoms, and that's what this chapter is about.

" ... so the first radioactive isotope says to the second, 'Half my life is over! I just hope the other halves don't go as fast.'"

Things to do before you read the science stuff

Topic: Half-Life
Go to: *www.scilinks.org*
Code: MCB017

For most subject areas in basic chemistry, you can base your understanding of concepts on easily observable things such as fizzing and color changes. The scientific concepts that help you understand the observations might be really abstract (ever seen an electron?), but at least you have something concrete (such as balloons exerting a force on a stream of water) to relate them to. Not so with nuclear chemistry. In the next two Things to Do sections, I will mainly have you do a few things that serve as analogies for the concepts I'll introduce later.

With that said, I'll show how consistent I can be by telling you about an activity you can do to observe something directly. Head to your local internet search engine and enter the term **cloud chamber**. You'll find a number of designs for building a cloud chamber. Because the procedure is quite a bit more involved than the kinds of activities I normally ask you to do, I'll leave it up to all of you Bob Vilas out there to build one. For the rest of us, I'll let you know what you can see in a cloud chamber. Even without a radioactive source nearby, you will see occasional "tracks" form in the mist of the chamber, indicating that something very small has passed through the mist. If you put a radioactive source nearby, you'll see many more tracks form. They look something like those in Figure 6.1.

Figure 6.1

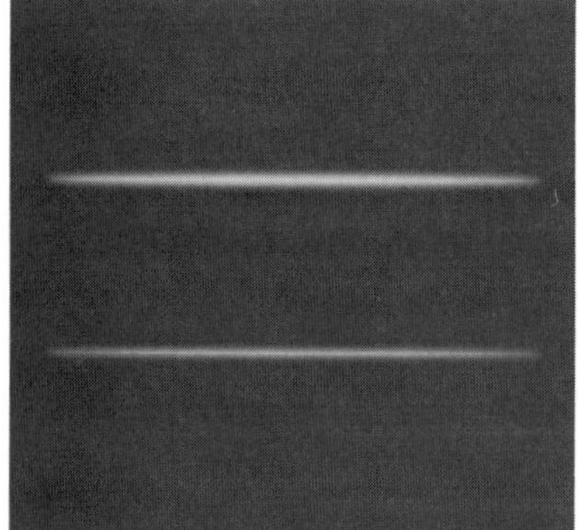

Now on to analogy-type activities. Gather 200 regular M&M'S, 200 pennies, 100 dice, or any other objects that can give one of two or more results when poured out on a table. For example, an M&M can randomly land letter side up or letter side down. A penny can randomly land tails up or heads up. A die can randomly land with between one and six dots facing up. For what you're about to do, I'll assume you're using 200 pennies.

Find a clear, smooth surface. Place all the pennies in a bag and mix them up thoroughly. Then empty the pennies out on the surface. Remove and set aside all the pennies that landed heads up and count the number of pennies remaining on the surface (the ones that landed tails up). Record this number. Place the pennies that landed tails up back in the bag and mix them thoroughly. Pour these out on the surface. Remove and set aside the pennies that landed heads up and count the pennies remaining on the surface (the ones that landed tails up). Record this number. Keep repeating this procedure until you have no more pennies left on the surface. When you're done, make a graph showing the number of pennies left on the vertical axis and the number of turns (each turn is when you throw the pennies on the surface and remove the heads) on the horizontal axis, as in Figure 6.2.

Figure 6.2

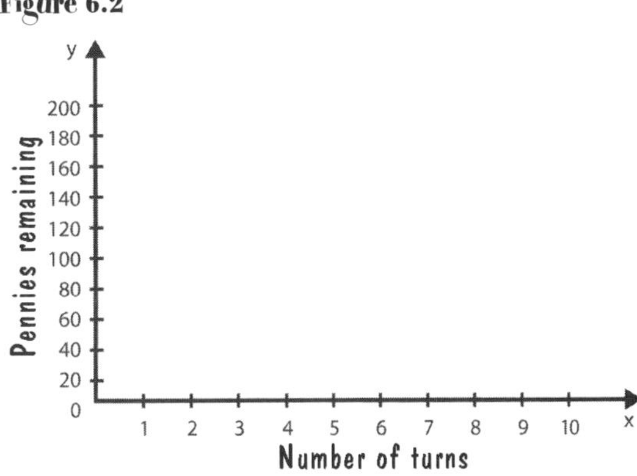

And a quick note if you use dice instead of pennies or M&M'S: Each time you throw the dice on the surface, remove just the dice that are showing two or the dice showing six (or any other number you choose). By removing, on average, only one-sixth of the dice, the procedure will take longer. You'll end up with a smoother graph, though. Also, whatever materials you use, you will get better results if you do the activity four or five times and average the results. Of course, if you have access to a room full of students, you can do the activity ten or more times, with each group doing it once.

The science stuff

I'm going to explain what kinds of things happen in radioactivity in this section. In the explanation section after this one, I'll address the all-important question of why radioactivity occurs.

A comment on the *why* question. When reviewing radioactivity for this book, I was reminded that too often in science resources, authors explain what happens without explaining why it happens. If you can only describe occurrences, then you really don't understand what's going on, and you end up only memorizing what happens. If you can figure out a mechanism for the occurrences, though, then you can build a lasting understanding of what's going on. Even though scientists often can only describe what happens when they first encounter a phenomenon, the ultimate goal is a mechanism for the phenomenon and the resultant understanding. You can compare this to mathematics, in which there are rules to follow. Only when you understand the reasoning behind the rules do you understand math.

Before you continue, you might benefit from a quick review of the structure of an atom. There is a central nucleus that consists of protons with a positive charge and neutrons with no charge. Surrounding this nucleus are negatively charged electrons. In this chapter, although electrons play a part as in the rest of chemistry, we'll find that they play a relatively small part in nuclear reactions. We'll also discover that there is a structure to the nucleus that goes beyond just the presence of protons and neutrons.

A cloud chamber contains supercooled, supersaturated alcohol vapor. If you send any tiny, charged object into this vapor, that charged object will cause ions to form in the vapor. These ions serve as places on which the vapor can condense (turn to liquid) and form tiny little "clouds." If the charged object moves really fast, it will leave trails of tiny clouds, which form tracks.

The charged objects that cause tracks in a cloud chamber are actually particles emitted from the nuclei of atoms. The nuclei of some atoms undergo changes, such as a neutron turning into a proton plus an electron, a proton turning into a neutron with the disappearance of an electron, a nucleus spitting out a neutron, and a nucleus spitting out an alpha particle (the nucleus of a helium atom—two protons and two neutrons). There is a whole range of particles you might or might not have heard of in these nuclear changes, such as neutrinos, anti-neutrinos, gamma particles, and positrons. As I said earlier, I'll explain why in the world such things might happen in a later section. For now, I'll just focus on one such change to illustrate the kinds of symbols and terminology used.

In alpha particle emission, a nucleus simply emits two protons and two neutrons (bound together). An example is the element radon-222, which has an atomic number of 86 (86 protons) and an atomic mass of 222 (222 total protons and neutrons together).[1] For this and other radioactive transitions, you can write an equation similar to a balanced chemical equation. Here it is:

radon → polonium + alpha particle (helium nucleus)

$$^{222}_{86}\mathrm{R} \rightarrow {}^{218}_{84}\mathrm{P} + {}^{4}_{2}\mathrm{He}^{2+}$$

or

$$^{222}_{86}\mathrm{Rn} \rightarrow {}^{218}_{84}\mathrm{Po} + \alpha$$

Notice that I've written each atom or particle with a new notation. The subscript in front of each symbol gives the atomic number (the number of protons in the nucleus) and the superscript in front of each symbol gives the atomic mass (the total number of protons and neutrons in the nucleus). This is common notation in radioactive decay, so you can keep track of the number of protons and neutrons. Also notice that because the radon lost a couple of protons, it transformed into a new atom—polonium.[2] The symbol for the helium nucleus is written ${}^{4}_{2}\mathrm{He}^{2+}$ with 2+ as a superscript because it has a charge of +2. Remember

[1] Just for practice, you might want to take a look at the Periodic Table and confirm these numbers.

[2] The number of protons in an atom determines its identity. You can change the number of neutrons or electrons and still have the same element, but changing protons results in a different element.

Topic: Radioactive Decay Process
Go to: *www.scilinks.org*
Code: MCB018

that it's just the nucleus, with the electrons that would make it a helium atom removed. Finally, I've replaced the symbol for the helium nucleus with the Greek letter α (pronounced *alpha*) because an alpha particle *is* a helium nucleus. The process above is called **radioactive decay** because the original radon lost part of its nucleus (the α particle) and became polonium, which has fewer overall particles in the nucleus. And yes, an α particle would leave a track in a cloud chamber.

Next let's look at the activity I had you do with pennies, M&M'S, or dice. The graph you made should have looked something like Figure 6.3.

Figure 6.3

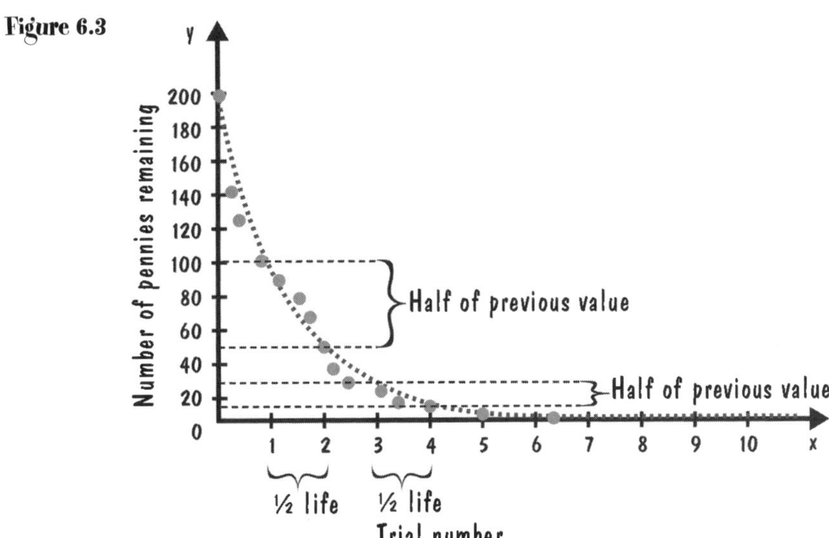

This graph is typical of any kind of situation in which a certain percentage of the number of existing objects decreases or increases with time. The name for this is **exponential decay** or **exponential growth**. For an example of exponential growth, look at any population growth curve and notice that it's the same curve as in Figure 6.3 with a different orientation. An example of exponential decay would be the amount of aspirin, or any other drug, left in the body over a period of time.

One characteristic of exponential decay is that the population of objects halves itself in a regular time interval. In the case of pennies or M&M'S, the number of remaining objects cuts in half about every turn. If you use dice and only remove, say, the dice that reads "3," then the population of dice halves itself over a time of several turns. Because all exponential decay curves do this, we use the term **half-life** to describe how fast the decay happens. Notice that two different half-lives are shown on the graph. In the second, the drop-off in number of pennies remaining is less than in the first. That's because in one half-life approximately half of the *existing* pennies are removed. Of course, the time for one half-life (one trial in this case, several trials if you use dice) is the same value throughout.

Because I seldom have you do activities just for the fun of it, you probably have guessed that the simulation models radioactive decay, and it does. When one atom changes into another via emission of a radioactive particle and a change inside the nucleus, the decay is exponential. The number of atoms that haven't decayed (like the number of pennies remaining) exhibits a graph similar to Figure 6.3, and there is an associated half-life. In fact, the half-life of a radioactive element is useful for determining how long the element will remain significantly radioactive—useful in everything from medicine to nuclear reactors.

There's a mathematical relationship, which I'll outline for you, that describes exponential decay. You start with a relationship between the change in a quantity (number of pennies removed, amount of a radioactive element that decays) and the amount of the quantity present at any time. In words, it looks like this:

change in quantity = (some constant)(amount of material remaining)

So, the amount of change, or the amount of stuff you lose, is directly related to the amount you have at any time. In symbols, we can write it as

$$\text{change in } N = (\text{a constant})\cdot N$$

where N represents the number of things you have at any time. This makes sense because how many things we lose in a given time period depends directly on the number of things we currently have. Now we invoke the magic of calculus (no, I'm not going to do any, so don't put the book down) to come up with a mathematical relationship that tells us how many things we have (this is N) after a time period (t), given that we start with a certain number of them (we use N_0 to represent that number we start with). Here's that relationship:

$$N = N_0 e^{-\lambda t}$$

In that equation as applied to radioactive decay, N stands for the number of atoms that have not yet decayed after a time (t), N_0 stands for the number of atoms you started with, e stands for a special number associated with natural logarithms that is approximately equal to 2.718, and λ stands for a decay constant that is different for different atoms. From this, you can determine the half-life of any radioactive element. It's a fairly simple derivation, but since we're not going to do any calculations with the above relationship, I'll spare you. Just remember that we can use the above equation to figure out how much of a substance has not decayed after a certain time, and that's a good thing to know. For example, we need to know when a radioactive substance used in a nuclear reactor is down to insignificant radiation levels for the purposes of storage. If you plan to use a radioactive dye (see the Applications section, p. 120) in the human body, you need to know that it will last long enough for you to make the necessary observations of body parts. All radioactive elements have distinctive half-lives, and it's pretty simple just to look them up when needed. Nice to know you don't have to make your own measurements each time.

Two final things before moving on to why some elements are radioactive. Because there are billions of individual atoms in a sample of radioactive material,[3] you never, in a practical sense, run out of radioactive material. You just keep taking halves of halves of halves and never getting to zero in any amount of time that matters to everyday life. So, if your understanding of half-lives is that after two half-lives everything is gone, then you don't have the concept.

That brings up the second thing, which is that there are acceptable levels of radiation. We are constantly bombarded with naturally occurring radiation from outer space and natural elements in the Earth. You've been bombarded with particles from radioactive decay since you were born. Of course, even naturally occurring radiation can be harmful. In my part of the country, it's wise to check the levels of radon underneath your home because its radioactive particles can cause health problems.

Just a few more things to do before you read more science stuff

Some of the activities in this section might seem to have nothing to do with radioactivity, but they do. It's important to try these activities so you can understand why elements are radioactive and how we use radioactivity to generate power. The first thing to do is pull two magnets apart and then let them snap back together, as in Figure 6.4 (p. 114). Then think about any energy transformations

[3] Just an aside if you're interested. There are exact numbers for the half-lives of elements, and we can get those exact numbers precisely because there are so many atoms in a radioactive sample. When considering individual atoms, though, we cannot predict exactly when the atom will decay or exactly how much energy the escaping particles will have. This is because of the uncertainty principle, discussed in Chapter 3. We cannot simultaneously know the energy of an interaction and the time over which the interaction takes place, so there is an inherent uncertainty in when this happens. As I said, though, the incredibly large number of atoms smoothes out this uncertainty and makes it possible to calculate accurate determinations of half-lives.

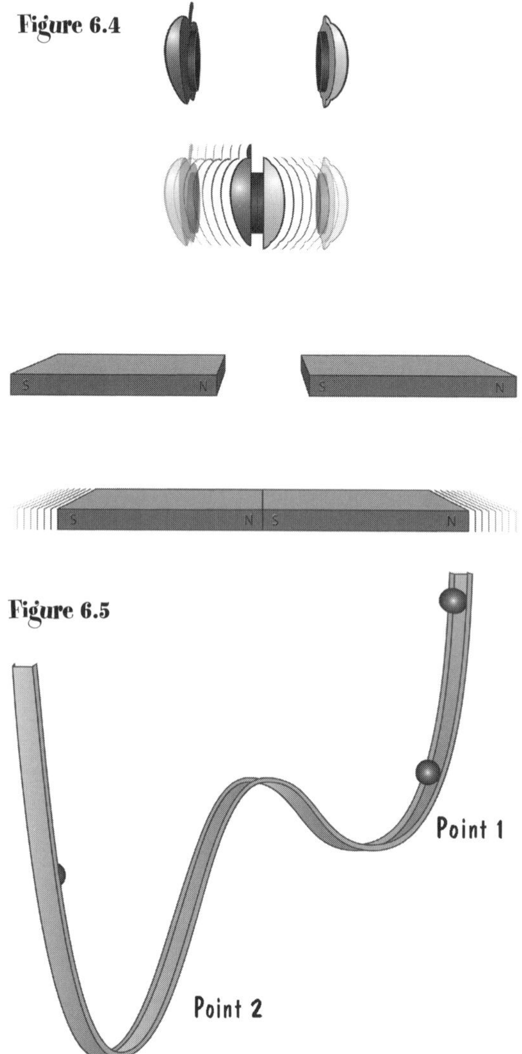

Figure 6.4

Figure 6.5

that might have taken place. When did the magnets have more energy—when they were apart or together?

Your next task is to get a marble or other ball and a length of Hot Wheels track or some other track on which the marble can roll freely. Shape the track as in Figure 6.5.

Start the marble at point 1. Push it up over the hump and let it come to rest at point 2. Where do you think the marble had more energy, at point 1 or at point 2? Did the marble ever have more energy than it did at these two points?

As you're wondering what in the world these activities have to do with nuclear chemistry, ponder this question: What holds the nucleus of an atom together? Shouldn't all those positively charged protons push one another apart? Next, take a look at the Periodic Table and see what happens to the number of protons and neutrons in an atom as the atoms increase in atomic number. In the smaller atoms, the numbers are equal. What happens after they are no longer equal?

Finally, I want you to watch a video. The video shows a bunch of Ping-Pong balls set on a bunch of mousetraps. One ball thrown onto the bunch causes all sorts of commotion. You can find such videos many places on the web, but the best one I found is at *http://natureofthechemicalblog.blogspot.com/2007/10/atomic-mousetraps.html.* If that link disappears for some reason, just plug "mousetraps chain reaction" into an internet search engine and you'll find a similar video.

More science stuff

I encourage you to take your time in this section. These are not necessarily easy concepts or concepts you will encounter unless you become a physics or chemistry major in college. However, I think they will greatly increase your understanding and perspective and greatly improve your ability as a teacher.

One of my pet peeves is that we hide from people the kinds of things in this chapter because the ideas aren't traditionally taught at lower levels. Yet these things are understandable and really help create a worthwhile view of science. No complicated math, so please don't shy away from this stuff.

Let's address the questions in the middle of the previous section first. It does seem that the positively charged protons in a nucleus should repel one another and break apart the nucleus. Remember that neutrons have no charge, so they don't exert an electric force. There's another force in play, though. Nucleons (protons and neutrons) exert a very strong force on one another when they get close. It's called the strong force (makes sense) or the **strong nuclear force**. This force is stronger than electric forces or gravitational forces but doesn't have an effect unless the nucleons are almost on top of one another. So, while the strong force is limited to the realm of the nucleus, it is more than enough to overcome the repulsive electric force between protons, and the nucleus holds together.

If you take a look at the Periodic Table, you'll notice that up to the element sulfur, with the exception of hydrogen and isotopes, the numbers of protons and neutrons in the element are equal (the atomic mass is roughly twice the atomic number). After that, the elements begin to have more neutrons than protons. Why? Because when you add neutrons to a nucleus, you increase the number of particles exerting a strong nuclear force without increasing the positive charge that tends to push the nucleus apart. So, the more neutrons, the better, right? Evidently not, because most of the heavier elements have protons and neutrons in the ratio of about 2 to 3 instead of having way more neutrons than protons. Figure 6.6 is a graph that you'll find in lots of chemistry resources; it shows how the ratio of protons to neutrons deviates from a ratio of 1 to 1.

Figure 6.6

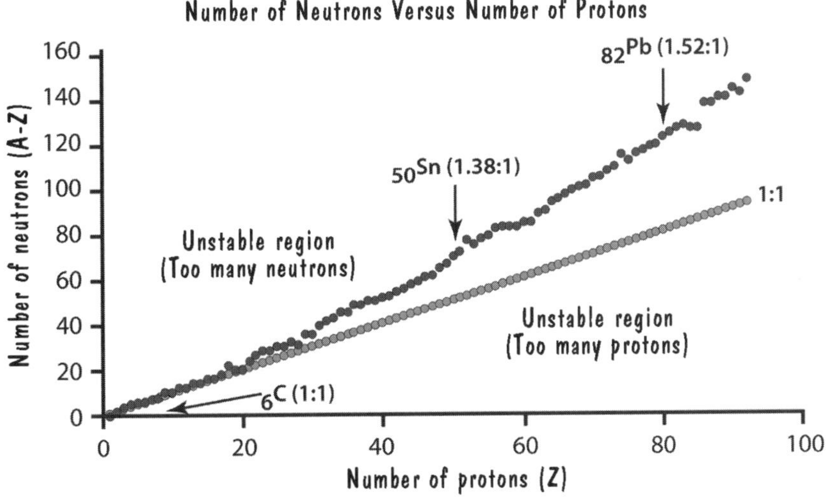

Okay, so what's going on? Why don't atoms have lots and lots of neutrons to create a strong bond and stability? The answer lies in the fact that neutrons and protons have a lot in common with electrons. No two electrons can have the exact same set of quantum numbers, and this leads to the whole concept of "shells" in which the electrons reside. Tap that memory again and recall that only two electrons could fit in the lowest energy shell, two in the next highest energy shell, six in the next highest energy shell, and so on. If you have an atom with shells completely filled with electrons, the next electron you try to add to this atom has to reside in the next highest energy level. That electron is typically easy to remove from the atom.

It turns out that neutrons and protons also have energy shells in which they reside. Therefore, the stability you get by adding extra neutrons and increasing the strong nuclear force can be offset by the fact that you can end up with an arrangement in which you're adding neutrons to higher, unfilled energy shells. Of course, as the energy of the shells gets higher and higher, adding more neutrons will definitely not be stable because all systems tend toward the lowest energy possible. So, we end up with an "optimal" ratio of protons to neutrons. Nuclear configurations that stray too far from that optimum tend toward nuclear change and radioactivity.

Now I'm going to tell you about a strange concept that's necessary for understanding radioactivity and other nuclear reactions. That concept is the equivalence of mass and energy. Mass can transform into energy, and vice versa. This is part of Einstein's theory of special relativity and is the source of that famous equation $E = mc^2$. Let's apply the theory to the activities you did in the previous section. When the two magnets are apart, we say that they have potential energy due to their separation. When you release the magnets, this potential energy transforms into kinetic energy (the motion of the magnets) and, finally, into heat and sound energy when the magnets collide. Just looking at the beginning and end of this process, you'll see that the magnets lose energy. They begin at rest with a certain amount of potential energy and end at rest without that energy. Because energy and mass are equivalent, then the lost energy of the magnets should show up as a loss of mass of the magnets. In fact, they do lose mass, as illustrated in Figure 6.7.

Figure 6.7

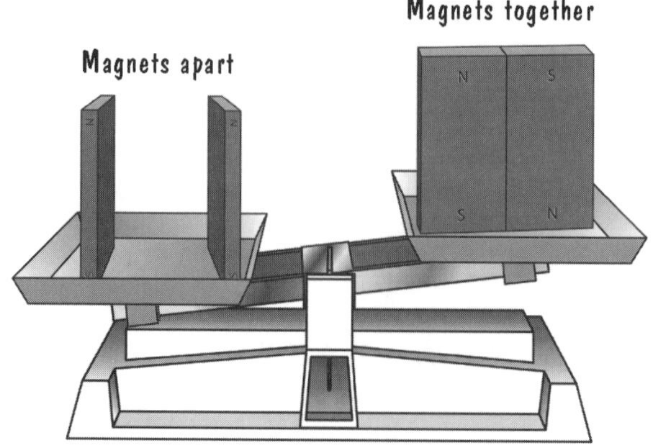

The magnets have more mass when separated than when together.

This figure is misleading and is not to be taken literally! No matter how sensitive a scale you have, you will not notice a difference in mass between magnets that are apart and magnets that are together. The difference in mass is way too small to measure in a conventional way.

The situation is similar with a marble on a track. When the marble is at Point 2, it has less energy than it does at Point 1.[4] Therefore, the mass of the marble at Point 2 is less than its mass at Point 1. Again, this mass difference isn't something we can actually measure with a scale, but picturing it that way helps (Figure 6.8).

Figure 6.8

Moving on to radioactive decay, take a look at our example of alpha particle emission.

radon → polonium + alpha particle (helium nucleus)

$$^{222}_{86}Rn \longrightarrow ^{218}_{84}Po + ^{4}_{2}He^{2+}$$

Radon-222 is unstable and spontaneously emits an alpha particle. The resulting polonium is more stable than the radon and has a lower energy state. In fact, there is a transformation of mass into energy (the kinetic, or motion, energy of the alpha particle accounts for most of this), so the radon has a greater mass than the sum of the masses of the polonium and the alpha particle. Cue the scales again in Figure 6.9.

Figure 6.9

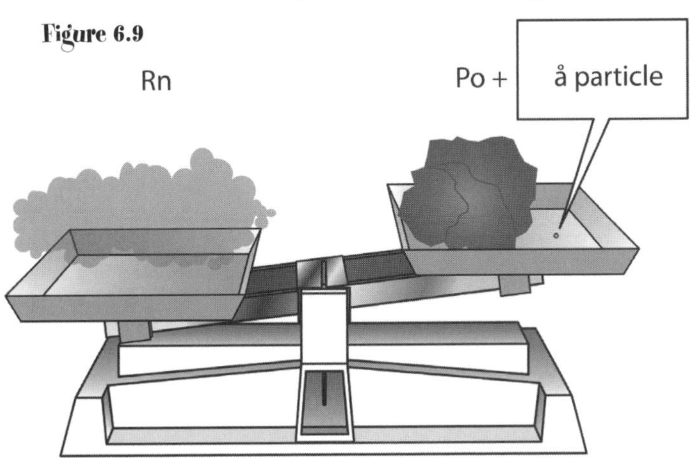

On to another nuclear interaction. Let's take a nucleus of deuterium (hydrogen with a neutron) and a nucleus of tritium (hydrogen with two neutrons) and slam

[4] This energy, which is gravitational potential energy, is actually shared with the Earth. Without the Earth, there is no difference in gravitational potential energy between Points 1 and 2.

Figure 6.10

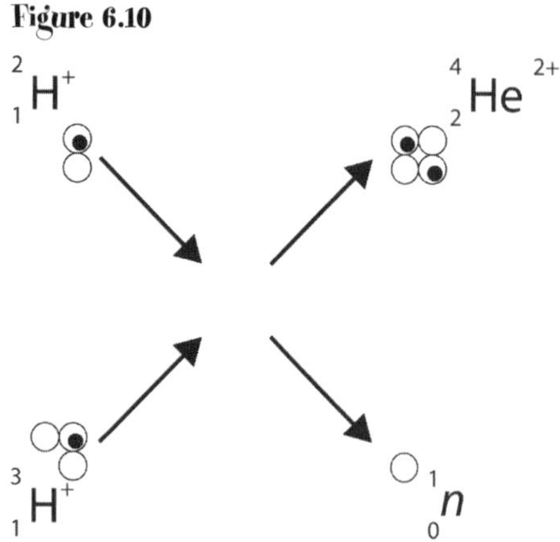

them together. As they approach each other, we have to overcome the electric repulsion caused by both of them being positive. Once they're close enough, the strong nuclear force takes over and they bind together to form a helium nucleus. In the process, a neutron is ejected. Look at Figure 6.10.

Because we have to overcome the electric repulsion, this collision is a lot like pushing a marble up a bump in a track in order for it to slide down into a lower depression, as in Figure 6.11.

The bottom line in all of this is that the mass of the deuterium and tritium is greater than the mass of the final helium nucleus and the extra neutron—this mass is converted into energy. Even though only about 0.4 percent of the mass is converted into energy, that's a lot of energy.[5] This process is known as **fusion**, and it's the nuclear reaction that fuels our Sun and other stars. In stars, this fusion is known as **hydrogen burning** (yes, fusion is what powers our Sun). In warfare, this fusion is known as the hydrogen bomb. In those cases, there are a couple of intermediate steps that I left out, but the principle is the same.

Figure 6.11

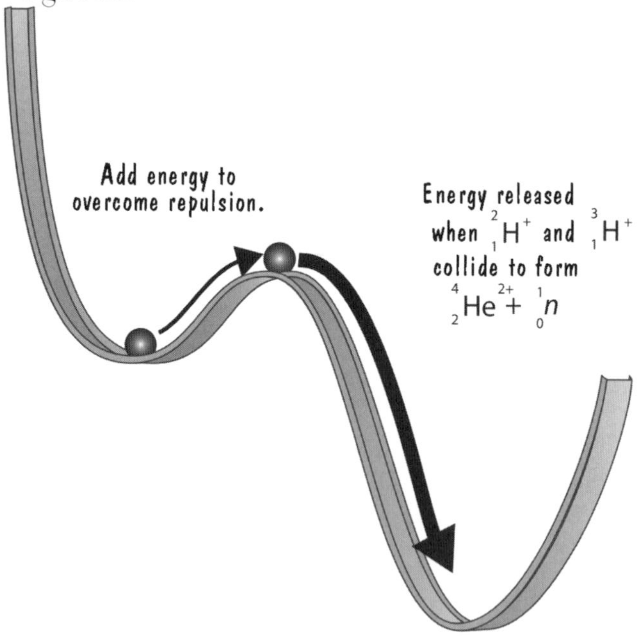

Add energy to overcome repulsion.

Energy released when ${}^{2}_{1}H^{+}$ and ${}^{3}_{1}H^{+}$ collide to form ${}^{4}_{2}He^{2+} + {}^{1}_{0}n$

Recall that sometimes adding neutrons and bringing protons and neutrons together results in more stability (as with our fusion example), and sometimes having too many neutrons and protons can result in instability. Uranium-235 is relatively stable, but if you fire a neutron at it, it captures the neutron and transforms into uranium-236. This new isotope isn't

[5] For example, if you have a tenth of a gram total of deuterium and tritium, and 0.4 percent of that mass is converted to energy, you get 9×10^{12} joules of energy (I used $E = mc^2$ to figure that out). That's easily enough energy to supply the typical household for about three years.

stable and spontaneously breaks apart into two smaller atoms, one possibility being krypton-89 and barium-144. Three neutrons also break off. If you were to determine the mass of all these things, you'd find that the mass of the original U-236 plus the mass of the incoming neutron is greater than the mass of the krypton plus the mass of the barium plus the mass of the three released neutrons (Figure 6.12).

Figure 6.12

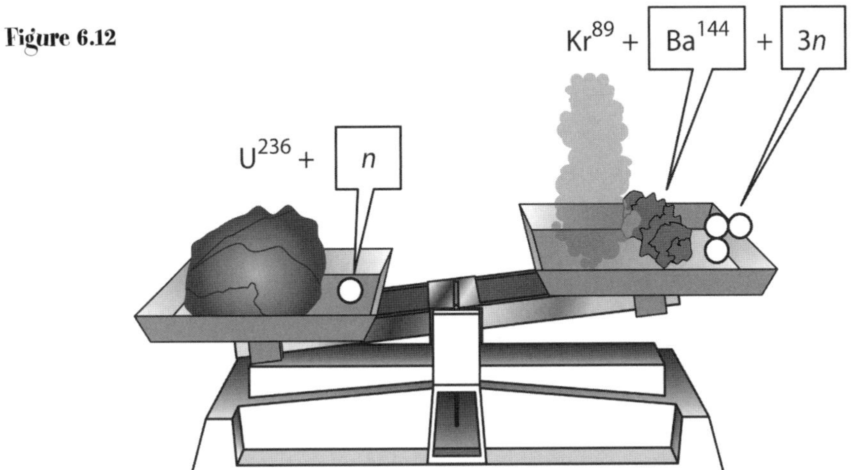

Again, mass has transformed into energy. When nuclei break apart rather than come together, it's called **fission**.

Topic: Fission/Fusion
Go to: www.scilinks.org
Code: MCB019

Here's where the Ping-Pong ball video comes in. Each mousetrap that you trigger releases its Ping-Pong ball along with a flying mousetrap. Each of these then triggers another mousetrap. With each release causing the release of at least two more traps, the traps begin to spring at a fast rate. This is known as a **chain reaction**. In our fission example, each of the three released neutrons can plow into a fresh U-235 atom and create another fission reaction. As with the mousetraps, the number of fission reactions increases rapidly (exponentially, in fact). If you have enough concentrated uranium, the chain reaction can result in a bomb. Hence the concern when certain countries start producing enriched uranium. If you can limit the number of neutrons that get produced, though, you have a controlled reaction that is suitable for a nuclear reactor. I'll discuss that in the Applications section (p. 120). I should also add one more thing. The products of an initial fission are often unstable and thus undergo radioactive decay. This leads to all that residual radiation that is potentially so dangerous in both nuclear weapons and nuclear power plants.

With most things in chemistry, if you understand what happens with energy, you understand a lot. If you understand the energy involved in radioactivity and nuclear reactions, you understand what's going on and why. Add in the conversion of mass to energy, and the picture is more or less complete. So, maybe the concepts in this section aren't so difficult after all.

Chapter summary

- Unstable nuclei decay spontaneously into more stable nuclei, usually with the release of various particles. This is known as radioactive decay.
- Radioactive elements have a half-life, which is the time it takes for half of a radioactive substance to decay. The substance doesn't completely decay after two half-lives because subsequent half-lives tell you how long it takes for half of the remaining material to decay.
- The strong nuclear force overcomes electric repulsion and holds neutrons and protons together in a nucleus.
- Protons and neutrons reside in energy shells, just as electrons do. This fact limits the number of protons and neutrons that a nucleus can have and still remain stable.
- There is an equivalence between mass and energy. Whenever a system transfers energy elsewhere, that system loses mass. Energy gains result in an increase in mass.
- Fusion is the joining of small nuclei to form larger nuclei along with the release of energy and/or particles. The energy released in the reaction is much greater than the energy needed to cause the reaction.
- Fission is the splitting of an unstable nucleus into smaller, usually more stable nuclei. Energy and/or collisions with particles cause fission, which results in the release of more energy and/or particles.

Applications

1. People sometimes think of radioactive material as something created by mad and crazy scientists. Although scientists can in fact produce new radioactive elements in the laboratory, the vast majority of radioactive materials we use occur naturally in the Earth. When you hear about gathering, say, fissionable uranium or plutonium, that doesn't happen in the laboratory. We mine these elements just as we mine coal, gold, and silver.
2. You've no doubt been to, or had a friend go to, a radiology department at your local hospital. Radiology used to consist of taking X-ray photographs but now includes much more. For example, some radioactive elements have an affinity for certain human organs or body parts. Radioactive iodine likes to hang out

in bones, so you can inject the stuff into a person, wait for it to accumulate in bone tissue, and then detect the radiation in order to find things such as stress fractures. Of course, you want radioactive elements with short half-lives for this process. Too many beta particles are not good for you!

3. Nuclear reactors are simply controlled fission. The reactor core has a large number of graphite rods that absorb neutrons and keep a chain reaction from happening. The rods can be added or removed to regulate the heat output of the reactor, and the heat output is what the reactor uses to create electricity. The core heats water, which turns to steam. The steam spins a turbine to generate electricity. So, a nuclear reactor is just a fancy way to heat water. Fusion reactions produce a lot more energy than fission reactions, but so far engineers haven't found a way to control a fusion reaction. Once that happens, it's cheap energy for everyone.

4. When carbon-based organisms die, they have roughly the same amount of radioactive carbon-14 in their systems as is present in the atmosphere. Over time, this carbon-14 decays into carbon-12. By measuring the amount of carbon-14 in a long-dead organism and knowing the half-life of carbon-14, we can determine how much has decayed and, therefore, how long ago the organism died. Not surprisingly, this is known as **carbon dating**, which has been a powerful way to date fossils for many years.

Topic: Carbon Dating
Go to: *www.scilinks.org*
Code: MCB020

5. In this chapter, I focused on alpha particle decay, fission, and fusion. There are, however, many other kinds of nuclear interactions that count as radioactive decay. Listed below are a few more.

   - Beta particle emission—A neutron turns into a proton and an electron. The new proton stays in the nucleus and the electron is emitted from the atom, and the electron is called a beta particle. Another subatomic particle, known as an antineutrino, is also produced.[6] An example is the decay of carbon-14 into nitrogen.

     carbon-14 → nitrogen + electron (beta particle) + antineutrino

     The electron, or beta particle, compensates for the increase in positive charge in the nucleus by the transformation of a neutron into a pro-

[6] For many years, scientists did not know of the existence of neutrinos and antineutrinos. Because they couldn't keep track of all the energy in this reaction and they believed strongly in the principle of conservation of energy, scientists invented the neutrino as a virtually undetectable particle that carried away some of the energy. All experiments since then have confirmed the existence of such particles.

ton. We don't expect positive charges to appear out of nowhere. The atomic mass remains at 14 because, although a neutron turns into a proton, the total number of protons and neutrons remains the same.

- Positron emission—A proton turns into a neutron plus a positively charged electron, known as a positron or beta-plus particle. As with electron emission, there's another particle included, this time a neutrino instead of an antineutrino. An isotope of fluorine decays into oxygen as follows:

fluorine-18 → oxygen + positron + neutrino

- Gamma particle emission—An atom emits a high-energy photon (particle of light) called a gamma particle (γ). No transformations take place in the nucleus except that it loses the energy the γ takes away.

excited nickel atom → lower-energy nickel atom + high-energy photon

This isn't a complete list of radioactive decay (electron capture by a nucleus and neutron emission are not included), but it's enough for you to get the idea of the transformations involved.

A Little Organic

You already know that the study of carbon atoms and the molecules they make has its own special place in chemistry. The reason for this is that carbon atoms combine to make a large list and wide variety of molecules. The reason for the wide variety is the sp^3 hybridization of the four valence electrons in carbon (see Chapter 3).

It would be impossible to investigate even a fraction of organic chemistry in this book, so I'll just go over a few things that will complement the limited organic chemistry in the first book. In other words, don't get upset because this isn't a comprehensive chapter on organic chemistry. In fact, you might not find this chapter all that useful (a few reviewers didn't!). Just look at it as a chance to find out a bit more about all things organic, and you can certainly use this chapter as an application of how hybrid orbitals behave. As with various other material in this book, I am not assuming you will necessarily have an opportunity to teach these concepts to students. You never know, however, when one of your students surprises you with a question about this stuff. It would be nice to know what the heck the student is talking about. Besides, Brian already did the artwork for this chapter, and he'd be really mad if I didn't use it.

Things to do before you read the science stuff

If you thought you could just forget all that stuff on bonding in Chapter 3, think again. I'm going to have you try to apply those concepts to a few organic molecules. Don't worry, I'll provide hints. The first molecule to consider is methane. Its formula is CH_4, with one carbon in the center attached to four hydrogen atoms. We can draw the structure as in Figure 7.1. In that figure, you can see that carbon forms a single bond with each hydrogen.

Figure 7.1

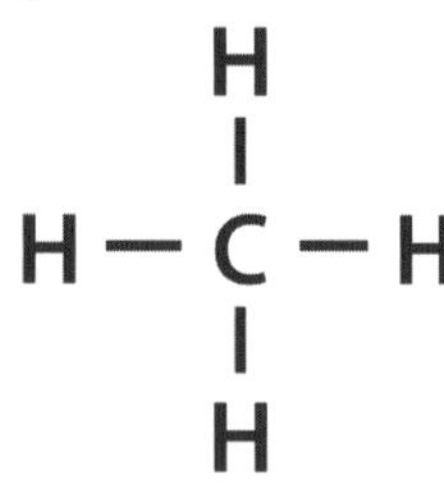

Your job is to figure out what the orbitals look like in these bonds. In other words, try to come up with a sketch similar to Figure 3.32 (p. 65). No, you don't have to worry about distortion of the molecule, as in Figure 3.32, but try to figure out what the hybrid bonding orbitals between the carbon and the hydrogens look like. Your hint is that the carbon atom exhibits sp^3 hybridization, so its orbitals look like Figure 3.24 (p. 59), which is reproduced here as Figure 7.2.

Figure 7.2

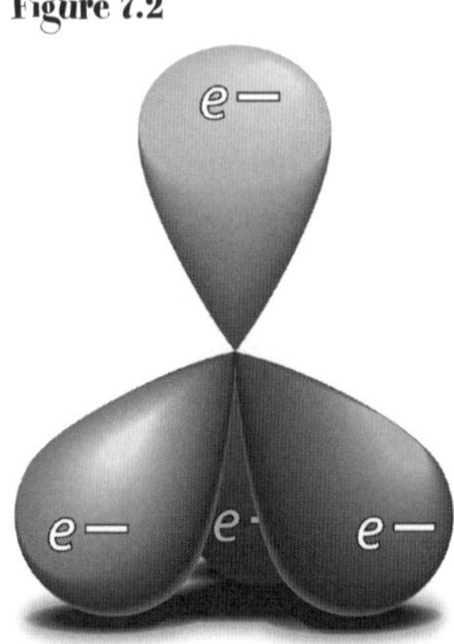

So your first task is pretty easy. Just determine what it looks like when four hydrogen atoms, with *s* orbitals, bond to the four sp^3 carbon orbitals in sigma (straight-on) bonds.

Figure 7.3

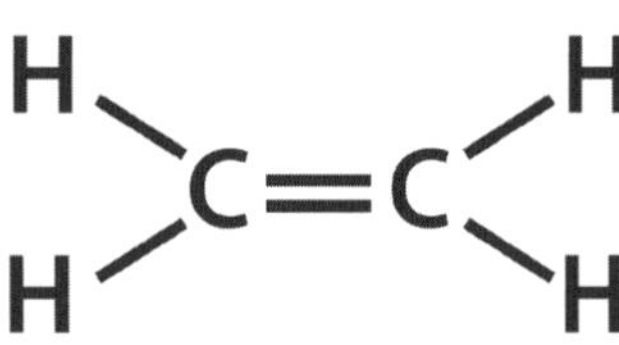

The next task is a bit more difficult. Look at the structure of ethene (C_2H_4) shown in Figure 7.3.

Notice that there is a double bond between the two carbon atoms, and recall from Chapter 3 that in a double bond you have one sigma bond and one pi bond (a sideways bond between *p* orbitals). It will also help you to know that in ethene the carbon molecules have sp^2 hybridization. That means that each carbon atom has three hybrid orbitals with one *p* orbital left over. This hybridization looks like Figure 7.4.

Figure 7.4

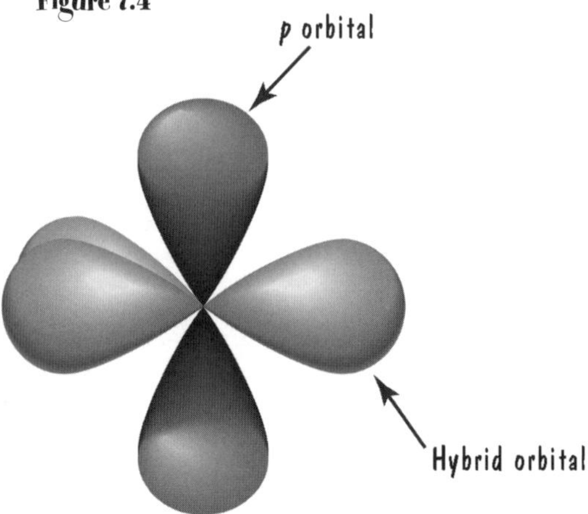

After you've figured that molecule out, or at least given it a shot, here's an extremely difficult one. In the molecule benzene (C_6H_6), the six carbon atoms bond together in a hexagon, and the six hydrogen atoms each bond to one carbon atom. The structure looks like Figure 7.5.

Figure 7.5

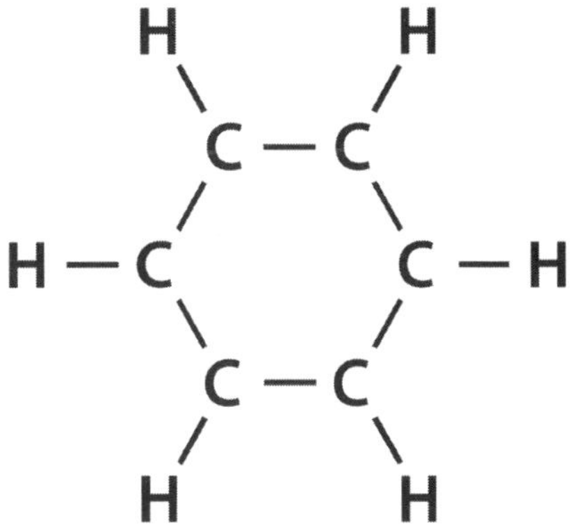

```
    H       H
     \     /
      C — C
     /     \
H — C       C — H
     \     /
      C — C
     /     \
    H       H
```

Now for a hint or two. The carbon atoms have sp^2 hybridization, just as in ethene. That means three hybrid orbitals and one regular *p* orbital. The carbons each make a single bond with a hydrogen and make single bonds with each carbon on either side. If you get that figured out, then ask yourself what might happen with the regular *p* orbitals that are left over. And no, I really don't expect complete success unless you already know the answer!

The science stuff

That was fun, wasn't it? Sort of like you're back in high school or college with a homework assignment that's really difficult. The nice thing about this homework assignment is that I'm going to provide the answers. The orbital diagram for methane (CH_4) is shown in Figure 7.6.

Figure 7.6

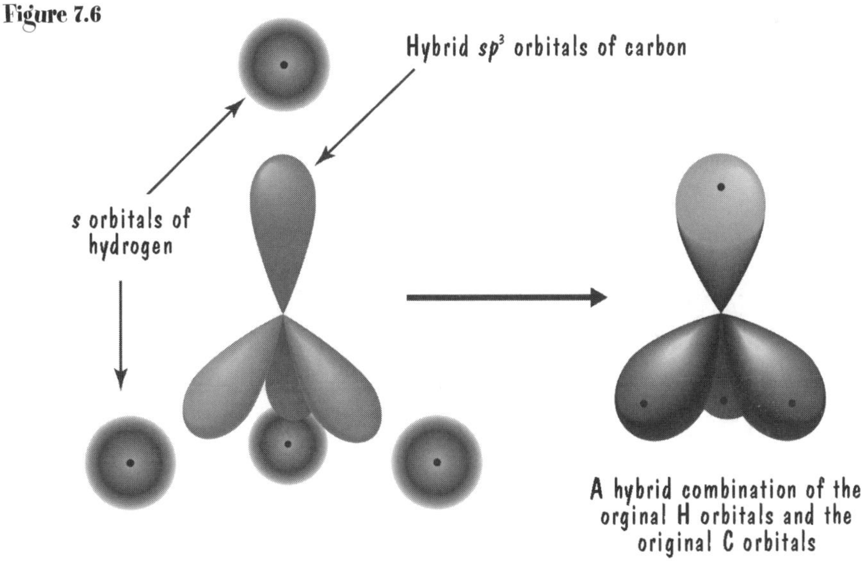

Figure 7.7

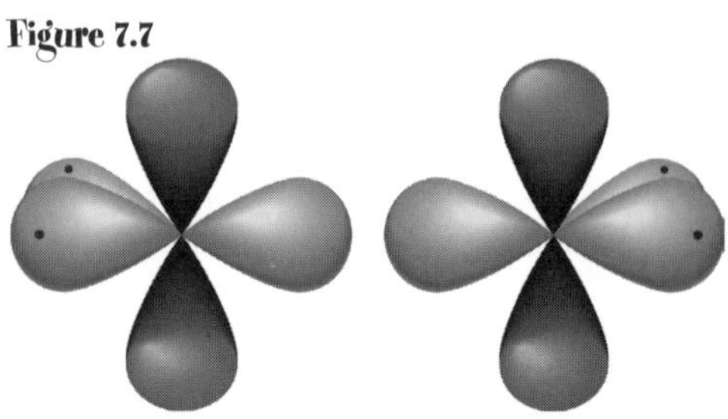

Now for ethene (C_2H_4). Figure 7.7 shows the situation before the two carbon atoms bond with each other. There are already bonds with carbon and hydrogen that are the same as the bonds shown in Figure 7.6.

Now we bring those two molecules together and form a double bond between the carbon atoms. The remaining sp^2 hybrid orbitals form a sigma bond, and then the regular *p* orbitals form a pi bond (a sideways bond). The result is Figure 7.8.

Figure 7.8

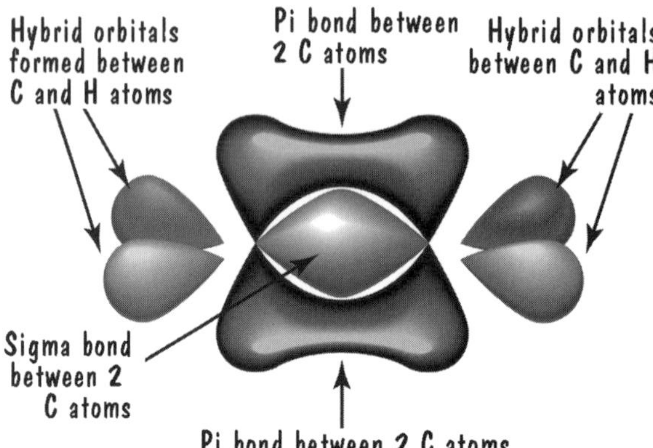

So, we have the double bond between the C atoms that consists of one sigma bond and one pi bond. Now for the final task. I told you benzene forms a ring. The bonds between the carbon atoms are single bonds, as are the bonds between the carbon and hydrogen atoms. It might not be too difficult for you to determine that with those bonds formed, you would get something like Figure 7.9. Notice that we have those leftover *p* orbitals that have one electron each. Shouldn't they just form pi bonds, as in ethylene? You would think so, but consider how that might happen. Two adjacent *p* orbitals would form a pi bond, meaning that with six carbon

Figure 7.9

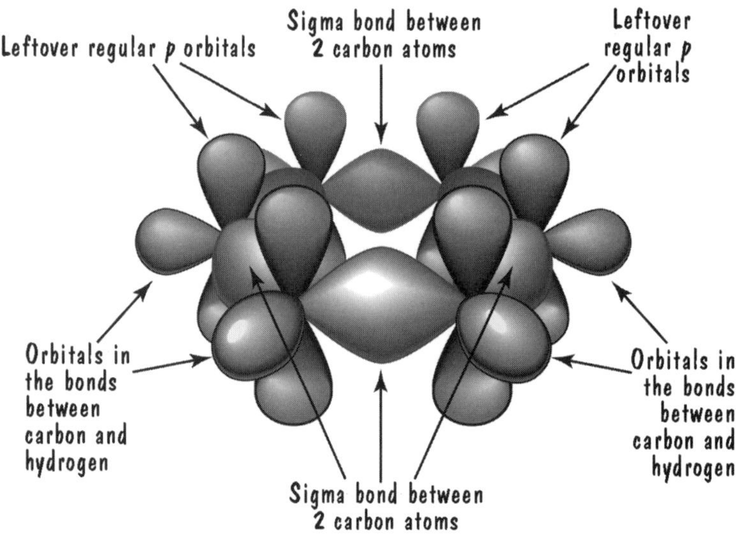

atoms, you would have three pi bonds between adjacent atoms. Certainly possible. But here we invoke the symmetry of the situation. All the carbon atoms in this ring of carbons are equivalent, with nothing special about any single one or any pair. So one has to ask,[1] "Why would a carbon form a pi bond with the carbon on one side of it when the carbon on the other side looks exactly the same?" The answer is that it doesn't work that way. All of the *p* orbitals in the **benzene ring** combine into one huge hybrid pi orbital, in which one electron from each carbon in the ring resides. This total of six electrons is shared by all of the carbons in the ring. We can represent that as shown in Figure 7.10. This kind of orbital is known as a **delocalized orbital** because it's not localized around one or two atoms.

Figure 7.10

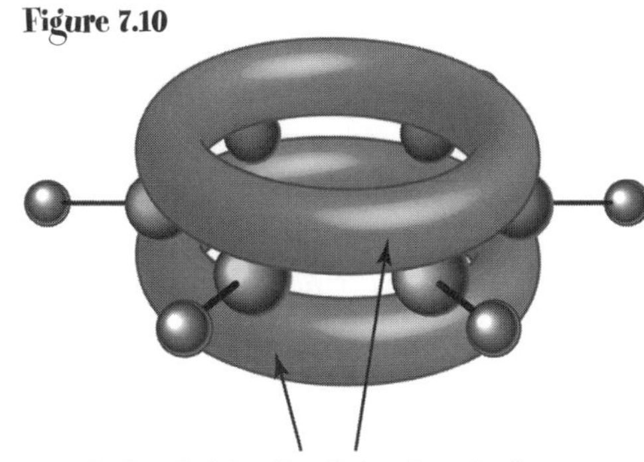

Delocalized pi bond that contains a total of 6 electrons, 1 from each carbon atom

In Figure 7.10, the sigma bonds shown in Figure 7.9 are now shown as just lines. This is to make the delocalized pi bonds clear. Too much clutter otherwise.

Now, why in the world did we go through all that? One reason is that it gives you more practice thinking about bonding in molecules and what happens in hybrid orbitals. The other is that benzene is such a special molecule in organic chemistry, it's good to know something about its structure. Plus, it shows up everywhere, in all kinds of molecules. For example, there are many benzene rings in the two versions of the phenolphthalein molecule I showed you in Chapter 5. Those are repeated in Figure 7.11.

Figure 7.11

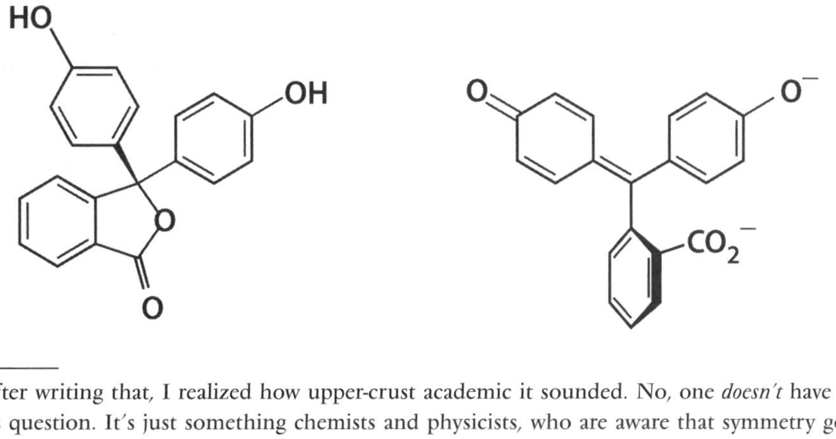

[1] After writing that, I realized how upper-crust academic it sounded. No, one *doesn't* have to ask this question. It's just something chemists and physicists, who are aware that symmetry governs much in the universe, would ask.

Figure 7.12

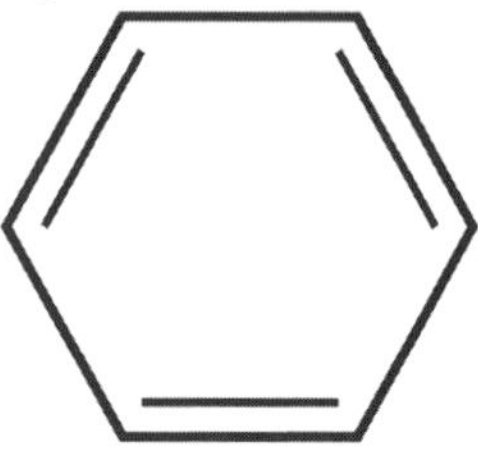

Figure 7.13

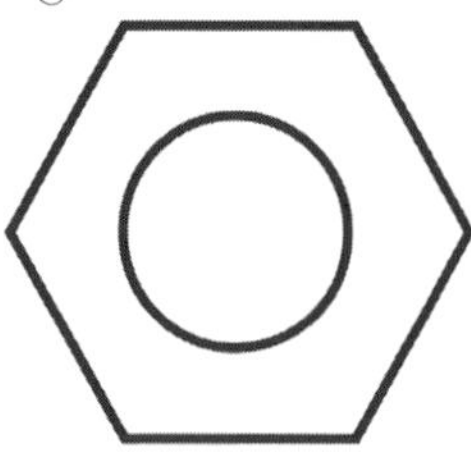

The benzene rings in those structures are represented as shown in Figure 7.12.

Figure 7.12 uses a bit of shorthand notation. First, each corner, or vertex, of the hexagon contains a carbon atom. It is also assumed that each corner has a hydrogen atom attached to it, as in Figure 7.5 (p. 125). So, any corner of a benzene ring in those phenolphthalein structures that doesn't have a line leading away to some other atom or molecule is assumed to have a hydrogen atom attached to it. Next notice the lines on the inside of the hexagon that seem to indicate double bonds. This is an old notation that hangs around today, and it's supposed to signify that there are both double and single bonds connecting the carbons in the hexagon. As we found out prior to this, though, in addition to the single sigma bonds connecting the carbons, there is one delocalized pi bond that contains six electrons. Thus, a better way to represent the benzene ring is shown in Figure 7.13.

More things to do before you read more science stuff

Get two identical clear glasses, a flashlight, about 10 grams of glucose powder dissolved in a glass of distilled water (this is the same glucose you used in Chapter 4), and a bottle of light corn syrup. (Karo brand works fine—make sure it's the clear stuff.) Finally, you need to find three polarizing filters. If you happen to have a copy of *Stop Faking It! Light,* then you have those filters in the pocket in the back of the book. If you don't have that book, you can obtain polarizing filters relatively cheaply from NSTA Press or a company called Rainbow Symphony.[2]

Figure 7.14

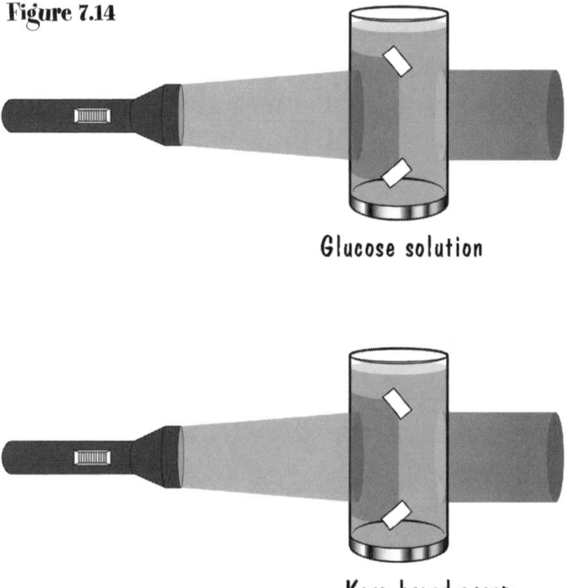

Once you have all the materials, set things up as shown in Figure 7.14. Tape the polarizing filters to the glasses.

[2] You can get individual packets of polarizing filters (the packet also contains colored filters and something called a diffraction grating) by going to *store.nsta.org* and searching for PB169X3L, and you can reach Rainbow Symphony at *www.rainbowsymphony.com.*

Look through the third polarizing filter (this is the filter that's not taped to either glass) at the light emerging from the light corn syrup. Rotate the filter as you look through it and notice the pretty colors. Do the same with the glucose solution. Notice the pattern of colors—which colors occur in which order? If all goes correctly, you'll see the same pattern of colors when you rotate the filter to the left when viewing through the corn syrup and when you rotate the filter to the right when viewing through the glucose solution.

More science stuff

I'd better start by explaining what polarizing filters do. One filter removes all light from the incoming light except that which is oscillating in a single direction. A second filter can let all, some, or none of that single-direction light (called **polarized light**) through, depending on the orientation of the two filters. Figure 7.15 shows how this works. The arrows indicate the direction of oscillation of the light waves.

Now let's apply our knowledge of polarizing filters to the corn syrup. When polarized light goes through corn syrup, the corn syrup rotates the direction of polarization. It also rotates different colors of light through different angles. Because the polarizing filter you have in your hand only lets light polarized in a given direction through, you will see different colors of the incoming light at different angles. As

Figure 7.15

Unpolarized light
Polarized light
Polarized filter

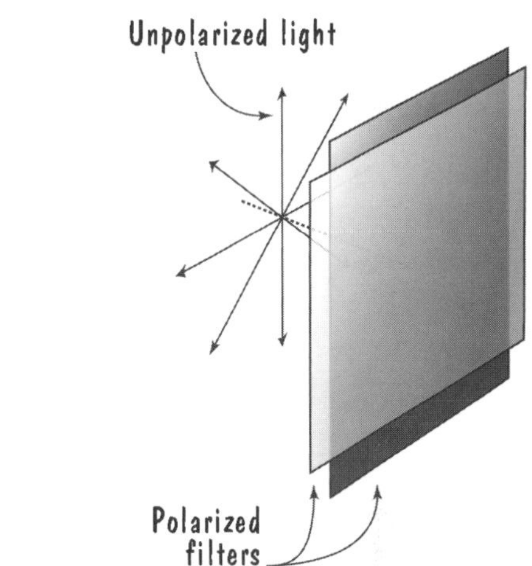

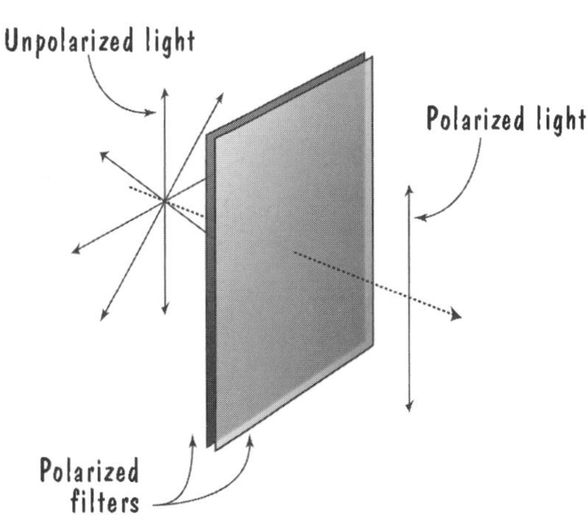

Depending on the orientation of the second filter, the light exiting the first filter does or doesn't get through the second filter.

you rotate your filter to the left, you should see red, orange, green, and blue in that order. See Figure 7.16.

Figure 7.16

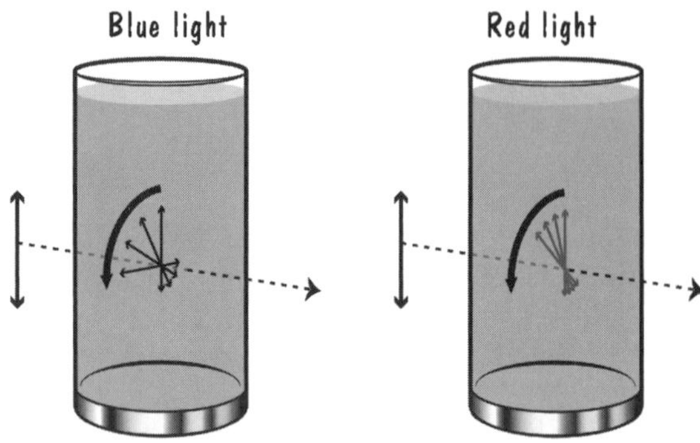

With glucose, the rotation of the polarized light is in the opposite direction—to the right as you look at the light coming at you. So as you rotate the filter in your hand to the *right*, you will see the same order of colors—red, orange, green, blue.

Okay, neat, but so what? To answer that, we have to investigate the molecules we're dealing with. There are two kinds of sugars—fructose (in the corn syrup) and glucose.[3] They both have the molecular formula $C_{12}H_{22}O_{11}$, but the atoms in the molecules are arranged differently. See Figure 7.17.

Figure 7.17

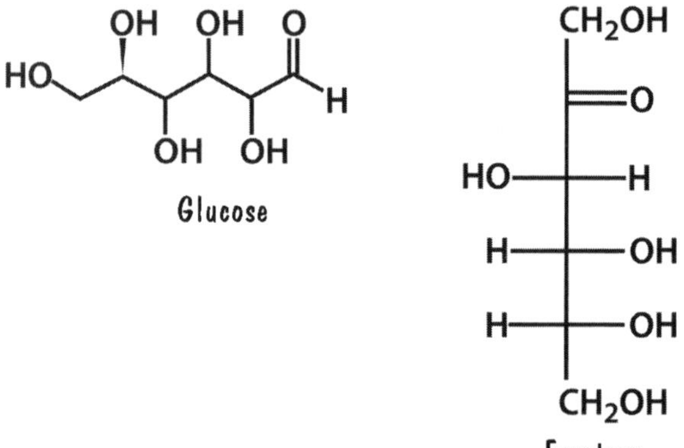

Glucose

Fructose

Molecules that are composed of the exact same atoms but have those atoms arranged differently are called **isomers** (the Greek word *isos* means *equal*, and the Greek word *meros* means *part*), and fructose and glucose are **structural isomers**. What that has to do with polarized light is that fructose rotates polarized light to the left (as you are looking at the oncoming light) and glucose rotates polarized light to the right (as you are looking at the oncoming light). Reflecting this property, fructose and glucose are also known as levulose (the Latin word *laevus* means *left*) and dextrose (the Latin word *dexter* means *right*).

Since this isn't a book about syrup, there better be a bigger lesson here, and there is. Because carbon atoms can combine in so many different ways, the world is full of isomers, and the different arrangements and orientations of atoms lead to molecules with the same molecular formula having very different properties. In our example, fructose has a sweeter taste than glucose, which is why many products use high-fructose corn syrup. So, the study of organic chemistry involves

[3] This is a small lie. Corn syrup has both kinds of sugar in it, but much more fructose than glucose, so it behaves a lot like a solution of pure fructose.

not just the composition of different molecules and how they interact but also the three-dimensional structures of those molecules and how those structures affect interactions.

Even more things to do before you read even more science stuff

An activity section for those who don't want to be that active. All I want you to do is head to the internet or a library (that's a place with lots of books you can use for free—people used to use it a lot) and find just about anything do to with organic chemistry. Look at the names of the molecules, such as 1,2-propanediol, 1,2-benzenedicarboxylic anhydride, or 1,3-dimethylpentane. See if you can make sense of those. If you do any amount of organic chemistry, are you supposed to memorize those complicated names? Is there a pattern to follow? Why yes, there is, and I'll explain it in the next section.

Even more science stuff

So, how does one go about naming all these organic molecules? To address that, let's look at the organic molecule pentane. Its molecular formula is C_5H_{12}, and Figure 7.18 shows three different ways to put those atoms together.

Figure 7.18

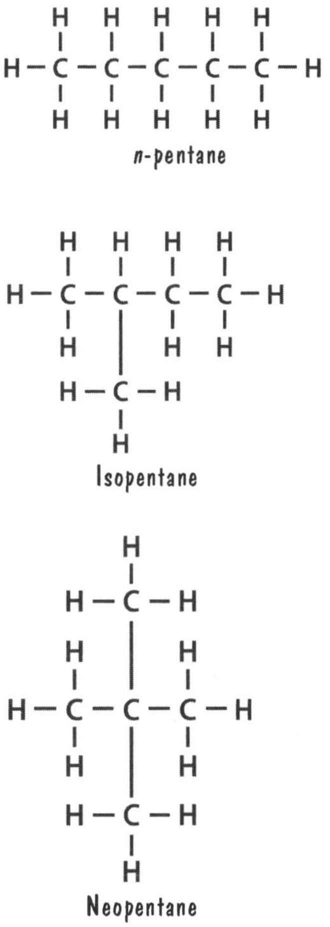

n-pentane

Isopentane

Neopentane

The first structure, with all of the carbon atoms in a straight line, is called *normal pentane,* or *n*-pentane. The second structure, clearly different from the first, is called *isopentane,* and the third, different still, is called *neopentane* (named after the guy who saved the universe[4]). That's not too complicated, but remember that organic molecules can contain many, many carbon atoms. With 10 carbon atoms, decane ($C_{10}H_{22}$) has 75 different possible structures. Using a different prefix for each structure would be a bit cumbersome. So, chemists came up with a different way of naming organic molecules besides using prefixes. This system, known as the **IUPAC system** (IUPAC stands for International Union of Pure and Applied Chemistry), uses names for basic structures and then numbers to explain the different orientations. For example, the molecule CH_3 is known as the **methyl group**. Pentane is the molecule C_5H_{12}. The isomer of

[4] Obscure movie reference. Yeah, I do that a lot.

Figure 7.19

```
    H   H   H   H   H
    |   |   |   |   |
H - C - C - C - C - C - H
    |   |   |   |   |
    H   H   H   H   H
```

Also drawn as

$H_3C - CH_2 - CH_2 - CH_2 - CH_3$

pentane in which all the carbon atoms are in a line is shown in Figure 7.19.

Figure 7.20 shows the pentane molecule with one of its hydrogen atoms replaced by a methyl group.

Now, in the prefix method of naming things, the molecule in Figure 6.12 (p. 119) would be called isohexane because there are six carbon atoms total and it's the first rearrangement you can create beyond having all six carbons in a row. In the IUPAC system, the molecule in Figure 6.12 is called 2-methylpentane. The number 2 indicates that the methyl group is attached to the second carbon after the start of the pentane chain. Similarly, the molecule in Figure 7.21 is called 3-methylpentane, because the methyl group is attached to the next carbon over in the chain.

Figure 7.20

```
    H   H   H   H   H
    |   |   |   |   |
H - C - C - C - C - C - H
    |   |   |   |   |
    H   |   H   H   H
        |
    H - C - H
        |
        H
```

Also drawn as

$H_3C - CH - CH_2 - CH_2 - CH_3$ (with CH_3 attached to the CH)

Adding a methylgroup (CH_3) to pentane

Figure 7.21

```
    H   H   H   H   H
    |   |   |   |   |
H - C - C - C - C - C - H
    |   |   |   |   |
    H   H   |   H   H
            |
        H - C - H
            |
            H
```

Also drawn as

$H_3C - CH_2 - CH - CH_2 - CH_3$ (with CH_3 attached to the CH)

3-methylpentane

We can add more than one methyl group to the pentane, as in Figure 7.22. The molecule shown there is called 2,4-dimethylpentane, with the numbers showing where the methyl groups attach and the *di* meaning there are two of them attached.

There's no way I can cover the complete naming system for organic compounds here, but maybe what I've presented will take the edge off when you see a molecule called 2-alkyl-4,4-dimethyl-2-oxazoline. Of course, scientists never make things easy, so you'll still see compounds called by their prefix naming convention. For example, we don't use the IUPAC system in naming isopropyl alcohol.

Figure 7.22

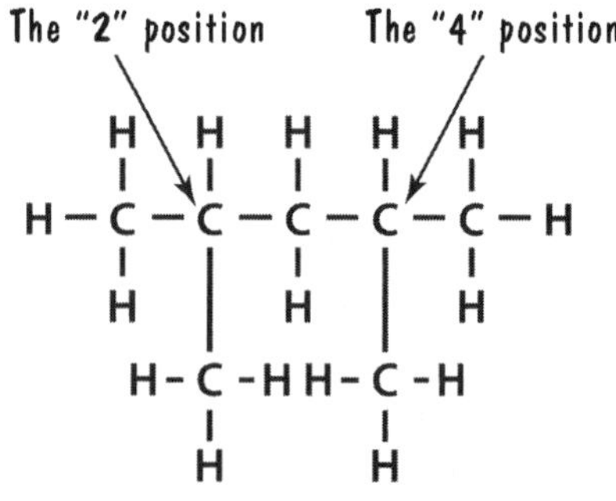

Also drawn as

$H_3C - CH - CH_2 - CH - CH_3$ (with CH_3 attached to each CH)

2, 4-dimethylpentane

As in the first chemistry book, I've given you just a taste of the subject of organic chemistry. It's just plain impossible to be more comprehensive and maintain the purpose of the books in this series. Hopefully, though, what you have learned in this and the previous chemistry book in the series will help you feel a bit less intimidated if and when you tackle more traditional resources on organic chemistry.

Chapter summary

- Organic chemistry is the study of molecules that contain carbon and hydrogen, among other atoms. The molecules formed in organic chemistry usually depend on the hybridization of electron orbitals in carbon.
- Benzene is a ring of carbon atoms, with hydrogen atoms attached, that forms a unique kind of hybrid orbital with all the *p* orbitals. The result is a "delocalized" ring orbital in which all six carbon atoms donate one electron but share all six electrons in the ring.
- Carbon atoms often are explicitly omitted from many drawings of organic structures. Each vertex in such drawings is assumed to contain a carbon atom plus a hydrogen atom.
- The arrangement of atoms in an organic molecule can dramatically alter the properties of the molecule. Molecules that have the same atoms but different organizations of those atoms are called isomers.
- There are several methods for naming organic compounds. The most complete and unambiguous method is the IUPAC method, which uses numbers for the location of basic molecular groups attached to other basic molecular groups.

Applications

1. Most structural isomers have different boiling points and sometimes have quite different properties. Ethyl alcohol and methyl ether (isomers with the formula C_2H_6O) differ in their interactions with other molecules. Ethyl alcohol interacts violently with sodium metal, and methyl ether doesn't interact at all with sodium.
2. Two isomers familiar to everyone involve carbon atoms only. Graphite and diamond contain nothing but carbon atoms (if you ignore impurities) in different structures, which are shown in Figure 7.23 (p. 134).

   These different structures lead to vastly different properties (and costs!) of the materials. You can see in Figure 7.23 that graphite forms layers. These layers flake off easily, which is why we use graphite in pencils. Diamond, on the other hand, has a much more stable structure, a structure so stable that

Figure 7.23

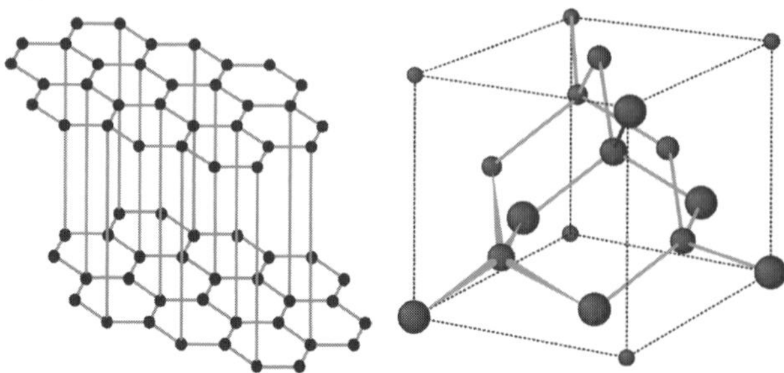

diamond is one of the hardest known substances. Diamonds are also a lesson in the interaction of light with matter. Varying amounts of impurities (atoms that substitute for carbon in the structure) lead to different colors of diamonds. And to ask the question you're dying to ask, you *can* turn graphite into diamond. The intense pressure under the Earth's crust is best for this, but it can also be done commercially, leading to manufactured diamonds that are commonly used for industrial purposes such as drill bits.

Topic: Diamond and Graphite
Go to: *www.scilinks.org*
Code: MCB021

3. We commonly think of crude oil as the substance we convert to gasoline, but it's also the source of materials for thousands of products we use every day. Crude oil is the starting point for plastics, polyesters, nylon, and any number of other things, and it's all about converting some organic molecules into others. So, the availability of oil affects not only gas prices but also the prices of lots and lots of common products.
4. The representations of organic molecules shown in, for example, Figure 7.22 are somewhat limited. They imply a completely flat molecule, but in reality most organic molecules are three-dimensional in shape. You will run across drawings that attempt to correct this inadequacy, such as that shown in Figure 7.24.

Figure 7.24

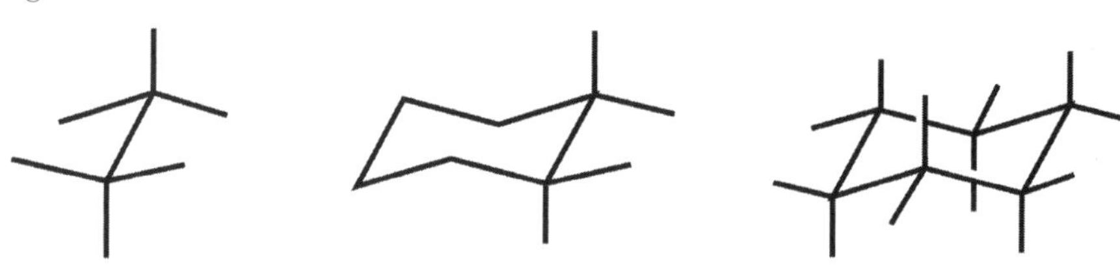

Perspective drawings like this make it easier to determine the difference in structural isomers, for example. Of course, with three-dimensional computer modeling, you can get an even better picture of what's going on.

Glossary

absolute zero. Absolute zero is the lowest temperature on the Kelvin scale. It is theoretically impossible to achieve absolute zero due to Heisenberg's uncertainty principle.

acid. An atom or molecule that donates one or more protons in a chemical reaction. Also, something in vats you should stay away from if you're an extra in a horror movie.

activation energy. The energy input necessary to cause a chemical reaction to occur on its own. Spontaneous reactions have a negligible activation energy. Also, the energy input necessary to get my son up in the morning. This is a large amount of energy.

anode. The negative terminal on a battery, or the terminal that attracts positively charged ions in an electrochemical reaction. Also, the part of your face that's stuffed up when you have a code.

Arrhenius theory of acids and bases. A theory of acids and bases in which an acid is defined as any substance that contributes protons or, more accurately, hydronium ions, in solution; and a base is defined as any substance that contributes a hydroxide ion (OH^-) in solution.

atmosphere. A unit of pressure. which is roughly the atmospheric pressure at sea level. Also, something generally lacking in fast food restaurants.

atomic mass. The mass of a single atom of an element, measured in atomic mass units. Also, where atoms go on Saturday night.

atomic mass unit. A unit of mass based on the mass of carbon-12 being exactly 12.0. With this system, the mass of each atom is approximately equal to its atomic number. Also, a military hospital for atoms. Think about it.

atomic number. The number of protons in an atom/element. For neutral atoms, the atomic number is also equal to the number of electrons in the atom.

atomic theory. The theory that all matter is composed of tiny things called atoms. The theory includes not just the atoms themselves, but what they're made of and how they interact with other atoms. The theory seems to be working pretty well.

atomic wedgie. Something you want to avoid in your school years. This has little to nothing to do with atoms.

Avogadro's number. The number 6.02214×10^{23}. This is the number of atoms or molecules contained in a mole. Also, what was up when Avogadro died.

base. An atom or molecule that accepts protons in a chemical reaction. Also a molecule that produces hydroxide ions when dissolved in water. Also, a white canvas thing used in baseball. Also, how some people refer to my sense of humor.

benzene ring. A closed structure containing six carbon atoms with six hydrogen atoms attached. Also, what benzenes give to one another when they get married.

bioluminescence. The process in which living organisms produce their own light. Think glowing fish and fireflies.

Boltzmann's constant. A constant used in a number of physics and chemistry applications, equal to 1.380×10^{-23} joules/(degree Kelvin). In this book, Boltzmann's constant is present in one version of the ideal gas law.

bond. A connection between atoms that involves the transfer or sharing of electrons. Also, something you can do with baby humans and baby ducks provided you want them following you around a lot.

Brönsted-Lowry theory of acids and bases. A theory that labels as an acid anything that donates one or more protons in a chemical reaction and labels as a base anything that accepts one or more protons in a chemical reaction.

carbon dating. A process in which scientists use the radioactive decay of carbon isotopes to determine the age of a substance. Also, when carbon atoms take in dinner and a movie.

catalyst. A molecule that facilitates chemical reactions between other molecules. Enzymes are catalysts.

catalytic converter. A device on automobiles that uses catalysts to convert unburned hydrocarbons into carbon dioxide and water.

catalyzed reaction. A chemical reaction that uses a catalyst to proceed in a certain direction.

cathode. The positive terminal on a battery, or the terminal that attracts negatively charged ions in an electrochemical reaction.

chain reaction. A process in which one nuclear reaction triggers two or more other nuclear reactions, leading rapidly to a whole bunch of nuclear reactions happening at once.

chemical equation. A statement using chemical symbols that represents a chemical reaction, with reactants on the left, followed by an arrow or two, followed by products on the right. A balanced chemical equation has equal numbers of each kind of atom on either side of the arrow(s), and can tell you how much of one thing reacts with how much of another thing to produce how much of a new thing or two or three.

chemical reaction. Any interaction between atoms and/or molecules in which molecules change structure with the addition, subtraction, or substitution of various atoms. Many textbooks make a big deal out of distinguishing between a chemical change and a physical change, but personally I don't see much value in it.

cloud chamber. A place where clouds meet. Not really. It's a device that allows you to see tracks left by charged particles.

combustion. A chemical reaction in which hydrocarbons combine with oxygen to produce carbon dioxide and water. We usually call this burning.

concentration. A number that tells you how much of a chemical is dissolved in a solution. Concentration is typically expressed as a molarity. Also, a game show I used to watch as a kid, which, now that I think of it, wasn't that great. Hugh Downs was the host.

covalent bond. A bond in which atoms share one or more electrons in a hybrid orbital.

cyalume. A special chemical involved in the glowing of glow sticks.

delocalized orbital. A hybrid orbital containing electrons that are shared among a number of atoms, across a fairly large region of space, atomwise. Also, an orbital that is "not from around here."

dissociated. A description of what happens when ionically bonded molecules dissolve in water or some other solution.

electrochemistry. A term that covers all sorts of chemical reactions that involve the movement of ions or electrons from one place to another, either in solutions or wires. Also, chemistry done by electros.

electron. A negatively charged object that is part of an atom. Electrons are really tiny, so tiny in fact that they are considered point objects, with no size at all.

electron spin. A property of electrons that can have a value of + 1/2 or −1/2, also referred to as up or down spin. This is a quantum mechanical construct that isn't associated with electrons actually spinning. Also, what electrons do when trying to promote a certain political cause.

electronegativity. A number that tells how much an atom tends to attract electrons. Also, something not encouraged in electron motivational seminars.

electroplating. The process of using a separation of charge or a voltage difference to deposit a film of metal on a given object. This can be done in a solution or in a vacuum. Also, what they do on *Top Chef* when they're serving electros.

energy level. An allowed energy for electrons in an atom or a molecule. Also, what you use to keep energies straight when hanging them on your wall.

energy shell. Another name for an energy level. Also, what energies pull into when scared.

Erlenmeyer flask. A funny-shaped flask used in chemistry. The narrow neck prevents spills when you're swirling the contents around. Clearly invented by a guy named Erlenmeyer.

exponential decay. A reduction in the number of any kind of thing in which the number of items that disappear is a function of the number of items that are present. Radioactive decay is exponential, and all forms of radioactive decay can be characterized by a half-life. Also, what apparently happens to your teeth if you use methamphetamine. My teeth are fine, thank you.

exponential growth. A growth in the number of any kind of thing in which the number of new items produced is a function of the number of items that already exists. Exponential growth generally starts slowly and eventually increases at a rapid rate.

fission. A nuclear reaction in which a relatively large, unstable nucleus breaks apart into smaller nuclei and/or particles, usually with the help of bombardment by other particles. This results in the release of a great deal of energy. Fission is the source of energy for nuclear power plants and for certain kinds of atomic bombs.

fluorescence. The process in which electrons in molecules are excited to high energy levels, usually by the input of ultraviolet light, and then emit visible light after losing a bit of energy through vibration. This is the process behind day-glo paints and posters, and is part of what happens in glo sticks.

force. Any push, pull, nudge, whack, or other such thing that changes the motion of an object. Yoda extolls the virtues of this.

fusion. A nuclear reaction in which relatively small atomic nuclei and/or particles come together to form larger nuclei. This results in the release of a great deal of energy. Fusion is the source of energy for the Sun and for hydrogen bombs. Also, a form of jazz.

gram molecular mass. The mass of a molecule in atomic mass units. One gram molecular mass of a substance contains one mole of molecules of that substance. This would also be a great name for an important British scientist.

half-life. The time it takes for half of the existing amount of a radioactive substance to decay. Each radioactive element has a characteristic half-life. Also, what you've reached at the age of 50, provided you're going to live a long time.

half reaction. The oxidation or the reduction part of an oxidation-reduction reaction. Half reactions focus solely on the gain and loss of electrons, and ignore substances that aren't oxidized or reduced even though those substances might be part of the overall chemical reaction.

Heisenberg's uncertainty principle. A mathematical statement regarding the limits of our simultaneous knowledge of an object's position and momentum. There is also a version of this principle involving our knowledge of the energy of a process and the time for the process to occur. For the purposes of the content of this book, this principle states that we are limited in our knowledge of what electrons are doing and where they are.

hybrid bubble. A new, different-shaped bubble that forms when two or more regular soap bubbles come together. This concept doesn't make much sense except when used as an analogy for what happens in hybrid orbitals in atoms and molecules. Also, a bubble on a Prius.

hybrid orbital. An electron orbital that is the mathematical combination of two or more separate electron orbitals. A simple covalent bond is an example of a hybrid orbital, and electron orbitals within a single atom can also form hybrid orbitals. Also, an orbital favored by electrons concerned about the environment.

hydrogen burning. The process in which hydrogen undergoes fusion to produce helium. We usually use this term in describing what happens inside stars, including our Sun.

hydronium ion. An ion produced when a free proton combines with a water molecule. Its chemical symbol is H_3O^+.

ideal gas constant. Also known as the universal gas constant, it's a constant number, represented by *R*, contained in the ideal gas law. The value of *R* is 0.0821 (L-atom)/(mol-K).

ideal gas law. A relationship between pressure, volume, and temperature for an ideal gas, stated $PV = nRT$. An ideal gas is one in which we ignore any energy lost in collisions of molecules and ignore the vibration and rotation of molecules in the gas. Also, the gas law that all other gas laws look up to.

inert gases. Another name for noble gases, the name deriving from the fact that inert gases have filled outer shells of electrons and thus do not readily interact with other atoms.

ion. An atom or molecule with a deficiency of or excess of electrons. Ions are either positively or negatively charged, and can carry an electric current when in solution. Also, a very, very long time for bad spellers.

ionic bond. A bond between atoms in which one atom grabs electrons from another atom, resulting in an electric attraction. For bad spellers, a bond involving a result that is the opposite of what is expected and usually amusing.

isomer. A molecule that contains the same exact atoms as another molecule, but in a different structural arrangement.

isotope. An atom that contains the same number of protons, but a different number of neutrons, as another atom. In other words, a more or less massive version of the same element. Also, the team name for a minor league baseball team in Albuquerque, which was stolen from the TV show *The Simpsons.*

IUPAC system. A system for naming organic compounds. IUPAC stands for International Union of Pure and Applied Chemistry.

kinetic energy. The energy an object has because of its motion. Kinetic energy is equal to $\frac{1}{2}mv^2$.

kinetic theory of gases. A model of the behavior of gases that makes a number of simplifying assumptions about energy involved in collisions and the independence of gas molecules.

law of conservation of mass. A law stating that in a chemical reaction, no mass is gained or lost. This law holds true as long as you don't concern yourself with extremely small changes in mass. In actuality, mass is converted to energy or vice versa in every chemical reaction, but these changes are negligible in most chemical applications.

LED. A light emitting diode, which is an electrical device that emits light using a small electric current.

logarithmic scale. A mathematical scale used to compare very large and very small numbers on the same graph. A change of 1 unit in a logarithmic scale corresponds to an actual change of a factor of 10. pH is a logarithmic scale. Also, a device used to determine the mass of logarithms.

magnetic field. A model used to explain magnetic interactions. In this book, magnetic fields are used only as an example of a model and aren't important for understanding the chemistry.

mass. A numerical measure of an object's inertia, which tells how difficult it is to change an object's motion with an unbalanced force. Also, a kind of hysteria.

methyl group. One carbon atom combined with three hydrogen atoms. Also, a therapy session for methyls.

model. In science, a construct that helps explain observations. Scientific models can be physical or mathematical. Also, someone who makes a lot of money, especially the "super" variety.

molar. A unit of concentration. Something that has a concentration of 1.0 molar has one mole of substance per one liter of solution. Also, a tooth in the back of your mouth.

molarity. The concentration of a substance dissolved in solution, measured in moles per liter.

mole. A quantity of atoms, molecules, or in fact anything else that is equal to 6.02×10^{23} of the thing. Also, a bad TV show that I think is no longer on the air. Also, a kind of rodent. Also, something you should get checked out by a doctor if it changes in appearance. Also, if you add an accent to this word, it's a great Mexican sauce.

neutron. An uncharged particle that usually hangs around the nucleus of an atom, but is sometimes found roaming around on its own, contributing to chain reactions. Also, the last name of a pretty funny cartoon character.

noble gas. Any of the elements on the far right side of the Periodic Table, which are all gases at room temperature and are all reluctant to interact with other elements. Also ... Nah, we got away with the cartoon in the first chapter, so I'm not going to push my luck with the editors.

nonpolar covalent bond. A covalent bond in which the charge is evenly distributed, so that no single part of the resulting molecule is charged positively or negatively.

nucleus. The center of an atom, containing protons and neutrons (with the exception of hydrogen, which doesn't contain any neutrons). The nucleus doesn't take up much space in an atom. The word is pronounced "nu-clee-us," not "nu-cu-lus." The wrong pronunciation is like fingernails on a chalkboard to me, so naturally my son loves to say it incorrectly around me. Mispronunciation of the word knows no intellectual, economic, or cultural bounds.

orbital. A mathematical probability distribution that describes where one is likely to find one or more electrons in an atom or molecule.

organic chemistry. The study of chemical reactions that involve primarily molecules containing carbon and hydrogen, along with other atoms.

organic molecule. A molecule that contains primarily carbon and hydrogen. Also, a molecule that likes granola.

oxidation. A process in which an atom or molecule loses electrons.

oxidation-reduction (redox) reaction. A chemical reaction in which one or more atoms or molecules lose electrons and one or more atoms or molecules gain electrons.

oxidation states. Numbers assigned to atoms or molecules that help one keep track of the gain and loss of electrons in a redox reaction.

Periodic Table. A big ol' chart that lists all the known elements along with information about each element. Many a middle school class has earned a pizza party when a certain percentage of students successfully memorize portions of this table. What a waste of pizza motivation power.

pH. A logarithmic scale used to measure the concentration of acid or base in a solution. When accompanied by the word *balanced,* this is a great selling point for shampoos, although most are pH balanced anyway.

phonon. A sound particle, analogous to a photon for light. Also, what people have when they're texting.

phosphorescence. A process in which electrons in molecules get excited to higher energies with incoming light and then fall down to lower energies over a long period of time, emitting light of their own. This is what's happening with glow-in-the-dark stickers and such.

photon. A light particle. This is a description of light that's an alternative to waves. Also, the name of a torpedo on *Star Trek.*

pi bond. A "sideways" covalent bond that forms between two *p* orbitals from separate atoms. Pi bonds are generally weaker than sigma bonds. Also, something that matures over time when you invest in pies.

polar. A description of molecules in which there is an overall separation of positive and negative charges. Also, a type of bear.

polar covalent bond. A covalent bond in which electrons spend more time on one side of the bond than on the other, leading to an overall separation of positive and negative charges. Also, a covalent bond formed between two white bears.

polarized light. Light in which the light's electric field vibrates in a specific direction. This is what you get when sending light through a polarizing filter. Many sunglasses are polarized because polarized filters eliminate roughly half of the light that's reflected from a surface.

polymers. Long chains of identical organic structures. These are essential ingredients in bad fashion statements.

pressure. Force divided by the area over which the force is exerted. Also, what a writer feels when he's extremely late in meeting a book deadline, which is what happened with this book.

probability distribution. A mathematical description of the probability of finding something in a given region of space. In chemistry, this applies primarily to electrons.

product. What's produced in a chemical reaction. Also, what you put in your hair if you're a metrosexual. Learned that term by watching *Queer Eye for the Straight Guy.*

proton. A positively charged particle that usually resides in the nucleus of atoms, though it can exist on its own.

radioactive decay. The process in which an element turns into another element with the release of various subatomic particles and energy.

radioactivity. Basically the same thing as radioactive decay.

reactant. A molecule or atom that reacts with another molecule or atom in a chemical reaction. Reactants are on the left side of a chemical equation.

reduction. A process in which an atom or molecule gains electrons. Also, a fancy name for gravy.

sea of electrons. A description of what electrons do in metals. Valence electrons in metals are shared among all the atoms in the metal.

shells. A name given to the different energy levels occupied by electrons in atoms and molecules. Also, something that adorns all sorts of household items such as lamps and toilet seats after a family has visited Florida.

sigma bond. A direct "head on" bond between various combinations of *s* and *p* orbitals from separate atoms.

solution. A chemical dissolved in a liquid, which is often water but can be other liquids including alcohol. Also, something you're looking for in your math homework.

s p d f. The labels for various electron orbitals.

speed. The distance traveled by something divided by the time it takes to travel that distance.

state. This can refer to many different situations in which a substance finds itself. In this book, it refers to solid, liquid, and gas as states of matter.

strong nuclear force. An extremely short range force that keeps the components of a nucleus together.

structural isomers. Isomers in which the arrangement of atoms in the molecules differs.

temperature. Something that tells you how hot or cold a substance is. More technically, it's a measure of the average kinetic energy of the molecules in a substance.

thermodynamics. The study of all things having to do with heat, temperature, thermal energy, and similar things. These quantities are often explained in terms of what various molecules are doing, which explains the presence of "dynamics" in the word.

thermoluminescence. A process in which electrons in molecules gain energy through the absorption of heat followed by those electrons losing energy and emitting light.

titration. A process in which one combines one solution with another, slowly adding them together until an "end point" is reached, often marked by the change in color of an indicator.

triboluminescence. A process in which electrons in molecules gain energy through mechanical means such as grinding things together, followed by those electrons losing energy and emitting light. Also, light produced by ancient cultures.

triple bond. A bond between atoms in which three separate pairs of orbitals combine for the purpose of sharing electrons. Triple bonds tend to be strong.

valence electron. An electron in the "outer shell" of an atom. This label is usually reserved for *s* and *p* electrons.

velocity. The speed of something with the addition of a direction in which the something is traveling.

volume. A specified amount of three-dimensional space. Also, a setting on an iPod that is usually way too high where my son is concerned.

Index

Page numbers in **boldface** type refer to figures.

P

T

U

V

W